COMMUNITY PROPERTY

ASPEN CASEBOOK SERIES

COMMUNITY PROPERTY

CHARLOTTE K. GOLDBERG

Professor of Law
Loyola Law School, Los Angeles

Wolters Kluwer
Law & Business

Published by Wolters Kluwer Law & Business in New York.

Wolters Kluwer Law & Business serves customers worldwide with CCH, Aspen Publishers, and Kluwer Law International products. (www.wolterskluwerlb.com)

To contact Customer Service, e-mail customer.service@wolterskluwer.com, call 1-800-234-1660, fax 1-800-901-9075, or mail correspondence to:

Wolters Kluwer Law & Business
Attn: Order Department
PO Box 990
Frederick, MD 21705

Printed in the United States of America.

1 2 3 4 5 6 7 8 9 0

ISBN 978-0-7355-9919-2

Library of Congress Cataloging-in-Publication Data
Goldberg, Charlotte K., 1946- author.
    Community property / Charlotte Goldberg, Professor of Law, Loyola Law School.
        pages cm. — (Aspen casebook series)
    Includes index.
    ISBN 978-0-7355-9919-2
1. Community property — United States. I. Title.
    KF526.G65 2014
    346.7301'664 — dc23

                            2013031256

About Wolters Kluwer Law & Business

Wolters Kluwer Law & Business is a leading global provider of intelligent information and digital solutions for legal and business professionals in key specialty areas, and respected educational resources for professors and law students. Wolters Kluwer Law & Business connects legal and business professionals as well as those in the education market with timely, specialized authoritative content and information-enabled solutions to support success through productivity, accuracy and mobility.

Serving customers worldwide, Wolters Kluwer Law & Business products include those under the Aspen Publishers, CCH, Kluwer Law International, Loislaw, ftwilliam.com and MediRegs family of products.

CCH products have been a trusted resource since 1913, and are highly regarded resources for legal, securities, antitrust and trade regulation, government contracting, banking, pension, payroll, employment and labor, and healthcare reimbursement and compliance professionals.

Aspen Publishers products provide essential information to attorneys, business professionals and law students. Written by preeminent authorities, the product line offers analytical and practical information in a range of specialty practice areas from securities law and intellectual property to mergers and acquisitions and pension/benefits. Aspen's trusted legal education resources provide professors and students with high-quality, up-to-date and effective resources for successful instruction and study in all areas of the law.

Kluwer Law International products provide the global business community with reliable international legal information in English. Legal practitioners, corporate counsel and business executives around the world rely on Kluwer Law journals, looseleafs, books, and electronic products for comprehensive information in many areas of international legal practice.

Loislaw is a comprehensive online legal research product providing legal content to law firm practitioners of various specializations. Loislaw provides attorneys with the ability to quickly and efficiently find the necessary legal information they need, when and where they need it, by facilitating access to primary law as well as state-specific law, records, forms and treatises.

ftwilliam.com offers employee benefits professionals the highest quality plan documents (retirement, welfare and non-qualified) and government forms (5500/PBGC, 1099 and IRS) software at highly competitive prices.

MediRegs products provide integrated health care compliance content and software solutions for professionals in healthcare, higher education and life sciences, including professionals in accounting, law and consulting.

Wolters Kluwer Law & Business, a division of Wolters Kluwer, is headquartered in New York. Wolters Kluwer is a market-leading global information services company focused on professionals.

Dedicated to
My mother, Rose Shusterman, Of Blessed Memory,
and
My mother-in-law, Sissy Goldberg, Of Blessed Memory.
They always had faith in me.

Summary of Contents

Contents

Preface

This book grew out of a love for community property law. For many years, I have taught a Marital Property lecture course focused on California law and a Community Property Seminar focused on law in the all the states that have adopted the community property system. The sharing concept of community property law is appealing to me and hopefully to others because it reflects the goals of an ideal marriage. Yet, there are only eight traditional community property states in the United States: Arizona, California, Idaho, Louisiana, Nevada, New Mexico, Texas, and Washington. Most of those states adopted community property law as a result of the Spanish or French legal background of those who originally settled there. More recently, Wisconsin and Alaska have adopted community property law through legislation.

Since the original adoption of community property law over one hundred years ago, each state has developed its own system. Although many of the basic concepts are the same, over the years there has been a divergence of views on many topics. Hence this book is both necessary and important for understanding the differences that have developed. It is especially relevant because two of the most populous states in the United States, California and Texas, have very different views on many issues. For instance, California prohibits the consideration of fault at divorce, while Texas allows fault to be a factor in the division of community property at divorce. Another example is that California considers the profits of separate property to be separate property, while Texas considers the profits of separate property to be community property. Finally, California and Texas have strikingly different views regarding the shared property rights of unmarried cohabitants, with California allowing oral and implied agreements regarding their property rights and Texas requiring written agreements only.

This book presents the similarities and differences among the traditional community property states regarding the property rights of couples, both married and unmarried. The chapters are structured around decisions that couples face before, during, and at the end of a marriage. Cases are chosen as representative of the differing views on each topic and issue. The book includes a substantial number of cases from every state. A table at the end of each chapter gives a snapshot of all states' view on that chapter topic. Discussion questions provide guidance to understanding the cases, and problems assist in application of the differing approaches. A separate chapter focusing on Wisconsin is included to highlight a state that has more recently adopted community property law. The reason is to delve more deeply into what is the essence of community property law and also to examine which view of the issues has been followed in Wisconsin.

This book can be used in various ways. It can be used as strictly a comparative law course to compare and contrast the views of all community property states. Alternatively, it can be used as a course on one state's law and, where relevant, with some notation of how other states treat the same issue. It can be taught in a seminar format, with students becoming experts in their own state and perhaps one or two other states. Seminar papers could include research on topics not covered in the book, such as the property rights regarding frozen embryos or copyrights and patents. It can also be taught in a lecture format with focus on one state only but highlighting, where relevant, other states' views.

Charlotte K. Goldberg

September 2013

Acknowledgments

I am grateful to Loyola Law School for supporting and encouraging the creation of this book. I also greatly appreciated the feedback of the reviewers of this book who assisted by offering much constructive criticism. Special thanks goes to Professor Thomas R. Andrews of the University of Washington School of Law. He took a chance on this book while it was still in manuscript form and used it to teach Community Property in Fall, 2012. His advice and assistance were invaluable. Thanks also to my friends and colleagues who also teach community property law: Grace Blumberg, Jan Costello, and Herma Hill Kay. Their collaboration on issues of community property law has informed my thinking on many issues and is appreciated.

This book could not have come to fruition without the able support of Loyola student research assistants: Malia Aberin, Mark Gray, Kaveh Keshmiri, Alice Kiureghian, Jennifer Misetich, Jenna Miyahara, Ryan Murray, Pearl Poon, Renee Pratt, Karen Tso, Tiffany Wu, and Saba Zafar. Special recognition goes to the Faculty Support Department at Loyola Law School, including Ruth Busch and Valda Hahn. The dedication of my Administrative Assistant, Elizabeth Luk, deserves special notice. She persevered through so many drafts and, actually, I do not know how the book would have been done without her help.

My deepest appreciation goes to Lynn Churchill and Roberta O'Meara at Aspen Publishers who always are so encouraging. Whenever I felt bogged down during the writing process, they exuded confidence that one day I could finish this project. Also, the patience and guidance of Kathy Langone, my editor, has been a large part in the creation of this book. Lastly, I am fortunate to have a supportive family. My husband Howard and our children Yehoshua, Ethan, Suri, and Dvora were always patient during the time when I said — "I have to go work on THE book."

COMMUNITY PROPERTY

Chapter 1

Introduction

A. OVERVIEW OF THE APPROACH OF THIS BOOK

The marital property system of eight western states is called community property. Those states derived their law from the civil law countries of France and Spain. For instance, Louisiana retains the character of its French history. California and the other community property states adopted their system from Spain via Mexico. The other traditional community property states include Arizona, Idaho, Nevada, New Mexico, Texas, and Washington.

What unites these states is the premise that property acquired by married couples is owned by both. This concept is one of sharing. The community of husband and wife shares in the efforts and labors of each spouse. For instance, if the husband works outside the home and earns a salary, the wife owns one-half of that salary by virtue of being part of the community. It is a concept that is attractive even in a society where men and women value their individuality. It is so attractive that it has been adopted in the state of Wisconsin through legislation[1] and in the state of Alaska.[2]

However, the main concept unifying the community property states does not guarantee identity of the laws in each state. Regarding division of community property at divorce, some states have mandatory 50/50 division while others allow judges to divide the property equitably using various factors. Regarding changing the character of property from community property to separate property of one spouse and vice versa, some states require a written document while others allow oral agreements. Regarding property rights of unmarried cohabitants, some states allow implied contracts to indicate sharing of property while others require written contracts.

The purpose of this book is to explore the differences among the community property laws of the bloc of community property states. This is particularly relevant if common law states follow the lead of Wisconsin and Alaska and decide to adopt a community property system. Also, since many spouses move from state to state, it is important for a lawyer to be aware of those differences when advising couples who want to plan their financial affairs.

This book will approach the issues of community property law through the use of three typical couples. The first will be called George and Martha, an older couple

---

1. See Wis. Stat. Ann. §§766.001–766.997.
2. See Alaska Stat. §§34-77.010–34.77-995, effective May 23, 1998.

who have established a number of assets and may soon be retiring. They are thinking of moving to a community property state and want to know how to arrange their affairs, mainly for estate planning purposes. The second couple will be Harry and Wilma, a middle-aged couple, who are beginning to think about investment of their growing savings and how to best hold any assets they acquire. The third couple will be Michael and Lisa, a young couple, who are just starting out married life, and are going to pursue professional careers and want to know how community property law will affect them.

The chapters of the book will be arranged to highlight various decisions that couples make in the course of marrying and acquiring property. Those decisions must be made within the context of the law of each community property state. Each chapter will explain the different approaches possible based on the laws of the eight traditional community property states. Discussion questions and problems will be included as well as relevant statutes and significant cases. Each chapter will include a chart for easy comparison of the states' laws.

B. WHAT ARE THE BASICS OF COMMUNITY PROPERTY DOCTRINE?

1.   *Characterization of Property as Community or Separate*

The term "community property" indicates that when a couple marries they form a community and any property would seem to be owned by the community. "Community property" encompasses the basic concept that when a couple marries they become equal owners of property that is acquired during that marriage. That concept is reflected in the California definition of community property: "all property, real or personal, wherever situated, acquired by a married person while domiciled in this state is community property."[3] However, within the parameters of the community property system, there is also respect for each spouse's property which is defined as separate property. For instance, in California, "Separate property of a married person includes all of the following: (1) All property owned by the person before marriage. (2) All property acquired by the person after marriage by gift, bequest, devise or descent."[4] The major distinctions are *when* property is acquired and *how* property is acquired. If acquired before marriage, the property is separate property, belonging to the spouse who acquired it. If acquired during marriage by a gift or inheritance, the property is also separate property of the spouse who receives it. Therefore, efforts and earnings by a spouse during marriage would constitute community property because they are not acquired by "gratuitous transfer," such as a gift or inheritance.

With only two categories, it would seem simple to determine in which category the property fits. But it is not simple and many disputes over property of a married

---

3. Cal. Fam. Code §760 (2012).
4. Cal. Fam. Code §770 (2012). California also includes the "rents, issues, and profits of separate property" as separate property. Some states considers those "rents, issues, and profits" as community property. See Chapter 9.

couple arise when the couple divorces or when one spouse dies. Thus, the "characterization" issue is often decisive in litigation. Certain devices have been created by courts and legislatures to aid in determining the disputed property's character. Two aids are (1) evidentiary presumptions and (2) tracing. Since the community property system as a matter of policy favors the "sharing concept" of community, property acquired during marriage is *presumed* to be community property. That presumption is rebuttable with the burden of proof falling on the party who is claiming that the property is his or her separate property. The most common way to rebut the community property presumption is to "trace" to the funds used to acquire the property. If the separate property proponent can demonstrate that the funds used to acquire the property came from a gift or an inheritance or were owned before the marriage, then the community property presumption can be successfully rebutted. Then the disputed property will be characterized as that spouse's separate property.

Another issue in characterizing a couple's property is whether the title to the property or the spouses' intentions should control. Under the common law systems of marital property, the title is often the determining factor of who owns the property. Community property systems differ in that title is less important, except in the case of joint titles. Also, it is recognized that the spouses' intentions regarding their property change when the marriage is faltering and divorce looms on the horizon. Courts and legislatures in community property states have struggled with the role of title and spousal intention when determining the character of the spouses' property.

Kraly v. Kraly, 147 Idaho 299, 208 P.3d 281 (2009), is a case that illustrates how a court will resolve the issue of characterizing a couple's property in divorce litigation. *Downer v. Bramet,* 152 Cal. App. 3d 837, 199 Cal. Rptr. 830 (1984), is a case that illustrates how a court will distinguish between community property and separate property.

KRALY v. KRALY

147 Idaho 299, 208 P.3d 281 (2009)
Supreme Court of Idaho

JONES, Justice.

Susan Kraly appeals from the district court's order concluding that a certain piece of real property was the separate property of her ex-husband, Stan Kraly. We affirm.

I.

On April 12, 2003, Stan and Susan were married in Florida. Shortly thereafter, Stan sold his primary residence in Palm City, Florida, which he had acquired as his separate property prior to the marriage, receiving over $500,000.00 in net proceeds. In March 2004, Stan used $167,500.00 of those separate proceeds to purchase sixty acres of unimproved property near Lightning Creek Road in Bonner County, Idaho (the Lightning Creek property). The warranty deed conveyed the property to "Stan Kraly and Susan Kraly, Husband and Wife." Stan also purchased other properties in Idaho with his separate funds, taking title to those in his name alone.

On October 5, 2004, less than one and a half years after getting married, Stan filed for divorce in an Idaho court on the grounds of irreconcilable differences. Without addressing property distribution issues, the court granted the divorce on August 17, 2005. The court limited its jurisdiction to the marriage itself and any assets located in Idaho; any assets located in Florida were to be distributed by a Florida court.

The trial for property issues occurred on March 1, 2006. The magistrate court entered a "final decree of divorce" on April 14, 2006, after hearing testimony on the disputed issues. It found that the Lightning Creek property was a community asset, but that Stan was entitled to reimbursement from the community for the $167,500.00 he spent purchasing the property because Stan had "proved by clear, convincing, and undisputed evidence that the source of funds to entirely purchase the property was from [Stan's] separate property." The magistrate court further held that "there was no evidence of any intent by [Stan] to gift his separate property purchase monies to [Susan] by the warranty deed alone." Nonetheless, the magistrate court held that any enhanced value of the Lightning Creek property in excess of the $167,500.00 was a community asset to be shared equally by the parties.

Stan appealed to the district court, arguing that because the Lightning Creek property was purchased with his separate funds, the property should be characterized as his separate property and its full value should be awarded to him. Susan cross-appealed, arguing that because the magistrate court found the Lightning Creek property to be community property, the court should have awarded her a full one-half community interest in the entire property. The district court reversed the magistrate court's decision, holding that the Lightning Creek property was Stan's separate property and that Susan was entitled to no part of its value. Susan appealed to this Court, arguing that the district court erred in reversing the magistrate court's decision.

II.

When reviewing the decision of the district court acting in its appellate capacity, this Court directly reviews the district court's decision. *Losser v. Bradstreet,* 145 Idaho 670, 672, 183 P.3d 758, 760 (2008). Thus, this Court considers whether the district court committed error with respect to the issues presented.

The trial court's findings of fact will not be set aside on appeal unless they are clearly erroneous such that they are not based upon substantial and competent evidence. *Stewart v. Stewart,* 143 Idaho 673, 676, 152 P.3d 544, 547 (2007). However, this Court exercises free review over the trial court's conclusions of law. *Id.* at 677, 152 P.3d at 548.

A.

The primary dispute in this case is whether the Lightning Creek property was Stan's separate property or property of the community. Stan argues that the property is his separate property because it was purchased in full with the proceeds from the sale of his separate home in Florida. Susan argues that because her name appears on the warranty deed, the Lightning Creek property is community property.

* * *

The District Court Properly Found the Lightning Creek Property to Be Stan's Separate Property

Susan claims that the Lightning Creek property was community property because, of the various properties Stan purchased with his separate funds, it was the only one which was titled in the names of both parties as a married couple. She reiterates that Stan testified that he purchased the property intending to live there with Susan as a married couple. Stan, on the other hand, argues that the parties had agreed that the property would belong to the community only after Susan contributed an equivalent amount of money to build a house on the Lightning Creek property. Until that occurred, Stan asserts that the property remained his separate property. Stan emphasizes the fact that the entire property was purchased with the proceeds from the sale of his separate property. Stan insists that even in cases where real property is deeded to both husband and wife the Court has examined other factors in order to determine the source of the funds used to purchase the property. *See Winn v. Winn,* 105 Idaho 811, 814, 673 P.2d 411, 414 (1983).

The characterization of property as either community or separate involves mixed questions of law and fact. *Krebs v. Krebs,* 114 Idaho 571, 573, 759 P.2d 77, 79 (Ct. App. 1988). The manner and method of acquisition of property are questions of fact for the trial court. *Batra v. Batra,* 135 Idaho 388, 391, 17 P.3d 889, 892 (Ct. App. 2001). The characterization of an asset in light of the facts found, however, is a question of law over which this Court exercises free review. *Id.*

Whether a specific piece of property is characterized as community or separate property depends on when it was acquired and the source of the funds used to purchase it. The character of property vests at the time the property is acquired. *Winn,* 105 Idaho at 815, 673 P.2d at 415. Property acquired during a marriage is presumed to be community property. *Reed v. Reed,* 137 Idaho 53, 58, 44 P.3d 1108, 1113 (2002). The presumption can be overcome if the party asserting the separate character of the property carries his burden of proving with reasonable certainty and particularity that the property acquired during marriage is separate property.[2] *Id.* at 59-60, 44 P.3d at 1114-15.

One way to prove that property acquired during marriage is separate property is to show that the asset was purchased with one spouse's separate property. *Worzala v. Worzala,* 128 Idaho 408, 412, 913 P.2d 1178, 1182 (1996). This Court has long recognized that the property acquired shares the same character as the property or funds used to acquire it. Therefore, the presumption that all property acquired during the marriage is community property can be overcome by showing that such property was purchased with one spouse's separate funds.

---

2. Separate property is defined as "[a]ll other property of either the husband or the wife owned by him or her before marriage, and that acquired afterward . . . either by gift, bequest, devise or descent, or that which either he or she shall acquire with the proceeds of his or her separate property, by way of moneys or other property, shall remain his or her sole and separate property." I.C. §32-903. Therefore, if property is purchased with separate funds, even if acquired during the marriage, the property maintains its separate character.

Because the Lightning Creek property was acquired during the marriage, the presumption arises that it was community property. Therefore, Stan bore the burden of overcoming that presumption with reasonable certainty and particularity. The evidence at trial clearly supported Stan's contention that the entire purchase price of the Lightning Creek property was paid with his separate funds from the sale of his pre-marital separate home in Florida. The magistrate court additionally found that Stan did not gift any part of the property to Susan. Therefore, the district court properly reversed the magistrate court's determination that the property was community property and correctly held that the Lightning Creek property was Stan's separate property.

* * *

In this case, the Court can easily understand why the magistrate court decided the case as it did. It is clear what facts it found and which ones it relied upon in reaching its decision. The magistrate court focused on the fact that Stan's separate funds paid for the property and that both parties were named in the deed. The magistrate court's only error was one of law.

III.

B.

The district court's decision is affirmed. Costs awarded to Stan.

Chief Justice EISMANN, and Justices BURDICK, W. JONES, and HORTON concur.

Discussion Questions

1. Examine the differing results if the magistrate's decision had been affirmed, if Susan's argument had been accepted and how the Supreme Court decided the case.
2. What role did the title and the intentions of the parties play in resolving this case?

The distinction between community property and separate property of one spouse often arises in the context of employment. Remuneration for efforts would ordinarily be considered community property, but it is possible that a spouse could receive a gift from the employer that would qualify it as that spouse's separate property. That was the issue in *Downer v. Bramet*.

DOWNER v. BRAMET

152 Cal. App. 3d 837, 199 Cal. Rptr. 830 (1984)
California Court of Appeal

KAUFMAN, Associate Justice.

Plaintiff Gloria Alice Bramet Downer (hereinafter referred to as former wife) appeals from a judgment of nonsuit on her complaint for the determination of her rights in certain property and for fraud. She claims a community property interest in the proceeds of sale of a one-third interest in a ranch conveyed to her former husband George Keith Bramet by his employer after the parties separated. At the close of former wife's case, former husband moved for nonsuit. The motion was granted and judgment entered accordingly.

FACTS

The parties were married in 1953, and separated in 1971. Former husband was an accountant and a tax expert. He worked for Chilcott Enterprises before, during and after the marriage, beginning in 1943. Chilcott Enterprises consisted of several businesses and corporations owned and operated by Edward Chilcott and his wife. Former husband was an officer of several of the corporations and acted as secretary-treasurer, accountant and recordkeeper for all of the Chilcotts' operations. Mr. Chilcott considered former husband his "righthand man."

Chilcott Enterprises had no retirement program of any kind for its employees. According to former wife's testimony, sometime in the mid-1960's former husband told her that Mr. Chilcott was going to give to him and two other employees a ranch in Oregon in lieu of retirement benefits. Nothing further was thereafter said about the ranch.

The parties separated in November 1971. In December 1972, after some exchange of drafts between the parties and their counsel, a marital settlement agreement was executed. The agreement, which was later incorporated in the judgment of dissolution, provided that all income and earnings of former husband or former wife after March 4, 1972, should be the separate property of the acquirer and that each party released any claim to such earnings or after acquired property. However, the agreement also contained a warranty "that neither party is now possessed of any property of any kind or description whatsoever, other than the property specifically mentioned in this Agreement" and a provision reading: "If it shall hereafter be determined by a Court of competent jurisdiction that one party is now possessed of any community property not set forth herein . . . such party hereby covenants and agrees to pay to [the other on demand an amount equal to one-half of the then] or present fair market value of such property, whichever is greater."

In August 1972, before the parties executed the agreement, but after the March 4 date specified in the settlement agreement, the Chilcotts deeded the W-4 Ranch in Oregon to former husband and two other employees. Former husband did not mention his interest in the ranch at the time he executed the settlement agreement in December 1972.

Former husband continued working for Chilcott Enterprises after the dissolution until he became disabled after suffering a stroke in 1976. In 1978, the ranch was sold for over $1,350,000 and former husband's interest in the sale proceeds was turned over to his conservator. This action was instituted in 1980 shortly after former wife learned of the conveyance of the ranch to former husband and the other employees.

Mr. Chilcott testified in essence that the conveyance to the three employees was a gift — the reason he deeded the ranch to the three employees was that he did not need the money and he just felt like giving it away.

Additional facts will be included in the discussion of the propriety of the nonsuit.

The Nonsuit

The question is thus whether there was substantial evidence that would have supported a verdict in favor of former wife on the issue of her interest in the ranch (or, more correctly, the proceeds from the sale of the ranch). Former wife contends there was substantial evidence the transfer of the ranch interest to former husband was in lieu of pension benefits, and is therefore community property. Former husband contends there is no substantial evidence the ranch constituted a retirement benefit and argues the transfer of the ranch interest was a gift, and thus, separate property pursuant to Civil Code section 5108. The trial court agreed with former husband that the transfer of the interest in the ranch to him was a gift and concluded therefore that it was his separate property.

We agree with the trial court and former husband that the Chilcotts' transfer of a one-third interest in the ranch to former husband was legally in the form of a gift. Civil Code section 1146 defines a gift as "a transfer of personal property, made voluntarily, and without consideration." The evidence establishes that that is precisely what was done in the case at bench. There is no evidence the ranch was transferred pursuant to a legal obligation to do so on the part of the Chilcotts. There is no evidence of any bargained-for contractual obligation nor of any detrimental reliance by former husband sufficient to invoke the doctrine of promissory estoppel. There is nothing to show, for example, that former husband was induced to stay in the Chilcotts' employ by the statement assertedly made by Mr. Chilcott that the ranch was going to be conveyed to the three employees in lieu of a pension program. There being no evidence of any legal obligation to convey the ranch, its conveyance can only have been a gift.

However, the conclusion the conveyance was legally a gift does not resolve the ultimate question of the characterization of the ranch interest or the proceeds of its sale as community or separate. Although Civil Code section 5108 provides that property acquired by the husband after marriage by gift is his separate property, the language of section 5108 must be read in the context of the entire marital property scheme. Earnings or property attributable to or acquired as a result of the labor, skill and effort of a spouse during marriage are community property. (Civ. Code, §5110; cf. Civ. Code, §5118.) Even though the transfer of the ranch interest was legally a gift, there is substantial, indeed strong, evidence the gift was made by former husband's employer in recognition of former husband's devoted and skillful services during his lifelong employment at Chilcott Enterprises.

The evidence shows former husband began working for Chilcott Enterprises in 1943. He became Mr. Chilcott's right hand man, did all the accounting for the various Chilcott operations, was responsible for all the tax planning, advice, and filing of returns, handled sales contracts and recordkeeping, served as officer in several of the corporate entities and supervised the ranch operations in California, Arizona and Oregon. For over 30 years, he was the Chilcotts' loyal and trusted employee. By contrast, there was no evidence of any social or personal relationship between former husband and the Chilcotts. The Bramets never went out socially with the Chilcotts, and former husband never played golf or other sports with Mr. Chilcott, never took a social trip, played cards or anything of that sort with the Chilcotts. The Bramets went to the Chilcotts' house once to attend the wedding of the Chilcotts' oldest daughter, and one time former husband took care of the Chilcotts' home while they were away on vacation. Otherwise, former husband never went to the Chilcotts' home socially. Mr. Chilcott testified that, except for their business relationship, he had practically no contact with former husband.

Thus, although the conveyance of the ranch interest to former husband was in the form of a gift, the evidence would support, indeed strongly suggests, that it was in whole or part a remuneratory gift in recognition of former husband's loyal and skilled efforts for and services to his employer. To the extent it was and to the extent the efforts and services were rendered during the marriage, the ranch interest conveyed to former husband and the proceeds of its sale were community property.

It was error therefore to grant the nonsuit as to the cause of action to establish former wife's interest in the proceeds of sale of the ranch interest.

If the ranch interest is ultimately determined to have been community property in whole or part, former wife will be entitled to her share of the proceeds of sale; if it should finally be determined to have been entirely former husband's separate property, former wife was never entitled to any part of it and has not been damaged.

The nonsuit was thus proper as to the cause of action for fraud and the judgment will be affirmed as to that cause of action.

DISPOSITION

The judgment of nonsuit is reversed as to the cause of action to establish plaintiff's interest in the proceeds of sale of the interest in the ranch property; as to the cause of action for fraud the judgment is affirmed. Plaintiff shall recover costs on appeal.

MORRIS, P.J., and RICKLES, J., concur.

Discussion Questions

1. Why was it significant that Keith Bramet never had a social relationship with his boss Mr. Chilcott?

2. On remand, could the trial court find that the proceeds of the ranch were part community property, part Keith Bramet's separate property? Explain.

---

2.   *Division of Community Property at Divorce: Equal or Equitable?*

Only three community property states have the rule of mandatory 50/50 division of community property at divorce: California, Louisiana, and New Mexico. The five remaining community property states give their courts the discretion to make an equitable division of community property. Those states — Arizona, Idaho, Nevada, Texas, and Washington — use various factors to decide whether the distribution of community property should deviate from equal division of community property. For more extensive discussion, see Chapter 14. In the mandatory 50/50 division states, the major issue is how to characterize the couple's assets to determine if they are community property, since separate property of each spouse is not divided at divorce. In the equitable distribution states, the question often revolves around which factors would allow one spouse to take more than one-half of the community property. Most of these states have a general formulation of what is "just" or "equitable" or "fair" under the circumstances. One significant issue is what role one spouse's "fault" that led to the divorce plays in unequal division of community property. The Texas Court of Appeals in *Marriage of Brown*, 187 S.W.3d 143 (Tex. Ct. App. 2006), addressed the role of "fault" when the divorce was based on "no fault" grounds.

MARRIAGE OF BROWN

187 S.W.3d 143 (2006)
Court of Appeals of Texas

Before Chief Justice GRAY, Justice VANCE, and Justice REYNA.

TOM GRAY, Chief Justice.
Donald R. Brown appeals the division of property made by the trial court. Because the trial court abused its discretion in making the division, we reverse and remand.

DIVISION OF PROPERTY

Donald presents two issues on appeal. They are as follows:

POINTS PRESENTED FOR REVIEW

Point Number One

"no fault" divorce

issue #1

When a dissolution of marriage is sought solely on the grounds of insupportability, evidence of fault becomes irrelevant as anylytical [sic] and may not be considered by the trial court in its just and right division of the community estate.

Point Number Two

issue #2

The trial court's division of the community estate awarding the wife 100% was arbitrary and unreasonable.

Donald's first point squarely presents the issue expressly left open by the Texas Supreme Court in *Young v. Young*, 609 S.W.2d 758, 761 (Tex. 1980). The issue in *Young* was:

> . . . whether the trial court may, in a fault-based divorce, consider the fault in breaking up the marriage as a factor in making a property division favoring one spouse.

Id. The Court went on to state it "is not necessary for us to express an opinion concerning the same issue in a 'no-fault' divorce, and we express none." *Id.* It is necessary for us to express an opinion on the very issue the Texas Supreme Court left open.

This Court has flirted with the issue in the past, but never squarely addressed it. When listing the factors a trial court may consider in making a just and right division of the community estate, we have included "benefits the innocent spouse would have received." *Roberts v. Roberts*, 663 S.W.2d 75, 77 (Tex. App. — Waco 1983, no pet.). By the use of the phrase "innocent spouse," the Court was necessarily referencing some allocation of fault in the break-up of the marriage.

Later, without any real analysis or discussion, a majority of this Court expressly listed "fault in the breakup of the marriage" as a factor the trial court could consider in making a just and right division of the community estate. *Smith v. Smith*, 143 S.W.3d 206, 213 (Tex. App. — Waco 2004, no pet.). "The factors most commonly used to support a disproportionate community property division are fault and disparity in income, earning capacity, business opportunities, and education." *Id.*

The only Texas court, that we have found, which has expressly addressed the issue is Beaumont. *Phillips v. Phillips*, 75 S.W.3d 564 (Tex. App. — Beaumont 2002, no pet.). *Phillips* is a plurality decision. In the lead opinion, Chief Justice Walker opined that because the legislature has authorized no fault divorce, fault could no longer be considered in dividing the community estate. Chief Justice Walker stated:

> . . . By reasonable and logical extension, the above finding permits us to hold that when dissolution of marriage is sought *solely* on the ground of insupportability, evidence of "fault" becomes irrelevant as an analytical construct and may not be considered by the trial court in its "just and right" division of the community estate.

Id. at 572. The lead opinion determined, however, that although the appellant had established error, the appellant had not established that the "trial court clearly abused its discretion in awarding Nancy a disproportionate share of the community estate. The trial court's division of the community estate was neither arbitrary nor unreasonable." *Id.* at 575.

In a concurring opinion, Justice Gaultney disagreed "with the assertion that a trial court has no discretion — under any circumstances, not just those at issue here — to consider conduct causing the divorce in making a just and right division of property when a divorce is granted under section 6.001 of the Family Code."

His analysis is as follows:

> Appellee pleaded fault as a basis for unequal division of the community property. Trial courts have wide discretion to consider a variety of factors in determining what is just and right in dividing community property. For example, in affirming a 72.9% award of community property to a wife one court noted "[a] key factor was [the husband's] abusive and violent nature, which ultimately contributed to the divorce." *Faram v. Gervitz-Faram,* 895 S.W.2d 839, 844 (Tex. App. — Fort Worth 1995, no writ). *See also Vautrain v. Vautrain,* 646 S.W.2d 309, 312 (Tex. App. — Fort Worth 1983, writ dism'd) (trial court may consider evidence of fault even if divorce granted on no fault grounds); *Clay v. Clay,* 550 S.W.2d 730, 734 (Tex.Civ.App.-Houston [1st Dist.] 1977, no writ) (cruelty considered in dividing property, even when the trial court granted divorce on insupportability).
>
> What is "just and right" in dividing the property should not depend on the ground on which the divorce is granted; the just and right division of property is separate from the dissolution issue. If one spouse's conduct causes the destruction of the financial benefits of a particular marriage, benefits on which the other spouse relied, a trial court should have discretion to consider that factor in dividing the community estate — regardless of the basis for granting the divorce.

Id. at 575-574.

In a dissenting opinion, Justice Burgess agreed with Chief Justice Walker that the trial court could not consider fault in the community property division in a divorce granted on a no fault basis. He also concluded, contrary to the lead opinion, that the trial court's error in considering fault in the property division resulted in harm to the appellant. *Id.* at 576.

We agree with Justice Gaultney, that "a trial court should have discretion to consider proven fault" in the break-up of the marriage when making a just and right division of the community estate. We overrule Donald's first issue.

Second Issue

Donald's argument under his second issue is somewhat less focused than his first. He phrases the issue as follows: "The trial court's division of the community estate awarding the wife 100% was arbitrary and unreasonable." His overall summary of argument, however, frames the argument regarding his contention that the trial court's disproportionate division of the marital estate awarding 100% of the estate to Darlene was made without "reference to any guiding rules or principles" and without "due regard for the rights of each party. TEX. FAMILY C. §7.001." Thus, he argues, the trial court's disproportionate division was an abuse of discretion.

As part of his argument, and Donald is representing himself on appeal, Donald "contends he was entitled to such a valuation [of the community estate] and further entitled to a share of the community assets given that he had spent all of thirty-five years loving, supporting, and contributing equally to their community." Donald believes a 50/50 division would be a just and right division. The trial court disagreed.

The Procedure

In an extraordinarily unusual procedure, the trial court conducted a hearing, knowing that Donald had not received notice and was not present. The trial court heard testimony subject to the possibility that Donald might appear for a subsequent hearing once Donald had been properly notified. But the trial court took no action to have Donald brought to court. The trial court had denied Donald's request for a bench warrant. And the trial court did not use any other procedures to allow Donald to present evidence or to otherwise participate in the hearing while yet incarcerated. The trial court scheduled a subsequent hearing and notified Donald thereof. It is clear from the record the trial court did not expect Donald to appear or otherwise participate. Donald was in prison. *See Brown v. State,* 54 S.W.3d 930 (Tex. App. — Corpus Christi 2001, pet. ref'd).

The Hearing (Without Notice to Donald)

Darlene testified that Donald was three years into a 50 year sentence for "molestation of a child."

She provided the testimony necessary to prove up the divorce. She testified generally that during the marriage certain property had been accumulated, including a house, a car, home furnishings, and retirement benefits. She was willing to assume any and all debts that existed against the property.

She also testified about what she thought Donald might do with his share of the marital estate if he received any property. This issue was of significance to his two adult children who testified that their mother should receive a disproportionate share of the community estate.

The adult daughter testified that she thought it was "a fair and reasonable disposition of the community assets" to award her mother, Darlene, the home, "the car, and retirement and stuff like that." She further testified this was necessary for "protection of the family estate."

The adult son likewise testified that he thought it was fair that "whatever is left now be awarded to her," Darlene. He felt "that this is necessary also to preserve the estate from maybe being conveyed away and/or given to some third person."

The trial court then asked Darlene about how Donald's representation in his criminal trial was paid for and how much it cost. Darlene did not know how much had been paid by Donald. She only knew she had paid $1,600 for something. The court and then counsel proceeded to question Darlene again about what Donald might do with any portion of the community estate awarded to him.

The Ruling

In announcing his prospective decision, the court stated "that he's [Donald] used some significant chunk of money out of the community estate to defend that — although he may be entitled to it, it was still a guilty plea — and that he seems, from your testimony, to be only inclined to waste any money he can get out of the community estate now, because everything that you've testified to [about how he intends to spend his portion] sounds like a complete waste."

The property division rendered by the trial court awarded to Donald all the personal property he was in possession of. He is in prison. There was no testimony he was in possession of any personal property.

He was also awarded all cash, retirement accounts, stocks and bonds, and insurance policies in his name. There was no testimony that any such items existed.

The Law

We do not write on a clean slate. This Court has held that the trial court errs in making a division of the community estate which is not supported by the evidence. In *Roberts,* we stated:

> . . . there was no evidence of the relative values of the properties awarded to the parties, and no evidence of the circumstances of the parties, upon which the division made might be justified. Since there was no evidence to support the determination that the division made was just and right, we hold the court abused its discretion in the matter.

Roberts v. Roberts, 621 S.W.2d 835, 838 (Tex. App. — Waco 1981, no pet.).

A majority of this Court has also stated that:

> . . . [b]ecause the debt owed by a spouse is a legally relevant factor in dividing the community estate, a trial court may abuse its discretion if it fails to consider such a factor. . . . The record does not disclose the amount of these debts, so the court could not have considered the amount of these debts in dividing the community estate. . . . Although the court need not divide the community estate equally, a disproportionate division must be supported by some reasonable basis. . . . Having reviewed the record, we find no reasonable basis for the disproportionate division of the community assets and the liabilities of the parties.

Smith v. Smith, 143 S.W.3d 206, 214 (Tex. App. — Waco 2004, no pet.).

Application

Turning back to the evidence presented in this case, the testimony was very general about the community estate. The focus was on three primary reasons justifying a disproportionate division. Those three reasons were 1) fault in causing the divorce; 2) use of community estate assets to pay for Donald's criminal defense; and 3) Donald's lack of need versus the general financial situation in which Donald's criminal conduct had left Darlene.

In essence, with only a sketchy listing of community assets, no discussion of the net value thereof, and affirmatively considering how Donald intended to spend his portion of the community property estate, the trial court awarded all identified net assets to Darlene and nothing to Donald. The problem revealed by this record is that the trial court was not provided adequate information about what was being divided; the value of assets, outstanding debts, and other relevant considerations like Donald's total defense cost. Further, the trial court improperly considered the uses for which Donald was apparently going to spend his community share as opposed to how his intended uses may have reflected on his financial needs and circumstances. In essence, if he intends to "waste" it, he must not have a current financial need for it.

"Although the trial court need not divide the community property equally, a disproportionate division must be supported by some reasonable basis." *Smith v. Smith,* 143 S.W.3d 206, 214 (Tex. App. — Waco 2004, no pet.). We find the trial court abused its discretion in the property division. Donald's second issue is sustained.

holding

Conclusion

We do not conclude that a just and right division could not result in this division, but rather, based upon this record, the trial court abused its discretion in awarding the entire net community estate to Darlene and nothing, or only de minimis assets, to Donald[The trial court's division of the community property estate is reversed and this case is remanded to the trial court for further proceedings consistent with this opinion.]

Discussion Questions

1. Why did the Court of Appeals conclude that "fault" could be considered in the division of community property even though the grounds for divorce were "insupportability" (no-fault)?

2. What does "fault" mean in some of the examples mentioned by the Court?

3. What were the reasons the trial court awarded wife Darlene 100 percent of the community property? Why did the Court of Appeals remand the case to the trial court?

In California, mandatory 50/50 division of community property is the rule at divorce. But in the following unusual case, *Marriage of Rossi*, 90 Cal. App. 4th 34, 108 Cal. Rptr. 2d 270 (2001), the Court of Appeal upheld the trial court's award of 100 percent of the community property lottery winnings to the husband Thomas. While reading the case, consider whether the case would have come out differently if the Court had accepted wife Denise's evidence about her relationship with Thomas.

MARRIAGE OF ROSSI

90 Cal. App. 4th 34, 108 Cal. Rptr. 2d 270 (2001)
Court of Appeal, Second District

Epstein, J.

Denise Rossi appeals from a postjudgment order in this dissolution case, awarding all the lottery winnings concealed by Denise during the dissolution proceedings to her ex-husband, Thomas Rossi.

We conclude that the family court's findings that Denise intentionally concealed the lottery winnings from Thomas and that her conduct constituted fraud within the meaning of Civil Code section 3294 are supported by substantial evidence and that there was no abuse of the court's discretion.

Factual and Procedural Summary

Denise and Thomas were married in 1971. In early November 1996, Bernadette Quercio formed a lottery pool with a group of her co-workers, including Denise. Each member of the pool contributed $5 per week. Denise contributed her $5 for a short time — three weeks — but, according to her papers, on December 1, 1996 or about that date, she withdrew from the pool.

In late December 1996, Ms. Quercio called Denise to say that their group had won the lottery jackpot. The jackpot prize was $6,680,000 and Denise's share was $1,336,000, to be paid in 20 equal annual installments of $66,800 less taxes, from 1996 through 2015. According to declarations by Denise and by Ms. Quercio, Ms. Quercio told her that she wanted to give Denise a share in the jackpot as a gift. Denise explained: "I was afraid to tell [Thomas] because I knew he would try to take the money away from me. I went to the Lottery Commission office and told them I was married but contemplating divorce. They told me to file before I got my first check, which I did. I believed that the lottery winnings were my separate property because they were a gift." In early January 1997, Denise filed a petition for dissolution of marriage in the Los Angeles Superior Court. She never told Thomas about the lottery jackpot. She used her mother's address to receive checks and other information from the California Lottery because it would be safer since Thomas would not see the lottery checks.

Thomas was served with the dissolution petition in January 1997. He and Denise talked about a settlement the same day. Thomas was not represented by counsel in the dissolution proceedings. He and Denise met with Denise's attorney. According to Thomas, he was given several papers to sign to finalize the dissolution. These included a marital settlement agreement and a judgment of dissolution.

Denise filled out a schedule of assets and debts dated January 27, 1997; a final declaration of disclosure; and an income and expense declaration dated January 30, 1997. She did not reveal the lottery winnings in any of these documents, either as community or separate property. Because Thomas did not have an attorney, Denise also filled out Thomas's schedule of assets and debts.

The marital settlement agreement was approved as part of the judgment of dissolution.

Judgment of dissolution was entered April 7, 1997. In 1998, Thomas filed for bankruptcy. In May 1999, a letter was sent to Thomas's home address, asking if Denise was interested in a lump-sum buy-out of her lottery winnings. This was the first Thomas knew about the lottery prize. He confirmed that Denise was a winner with the California Lottery. Thomas retained counsel, who contacted Denise's attorney. According to a declaration filed by Thomas's counsel, Denise's attorney confirmed that she had won a share of a lottery prize, "however, his client was unwilling to share any 'meaningful' amount of the Lottery proceeds. . . ."

In July 1999, Thomas filed a motion to set aside the dissolution of marriage based on fraud, breach of fiduciary duty and failure to disclose; for adjudication of the lottery winnings as an omitted asset; and sought the award of 100 percent of the lottery winnings pursuant to Family Code section 1101, subdivision (h).[2] Thomas also sought an award of his attorney's fees under section 1101, subdivision (g). Thomas sought ex parte orders for an accounting and a restraining order preventing the disposition of any of the lottery proceeds paid to Denise or of any assets obtained with lottery proceeds.

The trial court ordered an accounting of lottery proceeds received by Denise; restrained the disposition of lottery proceeds; and ordered that all lottery proceeds

---

2. All statutory references are to the Family Code unless otherwise indicated.

be placed in a money market account with no right of withdrawal without court order or joint consent of Thomas and Denise, except in the ordinary course of business or for necessities of life.

The trial court found that Denise intentionally failed to disclose her lottery winnings in the marital settlement agreement, the judgment, and her declaration of disclosure. It found that Denise breached her fiduciary duties under sections 721, 1100, 2100, and 2101 by fraudulently failing to disclose the lottery winnings and that she intentionally breached her warranties and representations set forth in the Marital Settlement Agreement. The court specifically found that Denise's failure to disclose the lottery winnings constituted fraud, oppression and malice within the meaning of Civil Code section 3294 and section 1101, subdivision (h). The trial court awarded Thomas 100 percent of the lottery winnings pursuant to Provision E of the Judgment of Dissolution, paragraph 9.1 of the Marital Settlement Agreement, and section 1101, subdivisions (g) and (h).

The trial court found that Denise's evidence that her share of the lottery winnings was a gift was not credible, and concluded that the lottery winnings were community property. Denise filed a timely notice of appeal.

DISCUSSION

We review factual findings of the family court for substantial evidence, examining the evidence in the light most favorable to the prevailing party. Because Civil Code section 3294 requires proof by "clear and convincing evidence" of fraud, oppression, or malice, we must inquire whether the record contains " 'substantial evidence to support a determination by clear and convincing evidence. . . .' " (*Shade Foods, Inc. v. Innovative Products Sales & Marketing, Inc.* (2000) 78 Cal. App. 4th 847, 891, 93 Cal. Rptr. 2d 364.)

The court found that Denise intentionally concealed her lottery winnings during the dissolution proceedings and that her conduct constituted fraud, oppression, and malice within the meaning of Civil Code section 3294 and section 1101, subdivision (h). On that basis, it awarded Thomas 100 percent of the winnings.

Section 721, subdivision (b) imposes a fiduciary duty on spouses in transactions between themselves: "This confidential relationship imposes a duty of the highest good faith and fair dealing on each spouse, and neither shall take any unfair advantage of the other. This confidential relationship is a fiduciary relationship subject to the same rights and duties of nonmarital business partners, as provided in Sections 15019, 15020, 15021, and 15022 of the Corporations Code, . . ."

Section 1101, subdivision (h) provides: "Remedies for the breach of the fiduciary duty by one spouse when the breach falls within the ambit of Section 3294 of the Civil Code shall include, but not be limited to, an award to the other spouse of 100 percent, or an amount equal to 100 percent, of any asset undisclosed or transferred in breach of the fiduciary duty."

Thomas argues that imposition of the 100 percent penalty under section 1101, subdivision (h) was mandatory, once the family court found that Denise acted with fraud, oppression or malice in concealing the lottery winnings during the dissolution proceedings.

The correctness of the family court's order awarding Thomas all of the lottery winnings is based on the finding that Denise's conduct constituted fraud within the meaning of Civil Code section 3294. Civil Code section 3294 provides in pertinent part: "(a) In an action for the breach of an obligation not arising from contract, where it is proven by clear and convincing evidence that the defendant has been guilty of oppression, fraud, or malice, the plaintiff, in addition to the actual damages, may recover damages for the sake of example and by way of punishing the defendant. [¶] .... [¶] (c) As used in this section, the following definitions shall apply: [¶] (1) 'Malice' means conduct which is intended by the defendant to cause injury to the plaintiff or despicable conduct which is carried on by the defendant with a willful and conscious disregard of the rights or safety of others. [¶] (2) 'Oppression' means despicable conduct that subjects a person to cruel and unjust hardship in conscious disregard of that person's rights. [¶] (3) 'Fraud' means an intentional misrepresentation, deceit, or concealment of a material fact known to the defendant with the intention on the part of the defendant of thereby depriving a person of property or legal rights or otherwise causing injury...."

The evidence established that Denise filed for dissolution after learning that she had won a share of a substantial lottery jackpot; that she consulted the Lottery Commission personnel about ways in which she could avoid sharing the jackpot with her husband; that she used her mother's address for all communications with the Lottery Commission to avoid notifying Thomas of her winnings; and that she failed to disclose the winnings at any time during the dissolution proceedings, despite her warranties in the marital settlement agreement and the judgment that all assets had been disclosed. The family court expressly rejected her evidence that the winnings constituted a gift and, as such, were her separate property. The record supports the family court's conclusion that Denise intentionally concealed the lottery winnings and that they were community property.

Denise argues she committed no fraud because the statutory definition of that term "denotes conduct much more malicious and vile in nature than the failure of a physically and emotionally abused woman to disclose an asset to her husband, whose gambling and money mismanagement problems detrimentally affected her life and caused her to file for bankruptcy and caused him to threaten to kill her. In not disclosing what Denise Rossi believed was her separate property, Denise Rossi did not intend to deprive Respondent of an asset that he was entitled to because she felt it belonged to her alone. Denise Rossi did not believe that she was misappropriating a community asset, and therefore did not have the requisite fraudulent intent to deprive Respondent of a community asset."

The problem with her argument is that the court expressly found her evidence was not credible. The record supports this finding. The court put it in the following clear terms: "I believe the funds used to purchase the ticket were community. I don't believe the story about the gift." The court expressly found that Denise intentionally failed to disclose her lottery winnings in the marital settlement agreement, the judgment and her declaration of disclosure. This case presents precisely the circumstance that section 1101, subdivision (h) is intended to address. Here, one spouse intentionally concealed a significant community property asset. She intentionally consulted with the Lottery Commission as to how to deprive Thomas of a share of the prize; used her mother's address for all communications with the lottery; and did not disclose the winnings in the dissolution proceedings. This supports a finding of fraud within the meaning of Civil Code section 3294. The family court properly concluded that under these circumstances, Thomas was entitled to 100 percent of the lottery winnings under section 1101, subdivision (h).

As we observed in *In re Marriage of Hokanson.* "The clear import of the language in subdivision (h) is that an award of attorney fees is discretionary, over and above the mandatory award of the entire asset at issue." The strong language of section 1101, subdivision (h) serves an important purpose: full disclosure of marital assets is absolutely essential to the trial court in determining the proper dissolution of property and resolving support issues. The statutory scheme for dissolution depends on the parties' full disclosure of all assets so they may be taken into account by the trial court. A failure to make such disclosure is properly subject to the severe sanction of section 1101, subdivision (h).

We find nothing in the language of the statute to justify an exception to the penalty provision of section 1101, subdivision (h) because of the supposed unclean hands of the spouse from whom the asset was concealed. Nor are we cited to legislative history which would suggest such an exception. None of the cases cited by Denise in support of her unclean hands defense is a family law case construing section 1101. This undercuts Denise's primary argument on appeal, that she was justified in concealing the lottery winnings because of Thomas's behavior. The plain meaning of section 1101, subdivision (h) disposes of Denise's argument that there should be a "downward departure in any remedy against Denise" because, as she claims, she was battered emotionally and physically by Thomas. She cites federal law to the effect that evidence of the battered woman's syndrome is a valid basis for a discretionary downward departure of criminal penalties otherwise applicable under federal criminal sentencing guidelines, and to California criminal cases addressing this syndrome. As we have discussed, no such exception is codified into section 1101. The cases cited are off point. The statute provides that, where a spouse conceals assets under circumstances satisfying the criteria for punitive damages under Civil Code section 3294, a penalty representing 100 percent of the concealed asset is warranted. The statute is unambiguous and no exception is provided.

DISPOSITION

The order of the family court is affirmed. Respondent is to have his costs on appeal.

CHARLES S. VOGEL, P.J., HASTINGS, J., concur.

Discussion Questions

1. Why did Denise conceal the lottery winnings from Thomas?
2. Why did the Court of Appeal uphold the award to Thomas of 100 percent of the lottery winnings?
3. Could a court in Texas have come to the same or different result?

PROBLEM 1.1

Our hypothetical couple George and Martha, who had been married many years, decided to move to Idaho. Soon after they moved, George received an inheritance from his father who owned a cherry orchard. They purchased a cabin in the mountains and used the funds from George's inheritance to pay for it. They take the title as "George and Martha, husband and wife, as community property." They were advised by their financial planner to take the cabin as "community property" because of the tax advantage if one of them died. Even though the property title said "community property," George thought that the cabin belonged to him because they used his inheritance to pay for it. Martha thought that since they now lived in a community property state and the title said community property, it belonged to both of them. How would an Idaho court characterize the cabin?

PROBLEM 1.2

Our hypothetical couple, Harry and Wilma, has accumulated a large sum of money from their jobs. They decided to use their savings to create a company that restores old photographs to present-day standards. Harry, who studied photograph restoration as a hobby, runs the company. The company is a success and is now worth over $1 million. Wilma has recently found out that Harry has been having a secret affair with one of his assistants in the company and has been supporting this assistant with funds from the company. She is considering filing for a divorce. She consults with an attorney about her rights to the company. What would be her rights if she was living in Texas? California?

Chapter 2

The Decision to Marry: Opting In or Out of the Community Property System

The community property system applies to married couples. It represents a system that exemplifies sharing. That means that when a couple marries, the state imposes a particular system on the property that they acquire during the marriage. The main concept is of shared ownership in the earnings of each spouse. Some may not buy into the system because they have in mind the stereotype of a wife who sits at home reading romance novels and eating bonbons or a husband who sits on the couch all day with the remote and drinks beer. Under either stereotype, under community property law, the at-home spouse shares in the earnings of the spouse working outside the home. One way to avoid the community property system is not to marry, but instead live with each other without a formal license and ceremony.

Consider three hypothetical couples. George and Martha are an older couple. They were both widowed after long marriages. They have arranged their affairs so that their children will be taken care of when they pass on. They decide that getting married would complicate their financial arrangements and decide instead to live together, sharing companionship and expenses, but not the obligations that marriage entails. Harry and Wilma are a couple that has experienced divorce in the past. They each have a negative view of the divorce process and decide that marriage is not for them. They think that living together would help them avoid the unpleasantness that might result if their relationship does not work out as anticipated. Michael and Lisa are the youngest of our hypothetical couples. They believe in independence and do not want the "strictures" of marriage. They had witnessed their own parents' divorces and are unwilling to commit to marriage, but have developed a relationship that led them to decide to live together.

These couples may live together for a period of years and some may believe that they have a "common law" marriage, even though they didn't formally marry. In most cases, if they live in a community property state, they are mistaken. All community property states have abolished common law marriage, except for Texas. The earliest to abolish common law marriage was Washington in 1892 and the most recent is Idaho in 1996. Common law marriage or informal marriage was widely accepted in the 19th century but gradually there has been a shift toward increased formality in the creation of a valid marriage. Even Texas, the only community property state recognizing common law marriage, has imposed stringent requirements to establish a common law marriage.

Estate of Wagner (1995) is a representative case of how Idaho treats common law marriage. Elizabeth Becker claimed that she was married to Bryan Wagner even though they lived together only from September 1992 until Wagner died in March 1993. The Supreme Court of Idaho found there was no common law marriage. Two Texas unreported cases, *Knight v. Volkart-Knight* (2001) and *Quinn v. Milanizadeh* (2008), explore the "representing to others" requirement to prove a common law marriage or informal marriage. *Quinn v. Milanizadeh* is illustrative of all the requirements of common law marriage.

A.   CRITERIA FOR ESTABLISHING A COMMON-LAW MARRIAGE: THE IDAHO AND TEXAS APPROACHES

1.   Idaho

ESTATE OF WAGNER
126 Idaho 848, 893 P.2d 211 (1995)
Supreme Court of Idaho

Silak, Justice.

This is an appeal from an order of the district court reversing the magistrate's finding that no common law marriage existed between the decedent and the respondent. We reverse the district court's decision, vacating its order, and reinstate the order of the magistrate.

I.

FACTS AND PROCEDURAL BACKGROUND

In approximately September 1992, the decedent, Bryan Rudolph Wagner (Wagner), and respondent, Elizabeth Becker (Becker), and her ten year old daughter from a previous marriage, Crystal Lee Becker, began living together in Becker's house in Lewiston, Idaho. In November 1992, Wagner proposed marriage to Becker and she accepted. Becker claims that she and Wagner consented to a common law marriage at the time he asked her to marry him in November 1992, and that they had an oral contract of marriage from that time on. A ceremonial marriage was planned for April 1993 in Reno, Nevada. Becker testified that even though they were common law married in November 1992, the couple wanted a ceremonial marriage for religious purposes.

Becker's Idaho driver's license expired in December 1992. She testified that she did not renew it under the name of Wagner because she did not know how to legally change it due to the common law marriage.

In January 1993, Wagner and Becker purchased wedding rings on layaway. The rings were paid off in early March 1993, and Becker immediately began wearing her ring.

In February 1993, Becker changed the name on her checking account at First Security Bank to Wagner. Although Becker received a letter from the bank informing her that in order for her to change the name on her account she was required to provide new signature cards and a copy of a marriage license, the checks were printed with the change. Becker wrote checks on this account, but not until after Wagner died. Wagner and Becker did not have a joint checking or savings account at any time.

Becker also ordered and received a First Security Cash Card in the name of Liz Wagner, and a Sprint Foncard in the name of Liz A. Wagner. The cash card was ordered at the same time she changed the name on her checking account, and the Sprint card was changed in early March 1993.

Becker testified that she and Wagner each contributed funds for groceries and each paid certain of the household bills. She also testified that they saved cash in a coffee can for the purchase of the wedding rings and the planned trip to Reno, Nevada in April 1993.

On March 19, 1993, Wagner died intestate. Thereafter, Becker filed an application for informal appointment as personal representative claiming that her interest in Wagner's estate was that of spouse at common law. Pursuant to her application, the magistrate, acting as registrar, appointed Becker personal representative of the decedent. At the same time, he issued letters of administration to Becker.

In April 1993, Appellant Terry Lynn Hall (Hall), the mother of the decedent, filed a petition for removal of personal representative, claiming that Becker either mistakenly or intentionally misrepresented in her petition for appointment that she was the common law wife of Wagner.

After a hearing on Hall's petition, the magistrate issued an opinion and order ruling that a common law marriage did not exist between Wagner and Becker. Hall's petition was therefore granted and letters of administration were issued to her.

On appeal, the district court reversed the magistrate's ruling, finding that a common law marriage existed between Wagner and Becker. Becker was thus reappointed personal representative of Wagner's estate. Hall appealed to this Court.

The issue on appeal is whether the magistrate court's findings are supported by substantial, competent evidence.

II.

ANALYSIS

* * *

B. The Trial Court Did Not Err in Ruling that No Common Law Marriage Existed Between Becker and Wagner

1. The Current State of the Law

A non-ceremonial marriage may be proven by a preponderance of the evidence in Idaho. Once a common law claimant proves the elements of a common law marriage by a preponderance of the evidence, this Court has held that a presumption of validity of the marriage arises and the burden of production shifts to the opposing party to show by clear and positive proof that the asserted marriage is invalid.

In deciding whether a common law marriage exists, we must first look to the pertinent statutory provisions. They are:

> I.C. §32-301. How solemnized. — Marriage must be solemnized, authenticated and recorded as provided in this chapter, but noncompliance with its provisions does not invalidate any lawful marriage.
>
> I.C. §32-201. What constitutes marriage. — Marriage is a personal relation arising out of a civil contract, to which the consent of parties capable of making it is necessary. Consent alone will not constitute marriage; it must be followed by a solemnization, or by a mutual assumption of marital rights, duties or obligations.
>
> I.C. §32-203. Proof of consent and consummation. — Consent to and subsequent consummation of marriage may be manifested in any form, and may be proved under the same general rules of evidence as facts in other cases.

These statutes set forth two general requirements for a finding that a common law marriage exists: 1) consent by the parties to enter into a contract of marriage, given at the time of contracting; and 2) the mutual assumption of marital rights, duties and obligations.

Although not separately designated elements of the doctrine under the statutory framework, proof of cohabitation of the parties and holding oneself out as being married are two of the best methods for proving that there was consent to the contract in the absence of a writing to that effect. With respect to the consent element, we have held that it need not be manifest by any identifiable conduct nor are there any magic words which must be spoken. Rather, consent may be express or implied from the parties' conduct. Evidence of conduct by and between the parties consistent with the existence of a common law marriage thus may be probative of consent. For example, when competent parties have held themselves out to be husband and wife and have gained the general reputation in the community as being such, or where they acknowledge they are husband and wife, a court may draw the inference that there was mutual consent between the parties to assume a marital relationship. Further, it is clear from this Court's prior cases that the element of consent found in I.C. §32-201 may be proven by circumstantial evidence such as cohabitation, reputation and the manner in which the couple characterize their relationship. Because frequently, questions as to the existence of such a marriage arise after the death of one party, common law marriage may be proven by the testimony of only the surviving party.

With respect to the present case then, Becker was required to make a prima facie showing of consent to marriage along with an assumption of marital rights, duties and obligations. This showing could have been made by evidence that she and Wagner assumed marital rights, duties, and obligations, cohabited, and held themselves out as being married. If she made such a showing, a presumption of the validity of the marriage would arise, shifting the burden to Hall to rebut the presumption by clear and positive proof of its invalidity.

2. The Magistrate Did Not Err in Concluding that Becker Failed to Make a Prima Facie Showing of Common Law Marriage and that the Presumption of Marriage Therefore Did Not Arise

In the present case, the magistrate found that Wagner and Becker began cohabiting in approximately September 1992. We hold that his finding is clearly supported by the record, and that the parties cohabited from September 1992 until Wagner's death in March 1993.

With respect to the element of the assumption of marital rights, duties and obligations, Hall argues that the magistrate correctly found that Becker had failed to offer sufficient proof of such assumption. We agree.

Becker claims that she and Wagner became common law husband and wife in November 1992 when Wagner proposed to her. However, for the year ending December 31, 1992, she filed a separate "Head of Household" income tax return. Wagner filed a "Single" tax return rather than a "Married" return even though, the magistrate found, he had recently had severe tax liability problems and the filing of a "Married" return would have affected both his and Becker's tax consequences for 1992. Additionally, between the date of the alleged marriage in November 1992, and Wagner's death in March 1993, Becker did not change her employment records. Although she did change the name on her checking account, ATM card and her Sprint Foncard from Becker to Wagner, these changes were not made until February and March 1993, and are more indicative of preparation for her upcoming April wedding.

Wagner and Becker did not commingle their funds. Although allegedly married in November 1992, they held no joint financial accounts at the time of Wagner's death, and neither deposited funds into the other's accounts. While the evidence shows that there was some commingling in the form of cash being set aside by both of them in a coffee can to pay for wedding rings and a trip to Reno, Nevada for the wedding ceremony, such commingling is too minimal to warrant a finding of assumption of the rights, duties and obligations of marriage. Further, the finding that Becker and Wagner were each responsible for certain household debts is evidence of non-commingling of funds. Thus, we hold that Becker failed to make an adequate showing that she and Wagner assumed the rights, duties and obligations of marriage.

With respect to the element of holding themselves out in the community as being married, the magistrate found the evidence to be conflicting. According to the record, there were a few occasions in which Wagner may have referred to

Becker in such a way that the listener could believe they were married. However, the instances in which both Wagner and Becker could have addressed the other as husband and wife, but did not do so, far outweigh the other. Indeed, Becker testifies that she never introduced Wagner as her husband and he never introduced her as his wife. In fact, there was evidence that Wagner introduced Becker as his "fiance" at a Christmas party in December 1992. We hold that the magistrate's findings are supported by substantial and competent evidence, even though conflicting. The magistrate is in the best position to judge the demeanor and credibility of the witnesses.

We do not place too much weight on the magistrate's finding that Becker and Wagner were not married because Becker did not change the name on her driver's license in December 1992 when she had an opportunity to do so due at its expiration. In our current times, many women for many reasons choose to retain their maiden names after they are married. This may not be the case here, however, since Becker did change her name on two accounts prior to the planned April 1993 wedding. In any event, we hold that the evidence on the element of Becker and Wagner holding themselves out as being married is conflicting, and therefore defer to the findings of the trial court.

III.

CONCLUSION

We hold that the magistrate's finding that the presumption of marriage did not arise in this case is supported by substantial and competent evidence. Although there is no question that Becker and Wagner cohabited from September 1992 until Wagner's death in March 1993, the evidence is conflicting with respect to whether the couple assumed marital rights, duties and obligations, and whether they held themselves out to the community as husband and wife. We will not disturb the trial court's factual findings where they are supported by substantial and competent, although conflicting, evidence. Because the presumption of a valid marriage did not arise, the burden never shifted to Hall to prove by clear and positive evidence that the marriage was invalid. Accordingly, the order of the district court is vacated, and the order of the magistrate is reinstated.

Discussion Questions

1. What were the main reasons that Becker was not found to have a common law marriage with Wagner?

2. Would the result have been different if Becker and Wagner had lived together for many years but never did have a ceremonial marriage?

3. Why do you think that the Idaho legislature decided to abolish common law marriage? Why didn't the new statute apply to invalidate common law marriages prior to 1996?

IDAHO CODE

§32-201. What constitutes marriage — No common-law marriage
after January 1, 1996

(1) Marriage is a personal relationship arising out of a civil contract between a man and a woman, to which the consent of parties capable of making it is necessary. Consent alone will not constitute marriage; it must be followed by the issuance of a license and a solemnization as authorized and provided by law. Marriage created by a mutual assumption of marital rights, duties or obligations shall not be recognized as a lawful marriage.

(2) The provisions of subsection (1) of this section requiring the issuance of a license and a solemnization shall not invalidate any marriage contract in effect prior to January 1, 1996, created by consenting parties through a mutual assumption of marital rights, duties or obligations.

2.   *Texas*

VERNON'S TEXAS STATUTES

§2.401. Proof of informal marriage
Effective: September 1, 2005

(a) In a judicial, administrative, or other proceeding, the marriage of a man and woman may be proved by evidence that:

(1) a declaration of their marriage has been signed as provided by this sub-chapter; or

(2) the man and woman agreed to be married and after the agreement they lived together in this state as husband and wife and there represented to others that they were married.

(b) If a proceeding in which a marriage is to be proved as provided by Subsection (a)(2) is not commenced before the second anniversary of the date on which the parties separated and ceased living together, it is rebuttably presumed that the parties did not enter into an agreement to be married.

(c) A person under 18 years of age may not:

(1) be a party to an informal marriage; or

(2) execute a declaration of informal marriage under Section 2.402.

(d) A person may not be a party to an informal marriage or execute a declaration of an informal marriage if the person is presently married to a person who is not the other party to the informal marriage or declaration of an informal marriage, as applicable.

KNIGHT v. VOLKART-KNIGHT

2001 WL 892250 (2001)
Court of Appeals of Texas

Before Hinojosa, Yañez, and Castillo, JJ.

Yañez.

appellant
appellee

Appellant, Oscar Knight, appeals the trial court's granting of a final decree of divorce in a suit brought by appellee, Reba Lavella Volkart-Knight,[1] to dissolve an alleged informal marriage. [A]ppellant challenges: the legal and factual sufficiency of the evidence supporting the trial court's determination that a common-law marriage existed; Because we find the evidence factually insufficient to support one of the required elements of a common-law marriage, we reverse.

BACKGROUND

Many of the facts in this case are in dispute; however, the following facts are not disputed. Between May and June, 1995, appellant began staying overnight at appellee's house. In July 1997, appellant purchased "The Koffee Klatch," a restaurant which appellee managed. On April 9, 1998, the parties ceased to be involved as a couple, and this action was filed by appellee on April 28, 1998. Following a bench trial, the trial court: (1) found that a common-law marriage existed; (2) granted a divorce; (3) found that a downpayment made by appellant on the restaurant was a gift to appellee, and awarded the restaurant to appellee; and (4) awarded certain property to each party, and allocated certain debts between the parties. This appeal ensued.

INFORMAL MARRIAGE

The three elements of a common-law marriage are: (1) an agreement to be married; (2) after the agreement, living together in Texas as husband and wife; and (3) representing to others in Texas that they are married. Tex. Fam. Code Ann. §2.401(a)(2) (Vernon 1998). A common-law marriage does not exist until the concurrence of all three elements. The burden of proof is on the one seeking to establish the existence of such a marriage. A proponent may prove an agreement to be married by circumstantial as well as direct evidence.

The statutory requirement of "representation to others" is synonymous with the judicial requirement of "holding out to the public." It is well-settled that "holding out" may be established by conduct and actions of the parties. Spoken words are not necessary to establish representation as husband and wife. Occasional introductions as husband and wife do not establish the element of holding out. The requirement of holding out may be established by evidence that the couple has a reputation in the community for being married.

DISCUSSION

Appellant argues that the evidence presented at trial is legally and factually insufficient to support the trial court's finding that an informal marriage existed. Appellant challenges the legal and factual sufficiency of all three

---

1. The record indicates that appellee never used the surname "Knight" in any manner prior to filing suit in district court to dissolve the alleged informal marriage.

elements: an agreement to be married, living together as man and wife, and representing to others that they were married. We begin by addressing the legal and factual sufficiency of the evidence supporting the implied finding that the parties represented to others that they were married.

Legal Sufficiency of Holding Out

In the present case, a friend of appellee and two of her employees testified that they heard appellant refer to appellee as his wife to several customers. A cook at the restaurant testified that he heard both employees and customers discussing the marriage between appellant and appellee. Appellee's daughter also testified that customers stated that appellant and appellee were married. This is more than a scintilla of evidence that the parties represented to others that they were married. We reject appellant's legal sufficiency challenge to the holding out requirement.

Factual Sufficiency of Holding Out

During direct examination, appellee testified that only close friends, family members, and some of the restaurant's customers were informed of the marriage between the parties. Additionally, those witnesses who testified that they were told of the alleged marriage consisted of close friends, employees, and family members. Occasional introductions as husband and wife do not establish the element of holding out. In her testimony during direct examination, appellee admitted that she and appellant did not seek a religious or civil marriage ceremony because they did not want public acknowledgment of their marriage.

In contrast to the testimony of appellee's witnesses, appellant presented friends, customers, and a former employee who testified that the couple never held themselves out as married. Appellant also presented the testimony of the couple's accountant and a loan officer. Both appellee and her accountant testified that during the period in which she claims to have been married to appellant, she filed income tax returns with the Internal Revenue Service listing her marital status as separate and single. On appeal, appellee argues that it is common practice for individuals to misrepresent information on their income tax returns for financial purposes. However, appellee cites us to no authority, and we have found none, providing an exception to the holding out requirement for the IRS. Additionally, appellee's accountant, an individual whom she knew in a professional capacity well before she met appellant, was first notified of the alleged marriage only after appellee's petition for divorce was filed.

The record also contains evidence that appellee represented herself as single when signing as a co-borrower with appellant on a loan. The loan officer testified that different procedures exist when a married couple applies for a loan as opposed to when two people apply for a loan as co-borrowers. Appellant and appellee did not apply for the loan as husband and wife, and did not protest when given loan applications for non-married individuals. Considering that appellee's evidence shows that she held out only to family, friends, and some customers, we afford great significance to the testimony regarding appellee's tax statements and loan application. Considering all the evidence, we hold that the evidence is factually insufficient to support the required element that the parties represented to others that they were married.

CONCLUSION

We hold that appellee's testimony as to the nature of her relationship with appellant, as well as the testimony of appellee's witnesses, provides more than a scintilla of evidence that the parties represented to others that they were married. Considering all the evidence, however, including appellee's representation of her status as "single" on a loan application and her tax returns, we conclude that the evidence supporting the implied finding that the parties represented to others that they were married is so weak and insufficient as to be manifestly unjust.

Because we find the evidence is factually insufficient to support the required element of an informal marriage that the parties represented to others that they were married, we hold that appellee failed to establish an informal marriage. We sustain appellant's first issue.

Because we have found that appellee failed to establish an informal marriage, the court's other orders concerning the granting of a divorce and the award of certain property and allocation of debts cannot stand.

We REVERSE the judgment of the trial court and REMAND for further action consistent with this opinion.

QUINN v. MILANIZADEH

2008 WL 828327 (2008)
Court of Appeals of Texas

Panel consists of Justices NUCHIA, HANKS, and HIGLEY.

LAURA CARTER HIGLEY, Justice.

This appeal arises from the divorce proceeding between appellant, Tyrone Michael Quinn, and appellee, Shaleh Rene Milanizadeh. Quinn challenges the trial court's "Final Decree of Divorce" by contending that the evidence did not show that a common-law marriage existed between Quinn and Milanizadeh. . . .

We affirm.

BACKGROUND

In June 1998, Quinn and Milanizadeh began dating. One year later, Milanizadeh moved to Atlanta to live with Quinn, who had taken a job there. In 2000, the couple separated and Milanizadeh moved back to Houston. Two weeks after she returned to Houston, Milanizadeh discovered that she was pregnant. After learning of the pregnancy, Quinn moved back to Houston. The couple's daughter, S.Q., was born on June 30, 2001.

Quinn and Milanizadeh purchased a home together in October 2001. Quinn resided in the home with Milanizadeh and his daughter. In April 2004, Quinn began working in Kuwait. Originally, Quinn had signed a one-year contract to work over-seas, but then signed another contract and stayed a second year in Kuwait. During that time, when Quinn returned on vacation, he would stay with Milanizadeh at their home. In August 2005, while working in Kuwait, Quinn purchased a high-rise condominium unit in Dubai for investment purposes.

After finishing his work in Kuwait, Quinn returned home in June 2006 to live with Milanizadeh. After learning that Quinn had engaged in infidelities, Milanizadeh filed for divorce on August 31, 2006. At that time, Quinn still resided with Milanizadeh.

The case was referred to and tried by an associate judge.

The issues tried to the associate judge were whether a common-law marriage existed between Quinn and Milanizadeh and, if so, the proper division of the marital estate. During trial, the associate judge first found that a marriage existed between Quinn and Milanizadeh. Trial then proceeded with respect to division of the marital estate.

Three weeks after trial, the associate judge sent the parties his written recommendations with respect to the marital estate. The associate judge made the following pertinent awards: (1) Milanizadeh was awarded the couple's home and the balances in all bank and savings accounts and (2) Quinn was awarded the condominium in Dubai.

Neither party requested a de novo review by the referring judge, and the referring judge signed a "Final Decree of Divorce" incorporating the associate judge's recommendations. Quinn now appeals the decree.

* * *

[A]

Common-Law Marriage

Appellant contends, "The trial court committed an abuse of discretion when it concluded a common-law marriage existed between the parties." Fairly considering his appellate arguments, we construe [this] issue to be a challenge to the legal and factual sufficiency of the evidence to support the finding that a common-law marriage existed between Quinn and Milanizadeh.

Common-Law Marriage: The Basic Principles

It is undisputed that no ceremonial marriage occurred between Quinn and Milanizadeh. Rather, the question presented at trial was whether they were married by virtue of an informal, or as known colloquially, a "common-law marriage." By finding that Quinn and Milanizadeh were married, the associate judge implicitly found that Quinn and Milanizadeh had entered into a common-law marriage.

In Texas, common-law marriage can be established by showing that the parties (1) agreed to be married; (2) cohabitated in Texas as husband and wife; and (3) represented to others that they were married. TEX. FAM. CODE ANN. §2.401(a)(2) (Vernon 2006). As the proponent of the marriage, Milanizadeh had the burden of proof on these elements. The existence of a common-law marriage is a question of fact to be resolved by the fact-finder.

C.   ANALYSIS

1.   AGREEMENT TO BE MARRIED

Quinn first challenges the associate judge's implied finding that he and Milanizadeh had an agreement to be married.

To establish an agreement to be married, "the evidence must show the parties intended to have a present, immediate, and permanent marital relationship and that they did in fact agree to be husband and wife." The agreement to be married may be established by direct or circumstantial evidence. The testimony of one of the parties to the marriage constitutes direct evidence that the parties agreed to be married. The conduct of the parties, evidence of cohabitation, and representations to others may constitute circumstantial evidence of an agreement, depending on the facts of the case.

At trial, Milanizadeh presented direct and circumstantial evidence supporting her claim that the parties agreed to be married.

Milanizadeh first testified that when she moved from Houston to Atlanta in June 1999 to live with Quinn, she and Quinn agreed that they were married. She testified that when she first arrived in Atlanta, Quinn said, "Hello, Mrs. Quinn."

Milanizadeh also presented evidence that the agreement to be married continued once the couple returned to Texas. The evidence showed that Quinn and Milanizadeh purchased a home together in October 2001 with a "VA loan." Milanizadeh testified that she was identified in the VA loan papers as Quinn's wife. The evidence further showed that the couple lived together in the home they purchased together. Quinn does not dispute that he resided with Milanizadeh in the home until April 2004, when he went to work in Kuwait. Milanizadeh testified that when Quinn came back to Houston on vacation while he worked overseas, he would stay at the home they purchased together. After his employment in Kuwait ended in June 2006, Quinn returned to Houston and again lived with Milanizadeh in the home they had purchased together. In July 2006, the couple went on a vacation together to Aruba and purchased a time share there together. Quinn testified that when he accepted a another job in Kuwait in the summer of 2006, he asked Milanizadeh to move there with him; however, Milanizadeh declined because she was in school to earn her master's degree.

Milanizadeh and Quinn both testified that Quinn had Milanizadeh on his health insurance plan for two years.

Milanizadeh also testified that Quinn's family referred to her as their daughter-in-law and her family referred to Quinn as their son-in-law. A friend of Milanizadeh, who testified at trial, stated that she thought Quinn and Milanizadeh were married. Quinn claims such evidence is insufficient to show an agreement because it is contradicted by other evidence in the record, most prominently his own testimony that he did not agree he and Milanizadeh were married. Quinn points out that Milanizadeh testified that she and Quinn had essentially ended their relationship in 2000 when she left Atlanta to return to Houston. But, Milanizadeh also testified that after she found out she was pregnant, Quinn moved to Houston, and the two bought a home together, indicating a reconciliation.

Quinn also cites the testimony of Milanizadeh's friend, who testified, although she heard Milanizadeh refer to Quinn as her husband, she never heard Quinn refer to Milanizadeh as his wife. Nonetheless, as mentioned above, the friend testified that she thought that Quinn and Milanizadeh were married.

In addition, Quinn points to a document, entitled "Contract Agreement," that he and Milanizadeh signed with respect to the purchase of their home. The document provided that, if after five years, either Quinn or Milanizadeh wished to sell the home, the other party must either agree to the sale of the home or must buy 50 per cent of the equity accrued in the home to the other party. The document also provided, "Common law marriage should not be taken in consideration with respect to this document."

Regarding the Contract Agreement, Milanizadeh testified that, though the document states that the parties were not signing under duress, she felt pressured by Quinn to sign it. She testified that Quinn asked her to sign the document on the day they were scheduled to close on the house. Milanizadeh stated that her daughter was only three months old, and they had already given notice on the apartment in which they had been living. She feared that if she did not sign the document, the closing would not take place, and they would have no place to live.

Quinn further points out that he and Milanizadeh had separate bank accounts and that he and Milanizadeh filed separate tax returns, filing as single persons. Milanizadeh testified that she and Quinn filed in this manner because it was more economically advantageous to them.

Quinn also asserts that Milanizadeh's claim that the couple had an agreement to be married is undermined by her own testimony that she knew that Quinn was "dating" other women. Despite Quinn's characterization, Milanizadeh testified that she learned that Quinn was engaging in infidelities, not that he was "dating" other women.

Quinn further cites evidence that, when the Dubai condominium was purchased, he purchased it alone. In contrast, Milanizadeh testified that Quinn used funds belonging to the marital estate to purchase the property. According to Milanizadeh, the two had discussed the purchase, and Quinn had told her that the purchase was an investment.

In sum, the evidence referenced by Quinn goes to the weight afforded the evidence and does not serve to negate a common-law marriage. Thus, any conflicts in the evidence did not preclude an implicit finding that Quinn and Milanizadeh had agreed that they were married; rather the conflicts go to the weight of the evidence and were for the fact-finder to resolve.

Lastly, Quinn contends that, because he ceased living with Milanizadeh on April 21, 2004 when he moved to Kuwait for work, Family Code section 2.401(b) operates to create a rebuttable presumption that there was no agreement between the couple that they were married. Section 2.401(b) provides that if the proponent of the marriage does not commence a proceeding to prove the marriage under Family Code section 2.401(a)(2) within two years of the date on which the parties to the alleged marriage separated and ceased living together, then there is a rebuttable presumption that the parties did not enter into an agreement to be married. Tex. Fam. Code Ann. §2.401(b). The undisputed record reveals that, after he returned from Kuwait in June 2006, Quinn lived with Milanizadeh for at least two months before she filed for divorce on August 31, 2006. Thus, the rebuttable presumption contemplated in section 2.401(b) has no application in this case.

2.   COHABITATION

Quinn next challenges the cohabitation element. He contends that he and Milanizadeh stopped living together on April 21, 2004, when he moved to Kuwait for a new job. As mentioned, Milanizadeh testified that, when he returned to Houston on vacation, Quinn stayed with her in the home that they had purchased together.

The evidence also showed that, when Quinn finished his job in Kuwait in June 2006, he moved back to the home he purchased with Milanizadeh. She did not file for divorce until the end of August 2006. Contrary to Quinn's position, this and other courts have held that evidence of similar living arrangements was sufficient to support a finding of cohabitation.

3.   HOLDING OUT TO OTHERS

Quinn urges that the evidence is legally and factually insufficient to support the implied finding that he and Milanizadeh held themselves out to the public as being married.

To satisfy this element of common-law marriage, parties must have represented to others that they were married. The requirement of "represented to others" is synonymous with the judicial requirement of "holding out to the public." It is well settled that "holding out" may be established by conduct and actions of the parties. Spoken words are not necessary to establish representation as husband and wife.

In this regard, as mentioned, evidence was presented that Quinn and Milanizadeh signed the VA loan to purchase their home as husband and wife. The evidence also showed that Quinn covered Milanizadeh on his health insurance for two years.

Milanizadeh testified that she heard Quinn refer to her as his wife to their friends and families. Milanizadeh's friend also testified that she thought that the couple was married. The friend heard Milanizadeh refer to Quinn as her husband and never heard Quinn deny that he was married to Milanizadeh. Testimony was also presented that the couple's families considered Quinn and Milanizadeh to be married. The evidence also showed that Quinn and Milanizadeh purchased a time share in Aruba together in July 2006.

Specifically, evidence was presented that Quinn and Milanizadeh held themselves out as being married when obtaining a VA loan. Milanizadeh also testified that Quinn referred to her publically as his wife.

Applying the appropriate standards of review, we hold that the evidence was legally and factually sufficient to support a finding that a common-law marriage existed between Quinn and Milanizadeh.

We overrule Quinn's issue.

CONCLUSION

We affirm the judgment of the trial court.

Discussions Questions

1. What is the purpose of the requirement that the couple "represented to others that they were married"?

2. Why did the court in *Knight* reverse the finding of a common-law marriage and the court in *Quinn* affirm the finding of a common-law marriage?

Table 2-1
Community Property States That Abolished Common Law Marriage

State	Common Law Marriage Yes/No	Date Abolished	Statute or Decision
Arizona	No	1913	Arizona Revised Statutes §25-111
California	No	1895	California Family Code §300
Idaho	No	1996	Idaho Code §32-201 (1996)
Louisiana	No	1927	Louisiana Revised Statutes 9:272
Nevada	No	1943	Nevada Rev. Statutes Ann. §122.010
New Mexico	No	1905	New Mexico Statutes Annotated §40-1-20
Washington	No	1892	*In re MacLaughlin's Estate*, 30 P. 651 (Wash. 1892)
Wisconsin	No	1949	*In re Van Schaick's Estate*, 256 Wis. 213, 40 N.W.2d 588 (1949)
Texas	Yes		Texas Family Code §2.401

B.   SHARED PROPERTY RIGHTS OF UNMARRIED COHABITANTS

Despite the abolition of common-law marriage, the courts have had to deal with property claims of unmarried cohabitants. In long-term relationships, where one cohabitant works outside the home and the other cohabitant takes care of the home and children, there may be an expectation that property accumulated during the relationship would be shared. Those expectations will be dashed if there is no common-law marriage available to the cohabitants who could have established the criteria of common-law marriage. Without marriage, either formal or informal, the earnings of a cohabitant belong to the earner. The courts have recognized the inequity of having one cohabitant of walk away with all the wealth from the relationship. The excerpt from the following article is an introduction to how the law will treat unmarried couples whose relationship would have qualified as a common-law marriage.

CHARLOTTE K. GOLDBERG, THE SCHEMES OF ADVENTURESSES: THE ABOLITION AND REVIVAL OF COMMON-LAW MARRIAGE

13 Wm. & Mary Journal of Women & the Law 483 (2007)

Common-law marriage is about to go the way of the buggy whip. In 2005, Pennsylvania abolished common-law marriage and other state legislatures are considering following Pennsylvania's lead. Even if common-law marriage is abolished in all states, the problem of unmarried cohabitants seeking property rights arising from their relationships will still challenge the courts. In particular, because most claimants are women, the perception of them as either an "adventuress" or a "virtuous wife" will often determine whether they will attain shared property rights. . . . The main impetus for abolishing common-law marriage was to prevent fraud by women perceived as adventuresses — women who were attempting to convert an illicit relationship into a marriage to gain monetary benefits. Another motivation reflected a completely opposite perception of women: women need protection from unscrupulous men who would take advantage of their youth and naivete. . . . Both these contrary perceptions of women — one who fraudulently sought the benefits of marriage and the other one who needed protection from fraud — led to the demise of common-law marriage.

1. The Contract Approach to Unmarried Cohabitants' Property Rights: Marvin v. Marvin, the Landmark Case

Even though common law marriage has been abolished in all but one community property state, the courts have dealt with the property rights of unmarried cohabitants. The landmark case involving those rights is *Marvin v. Marvin*, decided by the California Supreme Court in 1976. The Court recognized the "substantial increase in the number of couples living together without marrying" and that these relationships lead to legal controversies when the relationship ends in death or separation. The Court stated the principles that apply to unmarried couples. First, they are not covered by the law of marriage, and explained that "We do not seek to resurrect the doctrine of common law marriage. . . we hold only that [a cohabitant] has the same rights to enforce contracts and assert [an] equitable interest in property acquired through. . . effort as does any other unmarried person."

Second, the Court outlined the requirements to state what is today called a *Marvin* claim:

> "The courts should enforce express contracts between nonmarital partners except to the extent that the contract is explicitly founded on consideration of meretricious sexual services. In the absence of an express contract, the courts should inquire into the conduct of the parties to determine whether the conduct demonstrates an implied contract, agreement of partnership or joint venture, or some other tacit understanding between the parties. The courts may also employ the doctrine of quantum meruit, or equitable remedies such a constructive or resulting trust, when warranted by the facts of the case."

The rationale of the court was based "on the principle that adults who voluntarily live together and engage in sexual relations are nonetheless as competent as other persons to contract respecting their earnings and property rights. Of course, they cannot lawfully contract to pay for the performance of sexual services, for such a contract is, in essence, an agreement for prostitution and unlawful for that reason. But they may agree to pool their earnings and to hold property acquired during the relationship in accord with the law governing community property; conversely they may agree that each partner's earnings and the property acquired from those earnings remains the separate property of the earning partner. So long as the agreement does not rest upon illicit meretricious consideration, the parties may order their economic affairs as they choose, and no policy precludes the courts from enforcing such agreements."

The *Marvin* case itself did not represent the most promising case for proving either an express contract or one implied from conduct. The cohabitants, Lee Marvin, the famous movie actor, and Michele Triola Marvin, an entertainer and singer, cohabited for six years. Michele claimed that Lee had orally promised to "share equally any and all property accumulated as a result of their efforts whether individual or combined." At the trial, it was not surprising that he denied the agreement. In a "he said/she said" battle in court, Lee was the winner. Michele ended up with nothing other than the time spent with a prominent movie star.

Because of the parties' differing perceptions of the "agreement," it is difficult to prove an oral agreement to share property. It is more likely that the courts will examine the cohabitants' conduct that will demonstrate an implied agreement to share property. The facts that would be most successful in proving a *Marvin* agreement would involve a long-term relationship that looked like a marriage but for the marriage license. However, because courts are wary about reviving common law marriage, they often require other financial or business activity that shows the cohabitants' intent to share property. In *Maglica v. Maglica* (CA 1998), the court of appeal suggested that Claire Maglica, who worked in her cohabitant Anthony's business, would have a good case of proving an implied agreement sharing the business.

MAGLICA v. MAGLICA

66 Cal. App. 4th 442, 78 Cal. Rptr. 2d 101 (1998)
Court of Appeal

SILLS, P.J.

I. INTRODUCTION

[T]he finding that the couple had no contract in the first place is itself somewhat suspect because certain jury instructions did not accurately convey the law concerning implied-in-fact contracts. . . [P]laintiff was hindered in her ability to prove the existence of an implied-in-fact contract by a series of jury instructions which may have misled the jury about certain of the factors which bear on such contracts. The instructions were insufficiently qualified. They told the jury flat out that such facts as a couple's living together or holding themselves out as husband and wife or sharing a common surname did not mean that they had any agreement to share assets. That is not *exactly* correct. Such factors can, indeed, when taken together with other facts and in context, show the existence of an implied-in-fact contract. At most the jury instructions should have said that such factors do not *by themselves necessarily* show an implied-in-fact contract. Accordingly, when the case is retried, the plaintiff will have another chance to prove that she indeed had a deal for a share of equity in the defendant's business.

II.   FACTS

The important facts in this case may be briefly stated. Anthony Maglica, a Croatian immigrant, founded his own machine shop business, Mag Instrument, in 1955. He got divorced in 1971 and kept the business. That year he met Claire Halasz, an interior designer. They got on famously, and lived together, holding themselves out as man and wife — hence Claire began using the name Claire Maglica — but never actually got married. And, while they worked side by side building the business, Anthony never agreed — or at least the jury found Anthony never agreed — to give Claire a share of the business. When the business was incorporated in 1974 all shares went into Anthony's name. Anthony was the president and Claire was the secretary. They were paid equal salaries from the business after incorporation. In 1978 the business began manufacturing flashlights, and, thanks in part to some great ideas and hard work on Claire's part (e.g., coming out with a purse-sized flashlight in colors), the business boomed. Mag Instrument, Inc., is now worth hundreds of millions of dollars.

In 1992 Claire discovered that Anthony was trying to transfer stock to his children but not her, and the couple split up in October. In June 1993 Claire sued Anthony for, among other things, breach of contract, breach of partnership agreement, fraud, breach of fiduciary duty and quantum meruit. The case came to trial in the spring of 1994. The jury awarded $84 million for the breach of fiduciary duty and quantum meruit causes of action, finding that $84 million was the reasonable value of Claire's services.

III.   DISCUSSION

* * *

D. Certain Jury Instructions May Have Misled the Jury into Finding There Was No Implied Contract When in Fact There Was One

As we have shown, the quantum meruit damage award cannot stand in the wake of the jury's finding that Claire and Anthony had no agreement to share the equity in Anthony's business. But the validity of that very finding itself is challenged in Claire's protective cross-appeal, where she attacks a series of five jury instructions, specially drafted and proferred by Anthony. These instructions are set out in the margin.[11] We agree with Claire that it was error for the trial court to give three of these five instructions. The three instructions are so infelicitously worded that they might have misled the jury into concluding that evidence which can indeed support a finding of an implied contract could not.

The problem with the three instructions is this: They isolate three uncontested facts about the case: (1) living together, (2) holding themselves out to others as husband and wife, (3) providing services "such as" being a constant companion and confidant — and, seriatim, tell the jury that these facts definitely do not mean there was an implied contract. True, none of these facts *by themselves and alone* necessarily *compels* the conclusion that there was an implied contract. But that does not mean that these facts cannot, in conjunction with all the facts and circumstances of the case, establish an implied contract. In point of fact, they can.

In *Alderson v. Alderson* (1986) 180 Cal. App. 3d 450, 461, 225 Cal. Rptr. 610, the court observed that a number of factors, *including*

- direct testimony of an agreement;
- holding themselves out socially as husband and wife;
- the woman and her children's taking the man's surname;
- pooling of finances to purchase a number of joint rental properties;
- joint decisionmaking in rental property purchases;
- rendering bookkeeping services for, paying the bills on, and collecting the rents of, those joint rental properties; and
- the nature of title taken in those rental properties
- could all support a finding there was an implied agreement to share the rental property acquisitions equally.

We certainly do not say that living together, holding themselves out as husband and wife, and being companions and confidants, even taken together, are *sufficient in and of themselves* to show an implied agreement to divide the equity in a business

---

11. Here are the five:
  1. No Contract Results From Parties Holding Themselves out as Husband and Wife
       "You cannot find an agreement to share property or form a partnership from the fact that the parties held themselves out as husband and wife. The fact that unmarried persons live together as husband and wife and share a surname does not mean that they have any agreement to share earnings or assets.
  2. No Implied Contract From Living Together
       "You cannot find an implied contract to share property or form a partnership simply from the fact that the parties lived together[.]
  3. Creation of an Implied Contract
       ". . . The fact the parties are living together does not change any of the requirements for finding an express or implied contract between the parties.
  4. Companionship Does Not Constitute Consideration
       "Providing services such as a constant companion and confidant does not constitute the consideration required by law to support a contract to share property, does not support any right of recovery and such services are not otherwise compensable.
  5. Obligations Imposed by Legal Marriage
       "In California, there are various obligations imposed upon parties who become legally and formally married. These obligations do not arise under the law merely by living together without a formal and legal marriage."

owned by one of the couple. However, *Alderson* clearly shows that such facts, together with others bearing more directly on the business and the way the parties treated the equity and proceeds of the business, *can* be part of a series of facts which do show such an agreement. The vice of the three instructions here is that they affirmatively suggested that living together, holding themselves out, and companionship could not, as a matter of law, even be *part* of the support for a finding of an implied agreement. That meant the jury could have completely omitted these facts when considering the other factors which might also have borne on whether there was an implied contract.

On remand, the three instructions should not be given. The jury should be told, rather, that while the facts that a couple live together, hold themselves out as married, and act as companions and confidants toward each other do not, by themselves, show an implied agreement to share property, those facts, when taken together and in conjunction with other facts bearing more directly on the alleged arrangement to share property, can show an implied agreement to share property.

DISPOSITION

The judgment is reversed. The case is remanded for a new trial. At the new trial the jury instructions identified in this opinion as erroneous shall not be given. In the interest of justice both sides will bear their own costs on appeal.

WALLIN, J., and CROSBY, J., concurred.

Discussion Questions

1. How do the requirements of a *Marvin* agreement differ from the requirements of common-law marriage?

2. On remand, could Claire prove that she and Anthony had an implied-in-fact agreement?

3. If the Maglicas had lived in Texas, could Claire have succeeded in proving a common-law marriage?

------

2.   What Type of Agreement Will Succeed? The New Mexico, Nevada, Texas, and Louisiana Approaches

Not all community property states have whole-heartedly adopted the *Marvin* principles. In *Merrill v. Davis* (N.M. 1983), the New Mexico Supreme Court rejected implied agreements. In *Western States Construction, Inc. v. Michoff* (Nev. 1992), Justice Springer vigorously dissented to the Nevada Supreme Court's adoption of the *Marvin* principles. The Texas Legislature rejected *Marvin*'s oral and implied agreements by mandating that a contract "made on consideration of. . . nonmarital

conjugal cohabitation is not enforceable unless... in writing and signed...."
Vernon's Texas Statutes, Family Code §1.108. The case of *Zaremba v. Cliburn* (Tex.
1997) demonstrates the Texas courts' hostility to "palimony" suits. In Louisiana,
sharing of property by cohabitants (called paramour and concubine) depends on
the individual's contribution to its acquisition not the cohabitants' agreement.
Fairrow v. Marves (La. 2003).

MERRILL v. DAVIS

100 N.M. 552, 673 P.2d 1285 (1983)
Supreme Court of New Mexico

PAYNE, Chief Judge.

This appeal challenges the trial court's property settlement and denial of alimony
following the divorce of Pam Davis (Appellant) and Eddie Merrill (Appellee).

Appellant and Appellee were first married in November 1965 and divorced in
February 1973. Five months after the divorce, they began cohabiting. They remarried in February 1978, but permanently separated in November 1978. Their second
divorce was not entered until 1982.

During the period of cohabitation and prior to remarriage, the parties maintained a joint bank account. While cohabiting but before remarriage, Appellee
purchased one hundred percent of the stock of Davis Tractor Company and managed the retail tractor business.

Also during the period of cohabitation but before remarriage, Appellee began
construction of a house on property which he and Appellant had purchased as
tenants in common. Appellee paid $18,000 toward the price of the land and
material to construct the house. The money was proceeds of the sale of another
house which had been awarded to Appellee as separate property by the original
divorce decree in February 1973.

I.

Appellant argues that the conduct of the parties creates an implied agreement to
pool earnings and share accumulations acquired during cohabitation. Accordingly,
she alleges that she has a one-half interest in the Davis Tractor Company stock, and
that there should not be an $18,000 separate property lien on the land which was
purchased as tenants in common.

The trial court found that the joint bank account, living as husband and wife, and
Appellee's discontinuance of child support payments were not substantial evidence
of an implied agreement to pool their resources and share equally in the accumulated property. We do not recognize an implied agreement as grounds for granting
Appellant an interest in the property.

Appellant also argues that *Dominguez v. Cruz*, 95 N.M. 1, 617 P.2d 1322 (Ct. App.
1980) provides logical support for recognizing an implied agreement. In *Dominguez*,
the court of appeals stated that "[I]f an agreement such as an oral contract can exist
between business associates, one can exist between two cohabiting adults who are

not married if the essential elements of the contractual relationship are present."
Id. at 2, 617 P.2d at 1323. However, in *Dominguez*, there was an express oral agreement to hold property jointly. It is unnecessary for us to decide whether an express
agreement between cohabiting adults may create property rights similar to those
created by marriage. In this case, the issue is whether an agreement implied from
conduct as married partners creates the security and rights created by marriage.

Initially, we note that common-law marriage is not acknowledged in New Mexico.
For a marriage to be valid, it must be formally entered into by contract and solemnized before an appropriate official.

Common-law marriage is not recognized because of "the possibility of fraud
arising from claims of common-law marriage and the uncertainty which such claims
of marriage inject into the affairs of individuals. . . ." Recognition of the implied
agreement as argued by Appellant would inject even greater uncertainty than a
common-law marriage in such matters as wrongful death actions and estate settlements. As we have stated, the problem would be "the ease with which a mere adul-
terous relation may become, in the mouths of interested and unscrupulous
witnesses, a common-law marriage [or an implied agreement to share in the property acquired during cohabitation]." If we were to say that the same rights that
cannot be gained by common-law marriage may be gained by the implications
that flow from cohabitation, then we have circumvented the prohibition of
common-law marriage.

It is the policy of this state to foster and protect the institution of marriage.
The state's interest in marriage is recognized by statute which prescribes that the
contract of matrimony be solemnized. We agree with the court, in *Hewitt v. Hewitt*,
77 Ill. 2d 49, 31 Ill. Dec. 827, 394 N.E.2d 1204 (1979), where it stated:

> "[M]arriage is a civil contract between three parties-the husband, the wife, and the
> State. (Citations omitted.). . . [T]he State [has] a strong continuing interest in the insti-
> tution of marriage and prevents the marriage relation from becoming in effect a private
> contract terminable at will."

* * *

The judgment of the trial court is hereby affirmed.
IT IS SO ORDERED.

RIORDAN and STOWERS, JJ., concur.

WESTERN STATES CONSTRUCTION, INC. v. MICHOFF

108 Nev. 931, 840 P.2d 1220 (1992)
Supreme Court of Nevada

YOUNG, Justice.

Appellant Max Michoff ("Max") and respondent Lois Michoff ("Lois") cohabitated for approximately nine years, although they were never married. They formed
Western States Construction, Inc. during their relationship. Lois provided valuable
services in the operation of the business based on Max's representations that she was
a co-equal owner. When they terminated their relationship, Lois brought this action

seeking one-half of the parties' assets. The district court entered judgment in favor of Lois and against Max and Western States Construction, Inc. For the reasons discussed herein, we affirm the judgment against Max but reverse it against the corporation.

FACTS

In 1977, Lois and Max became romantically involved, even though Max was already married. At the time, Lois was employed as a prototype technician,[1] working forty hours per week and earning eleven dollars per hour. Their relationship continued, and Max divorced his wife. Lois and Max then decided to, and did, live together.

In 1979, Lois and Max moved from California to Carson City, Nevada. That same year, Lois legally changed her name to Lois Michoff.[2] The parties started a construction equipment rental business called L & M Rentals (named for Lois and Max). Lois obtained the business license and paid the licensing fees. The business license listed Lois as the sole owner. Max wanted Lois to be the sole owner so that his ex-wife could not make a claim against the business. Although Max contributed a large portion of the funds to start L & M Rentals, Lois and Max had agreed that they were co-equal owners of the business. Consequently, Lois devoted her efforts and time toward running the business, including such integral functions as bookkeeping and maintaining the equipment.

Approximately six months after starting L & M Rentals, Lois and Max discovered that they needed a contractor's license to operate the business. Lois therefore applied for such a license but listed the name of the business as Western States Construction. Lois was listed as the owner of the business and Max was listed as the "qualified employee." Lois testified that they had agreed that it was their company; thus, again, Lois provided much of the skill and labor necessary for the business' success. Her services included doing all of the office work (bookkeeping, payroll, and paperwork) and assisting in the maintenance, service, and running of the equipment. The profits from the business were either invested into the business or retained as savings.

In 1983, Lois and Max incorporated the business, naming it Western States Construction, Inc. ("Western States"). Lois testified that they agreed to hold the company as co-equal owners, each owning fifty percent of the company. The articles of incorporation listed Lois and Max as the Board of Directors and the Incorporators. Also, they were the sole officers of the corporation: Lois was treasurer, and Max was president and secretary. They opened checking and payroll accounts for Western States, and both Lois and Max had authority to withdraw funds from these accounts.

Lois continued to do the bookkeeping, and she also updated the records, reviewed bids, negotiated contracts and labored in the field-performing such jobs

---

1. A prototype technician builds printed circuit boards from scratch.
2. Lois claimed that she changed her name at Max's request; he believed that if they had a woman-owned, construction-type business, they would "fare better in getting jobs." For example, according to Lois, they could bid five percent over the low bid and nevertheless be classified as the low bidder. It is noteworthy that Max's attorney handled the name change.

as flagging and running heavy equipment. Whenever Western States sought a license increase, it was Lois who applied for the increase. In order to obtain the necessary contractor's bonds from the Contractor's Board, Lois personally guaranteed the bonds.

During their relationship, Max held Lois out as his wife. In fact, in 1984, Max entered a partnership agreement with Robert Frybarger and requested that Lois sign a consent of spouse. Max and Lois filed joint tax returns as husband and wife commencing in 1980 and continuing through 1986. For the years 1983 through 1986, they also filed tax returns under Western States, showing Lois as an officer and owner of the corporation. Moreover, Western States elected to file a sub-chapter S election on March 24, 1983. The election was signed by Lois and Max and designated the holdings of the corporation as community property.

After Lois and Max terminated their relationship (Lois apparently left Max because he had been physically abusing her), she brought this action, seeking a declaration and judgment that she owns one-half of the parties' assets, including Western States. She alleged that she had performed valuable services based on Max's representations that she owned one-half of the corporation. Specifically, the complaint provided:

> That at all times pertinent herein, Defendant, MAX MICHOFF, represented to [Lois] that she was entitled to one-half ($^1/_2$) of the assets held by Defendant, Western States Construction, Inc. In accordance with the representations, [Lois] has performed valuable services over many years last past, including those as set forth above.

* * *

> That based upon the representations as aforestated, [Lois] requests a determination by this Court that she is entitled to one-half ($^1/_2$) of the assets of the parties whether held solely in the name of MAX MICHOFF, Defendant Corporation, or [Lois].

After a trial, the district court found that there existed an express and an implied agreement between the parties to acquire and hold properties as if they were married. The court ruled that the community property laws should apply by analogy and thus entered judgment in favor of Lois and against Max and Western States for one-half of the net assets of the parties less the value of the property already taken.

DISCUSSION

Max contends that Lois did not plead any contractual claims against him. We disagree.

* * *

[W]e conclude that under Nevada's notice pleading rule, Max was given sufficient notice that Lois' complaint stated a cause of action for breach of an express and an implied contract to acquire and hold property as though the parties were married.

Max also contends that to allow unmarried cohabiting parties to hold their property as though they were married violates Nevada's strong public policy of encouraging legal marriages. We strongly disagree and emphasize that this court by no means seeks to encourage, nor does this opinion suggest, that couples should avoid marriage. Quite to the contrary, we reaffirm this state's strong public policy interest in encouraging legally consummated marriages. However, this policy is not furthered by allowing "one participant in a meretricious relationship to abscond with the bulk of the couple's acquisitions."

Unmarried couples who cohabit have the same rights to lawfully contract with each other regarding their property as do other unmarried individuals. Thus this court must protect the reasonable expectations of unmarried cohabitants with respect to transactions concerning their property rights. We therefore adopted, the rule that unmarried cohabitants will not be denied access to the courts to make property claims against each other merely because they are not married.

[W]e cited with approval the holding in *Marvin v. Marvin*, 18 Cal. 3d 660, 134 Cal. Rptr. 815, 557 P.2d 106 (1976), which provided:

> The courts should enforce express contracts between nonmarital partners except to the extent that the contract is explicitly founded on the consideration of meretricious sexual services. . . . In the absence of an express contract, the courts should inquire into the conduct of the parties to determine whether that conduct demonstrates an implied contract, agreement or partnership or joint venture, or some other tacit understanding between the parties. The courts may also employ the doctrine of *quantum meruit*, or equitable remedies such as constructive trust or resulting trusts, when warranted by the facts of the case.

We then expressly held that the remedies in *Marvin* are available to unmarried cohabitants. As stated in *Marvin*, adults who voluntarily live together "may agree to pool their earnings and to hold all property acquired during the relationship *in accord with the law governing community property*." (emphasis added).

Our brother Springer believes that the district court was misled by our statement in *Hay* that if unmarried cohabiting adults agree to hold their property as if they are married, "the community property laws of the state will apply by analogy." Justice Springer concludes that "[u]nmarried persons cannot own community property, by analogy or otherwise." *Marvin*, however, strongly supports our statement in *Hay* that the community property law may apply by analogy. While unmarried couples *cannot actually own* community property, this is so only because community property is a creature of statute which arises after a couple is legally married. Yet unmarried couples are not precluded from holding their property *as though* they were married. In such a case, the community property law can apply by analogy. Thus we hold that unmarried cohabiting adults may agree to hold property that they acquire as though it were community property.

Max next argues that Lois failed to prove the existence of a contractual agreement because she failed to show the basic elements of the contract, namely, that she did not allege a meeting of the minds and harmonious understanding as to the tenor and provisions of the agreement. [T]he terms of an express contract are stated in words while those of an implied contract are manifested by conduct.

There is no evidence that the parties expressly agreed to hold their property as though they were married. The district court erred in so finding. Nevertheless, we conclude that there is substantial evidence to support the district court's finding that Lois and Max impliedly agreed to hold their property as though they were married. In addition to living together and holding themselves out to be a married couple, this evidence included the parties filing federal tax returns as husband and wife, the parties designating that they held the Western States stock as community property in their Subchapter S election, and Max's insistence that Lois sign a consent of spouse to effectuate a partnership he wanted to enter. The district court's judgment against Max is therefore affirmed.[6]

However, the district court erred when it entered judgment against Western States, for Western States was not a party to the contract and therefore could not be liable for Max's breach thereof. Thus, we reverse the judgment against Western States and remand for further proceedings as to the disposition of the parties' property.

MOWBRAY, C.J., and ROSE and STEFFEN, JJ., concur.

SPRINGER, Justice, dissenting.

Lois and Max are not married; yet the trial court treated them as though they were married. The trial court heard and decided this case under our divorce statute. The trial court disposed of the property owned by each party as though it were community property, calling it "community property by analogy." The final decree in this case was entered in accordance with the divorce statute, which provides that "[i]n granting a divorce, the court ... [s]hall make such disposition of ... [t]he community property of the parties ... as appears just and equitable." I am so bold as to say that unmarried people cannot be treated by the courts like married people, that unmarried people do not have the legal capacity to hold community property, and that unmarried people are not entitled to property disposition decrees under our divorce statute. I almost stopped here; but then it occurred to me that the majority opinion might be taken seriously and that unmarried people like Lois and Max might start knocking on the doors of our divorce courts. This thought prompted me to write at some length on the novel legal principles announced by this court today, family law principles that I will refer to as the "Michoff Doctrine."[1]

The Michoff Doctrine permits "unmarried cohabiting adults" to enter into a kind of informal marriage contract which entitles them to have property that they acquire treated like community property and distributed by the divorce courts

---

6. With regard to Max, we commend the district court for its handling of this case. This case involved the sensitive area of property rights between unmarried cohabiting adults (an area which traditionally has been judicially tempered by moral views) and where the parties perhaps did not have the "cleanest" hands. The district court fairly applied the law of this state to reach an equitable result.

Lois wanted to formalize their relationship with a marriage ceremony, but Max balked. He apparently felt that his financial interests would be better served with a more informal arrangement. However, when the trial court sided with Lois, Max found that he had jumped from the frying pan of a prior marriage into perhaps the hotter fire of a contractual relationship. With hindsight, he may have fared better financially if he had been married. However, Max was, as the poet says, "The captain of [his] fate." We cannot see any benefit — except possibly to the lawyers — in remanding this action to be repled with the parties rehashing the same facts before the trial court.

1. My not wanting unmarried persons to come to our divorce courts seeking a "just and equitable" division of their supposed "community property by analogy" certainly does not mean that I have any quarrel with the well-established law in Nevada that permits people like Lois and Max to sue each other, not for divorce, but for contractual or equitable claims that they might have against each other.

"as though" they had been formally married. These "Michoff Marriages" will henceforth be governed by our Marriage and Divorce statutes.

The Michoff Doctrine is comprised of two principles:

1. *The As-Though-Married Principle.* This principle sanctions an informal marriage-by-agreement which permits unmarried cohabitants to sue and recover under the divorce statute.
2. *The Community-Property-by-Analogy Principle.* This principle allows "unmarried cohabiting adults"[2] to "hold property . . . as though it were community property" and "in accord with the law governing community property."

* * *

Permitting community property to be created by cohabitation or contract is a disincentive to marriage; it gives unmarried persons the rights of community property without imposing upon them the mutual assumption of duties that is attendant to the marital status. Unmarried persons will now be in a position to *choose* whether or not they wish to be governed by community property law; whereas, community ownership is thrust upon married persons at the time of their marriage unless they agree in writing not to hold property as community. The necessary result of today's judicial acceptance of "as-though" marriages and CPBA will be that married couples will automatically be controlled by community property laws unless they decide to "opt out"; whereas unmarried couples will now have the odd privilege of being able to choose (impliedly or expressly, orally or in writing) whether they wish to hold property regularly or as "community property by analogy." Such an arrangement is not only incongruous and disadvantageous to married persons, it is entirely inconsistent with the design and purpose of community property law. The legislature has accorded benefits, obligations, and protections to persons who have complied with the formal requirements of marriage. As noted by the California Supreme Court: "Formally married couples are granted significant rights and bear important responsibilities toward one another which are not shared by those who cohabit without marriage." I believe that we are constrained by our legislature's clear policy favoring formal marriage not to accord the same (or greater) protections to unmarried cohabitants that are accorded married individuals and that to do so constitutes judicial overreaching of a clear legislative purpose.

2. All of the marital privileges conferred upon unmarried persons by the Michoff Doctrine appear to be given to the rather large class of "unmarried cohabiting adults." I note that the majority places no restriction on the number or gender of these adults. I assume that application of the doctrine is not restricted to two cohabitants of opposite sex in order to avoid conflict with Nevada's prohibition against common-law marriages; still, the thought of a band of unmarried cohabiting adults suing each other under our Marriage and Dissolution chapter is not a pretty one. I can envision roommates Larry, Moe and Curly, unmarried cohabiting adults, deeply involved in divorce litigation. Any one of the three would be in a legal position to move out and sue the others claiming that the three had an implied agreement to share, per *Michoff,* property that they acquire as though it were community property. Larry could then take advantage of the community property laws and NRS Chapter 125 so that he could ask a divorce court to divide their CPBA interests, pursuant to NRS 125.150. This problem and the problem of creating community property rights by "implied" agreement through some undefined "conduct" on the part of cohabiting adults are problems enough; but the real problem in this case stems from its encouragement of informal marriage and in letting unmarried people create community property interests by merely agreeing to do so. Community property by nature and definition is created by operation of law. No other jurisdiction that I know of recognizes community property by agreement of unmarried parties.

I am strongly opposed to opening up our divorce courts to unmarried persons. The trial court was absolutely wrong to decide this case under our Marriage and Dissolution statute and, in a divorce-like decree, to divide a judicially-created, new species of property, "community-property-by-analogy." My disposition of this case would be to reverse the trial court decree and return the case to the trial court where, because of the strange way that this case has been handled, I would allow Lois to file a new complaint to state a contract claim if she has one. Lois is entitled to recover if she can prove, by a preponderance of evidence, that Max agreed to share with her the income and property that he acquired while he and Lois were living together.

Discussion Questions

1. What is the court's reasoning in *Merrill* for refusing to recognize implied agreements between cohabitants? Do you agree with that reasoning?
2. Do you agree with the majority or the dissent in *Michoff?*

ZAREMBA v. CLIBURN

949 S.W.2d 822 (1997)
Court of Appeals of Texas

Before DAY, BRIGHAM and HOLMAN, JJ.

DAY, Justice.

Appellant Thomas E. Zaremba filed suit in the 360th Family District Court against appellee Harvey Lavan Cliburn, Jr., aka Van Cliburn for claims arising from a relationship between Zaremba and Cliburn. Those claims included:

- An accounting of partnership assets
- Appointment of a constructive trust
- Breach of contract
- Breach of fiduciary relationship and bad faith
- Mismanagement of partnership property
- An appointment of a receiver
- Fraud
- Quantum meruit and unjust enrichment
- Intentional infliction of emotional distress

Zaremba alleged that on or about July 14, 1966, he and Cliburn became close friends and sexual partners and in 1977, Cliburn asked him to move in with him. He further alleged that at the same time he moved in with Cliburn, he, either orally or impliedly, agreed to provide services like shopping, doing the mail, paying the bills, drafting checks, co-managing the household, and dealing with accountants, creditors, and real estate agents in exchange for a share in Cliburn's income. He contended that 17 years later, Cliburn dissolved their alleged partnership and he received no partnership assets or income. The case was transferred to the 17th District Court of Tarrant County. Cliburn answered, generally denying the allegations and raising special exceptions:

> 1. Zaremba's petition failed to allege sufficient facts to state a claim for any cause of action based on an alleged partnership relationship because those actions must necessarily be based on an alleged partnership founded on an unwritten agreement concerning conjugal nonmarital cohabitation, unenforceable under the statute of frauds.

After a hearing on his special exceptions, Cliburn filed a motion for a "gag order." The trial court heard the gag order motion and entered an order regarding pretrial publicity. The trial court then entered a general order granting special exceptions. . . . The next day, the trial court entered a final judgment dismissing Zaremba's lawsuit with prejudice because the pleading defects raised in Cliburn's special exceptions were such that could not be cured by amendment. Zaremba appeals.

RECOVERY FOR SERVICES RENDERED IN CONSIDERATION OF NONMARITAL, CONJUGAL COHABITATION

Zaremba argues that the trial court erred as a matter of law by sustaining special exception one because it applied the 1987 amendment to the statute of frauds retroactively. Further, he argues that the clause at issue in the statute of frauds applies only to prohibit nonmarital, conjugal cohabitation as consideration and that he does not allege that the purported agreement was for consideration of nonmarital, conjugal cohabitation. Specifically the statute of frauds provides:

> (a) A promise or agreement described in Subsection (b) of this section is not enforceable unless the promise or agreement, or a memorandum of it, is
>   (1) in writing; and
>   (2) signed by the person to be charged with the promise or agreement or by someone lawfully authorized to sign for him.
> (b) Subsection (a) of this section applies to:
>   . . . .
>   (3) an agreement made on consideration of marriage or on consideration of nonmarital conjugal cohabitation. . . .

TEX. BUS. & COM. CODE ANN. §26.01(a), (b)(3) (Vernon 1987).

The stated purpose of the 1987 amendment to the statute of frauds was ending the "abusive filing of palimony suits." In public hearings before the Senate Jurisprudence Committee, Senator Caperton, the bill sponsor, described palimony lawsuits as "an embarrassment to the legal profession." He stated that the amendment would require "a deal . . . to live in a conjugal relationship . . . to be in writing" like an agreement made on consideration of marriage. Essentially, he said, the amendment would prohibit "palimony suits [like those] that have been read about in other states." Harry Tindall, chairman of the Family Law Section of the State Bar of Texas, testified as an individual supporting the legislation. He testified that promises made to induce someone to marry had to be written but promises made to induce someone to live with another need not be. "With the number of people living together today, these lawsuits are alive and well and they are usually grounded in the concept of breach of contract." Id. "Alfred Bloomingdale, Lee Marvin, Liberace, Billie Jean King, the litany is endless of people that have been involved in what I consider a strike suit . . . [but] [t]he[ ] claimants to [his] knowledge . . . never won"

On the Senate floor, Senator Caperton stated that the amendment would "do away with palimony lawsuits." He stated, "I'm killing palimony," and "we won't have to worry about the Lee Marvin kind of lawsuits in Texas if this bill passes." Before the House Committee on Business and Commerce, Tindall testified that promises made in consideration of nonmarital, conjugal relationships should be placed on an equal footing with promises made in consideration of marriage. By their nature, such promises are "not made as alleged." Such cases "create problems." "[T]hey are 9,999 times out of 10,000 a strike suit." And, the courts uniformly "rule for the defendants." The Legislature's intent in amending the statute of frauds was plainly to stop palimony suits.

This is a "palimony" suit by nature. Zaremba first filed this suit in a Tarrant County Family Court. This shows that although Zaremba has raised his claims as arising from a purported oral or implied partnership agreement, he considered the suit a "family" matter. Zaremba claims that he and Cliburn became close friends and sexual partners over 30 years ago. Zaremba alleges that when Cliburn asked him to move in with him in 1977, he agreed to provide services like shopping, doing the mail, paying the bills, drafting checks, dealing with accountants, creditors and real estate agents, and co-managing the household in exchange for a share in Cliburn's income. However, pleading ancillary items of consideration does not take the agreement outside the statute of frauds and render it enforceable. The performance of Zaremba's household services were collateral to a nonmarital, conjugal cohabitation agreement. Each claim put forth in Zaremba's petition as arising from a purported oral or implied partnership agreement is an attempt to disguise the palimonial nature of the suit and is, in actuality, founded on the principle that he was entitled to recover for alleged services rendered in consideration of nonmarital, conjugal cohabitation.

* * *

Thus, section 26.01(b)(3) bars Zaremba's claims for recovery under all causes of action that allege Zaremba was entitled to recover for services rendered in consideration of nonmarital, conjugal cohabitation, including his claims for equitable relief.

CONCLUSION

In summary, section 26.01(b)(3) bars all unwritten palimonial agreements concerning relationships that continued past the effective date of the amendment.

Consequently, it bars Zaremba's claims for recovery under all causes of action that allege Zaremba was entitled to recover for services rendered in consideration of nonmarital, conjugal cohabitation, including his claims for equitable relief.

Discussion Questions

1. Why does Texas require a written agreement between cohabitants?
2. Is it realistic to expect a written agreement between cohabiting couples?
3. How can the Texas law allowing common-law marriage be reconciled with the requirement of written agreements for cohabiting couples?

FAIRROW v. MARVES

862 So. 2d 1234 (2003)
Court of Appeal of Louisiana

PETERS, J.

SUMMARY OF FACTS

[This case involved a dispute between the heirs of Henry Fairrow and the heirs of Laura King. The dispute was over the ownership of 11 and $1/2$ acres of land in Rapides Parish, Louisiana. Henry Fairrow purchased the land in 1945 while he was living with Laura King. The deed stated that he was married to her. At that time, she was still married to another man, Mr. Marves. She had three children in that marriage. Even after she was divorced from Mr. Marves, she did not marry Henry Fairrow. After Henry and Laura "dissolved their relationship," Henry married Ora Dee and had three children with her.

Henry Fairrow died in 1968. In 1999, his surviving children, Ms. Fairrow and Ms. Park, sued to remove the cloud on their title because Laura King's name was on the original deed as married to Henry Fairrow. Summary judgment was granted in favor of his heirs. The legal wrangling continued because affidavits were produced that implied that even though Laura was not married to Henry, her funds were used to purchase the land. The Court of Appeal considered whether there should be a trial to determine whether those funds provided her and her heirs with an interest in the property.]

OPINION

Although these affidavits were submitted at only the February 24, 2003 hearing, it appears that both appeals currently before us rely on the assertions in the affidavits as establishing a genuine issue of material fact as to whether Ms. King made a contribution to the acquisition of the property through her own capital and industry. In support, the defendants cite jurisprudence to the effect that, as a matter of law, concubines are not prevented from asserting certain property claims against their paramours. *See Heatwole v. Stansbury*, 212 La. 685, 690, 33 So. 2d 196, 197 (1947) (holding that "concubines, although under certain disabilities, in the interest of good morals, are not prevented from asserting claims arising out of business transactions between themselves, independent of the concubinage"); *Lagarde v. Dabon*, 155 La. 25, 29, 98 So. 744, 745-46 (1923) (holding that "if a man and woman contract to carry on business together, their subsequent cohabitation does not destroy or lessen any right which she may have upon him for a remuneration for her services"); *Succession of LeBlanc*, 577 So. 2d 105, 108 (La. App. 4 Cir. 1991) (holding that "public policy does not prohibit a paramour and concubine from acquiring real property as co-vendees" but that "the acquisition must be independent of the concubinage; that is, the concubine must show that her contribution to the acquisition was obtained through her own capital and industry"); *LeDoux v. LeDoux*, 534 So. 2d 103, 106 (La. App. 3 Cir. 1988) (holding that "there is no public policy or legal impediment to a paramour and a concubine acquiring real property as co-vendees, and that when the concubine's name appears on the deed as a co-vendee there is a presumption that she is the owner of an undivided half interest"); *Broadway v. Broadway*, 417 So. 2d 1272, 1276 (La. App. 1 Cir.) (holding that "if the concubine can furnish strict and conclusive proof that her capital and industry, obtained independent of the concubinage, contributed a full share to the acquisition of the subject property, then equity dictates she be declared a one-half owner"), *writ denied*, 422 So. 2d 162 (La. 1982).

Ms. King did not sign the deed and nowhere on the deed did she appear as co-vendee; thus, there is no presumption that she owned an undivided one-half interest in the property. The deed itself shows that Mr. Fairrow acquired the property for $1,500.00, $1,100.00 of which was paid "cash in hand" with the remaining $400.00 to be paid in one installment due within six months of the date of the deed. Importantly, there is no evidence to show that Ms. King actually contributed to the *acquisition of the property* at issue through her own capital and industry. The defendants' evidence merely supports that Ms. King worked outside of the home and earned income at the time of the purchase of the property and that Mr. Fairrow was not working at the time of the purchase of the property. These premises, even if accepted as true, do not compel or even permit for that matter, without more, the conclusion that Ms. King had to have contributed to the acquisition of the property because she was the only one working at the time of the acquisition. Mr. Fairrow might have had other financial sources such as savings, investments, disability benefits, an inheritance, etc. One is left only to speculate. The fact that Ms. King worked outside of the home and earned income at the time of the purchase and the fact that Mr. Fairrow was not working at that time are simply not material facts because they are not determinative of the outcome of this dispute. Without more, these affidavits do not create a genuine issue of material fact so as to preclude summary judgment in favor of Ms. Fairrow and Ms. Parks. Thus, we find no error in the trial court's March 6, 2003 grant of their motion for summary judgment.

DISPOSITION

For the foregoing reasons, we affirm the judgments below at the appellants' cost. Affirmed.

WOODARD, J., dissenting.

I respectfully dissent from the majority's opinion.

Ms. King's heirs provided evidence, the inferences of which indicate that, more likely than not, it was her separate funds, not his, which were responsible for the property's purchase.

[W]e do not know from the record whether he knew that there was a legal impediment to their "marriage." All we know is that the two were living together and holding themselves out as husband and wife. Both were involved in co-habitation. Thus, we should not "punish" Ms. King's heirs and reward Mr. Fairrow's by denying her rightful and, apparently, well earned interest in this property because she "lived in sin," especially when we have no reason to believe that his behavior was no different from hers.

Indeed, the most reasonable factual inferences to draw from all of the evidence in this record is that Mr. Fairrow, not Ms. King, is the one who obtained an interest in the property because of the concubinage — that it was he who enjoyed the fruits of Ms. King's and her children's labor — and that it was her separate funds which actually purchased the property.

I submit that to discover the true ownership of this property and to do justice, we must look deeper than to the rebutted presumption, the majority relies on, and that inquiry requires a trial, rendering summary judgment inappropriate.

Discussion Questions

1. What supported the majority's rationale that the land belonged to Henry Fairrow's heirs? Was it a practical decision?

2. Why did Judge Woodward dissent?

---

3. The Expansion of the Marvin Approach: The Arizona and Washington Approaches

Other states have examined or expanded the reach of *Marvin*. The Supreme Court of Arizona, in *Carroll v. Lee* (Ariz. 1986), considered whether homemaking services can be adequate consideration for an implied agreement to share property.

CARROLL v. LEE

148 Ariz. 10, 712 P.2d 923 (1986)
Supreme Court of Arizona,
En Banc

GORDON, Vice Chief Justice.

Judith Carroll (Judy) has petitioned this Court for review of a decision of the court of appeals reversing the trial court's judgment granting her request of partition of certain real and personal property.

Judith Carroll, aka Judith Lee cohabited with Paul T. Lee for fourteen years ultimately settling in Ajo, Arizona. They went their separate ways in 1982. The couple did not marry nor ever seriously contemplate marriage. However, they did hold themselves out as husband and wife and Judy assumed Lee as her surname. Little personal property was owned by either party prior to the relationship and neither owned any real property. Throughout the course of the relationship the couple jointly acquired three parcels of real estate, several antique or restored automobiles, a mobile home and various personal property. The parties filed joint tax returns as husband and wife several times.

Paul is a mechanic by trade and operates an automobile repair shop in Ajo on a parcel of land acquired during the relationship. He supplied the vast majority of the money used to sustain the couple, while Judy kept the house (cleaning, cooking, laundry, working in the yard). Occasionally Judy helped Paul at the shop with billing and bookkeeping. The couple had a joint checking account out of which Judy paid the household bills. Paul did not utilize the account, preferring to deal in cash or money orders in his business.

The real property was titled to the couple in one of three ways. Title was held either, 1) as joint tenants with the right of survivorship, 2) as husband and wife, or 3) as husband and wife as joint tenants with the right of survivorship. The various automobiles and mobile home were all titled to Paul T. Lee or Judith E. Lee.

Judy was self-employed for approximately five years from 1978 to 1982 as a photographer/dark room technician. She made little money; most of it went back into the business. However, some was spent on the household. "Photos by Judy" had a separate business account with Judy the only signatory. After the parties "split up" Judy filed a partition action pursuant to A.R.S. §12-1211.

A bench trial was held and both parties testified. The trial court, in an amended judgment, essentially awarded each party a one-half interest in the real and personal property that was acquired by the couple during their relationship. The trial court found the following:

> "A contract existed and exists between the parties. While said contract is not in writing, the Court finds that the contract was assiduously and scrupulously adhered to by both parties in the repeated acquisition of properties and the repeated taking of title to properties in both names, pursuant to the contract. The Court further finds that gifts to and from each, to and from the other, pursuant to this same silent contract, of time, money, labor, sharing of duties, and the like constituted an equal sharing of the cost of the acquisitions of the various properties."

Paul appealed the decision of the trial court. The court of appeals reversed the award.

In *Cook v. Cook*, 142 Ariz. 573, 691 P.2d 664 (1984), we exhaustively reviewed agreements between non-married cohabitants. The agreement approved of in *Cook* was one between unmarried cohabitants to pool income, acquire assets and share in the accumulations. We compiled basic concepts of contract law [approving contracts oral, written or implied from conduct].

The court of appeals found that

> ". . . no evidence, in words or conduct, suggests *mutual* promises to contribute funds to a *pool* in the instant case. On the contrary, the implied agreement specifically described and delimited by the conduct of the parties in this case was an exchange of unlike services: one cohabitant's homemaking services for the other's monetary support."

Further the court stated,

> "There is no evidence of an agreement express or implied which could be read: he went to work, I stayed home, *and* we agreed to pool our assets and share our accumulations. Without the later element in the agreement we do not approach the *Cook v. Cook* situation."

at 935-936. (emphasis in original).

We disagree with the above reasoning and now reach the unanswered question from *Cook* as to whether an agreement between unmarried cohabitants with home-making services severable from a meretricious relationship as consideration can stand. In Arizona we recognize implied contracts, and there is no difference in legal effect between an express contract and an implied contract.

* * *

Paul received the cooking, cleaning and household chores he bargained for while Judy received monetary support. Together they were able to acquire property through their joint efforts. Clearly Judy's homemaking services can be valued and constituted adequate consideration for the couple's implied agreement.

We agree with the court in *Marvin v. Marvin*, 18 Cal. 3d 660, 134 Cal. Rptr. 815, 557 P.2d 106 (1976), in that "homemaking," severable from the meretricious rela-tionship can support an implied agreement as between two parties. It is important to note that Judy does not claim the parties had a "Marvin" agreement. In *Marvin*, Michelle Triola Marvin alleged an oral agreement under which the parties would pool property and earnings while holding themselves out as husband and wife; she would provide household services and he would support her for life. Judy has only requested partition to property which is jointly titled to her and did not request, for example, certain automobiles titled to Paul separately or Paul's repair shop (a subject to later be addressed). This situation is not nearly as potentially expansive as a case like *Marvin*.

We believe Judy proved the property requested to be partitioned was acquired through joint common effort and for a common purpose. It is not necessary for her to prove that she produced by her labor a part of the very money used to purchase the property. The parties had an implied partnership or joint enterprise agreement at the very least based on the facts and circumstances presented. Recovery for Judy should be allowed in accordance with these implied expectations. Paul's relevant testimony is as follows:

> Q Did you have a preference during your relationship, Paul, as to whether or not Judy should work or stay at home?
> A Yes.
> Q What was your preference?
> A I preferred that she stay home.
> Q All right. You wanted her to stay at home so that you had a nice home environment, meals were prepared on time —
> A Yes.
> Q — clothing was washed and cleaned and ready; correct?
> A Yes.
> Q The yard was nice; correct?
> A Yes.
> Q Dishes were washed?
> A Yes.
> Q Did she do all of those things in the early years, as far as the yardwork —
> A She kept, kept the home nice.
> Q She kept the home nice up until the time you split up; didn't she?
> A Yes.
> Q That included washing all of your clothes —
> A Yes.
> Q — preparing all of your meals?
> A Well, when she was there.
> Q When wasn't she there?
> A Trips out of, of town.
> Q How many trips did she take out of town annually?
> A It depended on her business.
> Q Talking about her photography business?
> A Yes.
> Q It's true, is it not, Paul, the majority of the time Judy stayed home and took care of that home —
> A Yes.
> Q — in the manner that I just went through; correct?
> A Yes.
>   . . . .
> Q Did you ever intend that she be an owner with you at that time, at the time that you were acquiring these properties that she be an owner of those properties at that time?
> A You mean a co-owner?
> Q Yes.
> A *I suppose at the time I had planned it that way.* (emphasis added)
> Q For her to be an equal, co-owner, or a co-owner with you at that particular moment, or at some time in the event that anything should happen to you?
> A Mostly it was in case anything happened to me.
> Q Is that what you told her?
> A Yes.
>   . . . .

Q Do you recall Mr. Aboud asking you that question about what your intention was, whether she would be a co-owner of that property at the time you took title to it?

A Yes, sir.

Q Do you recall pausing for quite a while before you answered?

A Yes, sir.

Q Wasn't your answer I guess at the time I did?

A At the time.

Q You've since changed your mind —

A Yes.

. . . .

Q But she did open up a joint account —

A Yes.

Q — for the two of you; correct?

A Yes.

Q She paid the household bills out of that account?

A Yes.

Q And you really have no quarrel with the way that she took care of the home as you wanted her to; didn't you?

A No, sir.

Q *That enabled you to work at your business and earn income —*

A Yes.

(emphasis added).

Judy's relevant testimony is as follows:

Q All right. What type of an arrangement, if any, did you and Paul discuss about what he expected from your relationship in terms of your contribution?

A We didn't really discuss it. *It just was there.* He went to work. I stayed home and kept the house and, mostly because that's what he wanted me to do.

Q He told you that's what he wanted you to do; didn't he?

A Oh, yeah.

Q And that, that included all the things that I went through with him, such as taking care of the laundry —

A Uh-huh, of course.

Q — doing the dishes —

A Yes.

Q — cleaning the house —

A Yes.

. . . .

Q Judy, were you ever paid for the services you provided Paul: the bookkeeping and the housekeeping, and yardwork, the —

A No, I didn't expect it. That was part of my job as his mate, I felt.

(emphasis added).

There was evidence from which the trial court could find the existence of an agreement for property to be acquired and owned jointly, as such was the method in which Paul took title in both the real and personal property. A reviewing court should not set aside the findings of the trial court unless such findings are clearly erroneous.

The finding of an agreement severable from a meretricious relationship is not so remarkable or a major change in the law. This was recognized in *Cook v. Cook, supra.* "The agreement . . . would be perfectly enforceable if made between parent and child, brother and sister, friend and friend or any other parties in a cohabitant relationship. The agreement would be enforceable if the parties had not lived together at all." 142 Ariz. at 577, 691 P.2d at 668.

The court of appeals found an agreement to exchange unlike services, but did not uphold the agreement based essentially on a failure of adequate consideration. Since we find a valid implied contract to combine efforts and jointly accumulate certain property . . . believe there was sufficient evidence to justify the trial court's finding that at the time the property was acquired Paul intended joint ownership, even though he may have since changed his mind.

This opinion does not discourage or shake the foundation of marriage in this state. Enforcement of the agreement is a logical extension of *Cook* and does not contravene public policy. This Court recognizes that community property rights derive solely from the marital relationship, and the law will not give non-marital cohabiting parties the benefit of community property. Community property is defined by A.R.S. §25-211 as follows:

> "all property acquired by either husband or wife during marriage, except that which is acquired by gift, devise or descent. . . ."

There is a strong legal presumption that all property acquired during marriage is community property. The spouse claiming particular property as separate must prove the separate nature by "clear and convincing" or nearly conclusive evidence. The presumption applies to property acquired during marriage even though title is taken in the name of only one spouse. Judy did not have the benefit of the marital presumption. She had to sustain a high burden of producing evidence in order to establish the agreement. Since Judy was a co-owner of the property under a contract theory, she had the right pursuant to A.R.S. §12-1211 to seek partition and divide the jointly owned assets. However, the award to Judy of any interest in the shop appears inconsistent with the parties' intentions. Judy made no claim to the shop and disavowed any interest in it during the proceedings.

We therefore vacate the opinion of the court of appeals and remand the case to the trial court for a redistribution of the property not inconsistent with this opinion.

HOLOHAN, C.J., and HAYS, CAMERON and FELDMAN, JJ., concur.

Discussion Questions

1. Why did the Court of Appeals reverse the trial court's finding of an implied agreement to share property? How did the Arizona Supreme Court clarify the law regarding cohabitants' agreements?

2. If Arizona allowed common-law marriage, could Judy succeed in proving she was married?

In Washington, despite the abolition of common law marriage, the courts have allowed unmarried cohabitants to share *community property*. The cohabitants must have a "meretricious relationship" which is defined as a "stable marital-like relationship where both parties cohabit with knowledge that a lawful marriage between them does not exist." Please note that the Washington definition of a "meretricious" relationship is the exact opposite of the California definition.

FENN AND LOCKWOOD

136 Wash. App. 1017 (2006)
Court of Appeals of Washington

BRIDGEWATER, J.

John B. Lockwood appeals: (1) the trial court's determination that he and M. Frieda Fenn were in a meretricious relationship; and (2) the trial court's equitable distribution of property, particularly the separate property (i.e., the family home), from that relationship. Fenn cross-appeals, arguing that the trial court abused its discretion when it equitably distributed 45 percent of the community property to her and 55 percent of the community property to Lockwood. We affirm in part, regarding the trial court's determination that the parties were in a meretricious relationship and the trial court's division of the community property to each party; but we reverse and remand for a just and equitable distribution of only the community property, without consideration of the parties' separate property.

FACTS

Fenn and Lockwood began dating in the summer of 1984. They developed an exclusive dating relationship and thereafter began living together in 1986. Six to eight months after living together, they hosted an "engagement party," during which they told family and friends that they wanted to start a family. In 1987, Fenn and Lockwood held a ceremony "to memorialize their lifelong commitment to each other and their goals." No officiant was present at the ceremony and neither party obtained a marriage license. Instead of rings, Fenn and Lockwood exchanged necklaces.

Before they lived together, Lockwood had quit his job and had started to design kayak kits. By the time of their commitment ceremony, Lockwood started selling these kits. In 1988, he obtained a business license for Pygmy Boats; in 1995, he incorporated the business, naming himself as the sole shareholder. During the early years of Pygmy Boats, Lockwood performed all the business functions, leaving him with little time for other things. And Fenn worked as a baker and a dishwasher for several employers.

Meanwhile, their daughter, Freya Fennwood,[1] was born in 1988. The parties agreed to raise her according to certain childrearing practices; but they soon

---

1. "The parties chose her last name to reflect their intent to be seen as a unit with a mixture of independence & dependence."

found that it was difficult to adhere to these practices in a modern workplace. As a result of these and other circumstances, Fenn primarily raised their daughter while Lockwood primarily ran the business.

In 1992, Fenn and Lockwood separated, living apart for 18 to 24 months. Fenn and Lockwood referred to this separation as their "two hut household." During this time, they continued to have "intimate relations, raise their child together, eat meals and sleep together three to five times a week." Thereafter the parties reconciled.

In 1997, Fenn and Lockwood acquired a house and real property on Jefferson Street in Port Townsend. In a written statement, they agreed that Fenn would own 41.5 percent as her separate property and that Lockwood would own 58.5 percent as his separate property.

But in 2002, the parties permanently separated. In 2003, Fenn filed for an equitable distribution of the property. The trial court concluded that Fenn and Lockwood were in a meretricious relationship. Thereafter, the trial court awarded 45 percent of the community property to Fenn and 55 percent of the community property to Lockwood. Within the award to Fenn, the trial court included Lockwood's "separate share" of the Jefferson Street property.

ANALYSIS

I.   MERETRICIOUS RELATIONSHIPS

A meretricious relationship is a "stable, marital-like relationship where both parties cohabit with knowledge that a lawful marriage between them does not exist." The use of such terms as "marital-like" or "marriage-like" are mere analogies because defining meretricious relationships as related to marriage would create a de facto common-law marriage, which our Supreme Court has refused to do. When a meretricious relationship terminates, the trial court must use a three-prong analysis for disposing of property.

First, the trial court must determine whether a meretricious relationship exists. Accordingly, the trial court analyzes five relevant factors: (1) the purpose of the relationship; (2) the pooling of resources and services for joint projects; (3) the intent of the parties; (4) the degree of continuous cohabitation; and (5) the duration of the relationship. These factors are neither "exclusive nor hypertechnical." These factors are meant to reach all relevant evidence helpful in establishing whether a meretricious relationship exists. Thus, whether a relationship is properly characterized as meretricious depends on the facts of each case.

Second, if such a relationship exists, the trial court evaluates the interest each party has in the property acquired during the relationship. "The critical focus is on property that would have been characterized as community property had the parties been married." Both the property owned by each party before the relationship and the property that would have been characterized as separate property had the couple been married should not be before the court for distribution at the end of the relationship.

While property acquired during a meretricious relationship is presumed to belong to both parties, this presumption can be rebutted.[3] If the presumption is not rebutted, the trial court may look to the dissolution statute, RCW 26.09.080, for guidance in fairly and equitably distributing the property acquired during a meretricious relationship.

Third, the trial court must make a just and equitable distribution of such property. The trial court may consider all relevant factors, including but not limited to, the nature and extent of the community property and the economic circumstances of each spouse at the time the division of the property is to become effective. Therefore, "The court may consider the health and ages of the parties, their prospects for future earnings, their education and employment histories, their necessities and financial abilities, their foreseeable future acquisitions and obligations, and whether ownership of the property is attributable to the . . . efforts of one or both spouses." Finally, when distributing the community property, the trial court's paramount concern should be the economic condition in which it leaves the parties.

Therefore, we review the trial court's conclusion that the parties were in a meretricious relationship.

II.   EXISTENCE OF A MERETRICIOUS RELATIONSHIP

Purpose of the Relationship

Lockwood claims that the "central aspect of marriage was distinctly absent from [their] relationship." Although he disputes the trial court's finding of fact that they participated in a "marriage-like relationship," he does not dispute the trial court's findings regarding the purpose of their relationship.

The trial court found that the purpose of the Lockwood and Fenn relationship included:

> companionship, love, sex, mutual support, having a child, raising their daughter, participating in a community to live like a marriage, but without state or religious involvement, to operate like — and present themselves to the world as — a family, and to share the joys and responsibility of parenting.

Lockwood and Fenn shared common goals for their family, business, and community. In fact, one of their goals was "to have a child and raise that child consistent with their common principles." Lockwood did not intend to be the "sole bread-winner" in the relationship; Fenn did not intend to be "financially dependent." And although both Lockwood and Fenn agreed to live in a "Pygmy Society," neither party could follow those ideals because they had to make accommodations for living in a first world country.

In addition, even after an attorney advised the parties in 1997 that the State of Washington had adopted the concept of meretricious relationships, Lockwood took no steps "to avoid operation of the legal consequence of being in a meretricious

---

3. The fact that title has been taken in the name of one of the parties does not, in itself, rebut the presumption of "common ownership."

relationship." Because Lockwood has not challenged these findings of fact, they are verities on appeal. And these findings assist us in our review of the trial court's conclusion.

Pooling of Resources

Lockwood claims that they never pooled their resources and services for joint projects. But he fails to observe that this factor is neither exclusive nor hypertechnical. The question is not simply whether they pooled their resources and services for joint projects; the question is whether they pooled and invested their time, effort, or financial resources enough to require an equitable distribution of property.

As Fenn notes, she and Lockwood "started with almost nothing. . . . They sacrificed, struggled, dreamed and thrived as a family." But Fenn and Lockwood "pooled their resources and services for joint projects, including work for Pygmy Boats, housekeeping, child rearing and breast[-]feeding." Ultimately, the community produced two significant "assets": Freya Fennwood and Pygmy Boats.

Shortly after beginning their relationship, Fenn and Lockwood shared a house in Seattle, which included a workshop for building kayaks. While the parties had separate bank accounts at this time, they each shared the household and living expenses.

And while the parties had many separate bank accounts, they also had joint bank accounts. "They mixed payment of expenses among these accounts. They moved money in and out of accounts. Both parties used credit cards for various meals and restaurants." Lockwood used his income "to pay community expenses, including meals eaten out by him, her or together."

The trial court found that Lockwood built his prototype kayak while the parties shared their house in Seattle. And it found that Lockwood did not acquire suppliers and did not begin selling the kayak kits until after he and Fenn had started their relationship. When Lockwood later started Pygmy Boats in Port Townsend, "Lockwood referred to Pygmy Boats as 'we' in order to make the business appear larger than a one man operation." Advertisements for the business referred to Pygmy Boats as a family business. Finally, newspaper and magazine articles about the business referred to Fenn and Lockwood as husband and wife.

In both Seattle and Port Townsend, the parties maintained a business office in their residence. Pygmy Boats paid rent to Fenn and Lockwood for use of the business office in their Port Townsend residence. The parties deposited the rent paid into either the parties' joint bank account or Lockwood's individual bank account. "There was no clear pattern of which account received the rent payment." In addition, the parties' personal phone number was the same as the business phone number. At either the business shop or the parties' home, all calls were answered, "Pygmy Boats."

After incorporating Pygmy Boats in 1995, Fenn and Lockwood jointly consulted with their accountant and their attorney for ways to minimize their taxes. On their professionals' advice, Fenn and Lockwood made Fenn an officer of the corporation and provided her a salary comparable to Lockwood's salary. And, depending on how they could most reduce their combined tax liability, either Fenn or Lockwood would claim Freya Fennwood as a dependent on his or her individual tax return.

Finally, although Lockwood paid the taxes on the family home out of his individual bank accounts, the community benefited from his actions.

Lockwood provided "the bulk of family labor" to Pygmy Boats, from which the community benefited. And Fenn provided "the bulk of family labor" to maintaining the household, caring for their daughter, and preparing the meals. CP at 29. Nevertheless, Fenn did work for Pygmy Boats. In particular, she managed the small business when Lockwood was on extended vacations. For some of these services, she was paid as an employee. For other of these services, she was not paid.

With regard to raising a family, Fenn and Lockwood agreed that their daughter:

> would be "worn," breast[-]fed for a long period of time, would not be placed in institutional day care, sleep in the "family bed", not eat food ground by a food mill, they would pre-chew her food, leave her undiapered when possible, receive infant massage, live like an "Eskimo Club," not be left in a playpen, be carried rather than strollered and would be home schooled.

Although both parties shared these values and tried to adhere to them, these childrearing practices conflicted with the environment of most workplaces. Because of this conflict, Fenn and Lockwood "made choices of how they would contribute to the community. Ms. Fenn's contribution was primarily through Freya. Mr. Lockwood's contribution was primarily through Pygmy Boats."

In fact, Lockwood denigrated Fenn for her contribution to the community. Although the trial court found that he was not deliberately unappreciative of her work, Lockwood measured contributions to the community "in dollars and cents." Because maintaining the household, caring for their daughter, and preparing the meals could not be measured "in dollars and cents," Lockwood did not recognize Fenn's contributions to the community. Lockwood did not provide, nor did he wish to provide, the labor and services necessary to maintain the household or care for their daughter.

Although Fenn's lack of financial contribution to the community was a source of conflict between the parties, Lockwood did not offer to care for their daughter part time so that Fenn could work part time. And Lockwood did not try to find child care for their daughter because "he was very busy at Pygmy Boats."

While Lockwood argues that these facts are no different from the facts in *Pennington*, the facts in this case, unlike in *Pennington*, show that Fenn substantially invested her time and effort for the mutual benefit of the parties. We agree with the trial court that Fenn and Lockwood jointly pooled their time, effort, and/or financial resources enough to require an equitable distribution of property, as contemplated by *Connell*.

Intent of the Parties

Lockwood argues that the trial court erred in finding that he and Fenn "decided to create and participate in a marriage-like relationship without participating in a state substantiated process." He also argues that the trial court erred in finding that he and Fenn "intended to have separate identities and accounts; but intended to be in a meretricious relationship."

But even assuming, without deciding, that the trial court erred in entering these findings of fact, numerous other findings of fact support the trial court's conclusion that the parties intended to form a meretricious relationship. The trial court found that Fenn and Lockwood had invited guests to an "engagement party," where they told family and friends that "they wanted to have a family together." According to Lockwood, the purpose of the party was " 'to present ourselves to persons who stood in the shoes of [ ] potential in-laws, letting them know this is a long term relationship, letting them be comfortable with the fact that each of us was going to be in the other person's life.' "

Thereafter, Fenn and Lockwood held a ceremony in which they memorialized "their lifelong commitment to each other and their goals." No officiant was present at the ceremony, and the parties had not obtained a marriage license. After the ceremony, Fenn and Lockwood "honeymooned at a friend's home on Lopez Island, then in the southwest Four Corners." Even though the ceremony was similar to a Quaker wedding, both parties knew that a legal marriage did not exist.

Both parties had discussed their "wishes" for what they intended to be a long term relationship. Lockwood did not want to be "the sole breadwinner," and Fenn did not want to be financially dependent.

The trial court found, "Regardless of the term used, they referred to their unit as a family." Lockwood referred to Fenn as his "wife." He also referred to his relationship with Fenn as a "domestic [p]artnership." And, although Fenn preferred the term "partners," she referred to Lockwood as her "husband" during her campaign for a position on the Port Orchard city council. And in her campaign material, she specifically referred to Pygmy Boats as a "family business." Finally, both Fenn and Lockwood remained monogamous throughout their relationship, even during their separation.

Unlike *Pennington*, both Fenn and Lockwood intended to be in a stable, long-term, cohabiting relationship. And as previously noted, even after an attorney advised the parties that the State of Washington had adopted the concept of meretricious relationships, Lockwood took no steps "to avoid operation of the legal consequences of being in a meretricious relationship," except with regard to the Jefferson Street property, as discussed below. This written agreement as to the separate ownership of the Jefferson Street property implies that all other property was community property. It also implies that the parties knew how to divide property into separate ownership, yet did so only with the Jefferson Street property.

Therefore, we agree with the trial court that Fenn and Lockwood "intended to memorialize their lifelong commitment to each other and their goals" and intended to be in a long term relationship with the other. And again, these findings assist us in our review of the trial court's conclusion.

Continuous Cohabitation & Duration of the Relationship

The trial court found, "The parties cohabitated continuously for over 16 years. This included a period of 18-24 months, during which they lived in separate homes; after which they reconciled." Furthermore, the trial court found, "The parties referred to that 18-24 month period as a 'two hut household.' During that time the[y] continued to have intimate relations, raise their child together, eat meals and sleep together three to five times a week." And even Lockwood concedes that he and

Fenn were in a continuous cohabitating relationship. Substantial evidence demonstrates that Fenn and Lockwood were in a stable cohabitating relationship.

Therefore, we agree with the trial court's conclusion that Fenn and Lockwood were in a meretricious relationship.

III. PROPERTY ACQUIRED DURING THE MERETRICIOUS RELATIONSHIP

Having concluded that the facts gave rise to a meretricious relationship, the trial court made a list of the parties' separate and community property. Lockwood's separate property totaled $472,559. Fenn's separate property totaled $158,135. The property that Fenn and Lockwood acquired during their meretricious relationship totaled $1,335,807.

The trial court then concluded that 45 percent of the community property should be awarded to Fenn and 55 percent of the community property should be awarded to Lockwood. Thus, the trial court distributed $601,113 of the community property to Fenn, including: (1) $82,367 in community assets; (2) Lockwood's $215,000 "share" of the Jefferson Street property; and (3) $303,746 from the Merrill Lynch Account. The trial court distributed $756,394 of the community property to Lockwood.

On appeal, Lockwood argues that the trial court erred in concluding that the Jefferson Street property was properly before it and subject to a just and equitable distribution. Fenn argues that Lockwood did not raise this issue below and that we should not consider his assignment of error. If anything, Fenn claims that Lockwood invited the error.

But separate property acquired during the meretricious relationship is not before the trial court for division. *Connell*, 127 Wn. 2d at 351. And we have no evidence, authority, or concession from either party that the trial court could dispose of the Jefferson Street property along with the community property upon termination of the meretricious relationship. Furthermore, because no finding of fact supports the conclusion of law that "[e]ven if the parties had an enforceable separate property agreement, enforcement of such an agreement would result in unjust enrichment," we strike it.

Nevertheless, Lockwood rebutted the presumption that the Jefferson Street property should be treated as community property. The trial court specifically found, "At the time of acquisition the parties entered a written agreement regarding their ownership interests in the Jefferson Street Property. They agreed that Mr. Lockwood would own 58.5 [percent] as his separate property and Ms. Fenn would own 41.5 [percent] as her separate property. The parties abided by this agreement."

Thus, the Jefferson Street property was never properly before the trial court for distribution, apart from declaring the parties to be joint tenants. *Connell*, 127 Wn. 2d at 352. And the trial court should not have treated this property as community property. Lockwood is correct that the trial court erred in distributing his separate "share" of the Jefferson Street property. On remand, the trial court should not place before it either party's separate property. It must treat the parties as joint tenants in the Jefferson Street property.

iv.   DISTRIBUTION OF PROPERTY

On cross-appeal, Fenn argues that the trial court abused its discretion in distributing the community property. Essentially, Fenn claims that there can be "no justification" for awarding Lockwood 55 percent of the community property when he owns more than three times the amount of separate property and earns more than 27 times the amount of income when compared with her. We disagree with Fenn.

The trial court has broad discretion in awarding property when a meretricious relationship terminates. *See In re Marriage of Fiorito*, 112 Wn. App. 657, 667, 50 P.3d 298 (2002). Absent an abuse of discretion, we will not reverse the trial court's decision. *Fiorito*, 112 Wn. App. at 668.

Here, the trial court considered many relevant factors, including the parties' economic conditions, in making a just and equitable distribution of the community property. As the trial court found, Fenn and Lockwood did not live an extravagant life style. Instead, they saved most of the money that they earned from Pygmy Boats for retirement. "They were frugal."

The trial court found, "In Mr. Lockwood's mind, Pygmy Boats was his creation. In many ways it was his vocation and avocation and his second family. This was recognized in the relationship." Fenn also knew that "Pygmy Boats was Mr. Lockwood's 'baby.'" At the time of trial, Lockwood received approximately $300,000 per year from his work at, and investments in, Pygmy Boats. But Lockwood is 62 years old and plans to retire or semi-retire. The trial court also found that Fenn is 48 and will have "10-15 years of a professional working life, if she chooses." Finally, the trial court found, "Awarding Pygmy Boats, Inc. to Mr. Lockwood fulfills the parties' intent that he retire and spend time in the wilderness."

Fenn argues that, given the findings of fact, "there is no tenable reason" to award Lockwood a disproportionate amount of community property. But based on such factors as the nature and extent of the community, the wishes of each party, and the economic circumstances of each party, the trial court awarded Fenn 45 percent of the community property and awarded Lockwood 55 percent of the community property. Such a distribution was not an abuse of discretion. Nevertheless, on remand, the trial court should make a just and equitable distribution that does not include either party's separate property; the trial court is free to dispose of the community property either in the same percentages or in different percentages when arriving at a just and equitable distribution.

Affirmed in part and remanded for a just and equitable distribution only of the parties' community property, not of the parties' separate property.

A majority of the panel having determined that this opinion will not be printed in the Washington Appellate Reports, but will be filed for public record pursuant to RCW 2.06.040, it is so ordered.

We concur: ARMSTRONG, J., and HUNT, J.

Discussion Questions

1. How similar is the Washington doctrine of "meretricious relationship" to common-law marriage?

2. Despite Fenn and Lockwood's intentions at the beginning of their relationship, did their relationship resemble a traditional marriage?

PROBLEM 2.1

Harry and Wilma met in 1995. Soon after, they began living together. They spoke about marriage, but they both said, "We don't need a piece of paper to confirm our commitment to each other." Harry worked as a civil engineer and Wilma worked as a receptionist in a doctor's office. Wilma took Harry's name and everyone thought that they were married. They placed their earnings in a joint bank account and filed income tax returns as a married couple.

After their first child was born in 1998, Wilma stayed at home. They had two more children. Wilma took care of all the family bookkeeping. In 2000, they had saved enough to buy a home. The title to the home was taken in Harry's name and the funds to buy the home came from Harry's earnings. According to Wilma, they had agreed that the home belonged to both of them. Over the years, they acquired other properties for investment. All the titles were in Harry's name. Some of the properties were rental apartments and Wilma took care of all the paperwork concerning the rentals. Recently, they have had financial troubles and they have separated. Harry is claiming that all the properties belong to him. Wilma consults an attorney to find out what her rights are regarding those properties. What would Wilma's rights be under the laws of each community property state?

Table 2-2
Unmarried Cohabitants Rights in Community Property States

State	Rule	Case/Statute
Arizona	Follows *Marvin v. Marvin*, allowing written, oral and contracts implied from conduct. Homemaking services are adequate consideration for an implied agreement to share property.	*Cook v. Lee*, 142 Ariz. 573, 91 P.2d 664 (1984), approving written, oral and implied contracts between unmarried cohabitants to pool income, acquire assets and share in accumulations. *Carroll v. Lee*, 148 Ariz. 10, 712 P.2d 923 (1986), homemaking services if severable from the meretricious can support an implied agreement
California	Written, oral and agreements implied from conduct allowed. Later cases require additional proof of sharing conduct beyond living together and holding out as husband and wife. Recognizes Same-Sex Domestic Partners	*Marvin v. Marvin*, 18 Cal. 3d 660, 557 P.2d 106, 134 Cal. Rptr. 815 (1976) *Alderson v. Alderson*, 180 Cal. App. 3d 450, 225 Cal. Rptr. 610 (1986), *Maglica v. Maglica*, 66 Cal. App. 4th 442, 78 Cal. Rptr. 2d 101 (1998) Ca. Fam. Code §297 (2005, as amended 2011)

Idaho	Idaho abolished common-law marriage as of 1996. Pre-1996 cases stated: "A court of equity will protect the property rights [during their relationship], either according to their agreement in respect to property, or according to principles of equity and justice."	Idaho Code §32-201 (1996) *Warner v. Warner,* 76 Idaho 399, 407, 283 P.2d 931, 935-36 (1955)
Louisiana	Unmarried cohabitants' relationship is referred to as concubinage. To share in real property, a concubine must be named on the deed and have contributed to its acquisition.	*Fairrow v. Marves,* 862 So. 2d 1234 (La. App. 2003)
Nevada	Follows *Marvin v. Marvin,* allowing contracts that are written, oral or implied from conduct.	*Western State Construction v. Michoff,* 108 Nev. 931, 840 P.2d 1220 (1992)
	Recognizes Same-Sex Domestic Partners	Nev. Rev. Stat. §122A.100 (2010)
New Mexico	Express oral contract between two cohabiting adults permitted, recognizing implied agreements would circumvent the prohibition of common-law marriage.	*Dominguez v. Cruz,* 95 N.M. 1, 617 P.2d 1322 (Ct. App. 1980), *Merrill v. Davis,* 100 N.M. 552, 673 P.2d 1285 (1983)
Texas	Rejection of *Marvin v. Marvin,* oral and implied from conduct contracts. Texas statute requires a written agreement.	Vernon's Texas Statutes, Family Code §1.108 (1987) *Zaremba v. Cliburn,* 949 S.W.2d 822 (Tex. App. 1997), indicates hostility to "palimony" suits
Washington	If cohabitants have a "meretricious relationship," courts will divide that property which would have been considered community property if they were married. A meretricious relationship is defined as a "marital-like relationship." It is not "meretricious" as defined in *Marvin v. Marvin,* which is a contract for prostitution. Requirements include "continuous cohabitation, duration of the relationship, purpose of the relationship, pooling of resources and services for joint projects and the intent of the parties." Recognizes Same-Sex Partners and Same-Sex Marriage	*In re Pennington,* 142 Wash. 2d 592, 14 P.3d 764 (2000) *Fenn and Lockwood* 136 Wash. 1017 (2006) Rev. Code Wash. §35.21.980 (2009), Same-Sex Marriage, Dec. 6, 2012
Wisconsin	No statutory right to property for unmarried cohabitants. Wisconsin Supreme Court has recognized protection for a cohabitant who relies on an express or implied in fact contract to share property. Claim must exist independently from the sexual relationship and is supported by separate consideration. Also available are claims for unjust enrichment and partition.	*Watts v. Watts,* 137 Wis. 2d 506, 405 N.W.2d 303 (1987) *Wis. Stat.* §770 (Domestic Partnership rights and obligations)

Chapter 3

Opting Out of the Community Property System: Standards for Premarital Agreements

A. VALIDITY/ENFORCEABILITY OF PREMARITAL AGREEMENTS

Premarital Agreements (also called antenuptial or prenuptial agreements) in community property states are used by couples to modify their rights and obligations in marriage. Early premarital agreements usually modified property inheritance rights upon death. By 1970, courts began to recognize premarital agreements in the event of divorce. Prior public policy objections to "contemplating" divorce in premarital agreements melted away, and instead these agreements were seen as positive developments because couples could decide in advance the details of a divorce settlement. For example, couples typically contract to opt out of the community property laws or to waive spousal support in the event of divorce.

For instance, consider our hypothetical couples. George and Martha are an older couple who are soon going to retire. If they decide to marry, they may want to clarify how their property would be divided if one spouse dies. This would be especially important if both have children from a prior marriage and they are bringing extensive property into the marriage that would be considered separate property. Harry and Wilma, a middle-aged couple, may have been married before and had experienced a difficult and contentious divorce. If they decide to marry, they may want to avoid the specter of possible divorce litigation by specifying that their earnings during marriage would be separate property and that they would waive spousal support in the event of divorce. Michael and Lisa, the youngest of our hypothetical couples, may believe that they should be financially independent even though they are committing to marriage. For them, a premarital agreement would spell out that their earnings would be separate property.

Until the 1980s, common law generally governed the community property states' approach to premarital agreements' validity and enforceability. Thus, there was great variance across the United States, including community property states, on these issues. Then, in 1983, the National Conference of Commissioners on Uniform State Laws promulgated the Uniform Premarital Agreement Act (UPAA) to encourage certainty and uniformity in the enforcement of premarital agreements. Most community property states have adopted the UPAA and use it as the basis for their statutory laws on premarital agreements. Louisiana and Washington are the only community property states whose laws are not based upon the UPAA.

1.   *Factors that Determine Validity: The Nevada Experience*

In *Buettner v. Buettner* (Nevada 1973), the couple signed a premarital agreement that established property rights and liabilities in the event of death or divorce. The court examined the validity of these provisions, and whether the agreement was signed under fraud, misrepresentation, material nondisclosure, or any other factor that would indicate unfairness or unconscionability. *Sogg v. Nevada State Bank* (Nevada 1992) and *Fick v. Fick* (Nevada 1993) both involved premarital agreements that were entered into prior to the state's adoption of the UPAA. In *Sogg*, the wife sought to declare the agreement unenforceable because it was signed shortly before the wedding and she was inadequately represented by independent counsel. In *Fick*, the wife sought to invalidate the premarital agreement because the husband did not fully disclose his assets and obligations prior to her signing.

BUETTNER v. BUETTNER

89 Nev. 39, 505 P.2d 600 (1973)
Supreme Court of Nevada

Zenoff, Justice:

The parties to this action, in contemplation of marriage, entered into an antenuptial agreement which provided, in pertinent part, as follows:

> 3. Both parties to this agreement, by execution hereof, do hereby agree and understand that they do completely and forever in the future relinquish all rights and claims, both legal and equitable, in the separate property estate of the other, except as otherwise set forth in this agreement.
>
> 4. That in consideration of said marriage and of the covenants of this agreement, JOHN A. BUETTNER and STELLA BEHNEN hereby promise and agree to give, devise and bequeath by their last wills and testaments to each other, one half of all property of whatever kind and wherever situated owned by each other at the time of their death, together with a contingent interest in the remaining one half of all such property as set forth in said wills which are to be executed after the marriage of the parties.
>
> * * *
>
> 5. In the event that either of the parties to this agreement obtain a decree of divorce in the future thereby terminating the contract of marriage of the parties, STELLA BEHNEN, in addition to one half share of the community property of the parties, shall receive from

JOHN A. BUETTNER in release and discharge of all rights, claims interests in law and equity which she might have or could have in/or to his estate or property, real or personal, or any part thereof, the following described property to have and to hold as her separate property to-wit:

(A) House and lot located at 1130 Ralston, Las Vegas, Nevada, together with all household goods and furniture located therein subject to the existing 1st Trust Deed.

(B) The sum of Five Hundred Dollars ($500.00) per month each and every month for a period of five years for a total amount of Thirty Thousand Dollars ($30,000.00).

Said money shall be paid to STELLA BEHNEN regardless of whether she remarries or not and shall commence on the first day of the month succeeding the issuance of the decree of divorce by a court of competent jurisdiction and continue thereafter on the first day of each succeeding month until paid in full.

The antenuptial agreement was silent as to the separate property if any, of Stella Behnen, but listed the separate property of John A. Buettner, which was later estimated by him to be worth approximately $400,000.00.

Subsequent to the execution of the contract, but on the same day (December 6, 1970), the parties were married. Both parties had been married previously and had children by prior marriages. On April 9, 1971 Mr. Buettner instituted divorce proceedings against his wife alleging fraud and misrepresentation in the inducement to sign the prenuptial agreement, mental cruelty and incompatibility. The wife in her answer advanced the antenuptial agreement and urged the court, in the event it should award plaintiff a divorce, to enter its decree as to property settlement and support in conformance with the agreement of the parties.

The judge, after trial to the court sitting without a jury, did not make any finding of fact as to plaintiff's allegation of fraud and misrepresentation by the wife to induce him to enter into the agreement. Nor did he make any finding as to the alleged mental cruelty of the wife. Instead, the divorce was granted upon the ground of incompatibility.

As to the antenuptial contract, the court entered its finding of fact as follows:

That said Pre-Marital Agreement, dated December 6, 1970, as entered into by and between the parties, is unfair and unjust to said parties.

As a conclusion of law, the court stated:

That the Pre-Marital Agreement . . . was made in derogation of marriage, is contrary to public policy and is therefore void. . . .

The court refused to honor the antenuptial agreement of the parties, where — under the wife would get the house, all household goods and furniture and $500.00 per month for 5 years, and instead awarded the wife a dining room set, a couch and $2,000 — payable at $166.67 per month for one year.

Mrs. Buettner has appealed from this decree claiming the trial court erred in refusing to give effect to the antenuptial agreement of the parties.

We are presented with two questions: (1) whether in this jurisdiction antenuptial contracts relating to property settlement and support in the event of divorce are void as contrary to public policy; and (2) if not, is this particular antenuptial contract so unconscionable or unfair that it should not be enforced?

1. While the court has never directly addressed itself to the question, a number of jurisdictions have announced the rule that contracts intended to promote or

facilitate the procurement of a divorce are void and unenforceable as contrary to public policy. See, e.g., *Posner v. Posner*, 233 So. 2d 381, 382 (Fla. 1970); *In re Cooper's Estate*, 195 Kan. 174, 403 P.2d 984, 998 (Kan. 1965).

The difficulty with the application of the rule is in determining when such a contract invites, promotes or encourages divorce. Agreements have been declared void which obligate one spouse to not defend or contest a divorce by the other spouse. Likewise, contracts under which there is an agreement to procure a divorce are invalid, as are those obligating the parties to conceal the true cause of the divorce by alleging another.

In addition, and by far the majority of the cases wherein such contracts are declared void, are those whereunder the husband sought to relieve himself of his duty to support the wife in the event of divorce, or to limit his liability for such support to a small fraction of that which a court would be likely to decree in light of the wife's needs and the husband's ability to pay. The reason such contracts tend to promote or encourage divorce is set forth in *Crouch v. Crouch*, 53 Tenn. App. 594, 385 S.W.2d 288, 293 (1964):

> Such contract could induce a mercenary husband to inflict on his wife any wrong he might desire with the knowledge his pecuniary liability would be limited. In other words, a husband could through abuse and ill-treatment of his wife force her to bring an action for divorce and thereby buy a divorce for a sum far less than he would otherwise have to pay.

While in the normal case the wife urges the invalidity of the contract, here, the husband, using a strange twist on the above rationale, argues that the contractual provision relating to the property settlement and support was so generous in favor of the wife that she was induced by the hope of financial gain to so abuse and mistreat her husband as to force him to bring an action for divorce.

We are unconvinced. We do not find, nor did the trial court find, that the prospective wife entered into the contract with the intent to obtain a divorce from Mr. Buettner and thereby profit financially. There was no finding that the wife caused the divorce. In fact, it is uncontradicted in the record that the serious acts of divorce were committed not by the wife, but by the husband, who, on at least two occasions, beat the wife severely because of her refusal to change her name to conform to that of his previous wife in order to commit a tax fraud. As a result of such beatings, appellant was hospitalized and required to undergo surgery. Similarly, we do not believe the agreement to be so generous in favor of the wife that she would be induced to seek a divorce as a source of financial gain. In fact, it seems clear, particularly in light of Section 4 of the agreement requiring reciprocal wills, that it would have been in the best financial interest of the wife to remain married, thereby sharing in her husband's moderate wealth during their joint lives, and standing to receive a large share of his estate at his death.

This case, then, does not stand on the same footing as those wherein certain types of antenuptial contracts are said to be violative of public policy because they induce, encourage or promote divorce.

Antenuptial contracts whereby the parties agree upon the property rights which each shall have in the estate of the other upon his or her death have long been held to be conducive to marital tranquillity and thus in harmony with public policy. We perceive no reason why a different rationale should apply where the parties have attempted to set contractually the property rights of each spouse and the amount of support due the wife in the event a prospective marriage fails.

Other jurisdictions do uphold antenuptial contracts relating to property settlement and support in case of divorce.

We quote with approval language of the Supreme Court of Florida in *Posner v. Posner*, 233 So. 2d 381, 384 (Fla. 1970):

> There can be no doubt that the institution of marriage is the foundation of the familial and social structure of our Nation and, as such, continues to be of vital interest to the State; but we cannot blind ourselves to the fact that the concept of the 'sanctity' of a marriage — as being practically indissoluble, once entered into — held by our ancestors only a few generations ago, has been greatly eroded in the last several decades. This court can take judicial notice of the fact that the ratio of marriages to divorces has reached a disturbing rate in many states. . . .
>
> With divorce such a commonplace fact of life, it is fair to assume that many prospective marriage partners whose property and familial situation is such as to generate a valid antenuptial agreement settling their property rights upon the death of either, might want to consider and discuss also — and agree upon, if possible — the disposition of their property and the alimony rights of the wife in the event their marriage, despite their best efforts, should fail. . . .
>
> We know of no community or society in which the public policy that condemned a husband and wife to a lifetime of misery as an alternative to the opprobrium of divorce still exists. And a tendency to recognize this change in public policy and to give effect to the antenuptial agreements of the parties relating to divorce is clearly discernible. Thus, in *Hudson v. Hudson*, Okl. 1960, 350 P.2d 596, the court simply applied to an antenuptial contract respecting alimony the rule applicable to antenuptial contracts settling property rights upon the death of a spouse and thus tacitly, if not expressly, discarded the contrary-to-public-policy rule.

The rule applicable to antenuptial contracts settling property rights upon the death of a spouse is set out by the Supreme Court of Kansas as follows:

> The general rule in this state is that contracts, made either before or after marriage, the purpose of which is to fix property rights between a husband and wife, are to be liberally interpreted to carry out the intentions of the makers, and to uphold such contracts where they are fairly and understandably made, are just and equitable in their provisions and are not obtained by fraud or overreaching. *In re Cantrell's Estate*, 154 Kan. 546, 119 P.2d 483, 486 (Kan. 1942).

We have given careful consideration to whether antenuptial contracts settling alimony and property rights upon divorce are to be viewed in this state as void because contrary to public policy, and hold that they are not. Nevertheless, as with all contracts, courts of this state shall retain power to refuse to enforce a particular antenuptial contract if it is found that it is unconscionable, obtained through fraud, misrepresentation, material nondisclosure or duress.

2. Having determined that antenuptial contracts settling property rights and alimony in the event of divorce are not per se void, we direct our attention to the question whether the particular contract in this case is unconscionable, unreasonable in amount or improperly obtained.

Respondent attaches much significance to the fact that the trial court made the following finding of fact:

> That said Pre-Marital Agreement . . . is unfair and unjust to said parties.

The finding, however, is merely conclusory. It indicates none of the indicia of unfairness or ultimate facts leading to the conclusion that the agreement was unfair and unjust. We therefore do not feel bound by the trial court's finding of fact that the contract was 'unfair and unjust.' The record does not reveal fraud, misrepresentation, material nondisclosure, duress or any other ultimate fact indicating unfairness or unconscionability of the contract.

The husband's own testimony from the record clearly shows the circumstances surrounding the execution of the contract:

> *Q:* And during the course of the discussion of marriage she wanted a pre-nuptial agreement; is that what you are telling us?
> *A:* It was mutually agreed.
> *Q:* What did he explain to you was the purpose of a antenuptial agreement?
> *A:* Protect both of our properties.
> *Q:* And that was your main desire, was it not?
> *A:* It was her, Stella and my desire.

* * *

> *Q:* But you didn't want to run a chance of just entering into a relationship where in the event that of your death that she might inherit your property or in the event of a divorce that you might have to divide half of your property with her, did you?
> *A:* No.
> *Q:* So, we can say, then, that you loved her with reservations.
> *A:* Well, to a certain extent.
> *Q:* But you wanted to retain your property rights and interest in your separate estate for the benefit of your children in case something happened, right?
> *A:* Right.
> *Q:* Because you had worked hard for your property, right?
> *A:* Right.
> *Q:* And it meant something to you, didn't it?
> *A:* Yes.
> *Q:* So, you didn't enter into this agreement down there recklessly, did you?
> *A:* No.
> *Q:* And you knew what it was all about and what you were about to do, your main purpose in going to Carelli's office was to be sure that your separate property was secure in the event anything occurred in the future as a way of divorce or separation; right?
> *A:* Right.

* * *

> *Q:* The amount that was arrived at was arrived at by you and Mrs. Buettner there in discussing it with Mr. Carelli, right?
> *A:* Right.
> *Q:* You are not claiming, of course, that your name was forged to this agreement.
> *A:* No.

Q: You freely and voluntarily signed it there in Mr. Carelli's office?

A: Yes.

Q: You are not claiming that Mr. Carelli or anybody else by duress induced you to sign this agreement?

A: No.

* * *

Q: . . . She never induced you to sign it?

A: It was just a mutual agreement.

In summary, we hold that the antenuptial contract should be enforced. It is not void as against public policy, and it was fair and reasonable in its provisions, understandably and intelligently entered into, and not obtained by fraud, misrepresentation or nondisclosure on the part of the wife.

Accordingly, we reverse and remand this matter to the trial court for proceedings consistent with this opinion.

THOMPSON, C.J., and MOWBRAY, GUNDERSON, and BATJER, JJ. concur.

Discussion Questions

1. The Court held that premarital agreements are not per se void as against public policy. Other community property states during this time period held that premarital agreements that induce divorce are void as against public policy. Can you think of provisions that might be void as against public policy? What reasons does the court cite for upholding premarital agreements that contemplate divorce?

2. Do you agree with the court's interpretation of the husband's testimony that the premarital agreement was neither unfair nor unconscionable? Why or why not?

Yes. he clearly wanted to protect himself

SOGG v. NEVADA STATE BANK

108 Nev. 308, 832 P.2d 781 (1992)
Supreme Court of Nevada

PER CURIAM

Victoria Sogg (Vicky) and Paul Sogg (Paul) met between 1972 and 1974, when both were married to other people. Paul was a successful general contractor, engaged in the business of acquiring and developing real estate. Vicky had been a professional country singer following her graduation from high school. In 1981, she left Las Vegas for Europe, where she was sporadically employed by her brother's company demonstrating wireless telephones to potential customers in various countries. While in Europe, Vicky also participated in DeForest, Inc., a partnership allegedly established to capitalize on differences in monetary exchange rates. Her participation in this partnership required an investment of $265,000, which she raised by securing a second mortgage on her house in Sherman Oaks, California, wrapped with a mortgage on her sister's house. Vicky returned to the United States in 1986, when the bank threatened to foreclose on the houses. She never received a return on her investment and was eventually unable to locate her "partners." She was told that the partnership went bankrupt in January of 1987, although she never received any documents to that effect and never consulted an attorney.

Vicky and Paul began dating in early 1987. Vicky was approximately fifty-five years old at the time, and Paul was approximately eighty-seven. Paul was divorced and Vicky was separated from her husband, Robert Fletcher (Fletcher). In April of 1987, Paul asked Vicky to marry him, and she obtained a divorce from Fletcher, which was paid for by Paul.

Prior to their marriage, Vicky was aware that Paul was a wealthy man. However, Vicky was never specifically informed of Paul's net worth, which was approximately twenty million dollars. Paul testified that prior to their wedding, he was aware that Vicky did not have substantial financial resources, but he believed Vicky was expecting to receive five million dollars from her European business venture.

The day before Paul and Vicky were to be married, Paul took Vicky to the office of his attorney, Mr. Avila (Avila), to sign a premarital agreement. Vicky testified that she was not given a copy of the agreement to read at the time. Avila told Vicky that she should review the agreement with her own attorney, and he took her to see a Mr. Cox (Cox), an attorney whose office was down the hall from Avila's. Avila had already arranged an appointment for Vicky with Cox. Cox met with Vicky alone and began reading parts of the agreement to her. He testified that she immediately had questions concerning certain provisions requiring her to return various items of jewelry that Paul had given her. After approximately twenty to thirty minutes, before Vicky and Cox had finished reviewing the agreement and before Cox had had the opportunity to offer Vicky his advice, Paul entered Cox's office unannounced. Paul testified that Cox and Vicky had been talking for an hour, and he wanted to know what was taking so long. Paul and Vicky began to argue and then left Cox's office, with Vicky in tears. At the time the couple left Cox's office, Paul was aware that Vicky was upset about provisions in the agreement concerning the jewelry he had given her and the payments he had made on her house, as well as the lack of a provision for her living expenses in the event of a divorce.

After the meeting in Cox's office, Paul called off the wedding and he and Vicky stopped talking to each other. Vicky returned the jewelry and the car that Paul had given to her. Several weeks later, the parties reconciled, and a new wedding date was set. Because the parties were in a hurry to get married prior to the date of their prearranged honeymoon, they did not discuss the premarital agreement again until shortly before the wedding. Vicky testified that she and Paul went to Avila's office to sign the agreement the day before their wedding. Avila was not present, but Paul and Vicky both signed the agreement in the presence of Avila's secretary. Vicky testified that she did not read the agreement at that time because Paul had told her that he had not had the opportunity to make any changes. In fact, she testified that she never actually read the document until after the marriage and honeymoon. Rather,

Vicky testified that she signed the agreement because Paul promised her that he would amend it when they returned from their honeymoon, to provide for her house in California and to allow her to keep the jewelry, furs, and car he had given her. Although an addendum to the agreement was eventually drafted, it was never signed by the parties.

Sometime after Vicky and Paul signed the premarital agreement and subsequent to the parties' marriage, Avila requested that Cox sign the attorney's certificate stating that he had counseled Vicky with respect to the agreement. Cox refused to sign the certificate after the marriage had taken place because he felt it would be misleading under the circumstances. Furthermore, Cox testified that he had not even seen the complete agreement prior to the parties' marriage, because the copy he had received did not contain any of the financial documents referred to as "attachments" in the agreement. Later, after Paul had initiated the divorce action, a second attorney, Mr. Swanson (Swanson), was also asked to review the agreement on Vicky's behalf. Swanson met once with both Paul and Vicky, but they never had the opportunity to review the entire agreement. Swanson's copy of the agreement was also missing the financial attachments, and he also refused to give his approval to the agreement.

Paul filed for divorce approximately eight months after the parties' marriage. The district court bifurcated the divorce action. During the first phase of the proceedings, the district court upheld the validity of the premarital agreement, finding that it had been voluntarily and knowingly entered into by both parties and that it was not unconscionable as a matter of law. During the second phase of the proceedings, the district court found that the jewelry, furs, and car given to Vicky by Paul were not gifts but were only for her use during the marriage, and that the mortgage payments he made on her house were a loan.

This court may review the validity of a premarital agreement de novo. *See also* NRS 123A.080(3). Because the premarital agreement in the instant case was adopted prior to this state's adoption of the Uniform Premarital Agreements Act (UPAA), this agreement will be found to be enforceable if it either conforms to the requirements of the UPAA or if it conforms to the common law, as interpreted by the courts of Nevada prior to enactment of the UPAA.

We have previously held premarital agreements to be enforceable unless "unconscionable, obtained through fraud, misrepresentation, material nondisclosure or duress." Other jurisdictions have held such agreements to similar standards. Because of the presumed fiduciary relationship existing between parties who are engaged to be married, a presumption of fraud has been found where the agreement entered into greatly disfavors one of the parties. This presumption may be overcome by a showing that the party claiming disadvantage was not in fact disadvantaged. Factors to consider include whether the disadvantaged party (1) had ample opportunity to obtain the advice of an independent attorney, (2) was not coerced into making a rash decision by the circumstances under which the agreement was signed, (3) had substantial business experience and business acumen, and (4) was aware of the financial resources of the other party and understood the rights that were being forfeited. Because, in the instant case, the premarital agreement signed by Vicky left her with no resources or means of support in the event of a divorce, and because Vicky probably would have received more under the community property laws of Nevada were it not for the premarital agreement, there is a presumption that the agreement was fraudulent. Therefore, the agreement should not be enforced unless this presumption is overcome by the aforementioned considerations.

The presumption of fraud may be overcome by a finding that the disadvantaged party had the opportunity to consult with an attorney of his or her own choosing.

[I]n the instant case, the premarital agreement was drafted by Avila, Paul's attorney. Avila had been Vicky's attorney during her previous divorce, so she had reason to trust him. On the day Vicky was first presented with the agreement, Avila had arranged an appointment for Vicky to meet with Cox. Vicky was never advised that she should select her own attorney. Cox spent less than an hour discussing the agreement with Vicky, and they were unable to discuss it in its entirety because Paul interrupted them. After the parties' marriage, when Cox was asked to sign the attorney's certificate, he refused because he felt that he had not been able to independently advise Vicky. Therefore, we conclude that Vicky did not receive the benefit of counsel from her brief meeting with Cox.

In addition, we reject Paul's contention that Vicky had ample opportunity to seek the advice of counsel between the time Paul called off the wedding and the time the parties reconciled. Because Vicky had no reason to know that the agreement would again become necessary, she had no reason to consult an attorney. Furthermore, she had not been given a copy of the agreement that she could show to an attorney. Finally, when Vicky was asked to sign the agreement a second time, shortly before the second wedding date, Paul's attorney was not present and Vicky was not given time to consult with her own attorney. Thus, we conclude that Vicky was not accorded an opportunity to obtain the assistance of counsel sufficient to overcome the presumption of fraud.

The circumstances surrounding the signing of a premarital agreement must also be considered in determining its enforceability.

In the instant case, Vicky was taken to Paul's attorney's office to sign the premarital agreement the day before their initial wedding date. While consulting with the attorney chosen for her by Paul, Paul interrupted Vicky, demanding to know the reason for the delay. Because she would not sign immediately, Paul called off the wedding. When Paul contacted Vicky several weeks later to attempt a reconciliation, he stressed that they had to get married immediately so that they would not miss the honeymoon cruise they had planned. Vicky was not presented with a copy of the agreement again until the morning of her wedding, when she was again under pressure to sign it because her wedding would be called off if she did not. We conclude that the circumstances surrounding the signing of the agreement prevented Vicky from adequately protecting her rights. Therefore, these circumstances support Vicky's contention that the agreement should not have been enforced.

Premarital agreements which seem unfair on their face will sometimes be upheld when the disadvantaged party to the agreement has substantial business experience.

[I]n this case, we find Paul's argument that Vicky was a sophisticated businesswoman tenuous. Paul argues that Vicky had substantial business experience because she (1) had managed her own finances during her career as a professional country singer, (2) had worked in Europe for five years, and (3) had been engaged in a business venture involving international currency arbitrage. In contrast, Vicky testified that the extent to which she managed her finances when she was a singer was that she cashed checks and deposited them into her bank account. Furthermore, her work in Europe consisted merely of demonstrating wireless telephone models for her brother's company. Finally, Vicky's involvement in "international currency arbitrage" consisted of her mortgaging her home to give money to four people who claimed to be engaged in this business, in exchange for the promise that she would receive five million dollars for her investment. Although she attended several meetings with this foursome while in Europe, she did not know whether a partnership or corporation had been formed, she was unable to locate her partners upon returning to the United States, and she did not know what had happened to the business when she left, except that someone had told her that it went bankrupt. Vicky took no action to protect her investment. We cannot but conclude that Vicky's business venture was a swindle in which she was the unwary prey, and that Vicky is in fact extremely unsophisticated with respect to business matters. Therefore, we conclude that the presumption that the premarital agreement is unfair is not overcome by the extent of Vicky's business experience.

Finally, premarital agreements will be enforced only where the party seeking to enforce the agreement fully disclosed his or her assets to the other party prior to signing.

In this case, the financial statement describing Paul's net worth was not attached to the agreement when Vicky signed it, although the agreement referred to this attachment. Paul testified that Vicky was familiar with his home, and that he had driven her around to see some of his other properties, although he had not told her their value. Although Vicky knew that Paul was wealthy, her testimony suggests that she underestimated the extent of his wealth. We conclude that Paul failed to make the disclosures necessary to permit Vicky to make an informed decision with respect to the premarital agreement, and that therefore, the agreement is invalid.

Because we conclude that the premarital agreement is invalid, we do not need to reach the issues arising from the second phase of the proceedings in this case. Accordingly, we reverse the judgment of the district court and remand this case with the instruction that it be retried before a different district court judge.

Discussion Questions

1. The court held that this premarital agreement was not enforceable. Why does the court presume that this premarital agreement was fraudulent? What are some of the factors that it considers in determining whether one party was disadvantaged? Do you agree with the court's assessment of Vicky's business acumen? *—yes*

2. Assume that you are Paul's attorney, how would you have counseled him with regard to the requirements for an enforceable premarital agreement?
• disclose all assets
• let her have ind. counsel
• don't contract for sub. less than court would order

FICK v. FICK

109 Nev. 458, 851 P.2d 445 (1993)
Supreme Court of Nevada

Per Curiam

THE FACTS

In 1981, appellant Robert N. Fick ("Robert") and respondent Bernice W. Fick ("Bernice") met and began living together. They married in 1984. Shortly before their wedding, the couple signed a prenuptial agreement drafted by Robert. The agreement set forth, among other things, a provision waiving Bernice and Robert's rights to alimony upon divorce. The corpus of the agreement acknowledged that each party attached a schedule of their various premarital assets and obligations. However, Robert did not attach his schedule until a year after they signed the agreement.

In 1986, the couple purchased a home in Las Vegas ("Las Vegas house") for approximately $55,000. In 1988, the couple also purchased an undeveloped lot in Cold Creek, Nevada (the "lot").

Bernice filed for divorce in 1989. After a bench trial, the district court entered a divorce decree and issued findings of fact and conclusions of law ("findings"). In the findings, the court: (1) characterized the lot as community property and ordered it sold; (2) valued the Las Vegas house at $60,000; (3) declared the alimony waiver provisions of the prenuptial agreement unenforceable; (4) granted Bernice $14,400 in unpaid support, $3,000 in rehabilitative alimony and $3,000 in attorney's fees.[1] Robert appealed.

On appeal, Robert argues that the district court: (1) improperly divided and characterized the lot as community property because the parties allegedly held the lot in joint tenancy; (2) erred in valuing the Las Vegas home at $60,000; (3) wrongly invalidated the couple's prenuptial agreement; and (4) incorrectly awarded rehabilitative alimony. We affirm.

DISCUSSION

The Lot's Characterization and Division

Generally, the law presumes that all property acquired during marriage constitutes community property. Spouses may also hold property as joint tenants.

A valid deed showing that a married couple holds title to property in joint tenancy qualifies as clear and certain proof to overcome the community property presumption. Such a deed raises a rebuttable presumption that the property is, in fact, a joint tenancy-the separate property of each spouse. Nevertheless, pursuant to NRS 125.150(1)(b), at divorce the district court "shall" justly and equitably divide a couple's community property assets *and* all property placed in joint tenancy after July 1, 1979.

---

1. At oral argument, Robert's attorney stated that Robert has failed to tender the awarded support, alimony and attorney's fees.

The district court found that the lot was community property and ordered it sold at fair market value with the proceeds divided equally between the parties.

On appeal, Robert argues that the district court erred in characterizing the lot as community property.

However, assuming that we address this issue and conclude that the Ficks possessed a valid deed registering the lot as joint tenancy, NRS 125.150 allows for the equitable division of community property and joint tenancies, and thus the district court's alleged error in characterizing the land is harmless. *characterized wrong but divided correctly*

The Prenuptial Agreement's Alimony Waiver Provisions

We review the validity of premarital agreements de novo. A premarital agreement entered into before October 1, 1989, is enforceable if the agreement conforms with either the requirements of NRS Chapter 123A, the Uniform Premarital Agreement Act ("UPAA"), or Nevada common law.

Pursuant to the UPAA, a premarital agreement is enforceable without consideration if it is in writing and signed by both parties. A premarital agreement may, among other things, eliminate alimony. However, a prenuptial agreement is unenforceable if it was unconscionable at execution, involuntarily signed, or the parties did not fully disclose their assets and obligations *before* the agreement's execution. Under the common law, a prenuptial agreement is enforceable unless it is "unconscionable, obtained through fraud, misrepresentation, material nondisclosure or duress." [O]ne overcomes the presumption of invalidity by showing that the disadvantaged party: (1) had ample opportunity to consult an attorney, (2) was not coerced, (3) possessed substantial business acumen, and (4) understood the financial resources of the other party and the rights being forfeited under the agreement.

In the instant case, the district court invalidated the alimony waiver provisions of Bernice and Robert's prenuptial agreement. We concur.

Although Bernice voluntarily signed the agreement, had an opportunity to consult with legal counsel, was not coerced and possessed the acumen to understand the transaction, we hold that the agreement is unenforceable because Robert did not fully disclose his assets and obligations before Bernice signed it.

Both parties agree that Robert attached his inventory of assets and that Bernice initialed that schedule long after the couple exchanged marital vows. In fact, at trial Robert testified that when he and Bernice signed the agreement, he had not finished compiling his schedule of assets. Notwithstanding that Robert and Bernice cohabitated and started a business together prior to marriage, we conclude that given the extensive list of Robert's possessions, Bernice could not have known the full magnitude of Robert's assets and obligations before marriage.

Indeed, Robert's late disclosure contravenes both the clear language of NRS 123A.080(1)(c) and the spirit of *Buettner* and *Sogg.* Additionally, we hold that Bernice's initialing of Robert's asset schedule does not satisfy the disclosure requirement because full disclosure *must* occur *before* contract execution. In this context, other jurisdictions also support our interpretation of full disclosure prior to signing.

Moreover, we have acknowledged that fiancés share a confidential, fiduciary relationship; each has a responsibility to act with good faith and fairness to the other. Such a responsibility contemplates that each party will make a full and fair disclosure prior to the execution of a premarital agreement. Robert shirked this responsibility.

Thus, we conclude that the district court properly declared the alimony provisions of the Ficks' premarital agreement unenforceable.

Rehabilitative Alimony Award

In determining whether to grant alimony, as well as the amount thereof, the district courts enjoy wide discretion. Specifically, the court may grant alimony pursuant to NRS 125.150(8) for re-education and re-training to facilitate a spouse's re-entry into the labor market. However, a grant pursuant to subsection (8) requires the court to establish a time frame for the recipient to commence re-education. NRS 125.150(9).

The district court awarded Bernice $3,000 of rehabilitative alimony to gain re-training in her pre-marital profession.

A review of the record reveals that the district court heard substantial evidence that Bernice no longer commanded the skills necessary to re-enter the labor market. The lower court also learned of the disparity between Bernice's and Robert's respective earning potential. Bernice possessed a high school education while Robert had obtained a Ph.D., M.B.A., M.P.A., M.A. in general studies, economics and business and a teaching credential. Thus we hold that the district court did not abuse its discretion in granting Bernice $3,000 to update her job skills.

Nonetheless, we conclude that the district court failed to establish a time frame for Bernice to commence her re-training as required by NRS 125.150(9). As a result, we remand this matter to the district court. On remand the district court is ordered to establish a time frame pursuant to NRS 125.150(9) for Bernice to commence her re-education.

We have carefully considered the other issues raised and conclude that they lack merit or need not be addressed given our disposition of this appeal. Accordingly, we affirm the district court's judgment in part and remand in part.

Discussion Questions

1. For premarital agreements signed prior to the UPAA, what does the court presume with regard to validity? How can this presumption be overcome?

2. Post enactment of the UPAA, what are the requirements to enforce a premarital agreement? Why did the court hold that this premarital agreement was invalid?

3. The court holds that the premarital agreement's alimony provision is unenforceable because the husband did not fully disclose his assets and obligations prior to its execution. Does this result trouble you since the wife voluntarily signed the agreement, had ample time to consult with independent counsel, was not coerced, and had the business acumen to understand the transaction? What are some of the reasons behind the court requiring fiancées to fully disclose their assets and obligations in such a situation?

Note: On July 23, 2012, the Uniform Law Commission approved an updated Act dealing with premarital and marital agreements, the Uniform Premarital and Marital Agreements Act (UPMAA), which clarifies the enforcement criteria of voluntariness and unconscionability. Legislation to adopt the UPMAA was introduced in Nevada early in 2013. See Brian H. Bix, *A New Uniform Law for Premarital and Marital Agreements*, 46 Fam. L. Q. 313 (2012).

2. Factors that Determine Validity: The Views of Texas, California, and Washington

(a) Texas

In *Marsh v. Marsh* (Texas 1997), decided after the state's adoption of the UPAA, the husband argued that the premarital agreement was unenforceable. The agreement was signed shortly before the wedding, and the husband, who was not represented by independent counsel, claimed to have not read the agreement prior to signing.

MARSH v. MARSH

749 S.W.2d 734 (1997)
Court of Appeals of Texas

Before MURPHY, C.J., and ANDERSON and O'NEILL, JJ.

ANDERSON, Justice.

In this appeal, we must determine whether the parties' premarital agreement is unconscionable as a matter of law. The trial court found that it was not, enforced the agreement, and ordered that appellant, William T. Marsh ("Bill"), is indebted to appellee, Juanita Jacobs Marsh ("Juanita") in the amount of $867,778, plus pre- and post-judgment interest and attorney's fees. In seventeen points of error Bill argues that the agreement is unenforceable because it is unconscionable, the trial court incorrectly calculated pre-judgment interest and erroneously excluded evidence. We affirm.

Bill and Juanita were married on March 19, 1991. At the time of the marriage, Bill was 78 and Juanita was 58. Both had been married previously. Juanita was reluctant to agree to marry because of the financial losses she incurred from the long illness and decline of her deceased husband. She agreed to marry Bill on the condition that he would provide for her financially.

On the morning before their evening marriage, Bill and Juanita executed an "Agreement in Consideration of Marriage" ("the premarital agreement"), a Trust Agreement, and a Release. The documents were prepared by Juanita's attorney, Robert Jarrard, and Bill was not represented by counsel. According to the premarital agreement, as consideration for Juanita's agreement to marry him, Bill agreed to pay to Juanita, as her separate property, one-half of his assets, which included several accounts in his name at Legg Mason Wood Walker, Inc. ("Legg Mason"). The assets were to be transferred to the Juanita Jacobs Trust ("the Trust") within thirty days of the marriage. The Trust Agreement provides that Juanita is the trustee and sole beneficiary of the corpus of the Trust. Bill and Juanita are equal income beneficiaries of the Trust, as long as both are living. The Trust terminates at Bill's death and the corpus is to be distributed to Juanita. The Release recites that Bill was "strongly requested to obtain counsel," but he elected not to do so. The Release further states that each party fully understood the terms of the premarital agreement, each entered it freely and with informed consent, and it was not procured by fraud, duress or overreaching.

After their marriage, Bill paid approximately $189,000 into the Trust, but thereafter refused to make further payments. Juanita filed suit to enforce the agreement.[2] Bill answered, claiming the agreement is unconscionable, he did not receive adequate disclosure of Juanita's assets, he had no way to acquire adequate knowledge of the property or financial obligations of Juanita, and did not waive this right. Alternatively, he claimed the agreement was achieved through fraud, duress, or overreaching, or that his performance was excused because of a failure of a predicate to his performance. He also counterclaimed, seeking return of the funds paid to the Trust. The trial court entered temporary orders which required Bill to maintain a minimum balance of $1,200,000 in his Legg Mason account through final hearing. The case was tried to the court, which ruled in favor of Juanita and incorporated its ruling in a written judgment dated August 15, 1995. The trial court entered a Supersedeas Order requiring Legg Mason to hold $1,282,249 in escrow to secure the judgment. On September 14, 1995, Bill filed a motion for new trial, which was overruled by operation of law. The trial court filed findings of fact and conclusions of law.[3]

I.   ENFORCEABILITY

Effective September 1, 1987, Texas adopted the Uniform Premarital Agreement Act, which is codified in Chapter 5 of the Texas Family Code. Section 5.46 of the Family Code, which governs the enforcement of premarital agreements, provides as follows:

(a) A premarital agreement is not enforceable if the party against whom enforcement is sought proves that:
(1) that party did not execute the agreement voluntarily; or
(2) the agreement was unconscionable when it was executed and, before execution of the agreement, that party:
(A) was not provided a fair and reasonable disclosure of the property or financial obligations of the other party;
(B) did not voluntarily and expressly waive, in writing, any right to disclosure of the property or financial obligations of the other party beyond the disclosure provided; and
(C) did not have, or reasonably could not have had, an adequate knowledge of the property or financial obligations of the other party.

2. At the time of trial, the parties were still married although they were separated. When the cause was submitted to this court, neither party had filed for divorce.
3. Although Bill requested findings of fact and conclusions of law timely, the trial court did not file them until October 31, 1995. Bill has not raised a point of error on appeal complaining about the late filing, however.

(b) An issue of unconscionability of a premarital agreement shall be decided by the court as a matter of law.

(c) The remedies and defenses in this section are the exclusive remedies or defenses, including common law remedies or defenses.

Bill has not raised the issue of voluntariness on appeal. Instead, he contends the agreement is unconscionable as a matter of law. In his points of error one, two, five, six and seven, Bill attacks the trial court's findings and conclusions which impliedly determined the agreement was not unconscionable. Specifically, the trial court determined in conclusion of law no. 2 that the premarital agreement is a valid and enforceable agreement pursuant to the Texas Family Code.

* * *

UNCONSCIONABILITY

The legislature and people of Texas have made a public policy determination that premarital agreements should be enforced. Therefore, premarital agreements are presumptively enforceable. According to the statute, Bill, as the party opposing enforcement, bore the burden of proof to rebut the presumption of validity and establish the premarital agreement is not enforceable. *Id.;* TEX. FAM. CODE ANN. §5.46(a) (Vernon 1993).

However, neither the legislature nor Texas courts have defined "unconscionable" in the context of marital or premarital property agreements. Instead, Texas courts have addressed the issue of unconscionability on a case-by-case basis, looking to the entire atmosphere in which the agreement was made. In the absence of clear guidance as to the definition of "unconscionability" in marital property cases, courts have turned to the commercial context. For example, the following general discussion of unconscionability, taken from a case involving a suit on a real estate listing agreement, is sometimes cited:

> In determining whether a contract is unconscionable or not, the court must look to the entire atmosphere in which the agreement was made, the alternatives, if any, which were available to the parties at the time of the making of the contract; the non-bargaining ability of one party; whether the contract is illegal or against public policy, and, whether the contract is oppressive or unreasonable. At the same time, a party who knowingly enters a lawful but improvident contract is not entitled to protection by the courts. In the absence of any mistake, fraud, or oppression, the courts, as such, are not interested in the wisdom or impolicy of contracts and agreements voluntarily entered into between parties compos mentis and sui juris. Such parties to contracts have the right to insert any stipulations that may be agreed to, provided they are neither unconscionable nor otherwise illegal or contrary to public policy. It has accordingly been said that, almost without limitation, what the parties agree upon is valid, the parties are bound by the agreement they have made, and the fact that a bargain is a hard one does not entitle a party to be relieved therefrom if he assumed it fairly and voluntarily. A contract is not unenforceable on the ground that it yields a return disproportionate to the expenditures in time and money, where there has been no mistake or unfairness and the party against whom it is sought to be enforced has received and enjoyed the benefits.

In our review of the evidence, we first consider the evidence supporting the trial court's conclusion that the agreement is not unconscionable.

Both the premarital agreement and the Release expressly state that each party entered the agreement freely and knowingly. Bill testified that there were no threats, fraud, overreaching, duress, or misrepresentations made to him to induce him to execute the agreement. He also acknowledged that he was free to consult an attorney and accountant before its execution. There was no evidence presented that Juanita took advantage of Bill. There was no evidence that Bill was senile, and he denied that he was. He was active in trading stocks. A letter Bill wrote to Legg Mason requesting specific transfers to the Trust from one of his accounts showed Bill appeared to be well aware of what he owned.

Juanita testified that Bill agreed to the transfer of one-half of his Legg Mason accounts to the Trust. She denied ever seeing the Legg Mason documents before they were attached to the agreements. She also stated she "thinks" Bill read the agreement before signing it. Juanita testified she never threatened or dominated Bill, and that the agreement was not procured through fraud or duress.

Jarrard, the attorney who prepared the agreement, testified that Bill provided all the financial documents needed to draft the premarital agreement, and that he dictated portions of the agreement. Specifically, Bill requested that he be a lifetime beneficiary of one-half of the income from the Trust. This provision was incorporated in the Trust. Jarrard also testified that he met with both parties over several hours in discussing the proposed agreement, including three visits with Bill alone. Jarrard stated he discussed the gift tax consequences with Bill, and Bill offered to have his accountant prepare any required tax return. Jarrard further testified he believed the parties were provided a copy of the documents to review before they were executed and he was sure that Bill understood the documents. Jarrard testified he "strongly" recommended Bill obtain counsel[5] Bill admitted Jarrard encouraged him to see a lawyer, but contends that he was not emphatic.

The Release contains similar language.

Clearly, there is some evidence supporting the factual basis for the trial court's conclusion that the agreement is not unconscionable. Therefore, we now consider all the remaining evidence in the record to evaluate whether the trial court's determination is against the great weight and preponderance of the evidence.

In reviewing the validity of a marital property agreement, this court has considered such factors as the maturity of the individuals, their business backgrounds, their educational levels, their experiences in prior marriages, their respective ages and their motivations to protect their respective children. Bill argues, however, that he established the following factors which make the agreement in this case unconscionable:

> (1) the onerous circumstances of its execution, including:
>   (a) the parties' disparate bargaining power;
>   (b) the agreement's proximity in time to the marriage;
>   (c) the absence of counsel representing Bill's interests;
> (2) the oppressive, one-sided nature of the agreement; and
> (3) the failure of the agreement to effect the parties' intent.

5. The Agreement provides: It has been strongly recommended, by the counsel of [Juanita], that [Bill] obtain counsel for representation in the negotiations of this "agreement," however, [Bill] has elected not to retain independent counsel. [Bill] represents that he enters into this "Agreement" with informed consent and that this "Agreement" was not procured by fraud duress or overreaching.

Our review of the entire record does not reveal that the evidence overwhelmingly established these factors. We disagree that the parties had disparate bargaining power. Both were mature, educated, and had business experience. Juanita had grown children to consider, and Bill was childless. Both Bill and Juanita had been married before, and Juanita had seen her assets diminished through the lengthy illness of her late husband. Only Juanita had previously executed a premarital agreement, however.

The fact that the premarital agreement was signed shortly before the wedding does not make the agreement unconscionable. Likewise, the fact that Bill was not represented by independent counsel is not dispositive. Moreover, Bill consulted his long-time attorney, James Baker, shortly after his marriage and admitted that Baker pointed out several problems with the agreement. Juanita testified Bill told her the agreement was worthless. Contrary to his attorney's advice, Bill requested transfers of approximately $189,000 from his Legg Mason account to the Trust.

We also do not accept Bill's assertion that the one-sided nature of the agreement strongly preponderates toward a finding of unconscionability. This court has found that even though a premarital agreement may be disproportionate, unfairness is not material to the enforceability of the agreement. A factual finding that a premarital agreement is unfair does not satisfy the burden of proof required to establish unconscionability.

Bill argues that when he wrote the check to pay for Jarrard's services, he made a mistake in writing the amount, demonstrating that he was "not thinking straight" when he executed the agreement. While Bill testified that he remembered very little about the events leading to the execution of the premarital agreement, that he did not know the contents of envelopes he delivered to Jarrard to draft the agreement, and that he did not read the agreement, he was quite clear as to the value of the assets he transferred to the Trust and corrected Juanita's counsel as to the total amount. Bill acknowledged that before the marriage, he and Juanita did not live together and had no access to each other's financial information. He denied seeing the documents before their execution and testified he only spent about twenty minutes in Jarrard's office that day. The fact that Bill denied reading the premarital agreement is not grounds for avoiding the contract. Absent fraud, one is presumed to know the contents of a document he has signed and has an obligation to protect himself by reading a document before signing it.

The trial court, as the trier of fact, was the sole judge of the credibility of the witnesses and the weight to be given to their testimony. The court may not have believed Bill's denial that he knowingly provided his financial documents and helped draft the premarital agreement because the testimony showed that only Bill had access to his personal financial documents and that Juanita had never seen the documents until they were attached to the premarital agreement. We cannot retry the case or otherwise substitute our judgment for that of the trier of fact.

Over objection to testimony on matters of law, the trial court permitted Bill to present expert testimony from Donn Fullenweider, a board certified family law practitioner, who concluded that the premarital agreement is unconscionable per se. He testified the agreement was suspect because it was executed the day of the marriage and that Juanita's lawyer should have insisted that Bill have independent counsel. He also faulted the agreement for failing to contemplate the divorce of the parties. He conceded, however, that the Trust did not terminate upon divorce, and the Trustee had a duty to care for Bill during his lifetime with the Trust income. However, only Juanita has the power to withdraw the corpus of the trust and may do so at any time. In rebuttal, Juanita's expert, Warren Cole, also board certified in family law, testified that in his opinion, the premarital agreement is an enforceable contract. He opined that the agreement was definitely not unconscionable. For an agreement to be unconscionable, it must be "so far one-sided that no reasonable person could consider it to be an arm's length transaction." He testified fairness is not determinative of unconscionability.

Bill contends that the effect of the premarital agreement is to create a heavy tax burden for both parties, which was not the parties' intent. While it is true that the premarital agreement states the parties intended the transfers to the Trust to qualify for the "unlimited marital deduction gift," the agreement is silent as to any other tax consequences. Bill provided testimony from Mickey R. Davis, an estate-planning expert, who testified about the adverse tax consequences of the agreement. Davis opined that the premarital agreement may result in taxes of $450,000 to $550,000, which includes gift taxes, income taxes and potential estate taxes. He testified there was no way the parties could have understood the tax problems after a brief reading of the documents. Juanita's expert testified that adverse tax consequences would not cause the agreement to be unconscionable and have nothing to do with the enforceability or validity of the agreement. Juanita contends that any adverse tax consequences could have been corrected by reformation of the contract, but Bill failed to plead alternatively for reformation. Bill's tax expert agreed that the adverse tax effects of the agreement could be corrected. The trial court requested the parties to agree to modify or reform the agreement to alleviate any potential tax problem, yet Bill refused. In addition, Juanita has agreed to pay any gift taxes that result from the agreement, although the testimony was that Bill was legally responsible for the taxes.

In the absence of any evidence that the premarital agreement was obtained through an unfair advantage taken by Juanita, we must conclude Bill has not sustained his burden to defeat the presumption of enforceability. "[T]he fact that a bargain is a hard one does not entitle a party to be relieved therefrom if he assumed it fairly and voluntarily." Having reviewed all the evidence in our record, we conclude the evidence is both legally and factually sufficient to support the trial court's implied finding that the agreement is not unconscionable. Therefore, the trial court's conclusion of law that the agreement is enforceable is correct. We hold that the premarital agreement is not unconscionable as a matter of law. Therefore, we overrule appellant's points of error.

Discussion Questions

1. Who has the burden of proof regarding the premarital agreement's enforceability? What factors did the court use to determine whether the burden had been met?

2. The court holds that even disproportionate or unfair premarital agreements may be enforced. How would a party go about establishing then that such a premarital agreement should not be enforced?

3. The husband elects to focus on the unconscionability aspect of the premarital agreement. Is there a strong case for arguing that the agreement was signed involuntarily? Why or why not?

4. Assume that the wife was independently wealthy, or that the economic roles of the parties had been switched (i.e., the wife was wealthy with no children), do you think the court would have held differently? What language in the holding might lead you to this conclusion?

(b) California

In *Bonds v. Bonds* (California 2001), the court assessed the voluntariness of a premarital agreement signed by the wife of a famous baseball player. The premarital agreement was signed immediately before the couple's Las Vegas wedding, and the foreign-born wife was not represented by independent counsel. There was evidence that neither party understood the agreement's significance, and that the wife lacked English language skills.

MARRIAGE OF BONDS

24 Cal. 4th 1, 5 P.3d 815, 99 Cal. Rptr. 2d 252 (2000)
Supreme Court of California

GEORGE, C.J.

In this case we consider whether appellant Susann (known as Sun) Margreth Bonds voluntarily entered into a premarital agreement with respondent Barry Lamar Bonds. We conclude that the Court of Appeal erred in determining that because Sun, unlike Barry, was not represented by independent counsel when she entered into the agreement, the voluntariness of the agreement must be subjected to strict scrutiny. Instead, we determine that the circumstance that one of the parties was not represented by independent counsel is only one of several factors that must be considered in determining whether a premarital agreement was entered into voluntarily. Further, as we shall explain, we conclude that substantial evidence supports the determination of the trial court that the agreement in the present case was entered into voluntarily.

I

Sun and Barry met in Montreal in the summer of 1987 and maintained a relationship during ensuing months through telephone contacts. In October 1987, at Barry's invitation, Sun visited him for 10 days at his home in Phoenix, Arizona. In November 1987, Sun moved to Phoenix to take up residence with Barry and, one week later, the two became engaged to be married. In January 1988, they decided to marry before the commencement of professional baseball's spring training. On February 5, 1988, in Phoenix, the parties entered into a written pre-marital agreement in which each party waived any interest in the earnings and acquisitions of the other party during marriage. That same day, they flew to Las Vegas, and were married the following day.

Each of the parties then was 23 years of age. Barry, who had attended college for three years and who had begun his career in professional baseball in 1985, had a contract to play for the Pittsburgh Pirates. His annual salary at the time of the marriage ceremony was approximately $106,000. Sun had emigrated to Canada from Sweden in 1985, had worked as a waitress and bartender, and had undertaken some training as a cosmetologist, having expressed an interest in embarking upon a career as a makeup artist for celebrity clients. Although her native language was Swedish, she had used both French and English in her employment, education, and personal relationships when she lived in Canada. She was unemployed at the time she entered into the premarital agreement.

Barry petitioned for legal separation on May 27, 1994, in California, the parties then being California residents. . . . The petition was amended to request dissolution, and the court bifurcated the trial proceedings, first adjudicating the issue of the validity of the premarital agreement and then reaching the remaining issues involving application of the agreement to the property held by the parties. . . . Only the first issue — the validity of the premarital agreement — is before this court.

Barry testified that he was aware of teammates and other persons who had undergone bitter marital dissolution proceedings involving the division of property, and recalled that from the beginning of his relationship with Sun he told her that he believed his earnings and acquisitions during marriage should be his own. He informed her he would not marry without a premarital agreement, and she had no objection. He also recalled that from the beginning of the relationship, Sun agreed that their earnings and acquisitions should be separate, saying "what's mine is mine, what's yours is yours." Indeed, she informed him that this was the practice with respect to marital property in Sweden. She stated that she planned to pursue a career and wished to be financially independent. Sun knew that Barry did not anticipate that she would shoulder her living expenses while she was not employed. She was not, in fact, employed during the marriage. Barry testified that he and Sun had no difficulty communicating.

Sun's testimony at trial differed from Barry's in material respects. She testified that her English language skills in 1987 and 1988 were limited. Out of pride, she did not disclose to Barry that she often did not understand him. She testified that she and Barry never discussed money or property during the relationship that preceded their marriage. She agreed that she had expressed interest in a career as a cosmetologist and had said she wished to be financially independent. She had very few assets when she took up residence with Barry, and he paid for all their needs. Their wedding arrangements were very informal, with no written invitations or caterer, and only Barry's parents and a couple of friends, including Barry's godfather Willie Mays, were invited to attend. No marriage license or venue had been arranged in advance of their arrival in Las Vegas.

Several persons testified as to the circumstances surrounding the signing of the premarital agreement.

* * *

The trial court observed that the case turned upon the credibility of the witnesses. In support of its determination that Sun entered into the agreement voluntarily, "free from the taint of fraud, coercion and undue influence . . . with full knowledge of the property involved and her rights therein," the trial court made the following findings of fact: "Respondent [Sun] knew Petitioner [Barry] wished to protect his present property and future earnings. Respondent knew . . . that the Agreement provided that . . . Petitioner's present and future earnings would remain his separate property. . . . Respondent is an intelligent woman and though English is not her native language, she was capable of understanding the discussion by Attorney Brown and Attorney Megwa regarding the terms of the agreement and the effect of the Agreement on each [party's] rights. [¶] . . . [¶] . . . Respondent was not forced to execute the document, nor did anyone threaten Respondent in any way. Respondent never questioned signing the Agreement or requested that she not sign the Agreement. Respondent's refusal to sign the Agreement would have caused little embarrassment to her. The wedding was a small impromptu affair that could have been easily postponed. [¶] Respondent had sufficient knowledge of the nature, value and extent of the property affected by the Agreement. Petitioner fully disclosed the nature, approximate value and extent of all of his assets to Petitioner, both prior to and on the day of the execution of the agreement. [¶] Respondent had sufficient knowledge and understanding of her rights regarding the property affected by the Agreement, and how the Agreement adversely affected those rights. Respondent had the opportunity to read the Agreement prior to executing it. Attorneys Brown and Megwa explained to both parties their rights regarding the property affected by the Agreement, and how the Agreement adversely affected those rights. Respondent never stated prior to execution that she did not understand the meaning of the Agreement or the explanations provided by Petitioner's attorneys. [¶] Respondent had sufficient awareness and understanding of her right to, and need for, independent counsel. Respondent also had an adequate and reasonable opportunity to obtain independent counsel prior to execution of the Agreement. Respondent was advised at a meeting with Attorney Brown at least one week prior to execution of the Agreement that she had the right to have an attorney represent her and that Attorneys Brown and Megwa represented Petitioner, not Respondent. On at least two occasions during the February 5, 1988, meeting, Respondent was told that she could have separate counsel if she chose. Respondent declined. Respondent was capable of understanding this admonition. The wedding was a small impromptu affair that could have been easily postponed."

The court also determined that Barry and Sun were not in a confidential relationship at the time the agreement was executed. The trial court also declared that pursuant to a pretrial stipulation the burden of proof rested upon Sun, but that even if the court were to place the burden of proof upon Barry, Barry had demonstrated by clear and convincing evidence "that the agreement and its execution [were] free from the taint of fraud, coercion or undue influence" and that Sun "entered the agreement with full knowledge of the property involved and her rights therein."

The Court of Appeal in a split decision reversed the judgment rendered by the trial court and directed a retrial on the issue of voluntariness. The majority opinion stressed that Sun lacked independent counsel, determined that she had not waived counsel effectively, and concluded that under such circumstances the evidence must be subjected to strict judicial scrutiny to determine whether the agreement was voluntary.

We granted Barry's petition for review.

II

We first consider whether the Court of Appeal majority applied the appropriate legal standard in resolving the question whether the premarital agreement was entered into voluntarily. We conclude it erred in holding that a premarital agreement in which one party is not represented by independent counsel should be subjected to strict scrutiny for voluntariness. Such a holding is inconsistent with Family Code section 1615, which governs the enforceability of premarital agreements.

* * *

A

There is nothing novel about statutory provisions recognizing the ability of parties to enter into premarital agreements regarding property, because such agreements long were common and legally enforceable under English law, and have enjoyed a lengthy history in this country. In California, a premarital agreement generally has been considered to be enforceable as a contract, although when there is proof of fraud, constructive fraud, duress, or undue influence, the contract is not enforceable.

At one time, a premarital agreement that was not made in contemplation that the parties would remain married until death was considered to be against public policy in California and other jurisdictions, but this court concluded in 1976 that the validity of a premarital agreement "does not turn on whether the parties contemplated a lifelong marriage."

Persons contemplating marriage began to enter into agreements setting out property rights in contemplation of marital dissolution — rights that differed from those that would accrue under applicable statutes — but there was some uncertainty and considerable lack of uniformity regarding the circumstances under which such agreements would be enforceable. In order to encourage enforcement of such agreements on a more certain and uniform basis, while, according to the drafters of the act, retaining some "flexibility," the Uniform Premarital Agreement Act (hereafter sometimes referred to as the Uniform Act) was promulgated in 1983.

In 1985, the California Legislature adopted most of the provisions of the Uniform Act. The only provisions of the Uniform Act omitted by the California Legislature were those permitting the parties to waive the right to spousal support and limiting the right to waive spousal support where such a waiver would result in a spouse's becoming a public charge. This legislative omission is examined in today's decision in *In re Marriage of Pendleton & Fireman* (2000) 24 Cal. 4th 39, 99 Cal. Rptr. 2d 278, 5 P.3d 839, but is not involved in the present case.

B

Pursuant to Family Code section 1615, a premarital agreement will be enforced unless the party resisting enforcement of the agreement can demonstrate either (1) that he or she did not enter into the contract voluntarily, or (2) that the contract was unconscionable when entered into *and* that he or she did not have actual or constructive knowledge of the assets and obligations of the other party and did not voluntarily waive knowledge of such assets and obligations. In the present case, the trial court found no lack of knowledge regarding the nature of the parties' assets, a necessary predicate to considering the issue of unconscionability, and the Court of Appeal accepted the trial court's determination on this point. We do not reconsider this factual determination, and thus the question of unconscionability is not before us.

[A] number of factors are relevant to the issue of voluntariness. In considering defenses proffered against enforcement of a premarital agreement, the court should consider whether the evidence indicates coercion or lack of knowledge . . . just as would be suggested by the dictionary definitions of voluntariness noted above. Specifically, the cases cited in the comment to the enforcement provision of the Uniform Act direct consideration of the impact upon the parties of such factors as the coercion that may arise from the proximity of execution of the agreement to the wedding, or from surprise in the presentation of the agreement; the presence or absence of independent counsel or of an opportunity to consult independent counsel; inequality of bargaining power-in some cases indicated by the relative age and sophistication of the parties; whether there was full disclosure of assets; and the parties' understanding of the rights being waived under the agreement or at least their awareness of the intent of the agreement.

We have considered the range of factors that may be relevant to establish the involuntariness of a premarital agreement in order to consider whether the Court of Appeal erred in according such great weight to one factor — the presence or absence of independent counsel for each party. [W]e do not believe that the terms or history of section 1615 of the Family Code support the conclusion of the Court of Appeal majority that a premarital agreement should be subjected to strict scrutiny for voluntariness in the absence of independent counsel for the less sophisticated party.

We conclude that although the ability of the party challenging the agreement to obtain independent counsel is an important factor in determining whether that party entered into the agreement voluntarily, the Court of Appeal majority erred in directing trial courts to subject premarital agreements to strict scrutiny where the less sophisticated party does not have independent counsel and has not waived counsel according to exacting waiver requirements.

* * *

III

Finally, we conclude that the trial court's determination that Sun voluntarily entered into the premarital agreement in the present case is supported by substantial evidence.

The Court of Appeal held the trial court erred in finding the parties' agreement to be voluntary. The appellate court stressed the absence of counsel for Sun, and, strictly examining the totality of the circumstances to determine voluntariness, pointed to Sun's limited English language skills and lack of "legal or business sophistication," and stated that she "received no explanation of the legal consequences to her ensuing from signing the contract" and "was told there would be 'no marriage' if she did not immediately sign the agreement." It also referred to typographical errors and omissions in the agreement, the imminence of the wedding and the inconvenience and embarrassment of cancelling it, and Sun's asserted lack of understanding that she was waiving her statutory right to a community property interest in Barry's earnings.

The trial court, however, determined that Sun entered into the premarital contract voluntarily, without being subject to fraud, coercion, or undue influence, and with full understanding of the terms and effect of the agreement. It determined that the parties did not stand in a confidential relationship. The trial court declared that although, pursuant to a pretrial stipulation, the burden of proof rested upon Sun, even if the burden were to rest upon Barry, he had demonstrated by clear and convincing evidence that the agreement had been entered into voluntarily.

The trial court made specific findings of fact regarding the factors we have identified as relevant to the determination of voluntariness. These findings are supported by substantial evidence and should have been accepted by the Court of Appeal majority — as they were by the dissenting justice in the Court of Appeal.

The trial court determined that there had been no coercion. It declared that Sun had not been subjected to any threats, that she had not been forced to sign the agreement, and that she never expressed any reluctance to sign the agreement. It found that the temporal proximity of the wedding to the signing of the agreement was not coercive, because under the particular circumstances of the case, including the small number of guests and the informality of the wedding arrangements, little embarrassment would have followed from postponement of the wedding. It found that the presentation of the agreement did not come as a surprise to Sun, noting that she was aware of Barry's desire to "protect his present property and future earnings," and that she had been aware for at least a week before the parties signed the formal premarital agreement that one was planned.

These findings are supported by substantial evidence. Several witnesses, including Sun herself, stated that she was not threatened. The witnesses were unanimous in observing that Sun expressed no reluctance to sign the agreement, and they observed in addition that she appeared calm, happy, and confident as she participated in discussions of the agreement. Attorney Brown testified that Sun had indicated a desire at their first meeting to enter into the agreement, and that during the discussion preceding execution of the document, she stated that she understood the agreement. As the trial court determined, although the wedding between Sun and Barry was planned for the day following the signing of the agreement, the wedding was impromptu — the parties had not secured a license or a place to be married, and the few family members and close friends who were invited could have changed their plans without difficulty. (For example, guests were not arriving from Sweden.) In view of these circumstances, the evidence supported the inference, drawn by the trial court, that the coercive force of the normal desire to avoid social embarrassment or humiliation was diminished or absent. Finally, Barry's testimony that the parties early in their relationship had discussed their desire to keep separate their property and earnings, in addition to the testimony of Barry and Brown that they had met with Sun at least one week before the document was signed to discuss the need for an agreement, and the evidence establishing that Sun understood and concurred in the agreement, constituted substantial evidence to support the trial court's conclusion that Sun was not subjected to the type of coercion that may arise from the surprise and confusion caused by a last-minute presentation of a new plan to keep earnings and property separate during marriage. In this connection, certain statements in the opinion rendered by the Court of Appeal majority — that Sun was subjected to aggressive threats from financial adviser Mel Wilcox; that the temporal proximity of the wedding was coercive under the circumstances of this case; and that defects in the text of the agreement indicate it was prepared in a rush, came as a surprise when presented, and was impossible to understand — are inconsistent with factual determinations made by the trial court that we have determined are supported by substantial evidence. . . .

The Court of Appeal majority rejected the conclusion of the trial court that Sun understood why she should consult separate counsel. This determination by the appellate court contradicts the specific finding of the trial court that Sun understood what was at stake. The trial court's finding is supported by the language of the agreement itself, including the indication in paragraph 10 that the earnings and accumulations of each spouse "during marriage" would be separate property, and additional language stating that "[w]e desire by this instrument to agree as to the treatment of separate and community property *after* the marriage. . . ." (Italics added.) The trial court's finding also was supported by evidence establishing that the attorneys explained to Sun the rights she would have under community property law. In addition, Barry testified that ever since the issue first came up at the beginning of the relationship, Sun had agreed that the parties' earnings and acquisitions should be separate. Further, the attorneys testified that during the February 5, 1988, meeting, Sun stated her intent to keep marital property separate. These circumstances establish that Sun did not forgo separate legal advice out of ignorance. Instead, she declined to invoke her interests under the community property law because she agreed, for her own reasons, that Barry's and her earnings and acquisitions after marriage should be separate property.

With respect to the question of inequality of bargaining power, the trial court determined that Sun was intelligent and, evidently not crediting her claim that limited English made her unable to understand the import of the agreement or the explanations offered by Barry's counsel, found that she was capable of understanding the agreement and the explanations proffered by Barry's attorneys. There is ample evidence to support the trial court's determination regarding Sun's English-language skills, in view of the circumstances that for two years prior to marriage she had undertaken employment and education in a trade that required such skills, and before meeting Barry had maintained close personal relationships with persons speaking only English. In addition, Barry and his witnesses all testified that Sun appeared to have no language problems at the time she signed the agreement. Brown and Megwa testified that Sun indicated at the February 5, 1988, meeting that she understood the agreement, and indeed the contract contains a paragraph indicating that the parties attest that they "fully understand[ ]" the terms of the agreement. The trial court's findings with respect to the notice and opportunity Sun received to obtain independent counsel at least one week before the agreement was executed, as well as evidence indicating Sun long had known and agreed that the marriage would entail separation of earnings and acquisitions, tend to undercut any inference that coercion arose from unequal bargaining power, including Barry's somewhat greater sophistication and the involvement of two attorneys and a financial adviser on Barry's behalf. In addition, although these persons represented Barry, there is substantial evidence that they did not pressure Sun or even urge her to sign the agreement. Further, although Barry had three years of college studies as well as some experience in negotiating contracts, while Sun had only recently passed her high school equivalency exam (in English) and had little commercial experience, there is evidence that Barry did not understand the legal fine points of the agreement any more than Sun did. In addition, the basic purport of the agreement — that the parties would hold their earnings and accumulations during marriage as separate property, thereby giving up the protection of marital property law — was a relatively simple concept that did not require great legal sophistication to comprehend and that was, as the trial court found, understood by Sun. Finally, we observe that the evidence supports the inference that Sun was intrepid rather than a person whose will is easily overborne. She emigrated from her homeland at a young age, found employment and friends in a new country using two languages other than her native tongue, and in two years moved to yet another country, expressing the desire to take up a career and declaring to Barry that she "didn't want his money." These circumstances support the inference that any inequality in bargaining power — arising primarily from the absence of independent counsel who could have advised Sun not to sign the agreement or urged Barry to abandon the idea of keeping his earnings separate — was not coercive.

With respect to full disclosure of the property involved, the trial court found that Sun was aware of what separate property was held by Barry prior to the marriage, and as the Court of Appeal noted, she failed to identify any property of which she later became aware that was not on the list of property referred to by the parties when they executed the contract. The trial court also determined that Sun was aware of what was at stake — of what normally would be community property, namely the earnings and acquisitions of the parties during marriage. Substantial evidence supports this conclusion, including Sun's statements to Barry before marriage, the terms used in the contract, and Brown's and Megwa's testimony that they painstakingly explained this matter to Sun.

With respect to the question of knowledge, as already explained it is evident that the trial court was impressed with the extent of Sun's awareness. The trial court did not credit her claim that before the premarital agreement was presented to her, the parties never had discussed keeping their earnings and acquisitions separate during marriage. Nor did the trial court credit her claim that the subject and content of the agreement came as a surprise to her, or that she did not understand that absent the agreement, she would be entitled to share in Barry's earnings and acquisitions during marriage. The finding that she was sufficiently aware of her statutory rights and how the agreement "adversely affected these rights" is supported by the testimony of Barry, Brown, and Megwa that the attorneys explained these matters before

Sun signed the agreement. In addition, as noted, Barry testified that he and Sun agreed long before their marriage that their earnings and acquisitions would remain separate.

The factors we have identified in assessing the voluntariness of the agreement entered into between Barry and Sun are not rigidly separate considerations; rather the presence of one factor may influence the weight to be given evidence considered primarily under another factor. In this respect, the trial court's finding that Sun had advance knowledge of the meaning and intent of the agreement and what was at stake for her is influential, as we have seen, in considering some of the other factors.

In considering evidence that Sun responded to Barry's suggestion that she secure independent counsel with the observation that she did not need counsel because she had nothing, the Court of Appeal majority drew the inference *least* in support of the judgment — namely, that this statement indicated Sun did not understand that she did have property interests at stake in the form of the community property rights that would accrue to her under applicable statutes, in the absence of a premarital agreement. We believe that this was error on the part of the appellate court, because substantial evidence supported the trial court's determination to the contrary. It is clear from the testimony of Brown and Megwa that, even if Sun did not peruse the entire document herself, they read it to her paragraph by paragraph, thoroughly explaining the matter to her. Barry's testimony further established that he and Sun had agreed from the beginning of their relationship that each would forgo any interest in the other's earnings and acquisitions during marriage.

Family Code section 1615 places on the party seeking to avoid a premarital agreement the burden of demonstrating that the agreement was involuntary. The trial court determined that Sun did not carry her burden, and we believe that its factual findings in support of this conclusion are supported by substantial evidence.

MOSK, J., KENNARD, J., BAXTER, J., WERDEGAR, J., CHIN, J., and BROWN, J., concur.

Discussion Questions

1. What factors did the Court consider in determining whether Sun voluntarily entered into the premarital agreement?

2. Do you agree with the California Supreme Court that Sun entered into the premarital agreement voluntarily?

The *Bonds* case led the California Legislature to amend the California Premarital Agreement Act by adding the following provisions. Consider how those provisions would have helped Sun to argue that she had not entered voluntarily into the premarital agreement. What is the most powerful protection for an economically inferior spouse?

CALIFORNIA FAMILY CODE

§1615. Unenforceable agreements; unconscionability; voluntariness
Effective: January 1, 2002

(a) A premarital agreement is not enforceable if the party against whom enforcement is sought proves either of the following:

(1) That party did not execute the agreement voluntarily.

(2) The agreement was unconscionable when it was executed and, before execution of the agreement, all of the following applied to that party:

(A) That party was not provided a fair, reasonable, and full disclosure of the property or financial obligations of the other party.

(B) That party did not voluntarily and expressly waive, in writing, any right to disclosure of the property or financial obligations of the other party beyond the disclosure provided.

(C) That party did not have, or reasonably could not have had, an adequate knowledge of the property or financial obligations of the other party.

(b) An issue of unconscionability of a premarital agreement shall be decided by the court as a matter of law.

(c) For the purposes of subdivision (a), it shall be deemed that a premarital agreement was not executed voluntarily unless the court finds in writing or on the record all of the following:

(1) The party against whom enforcement is sought was represented by independent legal counsel at the time of signing the agreement or, after being advised to seek independent legal counsel, expressly waived, in a separate writing, representation by independent legal counsel.

(2) The party against whom enforcement is sought had not less than seven calendar days between the time that party was first presented with the agreement and advised to seek independent legal counsel and the time the agreement was signed.

(3) The party against whom enforcement is sought, if unrepresented by legal counsel, was fully informed of the terms and basic effect of the agreement as well as the rights and obligations he or she was giving up by signing the agreement, and was proficient in the language in which the explanation of the party's rights was conducted and in which the agreement was written. The explanation of the rights and obligations relinquished shall be memorialized in writing and delivered to the party prior to signing the agreement. The unrepresented party shall, on or before the signing of the premarital agreement, execute a document declaring that he or she received the information required by this paragraph and indicating who provided that information.

(4) The agreement and the writings executed pursuant to paragraphs (1) and (3) were not executed under duress, fraud, or undue influence, and the parties did not lack capacity to enter into the agreement.

(5) Any other factors the court deems relevant.

(Stats. 1992, c. 162 (A.B.2650), §10, operative Jan. 1, 1994. Amended by Stats. 2001, c. 286 (S.B.78), §2.)

Current with all 2010 Reg. Sess. laws; all 2009-2010 1st through 8th Ex. Sess. laws; and all Props. on 2010 ballots.

(c) Washington

The State of Washington has not adopted the UPAA, but takes an approach that parallels the UPAA. In *Marriage of Matson,* 730 Wash. 2d 2479, 730 P.2d 668 (1986), the Supreme Court used a two-prong analysis that examined the substantive and procedural fairness of premarital agreements. In the case of *Marriage of Bernard* (Wash. 2009), that test was challenged, but the Supreme Court re-affirmed its earlier two-prong analysis. The emphasis in Washington is on procedural fairness, because the procedural requirements of full disclosure and voluntariness will validate an otherwise substantively unfair premarital agreement.

MARRIAGE OF BERNARD

165 Wash. 2d 895, 204 P.3d 907 (2009)
Supreme Court of Washington,
En Banc

STEPHENS, J.

Gloria Bernard filed for dissolution from Thomas Bernard. We are asked to determine the enforceability of their prenuptial agreement. We hold the agreement is not enforceable because it is substantively and procedurally unfair. We affirm Gloria's award of attorney fees and costs.

FACTS AND PROCEDURAL HISTORY

In 1995 Thomas hired Gloria to be the operations manager for Bernard Development Company. In late 1998, after the death of Thomas's first spouse, Thomas and Gloria began dating. Thomas asked Gloria to marry him but informed her he would require a prenuptial agreement because of the disparity in their relative wealth. At the time of their engagement, Thomas was 55 and a successful real estate developer with a net worth of approximately $25 million; Gloria was 49, held undergraduate and master's degrees in business administration, and had a net worth of approximately $8,000. The events surrounding the signing of the prenuptial agreement and its amendment are the subject of this litigation.

In January 2000, Thomas and his long-time attorney, Richard Keefe, began working on the prenuptial agreement. Thomas and Keefe repeatedly advised Gloria to obtain independent counsel but did not provide her with a draft of the proposed agreement. Lacking a draft, Gloria took no action to obtain representation. On May 24, Keefe prepared a prenuptial checklist for Thomas and Gloria and encouraged Gloria to obtain counsel. He provided her with the names of three attorneys but did not provide her with a draft agreement. On June 8, Keefe again encouraged Gloria to obtain independent representation, resending the prenuptial checklist. Gloria still did not have a draft of the agreement, however, and did not consult counsel at that time. Not until June 20, 18 days before the wedding, did Gloria receive a draft of the prenuptial agreement.

On July 5, Gloria met with Marshall Gehring, an attorney experienced in prenuptial negotiations. That evening Gehring received a working draft of the prenuptial agreement from Keefe. It was substantially different from the draft Keefe gave to Gloria on June 20.

Gehring testified at trial that he did not have sufficient time to conduct a full review of the agreement or draft a counteragreement. Instead, in a letter to Gloria dated July 7, the day before the wedding, he identified five areas of major concern with the prenuptial agreement. He indicated in his letter that he had additional minor concerns but did not specify what those were. Gehring's letter recommended that Gloria negotiate some kind of additional written instrument to address the concerns he outlined. In testimony, Gehring agreed that he had time to only "hit the high points" in his letter and said he would have reviewed the agreement "page by page" if he had been given more time. He further testified that during the short time he had to review the agreement, it was very difficult to talk directly with Gloria, as she was busy with guests, wedding details, and honeymoon preparations.

In addition, Thomas testified that he would have called off the wedding on its eve, or even the day of, had Gloria not signed the prenuptial agreement. Gloria testified that she believed Thomas would not have married her if she had refused to sign the agreement.

Gloria signed the prenuptial agreement the day before the wedding, on July 7, with the understanding that it would be amended. Thomas and Gloria's wedding took place at the Seattle Tennis Club on July 8 and included approximately 200 guests, some of whom had come from out of town.

Gloria and Thomas signed a "side letter" on the day of the wedding, agreeing to renegotiate the five areas of major concern Gehring noted in his July 7 letter. Both Gloria and Gehring testified that they believed the negotiations that followed the side letter were limited to the five areas identified by Gehring. The side letter required the anticipated amendment to be finalized no later than October 7, 2000, but the amendment would not be finalized until August 28, 2001. When it was eventually finalized, the amendment ratified the original prenuptial agreement and altered several provisions in accordance with each of Gehring's concerns.

Gloria filed for dissolution on February 4, 2005. Thomas demanded arbitration under the terms of the prenuptial agreement. Gloria moved for summary judgment, challenging the enforceability of the prenuptial agreement. The trial court bifurcated its analysis of the enforceability of the prenuptial agreement.

The court determined that the prenuptial agreement, as amended, was substantively unfair as a matter of law. The court directed a trial on the question of procedural fairness. After a four day trial, the court found the prenuptial agreement, as amended, was procedurally unfair. First, the court found that the draft sent to Gehring on July 5 was substantially different from the version Gloria received on June 20. The court further found that Gloria and Gehring received the revised draft of the agreement only a few days before the wedding, "too late to provide time for meaningful negotiation and full advise [sic]." The trial court also found that "[b]ecause of the impending wedding [Gloria] was faced with the choice of the humiliation of calling off a wedding or signing a substantively unfair document." Next, the court found the subsequent amendment did not cure the procedural defects of the original agreement because the terms of the side letter restricted the scope of renegotiation. Accordingly, "[a]s the scope of the negotiations allowed by the 'side letter' were so specifically limited, the fact that there was sufficient time for independent review and for the advice of counsel was insufficient to cure the defects of the first agreement." The trial court concluded that the agreement lacked procedural fairness.

Division One of the Court of Appeals affirmed. *In re Marriage of Bernard*, 137 Wash. App. 827, 155 P.3d 171 (2007). The Court of Appeals first held the agreement, as amended, was substantively unfair. The court then held the agreement, as amended, was procedurally unfair. The Court of Appeals reasoned that Gloria did not have the benefit of independent counsel, that her bargaining position was grossly imbalanced, and "at no time did [she] have full knowledge of her legal rights." Moreover, the court observed that because Gloria and Gehring believed the side letter dictated the subsequent amendment and because the side letter was entered into within 24 hours of the wedding, the subsequent amendment did not remedy the agreement's procedural unfairness.

We granted review. *In re Marriage of Bernard*, 163 Wash. 2d 1011, 180 P.3d 1290 (2008).

ANALYSIS

To determine the enforceability of a prenuptial agreement, this court undertakes a two-prong analysis. *In re Marriage of Matson*, 107 Wash. 2d 479, 482-83, 730 P.2d 668 (1986). The burden of proof lies with the spouse seeking enforcement.

Under the first prong, the court determines whether the agreement is substantively fair, specifically whether it makes reasonable provision for the spouse not seeking to enforce it. *Matson*, 107 Wash. 2d at 482, 730 P.2d 668. If the agreement makes a fair and reasonable provision for the spouse not seeking its enforcement, the analysis ends; the agreement is enforceable. This is entirely a question of law unless there are factual disputes that must be resolved in order for a court to interpret the meaning of the contract.

If, however, the agreement is substantively unfair to the spouse not seeking enforcement, the court proceeds to the second prong. Under the second prong, the court determines whether the agreement is procedurally fair by asking two questions: (1) whether the spouses made a full disclosure of the amount, character, and value of the property involved and (2) whether the agreement was freely entered into on independent advice from counsel with full knowledge by both spouses of their rights. *Matson*, 107 Wash. 2d at 483, 730 P.2d 668. If the court determines the second prong is satisfied, then an otherwise unfair distribution of property is valid and binding. *Id.* at 482, 730 P.2d 668.

Analysis under this second prong involves mixed issues of policy and fact, and accordingly review is de novo but undertaken in light of the trial court's resolution of the facts.

We note as an initial matter that both parties request this court reconsider the above two-prong analysis, which was expressly set out in *Matson* and has characterized our analysis for over 50 years. Gloria argues that this court should undertake an approach that requires both substantive *and* procedural fairness; that is, she argues that a substantively unfair agreement should not be saved by procedural fairness. On the other hand, Thomas argues the substantive fairness prong should be abandoned altogether because RCW 26.09.080 already directs courts to make a "just and equitable" distribution of property. We find it unnecessary to entertain these arguments because the prenuptial agreement at issue is both substantively and procedurally unfair, and the application of a different analysis would not alter the outcome here.

THE AGREEMENT

Turning to the agreement at issue, we apply the two-prong analysis to the prenuptial agreement as signed on the eve of marriage and subsequently amended 14 months later.[4] Thomas concedes the prenuptial agreement as originally executed on the eve of marriage was substantively and procedurally unfair; therefore, we must determine whether the later amendment cured the substantive or procedural deficiencies.

Under the first prong of our analysis, the agreement is enforceable if it is substantively fair. Here, the trial court concluded the agreement as amended was substantively unfair to Gloria. The Court of Appeals affirmed, reasoning that the amended agreement severely restricted the creation of community property, eliminating community property rights in the short term while permitting Thomas to enrich his separate property at the expense of the community. The Court of Appeals observed that the amended agreement provided nothing for Gloria from Thomas's separate property, nor reimbursed her for her contributions to Thomas's separate property, nor permitted maintenance, and it precluded any inheritance.

Thomas argues that because this was a short-term marriage there was no time to accumulate community property. He urges us to alter our analysis and evaluate substantive fairness at the time of enforcement, as opposed to at the time of execution, of an agreement. We refuse. To do so would change the test from one of fairness to fortuity. We adhere to the settled rule that "[t]he validity of prenuptial agreements in this state is based on the circumstances surrounding the execution of the agreement."

Moreover, Thomas's substantial labor in managing his separate assets produced revenue that is considered community property. Thus, the premise of Thomas's argument is incorrect; community property accumulated during the marriage.

To be sure, "[t]here is nothing unfair about two well-educated working professionals agreeing to preserve the fruits of their labor for their individual benefit." However, an agreement disproportionate to the respective means of each spouse, which also limits the accumulation of one spouse's separate property while precluding any claim to the other spouse's separate property, is substantively unfair.

Here, the community property consisted of half of Gloria's salary, which was controlled by Thomas, and in effect $100,000 of Thomas's earnings per year. In addition, the prenuptial agreement limited Gloria's inheritance rights, prevented Gloria from seeking spousal maintenance, prevented Gloria from using community property to assist her children, and sheltered Thomas from liability for any debts incurred by Gloria. The prenuptial agreement as amended remedied some of these problems, but overall made provisions for Gloria disproportionate to the means of Thomas, and limited Gloria's ability to accumulate her separate property while precluding her common law or statutory claims on Thomas's property.

---

4. That this case involves a prenuptial agreement, amended postnuptially, does not alter our analysis. See In re Marriage of Hadley, 88 Wash. 2d 649, 654, 565 P.2d 790 (1977) (analyzing three postnuptial agreements under the established two-prong approach).

The agreement as amended is substantively unfair. It can be enforced only if it was executed fairly, the second prong of our analysis.

Under the second prong of our analysis, we ask whether the spouses fully disclosed the amount, character, and value of the property involved and whether the agreement was entered into voluntarily and intelligently. The trial court found Gloria had full knowledge of the amount, character, and value of Thomas's assets, and Gloria does not dispute this finding. However, the trial court found that, given the timing of Gloria's receipt of the working agreement draft in relation to the wedding and her discussions with her attorney, the agreement was not entered into voluntarily or intelligently. The court further found that the subsequent side letter and amendment did not cure this defect, given the limited scope of negotiations.

Because the trial court made findings of fact about the agreement's lack of procedural fairness, we will uphold its findings if they are supported by substantial evidence. Here, substantial evidence supports the trial court's findings of fact regarding procedural unfairness. There was not enough time for Gloria or her attorney to adequately review the prenuptial agreement as evidenced by the late date at which a working draft was provided and the several distractions present for Gloria in the few days before the wedding. The evidence supports the trial court's finding that Gloria did not sign the July 7 prenuptial agreement "after receiving independent advice and with full knowledge of its legal consequences."

The trial court then considered whether the amendment to the agreement executed by Gloria and Thomas, contemplated by the July 8 "side letter," cured the deficiencies of the July 7 agreement. The trial court found that the scope of negotiation was so limited that the amendment did not cure the defects of the agreement. Substantial evidence supports this conclusion, as demonstrated by the testimony of Gloria and Gehring, who both understood that the terms of the amendment were limited to the five areas of concern set forth in Gehring's July 7 letter to Gloria. And the wording of the side letter is additional evidence that any amendment was limited to the matters set forth in the "side letter," CP at 1256,[5] supporting the trial court's finding that the terms of the side letter limited renegotiation. CP at 1816 (Finding of Fact 27).

The trial court observed that the side letter did not *expressly* limit the terms of the amendment to only the five areas of concern noted by Gehring and that the agreement as amended ultimately contained a matter outside the terms of the "side letter."[6] *Id.* Additionally, the deadline for renegotiation was abandoned. *Id.* But these observations do not negate the substantial evidence upon which the trial court based its finding regarding the limits of the amendment. Especially considering the trial court's ability to judge the weight and credibility of testimony, including Gloria's and her attorney's testimony that they understood the negotiations were limited, a fair-minded person would be persuaded that the side letter did not give Gloria a right to amend the prenuptial agreement beyond the few matters

---

5. The letter stated in pertinent part: "we and our attorneys will use their best efforts to negotiate in good faith and execute an amendment to the Agreement covering the following matters . . ." and then went on to discuss the five areas outlined in Gehring's letter. CP at 1256. It did not reference any other substantive changes to the prenuptial agreement.

6. The amendment included a provision not contained in the "side letter" that further isolated Thomas's earnings from the marital community. Br. of Resp't at 21.

specified in the "side letter." The trial court's findings of fact in this regard are amply supported, and we will not disturb them on review. *See Dickie*, 149 Wash. 2d at 879-80, 73 P.3d 369. We hold the agreement, as amended, was procedurally unfair.[7]

Because the prenuptial agreement was both substantively and procedurally unfair, it is unenforceable. We affirm the lower court's invalidation of the agreement.

Conclusion

We hold the prenuptial agreement, as amended, was substantively and procedurally unfair. We affirm the Court of Appeals. In addition, we affirm Gloria's award of attorney fees and costs, both at trial and on appeal.

I agree with the majority that the prenuptial agreement, as amended, is substantively unfair and "can be enforced only if it was executed fairly, the second prong of our analysis." However I disagree with the majority's conclusion that the amended agreement is also procedurally unfair (majority at 913) under the second prong. I would hold that the amended agreement is procedurally fair and thus enforceable. Therefore I dissent.

Under the second prong of our analysis we must determine whether a prenuptial agreement is procedurally fair by looking at (1) whether the spouses made a full disclosure of the amount, character, and value of the property involved and (2) whether the agreement was freely entered into on independent advice from counsel with full knowledge by both spouses of their rights. *In re Marriage of Matson*, 107 Wash. 2d 479, 483, 730 P.2d 668 (1986). If the second prong is satisfied then a prenuptial agreement is valid and binding. *Id.* at 482, 730 P.2d 668. I agree, as does the majority, with the trial court's finding, "Gloria had full knowledge of the amount, character, and value of Thomas's assets." However, I disagree with the majority's assertion that the trial court's finding that Gloria did not voluntarily and intelligently enter into the prenuptial agreement is supported by substantial evidence.

We review the totality of the circumstances to determine whether the spouse was "in a fair position to sign the agreement freely and intelligently." *Matson*, 107 Wash. 2d at 485, 730 P.2d 668. Instructive to our inquiry is *In re Marriage of Knoll*, 65 Or. App. 484, 671 P.2d 718 (1983), which *Matson* presented as an exemplar of the procedural fairness analysis. *Matson*, 107 Wash. 2d at 484, 730 P.2d 668.

> In *Knoll*, the wife challenged the validity of the prenuptial agreement. The court found the agreement valid judged in light of the circumstances in the case and the wife's range of experience. Important facts in the court's decision were: (1) the wife was advised of

---

7. The Court of Appeals appeared to rest at least some of its determination that there was procedural unfairness on a belief that Gloria's counsel was inadequate. *Bernard*, 137 Wash. App. at 836, 155 P.3d 171. Gloria did not make such an argument before this court or any court below. A discussion of counsel's adequacy is unnecessary to the resolution of this case because the trial court's findings are supported by substantial evidence without resort to consideration of the adequacy of counsel. We decline to entertain that question here.

the necessity of a prenuptial agreement at least 9 months before the wedding and knew and understood the purpose of the agreement; (2) she had been given a copy of the agreement at least 7 months before the wedding; (3) she was advised on numerous occasions by her husband's attorney to *seek* independent counsel; (4) she had an excellent understanding of her husband's assets because she handled the bookkeeping and payroll for her husband's businesses and was in charge of 10 of his business checking accounts; and (5) both parties had to reaffirm and sign the agreement 3 years later because they had lost the original document. The court decided that the failure to provide the wife with a detailed explanation of the agreement and her failure to follow advice and seek out independent counsel was offset by her knowledge and the procedural fairness provided her.

Id. at 484-85, 730 P.2d 668.

Similar substantive facts are present here: (1) Gloria was advised of the necessity of a prenuptial agreement from the outset of her betrothal to Thomas, (2) she had 14 months to renegotiate the agreement, (3) she was repeatedly advised to seek the advice of independent counsel and had independent counsel during the renegotiation period, (4) she had an excellent understanding of Thomas's assets because she worked for him, and (5) she reaffirmed the prenuptial agreement 14 months later. The only distinction is that in *Knoll* the spouse was given a copy of the agreement 7 months before the wedding, whereas Gloria had 14 months to renegotiate the agreement after the wedding. But this is a distinction without a difference because the entire prenuptial agreement was open to renegotiation. In sum that Gloria voluntarily and intelligently entered into the prenuptial agreement is supported by these facts.

Still the trial court found Gloria did not enter into the prenuptial agreement voluntarily or intelligently and that the amendment did not cure the defects of the agreement because the scope of the negotiation of the side letter was too limited. Clerk's Papers. The majority asserts these findings are supported by substantial evidence. However, the majority concedes that the trial court found "the side letter did not *expressly* limit the terms of the amendment to only the five areas of concern noted by Gehring and that the agreement as amended ultimately contained a matter outside the terms of the 'side letter.' " Additionally the deadline of the "side letter" was entirely abandoned. *Id.* The majority concludes, "a fair-minded person would be persuaded that the side letter did not give Gloria a right to amend the prenuptial agreement beyond the few matters specified in the 'side letter.'"

However the side letter provided Gloria and Thomas would "use their best efforts to negotiate in good faith and execute an amendment to the Agreement covering the following matters" but did not limit negotiation to *only* those matters. In fact the amendment to the agreement contained a matter *outside* the terms of the "side letter," which benefited Thomas. Gloria and her attorney should have realized that if Thomas amended the prenuptial agreement to contain a matter outside of the terms of the "side letter," then Gloria could have done so as well. That is what a fair-minded person would have surmised. The entire purpose of the "side letter" was to address Gloria's concerns with the prenuptial agreement, so substantial evidence does not support the trial court's finding that renegotiation was limited to the terms of the side letter.

Gloria did not use her best efforts to negotiate an amendment to the prenuptial agreement. A party to a prenuptial agreement must not keep back his or her reservations about the agreement. "Parties to a prenuptial agreement do not deal with each other at arm's length. Their relationship is one of mutual confidence and trust which calls for the exercise of good faith, candor and sincerity in all matters bearing upon the proposed agreement."

In *Cohn* spouses executed a prenuptial agreement and a settlement agreement. Later the wife challenged the enforceability of both agreements "on the grounds that [she] did not sign them on independent advice and with full knowledge of her rights, and that a full disclosure had not been made to her of the amount, character and value of the property involved." Rejecting the wife's challenge, the court observed the spouses had discussed the prenuptial agreement months prior to their wedding, and "[a]lthough [the wife] testified that she felt rushed into signing the agreement, . . . she did not at any point indicate to the lawyer who had drafted it that she felt she was being rushed or that she was signing anything that she did not fully intend to sign." The court reasoned if the wife did not understand the provisions or effect of the agreements "there [was] no evidence that she ever let her husband or the attorney know of her lack of knowledge. . . . [I]t would be unfair to penalize [the husband] for [the wife's] omission to request further information."

Similarly Gloria could have discussed her concerns about the prenuptial agreement while negotiating the terms of the amendment. But she did not. It is extremely unfair to Thomas to be penalized for Gloria's omission and failure to negotiate.

The prenuptial agreement, as amended, was substantively unfair but procedurally fair. As such I would hold the prenuptial agreement is enforceable and reverse the Court of Appeals.

Therefore, I dissent.

Discussion Questions

1. Consider whether procedural fairness should save an otherwise substantively unfair premarital agreement?

2. One factor that influences voluntariness is "proximity of signing of the agreement to the wedding." How important was that in *Bernard*? How does renegotiation during marriage change the dynamics of agreements between the spouses?

B. WAIVER OF SPOUSAL SUPPORT IN PREMARITAL AGREEMENTS

Premarital agreements that alter the property rights of spouses are universally accepted. Couples may opt out of the community property sharing concepts and adopt their own separate property scheme. The waiver of spousal support (also called alimony or maintenance) in the event of divorce is more controversial. Take the example of one of our hypothetical couples, Michael and Lisa. They enter marriage with the mindset of independence, each expecting to have successful careers. They are realistic enough to realize that marriages end in divorce and decide that independence should determine that they owe each other nothing if they divorce. Therefore, they enter into a premarital agreement that provides that their earnings will be separate property and that they waive any right each would have to spousal support. Although the marriage starts out that way, fate intervenes. Only Michael becomes successful in his career while Lisa is plagued with medical problems that prevent her from being employed. After a number of years, they decide to divorce. According to their premarital agreement, all of Michael's earnings are his separate property and there is no community property. Ordinarily, Lisa may be eligible for spousal support.

The issue of spousal support involves another interested party besides Michael and Lisa. It is the State. If Lisa is not supported by Michael, she would have to seek assistance in the form of welfare or some other form of state assistance. Therefore, the states are wary of relieving a spousal of the responsibility of spousal support even after the marriage has dissolved. Thus, provisions waiving spousal support in a premarital agreement may be treated differently from provisions dealing with characterization of property.

1.   Public Policy Considerations: The Arizona and Louisiana Experience

(a)   Arizona

Williams v. Williams (Ariz. 1926) involves a premarital agreement entered into in 1912, in which the husband argues that his obligation to pay spousal support was dissolved by agreement in exchange for $500. Nearly seventy years later, in *Williams v. Williams* (Ariz. 1990), a similar premarital agreement was entered into; the couple agreed that in the event of divorce neither party was entitled to an award of spousal maintenance.

WILLIAMS v. WILLIAMS
29 Ariz. 538, 243 P. 402 (1926)
Supreme Court of Arizona

LOCKWOOD, J.

Mattie L. Williams, hereinafter called appellee, instituted this action against John H. Williams, hereinafter called appellant, in the superior court of Maricopa county, asking for a limited divorce and suitable support. In her complaint appellee charged appellant with willful desertion and cruelty; also alleging that there was a large amount of community property, and that he had failed properly to support her for more than 2 years. Appellant answered by a general denial, and specially pleaded that, before the marriage of the parties, they had entered into a contract in writing which reads as follows:

'AGREEMENT

This agreement, made and entered into this 20th day of July, 1912, by and between John H. Williams, party of the first part, and Mattie L. Banks, party of the second part, both of Phoenix, Ariz., witnesseth:

* * *

It is further agreed by and between the parties hereto that in case the parties hereto should after said marriage at any time or for any cause or reason cease to live together or cease to maintain the relation of husband and wife, or in case said marriage shall be dissolved by the decree of any court, then and in such case or event, the party of the first part shall pay to the party of the second part the sum of five hundred ($500.00) dollars which shall be in full satisfaction and settlement of all claims and demands against the party of the first part, or his property.

* * *

In witness whereof the said parties have hereunto set their hands this 30th day of July, 1912.
John H. Williams.
Mattie L. Banks.

He alleged his readiness to pay the $500 set forth in said contract and denied there was any community property. The trial court made findings of fact and on these findings rendered judgment in favor of appellee for a limited divorce and for $100 a month to be paid by appellant for her support.

* * *

This brings us to the fourth and vital assignment. It is contended that the agreement above set forth is binding on the parties as to a settlement for all claims for support of appellee by appellant, and that since he has always been ready, able, and willing to pay the $500 set forth therein, the court has no right to award any further or greater sum. There is no question as to the terms of the agreement, nor that it was entered into by the parties without any fraud or undue influence being exercised. It was, however, urged at the trial that that portion which limits the amount which can be recovered by appellee from appellant to $500 is contrary to public policy and void, so far as support is concerned, and so the trial court found. It may be that such an agreement is perfectly valid in settling any rights which appellee acquired in the separate property of appellant by reason of the marriage. We, however, are decidedly of the opinion that it is void and contrary to public policy when the question of support to be adjudicated by a court in the case of either a limited or absolute divorce is involved. It is the duty of the husband to provide support for his wife during coverture. A contract in advance of the marriage whereby the wife waives such a right would certainly be contrary to public policy.

We think it is equally contrary to public policy for the parties to contract in advance that, if through the fault of the husband his wife is granted a divorce, he shall nevertheless be relieved under any and all circumstances from the burden of providing support for his wife in such amount as the court may deem proper. To hold to the contrary would be equivalent to holding that a man may contract in advance to be relieved from liability for his own negligence, tort, or even crime. We have examined the cases cited by counsel for appellant and we are satisfied that they are either not in point or are unsound in principle.

Discussion Questions

1. The court holds that the agreement was entered into without any fraud or undue influence, but still finds the $500 limitation of recovery as void as against public policy. The waiver is seen as equivalent to allowing a man to contract in advance to be relieved from liability for his own negligence, tort, or crime. Do you agree with this analogy?

2. What are some reasons that a couple might want to limit liability in the event of divorce? What are some reasons that society might not be willing to let them do so?

MARRIAGE OF WILLIAMS

166 Ariz. 260, 802 P.2d 495 (1990)
Court of Appeals of Arizona

EHRLICH, Judge.

This is an appeal from a trial court order entered in dissolution proceedings. The husband has appealed from the decree of dissolution and the denial of his motion for new trial. He alleges that the trial court erred in its conclusion of paternity and in its determination of his earning capacity.

FACTS

Kathy Ann Williams and Claude K. Williams, Jr., were married on November 3, 1984. *Prior to their marriage, they executed an antenuptial agreement as a part of which they agreed that all of the income received and obligations incurred during their marriage would be kept separate. They further agreed that in the event of divorce, neither would be entitled to an award of spousal maintenance.* [Italics added.]

The Williamses lived together from November 1984 until January 1986, when their relationship became estranged and the husband moved to Baltimore. In February 1986, the wife filed a petition for dissolution of their marriage. The following month, however, she visited her husband in Baltimore in a mutual effort to reconcile. After that visit, the wife discovered that she was pregnant. On November 23, 1986, she gave birth to a daughter.

The wife amended her petition for dissolution in July 1986 to include the fact of her pregnancy and a request for an award of child support. In the husband's response to the amended petition, he denied paternity of the child and denied that he had sufficient financial resources to support the child if, in fact, he was proven to be the child's father.

At the conclusion of the trial which then took place, the court held that the husband was the biological father of the child. It also found that the wife lacked sufficient property to provide for her reasonable needs and that she was unable to support herself through appropriate employment. It concluded that the provision contained in the antenuptial agreement by which the parties had waived spousal maintenance was against public policy and thus unenforceable. Based upon these findings, the trial court ordered the husband to pay spousal maintenance to the wife in the amount of $850 per month for a period of eighteen months, and child support in the amount of $823 per month. The husband thereafter filed a motion for a new trial, which was denied by the trial court. He then timely appealed to this court.

SPOUSAL MAINTENANCE

The husband alleges that the trial court erred in ordering him to pay spousal maintenance to the wife because the antenuptial agreement executed by the parties specifically provided that both parties waived an award of spousal maintenance upon divorce. The trial court held that this provision of the antenuptial agreement was void as against public policy, citing *Williams v. Williams*, 29 Ariz. 538, 544, 243 P. 402, 404 (1926).

Arizona recognizes the validity of certain antenuptial agreements: "Parties intending to marry may enter into agreements not contrary to good morals or law." A.R.S. §25-201(A). Clearly this statute was intended to sanction antenuptial agreements as long as they do not violate public policy.

The Arizona Supreme Court previously has held, however, in *Williams*, that an antenuptial agreement which purports to discharge a husband's duty of spousal support following divorce for a specific sum is contrary to public policy and void without reference to a particular agreement. The issue to be decided in this case, then, is whether the holding in *Williams*, that limitations on spousal maintenance contained in antenuptial agreements are against public policy *per se*, should be applied to void the waiver of spousal maintenance in this case, despite the changes in public policy regarding divorce that have occurred in Arizona in recent years. We agree with the husband's position that antenuptial agreements regarding spousal maintenance are no longer against public policy *per se*, and hold that such agreements must be considered individually to determine if the terms violate public policy.

The common law can and should be reformed when changed conditions and circumstances establish that it has become unjust or contrary to evolved public policy. Thus, this court is free to reevaluate previous decisions such as *Williams* in light of present facts and circumstances.

The decision in *Williams* was based upon two premises: Antenuptial agreements waiving spousal maintenance were considered to be against public policy first because they could result in a situation where the husband was relieved of his legal obligation to support his wife, although it was due to his fault that the wife sought and was granted a divorce. Such agreements also were against public policy because of the state's interest in the adequate support of its citizens; therefore, the husband's duty to support his wife could not be the subject of a contract between the parties.

The rationale articulated in *Williams* is less valid in light of the advent of "no-fault" divorce in Arizona. In so doing, the legislature eliminated the concept of fault from divorce proceedings. Under the new statutory scheme, either party to a marriage may seek a divorce based upon their "irreconcilable differences," without assessing blame against the other spouse.

While the state still has an interest in enforcing the support obligations that accompany marriage, this principle no longer necessarily leads to the conclusion that all antenuptial agreements concerning spousal maintenance are invalid. While, in *Williams*, the spousal support obligation was strictly enforced against the husband pursuant to the common law, the obligation is now statutory in nature, having undergone significant changes in recent years. Prior to the 1973 revisions which describe the spousal-maintenance obligation, it was clearly the husband's duty to support his wife during their marriage. This obligation arose out of the relationship itself and existed irrespective of the wife's separate estate or independent means. In fact, as it existed prior to 1973, an able husband who refused or neglected to support his wife was guilty of a felony.

A.R.S. §25-319 now says that either spouse may be ordered to pay maintenance to the other if certain contingencies are fulfilled. Additionally, A.R.S. §13-3611 provides that it is a class six felony for an able spouse, regardless of gender, to refuse to support the other during marriage if the need arises. Thus, the spousal-support obligation, both during marriage and after divorce, today is borne equally by both parties.

The state still has an interest in the support of its citizens, however. Consequently, antenuptial agreements which affect this obligation are still subject to scrutiny on public policy grounds. The majority of jurisdictions in this country which have considered this issue have adopted the view that antenuptial agreements affecting spousal maintenance are not *per se* against public policy, but that they must be considered on a case-by-case basis. These recent cases indicate that in order to be enforceable and comport with public policy, antenuptial agreements regarding spousal maintenance must be fair and equitable in their procurement and in their result. Specifically, the agreements must be fairly entered into upon full disclosure, and without fraud, overreaching or duress. Additionally, the results must not be made unconscionable by circumstances existing at the time of the marriage dissolution, such as when enforcement of the spousal maintenance waiver provision would render one spouse without a means of reasonable support or a public charge, either because of a lack of property resources or a condition of unemployability.

In specifically addressing the issue of antenuptial agreements regarding spousal maintenance and the state's interest in the support obligation, the court in *Gross* stated: In the review of provisions of antenuptial agreements regarding maintenance or sustenance alimony, a further standard of review must be applied — one of conscionability of the provisions at the time of the divorce or separation. . . .

We believe that the underlying state interest in the welfare of the divorced spouse, when measured against the rights of the parties to freely contract, weighs in favor of the court's jurisdiction to review, at the time of a subsequent divorce, the terms in an antenuptial agreement providing sustenance alimony for one of the parties. There is sound public policy rationale for not strictly enforcing such a provision which, even though entered into in good faith and reasonable at the time of execution, may have become unreasonable or unconscionable as to its application to the spouse upon divorce. It is a valid interest of the state to mitigate potential harm, hardship, or disadvantage to a spouse which would be occasioned by the breakup of the marriage, and a strict and literal interpretation of the provisions for maintenance of the spouse to be found in those agreements.

We find that the principles articulated above, as well as in the other cases previously noted, are persuasive and consistent with the Arizona legislature's intent in amending the laws pertaining to divorce. Therefore, we hold that it is no longer valid to simply reject an antenuptial agreement regarding spousal maintenance on general public policy grounds. An inquiry must be conducted regarding whether the agreement between the parties was fairly reached and whether it adequately provides for support of the spouse consistent with the needs and resources of both spouses at the time of dissolution.

Because the trial court relied upon *Williams* in holding that the spousal maintenance waiver provision of the antenuptial agreement was void, we remand this issue to be considered in light of the test we have articulated.

Based upon the testimony regarding the husband's past earning history and his future earning capacity, we do not believe that the trial court erred in attributing income to the husband in the amount of $4,000 per month.

This matter is remanded for proceedings consistent with this decision.

Discussion Questions

1. What are some reasons that the court cites as leading to the overruling of *Williams v. Williams* (1926) with regard to spousal support waivers?

2. Are there still some instances where a court may refuse to enforce a spousal support waiver? What might these be?

(b) *Louisiana*

The Supreme Court of Louisiana dealt with the issue of premarital agreements and spousal support in the case of *McAlpine v. McAlpine*, 679 So. 2d 85 (1996). In Louisiana, spousal support after divorce is called permanent alimony. Spousal support during divorce proceedings is called alimony *pendente lite*. The Court considered whether a waiver of permanent alimony in a premarital agreement is "null and void as against public policy." It is not. The opinion reflects the changing societal views of "fault" in divorce and whether "wives" need protection of the State.

McALPINE v. McALPINE

679 So. 2d 85 (1996)
Supreme Court of Louisiana

On Rehearing

Victory, Justice.

We granted rehearing in this case to reconsider the correctness of our original opinion in which we held that antenuptial agreements waiving permanent alimony are null and void as against public policy. After further review, we reverse our original opinion and hold that such antenuptial agreements are enforceable, but are subject to the same grounds for rescission as other contracts. Further, we agree with the trial court's determination in this case that Mrs. McAlpine entered into the antenuptial agreement freely and voluntarily and not under undue duress. Lastly, consistent with our original opinion, we agree with the trial court's holding that the Mercedes Benz was not a gift to Mrs. McAlpine.

Facts and Procedural History

About a week prior to their marriage in 1989, Michael McAlpine and Jonnie Fox signed an antenuptial agreement which provided for a separate property regime and for a waiver of alimony *pendente lite* and permanent alimony. The agreement provided, inter alia, that Jonnie Fox would receive $25,000 at divorce if the parties were married less than six years and $50,000 if they were married six years or more, regardless of fault or need on the part of Jonnie Fox. The parties were divorced on May 18, 1992. On October 5, 1992, Jonnie Fox McAlpine filed a rule to show cause why she (1) should not be awarded permanent alimony pursuant to article 112 of the Louisiana Civil Code, and (2) should not have a Mercedes Benz automobile returned to her, claiming it to be a gift to her from Mr. McAlpine.

The trial court held the antenuptial agreement to be enforceable, held that the Mercedes Benz was not a gift, and dismissed Mrs. McAlpine's rule. The Fourth Circuit Court of Appeal reversed the trial court's ruling in part, holding the antenuptial agreement void as against public policy, but affirmed the trial court with regard to the automobile, and remanded the case for further proceedings. Mr. McAlpine's writ of certiorari was granted, 94-1594 (La.9/30/94), 642 So. 2d 860, and on original hearing, with Justice Kimball dissenting, this Court affirmed, concluding that LSA-C.C. art. 112 was enacted to protect the public interest by preventing needy former spouses from having to seek public assistance and that any act in derogation of article 112 is void under LSA-C.C. art. 7. LSA-C.C. art. 7 provides that "[p]ersons may not by their juridical acts derogate from laws enacted for the protection of the public interest. Any act in derogation of such laws is an absolute nullity." LSA-C.C. art. 7.

We now conclude that permanent alimony was not enacted to protect the *public* interest, but for the benefit of *individuals*. Further, we conclude that if protection of the public interest was ever a proper consideration for permanent alimony, that day has long since passed.

[W]e see from the beginning of alimony in Louisiana that "fault" played an extremely important role, as Planiol said it did in French law.

In *Player*, we characterized alimony after divorce as a "pension," stating as follows:

> As the marriage is forever dissolved, there is no obligation arising from it. The law accords, not alimony in such a case, but a pension, to the unfortunate spouse who has obtained the divorce. This pension becomes revocable in case it should become unnecessary, and in case the wife should contract a second marriage.

Player was cited by this Court in 1940 for the proposition that alimony after divorce "is in the nature of a pension accorded by law to the wife without fault against whom a judgment of divorce has been rendered." The Court in *Fortier* went even further and called this alimony a "pure gratuity" to be granted "in the discretion of the court." *Id.*

In *Hays v. Hays*, 240 La. 708, 124 So. 2d 917 (1960), the husband argued that, since divorce dissolved the bonds of matrimony and thus his obligation to support his wife, and since permanent alimony was "a mere gratuity," an award of permanent alimony constituted a taking of his property for private purposes in violation of the federal and state constitutions. We disagreed and explained our definition of "gratuity" in the context of permanent alimony:

> By this statement this court meant that after divorce there no longer exists an obligation under the marriage contract for the husband to support and maintain his wife, as this contract has been dissolved. In other words, the court had in mind that the wife after divorce no longer has the absolute right to demand of her divorced husband support and assistance since the dissolution of the marriage contract relieved him of that obligation; that consequently the right of the wife to be awarded alimony under Article 160 does not flow from the marriage contract, and that insofar as this contract is concerned, the alimony is a gratuity in the nature of a pension. However, the court's statement cannot be construed to mean that there is no obligation on the divorced husband to pay alimony under certain circumstances.
>
> Divorce is not one of the inalienable rights granted by the federal or the state Constitution, and the lawmakers of the state may make laws regulating divorce and impose conditions under which a citizen of this state may obtain a divorce. Alimony is incidental and related to divorce, and its imposition is within the power which the lawmakers have to regulate and impose conditions for a divorce. Consequently, when the Legislature enacted Article 160 of the Civil Code, it was simply saying to a citizen of this state, as it had a constitutional right to do, *that if cause exists for a divorce, it may be had subject to the condition that the court may in certain specified circumstances require the husband to pay alimony.* By paying this alimony the husband is discharging an obligation imposed upon him by the court under authority of law, and his property is in no sense being unconstitutionally taken. (Emphasis added). *Id.*

The first time in the jurisprudence that we find permanent alimony described as a means to keep women off public assistance is Justice Barham's dissent in *Montz v. Montz*, 253 La. 897, 221 So. 2d 40 (1969). There, Justice Barham characterized permanent alimony as "socio-economic legislation . . . intended to assign responsibility for the dependency of such divorced women so as to relieve them from destitution and the State from their care." 221 So. 2d at 44 (dissenting opinion of Justice Barham). Likewise, relying on this statement, courts and commentators began to characterize permanent alimony as a means to keep divorced women from becoming wards of the state. Thus, commentators and courts, and in fact this Court on original hearing, base the proposition that permanent alimony was enacted to keep divorced spouses from becoming wards of the state on statements that were not law: *Loyacano*, which was vacated on rehearing and by the United States Supreme Court, and the dissenting opinion in *Montz*.

In light of the history of article 160, and courts' and commentators' interpretation of article 160, we must consider whether alimony after divorce is a "law enacted for the public interest" such that any waiver would be an absolute nullity. While other laws governing marriage and children are often enacted for the public interest and non-waivable, an examination and comparison of the laws in this area that have, and have not, been declared non-waivable provides valuable insight.

In *Holliday v. Holliday*, 358 So. 2d 618, 620 (La. 1978), we held prenuptial waivers of alimony *pendente lite* void as contrary to the public policy of this State, expressed in LSA-C.C. arts. 119, 120 and 148, that a husband should support and assist his wife during the existence of the marriage. We held that this legal obligation of support, as well as the fact that the conditions affecting entitlement to alimony *pendente lite* could not be foreseen at the time antenuptial agreements are entered, overrides the premarital anticipatory waiver of alimony. We noted that we expressed no opinion on the antenuptial waiver of permanent alimony, reserving it for another day.

Thus, alimony *pendente lite* is based on the statutorily imposed duty of the spouses to support each other during marriage. See LSA-C.C. art. 98 ("Married persons owe each other fidelity, support, and assistance."). We have historically noted the difference between alimony *pendente lite* and permanent alimony. *Player v. Player, supra*. Comment (e) to LSA-C.C. art. 98 states that "[t]he spouses' duties under this Article, as a general rule are matters of public order from which they may not derogate by contract." On the other hand, there is no corresponding statutory duty of support mandating permanent alimony between former spouses.

While we have held that alimony *pendente lite* is a law enacted for the public interest, the reasoning behind Justice Calogero's argument in the *Holliday* dissent, that alimony *pendente lite* is not a law of public order, is really applicable to permanent alimony. Justice Calogero dissented, stating as follows:

> Neither am I persuaded by relator's contention and the majority's inference that alimony pendente lite is, in the public interest, essential to avoid a wife's becoming a social burden and/or ward of the state. This attitude is a demeaning one which is inconsistent with the realities of the day. It is simply not correct to assume that all, or most, women are incapable of financial independence but must, instead, be wholly dependent upon either their husbands or the state.
>
> Furthermore, in this case, as in almost all marriages where the spouses have entered into an antenuptial agreement, there is no community of acquets and gains. The wife thus has the same control over her property between separation and divorce as she had prior to separation and prior to marriage. An antenuptial waiver by the wife of alimony pendente lite would make the wife no more of a burden on the state than she was prior to marriage. I therefore view alimony pendente lite as a right which is provided for the benefit of the individual and not for the protection of public order and good morals.

Id. at 622 (Calogero dissent). In today's world, more women than ever are in the workforce and are capable of financial independence. Further, a waiver of permanent alimony would make the spouse incapable of financial independence no more of a burden than he or she was before marriage.

The Civil Code limits spouses' rights, before and during marriage, to renounce or alter the marital portion or the established order of succession. LSA-C.C. art. 2330. The legislature determined that these rules were rules of public order that may not be derogated by agreement. LSA-C.C. art. 2330, comment (a). We believe that had the legislature intended to limit spouses' rights to waive post-divorce alimony in the same way, it would have made this clear. Instead, the Civil Code contains no prohibition against the waiver of post-divorce alimony.

Further, the Civil Code limits individuals' rights in other areas where a derogation of such rights would result in the individual becoming a public burden. An individual is forbidden from divesting himself of all his property by a donation inter vivos. LSA-C.C. art. 1497. Also, the right to contract not to compete is limited. LSA-R.S. 23:921. "Both of these situations demonstrate the underlying state concern that a person cannot by convention deprive himself of the ability to support himself." But, as stated in the above case note, alimony is distinguishable:

> To assume that a wife's waiver of alimony automatically occasions the danger that she will become a ward of the state is to assume that the only revenue which married women have is the salary earned by their husbands. Such an assumption is unrealistic in light of modern social trends. . . .
>
> Because waiver of alimony presents a severely limited likelihood that a spouse will become a ward of the state, this public interest should not be considered a public policy unlawfully contravened by the antenuptial waiver of alimony after divorce.

Clearly, a waiver of permanent alimony does not deprive a spouse of his or her ability to support herself.

In other situations involving spouses, waivers in certain areas are clearly allowed. The Civil Code gives spouses, before or during marriage, the right to enter into a matrimonial agreement as to all matters that are not prohibited by public policy. LSA-C.C. art. 2329. A "matrimonial agreement" is defined as "a contract establishing a regime of separation of property or modifying or terminating the legal regime." LSA-C.C. art. 2328. Thus, parties, before or during marriage, can waive their right to the legal regime. As with permanent alimony, this deprives a spouse of the other's earnings and property acquired during marriage that would otherwise become community property, and potentially involves greater consequences on the part of the non-earning spouse than would a waiver of permanent alimony, which is limited to one-third of the other spouse's income and is only to provide sufficient means for support.

[C]ourts have allowed post-separation waivers of permanent alimony and alimony *pendente lite*. Allowing a waiver of permanent alimony in return for a lump sum and treating it as a consent decree is in accordance with the provision of LSA-C.C. art. 112(B) that allows the court to award permanent alimony in a lump sum with the parties' consent.

To allow post-separation waivers of permanent alimony and not prenuptial waivers, as violative of the public order, would be incongruous. Either permanent alimony is a law established for the protection of the public interest, and, as such, a waiver of such is an absolute nullity under article 7, or it is not. On original hearing, "[w]e distinguish[ed] without overruling" most of the cases allowing waivers of permanent alimony in post-separation agreements because there, "unlike in an antenuptial agreement, the conditions which affect entitlement to alimony after divorce can be foreseen at the time of the contract." "Thus, the spouse who may be placed in necessitous circumstances by the agreement is in a much better position to protect him or herself and the risk that the spouse may become a ward of the state is significantly reduced." However, on reconsideration, we find that such a distinction is not justified under article 7 of the Civil Code, which decrees *any* act in derogation of a law enacted for the protection of the public interest is an absolute nullity. The concept of foreseeability is generally not a requirement for valid contracts.

Finally, to hold that antenuptial waivers of permanent alimony are invalid as a matter of public policy would be illogical because permanent alimony is granted only to spouses not-at-fault. Surely the grant of permanent alimony to "innocent" spouses and not "guilty" spouses cannot be a law enacted for the public interest under LSA-C.C. art. 7. Is it really arguable that the state has an interest in keeping not-at-fault divorced spouses off state support but has no such interest in keeping at-fault divorced spouses off the public dole? It is much more probable that the legislature in originally providing for permanent alimony did it not to keep needy ex-wives off public support, but to attempt to rectify the loss suffered by an innocent wife at the hands of an at-fault husband. If preventing divorced spouses from becoming a public burden was really a law enacted for the public interest it probably would have applied to all wives (now spouses), innocent or not.

Our holding today is in accordance with the majority of states that now hold that antenuptial waivers of permanent alimony are not per se invalid as against public policy. As stated by two family law commentators, since 1970, with the advent of no-fault divorce and the changes in society that such laws represent, public policy has changed and the traditional rule that prenuptial waivers of permanent alimony were void *ab initio* has given way to the more realistic view that such agreements are valid and enforceable under certain conditions. Rather than encouraging divorce, these agreements provide couples with the opportunity to plan for the future and safeguard their financial interests. Without this option, potential spouses may choose to live together informally without the benefit of marriage. Thus, these agreements may actually encourage marriage in some instances.

CONCLUSION

We conclude that permanent alimony is not a law enacted for the public interest. Rather, it was enacted to protect individuals, i.e., not-at-fault divorced spouses in need. Thus, the prohibition found in article 7 of the Civil Code does not apply.

Article 2031 of the Civil Code establishes that "[a] contract is relatively null when it violates a rule intended for the protection of private parties, as when a party lacked capacity or did not give free consent at the time the contract was made." LSA-C.C. art. 2031. The rules applicable to the validity of premarital agreements waiving permanent alimony are the same as for other contracts, namely, the Civil Code articles dealing with capacity, consent, error, fraud, and duress. The trial court in this case found that the antenuptial agreement was not the result of fraud, error or duress and, after careful review of the record, we agree with the court of appeal that these findings were not manifestly erroneous. In addition, the trial court was not manifestly erroneous in finding that the Mercedes Benz was not a gift to Mrs. McAlpine.

DECREE

For the reasons stated herein, the judgment of the court of appeal, reversing the trial court's dismissal of Mrs. McAlpine's claim for permanent alimony, is reversed and the trial court's judgment of March 24, 1993 is reinstated. The judgment of the trial court holding that the Mercedes Benz was not a gift to Mrs. McAlpine is affirmed.

REVERSED IN PART; AFFIRMED IN PART.

---

2. *Spousal Support Waivers: Statutory Variations*

Because of the controversy regarding the validity of spousal support waivers in premarital agreements, there is variation in how the community property states treat these waivers. For instance, New Mexico expressly prohibits spousal support waivers: A premarital agreement may not adversely affect the right of a . . . spouse to support. . . . N.M. Stat. Ann. §40-3A-4(B). The Arizona Legislature, when it enacted its version of the UPAA, provided an exception if the waiver of spousal support causes one party to the agreement to be "eligible for support under a program of public assistance at the time of separation or marital dissolution, a court, notwithstanding the terms of the agreement, may require the other party to provide support to the extent necessary to avoid that eligibility." A.R.S. §25-202(D). Idaho and Nevada enacted identical provisions. I.C. §32-925(2), N.R.S §123A.080(2). Texas allows premarital agreements to modify or eliminate spousal support. VTCA Family Code §4.003.

In 2001, the California Legislature amended its Premarital Agreement Act, to mandate representation by independent counsel when a premarital agreement includes a provision regarding spousal support. In addition, the amendment allows for the provision to be examined at the time of enforcement for unconscionability, even if there was representation by independent counsel. Cal. Fam. Code §1612(c).

Consider which formulations allow for certainty and enforceability. Which formulations provide the most protection for the spouse disadvantaged by the premarital agreement? The most protection for the State?

C. VALIDITY OF ORAL PREMARITAL AGREEMENTS: THE WASHINGTON AND CALIFORNIA EXPERIENCE

Generally, premarital agreements must be in writing. For instance, the California Premarital Agreement Act states that "a premarital agreement shall be in writing and signed by both parties." Cal. Fam. Code §1611. However, the question does arise when the premarital agreement is discussed and agreed to but never reduced to writing.

1. Washington

In *DewBerry v. George* (2003), the couple purportedly entered into an oral pre-marital agreement to treat earned income during the marriage as separate property. The wife sought to enforce this agreement with evidence of the couple's words and actions over the nine-year marriage that indicated they had entered into this agreement.

DEWBERRY v. GEORGE

115 Wash. App. 351, 62 P.2d 525 (2003)
Court of Appeals of Washington

COLEMAN, J.

At issue in this dissolution case is whether an oral prenuptial agreement to treat income earned during marriage as separate property is enforceable. Because the trial court found by clear, cogent, and convincing evidence supported by the record that the parties fully performed their separate property agreement during their marriage, we conclude that their oral prenuptial agreement is enforceable. The trial court did not err when it characterized the parties' property acquired during marriage as separate property in accordance with the agreement. In addition, we conclude that the trial court did not abuse its discretion by allocating the parties' separate property to the spouse who acquired it. Accordingly, we affirm the trial court's property division.

FACTS

Emanuel George, Jr. and Carla DewBerry started dating in 1980 while they were both living in California. DewBerry had just graduated from Boalt Hall School of Law and was working toward becoming a CPA at Arthur Andersen. George was a college-educated music industry executive.

In 1981, the parties were discussing marriage and George told DewBerry that, because a friend had been wronged in a divorce settlement and lost his house, he insisted on the following conditions of marriage: (1) DewBerry would always be fully employed; (2) each party's income and property would be treated as separate property; (3) each party would own a home to return to if the marriage failed; and (4) DewBerry would not get fat. DewBerry agreed to these conditions. This discussion took place in California, a community property state. Neither party was particularly wealthy at the beginning of their relationship. George and DewBerry married in 1986.

Between 1981 and 2000, George and DewBerry continually affirmed this agreement through words and actions. The record reflects painstaking and meticulous effort to maintain separate finances and property. During their marriage, DewBerry and George deposited their incomes into separate accounts which they used for their personal expenses and investments. In 1990, after the birth of their first child, they opened a joint checking account in order to handle certain agreed household expenses. George and DewBerry deposited a specified amount to the joint account, and they reimbursed their personal accounts from the joint account if they happened to use personal funds for household expenses. They took turns managing that account. By 2000, when George and DewBerry separated, they had accumulated minimal community property in the form of joint accounts and jointly purchased possessions. They held numerous investment, bank, and retirement accounts as individuals, and the spouse who had created and contributed to those accounts was considered the sole owner and manager of the assets in those accounts. The primary beneficiaries of their individual accounts were the parties' children, or alternatively, the estate of the spouse who funded them.

During their relationship, DewBerry purchased three houses as her separate property, securing financing separately in all instances by signing promissory notes or asking her sister to co-sign. The first house that she bought was a duplex in Oakland, which she purchased in 1982 in order to fulfill the third condition of the prenuptial agreement. The latter two houses, both located in Seattle, served as the family's primary residences. In accordance with the parties' agreement, DewBerry treated these houses as her separate property by paying for maintenance, improvements, and the down payment and mortgage with funds from her separate accounts. George paid DewBerry a set amount each month toward living expenses, such as utilities, and DewBerry repaid George for any maintenance costs he incurred. The only involvement George had with these properties was to sign documents at various times indicating either that he had no interest in the properties (the Oakland duplex and the first family home), or, in the case of the parties' most recent residence (the Thorndyke house), that he consented to being listed on the purchase documents as husband and wife per the bank's requirements. There was no intent that George be personally liable, however, for any of the indebtedness on the properties. George already owned real property in Texas and California that he had acquired before their marriage.

In 1985, DewBerry left Arthur Andersen to become an associate in a Seattle law firm. Meanwhile, George worked in sales and marketing in the entertainment and hospitality industries, and his salary was comparable to DewBerry's initial law firm salary, around $40,000 to $50,000 per year. By the 1990s, however, after DewBerry became a partner at her law firm, her annual salary increased rapidly, totaling over $1 million in 2000. Meanwhile, George's salary remained constant in the $40,000 to $50,000 range. Both parties worked full-time while sharing parenting responsibilities for their two children.

The trial court entered detailed findings of fact and conclusions of law regarding the parties' property and oral prenuptial agreement. Specifically, the trial court found by clear, cogent, and convincing evidence that the parties had entered into an oral prenuptial agreement, despite George's denial of the agreement's existence. The trial court also found that there had been "complete performance" of that agreement during the parties' marriage and, thus, the parties' property consisted primarily of separate property. The trial court ordered that the parties' property be divided roughly in accordance with its status as separate or community property. It awarded DewBerry $2.3 million, or approximately 82 percent of the parties' property, which consisted almost entirely of real and personal property that DewBerry had acquired during the marriage, as well as her pre-marriage separate property. George received property worth $600,000, consisting of his real and personal separate property from before and during the marriage, the bulk of the parties' community property, plus $300,000 cash from DewBerry's separate accounts. Part of the trial court's award to George consisted of a cash equivalent of 11 percent of the Thorndyke house value, or $74,250, based upon evidence of some commingling of property interests in the Thorndyke house (i.e., George's possible liability on the mortgage, his reliance on the house as a primary residence, and traceable community funds used for the down payment).

The trial court also found that George was voluntarily underemployed because he had not worked full-time hours from January 2000 through September 2001, the time of trial. After he was laid off from Eddie Bauer in 1999, George began working the early morning shift from 4 A.M. to 7 P.M. at UPS because it provided steady income and benefits. It also allowed him flexibility to pursue a career as a longshoreman and spend time with his children. The longshoring work was assigned on a daily basis at a dispatch hall, but because George lacked union membership and senior status, he worked only one to two shifts per week. The trial court ordered George to pay child support based upon imputed income of $48,000, which is more than he currently makes in his part-time jobs, but which is less than his salary at Eddie Bauer. George appeals the trial court's property division and the order of child support.

DECISION

George argues that the trial court erred when it found by clear, cogent, and convincing evidence that an oral separate property agreement had been made by the parties prior to marriage and that it had been fully performed during their marriage, making it an enforceable agreement. He claims that such an agreement is void under Washington's community property laws and the statute of frauds. He also disagrees with the trial court's conclusion that "almost all of the property the parties own is separate property and it should be awarded to the person who obtained it." We find no error and affirm.

There is nothing in Washington law that prohibits parties from entering into prenuptial agreements that alter the status of community property. Furthermore, there is substantial evidence to support the trial court's findings and conclusions regarding the existence and complete performance of the parties' oral prenuptial agreement. Thus, the part performance exception to the statute of frauds applies and the parties' oral agreement is enforceable.

Oral separate property agreements made *after* marriage have consistently been enforced by Washington courts when clear and convincing evidence shows both the existence of the agreement and mutual observance of the agreement.

But Washington courts have not yet addressed a situation where parties have orally agreed *prior* to marriage to have a separate property agreement during their marriage. Accordingly, this is a matter of first impression, and we address both the statute of frauds and Washington law concerning prenuptial agreements.

* * *

Although we hold that the statute of frauds applies to the agreement in question, we conclude that it is enforceable under the part performance exception to the statute of frauds. The doctrine of part performance is an equitable doctrine which provides the remedies of damages or specific performance for agreements that would otherwise be barred by the statute of frauds.

The first requirement of the doctrine of part performance of oral contracts is that the contract must be proven by clear, cogent, and convincing evidence. The second requirement is that the acts relied upon as constituting part performance must unmistakably point to the existence of the claimed agreement. If they point to some other relationship, such as that of landlord and tenant, or may be accounted for on some other hypothesis, they are not sufficient.

George contends that the trial court's findings are not supported by clear, cogent, and convincing evidence, but his argument is based solely on his perception that the trial court erred in finding that DewBerry's testimony regarding the creation of the agreement was more credible. The trial court's credibility findings are not subject to review on appeal. Here, the terms of the agreement were clear and simple. Several witnesses testified that the parties created an oral prenuptial agreement and that George and DewBerry acted in accordance with that agreement. Furthermore, despite George's denial of the agreement, the steps taken by the parties to avoid commingling of their assets were unusually strong evidence of a separate property agreement. It was undisputed that the parties meticulously accounted for and handled their individual incomes as separate property and created minimal joint accounts to handle certain family-related expenses and requirements. The husband and wife relationship cannot account for such painstaking efforts to establish and maintain separate property. We conclude that the trial court's determination that an oral agreement was made is supported by substantial evidence that is "highly probable."

Although Washington has never enforced an oral prenuptial agreement, several other jurisdictions have. These cases all involved partial or full performance of an oral prenuptial agreement. The case at bar is similar to the ones cited above because each of those cases involved complete performance of an oral prenuptial agreement during the parties' marriages.

We also reject George's contention that the oral prenuptial agreement is void because it is against public policy favoring creation of community property. Under Washington law, there is a presumption that all income earned during marriage will be community property. This presumption may be rebutted by entering into a separate property agreement, but proof of such an agreement is held to a higher evidentiary standard than a community property agreement.

George argues that Washington law prohibits parties from entering into an agreement to repudiate the community property system and that such an agreement is void because it conflicts with public policy favoring creation of community property. This is not an accurate statement of Washington law. Washington courts have long held that a husband and wife may contractually modify the status of their property. Public policy favors prenuptial agreements because they are "generally regarded as conducive to marital tranquility and the avoidance of disputes about property in the future." Prenuptial agreements are contracts subject to the principles of contract law.

Washington courts evaluate prenuptial agreements under the *Matson* two-prong test to determine whether the contract is substantively and procedurally fair. . . .

There is nothing unfair about two well-educated working professionals agreeing to preserve the fruits of their labor for their individual benefit. Indeed, as the one requesting the agreement, George apparently assumed that he had greater financial security, since he already owned some real estate and had a good job. Although in hindsight George may have been mistaken, this does not change the court's analysis. Both parties were aware of each other's education, assets, and income potential and had ample time to consider the agreement during their five-year engagement and fourteen-year marriage. We conclude that the agreement was both procedurally and substantively fair to both parties.

George's next contention is that the trial court erred by "failing to make a fair and equitable property division," as required by RCW 26.09.080. The record shows, however, that all of the parties' separate and community property was before the court, which did exercise its discretion to make an equitable division of property.

Moreover, "[t]he trial court has broad court has broad discretion in awarding property in a dissolution action, and will be reversed only upon a showing of manifest abuse of discretion." Just and equitable distribution does not mean that the court must make an equal distribution. In a well-reasoned oral opinion, the trial court fully set forth tenable grounds for dividing the parties' property in accordance with the parties' prenuptial agreement. The court's disposition relied in part on the fact that each party accumulated substantial separate property during the marriage and both parties are capable of working full-time and continuing to accumulate and manage their assets. Based upon the parties' agreement and expectations under that agreement, it cannot be said that the trial court's property distribution was an abuse of discretion.

We affirm.

Cox, A.C.J., and Grosse, J., concur.

Discussion Questions

1. The court upholds the enforceability of the couple's oral premarital agreement. What evidence was particularly persuasive in reaching this conclusion?

2. Assume that, in violation of the couple's oral premarital agreement, the wife "got fat" during the marriage or became employed part-time, do you think the court would have held differently? Why or why not?

2. *California*

Hall v. Hall (Cal. 1990) is another case in which the wife sought to enforce an oral premarital agreement that would have allowed her to live in her husband's house until she died in exchange for giving up her job, applying for Social Security at age 62, and giving him $10,000. The wife fulfilled her side of the bargain in full, but before title transferring documents were signed the husband died unexpectedly. The trial court held that the wife's partial performance of the couple's oral agreement qualified as an exception to the requirements of the Statutes of Frauds. The appellate court affirmed, holding that although the Premarital Agreement Act requires a premarital agreement to be in writing and signed by both parties, traditional exceptions to the Statutes of Frauds should be applied to premarital agreements as it does to all other contracts. The scope of *Hall*, however, is limited to where the party seeking enforcement "performed his/her part of the bargain and in so doing irretrievably changed his position." Thus, partial performance of acts typically common in marriage [e.g., the marriage itself] would not be sufficient to be considered "irretrievably changing position" for purposes of getting around the writing requirement.

HALL v. HALL

222 Cal. App. 3d 578, 271 Cal. Rptr. 713 (1990)
Court of Appeal

FROEHLICH, J.

David Allen Hall (David), as executor and trustee of the estate and trust of his father, Aubrey Milton Hall (Decedent), appeals from a judgment granting Carol Anita Hall (Carol), Decedent's second wife, a life estate in the residential property which she shared with Decedent. He contends any oral agreement Carol made with Decedent allowing her a life estate in the residence is unenforceable and that specific performance is improper.

FACTUAL AND PROCEDURAL BACKGROUND

The evidence viewed most favorably in favor of the judgment reflects that on February 5, 1986, some months after the death of his wife of 49 years, Decedent executed a revocable trust and a quitclaim deed transferring the fee interest in his residence to himself as trustee of the trust. Under the terms of the trust, during his lifetime Decedent was the sole beneficiary, and at his death his sons were to share equally in the property.

Decedent met Carol in March of 1986. They began dating, and in early May 1986 he asked her to marry him. She expressed concerns to Decedent about the marriage, about spending her money, and about not having a place to live for the rest of her life. Decedent convinced her to marry him, to give up her job so they could spend most of their time together, to apply for Social Security at age 62 so they would have additional money, and to give him $10,000 so they would have money to start the marriage. In exchange he promised she could live in his home for the rest of her life.

But for the agreement Carol would not have stopped working and would not have applied for early Social Security.

Carol and Decedent were married on July 16, 1986. In June she terminated her employment, moved in with Decedent, and applied for Social Security upon reaching age 62. She used her personal funds to finance a trip to Ohio soon after the marriage and gave Decedent other funds, aggregating more than the $10,000 they had agreed upon.

In October 1986, Decedent and Carol met with Pamela Ferrie Estabrook (Estabrook), the attorney who had prepared the trust document for Decedent. Carol testified that during the meeting Decedent authorized Estabrook to prepare an amendment to the trust which would allow Carol to live in the house for the rest of her life, and that he also asked Estabrook to prepare a new will for Carol. Estabrook testified that when the couple came to see her she was uncertain what Decedent wanted, but he said he wanted to provide a residence for Carol in the event of his death and also asked her to prepare a simple will for Carol. She testified that during a later telephone call he authorized her to prepare a trust amendment granting a life estate in his residence to Carol, and she prepared a draft amendment and sent it to him. She stated Decedent later told her he had some questions regarding the amendment and the will and would make an appointment with her sometime later. Decedent died unexpectedly on January 16, 1987, without signing the amendment.

On March 11, 1987, Carol filed a nine-count complaint against Decedent's sons, David and Aubrey Milton Hall, Jr. (Aubrey, Jr.), as individuals and in their capacities as cotrustees of Decedent's trust and co-executors of his estate, seeking a determination of her entitlement to a life estate in the residence and other relief. In trial before the court, David and Aubrey, Jr., were granted judgment at the close of Carol's case as to certain of her contentions related to personal property and on her claim to being a pretermitted spouse. After full trial, however, Carol prevailed in her action to establish a life estate in the realty, the court determining that the doctrine of partial performance was available to avoid statute of frauds problems otherwise applicable to the oral agreement the court found established by the evidence. David appeals as sole trustee and executor, Aubrey Jr., having resigned his positions.

DISCUSSION

I

David contends the oral agreement between Decedent and Carol is unenforceable because it was not in writing and signed by both parties. At the outset we should focus upon which of several possibly applicable statute of frauds provisions is pertinent to this case. David cites Civil Code section 5311 (premarital agreements must be in writing), section 5110.730 (transmutation of property between spouses must be in writing), and Probate Code section 150 (a)(3) (contract to make a will must be in writing). We believe the applicable statute of frauds provision is section 5311, dealing with premarital agreements. The evidence does not support, and the court did not find, any actual transmutation of property between Decedent and Carol.

The determination was that an agreement had been entered under the terms of which a transmutation *would* occur. Similarly, the factual determination of the court rules out a conclusion that this was an agreement to make transfers by way of will. It was an agreement to modify an existing trust so as to convey to Carol a life estate in the residential realty. We must, therefore, examine the provisions of sections 5300 through 5317, which constitute the codification in California of the Uniform Premarital Agreement Act, adopted in 1985.

II

The Uniform Premarital Agreement Act (the act) was added by the Legislature in 1985 and is effective as to any premarital agreement executed on or after January 1, 1986. (§5302.) The general purpose of the act is to make the law regarding premarital agreements uniform among the states adopting it. (§5301.) To date the act has been adopted in 14 states.

Under the act " '[p]remarital agreement' means an agreement between prospective spouses made in contemplation of marriage and to be effective upon marriage." " 'Property' means an interest, present or future, legal or equitable, vested or contingent, in real or personal property, including income and earnings." (§5310.)

"Parties to a premarital agreement may contract with respect to all of the following:

> (1) The rights and obligations of each of the parties in any of the property of either or both of them whenever and wherever acquired or located.
> (2) The right to . . . use . . . property. (§5312.)

Since the agreement between Carol and Decedent was made in contemplation of marriage and respected a right to property, it is governed by the act.

At the outset, we deal with Carol's contention that the act is actually not a statute of frauds. Acknowledging that the agreement she seeks to enforce was never committed to writing, she contends the act simply does not pertain to oral agreements. This argument is based on the following syllogism: (1) the act applies only to premarital agreements as defined in the act; (2) under section 5311 "[a] premarital agreement shall be in writing and signed by both parties"; and (3) therefore, definitionally, an agreement not in writing and signed by both parties is not a premarital agreement and not covered by the act. This somewhat startling argument finds some support in legislative materials generated by Senate and Assembly committees during consideration of the act which describe, among other things, situations excluded from the act. In several places these reports state the act does not deal with agreements between persons who cohabit but do not contemplate marriage or do not marry, "[n]or does [the act] provide for postnuptial or separation agreements *or oral agreements*." (Assem. Subcom. on Administration of Justice, Analysis of Sen. Bill. No. 1143 (1985-1986 Reg. Sess.) as amended July 18, 1985, p. 3; Assem. Office Research, 3d reading analysis of Sen. Bill No. 1143 (1985-1986 Reg. Sess.) p. 1., italics added.)

Literally, this comment suggests exclusion of all oral agreements from the act's coverage, relegating the scope of the new law to a governance only of the terms of written agreements. We cannot, however, accept this novel proposition. First, our research of authority from the several other states which have adopted the uniform act fails to reveal any similar interpretation. Second, nothing in the legislative or uniform commission reports expands upon or otherwise explains the comment about "oral agreements." Finally, the general tenor of all related materials leads to the conclusion that the new act was intended to be a statute of frauds law, replacing and not substantially changing the existing statute of frauds provision governing premarital agreements. For instance, the preamble to the Senate Committee Report on the bill states that the new act would replace existing statute of frauds provisions relative to premarital agreements, and that it would be "similar to existing law." The Report of the Assembly Subcommittee states that the new act "[r]equires a premarital agreement to be in writing and signed by both parties." The most detailed analysis of the law available to interested parties at the time it was being considered by the Legislature was a 23-page report prepared as of May 3, 1984, by the assistant executive secretary of the California Law Revision Commission. Nothing in this analysis suggests any intention that the act was not to preclude enforceability of oral agreements, generally. Typical of references to the issue is the simple statement in the prefatory note to the analysis that "Section 5312 requires that a premarital agreement be in writing and signed by both parties."

We do not, therefore, accept the proposition that in rewriting the California statute of frauds provision relating to premarital agreements the Legislature intended to regulate the effectiveness of agreements which to some extent had been reduced to writing, but to *deregulate* entirely the writing requirement in the case of agreements which were totally oral. We would need more than a "throw away" line in legislative materials to come to such a surprising conclusion. We rule that the act is a statute of frauds law, requiring that the agreement be in writing to be enforceable, and hence proceed to the core issue in this case, which is whether traditional exceptions to the statute of frauds remain viable in terms of the new act.

III

New section 5311, which provides that "[a] premarital agreement shall be in writing and signed by both parties," replaced former section 5134, which in turn was a reenactment without change of an earlier section enacted in 1872. Former section 5134 required: "All contracts for marriage settlements must be in writing, and executed and acknowledged or proved in like manner as a grant of land is required to be executed and acknowledged or proved." Exceptions "taking the case out of the statute" have traditionally been recognized as to all statute of frauds provisions. Thus, a substantial change of position in reliance on an oral agreement will estop reliance on the statute, and an actual transfer of realty constituting partial performance of the oral agreement will satisfy the proof element otherwise reflected in the requirement of a writing.

These exceptions were recognized in the enforcement of premarital agreements under the former law. It was well established that marriage itself or mere payment of money was not sufficient performance to take an oral prenuptial agreement out of the writing requirement of the statute, because these acts could reasonably be expected in any marriage. "Relief because of the partial or full performance of the contract is usually granted in equity on the ground that the party who has so performed has been induced by the other party to irretrievably change his position and that to refuse relief according to the terms of the contract would otherwise amount to a fraud upon his rights." For relief to be granted because of partial performance of an oral antenuptial contract, the acts which are relied upon must be unequivocally referable to the contract. Acts which, although done in performance of the contract, admit to an explanation other than the contract (such as the performance of husbandly or wifely duties) are not generally acts of partial performance which will take the agreement out of the statute of frauds.

The trial court, on the basis of substantial evidence, held that the oral agreement to transfer a life estate to Carol was enforceable, and taken out of the statute of frauds, because of partial performance of the agreement by Carol. It found that Carol would not have married without some agreement with respect to her financial security; that she quit working and took early Social Security in performance of her part of the bargain; and the payments she made to Decedent were consistent with their agreement.

Certainly under the former law this finding is sustainable. Marrying Decedent and paying him $10,000 in accordance with the agreement would not, standing alone, have been sufficient performance to take the case out of the statute of frauds. But by her additional acts of stopping work and applying for early Social Security Carol irretrievably changed her position in reliance on Decedent's promise to provide her a house for the rest of her life. Her performance constituted detrimental reliance on his promise sufficient to allow enforcement of the contract under the former law.

The issue, then, is whether the partial performance exception remains applicable under the act. We rule that the exceptions to the statute recognized under the former law are equally applicable to the Uniform Premarital Agreement Act. It is true that the act does not specifically reference any of the traditional exceptions to the statute of frauds. Equally true, however, is that the act does not preclude them. Also, nothing in any of the legislative materials nor in the reports of the Commissioners on Uniform State Laws makes any reference to the exclusion of traditional exceptions. To the contrary, the report of the executive secretary of the California Law Revision Commission recognized the continued viability of exceptions to the statute of frauds: "It appears that acts that take the agreement out of the writing requirement of Section 5312 are recognized. We must assume the framers of the uniform act were well versed in the statute of frauds and knew about the exceptions applied to the writing requirement. Since the Commissioners on Uniform State Laws apparently recognized the existence of traditional exceptions, and the reports of legislative committees commenting on the law make no suggestion of exclusion of the exceptions, we must assume it was intended such exceptions continue to be viable. We therefore find the trial court's reliance upon partial performance as removing the case from the statute to be justified.

IV

David argues allowing a life estate for Carol is harsh and inequitable to innocent third parties since the trust's beneficiaries may be denied their inheritance for many years, whereas Decedent and Carol were only married for a few months.

"It is to be presumed that the breach of an agreement to transfer real property cannot be adequately relieved by pecuniary compensation. In the case of a single-family dwelling which the party seeking performance intends to occupy, this presumption is conclusive." "It is settled that the fairness and reasonableness of a contract is determined from the circumstances as they existed at the time of the making of the contract." At the time Decedent and Carol entered into their agreement they surely anticipated more time together than the few months they enjoyed. Carol detrimentally relied on Decedent's promise that she could continue to live in his home if he predeceased her. Her expectancy interest can only be protected by an order of specific performance. Enforcement of the life estate is not excessive or inequitable to the individuals who will ultimately inherit the property.

DISPOSITION

The judgment is affirmed.

KREMER, P.J., and NARES, J., concurred.

Discussion Questions

1. Why did Anita Hall think that she needed a premarital agreement? What acts would not fall within "irretrievably changing position"?
2. The *Hall* case dealt with a widow. How does that differ from a scenario involving divorce?

PROBLEM 3.1

George and Martha are an older couple that would like to marry, but desire to protect their respective separate property. They come to you for legal advice in drafting their premarital agreement. What key information would you provide to them, or ask of them, during your initial consultation?

PROBLEM 3.2

Harry and Wilma are both middle-aged divorcés. The couple signed a premarital agreement waiving spousal support and community property claims. During their marriage, Wilma wins the state lottery and the couple both retire early at the age of 50. Unfortunately, the constant company of one's spouse leads to marital discord for these two. Harry files for divorce, and comes to you for legal advice regarding the enforceability of the signed premarital agreement. He is particularly concerned that the lottery winnings will be declared Wilma's separate property because she used separate property funds to purchase the winning ticket. Harry is retired and would be living at near poverty level due to the steep decline in his real estate and stock portfolio, and diminished retirement payout. What arguments will you advise Harry to make in this dispute? What will Wilma likely argue? How will a court most likely rule?

PROBLEM 3.3

Michael and Lisa are young professionals who believe in economic independence. Lisa has just finished law school and is a first-year associate in a local law firm. Michael is a tax consultant with four years of professional experience. Lisa has drafted a premarital agreement that she insists that Michael sign. The agreement specifies that the couple will not be subject to community property law upon marriage, instead all income will be the separate property of the parties. The agreement also waives spousal support in the event of divorce. Assume that Michael signs the premarital agreement. In ten years, both are successful professionals, but the marriage has begun to deteriorate. Then, Lisa is diagnosed with a serious illness; the expensive experimental treatment costs take a great toll on their finances and relationship. Michael wants to end the marriage. Lisa is now unemployed, and would rely on State aid should the couple divorce. Michael comes to you for legal advice. He wants to know if the premarital agreement's spousal support waiver is enforceable. What do you advise him? What will Lisa likely argue? How will a court most likely rule in the differing community property states?

PROBLEM 3.4

Now assume that both Lisa and Michael are healthy, successful professionals, but their marriage has failed. Also assume that at the time the premarital agreement was signed, they had been living together for one year. They drafted schedules disclosing their premarital assets and obligations that were attached to the premarital agreement. However, Lisa failed to include the 1962 Porsche 356B convertible (a graduation present) that was frequently driven by the couple on weekends but stored in Lisa's parents' classic car garage. Assume that the couple both consulted independent counsel prior to signing the agreement. How will a court most likely rule with regard to the agreement's enforceability? Why?

Table 3-1
Premarital Agreements in Community Property States

State	Rule	Case/Statute
Arizona	Follows UPAA, Unenforceable if involuntary or unconscionable at time of execution Unconscionable and lack of fair and reasonable disclosure or voluntary and express waiver of disclosure AND did not have adequate knowledge of property/financial obligations of other party	Arizona Revised Statutes §25-201-203

California	Follows UPAA with amendments in 2001 that specify requirements re spousal support waivers and voluntariness.	Family Code §§1612 and 1615
Idaho	Follows UPAA, Unenforceable if involuntary or unconscionable at time of execution Unconscionable and lack of fair and reasonable disclosure or voluntary and express waiver of disclosure AND did not have adequate knowledge of property/financial obligations of the other party	Idaho Code §§32-923-927
Louisiana	Does not follow UPAA, PMAs invalid if against public policy. Requires a notary and two witnesses. May not renounce or alter marital portion or established order of succession. May not limit one spouse's ability to obligate the community or to alienate, encumber or lease CP.	Louisiana Civil Code §§2329-2330
Nevada	Follows UPAA, Unenforceable if involuntary or unconscionable at time of execution Unconscionable and lack of fair and reasonable disclosure or voluntary and express waiver of disclosure AND did not have adequate knowledge of property/financial obligations of other party	Nevada Revised Statutes §123A.010–123A.100
New Mexico	Follows UPAA, Unenforceable if involuntary or unconscionable at time of execution Unconscionable and lack of fair and reasonable disclosure or voluntary and express waiver of disclosure AND did not have adequate knowledge of property/financial obligations of other party	New Mexico Statutes Annotated, §§40-3A-1–40-3A-10
Texas	Follows UPAA, Unenforceable if involuntary or unconscionable at time of execution Unconscionable and lack of fair and reasonable disclosure or voluntary and express waiver of disclosure AND did not have adequate knowledge of property/financial obligations of other party	Vernon's Texas Statutes, Family Code §§4.001–4.009
Washington	Does not follow UPAA, Courts use a two-prong analysis to determine (1) if the PMA is substantively fair. If fair and reasonable provision for spouse not seeking enforcement, analysis ends. If substantively unfair, (2) the court asks if there was full disclosure and whether the agreement was freely entered into on independent advice from counsel with full knowledge by both spouses of their rights. If (2) satisfied, then a substantively unfair provision is valid and binding.	*Marriage of Matson,* 107 Wash. 2d 479, 730 P.2d 668 (1986), *Marriage of Bernard,* 165 Wash. 2d 895, 204 P.3d 907 (2009)

| Wisconsin | Any agreement made by the parties before or during the marriage concerning any arrangement for property distribution; such agreements shall be binding upon the court except that so such agreement shall be binding where the terms of the agreement are inequitable as to either party. Modification or elimination of spousal support is permitted but may not result in a spouse having less than necessary and adequate support. | Wis. Stat. §§767.61(3)(L) (formerly §767.255(3)(L)), 766.68 (3)(d), (9), *Levy v. Levy*, 388 Wis. 2d 523, 388 N.W.2d 170 (1986) (premarital agreement intended to apply at death did not apply at divorce), *Krejci v. Krejci*, 266 Wis. 2d 284, 667 N.W.2d 780 (Ct. App. 2003) (enforcement of agreement would be inequitable) |

Chapter 4

Opening a Bank Account: Commingling Community and Separate Funds

When a couple marries, they enjoy the wedding ceremony, reception, and gifts. After the honeymoon, they will return to the reality of their jobs. They may decide to open a new checking account in both their names for their salaries. They may decide to keep the individual checking accounts they had prior to their marriage. They may also decide to open a savings account to begin a nest egg in order to buy a home. They will rarely think about keeping separate accounts for community property and separate property money. Let's take the example of Michael and Lisa. Michael had a savings account in his name in which he puts $100 a month from his salary. At the time they married, the bank account had $5,000. That $5,000 was separate property because he earned it before their marriage. After marriage, his salary is community property. If he continues to deposit $100 a month from his salary, he has now "commingled" community property funds with his separate property funds. Once commingling occurs and the marriage lasts for a significant period of time, it is usually difficult to untangle the mass of funds in the bank account. There is nothing about the $100 that identifies it as separate or community. Yet it is possible to keep records to know when and what type of funds were deposited and withdrawn from a commingled account. However, often married people do not realize that it is necessary to keep records regarding the funds until their marriage has come to an end and they have consulted with a lawyer. At that point, wrangling can begin about (1) the ownership of the funds in the bank account itself and (2) about the ownership of property purchased using funds from the commingled bank account.

A. DETERMINING THE CHARACTER OF THE FUNDS IN A COMMINGLED BANK ACCOUNT

1. Louisiana Approach

The Louisiana case of *Cutting v. Cutting* (1993) deals with a dispute over the husband's retirement savings plan at his job. The savings plan had more than

$7,000 in his account at the time of marriage and had more than $40,000 at the time of divorce. Because the savings plan contained commingled funds, the $7,000 from before marriage and community property funds earned during marriage, the court had to determine whether at the time of divorce the savings plan contained any separate property funds or was all community property.

CUTTING v. CUTTING

625 So. 2d 1112 (1993)
Court of Appeal of Louisiana

KNOLL, Judge.

This is an appeal from a judgment partitioning the community that formerly existed between Gail and Jack E. Cutting.

Gail appeals, asserting that the trial court erred in: (1) its valuation of the disputed community assets; (2) characterizing certain community liabilities as her separate debts; and, (3) determining the reimbursements owed by the parties concerning the community residence. Jack also appeals the trial court's ruling that Gail was entitled to elect the method of payment to her of her portion of the Reynolds Metals Company Savings and Retirement Plan (Reynolds Metals Plan). For reasons which follow, we affirm the trial court's judgment as amended.

FACTS

The Cuttings married in Arkansas on May 13, 1981. Both had children from previous marriages. In January of 1984, the couple moved to Lake Charles, Louisiana where they purchased a home. Gail, Jack, and Gail's two minor children from her previous marriage, lived in the home until the Cuttings' physical separation on February 9, 1989. From that date, Jack retained the sole use and occupancy of the house until it was sold on April 30, 1991. The Cuttings legally separated on March 7, 1989, and were divorced on June 27, 1990. On April 25, 1990, Gail requested a partition of the community property.

The trial court heard the partition proceeding on December 10, 1990. On October 24, 1991, in written reasons, the trial court assigned values to and apportioned the assets and debts of the community. On May 4, 1992, Gail moved to reopen the matter for the limited purpose of adducing evidence pertinent to the entry of a Qualified Domestics Relations Order (QDRO) disposing of the parties' proportionate shares of the Reynolds Metals Plan in accordance with the trial court's written reasons for judgment. The trial court granted the motion and accepted additional evidence via joint offerings and stipulations. The trial court entered written reasons concerning the QDRO on September 8, 1992.

On September 24, 1992, after valuing and apportioning the assets and liabilities, the trial court signed a judgment which allocated the assets and debts between the parties. This original judgment erroneously ordered Gail to pay $104.79 to Jack. On the same day, the trial court corrected the judgment to order Jack to pay Gail $192.70. It also declared Gail to be entitled to a $1/2$ interest in that portion of the benefits ultimately payable under the Reynolds Metals Plan which are attributable to

Jack's employment during the existence of the community property regime, a period of 8.203 years. From this judgment, both parties bring this appeal.

VALUATION OF COMMUNITY ASSETS

Gail attacks the trial court's valuation of three disputed community assets, namely, the 1984 Nissan Maxima, the 1987 Nissan Pathfinder, and the Reynolds Metals Plan.

At trial, Jack submitted an appraisal from Lakeside National Bank which valued the Pathfinder at $10,475 and the Maxima at $4,250. Gail submitted an appraisal from National Bank of Commerce which valued the Pathfinder at $11,000 and the Maxima at $3,100. Neither party called the appraisers as witnesses at trial. Gail contends that the trial court erred because the LNB appraisal contained a high mileage deduction for the Pathfinder, which had 55,000 miles, but did not contain a high mileage deduction for the Maxima, which had over 100,000 miles.

LSA–R.S. 9:2801(4)(c) provides in pertinent part that, "[i]n allocating assets and liabilities, the court may divide a particular asset or liability equally or unequally or may allocate it in its entirety to one of the spouses. . . ." The trial court has great discretion in partitioning community property, and it is not required to accept at face value a spouse's valuation of assets or debts, or claims against the community. *Breaux v. Breaux*, 555 So. 2d 1001 (La. App. 3rd Cir. 1990). Confronted with the appraisals and in absence of live testimony concerning the method of calculating appraised values, the trial court valued the Pathfinder at $10,737.50 and the Maxima at $3,675. We cannot say that this median figure constituted an abuse of the trial court's discretion.

Next, Gail attacks the trial court's valuation of the Reynolds Metals Plan. The record shows that Jack had participated in the savings plan since its inception in 1976 or 1977. Prior to his marriage on May 13, 1981, he had invested $7,171.57 of separate funds. This figure is supported by Jack's testimony and a joint exhibit reporting a balance of $7,171.57 as of June 30, 1981, approximately 48 days after the marriage. To ascertain the value of the plan as of the date the community terminated, March 7, 1989, the parties introduced one report showing a value of the plan of $42,806.77 as of December 31, 1988, 66 days prior to the termination of the community regime, and one showing a value of $46,718.07 as of June 30, 1989, 115 days after the termination of the community regime.[1]

The trial court accepted Jack's argument that the $7,171.57 value as of June 30, 1981, represented a separate property contribution and subtracted that amount to calculate community property contributions to the plan. In doing so, the suggested valuation would be between $35,635.50 and $39,546.50. The trial court apparently valued the account at a median figure of $37,581.81.

Gail contests this valuation. First, she contends that the $7,171.57 should not be subtracted because under Louisiana law, separate funds commingled with community funds are deemed as a matter of law to be the first funds withdrawn. She maintains that because Jack withdrew $12,000 to $13,000 during the marriage, he necessarily removed the entirety of the separate property funds from the plan.

---

1. Valuations were reported every 6 months.

Our jurisprudence shows that when separate funds are commingled with community funds to the extent that the separate funds are no longer capable of identification, and it is impossible to trace the origin of the funds, then all of the funds are considered community. See, e.g., *Thibodaux v. Thibodaux*, 577 So. 2d 758 (La. App. 1st Cir. 1991). Jack argues that the funds are clearly traceable and were not commingled to the extent that it is impossible to establish which funds belong to the separate and community estate and, thus, *Succession of Sonnier*, 208 So. 2d 562 (La. App. 3rd Cir. 1968), is inapplicable and the court need not allocate the $12,000-$13,000 from the separate funds first.

In *Sonnier*, a deposit of $17,500 was made from Jean Batiste Ardoin's separate funds. Subsequently withdrawals amounting to $8,645.36 were made from the account before the death of his wife, Evangeline Sonnier. The Third Circuit stated at page 569:

> "Since there is a presumption that all of the funds in the checking account belonged to the community, and the burden rests on Ardoin to establish the contrary, it seems proper to us to regard all of the withdrawals made from this account during the period beginning November 10, 1965, and ending May 22, 1966, as having come from Ardoin's separate funds. This leaves a balance of $8,854.64 in the checking account at the time of Evangeline Sonnier's death which the evidence establishes as belonging to the separate estate of Ardoin. The remaining balance of $2523.87 which was in the checking account at the time of her death must be classified as community property." (Citation omitted.)

We are further persuaded by Professor Katherine Spaht's comments[2] concerning the presumption in *Sonnier:*

> ". . . [There is a] presumption that withdrawals from an account in which community and separate funds are commingled are presumed to come first from separate funds. This may or may not have a basis in reality, but it would seem to be a corollary consistent with the presumption of community; what remains in the account is subject to the presumption. At least one author suggests this approach is a reasonable one: 'There is a problem, of course, when community and separate fungibles or funds have been placed in a single pool or account from which withdrawals have been made without records over so long a period as to make a tracing of values impossible. In that case it may be legitimate to have a presumption in favor of the community character of the thing, for in this way the most any spouse could lose under the formula is half of that to which he would have been entitled." (Footnotes omitted.)

In *Succession of Russo*, 246 So. 2d 26 (La. App. 4th Cir. 1971), writ denied, 258 La. 760, 247 So. 2d 861 (1971), Mrs. Russo had opened an account with $8,966.32 of separate funds. With the exception of credits to the account for interest earned, the only other deposits made were two totaling $343 of admittedly community funds. As of the date of her death, the balance in the account, after various withdrawals, was $7,521.09. The Fourth Circuit found it clear that the commingling of the amount deposited originally by Mrs. Russo and the $343 of community funds is inconsequential and did not cause the funds to lose their separate identities. The court then recognized that in conformity with the rationale of *Sonnier*, all subsequent withdrawals from such an account are made from separate funds. The court found

---

2. K. Spaht & W. Hargrave, 16 Louisiana Civil Law Treatise, Matrimonial Regimes §4.5 at 131 (1989).

that the withdrawals came first from Mrs. Russo's separate funds, the $343 community property was preserved, and the remaining sum was Mrs. Russo's separate property.

We find the present case analogous to the *Russo* case. In the present case, the separate and community funds were commingled, but not to the extent as to cause the funds to lose their identities.[3] Under the rationale of *Russo*, the withdrawals come first from separate funds. Thus, without evidence to the contrary, we presume that the $12,000 to $13,000 withdrawn by Jack first depleted his separate funds of $7,171.57. As such, we conclude that the trial court erred in deducting the $7,171.57 from the total amount of funds in the account when the community regime terminated. Thus, we find that the savings plan should be valued at $42,806.77 as of December 31, 1988, and $46,718.07 as of June 30, 1989.

Gail also contends that the trial court should have prorated to determine the value of the account instead of dividing the difference between the values as of December 31, 1988, and June 30, 1989, to determine its value as of March 7, 1989. We agree and prorate to recalculate the value of the account as of March 7, 1989. We determine that this value equals $44,232.37 ($21.60 per day for 66 days [$1,425.60] plus the beginning balance, $42,806.77) as of March 7, 1989, the date the community terminated.

* * *

For the above and foregoing reasons, the judgment of the trial court is affirmed as amended. Costs of this appeal are assessed equally between Jack and Gail Cutting. Affirmed as amended and rendered.

Discussion Questions

1. When funds are commingled in a bank account, who should have the burden of proving whether there are separate property funds in the account?

2. Do you agree that when a withdrawal is made from a commingled account, the separate property funds should be presumed to be withdrawn first?

3. What would have been the result if the court had decided that the community property had been withdrawn first?

[handwritten: LA is only 1st in 1st out rule. rest are "last in 1st out"]

---

2. Washington and California Approaches

In the Washington case of *Marriage of Skarbek* (2000), the husband John opened a joint savings account when he married Dina in 1994. In that savings account, he deposited his separate property funds and community property funds. Gifts, tax refunds, and presents were also deposited into the account. The account total at divorce was $84,400. Originally, the judge determined that $46,000 was John's separate property that he had traced and the remaining $38,400 in the account

---

3. The record does not show specifically how the funds were used, but merely states that the funds were ultimately exhausted.

was community property to be split between John and Dina. John would receive $65,200 ($46,000 plus half of $38,400) and Dina would receive $19,200 (half of $38,400). The judge reversed his ruling because the savings account was held jointly. Therefore John's separate property was presumed to be a gift to the community and John had not rebutted that gift presumption. Thus, the entire account was community property and split between John ($42,200) and Dina ($42,200).

MARRIAGE OF SKARBEK

100 Wash. App. 444, 997 P.2d 447 (2000)
Court of Appeals of Washington

SWEENEY, J.

A rebuttable presumption arises that property acquired during marriage with separate funds is a gift to the community. *In re Marriage of Hurd*, 69 Wash. App. 38, 51, 848 P.2d 185 (1993). But depositing separate funds in a joint bank account is not an acquisition of property; therefore, no presumption attaches. John Skarbek deposited separate funds in a joint account. But he then traced and identified the separate funds. The court classified those funds as community property. This was error and so we reverse and remand.

FACTS

John and Dina Skarbek were married in 1994 and separated in 1997. In between, the couple moved to Walla Walla, Washington.

When he got married, Mr. Skarbek had deposits in three bank accounts. When they moved across country, he closed these accounts and transferred $4,000 into a joint checking account and $30,059.21 into a joint savings account in Washington. An additional $18,000 in community funds was deposited in the joint savings account.

Ms. Skarbek did not work outside of the home. Mr. Skarbek's paycheck was deposited in the joint savings account. The couple paid most of their living expenses by credit card, and transferred funds monthly from savings to checking to pay the bills. Gifts, tax refunds, and presents were also deposited into the joint savings.

A hearing was held to divide the property. Mr. Skarbek claimed the start-up funds for these joint accounts were his separate property. He traced $46,000 of his separate funds to the court's satisfaction. The court characterized this amount as Mr. Skarbek's separate property and awarded it to him in the property distribution. The court characterized the remainder as community property and awarded Ms. Skarbek half, or $19,200.

Ms. Skarbek moved for reconsideration, asserting the entire amount in both accounts was community property and requesting an equal division.

In a letter opinion, the judge reversed his ruling. Relying on *Hurd*, the court determined that, by transferring his separate funds into joint accounts, Mr. Skarbek created the presumption of a gift to the community, and that Mr. Skarbek had failed to produce sufficient evidence to rebut the presumption.

The court issued amended findings of fact, conclusions of law, and decree awarding Ms. Skarbek an additional $23,000, half of the traced funds.

Mr. Skarbek appeals. This court is asked to determine whether Mr. Skarbek can claim as his separate property traceable funds in a joint account.

DISCUSSION

The funds were community property is not a finding of fact, it is a conclusion of law. *Id.* at 94-95, 645 P.2d 1148.

PROPERTY ACQUIRED BEFORE MARRIAGE

The character of property as separate or community is established at the point of acquisition. Property acquired by the husband before marriage is his separate property. RCW 26.16.010; *Hurd*, 69 Wash. App. at 50, 848 P.2d 185.

Once established, separate property retains its separate character unless changed by deed, agreement of the parties, operation of law, or some other direct and positive evidence to the contrary. Separate property will remain separate property "through all of its changes and transitions" so long as it can be traced and identified. The burden is on the spouse asserting that separate property has transferred to the community to prove the transfer by clear and convincing evidence, usually a writing evidencing mutual intent.

COMMINGLED FUNDS

Separate property retains that character when it is brought to Washington from another state. Separate property brought to this state by a married man and intermingled with funds accumulated here, with no effort to keep them separate, becomes community property. *Mumm v. Mumm*, 63 Wash. 2d 349, 352, 387 P.2d 547 (1963). Commingled funds are thus presumed to be community property. And the burden is on the spouse claiming separate funds to clearly and convincingly trace them to a separate source.

However, only when money in a joint account is hopelessly commingled and cannot be separated is it rendered entirely community property. If the sources of the deposits can be traced and identified, the separate identity of the funds is preserved.

The name under which property is held does not constitute direct and positive evidence determinative of whether the property is community or separate. Making a spouse a signatory on a bank account does not automatically convert separate funds therein into community property.

Nothing in *Hurd* is in conflict with this well settled law:

> Funds are characterized as separate or community at acquisition. *Hurd*, 69 Wash. App. at 50, 848 P.2d 185.
>
> Separate property acquired before marriage remains separate unless its character is changed. *Id.*

Commingled funds become community property when they cannot be traced or identified. *Id.*

The name under which property is held is not determinative of a change of character. *Id.* at 51, 848 P.2d 185.

PROPERTY ACQUIRED DURING THE MARRIAGE

Property acquired during the marriage has the same character as the funds used to buy it. The presumption is that it is community property. And the party asserting otherwise has the burden of proving it was acquired with separate funds.

What we have here is property acquired before, not during, the marriage. Ms. Skarbek does not dispute that Mr. Skarbek accumulated these funds prior to the marriage. The money was, therefore, his separate property at the date of acquisition. It, therefore, remained his separate property unless its character was changed by mutual agreement. But Mr. Skarbek lost the benefit of the presumption and assumed the burden of proving the separate character of the funds when he put the money into an account where it was commingled with community funds. He then met this burden by establishing and tracing, clearly and convincingly, the separate source of the funds.

He did this by exhaustively documenting the details of the bank account activity. The court was satisfied with his accounting and his tracing of $46,000 as continuously separate property. The court correctly characterized this money as Mr. Skarbek's separate property in its findings of fact, conclusions of law, and decree of September 25, 1998.

NO PRESUMPTION OF A GIFT

A rebuttable presumption arises that property acquired with separate funds during the marriage is presumed to be a gift to the community. The parties and the trial court mischaracterize the bank accounts as property acquired during the marriage and put in joint names. The Skarbeks are fighting over money, not bank accounts. The transaction here is not the same as buying stocks or bonds or land. They did not "buy" a bank account. He deposited money in an account. The accounts were established during the marriage. But the money in those accounts was acquired before the marriage. . . .

The property in dispute is the traceable funds acquired before the marriage. Mr. Skarbek does not dispute the community character of all funds earned and deposited in the account after the marriage. The $46,000 Mr. Skarbek brought to the marriage remains his separate property.

REMAND IS REQUIRED

Remand is required when it appears the trial court's division of the property was dictated by a mischaracterization of the separate or community nature of the property. Here, the court reversed its ruling based on its characterization alone.

We reverse and remand for further proceedings.

BROWN, A.C.J., and SCHULTHEIS, J, concur.

Note: Part of the *Marriage of Hurd* case was disapproved by the Washington Supreme Court in *Estate of Borghi*, 167 Wash. 2d 480, 486, 219 P.3d 932, 936 (2009) (A gift presumption does not arise when title to property is changed from the name of a single spouse to both spouses). Since the Court of Appeals in *Skarbek* did not rely on the gift presumption, it is still good law on funds in a joint bank account.

Discussion Questions

1. Should putting the title to a bank account in joint names change the character of the funds in the bank account?

2. The court explained that the Skarbeks paid for their living expenses by credit card and then transferred funds from the savings account to pay those bills. Can you tell from the court's analysis whether Washington uses FIFO (First In First Out) or LIFO (Last In First Out) to determine which funds pay for community expenses?

3. Why should the bank account be treated differently from property acquired using funds from the bank account?

In California, the *Skarbek* view of bank accounts is mandated by Probate Code §5305:

PROBATE CODE

§5305. Pro-Community property presumption for sums on deposit in accounts

(a) If parties to an account are married to each other, whether or not they are so described in the deposit agreement, their net contribution to the account is presumed to be and remain their community property.

(b) The presumption. . . may be rebutted by proof of either of the following:

   (1) The sums on deposit that are claimed to be separate property can be traced from separate property unless it is proved that the married persons made a written agreement that expressed their clear intent that the sums be their community property.

   (2) The married persons made a written agreement, separate from the deposit agreement, that expressly provided that the sums on deposit, claimed not to be community property, were not to be community property.

Assuming there is no written agreement between John and Dina, how would their dispute have been resolved by a California court applying Probate Code §5305? Or applying the Louisiana or Washington approach?

B.   CHARACTER OF PROPERTY ACQUIRED FROM A COMMINGLED BANK ACCOUNT

When property is acquired from a commingled bank account, the presumption is that the property is community property. This presumption is rebuttable. The separate property proponent bears the burden of proof to show that the acquired property is separate property. That burden is either "preponderance of the evidence" or a higher standard such as "clear and convincing." There are differing views about the proper method that can be used to meet the burden of proof. There are actually three different methods. The first method is called the "exhaustion method" or the "family expense method." That method requires the separate property proponent to prove that at the time of acquisition of the property, community property funds in the commingled account had been used (exhausted) for community expenses and only separate property was available to acquire the property. The second method is called "direct tracing." That method requires the separate property proponent to prove that at the time of acquisition that even though there were both types of funds in the commingled account, the separate property proponent intended to use separate property funds to acquire the property and can show that those funds were actually used.

The third method is called "total recapitulation" or "accounting" or "indirect tracing." This method differs from the other two because it does not focus on the bank account at the time of acquisition. Instead, this method allows the separate property proponent to prove that property acquired during the marriage was separate property because over the course of the marriage community expenses exceeded community income, therefore all property acquired from the commingled account was separate property.

In all cases, proof requires record keeping. Therein lies the danger of commingling. Most couples are very casual about keeping separate accounts for separate property and community property funds. It is mainly at divorce, that commingling represents a peril for the separate property spouse.

The Louisiana case of *Granger v. Granger* (1998) is an example of how the presumption regarding property acquired from a commingled account can be rebutted.

GRANGER v. GRANGER

722 So. 2d 107 (1998)
Court of Appeal of Louisiana

Cooks, Judge.

This appeal arises from a community property partition suit between Julie Ann Mouiller Granger and Carl Douglas Granger, Jr. Mrs. Granger appeals the trial court's decision characterizing the family residence as Mr. Granger's separate property.

For the reasons which follow, we affirm the judgment of the trial court.

BACKGROUND FACTS

Doug and Julie Granger were married on June 8, 1984. On April 23, 1991, Mrs. Granger filed a petition for divorce which was granted on February 25, 1992. Following the divorce, she filed a petition for a partition of the community assets, along with a detailed description listing the items she alleged was community property. Among other things, she alleged that the brick home the parties purchased during the marriage was community property. Further, she alleged that all improvements on the home were also acquired by using community funds.

Mr. Granger filed an answer to the petition and also filed a detailed descriptive list. He alleged, among other things, that the brick home purchased during the marriage was his separate property.

After a trial on the merits, the trial court classified the various properties and debts as either being separate or community. Specifically, the trial judge found the home and all improvements purchased with the home was Mr. Granger's separate property.

ASSIGNMENT OF ERROR

She now assigns the following error for review:

Whether the appellee commingled community property and separate funds that were in Certificates of Deposit and Money Market Accounts listed in both appellant's and appellee's names; which funds were deposited in a joint checking account and used to purchase the community brick home, so as to make the home community property.

LAW AND ANALYSIS

THE BRICK HOME

Mrs. Granger contends the trial court committed manifest error in holding that the brick home and the improvements were the separate property of Mr. Granger. We disagree.

On May 30, 1993, the Grangers purchased a purchased a brick home for $30,000 from the father and sister of Mr. Granger. The Act of Cash Sale listed the purchasers as "Carl Douglas Granger and Julie Ann Granger, husband and wife." The funds used to purchase the brick home came from the appellee's and appellant's joint Certificates of Deposit and Money Market Accounts. These funds were eventually placed in the appellee's and appellant's joint checking account from which checks in the amount of $20,000 and $10,000 were issued to the appellee's father and sister. Mr. Granger points out the vast majority of these funds represents a portion of his mother's estate which he acquired by succession. Mrs. Granger argues that the $30,000 is comprised of community funds commingled with separate funds, making all of the funds community property. She urges that the brick home and its improvements are community assets.

La. Civ. Code art. 2338 provides:

> The community property comprises: property acquired during the existence of the legal regime through the effort, skill, or industry of either spouse; property acquired with community things or with community and separate things, unless classified as separate property under Article 2341; property donated to the spouses jointly; natural and civil fruits of community property; damages awarded for loss or injury to a thing belonging to the community; and all other property not classified by law as separate property.

"Things in the possession of a spouse during the existence of a regime of community acquets and gains are presumed to be community, **but either spouse may prove that they are separate property**." La. Civ. Code art. 2340 (emphasis added).

La. Civ. Code art. 2341 states in pertinent part:

> The separate property of a spouse is his exclusively. It comprises: property acquired by a spouse prior to the establishment of a community property regime; property acquired by a spouse with separate things or with separate and community things when the value of the community things is inconsequential in comparison with the value of the separate things used; property acquired by a spouse by inheritance or donation to him individually. . . .

"Funds are not community by virtue of the fact that they are in a joint account." In *Curtis v. Curtis*, 403 So. 2d 56 (La. 1981), the Supreme Court held:

> We have stated in cases involving bank accounts that the mere mixing of separate funds and community funds in the same account does not itself convert an entire account into community property; only when separate funds are commingled with community funds indiscriminately so that the separate funds cannot be identified or differentiated from the community funds are all the funds characterized as community funds. Where separate funds can be traced with sufficient certainty to establish the separate ownership of property paid for with those funds, the separate status of such property will be upheld.

Furthermore, "[t]he party alleging the separate character of property must prove that the property was acquired and paid for with separate funds by proof that is fixed, clear, positive and legally certain." This level of proof is greater than a preponderance of the evidence, but less than a reasonable doubt.

The trial judge found Mr. Granger met his burden of proof, thereby sufficiently rebutting the presumption that the brick home is community property. Mr. Granger testified $24,000 of the certificates of deposit used to purchase the home were proceeds from the sale of the Grangers' previous home. This home was conveyed to Mr. Granger by his father in exchange for an agreement that he would take $25,000 less in cash owed to him from his mother's estate. Mr. Granger testified the listed certificates of deposit were also purchased with succession money disbursed to him from his mother's estate. This claim was substantiated by a check, introduced at trial, made payable to Mr. Granger in the amount of $11,750.00, representing his balance of the succession owed to him. Under the principle of real subrogation, funds acquired through the sale of separate property remain separate. Also, "[t]he separate property of a spouse is his exclusively. It comprises . . . property acquired by a spouse by inheritance or donation to him individually." La. Civ. Code art. 2341.

Mrs. Granger did not present any evidence refuting Mr. Granger's testimony. She argues that once the separate funds were deposited in the joint checking account, they became indiscriminately mixed with community funds, thus making all of the funds community property. Her argument is without merit. Mr. Granger's separate funds were not mixed with community funds such that they are no longer capable of identification. The only community funds which were commingled with Mr. Granger's separate money was the interest earned from his certificates of deposit and a small amount of earnings from the couple's jobs, both of which were minute in comparison to the amount of separate funds in the account. We cannot say, under the circumstances, the trial judge erred in finding the home was purchased with funds substantially derived from Mr. Granger's separate property and thus remained a part of his separate estate.

Decree

For the foregoing reasons, the judgment of the trial court is affirmed. All costs of this appeal are assessed to plaintiff-appellant.

Affirmed.

Discussion Questions

1. Which method did Mr. Granger use to rebut the community property presumption?
2. Even though the proof is a high one, "fixed, clear, positive and legal certain," why did Mr. Granger succeed in proving the Brick Home was his separate property?

The most controversial methods are the total recapitulation method and the direct tracing method. Before delving further into the tracing methods, the following examples highlight the differences between the methods. Let's say that John and Dina marry. John has a bank account with separate property funds totaling $40,000. John puts his monthly paycheck of $2,000 in the same account. He has now commingled his paycheck which is community property with the separate property funds. After six months, there is $12,000 of community property and $40,000 of separate property. So far there are only deposits. If John pays $2,000 a month for community expenses for the next six months, what will be left in the account? If the family expenses were paid from the community funds, then the $40,000 will always remain in the account. If John buys stock for $20,000, the question is how to characterize the stock that is presumed to be community property because it was purchased during marriage. Because he has commingled, he would have the burden of proof by tracing to his separate property funds. Under these facts, he could succeed under the exhaustion method. If he had kept good records, he could prove that at the time of acquisition of the stock, all community property was exhausted by paying for community expenses and therefore the only funds in the account were his separate property. Therefore the stock would be characterized as John's separate property. The exhaustion method is the most certain for John, the separate property proponent, to succeed in rebutting the community property presumption.

Let us change the facts and say the John used only $1,000 a month for family expenses. Then $1,000 of community funds would accumulate monthly in the commingled account. At the time of acquisition of the stock, he would not be able to prove that all the community funds were exhausted by community expenses like rent or food, so there is a question of whether a $20,000 stock purchase came from his separate property or community property or both. Under the direct tracing method, if he had kept good records, he could show that separate property funds were available and he intended to use them to buy the stock. Thus, he would have rebutted the presumption that the stock acquired during marriage was community property. In this scenario, if $5,000 of community property funds were in the account, it is possible that a court could use a version of the exhaustion method and determine that the stock was 1/4 community property ($5,000/20,000) and 3/4 John's separate property ($15,000/20,000). The court has "exhausted" the community funds to buy the stock and at that point the only remaining funds would be John's separate funds. The direct tracing method also requires good record keeping, but does not require exhaustion of community property funds for the separate property proponent to succeed in rebutting the community property presumption.

Under the total recapitulation method or accounting method, John could rebut the community property presumption regarding property acquired during marriage, by showing that throughout the marriage, community expenses exceeded community funds that were deposited in the commingled account. There would be no need to look at the state of the bank account at the time of acquisition. This method favors the separate property spouse when there is a far greater amount of separate property wealth in comparison to community property earnings.

One corollary that has been assumed in describing the tracing methods is that when there is commingling, community expenses are paid from community funds before dipping into separate funds. Most community property states have adopted the view that generally community funds are withdrawn first from a commingled account or the view that community expenses are presumed to be paid first from community funds.

1. The California Approaches: Exhaustion and Direct Tracing Methods

In the landmark California case of *See v. See* (1966), the California Supreme Court rejected the total recapitulation method and adopted the exhaustion method. Later, the same court approved the direct tracing method in *Marriage of Mix* (1975).

SEE v. SEE

64 Cal. 2d 778, 415 P.2d 776, 51 Cal. Rptr. 888 (1966)
Supreme Court of California,
En Banc

TRAYNOR, Chief Justice.

Plaintiff Laurance A. See and cross-complainant Elizabeth Lee See appeal from an interlocutory judgment that grants each a divorce. Laurance attacks the finding that he was guilty of extreme cruelty, the granting of a divorce to Elizabeth, and the award to her of permanent alimony of $5,400 per month. Elizabeth attacks the finding that there was no community property at the time of the divorce. Neither party contests the provisions regarding custody and support of the three minor children.

The parties were married on October 17, 1941, and they separated about May 10, 1962. Throughout the marriage they were residents of California, and Laurance was employed by a family-controlled corporation, See's Candies, Inc. For most of that period he also served as president of its wholly-owned subsidiary, See's Candy Shops, Inc. In the twenty-one years of the marriage he received more than $1,000,000 in salaries from the two corporations.

Laurance had a personal account on the books of See's Candies, Inc., denominated Account 13. Throughout the marriage his annual salary from See's Candies, Inc., which was $60,000 at the time of the divorce, was credited to this account and many family expenses were paid by checks drawn on it. To maintain a credit balance in Account 13, Laurance from time to time transferred funds to it from an account at the Security First National Bank, hereafter called the Security Account.

The funds deposited in the Security Account came primarily from Laurance's separate property. On occasion he deposited his annual $15,000 salary from See's Candy Shops, Inc. in that account as a "reserve against taxes" on that salary. Thus there was a commingling of community property and separate property in both the Security Account and Account 13. Funds from the Security Account were sometimes used to pay community expenses and also to purchase some of the assets held in Laurance's name at the time of the divorce proceedings.

Over Elizabeth's objection, the trial court followed a theory advanced by Laurance that a proven excess of community expenses over community income during the marriage establishes that there has been no acquisition of property with community funds.

Such a theory, without support in either statutory or case law of this state, would disrupt the California community property system. It would transform a wife's interest in the community property from a "present, existing and equal interest" as specified by Civil Code section 161a, into an inchoate expectancy to be realized only if upon termination of the marriage the community income fortuitously exceeded community expenditures. It would engender uncertainties as to testamentary and inter vivos dispositions, income, estate and gift taxation, and claims against property.

The character of property as separate or community is determined at the time of its acquisition. If it is community property when acquired, it remains so throughout the marriage unless the spouses agree to change its nature or the spouse charged with its management makes a gift of it to the other.

Property acquired by purchase during a marriage is presumed to be community property, and the burden is on the spouse asserting its separate character to overcome the presumption. The presumption applies when a husband purchases property during the marriage with funds from an undisclosed or disputed source, such as an account or fund in which he has commingled his separate funds with community funds. He may trace the source of the property to his separate funds and overcome the presumption with evidence that community expenses exceeded community income at the time of acquisition. If he proves that at that time all community income was exhausted by family expenses, he establishes that the property was purchased with separate funds. In *Thomasset v. Thomasset*, 122 Cal. App. 2d 116, 264 P.2d 626, the court made clear that the time of acquisition of disputed property is decisive. "An accountant testified that at the time the various items adjudged to be defendant's separate property were purchased, there were no community funds available. . . . The evidence (shows) that at the time the property was purchased the community funds had been exhausted. . . ." (*Id.* at p. 127, 264 P.2d at p. 633)

A husband who commingles the property of the community with his separate property, but fails to keep adequate records cannot invoke the burden of record keeping as a justification for a recapitulation of income and expenses at the termination of the marriage that disregards any acquisitions that may have been made during the marriage with community funds. If funds used for acquisitions during marriage cannot otherwise be traced to their source and the husband who has commingled property is unable to establish that there was a deficit in the community accounts when the assets were purchased, the presumption controls that property acquired by purchase during marriage is community property. The husband may protect his separate property by not commingling community and separate assets and income. Once he commingles, he assumes the burden of keeping records adequate to establish the balance of community income and expenditures at the time an asset is acquired with commingled property.

The trial court also followed the theory that a husband who expends his separate property for community expenses is entitled to reimbursement from community assets. This theory likewise lacks support in the statutory or case law of this state. A husband is required to support his wife and family. Indeed, husband and wife assume mutual obligations of support upon marriage. These obligations are not conditioned on the existence of community property or income. The duty to support imposed upon husbands by Civil Code section 155 and upon wives by Civil Code section 176 requires the use of separate property of the parties when there is no community property. There is no right to reimbursement under the statutes.

Plaintiff has not met his burden of proving an excess of community expenses over community income at the times the other assets purchased during the marriage were acquired. The part of the judgment finding them to be his separate property is therefore reversed. Since the property issues were tried on the theory that the nature of the property could be determined by proving total community income and expenditures and since the parties may have additional evidence that would otherwise have been presented, plaintiff's failure to overcome to presumption that the assets are community property is not conclusive. We therefore remand the case for retrial of the property issues.

The judgment is affirmed in all other respects. Elizabeth shall recover her costs on both appeals.

McComb, Peters, Tobriner, Peek, Mosk, and Burke, JJ., concur.

Discussion Questions

1. What is the Court's rationale for rejecting Laurance See's reliance on the Total Recapitulation Method?
2. Why is it correct to place the burden of proof on the separate property proponent?

MARRIAGE OF MIX

14 Cal. 3d 607, 536 P.2d 479, 122 Cal. Rptr. 79
Supreme Court of California,
En Banc

Sullivan, Justice.

In this action for dissolution of marriage, appellant Richard Mix (Richard) appeals from an interlocutory judgment of dissolution declaring that appellant and respondent Esther Mix (Esther) are entitled to have their marriage dissolved, awarding custody of the minor child of the parties to Esther, and dividing their community property. Richard attacks the finding that, except for the property specifically found to be community, all property both real and personal standing in Esther's name or being in her possession at the time of the separation was her separate property.

Richard and Esther were married on September 4, 1958, and separate on December 14, 1968. There is one child of the marriage, a boy born February 24, 1960. At the time of marriage Esther was an attorney admitted to practice in California and Richard a musician and part-time teacher. Thereafter, they continued to pursue their respective careers. At the start, Esther was an associate in a law firm earning approximately $400 a month; by the time of her separation, she had become a 40 percent partner in the firm and earned about $25,000 annually. Richard's career as a musician, including regular employment with the Sacramento Symphony Orchestra, proved to be a good deal less remunerative; his annual income was generally between $1,000 and $3,000.

At the time of her marriage Esther owned considerable property. This included interests in income producing real property, a residence, a life insurance policy and bank accounts of indeterminate amounts. At that time Richard closed his savings account and the parties changed his checking account at the Bank of America into their joint account. In this new checking account, the parties deposited all their earnings as well as Esther's income from her separate property. This practice continued until 1963 when Esther opened an account in her name alone at the

California Bank. In this account she deposited most of her income both from her law practice and her various investments.

[T]he court found that all other property, both real and personal, standing in Esther's name or being in her possession was her separate property. This is the finding upon which the present controversy centers.

After making a general finding that all of the property which stood in Esther's name was her separate property, the trial court went on to state: "All of such property which was acquired during the marriage of the parties in the name of petitioner (Esther) was taken in petitioner's name with the knowledge of respondent (Richard) and with the understanding of the parties that it was to be held as petitioner's separate property. Said property was purchased with petitioner's separate funds which were identified and traced by petitioner. Any improvement made during marriage to petitioner's separate property, and any separate property purchased with funds from any bank account in which both separate and community funds were comingled (sic), were made either by respondent or with his knowledge and consent with the intent that such improvements or property would belong to petitioner, and there was at all times a sufficient balance of separate property deposited to such accounts to cover all such amounts withdrawn. All borrowed funds used to improve petitioner's separate property were the proceeds of loans obtained upon the hypothecation of such separate property, and in making such loans the lender did not rely on the credit of the community. Such funds are the separate property of petitioner."

It thus appears that the trial court rested its finding as to Esther's separate property on two independent bases: (1) that Esther had adequately traced the source of the funds withdrawn from the commingled bank accounts for use in connection with the aforementioned properties to her separate funds; (2) that there was an agreement between Richard and Esther that all property purchased by the latter in her own name during marriage was to be her separate property.

The following legal principles apply: "All property of the wife, owned by her before marriage, and that acquired afterwards by gift, bequest, devise, or descent, with the rents, issues, and profits thereof, is her separate property." Property purchased with the wife's separate property funds is her separate property. The wife's earnings during the marriage are community property and are subject to her management and control.

[P]roperty acquired by purchase during a marriage is presumed to be community property, and the burden is on the spouse asserting its separate character to overcome the presumption. This presumption applies to property purchased during the marriage with funds from a disputed source, such as an account or fund in which one of the spouses has commingled his or her separate funds with community funds. The mere commingling of separate with community funds in a bank account does not destroy the character of the former if the amount thereof can be ascertained.' "If the property, or the source of funds with which it is acquired, can be traced, its separate property character remains unchanged. But if separate and community property or funds are commingled in such a manner that it is impossible to trace the source of the property or funds, the whole will be treated as community property. . . ."

We conclude therefore that the controlling presumption in this case is the one that property acquired during marriage is community property.

The presumption that all property acquired by either spouse during the marriage is community property may be overcome. Generally speaking such post-marital property can be established to be separate property by two independent methods of tracing. The first method involves direct tracing. As the court explained in *Hicks*: "[S]eparate funds do not lose their character as such when commingled with community funds in a bank account so long as the amount thereof can be ascertained. Whether separate funds so deposited continue to be on deposit when a withdrawal is made from such a bank account for the purpose of purchasing specific property, and whether the intention of the drawer is to withdraw such funds therefrom, are questions of fact for determination by the trial court." The second method involves a consideration of family expenses. It is based upon the presumption that family expenses are paid from community funds. If at the time of the acquisition of the property in dispute, it can be shown that all community income in the commingled account has been exhausted by family expenses, then all funds remaining in the account at the time the property was purchased were necessarily separate funds.

The effect of the presumption and the two methods of overcoming it are succinctly summarized in *See*: "If funds used for acquisitions during marriage cannot otherwise be traced to their source and the husband who has commingled property is unable to establish that there was a deficit in the community accounts when the assets were purchased, the presumption controls that property acquired by purchase during marriage is community property." Throughout the marriage Esther commingled her community property earnings from her law practice with the rents, issues and proceeds from her separate property in several bank accounts. She concedes that she made no attempt to trace the source of the property by resorting to the "family expense method." We are satisfied from our review of the evidence that Esther failed to keep adequate records to show that family expenses had exhausted community funds at the time of the acquisition of any of the property here in dispute.

Esther contends, however, that she introduced sufficient evidence to trace the source of the funds used to acquire each item of disputed property to her separate property in accordance with the "direct tracing test" described in *Hicks v. Hicks*, and that therefore the trial court's finding to that effect is supported by substantial evidence. In *Hicks* the husband introduced evidence of separate property deposits amounting to $267,580.81, consisting of $91,610.90 from dividends, $66,266.70 in proceeds from sales of separate property assets, and $109,703.21 from loans secured by the credit of his separate property. He also introduced evidence of separate property withdrawals in the amount of $172,931.80 and an excess of total separate property deposits over separate property withdrawals in the amount of $94,649.01. The court held that this evidence in combination with evidence showing that the questioned withdrawals were intended to purchase the disputed property as separate property, supported the trial court's finding of separate property.

Esther introduced into evidence a schedule compiled by herself and her accountant from her records which itemized chronologically each source of separate funds, each expenditure for separate property purposes, and the balance of separate property funds remaining after each such expenditure. She received $99,632.02 attributable to her separate property; expended $42,213.79 for separate property purposes, leaving an excess of separate property receipts over separate property expenditures in the amount of $57,418.23 throughout the course of the marriage. Each year from 1958 to 1968, excepting the year 1961, there was an excess of separate property receipts over separate property expenditures, leaving a balance of separate funds. The 1961 deficit did not, however, exhaust the balance of separate funds carried forward from prior years. The schedule demonstrated that Esther's expenditures for separate property purposes closely paralleled in time and amount separate property receipts and thus established her intention to use only her separate property funds for separate property expenditures.

Richard contends that the schedule contains a fatal flaw in that the entries of receipts and expenditures are not tied to any bank account or bank accounts. Therefore, he argues, the schedule shows merely the availability of separate funds on the given dates but fails utterly to demonstrate the actual expenditures of those funds for the enumerated separate purposes. Esther concedes that she was unable to support the schedule by correlating each itemized deposit and withdrawal on the schedule with an entry in a particular bank account due to the unavailability of various bank records as well as to the lack of such records of her own. Richard urges that this state of the evidence demonstrates that Esther has failed to meet her burden, that she has therefore not overcome the community property presumption, and that her claims to specific property as being her separate property must fall.

We agree that the schedule by itself is wholly inadequate to meet the test prescribed by *Hicks v. Hicks*, and to support the trial court's finding that Esther "identified and traced" the separate property. However, the schedule was not the only evidence introduced by Esther to effect the tracing. She personally testified that the schedule was a true and accurate record, that it accurately reflected the receipts and expenditures as accomplished through various bank accounts, although she could not in all instances correlate the items of the schedule with a particular bank account, and that it accurately corroborated her intention throughout her marriage to make these expenditures for separate property purposes, notwithstanding her use of the balance of her separate property receipts for family expenses.

The trial court evidently believed Esther. "The testimony of a witness, even the party himself, may be sufficient." Viewing this evidence in the light most favorable to Esther, giving her the benefit of every reasonable inference, and resolving all conflicts in her favor, as we must under the rules of appellate review, we conclude that there is substantial evidence to support the trial court's finding that Esther traced and identified the source and funds of her separate property. We are satisfied that the trial court was warranted in inferring from this evidence that the bank records if introduced would fully verify the schedule as supported by Esther's testimony to the effect that "separate funds . . . continue(d) to be on deposit when a withdrawal (was) made . . . for the purpose of purchasing specific property, and . . . (that) the intention of the drawer . . . (was) to withdraw such funds therefrom. . . ."

Since we conclude that the judgment can be upheld on the basis of an adequate tracing of Esther's separate property, it is unnecessary for us to consider whether it can also be upheld on the independent basis of an agreement between Richard and Esther as to the separate character of the properties in controversy.

The judgment is affirmed.

WRIGHT, C.J., AND McCOMB, TOBRINER, MOSK, CLARK and BURKE, JJ., concur.

Discussion Questions

1. Esther Mix created a schedule that showed separate property sources and separate property expenditures from the years 1958 to 1968. What were the weaknesses in this evidence? Why did Esther succeed in proving the acquisitions were her separate property?

2. What is problematic about the direct tracing method? Is it similar or different from the total recapitulation method?

---

2.   The Idaho Approach: Total Recapitulation Method

Although rejected by the California Supreme Court, the total recapitulation method was adopted in Idaho in 1969, *Evans v. Evans,* 92 Idaho 911, 453 P.2d 650 (1969), and more recently in New Mexico in 1993, *Zemke v. Zemke,* 116 N.M. 114, 860 P.2d 756 (Ct. App. 1993). While reading the *Weilmunster* case from Idaho, do not be confused by the terminology used by the Court of Appeals. "Direct tracing" refers to both the exhaustion method and direct tracing and "accounting" refers to the total recapitulation method.

WEILMUNSTER v. WEILMUNSTER

858 P.2d 766 (1993)
Court of Appeals of Idaho

The Court's prior opinion, dated July 30, 1992, is hereby withdrawn.

SILAK, Judge.

This appeal concerns the classification and distribution of the parties' property upon divorce. Donald and Lana Weilmunster sued each other for a divorce and a decree classifying and distributing their separate and community assets. During the marriage, Donald commingled his separate funds with the funds of the community. At trial, Donald sought to prove by indirect tracing, or accounting, that many of the assets purchased with the commingled funds were proceeds of his separate funds, and, thus, his separate property. After trial, the magistrate awarded Lana a divorce against Donald. In classifying the parties' property, the magistrate determined that Donald had satisfactorily traced many of the commingled assets to his separate property, and, therefore, the magistrate attributed those assets to Donald's separate estate. The magistrate also concluded that the community's expenses during the marriage exceeded its income, leaving no community interest in the commingled funds. Lana appealed to the district court, claiming that the magistrate had wrongfully characterized much of the parties' property as Donald's separate property rather than as part of the community estate, which characterization not only led the magistrate to improperly award much of the community's property to Donald, but also to the erroneous conclusion that the community had no interest in the account's residual funds.

The district court substantially reversed the magistrate, holding that the magistrate erred in permitting Donald to prove his separate property by the use of accounting evidence when direct tracing of the parties' property was objectively possible, and in classifying much of the property as Donald's separate property rather than as community property. Donald now appeals to this court, and Lana cross-appeals. For the reasons set forth below, we reverse the district court in part and reinstate the findings and conclusions of the magistrate.

FACTS AND PROCEDURAL BACKGROUND

Prior to and at the time of their marriage, both Lana and Donald had substantial separate estates. Donald's premarital estate included four ranches; some mining claims; equipment used to run his various ranching, farming, and logging operations; a cattle herd of about 500 head plus calves; contracts receivable from the sale of real properties; and a bank account containing $25,000. The debts pertaining to Donald's premarital estate included contracts payable on real estate purchased for Donald's farming and ranching operations; various other loan obligations; and $60,000 in personal debt to a Mr. Blackeby. Lana's premarital estate included a number of rental properties, a one-sixth interest in a farm in Arizona, and a contract receivable on some real estate. The total debt Lana owed on these properties was approximately $130,000. At the time of the marriage, Lana had no money in any accounts.

On June 16, 1981, Lana and Donald were married. During the marriage, Donald commingled proceeds and income from his separate property in the same accounts which contained the parties' community assets.

Throughout the marriage, Donald received interest income from his contracts receivable in the amount of $182,329. Donald used this separate income to pay interest charges on his various separate debts.

As mentioned above, Donald owned a cattle herd prior to the marriage. Both parties have characterized the calves which were born into the herd during the marriage as community property. During the marriage the parties did not distinguish between those cattle which were Donald's separate cattle, and those cattle which, being born into the herd during the marriage, were the community's. All of the cattle, both separate and community, were pastured on Donald's separate ranches throughout the marriage.

Also during the marriage, an interest in a W & W Land Partnership was purchased with funds from the commingled account.

On September 6, 1985, after approximately four years of marriage, Donald filed a complaint seeking a divorce against Lana on grounds of irreconcilable differences. Lana subsequently filed a counterclaim seeking a divorce against Donald on the same grounds and on the additional ground of extreme cruelty by infliction of grievous mental suffering.

The matter was tried to a magistrate over eight days of proceedings which concluded on June 19, 1987. The magistrate received extensive evidence regarding the alleged grounds for divorce and the proper classification and distribution of the parties' property. On June 26, 1987, the magistrate entered a partial summary judgment pursuant to a stipulation of the parties, which granted the parties a divorce and restored Lana to the use of her former name, Lana D. Hale. The magistrate reserved his determination as to the classification and distribution of the parties' property until further documentation and information had been submitted by the parties.

On September 30, 1987, after the parties had submitted post-trial motions, documentation and arguments, the magistrate filed his findings of fact and conclusions of law. The magistrate concluded that during the marriage both parties sustained net operating losses with respect to their separate estates; the community spent more money than it earned; proceeds from Donald's separate property and loans made up the community shortfall; the community estate did nothing to enhance the separate estate of either party; and the community had insufficient funds in the commingled account to have been able to purchase the interest in the W & W Land Partnership. Based on these findings, the magistrate concluded that the community had no interest in the funds which remained in the commingled account, and ordered an equitable distribution of the parties' remaining assets. Subsequently, Lana moved to amend and add to the magistrate's findings and conclusions. On April 21, 1988, the magistrate filed amended and additional findings and conclusions, pursuant to which an Amended Judgment and Decree was entered on May 31, 1988.

On appeal to the district court, Lana contended that the magistrate erred in characterizing a number of the parties' assets as Donald's separate property, rather than attributing the assets to the community estate. She asserted that had the magistrate properly characterized these assets as community property, the magistrate would have found that the community's deposits in the account actually exceeded its expenditures. Specifically, Lana claimed that the magistrate should have credited the community estate with: (1) the interest income Donald received from his separate property during the marriage; (2) the pasturage value of Donald's separate ranches; and (3) more than 20% of the remaining cattle herd. She also claimed that had the magistrate correctly characterized these assets as community property, the magistrate would have found that the community had sufficient funds in the commingled account to purchase the disputed interest in the W & W Land Partnership.

In its memorandum decision on appeal, the district court substantially reversed the magistrate, holding: (1) that Donald should not have been allowed to use indirect tracing evidence to prove his separate property which he had commingled with community funds; (2) that the community was entitled to be credited with the amount of Donald's separate interest income which he used to pay the interest on his separate debts; (3) that the community should not have been charged with the cost of using Donald's separate property pastures to maintain the community's cattle during the marriage; and (4) that, on remand, the magistrate should reclassify the parties' assets pursuant to its holding, and reevaluate whether the community had sufficient funds in the commingled account to have been able to purchase the interest in the W & W Land Partnership. The district court affirmed the magistrate's finding that the community had a 20% interest in the remaining cattle herd. Donald has appealed, and Lana has cross-appealed, from the district court's decision.

Issues on Appeal

Donald raises the following issues on appeal:

Whether the magistrate correctly exercised his discretion in admitting and applying the accounting, or indirect tracing, evidence presented by Donald to prove his separate property from the parties' commingled assets. . .

Whether the magistrate correctly decided that the community lacked sufficient funds to have been able to invest in the W & W Land Partnership, and therefore that the investment was Donald's separate property.

In her cross-appeal, Lana raises the issue whether the magistrate erred in finding that 80% of the cattle in the herd at the time of divorce were Donald's separate property, having been owned by him prior to the marriage.

Analysis

1. admission and application of accounting evidence to prove donald's separate estate

A. Admission of Accounting Evidence

During the course of the parties' marriage, Donald commingled his separate funds with the parties' community funds in a bank account. The funds from this account were used to pay for Donald's separate operations as well as the community's operations and expenses. At trial, Donald sought to prove which funds in the commingled account, and proceeds from funds in the commingled account, were his separate property. To accomplish this he offered accounting, or indirect tracing, evidence in the form of bank statements, deposit slips, checks, tax returns, and the testimony and reports of his accountant who summarized the parties' financial transactions during the marriage. Lana contends that the magistrate erred in allowing Donald to present this accounting evidence without first showing that it was impossible to use direct tracing to prove the separate character of the disputed assets.

Whether a party must show that direct tracing is impossible before the party is allowed to use accounting evidence to prove the separate character of assets is a question of law, which we review freely. For the following reasons, we hold that a party attempting to prove the separate character of assets derived from commingled funds is not required to demonstrate that direct tracing is impossible before employing accounting evidence to prove that the assets were purchased with separate funds.

Our Supreme Court has established legal principles governing the classification of property upon the dissolution of marriage where the parties have commingled their separate and community estates. In *Stahl v. Stahl*, 91 Idaho 794, 430 P.2d 685 (1967), the parties disputed the character of the husband's separate funds which he had commingled in an account with the parties' community funds. In resolving the dispute, the Supreme Court stated:

> [T]here is a presumption that all property acquired by the spouses during coverture is community property; however, when the source of the property can be established

with reasonable certainty and particularity as the separate property of one or the other, the effect of such presumption is overcome, and the property so traced retains its character as separate property.

* * *

So long as the separate property of either spouse is identifiable and traceable, commingling of such separate property with community property does not convert the separate property into community property. *Stahl,* 91 Idaho at 797-98, 430 P.2d at 688-89 (citations omitted). It is significant that while the Court held that separate property which is commingled with community property retains its separate character so long as it can be traced "with reasonable certainty and particularity" to its separate source, the Court did not make any distinction between the direct and indirect tracing methods.

In *Evans,* the trial court found that the husband's separate estate had not been commingled with the community's assets to such an extent that it had lost its separate identity. On appeal, the Court stated:

> It is true that there is a presumption that property acquired during marriage is community but only when it is impossible to trace the source of the specific property. Further, so long as the separate property of either spouse is identifiable and traceable, commingling of such property with community property does not convert the separate property into community property.

Evans, 92 Idaho at 918, 453 P.2d at 567. The Court then recited the same language quoted above from *Stahl,* and, after reviewing the accounting evidence presented by the husband, upheld the trial court's findings. Thus, in *Evans,* the Court upheld the husband's use of accounting evidence without requiring any showing that direct tracing was impossible.

Our refusal to impose a requirement that parties show the impossibility of direct tracing before they can use accounting evidence is supported by sound policy considerations. The lack of such a prerequisite does not improperly encourage parties to employ accounting evidence when direct tracing is possible and feasible. This is because even though accounting evidence is admitted, the party asserting the separate character of the property still carries the burden of proving that fact with certainty and particularity, and it remains for the finder of fact to determine whether that burden has been met. Thus, parties asserting the separate character of commingled property will naturally be motivated to use direct tracing over indirect tracing evidence because direct tracing is generally more persuasive, if not conclusive, in proving the separate character of commingled property.

Based on our analysis of the above cases, we hold that a party asserting the separate character of property must prove the property is separate with reasonable certainty and particularity. The party may accomplish this by use of accounting evidence as well as direct tracing. A showing that direct tracing is impossible is not required before accounting evidence can be used. Accordingly, we hold that the magistrate did not err in admitting and considering Donald's accounting evidence without first requiring him to show the objective impossibility of directly tracing the disputed assets.

B. *Classification of Property and Application of Accounting Evidence*

The magistrate determined that the great weight of the evidence supported Donald's theory of the financial history of the marriage; that during the marriage the community spent more money than it received; and that proceeds from Donald's separate property and loans made up for the community's deficit. Based on these findings, the magistrate concluded that the community's interest in the commingled assets had been entirely consumed during the marriage, and thus no community interest remained in the commingled assets at the time of divorce.

* * *

(iii) *Application of Accounting Evidence and Classification of the Interest Purchased in the W & W Land Partnership.* The evidence in the record shows that all of the community's funds were maintained in an account into which Donald commingled his separate funds. Based on the tax returns of the parties, the magistrate found that the community spent more money than it received during the marriage. The magistrate also found that Donald, through documentary evidence and the testimony of his accountant, had met his burden of tracing and accounting for all funds received during the marriage. From the accounting evidence presented by Donald, the magistrate was able to identify those deposits and expenditures which pertained to the community and those which pertained to Donald's separate estate. This accounting evidence also supports the magistrate's finding that the community's expenditures exceeded its deposits. The record also supports the magistrate's finding that Donald's separate funds in the commingled account made up for the community's shortfall.

The record shows that the disputed interest in the W & W Land Partnership was purchased with funds from the commingled account. The magistrate concluded that because the community had exhausted its share of the commingled account, the interest in the W & W Land Partnership must have been purchased with Donald's separate funds, and thus according to the accounting method of tracing, the asset pertained to Donald's separate estate. We note that the evidence in the record does not show that, at the time the interest in the W & W Land Partnership was purchased from the commingled funds, the community's share of those funds had been exhausted. However, our Supreme Court has stated that "a requirement of showing that community funds were exhausted at the date of purchase of each disputed asset, imposes too heavy a burden of record keeping on the average spouse." As noted above, the factual findings which underlie the magistrate's conclusions are supported by substantial competent, although conflicting, evidence. Accordingly, we can find no error in the manner in which the magistrate classified the separate and community property of the parties and the magistrate's findings and conclusions regarding the classification and distribution of the parties' commingled funds are affirmed.

2. CLASSIFICATION OF THE CATTLE HERD

The magistrate determined that 80% of the cattle at the time of divorce were Donald's separate property, having been owned by him prior to the marriage. The magistrate credited the remaining 20% of the cattle to the community estate.

Lana contends that this finding is clearly erroneous because it is not supported by substantial evidence.

In a divorce proceeding, the trial court, not this Court on appeal, resolves the conflicting evidence and determines the weight, credibility, and inferences to be drawn from such evidence, and, where the evidence is substantial and competent, although conflicting, the trial court's findings will not be disturbed. *Gapsch,* 76 Idaho at 48-49, 277 P.2d at 280.

At trial, Donald testified that at the time of the divorce approximately 80% of the cattle in the herd were cattle that he had owned prior to the marriage. Donald also testified that during the marriage he sold the younger animals which had been born into the herd because he could not afford to sell and replace the older cattle. The testimony of a Mr. Beckman indicated that he purchased most of Donald's older cows in the spring of 1981, before the parties were married, leaving Donald with a relatively young herd at the beginning of the marriage. This testimony constitutes substantial competent evidence supporting the magistrate's finding that 80% of the cattle at the time of divorce were Donald's separate property, having been owned by him prior to the marriage. Because this finding is supported by substantial competent evidence, we will not disturb it on appeal.

CONCLUSION

Based on the facts and reasoning set forth above, we hold that the magistrate did not err in: admitting and considering the accounting evidence presented by Donald; classifying the interest purchased in the W & W Land Partnership; and determining the community's interest in the parties' cattle herd.

WALTERS, C.J., and SWANSTROM, J., concur.

Discussion Questions

1. What advantage did the wife Lana think would be gained by requiring her husband Donald to prove that direct tracing was impossible?

2. Why did the Court of Appeals think that the accounting method should be an alternative to the direct tracing method?

3. How did Donald prove that the commingled "cattle" were 80 percent his separate property?

PROBLEM 4.1

Ann was married to Bob in 2008. Soon after the marriage, she inherited $20,000 from her Aunt Carol. She opened a savings account in her name with the $20,000. She also decided to have the bank automatically transfer $100 every month from her checking account to her savings account. The checking account contained deposits from her salary at her job. No other deposits were made to the account. In 2011, she withdrew $2,500 for a trip that Bob and she took to Europe. That was the only withdrawal from the bank account. Recently, their marriage has deteriorated and they are considering divorce. Ann has consulted with an attorney who questioned her about their assets, including the savings account. If Ann and Bob live in Louisiana, how would a court treat the bank account? If Ann and Bob live in California or Washington, how would a court treat the bank account?

PROBLEM 4.2

Earl and Fran married in 2000. Earl came from a wealthy family and his father set up a trust fund for him. Earl also worked in his father's business and received a salary of $10,000 a month. At the time of their marriage, there was a balance of $100,000 in his bank account. After they married, Earl's salary was deposited into his account.

Fran worked in the accounting department of a national retail chain. After they married, Fran quit her job at Earl's request. He told her that she didn't need to work, since his trust fund and his salary were sufficient to live on. Earl was used to spending money freely, but his father had taught him to keep meticulous records of every penny he spent. Earl continued to spend freely and keep meticulous records during their marriage. Some months, they spent more than $10,000 a month on food, entertainment, and travel. During the busy season for his father's business which was the last three months of the year, they spent about $5,000 a month on family expenses. In 2006, as an investment, Earl purchased a small local farm that grew organic produce. The purchase price of the farm was $50,000. In 2010, Earl purchased stock in a biotech company for $25,000.

Recently, Earl and Fran have had marital problems and are considering a divorce. Earl has consulted an attorney about his rights to the farm and the stock he purchased. The attorney explained to him that depositing his salary into the same bank account with the trust fund money resulted in commingling. Earl still thinks that the farm and stock are his separate property and asked how a court would decide. If Earl and Fran lived in California, could Earl succeed in proving that the farm and stock are his separate property? What if they lived in Idaho?

Table 4-1
Commingling Separate and Community Funds In Community Property States

State	Rule	Case/Statute
Arizona	"Where community property and separate property are commingled, the entire fund is presumed to be community property unless the property can be explicitly traced." Burden of proof on the separate property proponent to prove that the funds or a portion of them are separate property by clear and satisfactory evidence.	*Cooper v. Cooper,* 130 Ariz. 257, 259, 635 P.2d 850, 852 (1981), *Porter v. Porter,* 67 Ariz. 273, 195 P.2d 132 (1948)

California	Commingled bank accounts presumed to be community property, separate property proponent has burden of proof to trace to separate property funds. Acquisitions from a commingled bank account are presumed to be community property. If all community income was exhausted by family expenses at the time of acquisition, the property acquired is separate property. Alternatively, when both separate and community funds are in a commingled account, if the separate property proponent intended to use separate property funds and did use those funds, the property acquired is separate property. Spouse who commingles has burden of record keeping. Burden of proof is preponderance of the evidence. Total recapitulation method rejected.	Probate Code §5305 (2009). *See v. See*, 64 Cal. 2d 778, 415 P.2d 776, 51 Cal. Rptr. 888 (1966) (exhaustion method), *Marriage of Mix*, 14 Cal. 3d 604, 536 P.2d 479, 122 Cal. Rptr. 79 (1975) (direct tracing), *Estate of Murphy*, 15 Cal. 3d 907, 544 P.2d 956, 126 Cal. Rptr. 820 (1976)
Idaho	Property acquired from commingled funds is presumed to be community property. Burden of proof on party asserting that the assets are separate property. Proof is reasonable certainty and particularity. Total recapitulation method adopted (called accounting): proof that throughout the marriage, community living expenses consumed or exceeded the community income results in acquisition characterized as separate property. Direct tracing (exhaustion or direct tracing) also allowed.	*Houska v. Houska*, 95 Idaho 568, 512 P.2d 1317 (1973), *Evans v. Evans*, 92 Idaho 911, 453 P.2d 560 (1969), *Stahl v. Stahl*, 91 Idaho 704, 430 P.2d 685 (1967)
Louisiana	Commingled bank accounts presumed to be community property, separate property proponent has burden of proof by tracing to separate property funds. Presumption that withdrawals come first from separate property funds. For acquisitions from a commingled fund, separate property proponent must prove property acquired and paid for with separate funds. Proof must be "fixed, clear, positive and legally certain."	*Cutting v. Cutting*, 625 So. 2d 1112 (La. App. 1993), *Granger v. Granger*, 722 So. 2d 107 (La. App. 1998)
Nevada	Commingled bank accounts presumed to be community property, separate property proponent has burden of proving that acquisition is separate property by (1) direct tracing to the timing and amounts of separate property deposits and withdrawals or by (2) at the time of purchase community income was	*Malmquist v. Malmquist*, 106 Nev. 372, 792 P.2d 372 (1990)

	exhausted by family expenses. Direct tracing requires separate property proponent establish timing and amounts so separate property deposits and withdrawals as well as intent to use those funds.	
New Mexico	Permits total recapitulation method, which determines whether community expenditures have depleted community income to ascertain if property acquired from a commingled fund is separate property. Separate property proponent has burden of proof by a preponderance of evidence. Direct tracing method also permitted.	*Zemke v. Zemke*, 116 N.M. 1114, 860 P.2d 756 (1993)
Texas	Property possessed by either spouse during marriage is presumed to be community property. If separate property can be definitely/clearly traced and identified, it remains separate property. Community-out-first presumption applies. Burden of proof on separate property proponent is "clear and convincing evidence."	*Welder v. Welder*, 794 S.W.2d 420 (Tex. Ct. App. 1990), *Smith v. Smith*, 22 S.W.3d 140 (2000)
Washington	Commingled funds in a bank account are presumed to be community property. Burden on the spouse claiming separate funds to clearly and convincingly trace them to a separate source. If the sources of the deposits can be traced and identified, the separate identity of the funds is preserved. Improvements to separate property from a commingled account presumed to be from separate property if traced.	*Marriage of Skarbek*, 100 Wash. App. 444, 997 P.2d 447 (2000), *Marriage of Pearson-Maines*, 70 Wash. App. 860, 855 P.2d 1210 (1993)
Wisconsin	Non-divisible property (separate property) includes inherited and gifted property. At divorce, a party who asserts that the property is non-divisible has the burden of showing that it remains non-divisible at the time of divorce. That party must show that the property has retained its character and identity through tracing and lack of donative intent.	Wis. Stat. §767.255(2)(a), *Derr v. Derr*, 289 Wis. 2d 671, 696 N.W.2d 170 (Ct. App. 2005) (apartment building gifted to husband during marriage was non-divisible asset), *Steinmann v. Steinmann*, 309 Wis. 2d 19, 749 N.W.2d 145 (2008) (tracing and transmutation can be used to characterize non-divisible property)

Chapter 5

Buying a Home: Joint Tenancy or Community Property Titles

A. ONLY TWO CATEGORIES: COMMUNITY PROPERTY OR SEPARATE PROPERTY

The community property system did not derive from the common law system so familiar to American lawyers and law students. For this reason, the common law property concepts, based strictly on title, clash with the community property concepts of separate and community property. The clash of concepts is most dramatic when the courts and legislatures of community property states are confronted with the practice of many married couples who take their property in the form of joint tenancy with right of survivorship. That form of title will be referred to in this Chapter by the short-hand term "joint tenancy." The drama is heightened because married couples will often designate the title of their most valuable asset, their home, as held in joint tenancy.

In community property law there are only two categories: separate property and community property. The clash occurs when it must be determined whether joint tenancy fits within either category. Where *does* the common law title joint tenancy fit in a community property system? From a common-sense viewpoint, one would assume that joint tenancy is like community property, since the term "joint" seems to reflect the "joint" ownership concept of community property. But common sense does not lead to the correct answer. The reason is that joint tenancy and community property differ at the very core of their characteristics — how they are treated at death of one of the spouses. The major distinguishing characteristic of joint tenancy is "the right of survivorship." That means that on the death of one of the spouses, the property passes to the surviving spouse by operation of law. The property does not go through probate; the property cannot be devised by one of the spouses to a child or other relative. On the other hand, community property differs at the death of one of the spouses. It does not automatically pass to the surviving spouse. A spouse has a right to devise one-half of that property to a child or other relative. So far, the initial assumption is that joint tenancy falls into the category of community property. However, because they differ at death, joint tenancy cannot be community property. The only category left under community property law is separate property. Therefore, joint tenancy must fall into the category of separate property, the undivided separate property of each of the spouses that passes to the surviving spouse upon death of the other spouse.

Since joint tenancy does not fit the definition of community property regarding the death of one spouse, the corollary issue is how joint tenancy should be treated at divorce. Again, a common-sense view would be that since "joint" has the connotation of "equal" ownership, joint tenancy property should be divided equally at divorce. It is true that joint tenancy is split equally when it is severed or partitioned and then becomes the common law form of tenancy in common. Therefore, in those community property states where there is mandatory 50/50 split of community property at divorce, joint tenancy could be treated exactly like community property. However, in those community property states where there is equitable division of community property, community property will not always be split equally and in some scenarios will differ from joint tenancy that must be partitioned equally. Thus, again the common-sense view must yield and it is again evident that joint tenancy is not community property.

To illustrate how these differences in concepts work, let us take our hypothetical couple, Harry and Wanda. For several years, they have been renting an apartment because they could not afford to buy a home. When Wanda receives an inheritance from her father, they use those funds to buy a condominium. They found one that they feel is perfect for them and the real estate agent asks how they would like to hold the title. They ask what the real estate agent suggests. At that point, the real estate agent explains that joint tenancy is a good idea because at death, the home will go to the survivor without going through probate. Since Harry and Wanda and the real estate agent are not familiar with community property law, the title is taken in joint tenancy. There are two possible scenarios.

In the first scenario, Harry and Wanda could have a long marriage and when one of them dies, the condo will pass to the survivor without probate. In that instance, it is likely that Wanda would want Harry to have the condo. In the second scenario, Harry and Wanda's marriage is not long lived and they decide to divorce. When Wanda consults an attorney, she will explain that it was her inheritance that was used to purchase the condo. She feels that despite the title being in a joint tenancy, she thinks the condo is hers because of the funds used to buy the condo, her separate property. Harry would feel differently. He will note that the title says "joint" and to him that indicated that they owned the condo together and that he has a right to one-half. Wanda does not think that Harry deserves to own one-half of the condo when her separate property funds paid for the condo. So the legal dilemma is how to treat a joint tenancy at divorce when the spouses' only intention at the time they acquired the condo was to provide a right of survivorship upon one of their deaths. Another issue arises if the condo is considered "joint" property or community property by way of legislative fiat: whether Wanda should have a right to reimbursement of her separate property funds upon divorce.

The following case, *Estate of Ashe* (Idaho 1988), illustrates the potential consequences at death of spouses taking community property funds and designating those funds as joint tenancy. Although the facts did not involve a home, it does show the tension between the common-law title joint tenancy and the community property concept of community property.

ESTATE OF ASHE

114 Idaho 70, 753 P.2d 281 (1988)
Court of Appeals of Idaho
Affirmed, 117 Idaho 266, 787 P.2d 252 (1990)
Supreme Court of Idaho

SMITH, Judge Pro Tem.

This is an appeal from an order made in the administration of a decedent's estate, with respect to the inclusion, and exclusion, of certain property in the estate. The order was entered in the magistrate division in Owyhee County, in the estate of Esther Ashe, deceased. The petition of Sam Ashe, surviving husband of the decedent, to classify a Merrill-Lynch brokerage account as his separate property pursuant to a joint tenancy agreement, and to classify as community property an acreage in Idaho formerly shared with his wife, Esther Ashe, was denied by the magistrate. On appeal, Mr. Ashe asserts the magistrate applied an incorrect standard of proof to the question of joint tenancy. He also contends that as a matter of law a deed to the Idaho property was never delivered. We affirm.

Esther Ashe died on December 26, 1983. She left a surviving spouse, Sam Ashe; a son from a prior marriage, Jack Hurt; and Jack's sons and grandsons. After Jack Hurt was appointed as special administrator, he filed a petition for formal probate of the will of Esther Ashe, and for his appointment as personal representative. Sam Ashe objected, alleging that duress and mental incapacity of the decedent rendered the will invalid. That contest was resolved by a stipulation in which the will was admitted to probate, another person (James Schiller) was appointed as personal representative, and the contested issues were delineated.

Later, Sam Ashe filed a petition seeking an order declaring (1) that a cash management account at Merrill-Lynch, Boise, Idaho, was his property and was not to be included in the estate and (2) that a parcel of real property previously deeded to Jack Hurt was to be included in the estate as community property. Jack Hurt responded, petitioning for a determination that the Merrill-Lynch account was community property and that the real estate in question had been disposed of by the deed and therefore was not a part of the estate. Following trial before a magistrate, the court entered findings of fact and conclusions of law, and an order denying Sam's petition and granting Hurt's petition. The magistrate's decision was affirmed on appeal to the district court.

I. BACKGROUND

The facts leading to the controversy in this case are not materially in dispute. Sam and Esther were married in Santa Rosa, California, in 1938. Esther's son by a prior marriage, Jack Hurt, was then about fourteen years of age. He lived with Sam and Esther for about four years after the marriage. Sam and Esther had no children during their marriage.

Sam and Esther accumulated considerable wealth during their marriage. Sam "bucked" the oil fields for a few years and then started speculating in houses, buying and building in Bakersfield, California and the environs. They each inherited some assets from their respective families. Sam gave real estate he inherited to his family members. Securities inherited by Esther in 1960 in the amount of about $19,000 were either sold or reinvested by the couple. Esther was an osteopath, but apparently did not practice her profession. Accordingly, it is apparent from the record that the wealth of Sam and Esther came from Sam's expertise as a speculative builder, from their investments and from the construction business.

The couple established a joint tenancy stock brokerage account at the E.F. Hutton office in Bakersfield in 1963. According to Mr. Ashe's testimony, after Esther had attended a businesswomen's meeting, she took Sam to confer with an investment advisor who had aroused her interest in the manner of making investments. Sam recalled that the investment advisor told them there were two ways to avoid inheritance taxes, i.e., to give the property away or to spend it. The investment advisor also talked to Sam and Esther about holding property in joint tenancy with right of survivorship.

As a result of this advice and other contacts, Sam deduced that in joint tenancy with right of survivorship, two people own the property, and if one survives the other, the survivor takes the ownership of the total property. He also understood that one cannot "will away" property that is held in joint tenancy.

Thus, according to Sam's understanding of the meaning of joint tenancy, Sam and Esther accumulated their wealth in joint tenancy with right of survivorship. However, the evidence does not clearly establish whether Esther fully understood all of the ramifications of joint tenancy with right of survivorship. It does appear that Esther for years incorrectly believed that a married person could not make a will at all without the consent of the other spouse. So from time to time during the marriage, Esther asked Sam about making a will. Sam would respond "lets get together and see what we want." However, they never did get together in the making of a will.

At some time just prior to 1972, Sam became interested in residing in Idaho. In 1972 and 1973, he and Esther liquidated their real estate holdings in California and moved to the vicinity of Marsing, Idaho. The E.F. Hutton brokerage account was left in California. They acquired a home and acreage in the Marsing area which came to be known to them as the "Home Place."

While Sam and Esther lived in the Marsing area, they met people, made friends and became a part of the community. Esther continued to be concerned about the disposition of their estate, as was Sam. In April of 1981, Sam gave some Owyhee County lots to his brother, Tillman Ashe. Esther reluctantly joined in this conveyance. That same month, Sam joined with Esther in deeding the Home Place to Esther and Jack. The deed was delivered to Esther by Sam with the admonition that the deed should not be recorded. Jack was not told about this deed at that time. Sam and Esther contemplated they would have the use of the Home Place so long as they needed it. However, no language reserving a life estate was contained in this deed. Jack did not become aware of this deed until October, 1981.

In May, 1981, Jack Hurt moved from Arkansas to Idaho. Jack testified that his mother had invited him to move to Marsing. Sam testified that, prior to this move, Esther asked Sam if he wanted Jack and Ina, Jack's wife, to move to Marsing. Sam did not want them to move to Idaho, but the next thing he knew they had moved in. Actually, Jack and Ina lived in Ina's travel trailer parked on the Home Place. After that Sam felt like a stranger in his own home. Following Jack and Ina's move onto the property, all of the parties were living "pretty close" together and, according to Sam, Jack was showing his mother great "familial" affection for the first time. It is clear from Sam's deposition that he thought Jack was trying to ingratiate himself, particularly with Esther, in order to gain from the newly "cultivated" close relationship.

Later in September, 1981, because of the way Jack was acting, Sam felt uncomfortable. He decided to take a trip to Europe. He stayed about thirty days. He then returned to the United States having decided not to return home to Marsing. Sam was concerned Esther might cash out the brokerage account in California and "leave him in the cold." He decided to take the money himself. He cashed in the E.F. Hutton account, and obtained $329,000 in checks. He then returned to Marsing, found $28,000 in his bank account there, put $4,000 with it, obtained cashier's checks amounting to $325,000 and took the cashier's checks with him to San Francisco where he opened a new brokerage account in his own name with Merrill-Lynch. The cashier's checks, two in number, were dated October 29, 1981. The Merrill-Lynch account was established on or about the next business day.

On October 30, 1981, Esther and Jack consulted with an attorney, Terry Coffin. Esther had learned that Sam was back from Europe and that he had cashed in the E.F. Hutton account. She also was concerned about the state of Sam's health. She had heard he was ill. She believed Sam was going to take the money to Arden Woods Benevolent Society in San Francisco and use those funds to acquire a place to live for the rest of his life. She wanted Terry Coffin to make sure her share of the money was protected. After discussing several possibilities, Coffin recommended divorce proceedings be filed so she could obtain a restraining order to tie up the money.

On November 2, 1981, the divorce action was filed. Also, the deed of the Home Place to Jack and Esther was recorded. About the same time, David Stecher, another attorney in the same firm with Terry Coffin, was instructed by Esther to prepare a will for her. She executed the will on November 5, 1981. The will gave all of her property to Jack, his children and his grandchildren. This will was the one later admitted, by stipulation, to probate in this case.

Toward the latter part of November, 1981, Sam returned to Marsing to contest the divorce or at least the settlement thereon. While in Marsing Sam and Esther reconciled at the urging of a friend, John Larsen.

In January, 1982, while Sam and Esther were traveling in California, they went to San Francisco where Sam transferred the Merrill-Lynch account to himself and Esther as joint tenants with right of survivorship. Sam and Esther were still residing at the Home Place in Marsing. In March, 1982, the Merrill-Lynch account in San Francisco was transferred to Merrill-Lynch in Boise, Idaho. Brokers James Steele and Louise Schneider discussed joint tenancies with the Ashes. The Boise account was set up in the same manner as was accomplished previously for the California account.

Then, on June 21, 1982, the Home Place (which earlier had been deeded to Jack and Esther outright) was again transferred so as to make them joint tenants with right of survivorship. The mechanics of this involved conveyances by Jack and Esther to attorney Stecher, as a straw man, who then reconveyed the Home Place to Jack and Esther as joint tenants with right of survivorship.

In late 1982, Sam and Esther again travelled to California. They stayed in Santa Barbara for about a year, visited in Bakersfield and attended a summer educational session in St. Louis, Missouri, returning to Marsing in 1983. Esther died in December. The proceedings in the courts below then began.

The findings of fact and conclusions of law entered by the magistrate included procedural facts, general facts, ultimate facts and conclusions of law. The "Conclusions of Law," essentially state as follows:

1. The law of Idaho applied.
2. In reference to the Merrill-Lynch account, Sam Ashe had the burden to prove by clear and convincing evidence that Esther Ashe intended the creation of a joint tenancy with right of survivorship; that Sam Ashe did not meet that burden of proof; that therefore the account did not pass to Sam Ashe by right of survivorship but in fact passed under the last will and testament of Esther Ashe.
3. The deeds on the Home Place transferred that property to Jack Hurt, as the survivor of the joint tenancy created by the deeds.
4. The burden of proof was not met by the petitioner, Sam Ashe, to set aside the deeds, and the real estate at the time of the death of Esther Ashe was not community property.

As stated, the magistrate made an order based on his findings and conclusions. On appeal, the district court concluded there was sufficient evidence in the record of the case to affirm the findings and legal conclusions of the magistrate.

II. Issues

On his appeal to this Court, Sam Ashe presents the following issues and contentions:

(a) Whether, with regard to the stock brokerage account, the magistrate erred in requiring that joint tenancy with right of survivorship be proved by clear and convincing evidence. Ashe contends the magistrate erred in this respect because the Ashes originally maintained the brokerage account in California and therefore California law and not Idaho law is applicable to the account.

(b) Whether the magistrate erred in applying the presumption of community property to the account, thereby requiring proof by clear and convincing evidence that the account was held by the Ashes in joint tenancy with right of survivorship. Ashe claims that the adoption of Idaho Rule of Evidence 301 has modified that judicially created presumption.

(c) Whether the magistrate's finding that Esther did not intend to create a joint tenancy in the brokerage account was supported by substantial, competent evidence. Ashe contends the evidence indicated clearly that Esther understood the effect of a joint tenancy and the finding of a lack of intent was therefore not supported by the evidence.

III. Discussion

The action of Sam when he returned from Europe in late October, 1981, is a crucial fact in the case. At that time, he terminated the E.F. Hutton account, and placed all of the proceeds in his own name in a Merrill-Lynch account. Any act of a joint tenant which destroys one or more of its necessary co-existent unities of interest, time, title and possession operates as a severance of the joint tenancy and extinguishes the right of survivorship; the act of one joint tenant in severing his interest in the property severs the joint tenancy, thereby terminating the joint tenancy. Thus, when Sam cashed out the E.F. Hutton account, he terminated the joint tenancy. But when Sam and Esther reconciled in December, 1981, and reestablished the brokerage account in January of 1982, in San Francisco, they were domiciled in Idaho.

It is well settled that personal property acquired during coverture is governed and controlled by the law of the marital domicile. Therefore, we conclude that, since Sam and Esther were domiciled in Idaho at the time the Merrill-Lynch brokerage account was created in California as a joint tenancy account, the magistrate was correct in deciding to apply the law of Idaho.

B

Mr. Ashe acknowledges the rule that a survivor of a joint account is required to show by clear and convincing evidence the deceased party to the account intended that the corpus of the account pass to the survivor by right of survivorship. *See In re Estate of Bogert,* 96 Idaho 522, 531 P.2d 1167 (1975). However, Ashe contends that adoption of I.R.E. 301 has changed the *Bogert* ruling.

We disagree. Therefore, we hold the magistrate did not err in requiring proof by clear and convincing evidence that Esther intended the creation of a joint tenancy with right of survivorship on the Merrill-Lynch account.

C

We turn next to the magistrate's finding that Esther did not intend to create a joint tenancy with respect to the brokerage account. Ashe contends there was not substantial and competent evidence produced at trial to support that finding. He maintains there was uncontradicted evidence by three disinterested witnesses who said they had explained to Esther and she understood the effect of a joint tenancy with right of survivorship. We disagree with Ashe's position. The magistrate did not find Esther lacked the intent. Instead, the magistrate held that Ashe had failed to carry his burden to show the existence of such an intent.

Ashe has cited *Kreiensieck v. Cook,* 108 Idaho 657, 660, 701 P.2d 277, 280 (Ct. App. 1985), for this rule:

When a trial court finds facts that must be established by clear and convincing evidence, the question on appeal remains whether the findings are supported by substantial and competent evidence.

As applied to this case, the rule placed the burden on Ashe to prove by clear and convincing evidence Esther intended to create a joint tenancy account. The magistrate made his findings on the basis he was not convinced by Ashe's evidence that Esther intended to create a joint tenancy when Sam and Esther travelled to San

Francisco in 1981 after they reconciled. It is not required that there be evidence on which the magistrate must rely to find that Esther did not intend the creation of a joint tenancy. Rather, in finding no joint tenancy was created, the magistrate may — even in the face of uncontroverted evidence to the contrary — rely on the presumption favoring community property in finding no joint tenancy was created.[2]

In any event, Ashe is not correct in his assertion that the evidence was uncontroverted on the issue of whether Esther intended and understood the effect of joint tenancy with right of survivorship. The record describes instances where Esther merely acquiesced in events which were taking place. The stockbrokers' testimony on which Ashe relies disclosed the brokers did not inquire into Esther's intentions. The testimony of her friend, Betty Ashe, and others indicated Esther always intended to maintain her one-half interest in the joint account. For example, Esther's reluctant filing of a divorce was undertaken to protect and preserve her one-half interest in the brokerage account.

The *Bogert* case, *supra*, is factually similar and on point with this case. In *Bogert*, the Idaho Supreme Court held:

> (1) Spouses can transmute community property into joint tenancy in the state of Idaho, with right of survivorship, but the intention to so transmute the property must be shown by clear and convincing evidence.
>
> (2) When spouses attempt to transmute community property to property owned by joint tenancy, each thus makes a gift to the other of his or her interest in the community property, including the right to devise one-half of the community property at death, and in return receives as a gift a separate property interest in joint tenancy. The intent of a party to a joint account to have made an inter vivos gift must be proved by clear and convincing evidence.
>
> (3) The decedent's intention to make a gift must be demonstrated by a quantum of proof greater than a preponderance of the evidence, i.e., an intent to make such a gift clearly and unequivocally.
>
> (4) Whether a clear and convincing burden of proof has been met is a question for the trier of fact to decide.

It is not clear from the record that Esther intended a gift to Sam of her interest in the account. Instead, consistent with the magistrate's determination, it appears the basic intent of Sam and Esther in creating the joint account was an ill-advised attempt to avoid probate and not the making of gifts to each other. Accordingly, the decision of the magistrate that Sam had not met his burden of proof must be affirmed as to the Merrill-Lynch account.[3]

---

2. We have not found any authority explicitly holding that a trial court may rely upon the community property or a status quo presumption in the face of uncontroverted evidence of an intent to transmute property to separate property status. However, given the heavy burden on the proponent of transmutation, such a rule appears to be consistent with prior cases. *See, e.g.,* Griffin v. Griffin, 102 Idaho 858, 642 P.2d 949 (Ct. App. 1982) (signature on loan application supportive of transmutation intent, but not conclusive — finding of no transmutation affirmed despite no contrary evidence); *Hooker v. Hooker,* 95 Idaho 518, 511 P.2d 800 (1972) (first reported Idaho transmutation case — "isolated testimony" was sufficient to create "substantial conflict" in evidence upon which trial court could find no intent to transmute).

Our decision rests on the theory that the trial judge must be "convinced" by the evidence, the burden is not simply one of going forward ("production"). Here the judge was not convinced, i.e., Ashe did not meet his burden of persuasion.

3. We readily recognize that if the burden of proof in this case had been less than "by clear and convincing evidence," (for example, by a simple preponderance of the evidence) the result in this case could have been entirely different.

D

We turn next to the conveyance of the Home Place by Sam and Esther to Esther and Jack in April, 1981. Ashe asserts the magistrate erred in reaching the following finding and conclusion:

> Sam and Esther executed a deed . . . conveying the property to Esther and Jack as grantees. The court finds that was a voluntary act and that Sam "did it to make her happy." The Court finds a valid consideration was given — that Sam had previously conveyed real estate to his brother and nephews. Secondly, the Court further finds that the delivery of the warranty deed to one of the grantees constituted delivery to both grantees. The Court concludes that the burden of proof to set aside the conveyance has not been sustained.

The magistrate held that Ashe had made an effective gift of the Home Place.

* * *

As the magistrate determined, Sam intended to make the conveyance, and the deed was delivered to and accepted by Esther. Upon the record of this case, the delivery of the deed to Esther constituted a delivery to Jack as well. Esther thought she was acting in Jack's behalf in procuring the deed and accepting it. As a cograntee, Jack's actual knowledge of the conveyance was not required. To act in Jack's behalf, Esther did not need to have express authority from him to accept the delivery of a deed for him. Therefore, we agree that the magistrate reached the correct conclusion in finding the Home Place was validly conveyed to Esther and Jack.

Discussion Questions

1. What right is given up if community property funds are transmuted into joint tenancy? *-the right to devise the prop. @ death*
2. Who should be favored in this scenario, the surviving spouse or a child from a prior marriage?

B. DIVISION OF JOINT TENANCY AT DIVORCE: THE ARIZONA APPROACH

In Arizona, the courts are given discretion to divide community property and joint tenancy property "equitably." Arizona Revised Statutes §25-318(A) provides that the court shall "divide the community property, joint tenancy and other property held in common equitably, though not necessarily in kind, without regard to marital misconduct." The *Marriage of Inboden* case (Arizona 2010) is an example of how an equitable division state determines how to divide joint tenancy property at divorce. It is important to note (1) how Arizona views a joint tenancy and (2) what role the contribution of separate property funds plays in the division of joint tenancy property at divorce.

MARRIAGE OF INBODEN

223 Ariz. 542, 225 P.3d 599 (2010)
Court of Appeals of Arizona

BROWN, Judge.

Lowell Inboden ("Husband") appeals from the family court's decree of dissolution. He argues that the court erred in ordering an unequal distribution of the marital home in favor of Carolyn Inboden ("Wife"). For the following reasons, we vacate the court's decree in part and remand for further proceedings.

BACKGROUND

Husband and Wife married in July 2005. Shortly before the marriage, Wife used $90,000 of her separate funds to buy an undeveloped lot in Yuma and the couple took title to the lot as joint tenants. After they married, the parties built a house on the lot and executed another deed transferring the lot and house (collectively "the property") from themselves as separate persons to themselves as married persons as joint tenants with rights of survivorship. Acting as their own general contractor, the couple did the majority of the work on the house. They prepared plans for the house, framed it, and did the interior work. They used subcontractors only for specialty jobs. In addition to their labor, each spouse contributed financially toward construction costs, with Wife paying $67,000 from her separate funds and Husband paying $46,500 of his separate funds. The couple also obtained a loan against the property to complete the construction, pay off some debts, and furnish the house. Ongoing expenses during the marriage were paid from their monthly retirement funds.

The house was ready for occupancy in June 2006. Two months later, however, Husband moved out of the house and, apart from a three-week visit in December, he never returned. Wife petitioned for dissolution of the marriage in April 2007.

Following a trial regarding the division of the marital assets and liabilities, the family court concluded that the house was jointly held marital property subject to equitable division, citing *Toth v. Toth*, 190 Ariz. 218, 946 P.2d 900 (1997). The court found the value of the property was $310,000. After deducting the amount of the lien, the equity totaled $216,029. The court then determined the parties were entitled to reimbursement for their financial contributions from their separate property funds: $157,000 for Wife and $46,500 for Husband. The court further divided the remaining $12,529 equity in the house in proportion to each party's contribution of separate funds. The court awarded Wife possession of the house and ordered her to make an equalization payment to Husband. Husband timely appealed and we have jurisdiction pursuant to Arizona Revised Statutes ("A.R.S.") section 12-2101(B) (2003).

DISCUSSION

Husband contends that the family court erred as a matter of law and abused its discretion in dividing the house's equity based solely on the relative contributions of separate property. Wife counters that the court's allocation of the marital home is a "sound discretionary exercise" of the court's equitable jurisdiction.

The division of marital property upon dissolution is governed by A.R.S. §25-318(A) (Supp. 2009), which provides that each spouse be assigned his or her separate property and all jointly held property be divided equitably. In most cases, dividing jointly held property substantially equally will be the most equitable unless there exists a sound reason to divide the property otherwise. *Toth*, 190 Ariz. at 221, 946 P.2d at 903 (citing *Hatch v. Hatch*, 113 Ariz. 130, 133, 547 P.2d 1044, 1047 (1976)).

The family court has broad discretion in determining what allocation of property and debt is equitable under the circumstances. In considering the equities, courts might reach different conclusions without abusing their discretion. Thus, we will not disturb a court's ruling absent a clear abuse of discretion.

A.   MARITAL JOINT TENANCY PRESUMPTIONS

As an initial matter, Husband contends that by placing the property in joint tenancy, both parties made a gift of their separate property interests to the community, resulting in each party holding an undivided one-half interest in the property. Based on this presumption, Husband argues that the family court erred by not recognizing and considering his equal interest in the property when making the division. Husband suggests that because he owned a one-half interest in the property, a less than one-half share in the division would be inequitable. We disagree with Husband's reasoning.

It is well established that when a spouse places separate property in joint tenancy with the other spouse a presumed gift occurs and the presumption can only be overcome by clear and convincing evidence. *Valladee v. Valladee*, 149 Ariz. 304, 307, 718 P.2d 206, 209 (App. 1986). However, such gifts merely represent equitable rights in the jointly held property, they do not constitute irrevocable gifts of a one-half interest. *Toth*, 190 Ariz. at 221, 946 P.2d at 903.

Here, when Husband and Wife executed a deed after their marriage, transferring the property from themselves as single persons to themselves as married persons, a presumption arose that each spouse gifted his or her respective separate property interests to the other. Further, Wife does not argue, nor does anything in the record suggest, that an interspousal gift was not intended. But acknowledging the equal ownership interest in the property does not end the inquiry. All jointly held marital property, whether acquired by interspousal gift or otherwise, is subject to equitable division under A.R.S. §25-318(A).

B.   CONTRIBUTIONS OF SEPARATE PROPERTY

Although the family court has broad discretion in how to allocate assets and liabilities upon dissolution, absent an agreement to the contrary or the presence of other relevant factors, an unequal division of jointly held property may not be made solely to reimburse a spouse for separate funds used to buy jointly held property. *Toth*, 190 Ariz. at 222, 946 P.2d at 904 (citing *Whitmore v. Mitchell*, 152 Ariz. 425, 733 P.2d 310 (App. 1987)) (recognizing that a court may not order a substantially unequal division of jointly held property solely to reimburse one of the spouses for spending his or her separate funds to acquire the property); *Valladee*, 149 Ariz. 304, 718 P.2d 206 (finding that family court abused its discretion in making a substantially unequal division of the jointly held property solely to reimburse husband for expending his separate funds to initially acquire the property).

In this case, the family court found that Wife was entitled to $157,000 "as and for reimbursement of her separate property contributed to the joint tenancy property" and Husband was entitled to $46,500 "as and for reimbursement of his separate property contributed to the joint tenancy property."[1] A reasonable reading of the court's order indicates that its property division was based *solely* on the relative contributions of separate property each spouse made toward the purchase of the jointly held property. Nothing in the court's order suggests that it relied on any other factors nor does the record provide a reasonable basis to conclude otherwise. Thus, we must conclude that the court abused its discretion when it ordered a substantially unequal distribution of the jointly titled marital property only for the purpose of reimbursing each spouse for their respective financial contributions to the purchase of the property.

C. EQUITABLE DIVISION OF JOINTLY HELD PROPERTY

Even if the family court's order was not made solely to reimburse Husband and Wife for their respective contributions of separate property, the court was nonetheless obligated to divide the property equitably. The touchstone of determining what is "equitable" is a "concept of fairness dependent upon the facts of particular cases." *Toth*, 190 Ariz. at 221, 946 P.2d at 903. Wife argues that a division of the property based on the parties' relative contributions provides the only fair result. Husband, on the other hand, contends that even under *Toth* the property should be divided substantially equally because this is not one of the "rare occasions" contemplated by *Toth* where equal is not equitable.

In general, upon dissolution of a marriage, an equitable division of jointly held property should be substantially equal absent facts to support a contrary result. *See Valladee*, 149 Ariz. at 309, 718 P.2d at 211. Under A.R.S. §25-318(C), a court may consider excessive or abnormal expenditures and the destruction, concealment, or fraudulent disposition of property when making equitable divisions of property. But a court is not limited to considering these statutory factors; instead, any other factors that bear on the equities of a case may properly be considered. *Toth*, 190 Ariz. at 221-22, 946 P.2d at 903-04.

1. The family court cited *Nw. Fire Dist. v. City of Tucson*, 185 Ariz. 102, 103, 912 P.2d 1331, 1332 (App. 1995) for the proposition that joint tenants own a proportional undivided interest in joint tenancy property. The court then proceeded to reimburse the parties for their proportional contributions. As discussed *infra*, when making an equitable division of jointly held property upon dissolution of a marriage, the family court's obligation is to consider all factors that bear on the equities of the division, not merely the contribution of each spouse to the jointly titled property.

Our supreme court in *Toth* analyzed the meaning of "equitable" under A.R.S. §25-318 and concluded that an equal division of jointly held property was not equitable in a two-week marriage when one spouse used separate funds to acquire the property, the non-purchasing spouse had "made no contribution — pecuniary or otherwise — to the purchase of the [property,]" and the extremely short union allowed "no time for a marital relationship to develop, or for other equities to come into play." *Id.* at 221, 946 P.2d at 903.

[A] determination of what constitutes an equitable division of marital property may include consideration of contributions made by each spouse to the community, in whatever form. This inquiry is based on the recognition that under community property principles, spouses work together to accumulate property. Thus, if a spouse contributes to the marital relationship as a whole or improves the value of the specific property in question, e.g., using either money or labor, then an unequal property division would not be justified so long as these contributions were not completely negligible.

In sum, when making an equitable division of community property upon dissolution of a marriage, the family court should consider all factors that bear on the equities of the division, including the length of the marriage; the contributions of each spouse to the community, financial or otherwise; the source of funds used to acquire the property to be divided; the allocation of debt; as well as any other factor that may affect the outcome. As noted above, the record in this case reflects that the family court reimbursed each spouse for their respective contributions, without considering these equitable factors. Thus, we remand to allow the family court to make an equitable distribution of the property under A.R.S. §25-318(A), consistent with the principles explained in this decision. In doing so, the court may receive additional evidence to evaluate the equitable factors, including evidence relating to the current value of the property.

CONCLUSION

For the foregoing reasons, we vacate the portion of the dissolution decree relating to the division of the property held in joint tenancy by the parties and remand for further proceedings.

Concurring: PHILIP HALL, Presiding Judge, and MAURICE PORTLEY, Judge.

Discussion Questions

1. When a spouse places separate property in joint tenancy, is that a gift to the community as claimed by Husband in this case?

2. What was wrong with the trial court's division of the property, and what evidence would be relevant on remand?

C. CHARACTERIZATION OF JOINT TENANCY AS COMMUNITY PROPERTY AT DIVORCE: CALIFORNIA AND NEW MEXICO APPROACHES

Many states recognize that joint tenancy cannot be community property. However, most community property states choose to either treat joint tenancy as community property at divorce or create a presumption that joint tenancy is community property at divorce. In those states that have equitable division at divorce, like Arizona and Nevada, treating joint tenancy as community property avoids the necessity of partitioning the property 50/50. In the case of Harry and Wanda, that would mean that an Arizona or Nevada court could give Wanda more than one-half of the property, perhaps even all. In those states that have mandatory 50/50 division of community property at divorce, the question becomes whether the title or the funds control the characterization of the property. Because both spouses sign the joint tenancy deed or title, it can be viewed as a written agreement about how to hold the property. That designation may be respected throughout the marriage and at death, but may be contested at divorce.

1. *California Legislation*

California, a state that has moved toward requiring formal written agreements between spouses, has legislatively enacted a presumption that joint tenancy deeds and titles are community property at divorce unless the spouses provide otherwise in writing. Thus, joint tenancy titles are in essence a written agreement to hold property as community property in the event of a divorce. However, California has also attempted to provide for the spouse who has contributed separate property funds to the acquisition of the property. California even tried to make this legislation retroactive to all property, even to property acquired prior to the date of the enactments. That attempt was unsuccessful.

CALIFORNIA FAMILY CODE
§2581(formerly Civil Code §4800.1). Community property presumption for property held in joint form

For the purpose of division of property on dissolution of marriage . . . property acquired by the parties during marriage in joint form including property held in tenancy in common, joint tenancy, tenancy by the entirety, or as community property, is presumed to be community property. This presumption is a presumption affecting the burden of proof and may be rebutted by either of the following:

(a) A clear statement in the deed or other documentary evidence of title by which the property is acquired that the property is separate property and not community property.
(b) Proof that the parties have made a written agreement that the property is separate property.

CALIFORNIA FAMILY CODE

§2640(b) (formerly Civil Code §4800.2). Separate property contributions
to community estate property acquisition

In the division of the community estate . . . the party shall be reimbursed for
the party's contributions to the acquisition of the property to the extent the
party traces the contributions to a separate property source.

MARRIAGE OF BUOL

39 Cal. 3d 751, 705 P.2d 354, 218 Cal. Rptr. 31 (1985)
Supreme Court of California

REYNOSO, Justice.

May legislation requiring a writing to prove, upon dissolution of marriage, that
property taken in joint tenancy form is the separate property of one spouse constitutionally be applied to cases pending before its effective date? We conclude that it
may not. Applied retroactively, the statute impairs vested property rights without
due process of law.

Esther and Robert Buol married in 1943 and separated in 1977. The Buols had
three children together and Esther had one child from a previous marriage.

Robert worked as a laborer until 1970 when he was fired, at least in part, due to
alcoholism. He began receiving Social Security total disability payments in 1973.
Esther began working in 1954 as a housekeeper, a babysitter and an attendant to
elderly women. Since 1959 she has been employed as a nursing attendant at a local
hospital.

With Robert's knowledge and consent, Esther put her earnings in a separate bank
account. Esther used the money to support the family, and in 1963, purchased a
home in San Rafael. Although title was taken in joint tenancy on the advice of the
realtor handling the sale, Esther made all mortgage, tax, insurance and maintenance payments out of her separate account. Robert contributed nothing. The
original purchase price was $17,500. The home is now valued at approximately
$167,500.

The sole issue at trial was the status of the home as separate or community
property. Esther testified that she purchased the home with her earnings which
Robert had emphasized numerous times were hers to do with what she pleased.
She also testified that she never would have gone to work without such an agreement
because "that would be more money for him to put into gambling and drinking."
In addition, she testified that he had always maintained that the house was hers and
that he wanted no responsibility for it, until after he moved out and started demanding that she sell it so that he could have a share of the proceeds.

Esther's testimony was corroborated by two of the Buols' children, Roy and
Judith, Judith's husband, and Esther's brother-in-law. Each remembered many conversations with Robert, alone or in family gatherings, in which he confirmed that the
house was Esther's. Robert offered conflicting testimony, but conceded that he
considered Esther's earnings to be hers alone, that he borrowed from her occasionally and that she made all the house payments out of her separate account.

Finding that the parties had an enforceable oral agreement (*In re Marriage of Lucas* (1980) 27 Cal. 3d 808 [166 Cal. Rptr. 853, 614 P.2d 285]) that the earnings and the home were Esther's separate property, the court entered judgment awarding the home to Esther. Robert appealed, contending that there was insufficient evidence to support the finding of an oral agreement.

While the appeal was pending, Civil Code section 4800.1 was enacted. Under that section the only means of rebutting the presumption that property acquired during marriage in joint tenancy is community property is by providing evidence of a written agreement that the property is separate property. No writing exists in the instant case.

I

We must determine whether section 4800.1 may be given retroactive effect without offending the state Constitution. It appears that the Legislature intended section 4800.1 to apply retroactively to cases such as the one at bench. Section 4 of Assembly Bill No. 26 states, "This act applies to the following proceedings: [¶] (a) Proceedings commenced on or after January 1, 1984. [¶] (b) Proceedings commenced before January 1, 1984, to the extent proceedings as to the division of property are not yet final on January 1, 1984." As the trial court's judgment awarding the $167,500 residence to Esther as her separate property was on appeal as of section 4800.1's January 1, 1984, effective date, the division of property was not yet final. Presumably, therefore, section 4800.1 would operate to defeat Esther's separate property interest to the extent it is unprotected by section 4800.2's formula for reimbursing separate property contributions to community assets. Under section 4800.2, only $17,500 would be credited as Esther's separate property; the remaining $150,000 would be attributed to the community.

Legislative intent, however, is only one prerequisite to retroactive application of a statute. Having identified such intent, it remains for us to determine whether retroactivity is barred by constitutional constraints. We have long held that the retrospective application of a statute may be unconstitutional if it is an ex post facto law, if it deprives a person of a vested right without due process of law, or if it impairs the obligation of a contract. See *In re Marriage of Bouquet* (1976) 16 Cal. 3d 583, 592 [128 Cal. Rptr. 427, 546 P.2d 1371].

Retroactive application of section 4800.1 would operate to deprive Esther of a vested property right without due process of law. (Cal. Const., art. I, §7.) At the time of trial, Esther had a vested property interest in the residence as her separate property. (Cf. *Bouquet, supra*, 16 Cal. 3d at p. 591; *Addison v. Addison* (1965) 62 Cal. 2d 558, 566 [43 Cal. Rptr. 97, 399 P.2d 897, 14 A.L.R.3d 391].) The law had long recognized that "separate property . . . [might] be converted into community property or *vice versa* at any time by oral agreement between the spouses. [Citations.]"

The Buols had such an agreement as to Esther's earnings and the home she purchased and maintained with those earnings. "The status of property as community or separate is normally determined at the time of its acquisition." Such status is not dependent on the form in which title is taken.

At all relevant times — when Esther purchased the home, during trial and when the trial court entered judgment for Esther — proof of an oral agreement was all that was required to protect Esther's vested separate property interest. Section 4800.1's requirement of a writing evidencing the parties' intent to maintain the joint tenancy asset as separate property operates to substantially impair that interest.

While the Legislature generally is free to apply changes in rules of evidence or procedure retroactively when no vested rights are involved, it is not so unrestrained when these changes directly affect such rights. (See, e.g., *Augustus v. Bean* (1961) 56 Cal. 2d 270 [14 Cal. Rptr. 641, 363 P.2d 873] [no vested right in remedy in place prior to contribution by joint tortfeasors]; *Owens v. Superior Court* (1959) 52 Cal. 2d 822 [345 P.2d 921, 78 A.L.R.2d 388] [no vested right in more limited scope of preamendment long arm statute]; *San Bernardino County v. Indus. Acc. Com.*, *supra*, 217 Cal. 618 [amendment designed to prevent injured employee from realizing double recovery impairs no substantive right]; *Los Angeles v. Oliver* (1929) 102 Cal. App. 299 [283 P. 298] [vested right to just compensation in condemnation proceeding not affected by change in method of computing amount due].)

Applied retroactively, section 4800.1 unquestionably is substantive. A statute is substantive in effect when it "imposes a new or additional liability and substantially affects existing rights and obligations." Section 4800.1 imposes a statute of frauds where there was none before, penalizing the unwary for relying upon the law as it existed at the time the property rights were created rather than at the time dissolution proceedings were already underway. This paradoxical approach is aptly illustrated by the *Martinez* court's gratuitous offer to remand that case "in fairness to [the husband] . . . for a hearing at which he shall have the opportunity to prove a written agreement in accordance with section 4800.1." (*Id.*, 156 Cal. App. 3d at p. 30.) Understandably, the court refrains from suggesting just how the husband might go about creating the document that is missing solely because it was never required to prove a separate property interest under former law.

The statute does much more than simply articulate the means by which the community property presumption might be rebutted. Insofar as it applies retroactively, the statute imposes an irrebuttable presumption barring recognition of the vested separate property interest. In the case at bar, and all similar proceedings instituted prior to January 1, 1984, the time for executing a written agreement as to the character of joint tenancy marital property has long passed. By eliminating the means by which one might prove the existence of the vested property right, imposing instead an evidentiary requirement with which it is impossible to comply, section 4800.1 affects the vested property right itself.

In this respect, section 4800.1 is virtually indistinguishable from the "substantive" measure considered in *Vegetable Oil Products Co.* v. *Superior Court* (1963) 213 Cal. App. 2d 252 [28 Cal. Rptr. 555], which also purported to impose a writing requirement after the fact. In that case, a worker, injured while completing a project on Vegetable Oil's premises, brought suit against Vegetable Oil for personal injury. The trial court denied Vegetable Oil's motion to file a cross-complaint against the employer for indemnification based on the employer's contributory negligence, because Labor Code section 3864, adopted after the injured worker filed suit, barred such indemnity absent a written indemnification agreement predating the injury.

The Court of Appeal reversed, concluding that retroactive application of the statute would contravene due process. (*Id.*, at p. 258.) Because the parties' legal relationship was established on the date of the injury, Vegetable Oil's indemnification rights accrued before the legislation became effective. "'Where a statute operates immediately to cut off an existing remedy and by retroactive application deprive a person of a vested right, it is ordinarily invalid because it conflicts with the due process clauses of the federal and state constitutions.'" (*Ibid.*, quoting *California Emp. etc. Com. v. Payne* (1947) 31 Cal. 2d 210, 215 [187 P.2d 702]. Accord *Wells Fargo & Co. v. City etc. of San Francisco* (1944) 25 Cal. 2d 37, 41 [152 P.2d 625]; *Wexler v. City of Los Angeles* (1952) 110 Cal. App. 2d 740, 747 [243 P.2d 868].)

Notwithstanding the language used in section 4800.1, that measure imposes the same impossible burden declared to be unconstitutional in *Vegetable Oil Products*. In each instance, the party attempting to assert a vested right is precluded from doing so by imposition of a writing requirement long after any opportunity to obtain such a writing has passed. To the extent that section 4800.1 makes such insurmountable demands on vested property rights, that it does so under the guise of an evidentiary rule is of little avail. Applied retroactively, section 4800.1 is a substantive measure which directly impairs vested property rights.

Section 4800.2's provision for reimbursement of the separate property contributions to what now is conclusively presumed to be community property regardless of the parties' intent, does little to neutralize section 4800.1's adverse effect on vested property rights. In the instant case, the trial court ruled that the $167,500 home was Esther's separate property. Retroactive application of the new statutory scheme would decrease that separate property interest to only $17,500. Esther would not be reimbursed for interest payments on the mortgage (which would have constituted virtually all of her monthly payments during the early years of the loan), taxes, insurance payments or maintenance costs. The remaining $150,000 would be credited to the community, an interest which arose only after judgment was entered by the trial court. Robert would thus receive a windfall of $75,000. Moreover, because the house represents the full extent of Esther's property, she would be forced to sell it to satisfy Robert's claim. As this case all too painfully demonstrates, section 4800.2 may provide only superficial protection against section 4800.1's potentially devastating impact upon vested property rights.

II

We turn to the question whether impairment of Esther's vested property right violates due process of law. Vested rights are not immutable; the state, exercising its police power, may impair such rights when considered reasonably necessary to protect the health, safety, morals and general welfare of the people. (*Bouquet, supra,* 16 Cal. 3d at p. 592.) In determining whether a given provision contravenes the due process clause we look to "the significance of the state interest served by the law, the importance of the retroactive application of the law to the effectuation of that interest, the extent of reliance upon the former law, the legitimacy of that reliance, the extent of actions taken on the basis of that reliance, and the extent to which the retroactive application of the new law would disrupt those actions." (*Ibid.*)

Where "retroactive application is necessary to subserve a sufficiently important state interest," the inquiry need proceed no further. In *Bouquet,* where we validated retroactive application of an amendment to Civil Code section 5118 making the postseparation earnings of both spouses, not just those of the wife, separate property, we emphasized that "[t]he state's interest in the equitable dissolution of the marital relationship supports this use of the police power to abrogate rights in marital property that derived from the patently unfair former law."

In *Bouquet* we identified an important state interest in the "equitable dissolution of the marital relationship" and stressed that retroactive application was necessary to remedy "the rank injustice of the former law." Thus, these cases support the proposition that the state's paramount interest in the equitable dissolution of the marital partnership justifies legislative action abrogating rights in marital property where those rights derive from manifestly unfair laws. ([2d]) No such compelling reason exists for applying section 4800.1 retroactively. Section 4800.1 cures no "rank injustice" in the law and, in the retroactivity context, only minimally serves the state interest in equitable division of marital property, at tremendous cost to the separate property owner.

[W]e can infer that the Legislature's primary motivation in enacting section 4800.1 was to promote the state's interest in equitable distribution of marital property upon dissolution. We are at a loss to explain, however, how retroactive application of the statute is "necessary to subserve" that interest.

Retroactive application of the writing requirement does not advance the goal of insuring equitable division of community property where, as here, the asset in question is the separate property of one spouse. Moreover, because the writing requirement only applies to joint tenancy property, it fails to achieve uniformity in the division of marital property. ([9]) The presumption that property taken as "husband and wife" is community property (§5110) may still be rebutted by evidence of a contrary oral agreement. Nontitle property acquired during marriage is presumed to be community property (§5110), but may be proved otherwise by tracing alone.

Thus, whether or not a spouse will be able to prove that certain property is separate may well depend on happenstance alone. The Legislature and the courts have long been aware that "'husbands and wives take property in joint tenancy without legal counsel but primarily because deeds prepared by real estate brokers, escrow companies and by title companies are usually presented to the parties in joint tenancy form. . . .' [Citation.]" (*Lucas, supra*, 27 Cal. 3d at p. 814.) ([2e]) Given the lack of uniformity in treatment of marital property presumptions, it seems manifestly unfair to apply section 4800.1 to penalize one marital partner after all is said and done, for making an uninformed legal decision at the insistence of a real estate agent, where retroactivity of the statute advances no sufficiently compelling state interest.

We conclude that retroactive application of section 4800.1 would substantially impair Esther's vested property right without due process of law. The state interest in equitable dissolution of the marital partnership is not furthered by retroactive effect. Retroactivity only serves to destroy Esther's legitimate separate property expectations as a penalty for lack of prescience of changes in the law occurring after trial. Due process cannot tolerate such a result.

The judgment is affirmed.

BIRD, C.J., MOSK, J., KAUS, J., BROUSSARD, J., GRODIN, J., and LUCAS, J., concurred.

Discussion Questions

1. How would the Buols' home be characterized if their oral agreement was recognized? What if a written agreement were required?

2. If the home was characterized as community property, would the right to reimbursement in §2640(b) help Esther Buol?

3. Why is it unconstitutional to apply the writing requirement and the reimbursement right retroactively?

---

2. New Mexico Legislation

In the case of *Swink v. Fingado,* the New Mexico Supreme Court was asked by the United States Court of Appeals to resolve the question of the retroactivity of legislation that changed to the definition of community property to included joint tenancy. That legislative amendment stated that "property acquired by a husband and wife by an instrument in writing . . . as joint tenants . . . will be presumed to be held as community property unless such property is separate property. . . ." The issue certified to the New Mexico Supreme Court would determine the extent of the property subject to the bankruptcy court's jurisdiction and thus the creditors of the married couple, the Fingados. The New Mexico decision highlights the differences between joint tenancy and community property and explains how to determine whether a change in the law should be applied retroactively.

SWINK v. FINGADO

115 N.M. 275, 850 P.2d 978 (1993)
Supreme Court of New Mexico

MONTGOMERY, Justice.

The United States Court of Appeals for the Tenth Circuit certified to this Court the following question of New Mexico law:

> Do the 1984 amendments to §40-3-8 N.M.S.A.1978 (as enacted), apply retroactively so as to convert property acquired by husband and wife as joint tenants prior to the passage of the amendments, and thus originally held as separate property, into community property which would be included in the bankruptcy estate?

Swink v. Sunwest Bank (In re Fingado), 955 F.2d 31, 32 (10th Cir. 1992).

The 1984 amendments referred to in the question were contained in an act passed by the legislature that year, 1984. Section 1 of the act ("the 1984 Act") amended NMSA 1978, Subsection 40-3-8(A) (Repl. Pamp. 1983), to delete from the definition of "separate property" the phrase "each spouse's undivided interest in property owned in whole or in part by the spouses as co-tenants in joint tenancy or as co-tenants in tenancy in common." Section 1 of the 1984 Act also amended Subsection 40-3-8(B) by adding the following sentence to the definition of "community property" in that subsection: "Property acquired by a husband and wife by an instrument in writing whether as tenants in common or as joint tenants or otherwise will be presumed to be held as community property unless such property is separate property within the meaning of Subsection A of this section."

Section 2 of the 1984 Act amended one of the sections of Article 2 of the Probate Code, dealing with the subject of intestate succession and wills. That section, NMSA 1978, Section 45-2-804, is headed "Death of spouse; community property" and provides that upon the death of either spouse one-half of the community property belongs to the surviving spouse and the other half is subject to the testamentary disposition of the decedent. The 1984 amendment added this clause: "except that *community property that is joint tenancy property* under Subsection B of Section 40-3-8 NMSA 1978 shall not be subject to the testamentary disposition of the decedent." Subsection 45-2-804(A).

The effect of the 1984 amendments, then, was to make clear that marital property which is not separate property under Subsection 40-3-8(A), even though acquired by the spouses through an instrument designating them as joint tenants, is presumed to be held as community property and that such property may be *both* community property *and* joint tenancy property, in which case it is not subject to the testamentary disposition of either spouse. In other words, under the 1984 amendments the right of survivorship — the principal attribute of joint tenancy property, *Trimble v. St. Joseph's Hospital (In re Trimble's Estate)*, 57 N.M. 51, 54, 253 P.2d 805, 807 (1953) — continues to inhere in community property that is joint tenancy property.

For the reasons explained and subject to the qualification noted in this opinion, we answer the Tenth Circuit's question in the affirmative. We hold that property acquired before 1984 by a husband and wife through an instrument designating them as joint tenants is presumed to be held as community property, even though it may also be held as joint tenancy property.

I

The properties in question were acquired by Mr. and Mrs. Fingado in 1964 and 1969. The parcel acquired in 1964 was located on Vermont Street in Albuquerque, New Mexico, and was purchased for rental purposes; the other parcel was located on Rio Grande Boulevard in Albuquerque and was purchased as the Fingados' residence. Both properties were conveyed to "H.S. Fingado and Valetta Ruth Fingado, his wife, as joint tenants." The record contains no evidence as to whether the funds used to make the purchases were community or separate in character.

In 1987, an involuntary petition in bankruptcy was filed against the Fingados under Chapter 7 of the United States Bankruptcy Code. The petition was later dismissed as to Mrs. Fingado. In October 1989, the Trustee in bankruptcy, Harley H. Swink, sold the property on Vermont Street but retained the proceeds pending an adjudication of the rights of the parties to those proceeds.

Two months later, the Trustee petitioned the bankruptcy court for authority to sell the property on Rio Grande Boulevard. Mrs. Fingado objected to this sale, claiming a one-half interest in the property. She also claimed one-half of the proceeds from the sale of the Vermont Street property. She asserted that both properties were joint tenancy properties and that, under Bankruptcy Code Subsections

363(h) and (j), her one-half interest as a joint tenant in the proceeds from the sales of the properties was her separate property and not property of the bankruptcy estate.

The Trustee, on the other hand, alleged that both properties were community property of the bankrupt debtor, Mr. Fingado, and his spouse and that the interests of both spouses were therefore property of the bankruptcy estate under Subsection 541(a)(2) of the Bankruptcy Code. Mrs. Fingado concedes that if she and her husband held the properties as community property, both her interest and his became the property of the bankruptcy estate under Subsection 541(a)(2) and the proceeds from the sales of the property are distributable, under Subsection 726(c) of the Bankruptcy Code, to holders of community claims against the Fingados. It is now undisputed that all creditors asserting claims against Mr. Fingado are creditors of the community.

In asserting that the Vermont Street and Rio Grande Boulevard properties were community property, the Trustee relied on Subsection 40-3-8(B), as amended by the 1984 Act. Mrs. Fingado disputed the applicability of this statute; she argued that the 1984 amendment did not apply retroactively to change the status of the properties, which, at the time of their acquisition (she maintained), were separate, not community, property.

The United States Bankruptcy Court for the District of New Mexico applied Subsection 40-3-8(B), as amended; determined that Mrs. Fingado had failed to overcome the presumption in the subsection that the properties, although held in joint tenancy, were community property; and held that, as community property, they were part of the bankruptcy estate and not subject to any claim that Mrs. Fingado would otherwise have as a co-owner. The bankruptcy court accordingly authorized the sale of the Rio Grande Boulevard property, which, pursuant to Bankruptcy Code Subsection 363(i), Mrs. Fingado purchased for $320,000 less her homestead exemption of $20,000, for a net purchase price of $300,000.

Mrs. Fingado appealed to the United States District Court for the District of New Mexico, which reversed the bankruptcy court's judgment and ordered payment to Mrs. Fingado of one-half of the net sales proceeds from both properties. The district court did not issue an opinion in connection with its judgment, but apparently took the view that the New Mexico Legislature had not intended that the 1984 amendments to Subsection 40-3-8(B) would operate retroactively. The court therefore held that the properties were each spouse's separate property when acquired and remained such at the time they were sold. The Trustee appealed to the Court of Appeals for the Tenth Circuit, which certified to us the question noted at the beginning of this opinion.

In their briefs to the Tenth Circuit (which have been submitted to us) and in their arguments here, the parties take essentially the same positions that they argued before the bankruptcy court and the federal district court. Mrs. Fingado relies principally on the thoroughly entrenched principle of New Mexico community property law that property acquired by a married couple takes its status as community or separate property at the time of its acquisition, and on the similarly well-accepted propositions that a statute applies retroactively only when there is clear legislative intent that it should do so, and that when a statute affects vested or substantive rights, it is presumed to operate prospectively only. The Trustee responds that this Court's task is the familiar one of construing a statute — *i.e.*, determining legislative intent — so that we must answer the question: Did the 1984 legislature intend that the 1984 Act would operate retrospectively when it created a new presumption that, even when property is acquired and held in joint tenancy, the property is *both* community *and* joint tenancy property? The Trustee points to various indicia of legislative intent which, he asserts, demonstrate an intent to apply the 1984 amendments retroactively to property previously acquired by a husband and wife as joint tenants.

[1] For the reasons that follow, we basically agree with the Trustee's position. Property acquired through an instrument establishing, or indicating ownership in, joint tenancy, even though acquired before 1984 and even though having the legal incident of the right of survivorship, is nonetheless presumed to be community property — a presumption which can be rebutted by showing that the property is properly characterized as separate property as defined by Subsection 40-3-8(A).

II

We begin by discussing some of the history of the 1984 amendments. In 1972, effective July 1, 1973, the people of New Mexico adopted the Equal Rights Amendment to our Constitution: "Equality of rights under law shall not be denied on account of the sex of any person." N.M. Const. art. II, §18. In order to implement the amendment with respect to our community property laws, the legislature enacted the Community Property Act of 1973. *See generally* Anne K. Bingaman, *The Community Property Act of 1973: A Commentary and Quasi-Legislative History*, 5 N.M. L. Rev. 1 (1974). To comply with the Equal Rights Amendment, the 1973 Act significantly changed several of this state's community property laws by eliminating property-law distinctions based on gender.

* * *

[W]e see that the 1973 New Mexico Legislature enacted several measures dealing with a spouse's interest in property held in joint tenancy form. First, that interest was defined as the spouse's separate property, even though the asset in which he or she held the interest may have been acquired with community funds or may have been otherwise traceable to community property. Second, to forestall any possible argument that this characterization of the interest had all of the characteristics of true separate property, the legislature expressly preserved the survivorship incident of joint tenancy property. Third, recognizing that, owing to the practices of banks, title companies, and others — as well perhaps as to the preference of many married couples to hold their assets in a form enabling the survivor to receive full ownership without the intervention of probate in the event of one spouse's death — the legislature treated as community property, for debt satisfaction purposes, *all* property in which the spouses held equal undivided interests as joint tenants (or tenants in common) and, for purposes of transfers of property, likewise required joinder by each spouse for *all* property in which the spouses were cotenants. Thus, the 1973 legislature came close to recognizing the "hybrid" form of property ownership (community property in joint tenancy form) that had been advocated in California several years before. The stage was thus set for adoption of the amendments in the 1984 Act.

As we have seen in the introduction to this opinion, the 1984 legislature deleted from the definition of "separate property" in Subsection 40-3-8(A) the phrase "each spouse's undivided interest in property owned in whole or in part by the spouses as cotenants in joint tenancy or as cotenants in tenancy in common." The subsection now reads:

> A. "Separate property" means:
>
> . . . .
>
> (5) property designated as separate property by a written agreement between the spouses, including a deed or other written agreement concerning property held by the spouses as joint tenants or tenants in common *in which the property is designated as separate property.*

NMSA 1978, §40-3-8(A) Then, as also noted at the beginning of this opinion, the 1984 legislature added this sentence to Subsection (B) of Section 40-3-8:

> Property acquired by a husband and wife by an instrument in writing whether as tenants in common or as joint tenants or otherwise will be presumed to be held as community property unless such property is separate property within the meaning of Subsection A of this section.

1984 N.M. Laws, ch. 122, §1. And finally, the legislature in the 1984 Act made the other changes referred to at the beginning of this opinion and that will be referred to below.

The question, as certified to us by the Tenth Circuit Court of Appeals, is: Were these changes intended to operate retroactively so as to apply to property acquired before their enactment?

III

We begin with the proposition, stressed by Mrs. Fingado, that "New Mexico law presumes a statute to operate prospectively unless a clear intention on the part of the legislature exists to give the statute retroactive effect." The very statement of this proposition demonstrates (by use of the word "presumes") that it is a rule or canon of statutory construction, not an inflexible determinant of legislative intent. Several reiterations of the principle by our Court of Appeals confirm this view of the rule as one of statutory construction.

If the statute expressly declared that it was to be applied prospectively only, we would of course give it that effect. Conversely, if it expressly stated that it was to operate retroactively, we presumably would abide by that statement (absent some constitutional objection). The 1984 Act does not declare the legislature's intent, one way or the other. Legislative silence is at best a tenuous guide to determining legislative intent, so we start with a presumption that the legislature intended the 1984 Act to operate prospectively only — but our search cannot, or should not, end there.

"[T]he prospective application of a newly enacted act to [a preexisting and ongoing transaction] must also be determined by the words of the statute, the legislature's intent in enacting the statute, and by the public policy considerations which are evident from the statute." We interpret "the legislature's intent in enacting the statute" to mean the purpose of the new law — the objective the legislature has sought to accomplish. Other state courts have applied a similar approach in construing a statute not expressly declared to be either retroactive or prospective in effect.

Based on our review of the legislative history preceding the 1984 Act and of the parties' briefs in this case, we discern two primary purposes of the 1984 Act. The first purpose, as indicated by the title of the Act, was to "clarify" kinds of property under the community property laws then in effect. The second purpose—a much narrower and more specific purpose—was to make it clear that, under the law as so clarified, joint tenancy property held by spouses could be characterized as community property so that, upon the death of either, the survivor's tax basis in the entire property would increase (or decrease, as the case might be) to the fair market value of the property at the time of the deceased spouse's death.

A

As to the first purpose, we have already seen how the Community Property Act of 1973 created something of an amalgam between community property and joint tenancy concepts. We have nothing but high praise for the drafters of the 1973 Act in implementing the Equal Rights Amendment, but the result of their efforts to accommodate revised community property law concepts with the realities of the ways in which married people hold property in modern society left certain questions unanswered.

If most marital property held in joint tenancy was subject to the same strictures as applied to community property, did not the 1973 Act create—or come close to creating—a "hybrid" form of community property in joint tenancy form? Given the ways in which most married couples acquire and hold property—not just real property, but bank accounts, stocks and bonds, and other assets commonly held in the names of both spouses and joined by the word "or"—was there any reason not to give legal recognition to an undeniable fact of modern life: that many married couples hold their community assets in joint tenancy form so as to achieve the objective, if one of them dies, of vesting ownership of those assets in the survivor?

We believe that the legislature intended to answer these and similar questions, at least in part, by recognizing a new species of community property called, "community property that is joint tenancy property."

It is an accepted principle of statutory construction in other states that a statute which clarifies existing law may properly be regarded as having retroactive effect. Although we have found no New Mexico cases enunciating this principle, it is articulated in several opinions of our sister states. *See, e.g., Tomlinson v. Clarke,* 118 Wash. 2d 498, 825 P.2d 706, 713 (1992) (en banc) ("When an amendment clarifies existing law and where that amendment does not contravene previous constructions of the law, the amendment may be deemed curative, remedial and retroactive."); *GTE Sprint Communications Corp. v. State Bd. of Equalization,* 1 Cal. App. 4th 827, 2 Cal. Rptr. 2d 441, 444-45 (1991) ("Where a statute or amendment clarifies existing law, such action is not considered a change because it merely restates the law as it was at the time, and retroactivity is not involved.").

Applying this principle in the present case is somewhat problematic, because the law in New Mexico at the time the 1973 Act was enacted, and probably afterwards, seems to have differentiated fairly sharply between the civil-law form of property

ownership known as community property and the common-law estates of joint
tenancy and tenancy in common. . . .

[T]his Court and our Court of Appeals have frequently expressed the view, or
taken it for granted, that joint tenancy property is a species of separate property and
that to convert community property into separate property, including joint tenancy
property, and vice versa, a husband and wife must "transmute" their property from
one form into the other.[14]

On principle, however, and as a practical matter, there is no good reason why the
incidents of community property should be regarded as altogether inconsistent with
the incidents of joint tenancy property. In fact, our statutes, while perhaps not
expressly or impliedly recognizing that these two forms of ownership may overlap,
certainly do not preclude their coexistence in the same property at the same time.
Although, as noted earlier, joint tenancy is one of the common-law estates incorporated into the law of this state from English law, it is now, and has been since 1971,
defined by statute:

> A joint tenancy in real property is one owned by two or more persons, each owning the
> whole and an equal undivided share, by a title created by a single devise or conveyance,
> when expressly declared in the will or conveyance to be a joint tenancy, or by
> conveyance . . . from husband and wife when holding as community property or otherwise
> to themselves or to themselves and others, when expressly declared in the conveyance to
> be a joint tenancy. . . .

This statute, which embraces the classical "four unities" of time, title, interest,
and possession, certainly covers a deed to a husband and wife conveying real property, acquired by them with community funds and intended to be part of their
community estate, even though the same instrument conveys title in joint tenancy.
Each spouse owns the whole and an equal undivided share, and each has taken a
single title through a single conveyance.

Can it be seriously contended that a married couple who have placed their community funds in a joint checking or savings account, or who have invested in stocks
or bonds carrying the familiar "JTWROS" designation, or who have registered a
family automobile in joint tenancy, have thereby "transmuted" those funds from
community property into the separate property of each of them, so that legal principles relating to community property no longer apply to that property?

The chief incident of joint tenancy is the right of survivorship. The chief, or one
of the chief, incidents of community property lies in the duty of the district court on

---

14. The terms "transmute" and "transmutation" are thoroughly embedded in our community property law and the law of other community property states, but the terms have unfortunate connotations.
Although the word "transmute" is defined simply as "to change or alter in form, appearance, or nature:
convert," another definition is "to change into another substance or element" especially gold or silver.
Webster's Third New International Dictionary 2430 (Philip B. Gove, ed. 1976). The dictionary definitions refer
to the efforts of ancient alchemists to transform base metals into gold or silver, and in this sense the term
"transmutation" has acquired an almost metaphysical or "mystical sounding" connotation. *See* Robert
E. Clark, *Transmutations in New Mexico Community Property Law,* 24 Rocky Mtn. L. Rev. 1, 2 (1952). It is as
though community property were some kind of substance into which (or from which) another
substance — separate property — could only be converted by some kind of mysterious process. We
expressly disclaim any such "mystical" use of the term. Transmutation is simply "a general term used
to describe arrangements between spouses to convert property from separate property to community
property and vice versa." *Allen v. Allen,* 98 N.M. 652, 654, 651 P.2d 1296, 1298 (1982) (citing William
A. Reppy & William de Funiak, *Community Property in the United States* 421 (1965)).

dissolution of the spouses' marriage to divide the property equally. This has always been the law in New Mexico, *see Beals v. Ares, 25 N.M. 459, 499-500, 185 P. 780, 793 (1919)*; community property is not the separate property of either or both spouses, whether it is held in joint tenancy or not. The 1984 legislature was on sound ground in clarifying this as the law in New Mexico and, we believe, intended to apply the 1984 amendments to *all* community property acquired by spouses as joint tenants, no matter when acquired.

[Discussion of Tax Purpose Omitted]

D

The subject of possible constitutional infirmity of applying the 1984 Act retroactively brings us to Mrs. Fingado's other principal criterion for determining legislative intent: the rule that when a statute affects vested or substantive rights, it is presumed to operate prospectively only. Citing *Ranchers State Bank v. Vega* and *Ashbaugh v. Williams*, 106 N.M. 598, 599, 747 P.2d 244, 245 (1987), Mrs. Fingado points out that the presumption of prospective-only effect may be constitutionally required, especially if applying a newly enacted law retrospectively would diminish rights or increase liabilities that have already accrued. *See also Rubalcava v. Garst*, 53 N.M. 295, 206 P.2d 1154 (1949) (statute requiring writing cannot be constitutionally applied to bar cause of action based on oral contract formed prior to statute's enactment).

We note first that the presumption of prospective-only effect when "vested" or "substantive" rights are affected, like the presumption obtaining when the legislature does not clearly express its intent, is just that-a *presumption*, a rule or canon of statutory construction to aid in determining legislative intent when that intent is not specifically declared. Therefore, all of the indicia of the legislature's intent discussed earlier in this opinion apply to the presumption now under consideration. However, if a valid constitutional objection exists to applying the 1984 Act retroactively, our inquiry is at an end; obviously we cannot construe the Act as applying retroactively if that construction would run afoul of the Constitution.

But we do not think that the 1984 Act violates the Constitution, and this for two reasons: First, we do not believe that the 1984 amendments, if applied retroactively to Mr. and Mrs. Fingado's properties acquired in 1964 and 1969, diminished or otherwise altered Mrs. Fingado's rights in the properties. Second, even if some diminution or alteration occurred, it is an accepted principle of constitutional law that the legislature can alter, retroactively, the incidents of marital property in the exercise of its police power and in recognition of the state's strong interest in governing the relationships between married persons.

When the Fingados acquired the properties, assuming they had all of the characteristics of true joint tenancies and none of the characteristics of community property, either joint tenant could have conveyed his or her fractional interest without the consent of the other. There is no question that characterizing the Fingados' properties as community property under the 1984 amendments, even though those properties were held in joint tenancy for purposes of survivorship, altered Mrs. Fingado's rights in this respect. However, that alteration had already occurred, years before passage of the 1984 Act. As we have seen, under the 1973 Act

Mr. Fingado's joinder was required for all transfers or mortgages, or contracts to transfer or mortgage, "any interest in community real property and separate real property owned by the spouses as cotenants in joint tenancy or tenancy in common." Subsection 40-3-13(A).

Similarly, there might have been a question in 1964 or 1969 whether Mrs. Fingado's interest in the joint tenancy properties would have been liable for her and her husband's community debts. Again, however, this question was answered expressly in the 1973 Act, as amended in 1975, under which "[c]ommunity debts [are] satisfied first from all community property and all property in which each spouse owns an undivided equal interest as a joint tenant or tenant in common. . . ." Subsection 40-3-11(A).

Mrs. Fingado suggests that the 1973 Act might have unconstitutionally altered her rights, and possibly increased her liabilities, as a joint tenant in property acquired before 1973. The constitutionality of the 1973 Act, however, is not before us in connection with the question certified by the Tenth Circuit; and, even if it were, we would be loath to hold that the 1973 Act, which had the purpose and effect of ridding our law of unconstitutional distinctions (perhaps under the Equal Protection Clause and certainly under the Equal Rights Amendment) between property owners based on their sex, was itself unconstitutional. We believe that the 1973 Act, as well as the amendments thereto in the 1984 Act, represented competent and proper exercises of the legislature's lawmaking power to prescribe the incidents of marital property, as we shall now explain.

Professor Bingaman notes that a California commentator has concluded that "there is no substantial constitutional objection today to retroactive amendment of presumptions in community property law. . . ." In the *California Law Review*, Barbara N. Armstrong, *"Prospective" Application of Changes in Community Property Control — Rule of Property or Constitutional Necessity?*, 33 Cal. L. Rev. 476 (1945), Professor Armstrong's basic thesis was:

> "Vested rights, of course, may be impaired 'with due process of law' under many circumstances. The state's inherent sovereign power includes the so called 'police power' right to interfere with vested property rights whenever reasonably necessary to the protection of the health, safety, morals, and general well being of the people. . . .
>
>   . . . .
>
> "The constitutional question, on principle, therefore, would seem to be, not whether a vested right is impaired by a marital property law change, but whether such a change reasonably could be believed to be sufficiently necessary to the public welfare as to justify the impairment."

[Many] of the principles espoused in the theory find strong support in New Mexico law and that the theory therefore provides still another basis for our holding that the 1984 Act applies retroactively to property acquired before its passage. In *Wiggins v. Rush*, for example, we said:

> The State of New Mexico has a vital interest in the marital status. This interest is clearly expressed in our statutory framework concerning the marital status, including its creation, dissolution, and the methods by which the parties to the marriage can hold property. It is this vital state interest in the marital status that distinguishes the marriage relationship from other contractual relationships. . . .

. . . New Mexico's interest in the protection of the family relationship, as expressed in our statutes, indicates that the state deems itself an interested party when the community estate and the marriage itself are affected.

83 N.M. at 138, 489 P.2d at 646.

It is, after all, in large part a *presumption* we are dealing with in this case-the presumption added by the 1984 amendment as the second sentence in Subsection 40-3-8(B); and presumptions and other remedial measures are the stuff of which retroactivity is made. The presumption is consistent with and reinforces the long-standing, basic presumption of New Mexico community property law, now contained in Subsection 40-3-12(A), that property acquired during marriage is community property. The presumption established by the 1984 amendment is rebuttable by showing that property is separate property under Subsection 40-3-8(A), that it was acquired by either spouse before marriage or by gift, bequest, devise, or descent.

It is well settled that when a spouse merely places his or her separate property into joint tenancy with the other spouse, without an intention to make a gift or otherwise transmute the separate property into a true joint tenancy in which each spouse has an undivided one-half interest, the property retains its character as separate property. By the same token, property which *is* community property-because it has been acquired during marriage and is attributable, for example, to the earnings of one or both spouses, retains its character as such and is not "converted" from the community property of both spouses into the separate property of either or both,[21] absent persuasive evidence that the parties intended to transmute their community property into separate property. The presumption in the second sentence of Subsection 40-3-8(B) reaffirms this basic tenet of community property law, while recognizing that such community property can be held in joint tenancy to achieve the survivorship feature of that form of ownership.

IV

We do not perceive our holding as working any injustice upon Mrs. Fingado. Under Subsection 40-3-11(A), her interests in the Vermont Street and Rio Grande Boulevard properties were subject to payment of the Fingados' community debts (subject to applicable exemptions), whether those properties were deemed community property or property in which each spouse owned an undivided equal interest as a joint tenant. Our holding is that under the 1984 amendments to this state's community property statutes, the properties were properly characterized as

---

21. It is in this sense that we qualify our affirmative answer to the Tenth Circuit's question. The 1984 amendments to §40-3-8 did not necessarily "convert" property originally held as separate property into community property; in a very real sense, the property may be regarded as having been community property all along. No evidence was adduced in the bankruptcy court or the district court as to the source of the funds used to acquire the properties or that the properties may have been classifiable as separate property under §40-3-8(A), so the presumption in §40-3-8(B) was applicable and the properties were properly regarded as the Fingados' community property.

community property and were therefore included in the bankruptcy estate under Subsection 541(a)(2) of the Bankruptcy Code.

IT IS SO ORDERED.

BACA and FROST, JJ., concur.

Discussion Questions

1. How did New Mexico Legislature treat joint tenancy property before the 1984 Act? How did the 1984 Act change the treatment of joint tenancy property?

2. What was the New Mexico Supreme Court's rationale for applying the 1984 Act retroactively? How does that differ from the California Supreme Court's rationale in *Marriage of Buol*?

3. How does the New Mexico Supreme Court resolve the constitutional issue of retroactive application diminishing Mrs. Fingado's substantive rights or increasing her liability?

D. COMMUNITY PROPERTY WITH RIGHT OF SURVIVORSHIP

The tension between the concepts of common law title joint tenancy and community property has led to an increasing number of community property states to recognize a "hybrid" form of property: "community property with right of survivorship" or the short-hand term "survivorship community property." In 1987, the Texas Legislature passed legislation that recognized that "spouses may agree between themselves that all or part of their community property, then existing or to be acquired, becomes the property of the surviving spouse on the death of a spouse."[2] Earlier, Nevada has passed legislation mandating that community property with right of survivorship could arise through "an instrument expressly declaring" that form of title.[3] Arizona and California followed with Idaho being the most recent to enact legislation recognizing survivorship community property in real property in 2008.[4]

The reasons for the legislation recognizing this new form of community property go beyond the differences between common law and community property.

---

2. Act of August 28, 1987, ch. 297, 1987 Tex. Laws 715. See Tex. Probate Ann. Code §439 (Vernon 2003). Since 1881, Washington has permitted spouses to create, by a standard community property agreement, survivorship community property. Rev. Code Wash. §26.16.120.

3. Nev. Rev. Stat. §111.064 (1981).

4. Idaho Code Ann. §15-6-401 (effective July 1, 2008), Ariz. Rev. Stat. §14-1201(28), Cal. Civ. Code §682.1 (2001).

Traditionally, joint tenancy was a way of avoiding probate because the property passed by operation of law to the surviving spouse. Survivorship community property would also avoid probate by the right of survivorship. With the increased value of homes before the "housing bubble" burst in 2008, there was a realization that there was a distinct tax disadvantage to holding property as joint tenancy. Since community property at death held a tax advantage, state legislatures moved to provide that tax advantage through the creation of survivorship community property.

As explained by retired Probate Commissioner Don Ashworth who was involved in passage of Nevada's survivorship community property legislation, "The big advantage of the Community Property with Right of Survivorship is that there is no probate and in the event the property has appreciated in value, there will be a step up in basis for Federal Income Tax purposes on both halves of the real property equal to the fair market value of the property at that time. When dealing with joint tenancy property however, there will be only a step up in basis on one-half of the fair market value of the entire property of the first joint tenant, instead of the full value."[*] He explains this in an example which we can apply to our hypothetical couple, Harry and Wanda, who purchases a condo for $100,000, paying cash. The basis for income tax purposes (for determining capital gains tax) is $100,000. Assume that the condo appreciates to $180,000. Assume that Harry dies at that time. If the condo is titled as survivorship community property, the condo is not subject to probate and also because it is community property, the basis for the property is stepped up to $180,000 which is the value at Harry's death. If Wanda then sells the condo for $180,000, she does not have to pay capital gains tax on the $80,000 appreciation. If the condo is titled as joint tenancy, the step up is based on Harry's portion of the condo, which is one-half. Since the appreciation was $80,000, only $40,000 will be stepped up, making the value at the time of Harry's death, $140,000. The other $40,000 of appreciation will be subject to capital gains tax. Thus, survivorship community property represents a significant tax advantage over joint tenancy for a surviving spouse.

Because joint tenancy and community property cannot actually exist in the same property at the same time, the Texas legislature, courts, and voters struggled with how to resolve the conceptual conflict. The conflict was resolved through a constitutional amendment allowing community property to pass upon death to the surviving spouse and subsequent legislation to set standards for how spouses could establish that right of survivorship. Unintended consequences of those actions are played out in the case of *Holmes v. Beatty*, 290 S.W.3d 852 (Tex. Sup. Ct. 2009).

HOLMES v. BEATTY

290 S.W.3d 852 (2009)
Supreme Court of Texas

Chief Justice JEFFERSON delivered the opinion of the Court.

After decades of debate in the bench, bar, and the Legislature about the ability of spouses to obtain rights of survivorship in community property, Texas citizens

---

[*]Don W. Ashworth, "Perspectives from the Retired Probate Commissioner: Nevada Laws and Procedures in a New Light," 15 April Nev. Law 10 (2006).

changed the constitution to confirm that right. The 1987 amendment provides that "spouses may agree in writing that all or part of their community property becomes the property of the surviving spouse on the death of a spouse." TEX. CONST. art. XVI, §15. Two years later, the Legislature enacted Probate Code sections 451 through 462 to address the formalities necessary to the create a survivorship arrangement. *See* TEX. PROB. CODE §§451-62. Today we are asked to determine how these sections operate with respect to rights of survivorship in certain brokerage accounts and securities certificates issued from those accounts. We conclude that the account agreements and certificates at issue here created rights of survivorship. Accordingly, we reverse and render in part and affirm in part the court of appeals' judgment.

I.   FACTUAL AND PROCEDURAL BACKGROUND

Thomas and Kathryn Holmes married in 1972. During their marriage, Thomas and Kathryn amassed over ten million dollars in brokerage accounts and acquired securities certificates issued from those accounts. Kathryn died in 1999. Her will appointed Douglas Beatty, her son from a previous marriage, as the independent executor of her estate. Thomas died approximately nine months later. His son, Harry Holmes II ("Holmes"), also from a previous marriage, was appointed independent executor of his estate. The accounts and certificates were variously listed as "JT TEN"; "JT TEN *defined as* 'joint tenants with right of survivorship and not as tenants in common'"; "JTWROS"; and "Joint (WROS)." If those acronyms and definitions establish a right of survivorship, then Thomas acquired 100% upon Kathryn's death, and upon his death, the holdings would have passed under his will, which left nothing to Kathryn's children. If those designations were insufficient to create survivorship interests then, as community property, only 50% would have passed to Thomas, with the remaining 50% of the accounts and certificates passing under Kathryn's will, which left nothing to Thomas's children.

Beatty sought a declaration that all of the assets were community property; Holmes countered that the assets passed to Thomas through survivorship, and then to Thomas's beneficiaries following his death. On competing motions for summary judgment, the trial court concluded that some of the assets were held jointly with survivorship rights and others were community property. In two opinions, the court of appeals affirmed in part, reversed and rendered in part, and remanded for further proceedings. 233 S.W.3d 475, 494; 233 S.W.3d 494, 522-23. Holmes and Beatty petitioned this Court for review, which we granted. 52 Tex. Sup. Ct. J. 149 (Dec. 4, 2008). Because these two appeals involve "substantially similar facts, arguments, and briefing," we have consolidated them into a single opinion and judgment.

II.   DEVELOPMENT OF RIGHTS OF SURVIVORSHIP IN COMMUNITY PROPERTY IN TEXAS

A.

The Hilley *Era*

Texas has not always allowed spouses to create rights of survivorship in community property. In *Hilley v. Hilley*, 161 Tex. 569, 342 S.W.2d 565, 568 (1961), we held that it was unconstitutional for spouses to hold community property with rights of survivorship. The dispute in *Hilley* concerned whether stock purchased with community funds and "issued in the names of the husband and wife 'as joint tenants with rights of survivorship and not as tenants in common'" actually conferred rights of survivorship. *Id.* at 566. We reasoned that because this property was acquired during marriage with community funds and thus "by definition became community property," it was required to pass either under the decedent's will or under the intestacy statutes, absent a written agreement signed by the spouses partitioning the stock from their community property, thereby making it separate property. *Id.* at 568. We noted that to hold otherwise would directly contravene the constitution's community property provision. *Id.*

After *Hilley*, the Legislature amended the Probate Code in an attempt to recognize survivorship rights in community property. Act of April 27, 1961, 57th Leg., R.S., ch. 120, §1, 1961 Tex. Gen. Laws 233, *amended by* Act of May 22, 1969, 61st Leg., R.S., ch. 641, §3, 1969 Tex. Gen. Laws 1922, 1922 ("It is specifically provided that any husband and his wife may, by written agreement, create a joint estate out of their community property, with rights of survivorship."). In *Williams v. McKnight*, 402 S.W.2d 505, 508 (Tex. 1966), we considered the amendment's constitutionality. Citing *Hilley*, we held that any statutory attempt to grant survivorship rights in community property would be unconstitutional. *Id.* ("Constitutional limitations are as binding upon the Legislature as they are upon the Judiciary."). We reaffirmed that the only way for a couple to create survivorship rights was to partition their community property into separate property, then execute survivorship agreements for that separate property. *Id.* at 508. This process came to be known among practitioners as the "Texas Two-Step." *See, e.g.,* Robert N. Virden, *Joint Tenancy with Right of Survivorship & Community Property with Right of Survivorship*, 53 Tex. B.J. 1179, 1179 (1990). Subsequent decisions echoed this result. *See, e.g., Allard v. Frech*, 754 S.W.2d 111, 115 (Tex. 1988) ("This holding is based on a firmly rooted principle of community property law which requires the actual partition of community property before a valid joint tenancy with the right of survivorship can be created."); *Maples v. Nimitz*, 615 S.W.2d 690, 695 (Tex. 1981) (same).

B.

The 1987 Constitutional Amendment and Subsequent Legislation

In 1987, the Legislature passed, and the Texas voters approved, a constitutional amendment authorizing rights of survivorship in community property. Tex. S.J. Res. 35, 70th Leg., R.S., 1987 Tex. Gen. Laws 4114, 4114-15. The amendment provided that "spouses may agree in writing that all or part of their community property becomes the property of the surviving spouse on the death of a spouse." Tex. Const. art. XVI, §15. Two years later, the Legislature passed Senate Bill 1643, which added Part 3 to Chapter XI of the Probate Code concerning non-testamentary transfers. This new section governs "[a]greements between spouses regarding rights of survivorship in community property." Tex. Prob. Code §46(b).

Probate Code sections 451 and 452 are at issue in this case. Section 451 states: "At any time, spouses may agree between themselves that all or part of their community property, then existing or to be acquired, becomes the property of the surviving spouse on the death of a spouse." *Id.* §451. Section 452 lays out these requirements:

An agreement between spouses creating a right of survivorship in community property must be in writing and signed by both spouses. If an agreement in writing is signed by both spouses, the agreement shall be sufficient to create a right of survivorship in the community property described in the agreement if it includes any of the following phrases:

1. (1) "with right of survivorship";
2. "will become the property of the survivor";
3. "will vest in and belong to the surviving spouse"; or
4. (1) "shall pass to the surviving spouse."

An agreement that otherwise meets the requirements of this part, however, shall be effective without including any of those phrases. *Id.* §452. The Legislature stated that these agreements do not change the nature of community property: "Property subject to an agreement between spouses creating a right of survivorship in community property remains community property during the marriage of the spouses." *Id.* §453. With this constitutional amendment and legislation, the Legislature hoped to finally resolve the battle over survivorship rights in community property. The proponents urged that these sorts of agreements were common in other states and simplified the transfer of certain assets to surviving spouses. *See* Gerry W. Beyer, 10 Texas Practice Series: Texas Law of Wills §60.1 (3d ed. 2002). As Professor Beyer noted, a community property survivorship agreement "is a simple, convenient and inexpensive method for many married people to achieve an at-death distribution of their community property that is in accord with their intent." *Id.* §60.9.

As the amendment's drafters noted at the time, "[m]any Texas spouses hold a substantial amount of assets in a form that is ineffective to achieve their desired purpose." Senate Judiciary Comm., Resolution Analysis, Tex. S.J. Res. 35, 70th Leg., R.S. (1987). Supporters argued that the proposed constitutional amendment would "eliminate a trap for the unwary married couple who would execute a signature card provided by a financial institution and believe, mistakenly, that they have created an effective joint tenancy with right of survivorship in relation to their community property." Texas Legislative Council, Analyses of Proposed Constitutional Amendments And Referenda, Info. Report, No. 87–2 at 36 (Sept. 1987).

The purpose of the amendment and accompanying legislation, then, was to provide "[a] simple means . . . by which both spouses by a written instrument can provide that the survivor of them may be entitled to all or any designated portion of their community property without the necessity of making a will for that purpose." Senate Judiciary Comm., Resolution Analysis, Tex. S.J. Res. 35, 70th Leg., R.S. (1987). As the committee observed, "many banks and savings and loans associations have often failed to provide forms by which their customers can create effective joint tenancies out of community property." *Id.* The amendment addressed these concerns by removing the constitutional hurdles to creating rights of survivorship in community property.

III. Application

The assets at issue in this case fall into two categories: (1) securities accounts and (2) securities certificates issued from those accounts. These two categories of assets are affected by distinct legal analyses, so we address each in turn.

A. THE SECURITIES ACCOUNTS

Thomas and Kathryn Holmes maintained investment accounts with multiple financial institutions. Each of them was governed by an account agreement that dictated terms, such as who could manage the accounts and whether the accounts were held with rights of survivorship.

1. Accounts Agreements With a "JT TEN" Designation

At the time of Kathryn's death, the Holmeses held two investment accounts whose agreements included the designation "JT TEN": one with Dain Rauscher, Inc. and another with First Southwest Company. Thomas and Kathryn opened the Dain Rauscher account in 1994. The account agreement, titled "JOINT ACCOUNT AGREEMENT" was styled "THOMAS J. HOLMES AND KATHRYN V. HOLMES, JT TEN." The agreement gave the account holders an option to strike through "paragraph (a) or (b) whichever is inapplicable." Paragraph (a) stated "it is the express intention of the undersigned to create an estate or account as joint tenants with rights of survivorship and not as tenants in common." Paragraph (b) gave the account holders the option to designate who would receive the interest in the account upon their death and the percentages each recipient would receive. The Holmeses struck neither provision. They both signed the agreement, and "Jt. Ten" appeared next to Kathryn's name on the signature line.

The Holmeses opened the First Southwest Account in 1997. The account agreement listed their names as "THOMAS J. HOLMES, KATHRYN V. HOLMES JT TEN." The agreement did not define "JT TEN" and did not include any further discussion of survivorship rights. Both Thomas and Kathryn signed the First Southwest account, as well.

The court of appeals held that neither of these agreements "clearly reflect[ed] intent to own the account with a right of survivorship." 233 S.W.3d 475, 481; *see also* 233 S.W.3d 494, 505. As to the Dain Rauscher account, the court noted that because the couple did not strike through paragraph (a) or (b), the agreement "did not affirmatively reflect any intent to effect a non-testamentary transfer — through a right of survivorship or otherwise." 233 S.W.3d 475, 481. The court also rejected Holmes's argument that the "JT TEN" designation on the agreements satisfied section 452's requirements: the "mere inclusion of 'JT TEN' next to Kathryn's and Thomas's names in the account title did not sufficiently convey intent to create a right of survivorship." *Id.* at 483. The court agreed with Beatty's argument that "parties may own property as joint tenants without being subject to a right of survivorship." *Id.*; 233 S.W.3d 494, 505.

We disagree with the court of appeals on each point. A joint tenancy carries rights of survivorship. *See, e.g., U.S. v. Craft,* 535 U.S. 274, 280, 122 S. Ct. 1414, 152 L. Ed. 2d

437 (2002) ("The main difference between a joint tenancy and a tenancy in common is that a joint tenant also has a right of automatic inheritance known as 'survivorship.' Upon the death of one joint tenant, that tenant's share in the property does not pass through will or the rules of intestate succession; rather, the remaining tenant or tenants automatically inherit it."). Contrary to Beatty's and the court of appeals' assertion then, a joint tenancy cannot be held without rights of survivorship; such a joint agreement would be a tenancy in common. *See Craft*, 535 U.S. at 280, 122 S. Ct. 1414; 7 POWELL ON REAL PROPERTY §51.01[1] ("[A joint tenancy] is distinguished from a tenancy in common principally by the right of survivorship."). The financial industry's use of "joint tenancy" is also consistent with this view. *See, e.g.*, SEC. TRANSFER ASSOC., *Guidelines of the Securities Transfer Association* AV-1 (Oct. 2005) (defining "Joint Tenancy" as a "[f]orm of ownership where two or more individuals hold shares as joint tenants with right of survivorship. When one tenant dies, the entire tenancy remains to the surviving tenants. JOHN BROWN & MARY BROWN JT TEN.").

* * *

Section 439(a) requires that a survivorship agreement between non-spouses use either the statute's language or a substitute that is "in substantially the [same] form." TEX. PROB. CODE §439(a). Section 452 is less restrictive, presumably because agreements between spouses are less vulnerable to fraud. The constitutional amendment permitting survivorship agreements in community property was intended to facilitate the creation of such agreements, and the Legislature's use of less confining language comports with that goal.

Precedent, trade usage, and seminal treatises make clear that joint tenancies carry rights of survivorship, and the Holmeses' agreement included this designation. This does not fully answer, however, the inherent tension in owning community property as "joint tenants." Professor Reed Quilliam noted in an article published shortly after the constitutional amendment and statutes were adopted that "[j]oint tenancy is a form of separate property ownership and is wholly incompatible with community property concepts." *See* W. Reed Quilliam, Jr., *A Requiem for* Hilley: *Is Survivorship Community Property a Solution Worse than the Problem?*, 21 TEX. TECH L. REV. 1153, 1167 (1990). In the same discussion, though, Professor Quilliam predicted that situations like this case were likely to arise:

> It is likely that misconceptions about the new form of property ownership will result in instances of spouses agreeing to hold community property "as joint tenants with right of survivorship" rather than merely "with right of survivorship." What will be the effect of such designation?
>
> Manifestly the property will remain community, although the spouses' agreement to hold with right of survivorship should be given effect to impress *this* characteristic on it. The property *cannot* be joint tenancy property, a form of separate property ownership, unless it has first been rendered separate by partition. The agreement of the spouse violates the constitution insofar as it seeks to establish a joint tenancy in community property. But the agreement to hold such property with right of survivorship is now constitutionally sanctioned.

Id. at 1168-69 (emphasis in original). We agree with Professor Quilliam. A "joint tenancy" or "JT TEN" designation on an account is sufficient to create rights of survivorship in community property under section 452. The Dain Rauscher and First Southwest accounts included this designation, and we "give effect to the written expression of the parties' intent." *Balandran v. Safeco Ins. Co. of Am.*, 972 S.W.2d 738, 741 (Tex. 1998). Because the "JT TEN" designation was sufficient to indicate the Holmeses' intent to hold those accounts with rights of survivorship, we reverse the court of appeals' judgment on the Dain Rauscher and First Southwest accounts.

B. THE SECURITIES CERTIFICATES

At the time of Kathryn's death, the Holmeses also held securities in certificate form issued from accounts once held with Kemper Securities and Principal/Eppler, Guerin & Turner. We must determine, then, whether the Kemper Securities and Principal account agreements established rights of survivorship. The Kemper account agreement was titled "JOINT ACCOUNT WITH RIGHT OF SURVIVOR-SHIP" and was signed by both spouses. This meets the test we established above to create rights of survivorship in an investment account. The agreement for the account held with Principal/Eppler, Guerin & Turner listed the Holmeses' names as "Thomas J. Holmes & Kathryn V. Holmes JTWROS" and was signed by both. This agreement, too, established rights of survivorship in the account. Because both of these accounts were held with rights of survivorship, so too were the certificates issued from those accounts. Accordingly, we reverse the court of appeals' judgment as to these securities.

IV. CONCLUSION

The 1987 constitutional amendment and accompanying legislation sought to facilitate the creation of rights of survivorship in community property and eliminate the constitutional hurdles spouses faced when attempting to establish such rights. The Holmeses' account agreements clearly indicated their intent to create rights of survivorship in those accounts. The rights were not lost when the Holmeses later obtained some of their investments in certificate form. Pursuant to these survivorship agreements, each of the accounts and certificates at issue in this case passed to Thomas upon his wife's death, and then by will to Thomas's beneficiaries when he died. If the Holmeses had wished an alternate devise, they could have made appropriate provisions in their respective wills. As they did not, we reverse and render in part and affirm in part the court of appeals' judgment. TEX. R. APP. P. 60.2(a), (c).

Discussion Questions

1. What was the Texas Supreme Court's constitutional objection to legislative attempt to create survivorship community property?

2. Under the present survivorship legislation, Tex. Probate Code, §§451-452, how can spouses create survivorship community property? *written agreement signed by both phrases or the like*

their intent was clearly communicated

3. Why did the Court determine that Thomas and Kathryn Holmes had complied — with the requirements for creating survivorship community property and was the result fair? *-not really*

The final issue is how survivorship community property should be treated during marriage and at divorce. The most logical way for courts to treat this new form of property title is to ignore the "right of survivorship" during an ongoing marriage. The right of survivorship does not become effective until death and therefore should not change the way the property is treated during marriage.

↳ @ divorce, community property

PROBLEM 5.1

Philip and Estelle met at a get-together for widowers and widows. Philip had two adult children and Estelle had an adult daughter. When they married, Philip sold his home. With the proceeds, they bought another home which they took in joint tenancy. However, Philip wanted to make sure that his adult children would receive the home if he died before Estelle. If Estelle died first, he wanted to receive the home via the right of survivorship. Therefore, in his will he specified that "all interests in my property, both community and separate, will go to my children." Recently, Philip died. His children claim that under Philip's will, they have a right to one-half of the home if community property and the whole home if it is separate property. Estelle claims that she owns the home because of the survivorship provision of joint tenancy. How would an Idaho court resolve this dispute? Who will receive the home?

PROBLEM 5.2

Frank and Gwen met at art exhibition of Gwen's paintings. Gwen was a successful artist and Frank was an aspiring jazz pianist. They were attracted by their mutual creative talents. They married soon after and found a wonderful condo where they could both pursue their careers. It already had great light for painting and Frank, who was very handy, made one room soundproof so he could practice without bothering Gwen or their neighbors. Since Gwen had sold one of her paintings for $500,000 before they married, they were able to buy the condo for cash. They were advised that the best way to take the title was "joint tenancy" so that if either died, the survivor would receive the condo without going through probate. They took the title as suggested. After about two years, their marriage suffered because Frank was often away on a concert tour. They are contemplating divorce. How would an Arizona court characterize and divide the condo? How would a California court characterize and divide the condo?

PROBLEM 5.3

The California Legislature passed an amendment to Family Code §2640. The amendment provided that there was a right to reimbursement of the separate property contributions of one spouse to improve the separate property of the other spouse. The right to reimbursement could be established by tracing to the separate property funds used for the improvement. The purpose of the amendment was (1) to make it consistent with the right to reimbursement of separate funds to community property and (2) to be consistent with the expectations of married couples upon divorce. The amendment reversed prior law that separate property funds were a gift to the other spouse. The amendment went into effect January 1, 2011, and is silent on retroactivity.

Mark and Nancy married in 2005. At that time, Nancy owned a home in Palm Desert, California. Mark loved to swim and in 2006 he received an inheritance from his grandfather of $25,000. They decided to use the money to put a swimming pool at the Palm Desert home. They have recently decided to divorce. Mark is claiming reimbursement of the funds used for the swimming pool based on the 2011 amendment. Nancy is claiming that the 2011 amendment is not retroactive and the funds used for the swimming pool were a gift to Nancy. How would a California court decide? A New Mexico court?

Table 5-1
Joint Titles in Community Property States

State	Rule	Case/Statute
Arizona	Joint tenancy is considered separate property but is treated as community property at divorce and can be divided equitably Title can be held as "community property with right of survivorship"	A.R.S §25-318(A). *Toth v. Toth*, 190 Ariz. 218, 946 P.2d 900 (1997). A.R.S. §14-1201(28)
California	Joint tenancy is presumed to be community property at divorce, the community property presumption can be rebutted by a written agreement or a clear statement in the deed Title can be held as "community property with right of survivorship"	Cal. Family Code §2581. Cal. Civil Code §682.1 (2001)
Idaho	Title can be held as "community property with right of survivorship"	*Estate of Ashe*, 753 P.2d 281 (1988), Idaho Code §15-6-401 (2008)
Louisiana	No recognition of joint titles, joint ownership is designated as "ownership in indivision"	La. Civil Code, art. 797 (1991)
Nevada	Joint tenancy deed is presumed to be joint tenancy, separate property of each spouse, but can be justly and equitably divided at divorce, Title can be held as "community property with right of survivorship"	Nev. Rev. Stat. §125.150(1(b), Nev. Rev. Stat. §111.064, *Fick v. Fick*, 109 Nev. 458, 851 P.2d 445 (1993)
New Mexico	Joint tenancy is presumed to community property, unless there is a deed or written agreement in which property is designated as separate property.	West's N.M. Stat. §40-3-8

Texas	Community property may be held as joint tenancy and will carry the right of survivorship	Texas Const. art. XVI, §15 (1987), Texas Probate Code §451-452 (1989), *Holmes v. Beatty*, 290 S.W.3d 852 (2009)
Washington	Joint tenancy interests are presumed to be community property, a joint tenancy that is severed is presumed to be community property. Survivorship community property allowed by agreement.	Wash. Rev. Code §64.28.040, §26.16.120
Wisconsin	Transfer of separately owned property into joint tenancy changes the character of ownership in the entire property into marital property that is subject to division at divorce. Joint tenancy and survivorship marital property are available in Wisconsin. Creation of joint tenancy requires a marital agreement.	Wis. Stat. §§767.255(2), 766.58-766.60, *Steinmann v. Steinmann*, 309 Wis. 2d 29, 749 N.W.2d 145 (2008)

Chapter 6

Pursuing an Advanced Degree: Ownership or Equity?

A. EDUCATIONAL DEGREES

Let us return to our hypothetical couple Michael and Lisa. They both have jobs in the healthcare field. Lisa is a nurse and Michael works in a hospital in medical records. Lisa decides to pursue a medical degree with the hopes of becoming a pediatrician. Michael supports the idea and they agree that he will continue working to support them while Lisa goes to medical school. Fast forward to the time after Lisa receives her medical degree and finishes her internship and residency. Her rigorous schedule has taken a toll on their marriage. They have separated and Lisa files for divorce. Michael comes to an attorney for advice. He feels that he has sacrificed so that they could share in the increased earnings that Lisa will be able to receive as a doctor. He feels that it is unfair that the time and effort and work that he expended to pursue their joint dream of a better life will not be realized.

This common scenario represents two major issues in community property: (1) whether the degree is community property that can be divisible at divorce; and (2) whether the supporting spouse receives reimbursement for his or her contributions while the student spouse was obtaining the degree. The former has essentially been resolved by all of the community property states. Although an educational degree may enhance the earning capacity of the student spouse, and ultimately the community, courts have determined that since an educational cannot be sold, transferred, or assigned to anyone else, it is personal to the holder and therefore cannot be considered divisible property at divorce. For example, in *Wisner v. Wisner* (Arizona 1981), the Arizona Court of Appeals held that education is considered an intangible property right, and as such, is not characterized as property that can be divided at divorce. Similarly, California, Louisiana, New Mexico, and Texas hold that educational degrees are not subject to community property distribution. Washington has gone the furthest, and in fact declined to determine whether an educational degree is even property. Instead, Washington employs an equitable remedy not based upon the characterization of the property, but rather on what is just and fair at divorce in the division of property and an award of maintenance. See *Washburn v. Washburn* (Washington 1984).

In *Muckleroy v. Muckleroy*, 84 N.M. 14, 498 P.2d 1357 (1972), the New Mexico Supreme Court was faced with determining whether the husband's medical license was separate or community property. For the license to be considered community property, the court noted that it must possess the attribute of joint ownership. Because a medical license is only earned and issued to one spouse, authorizing only that individual to practice medicine, it is not the subject of joint ownership, and therefore is separate property. An educational degree falls into the same category. In fact, no community property state has held that an educational degree or license is property divisible at divorce.

The more difficult challenge facing courts is how to fashion a remedy for the supporting spouse who contributed long hours and hard work so that the student spouse could receive the degree. Because the degree follows the holder, if divorce occurs soon after the degree is attained, the supporting spouse basically receives nothing at divorce. While the student was in school, it is highly unlikely that they have accumulated any significant community property. In addition, the supporting spouse would probably not be eligible for spousal support because that spouse was already working during the marriage. So there have been several approaches to solving this particular inequity. In those states that have equitable division of community property at divorce, the supporting spouse's efforts are a relevant factor in dividing their property at divorce. Unfortunately, that remedy is often inadequate due to the lack of accumulated property. The courts then struggle to find alternative ways to compensate the supporting spouse's contribution to the student spouse's education. For instance, Washington notes that maintenance may be an option if there is little property to divide. Arizona, Idaho, Nevada, and Texas also consider education as a factor in dividing community property.

Other states have used a "reimbursement" mechanism to compensate the supporting spouse for contributions made to enable the student spouse to attain a degree or training. Louisiana authorizes an award to the supporting spouse for the financial contributions made during the marriage to the education or training of his spouse that increased that spouse's earning power. California has devised a similar method that reimburses the community for community contributions to the education or training of the spouse whose education substantially enhanced the earning capacity of the student spouse.

Arizona and Texas are at opposite extremes of the equity scale. Although both take the education into account when equitably dividing community property, Arizona goes beyond that to fashion a remedy based on unjust enrichment. If the student spouse is unjustly enriched, Arizona courts have authorized restitution to the supporting spouse for financial contributions for both living expenses and direct educational expenses. Since Texas does not recognize an educational degree as property divisible at divorce, reimbursement of contributions to that degree is unavailable. Contributions have to be to property to be reimbursed. Therefore, in Texas, only property division is available as a remedy and that may be limited in the scenario of divorce soon after the degree is attained.

A lawyer advising Michael would have to research the remedy available in the state where the spouses lived. If they were in an equitable division state like Arizona, Idaho, Nevada, Texas, and Washington, support of the student spouse who attained an educational degree that enhanced earning capacity would be a factor that may result in an additional share of community property to the supporting spouse.

However, it is unlikely to be sufficient if the divorce occurred soon after the student spouse received the degree. Michael could then attempt other remedies to balance the inequity because of Michael's dashed expectations of sharing in Lisa's enhanced earning capacity. Reimbursement of financial contributions to expenses for the education might be a possibility in some states like California and Louisiana. In Arizona, restitution of financial contributions for living expenses may be available as well. When reading the cases in this Chapter, consider whether any of the remedies are a substitute for sharing in the enhanced earning capacity that an advanced degree promises.

B. CONTRIBUTION OF SUPPORTING SPOUSE A FACTOR IN EQUITABLE DISTRIBUTION: THE WASHINGTON REMEDY

Washburn v. Washburn (Washington 1984) reflects how Washington treats educational degrees. In this consolidated case, both wives, who supported their families while their husbands attended veterinary school, sought compensation for their financial contributions. The Supreme Court of Washington ruled that the wives' contributions to their husbands' educations were relevant considerations in making an equitable distribution of property under Wash. Rev. Code §26.09.080. This code allows courts to divide property not by their character as separate or community, but instead by what is just and equitable, taking into account relevant factors.

WASHBURN v. WASHBURN

101 Wash. 2d 168, 677 P.2d 152 (1984)
Supreme Court of Washington,
En Banc

DIMMICK, Justice.

When one spouse supports the other through professional school in the mutual expectation that the community will enjoy the financial benefit flowing from the resulting professional degree, but the marriage is dissolved before that benefit can be realized, should the supporting spouse be compensated? Our answer is yes. The contribution of the supporting spouse to the attainment of a professional degree by the student spouse is a factor to be considered in dividing property and liabilities pursuant to RCW 26.09.080, or in awarding maintenance pursuant to RCW 26.09.090. The Washburn court failed to consider Mrs. Washburn's contribution to her husband's education in any respect. We thus reverse and remand for consideration of the appropriate compensation due Mrs. Washburn. The Gillette court did value Mrs. Gillette's contribution to Mr. Gillette's education and supplemented its property division with a lump-sum award of $19,000, to be paid over time. We affirm this award.

I

A.   WASHBURN

The parties were married in 1971 while they were juniors at the University of Idaho. Upon their graduation in 1973, both parties worked. In the fall of 1974 they moved to Pullman, Washington so that Mr. Washburn could attend veterinary school at Washington State University. From the fall of 1974 until February 1978 Mr. Washburn attended classes and held summer and part-time employment. During this same period Mrs. Washburn worked full time. The parties then moved to Kentucky to allow Mr. Washburn to participate in an internship. Mr. Washburn received his degree in June 1978.

Upon Mr. Washburn's graduation the parties moved to Michigan where Mr. Washburn served an internship. Mrs. Washburn worked full time until their child was born in April 1979. In July 1979 the parties returned to Snohomish, where Mr. Washburn began practice as a veterinarian. They separated in January 1981 and a decree of dissolution was entered in June.

The trial court found that the parties' family home had been sold during the separation and the $4,400 proceeds equally divided. It awarded the remaining community property to the party in possession thereof (approximately $3,500 to Mrs. Washburn and $5,700 to Mr. Washburn) and required Mr. Washburn to pay all community debts, including educational loans. The trial court denied Mrs. Washburn's request for maintenance. The court also declined to characterize Mr. Washburn's degree as property, and refused to admit expert testimony which would have established the value of the degree through comparison of Mr. Washburn's earning potentials with and without it. Finally, it concluded that a judgment in favor of one spouse as against the other as compensation for contribution towards the cost of an education was impermissible.

Mrs. Washburn appeals that portion of the court's conclusion of law relating to Mr. Washburn's degree.

B.   GILLETTE

The parties were married in 1968. In 1970 they both contributed equally to the purchase of a ranch. The ranch operation, however, failed. In 1974 the parties agreed that Mr. Gillette should obtain a degree in veterinary medicine. The trial court, in an unchallenged finding of fact, found that at this time the parties both anticipated they would share equally in the expected increased earning capacity of Mr. Gillette and agreed to undertake the effort. The court in addition found that Mr. Gillette promised Mrs. Gillette that if she would support him during his years in school, she would never have to work again.

Mr. Gillette obtained his undergraduate degree in biology in 1978 from Eastern Oregon State College and was accepted into the veterinary college at Washington State University. The parties separated in October 1981. During Mr. Gillette's schooling and while the parties were together, Mrs. Gillette worked full time, contributing her income and money from a personal injury settlement. She turned down offers of job promotions so that she could move with her husband to

Washington State University. Mr. Gillette worked part time, and also received gifts from his father and disability payments. Mr. Gillette obtained his degree in veterinary medicine in 1982. A decree of dissolution was entered in March 1983.

The trial court found that the parties' lifestyle had been modest and their net worth diminished during the time Mr. Gillette had attended school. It affirmed the parties' own division of their community property (approximately $13,295 to Mrs. Gillette and $7,540 to Mr. Gillette). It charged Mr. Gillette with the educational loans incurred prior to and after separation. Mrs. Gillette agreed to pay past taxes.

The trial court concluded that neither the professional degree nor the increased earning capacity resulting from that degree were property subject to division. However, it awarded Mrs. Gillette a judgment of $19,000 as an "equitable right to restitution," which it calculated as follows:

> During the 7½-year period the Petitioner was in school, the Respondent contributed an excess of $24,000.00 to the community. It is reasonable to assume that she consumed one-half that amount. During that time she lived a more spartan life than would have otherwise been necessary. There is no source of funds at present from which to order immediate repayment. Inflation had a very dramatic effect upon the value of the dollar during the period of the Petitioner's schooling. Petitioner has therefore benefited from the $12,000.00 excess contribution. The wife is receiving property and liabilities with a net value of $8,800.00 more than one-half of the parties' net worth and that sum is therefore subtracted from $12,000.00, leaving a $3,200.00 deficit. An additional sum of $12,000.00 should be added to reimburse the wife for 7½ years of reduced living standards and a reduced opportunity to accumulate property. This is based upon the theory that if the Petitioner had worked full-time instead of going to school he would have at least equaled Respondent's earnings, and the Respondent would have benefited from one-half of that increased earning ability. In addition, the wife would have had better working conditions and security had she taken the promotions offered at the time. The $12,000.00 added to $3,200.00 equals $15,200.00. To adjust for inflation, the figure should be increased by 25%, which adds $3,800.00 for a total of $19,000.00.

Conclusion of Law 4, CP 75-76.

The trial court also found Mrs. Gillette was entitled to maintenance in the amount of $1 per year.

Mr. Gillette appeals from the portion of the decree requiring him to pay $19,000 and maintenance. Mrs. Gillette cross-appeals contending Mr. Gillette's increased earning capacity resulting from the education is property which should be valued and divided.

II

The cases at bar are representative of a situation which is so familiar as to be almost a cliche. A husband and wife make the mutual decision that one of them will support the other while he or she obtains a professional degree. The educational years will be lean ones for the family not only because of heavy educational expenses, but also because the student spouse will be able to earn little or nothing. Moreover, the supporting spouse may be called upon to postpone his or her own education or forgo promotions and other valuable career opportunities in order to find a job near the student spouse's school. These sacrifices are made in the mutual expectation that the family will enjoy a higher standard of living once the degree is obtained. But dissolution of the marriage intervenes. Because the family spent most of its financial resources on the degree, there may be few or no assets to be distributed. The student spouse has the degree and the increased earning potential that it represents, while the supporting spouse has only a dissolution decree.

A.

Other courts have responded to this all too common situation in a variety of ways. Some courts simply deny any recovery to the supporting spouse. Generally, these courts deny recovery because they cannot find a legal label for the requested award which seems to fit. Designation of the degree as "property" which may be valued and equitably divided is rejected because the degree, which cannot be sold, assigned or inherited, lacks the traditional attributes of property. Unjust enrichment, which would place a value on the supporting spouse's contribution, is rejected as inappropriate in the context of marriage, which is "more than an economic undertaking." Maintenance is rejected because the supporting spouse is capable of self-support. The ability to consider the supporting spouse's contribution in dividing marital assets is acknowledged, but proves useless because there are no assets.

B.

In view of the fact that fault is an impermissible consideration in a dissolution proceeding in this state, we are disinclined to compensate the supporting spouse under the theory of unjust enrichment. Unjust enrichment is a contract implied at law requiring a person to make restitution to the extent he has been unjustly enriched. Not only must the person be enriched, but the enrichment must be unjust. To require trial courts to determine whether the student spouse had been *unjustly* enriched by the efforts of the supporting spouse would invite the introduction of evidence as to who was at fault in the termination of the marriage before the fruits of the degree could be realized. Nor are we inclined to address at this time the somewhat metaphysical question of whether a professional degree is "property." However, we need not join the ranks of those courts which deny recovery. The liberal provisions of our Dissolution of Marriage Act, codified in RCW 26.09, provide a flexible way for courts to fairly compensate supporting spouses in the state of Washington.

When a person supports a spouse through professional school in the mutual expectation of future financial benefit to the community, but the marriage ends before that benefit can be realized, that circumstance is a "relevant factor" which must be considered in making a fair and equitable division of property and liabilities pursuant to RCW 26.09.080, or a just award of maintenance pursuant to RCW 26.09.090. A professional degree confers high earning potential upon the holder. The student spouse should not walk away with this valuable advantage without compensating the person who helped him or her obtain it.

We have said that the supporting spouse may be compensated through a division of property and liabilities. In many cases, however, the wealth of the marriage will have been spent towards the cost of the professional degree, leaving few or no assets to divide. Where the assets of the parties are insufficient to permit compensation to be effected entirely through property division, a supplemental award of maintenance is appropriate.

With respect to maintenance, we recognize that the spouse who is capable of supporting someone through school will in most cases also be capable of supporting him or herself after the marriage is dissolved. However, under the extremely flexible provisions of RCW 26.09.090, a demonstrated capacity of self-support does not automatically preclude an award of maintenance. Indeed, the ability of the spouse seeking maintenance to meet his or her needs independently is only *one* factor to be considered. RCW 26.09.090(1)(a). The duration of the marriage and the standard of living established during the marriage must also be considered, making it clear that maintenance is not just a means of providing bare necessities, but rather a flexible tool by which the parties' standard of living may be equalized for an appropriate period of time. RCW 26.09.090(1)(c), RCW 26.09.090(1)(d). Moreover, the factors listed in the statute are not exclusive. The trial court may consider the supporting spouse's contribution and exercise its broad discretion to grant maintenance, thereby in effect allowing the supporting spouse to share, temporarily, in the lifestyle which he or she helped the student spouse to attain.

In making an equitable property division or awarding maintenance, the trial court exercises broad discretionary powers. Its disposition will not be overturned on appeal absent a showing of manifest abuse of discretion. We are reluctant to encroach upon this discretion by providing a precise formula prescribing the amount of property to be distributed or maintenance to be awarded to the supporting spouse.

Instead, we direct the trial court to consider the following factors, among others, in determining the proper amount of compensation for the supporting spouse:

(1) The amount of community funds expended for direct educational costs, including tuition, fees, books, and supplies. We do not include living expenses incurred by the student spouse as a factor because those expenses would have existed regardless of whether the student spouse pursued a professional education.

(2) The amount which the community would have earned had the efforts of the student spouse not been directed towards his or her studies. By including this factor, we do not imply that parties to a marriage have a general duty to the community to realize their full economic potential. However, when the parties to a marriage make the joint decision that one spouse should obtain a professional degree or license, the community sacrifices not only the funds spent for direct educational or training costs, but also the earnings of the student spouse, if he or she would otherwise have been working. These sacrifices were made in the expectation that the community would receive financial benefit in the form of increased future earnings. When this expectation is frustrated by dissolution of the marriage, it would be inconsistent to permit the trial court to compensate the supporting spouse for the funds spent, but not the funds forgone.

(3) Any educational or career opportunities which the supporting spouse gave up in order to obtain sufficiently lucrative employment, or to move to the city where the student spouse wished to attend school.

(4) The future earning prospects of each spouse, including the earning potential of the student spouse with the professional degree.

Factors (1) and (2) reflect funds sacrificed by the community in order to obtain the education or training; accordingly, the supporting spouse should be awarded no more than his or her one-half interest therein. The trial court may take the effect of inflation during the educational years into account. Factor (3) is included to permit the trial court to adjust the property division or maintenance award as appears just and equitable, in light of the opportunities forfeited by the supporting spouse. Factor (4) simply applies to the present context the long-standing rule that the economic condition in which a dissolution decree leaves the parties is a paramount concern in determining issues of property division and maintenance.

We point out that where a marriage endures for some time after the professional degree is obtained, the supporting spouse may already have benefited financially from the student spouse's increased earning capacity to an extent that would make extra compensation inappropriate. For example, he or she may have enjoyed a high standard of living for several years. Or perhaps the professional degree made possible the accumulation of substantial community assets which may be equitably divided. However, our attention today is centered on the more difficult case of the marriage that is dissolved before the supporting spouse has realized a return on his or her investment in family prosperity.

Some might object that by recognizing the supporting spouse's right to compensation, we are treating marriage as a commercial enterprise. That is not our intent nor the result of this decision. Rather, as was well stated by the court in *Mahoney v. Mahoney*, 91 N.J. 488, 500, 453 A.2d 527 (1982):

> This Court does not support reimbursement between former spouses in alimony proceedings as a general principle. Marriage is not a business arrangement in which the parties keep track of debits and credits, their accounts to be settled upon divorce. Rather, as we have said, "marriage is a shared enterprise, a joint undertaking . . . in many ways it is akin to a partnership." But every joint undertaking has its bounds of fairness. Where a partner to marriage takes the benefits of his spouse's support in obtaining a professional degree or license with the understanding that future benefits will accrue and inure to both of them, and the marriage is then terminated without the supported spouse giving anything in return, an unfairness has occurred that calls for a remedy. (Citations omitted.)

Turning to the cases before us today, we note that Mrs. Gillette supported her husband through undergraduate and veterinary school in the mutual expectation that they would both share in the increased earnings which the veterinary degree would produce. Indeed, Mr. Gillette promised his wife that once he received his degree, she would never have to work again. These expectations were shattered when the parties separated only months before Mr. Gillette received his veterinary degree.

The parties agreed upon a division of community assets, leaving the trial court little opportunity to compensate Mrs. Gillette entirely through property division. To supplement the property division, the court awarded Mrs. Gillette $19,000 as an "equitable right to restitution," based upon her contribution to the attainment of the veterinary degree. The court made this lump-sum award payable over time, thereby reducing the burden on Mr. Gillette.

The trial court labeled its $19,000 award "restitution." However, because the award will be paid in installments, thereby equalizing the parties' standard of living for a limited time, it is in effect an award of lump-sum maintenance. Our concern is not the particular label applied to this award, but rather its fairness as determined by those factors set out in RCW 26.09.090.

The trial court calculated the amount of its award to Mrs. Gillette without the benefit of the four factors set forth as guidelines herein. However, RCW 26.09.090 places emphasis on the justness of an award, not its method of calculation. Here, Mrs. Gillette supported her husband through 7 1/2 years of school. She turned down offers of job promotions to follow him to Washington State University. Under these circumstances, we cannot say that the trial court's award of $19,000 was a manifest abuse of discretion.

Because the $19,000 award is in effect maintenance, the trial court's order requiring Mr. Gillette to pay maintenance in the amount of $1 per year is unnecessary and is reversed. We affirm, however, the portion of that same order which provides that the award shall not terminate upon Mrs. Gillette's remarriage or death, so that her right to receive the full $19,000 may be preserved.

We turn next to the Washburn case. Mrs. Washburn worked full time to support Mr. Washburn while he attended veterinary school. Less than 2 years after Mr. Washburn began practice as a veterinarian, the marriage was dissolved. Nevertheless, the trial judge concluded he was unable to compensate Mrs. Washburn for her contribution to her husband's education, stating:

> I don't believe that I am prepared, nor am I convinced I'd be authorized to make, enter a judgment in favor of one spouse as against the other as compensation, and that's really what we are speaking of, compensation for the broken, lost, destroyed hopes and aspirations that the parties had, either when they got married or during the early years of their marriage.
>
> In this case there is just nothing, no asset to divide. When and if our Supreme Court comes to the point of holding that I can make a division or can in effect make a division of future earning potential, separate and apart from any physical or tangible asset of the parties, maybe we will have a new approach to the dissolution, I do not feel prepared to innovate that type of approach. Oral Ruling of the court. CP 29-30.

Under our opinion today, Mrs. Washburn may be entitled to an award as compensation for her contribution to her husband's education. Such compensation may be effected through property division, maintenance, or a combination of both. Although Mrs. Washburn did not appeal from the trial court's denial of maintenance, she did appeal the broader issue of whether she was entitled to a judgment as compensation for her contribution towards the cost of her husband's education. We reverse the Washburn court's conclusion of law that a judgment as compensation for contribution towards the cost of an education is impermissible, and remand for consideration of the compensation due Mrs. Washburn.

Gillette is affirmed. Washburn is reversed in relevant part and remanded.

WILLIAM H. WILLIAMS, C.J., and STAFFORD, UTTER, BRACHTENBACH, DOLLIVER, DORE and PEARSON, JJ., concur.

This case involves the twin issues of characterization and valuation of a spouse's professional education. The majority declines to address whether the professional degree should be characterized as property, and simply holds that the expectation of future financial benefit derived from supporting a spouse through professional school is a relevant "factor" which must be considered in making a just and equitable division of property and liabilities or a just maintenance award. While I am in general agreement with this holding, I would characterize this interest as a marital asset in the context of increased earning capacity subject to distribution.

The majority's holding on the issue of valuation/recovery is limited to an award to the supporting spouse in the form of reimbursement and/or rehabilitative maintenance or property distribution. I do not agree that such an award is a just and equitable distribution of the assets of the community. I would hold that the value of the educational degree is measured by the increased earning capacity inherent in the particular education and as such is subject to a just and equitable distribution.

I

Support for characterizing the professional education degree as a divisible asset is found in other areas of intangible and speculative property rights considered to be divisible upon dissolution.

The accounting concept of goodwill, like an advanced professional degree, is by nature an asset with an elusive value. However, this court and the lower appellate courts have held that professional goodwill, although intangible and commonly defined as the expectation of continued public patronage, is a factor which has a value and should be included among the assets distributed upon a marriage dissolution. While the goodwill of a particular professional practice may not be marketable and the determination of its value difficult, it is nonetheless an asset of the community because it has a value to the professional spouse. The nonprofessional spouse, having contributed to the building of the professional practice through the provision of services, financial, domestic, or otherwise, has a valuable interest in the goodwill of the professional spouse's practice. The mere fact that goodwill is an amorphous asset and a value cannot be precisely determined is an improper basis for a court's refusal to acknowledge and to consider the existence of the goodwill value when dividing the value of a professional practice between spouses in a marital dissolution proceeding.

Methods of placing a value on professional goodwill vary according to the circumstances of each case. Factors considered when valuing the goodwill of a professional practice include the length of time that the professional spouse has practiced, the comparative success of the spouse's professional practice, the professional spouse's age and health, the past profits of the practice, the fixed resources of the practice, and the physical assets of the practice.

The crucial point for our inquiry is not the means by which goodwill is valued, but that a property interest is found in an intangible.

The divisibility of pension and retirement benefits of an employed spouse upon dissolution provides another analogy to support the proposition that the professional degree be considered an asset subject to distribution. Even though pension and retirement benefits normally are not mature, but are future interests, contingent future interests, or even expectancies, the benefits may have a value to both spouses that is capable of division as property.

In a wrongful death or a personal injury action, courts consistently have recognized the need to determine the value of a professional education in order to compensate fully a plaintiff for loss of future income. Damages in a personal injury or wrongful death action are unliquidated; no one fixed mathematical formula is used to decide each case. Rather, each case involves different facts, considerations, and probabilities to which courts cannot attempt to apply a formula. Instead, courts must assume that each situation is unique and recognize that a determination of damages involves some speculation, uncertainty, and arbitrariness. Courts, however, rarely deny a remedy for lost future earning capacity in a personal injury or wrongful death action merely because assessing future earning capacity involves the court in some speculation. We should be equally hesitant to deny relief to a nonstudent spouse who has lost the economic potential of the partial value of the education that she helped to provide.

A court easily can extend the tort concept of valuation of future earning capacity to a situation in which the supporting spouse will lose the economic benefits of the degreed spouse's education upon dissolution of the marriage. The nonstudent spouse will lose the same expectancy as the plaintiff will in the personal injury or wrongful death action.

A number of recent cases from sister jurisdictions have held that the supporting spouse is entitled to a distribution of increased earning potential for his or her support of the family while the other spouse obtained an education.

The leading case cited most often for the proposition that a professional degree is not property is the Colorado Supreme Court decision of *Graham v. Graham*, 194 Colo. 429, 574 P.2d 75 (1978), where by a sharply divided vote (4-3) that court held that an educational degree was not property capable of division in marriage dissolution proceedings. Nonetheless, the majority in *Graham* did conclude that a spouse's contributions to the acquisition of a professional degree could be considered in matters of alimony for support and maintenance and for property settlement where marital property existed to be divided. It should further be noted that the *Graham* majority, unlike Washington, appears to consider goodwill as not a community asset subject to distribution.

In *In re Marriage of Horstmann*, 263 N.W.2d 885 (Iowa 1978), the Iowa Supreme Court agreed with the pronouncement of the Colorado Supreme Court in *Graham* that a professional degree is not an asset to be considered in the distribution of the marital property. However, the court held that the increased earning potential made possible by the degree was an asset for distribution by the court. The court said, at page 891:

> We hold a trial court in a dissolution case where proper evidence is presented may consider the future earning capacities of both parties and in determining those capacities it may consider the education, skill or talent of both parties. This statement of principle, articulated in *Schantz* [*v. Schantz*, 163 N.W.2d 398 (Iowa 1968)], applies to the court's determination of an equitable distribution of assets and property and to a determination of whether alimony should be awarded and, if so, to the amount to be awarded. *In re Marriage of Beeh*, 214 N.W.2d 170, 174 (Iowa 1974).

ROSELLINI, Justice (dissenting).

In *Wisner v. Wisner*, 129 Ariz. 333, 631 P.2d 115, 122-23 (Ct. App. 1981), the court held that while an education itself is not properly subject to division in a dissolution of marriage proceeding, it is still a factor to be considered, in addition to others, in arriving at an equitable property division and in determining manner of spousal maintenance and child support:

> We agree with the majority opinion in *Graham* that education is an intangible property right, the value of which, because of its character, cannot properly be characterized as property subject to division between the spouses. In our opinion, the marital property concept simply "does not fit." However, while an *education* itself is not property subject to division, it is still a factor to be considered, in addition to others, in arriving at an equitable property division and in determining matters of spousal maintenance and child support. Thus, while education, along with the potential for greater earning capacity which can accompany it, is doubtless a factor to be considered by the trial judge in determining what distribution of property would be "equitable", and is even more obviously relevant upon the issue of spousal maintenance, it cannot be deemed property as such within the meaning of the Arizona statute.

(Citations omitted.) *Wisner*, at 340-41, 631 P.2d 115.

In *In re Marriage of Vanet*, 544 S.W.2d 236 (Mo. Ct. App. 1976), the court held that a professional education and right to practice in a particular field are in the nature of a financial resource and a realistic assessment properly entails consideration of anticipated earning capacity.

Recently the Court of Appeals of Michigan in *Woodworth v. Woodworth*, 126 Mich. App. 258, 337 N.W.2d 332, 334 (1983) held that the husband's law degree, which was the end product of a concerted family effort, was marital property subject to distribution upon dissolution of the marriage:

> The facts reveal that plaintiff's law degree was the end product of a concerted family effort. Both parties planned their family life around the effort to attain plaintiff's degree. Toward this end, the family divided the daily tasks encountered in living. While the law degree did not preempt all other facets of their lives, it did become the main focus and goal of their activities. Plaintiff left his job in Jonesville and the family relocated to Detroit so that plaintiff could attend law school. In Detroit, defendant sought and obtained full time employment to support the family.
>
> We conclude, therefore, that plaintiff's law degree was the result of mutual sacrifice and effort by both plaintiff and defendant. While plaintiff studied and attended classes, defendant carried her share of the burden as well as sharing vicariously in the stress of the experience known as the "paper chase."

We believe that fairness dictates that the spouse who did not earn an advanced degree be compensated whenever the advanced degree is the product of such concerted family investment. The degree holder has expended great effort to obtain the degree not only for him- or herself, but also to benefit the family as a whole. The other spouse has shared in this effort and contributed in other ways as well, not merely as a gift to the student spouse nor merely to share individually in the benefits but to help the marital unit as a whole.

Numerous other states have also granted relief to the supporting spouse based in part on increased earning capacity. *See, e.g., Moss v. Moss*, 639 S.W.2d 370 (Ky. Ct. App. 1982);

DeLa Rosa v. DeLa Rosa, 309 N.W.2d 755 (Minn. 1981); *Hubbard v. Hubbard*, 603 P.2d 747 (Okl. 1979); *O'Brien v. O'Brien*, 114 Misc. 2d 233, 452 N.Y.S.2d 801 (1982); *Daniels v. Daniels*, 20 Ohio Ops. 2d 458, 185 N.E.2d 773 (Ct. App. 1961). *See also* Ind. Code §31-1-11.5-11(c) (1980), *overruling Wilcox v. Wilcox*, 173 Ind. App. 661, 365 N.E.2d 792 (1977).

Accordingly, I would characterize the professional education as a marital asset in the context of increased earning capacity subject to distribution.

II

Having determined that the professional degree is an asset of the marital community, we must next determine in what method of valuation should be used to compensate the supporting spouse.

I reject the restitution and rehabilitation methods adopted by the majority. Application of these methods can be seen in the New Jersey decisions of *Mahoney v. Mahoney*, 91 N.J. 488, 453 A.2d 527 (1982); *Hill v. Hill*, 91 N.J. 506, 453 A.2d 537 (1982); *Lynn v. Lynn*, 91 N.J. 510, 453 A.2d 539 (1982).

An assumption that a professional education is solely a monetary purchase underlies the restitution and rehabilitation method of valuation. The court merely measures the supporting spouse's recovery by the amount of contributions to attainment of the degree and loss of earnings to the community while the student spouse is attaining an education, together with opportunities the supporting spouse has forgone.

This measure of recovery undercompensates the supporting spouse by completely ignoring the value of the professional education as a marital asset. Acquiring an education represents more than a mere monetary contribution and forfeiture of opportunity. Limiting the recovery to restitution and rehabilitation (lost opportunity) does not provide the supporting spouse his/her expectation of economic benefit from the career for which the education laid the foundation. The degree was a family investment, rather than a gift or benefit to the degree holder alone. *See Woodworth v. Woodworth*, 126 Mich. App. 258, 337 N.W.2d 332 (1983); Pinnel, *Divorce After Professional School: Education and Future Earning Capacity May Be Marital Property*, 44 Mo. L. Rev. 329, 335 (1979); Loper, *Horstmann v. Horstmann: Present Right to Practice a Profession as Marital Property*, 56 Den. L.J. 677, 689 (1979). A just and equitable distribution of this asset requires valuation of the increased earning capacity inherent in a professional education.

Placing a value on an individual's earning potential is not compensation for a failed expectation that the professional spouse would realize his/her full economic potential. Rather the valuation is upon the effect of the present right to practice a particular profession on the spouse's earning capacity. *See*, Note, *Family Law: Ought a Professional Degree Be Divisible As Property Upon Divorce?*, 22 Wm. & Mary L. Rev. 517 (1981); Comment, *The Interest of the Community in a Professional Education*, 10 Cal. W. L. Rev. 590 (1974).

The Michigan Court of Appeals set forth the relevant factors in valuing a professional degree:

[T]he length of the marriage after the degree was obtained, the sources and extent of financial support given plaintiff during his years in law school, and the overall division of the parties' marital property. In determining the degree's present value, the trial court should estimate what the person holding the degree is likely to make in that particular job market and subtract from that what he or she would probably have earned without the degree. *Recompense for Financing Spouse's Education: Legal Protection for the Marital Investor in Human Capital,* 28 Kan. L.Rev. 379, 382-384 (1980).

(Footnote omitted.) *Woodworth v. Woodworth,* 337 N.W.2d at 337.

The Supreme Court of Kentucky in *Inman v. Inman,* 648 S.W.2d 847 (Ky. 1982) indicated that if the issue were before the court, the proper formula to be followed in placing a value on an educational degree secured by a spouse, to which the other spouse contributed financially, is to measure the recovery by the amount of money the nonstudent spouse contributed toward living expenses, the amount of money contributed for educational costs, and the potential for increase in future earning capacity made possible by the degree, thus not treating the degree as marital property.

The method for valuation of the increased earning capacity should require a comparison of the student spouse's earning capacity at the time of marriage with that at the time of dissolution or permanent separation. From this value a just and equitable distribution should be made between the parties. Where a marriage has endured for some time after the degree is obtained, the supporting spouse may already have been benefited from the increased earning capacity and such be taken into account in making a just and equitable distribution. Because this method of calculation is akin to the method used to ascertain damages for loss of earnings in a tort or wrongful death action, a body of knowledge already exists in the field of economics to make this type determination.

III

Turning to the cases before the court, I would reverse and remand both decisions for a valuation of the professional education and a just and equitable distribution in accordance with the mandate of RCW 26.09.080. In the event that there is insufficient property to make a just and equitable award to the supporting spouse, the trial court may award a lump sum payment to be distributed by the professional spouse in periodic payments over a reasonable period of time.

Discussion Questions

1. What factors does Washington require trial courts to use when determining if a supporting spouse should receive compensation? Why do you think the court requires all of these factors to be considered?

2. What is the purpose of considering whether the spouses had a mutual expectation of future financial benefit to the community, but the marriage ends before that benefit can be realized?

3. Would the result have been different if the marriages lasted ten years after the veterinary degrees were obtained?

C. AWARD FOR FINANCIAL CONTRIBUTIONS: THE LOUISIANA REMEDY

Louisiana's remedy to the supporting spouse is statutory in nature. La. Civ. Code art. 121 allows a court to award a party a sum for his or her financial contributions made during the marriage to education or training of the spouse that increased the spouse's earning power, as long as the claimant did not benefit from the increased earning power during the marriage. In *Clemons v. Clemons* (Louisiana 2007), the court held that under La. Civ. Code art. 121, the wife was not entitled to compensation for her financial support of the husband during veterinary school because she received sufficient benefits due to the accumulated community property. By contrast, *Shewbridge v. Shewbridge* (Louisiana 1998) reflects the type of situation where recovery was allowed because the marriage ended shortly after the husband completed his schooling and obtained his commercial pilot's license.

CLEMONS v. CLEMONS

960 So. 2d 1068 (2007)
Court of Appeal of Louisiana

Before GASKINS, PEATROSS and LOLLEY, JJ.

PEATROSS, J.

These appeals arise from the partition of community property between Patricia Clemons and Tony Clemons. Both parties appeal several aspects of the trial court's judgment. For the following reasons, we amend and, as amended, we affirm.

FACTS

The parties physically separated in April 2002. A Judgment of Divorce was rendered on November 5, 2002, and was signed and filed December 2, 2002. A trial to partition the community property was held in November 2005. The Judgment of Partition divided the assets and liabilities between the parties and awarded Ms. Clemons an equalization payment of $165,216.61 less one-half of the value of their mobile home.

In addition, under La. C.C. art. 121, the trial court awarded Ms. Clemons $17,500 for her financial support of Dr. Clemons while he was in veterinarian school.

Dr. Clemons appeals . . . the La. C.C. art. 121 award to Ms. Clemons for financially supporting him through veterinarian school.

EDUCATIONAL SUPPORT AWARD

Both parties challenge the trial court's award under La. C.C. art. 121 for Ms. Clemons' financial support of Dr. Clemons during veterinary school after they were married. Dr. Clemons appeals both the propriety of granting the award and the amount, while Ms. Clemons argues for the amount of the award to be increased.

A professional degree or license is not community property and is not subject to community property distribution. *Gill v. Gill*, 39,406 (La. App. 2d Cir. 3/9/05), 895 So. 2d 807; La. C.C. art. 121, 1990 revision comment (f). Article 121, instead, provides that:

> In a proceeding for divorce or thereafter, the court may award a party a sum for his financial contributions made during the marriage to education or training of his spouse that increased the spouse's earning power, to the extent that the claimant did not benefit during the marriage from the increased earning power.
>
> The sum awarded may be in addition to a sum for support and to property received in the partition of community property.

Dr. Clemons argues that Ms. Clemons does not qualify for this provision because, in their eight years of marriage, six years of which were after his graduation, she benefitted from his increased earning power. Ms. Clemons responds that she worked hard in the veterinarian practice of Dr. Clemons and contributed to its growth. She further asserts that the family residence, a mobile home worth no more than $8,000, is proof that she did not benefit from his increased earning power during their marriage. She claims that the award was proper considering her contributions to the growth of the business and that the parties separated just as Dr. Clemons was about to enjoy the greater earning potential of his degree by opening a new building for his veterinarian clinic.

In determining whether an award is warranted under article 121, a court should consider: (1) the claimant's expectation of shared benefit when the contributions were made (2) the degree of detriment suffered by the claimant in making the contributions, and (3) the magnitude of the benefit the other spouse received. Benefits from the increased earning power may be in the form of an improved lifestyle or an increase in community assets. "A spouse who contributed financially to the education or training of the other spouse in a marriage of significant duration may have already benefitted during the existence of the marriage by an improved standard of living or an accumulation of community property."

In reviewing the few cases that have addressed this provision, we find that cases which upheld an article 121 award were for separations that occurred shortly after the graduation of the supported spouse. This is the situation contemplated in the comments to article 121.

> The usual situation that has prompted the making of awards of this kind in other states has involved a wife who supported her husband through professional school, only to be divorced by him shortly after his graduation. Usually the wife has had little opportunity to share in the husband's enhanced income, and ordinarily little or no community property has accumulated to be divided between them.

Based on this language, one court denied the wife an article 121 award for her financial support of her husband during law school three years prior to their separation. The court held that, in those three years, the wife had benefitted from the husband's substantial increase in income focusing on her improved lifestyle; and, as such, she was not entitled to an award under article 121.

Under this analysis, we find that the trial court improperly awarded Ms. Clemons money under article 121. While in both the trial testimony and argument before this court counsel for Ms. Clemons stresses her lack of an improved lifestyle, this focus overlooks the total community assets accumulated during the Clemons' marriage. Most notably, the agreed value of their community business of Rocking Rooster was $161,883. Although Ms. Clemons contributed to this business with her own hard work, it was only made possible by Dr. Clemons' veterinarian degree and license. In addition, the parties had various accounts and other assets that amounted to significant community property. As indicated by the comments of article 121, this is not the situation that this article was designed to remedy.

Ms. Clemons further argues that an article 121 award is due because the marriage terminated just before Dr. Clemons was about to enjoy a higher earning level. The analysis under article 121 is not whether a spouse has reached his full earning potential at the time of the separation, but to what extent the supporting spouse did not enjoy the benefits of the other spouse's increased earning power. While Ms. Clemons had possibly anticipated greater financial benefits from Dr. Clemons' degree at the time she was supporting him through school, she received such sufficient benefits based on the accumulated community property. This is simply not a case where the supporting spouse, Ms. Clemons, has received little or no benefit from supporting the other spouse, Dr. Clemons, through his education. We, therefore, reverse the trial court's award under La. C.C. art. 121.

Discussion Questions

1. What factors are considered when determining whether a compensation award is warranted under La. Civ. Code art. 121?

2. Why did the court find it irrelevant that the wife contributed her own hard work to the business, which added to its success?

SHEWBRIDGE v. SHEWBRIDGE

720 So. 2d 780 (1998)
Court of Appeal of Louisiana

Before MARVIN, WILLIAMS and GASKINS, JJ.

GASKINS, Judge.

Anthol William Shewbridge, Jr., appeals from a trial court judgment awarding his former wife, Beverly D. Nugent Shewbridge, the sum of $15,314.30 for contributions she made to his education and training during their marriage. We amend the judgment and, as amended, affirm.

FACTS

The parties were married in December 1987. Prior to their marriage, Mr. Shewbridge was a student at Northwestern State University (NSU) studying in the area of aviation science. He was not employed. His father, Dr. Anthol Shewbridge, supported him providing money for education and living expenses. Once married, Mr. Shewbridge continued his studies at NSU, and Mrs. Shewbridge worked. Dr. Shewbridge continued to provide monthly financial support to his son. The financial support provided by Dr. Shewbridge ended in August 1992 after Mr. Shewbridge received his commercial pilot's license and moved with his wife to Harper's Ferry, West Virginia. The couple separated in 1993.

During their divorce proceedings, Mrs. Shewbridge asserted a claim under La. C.C. art. 121 for her contributions to her husband's education and training. At the hearing on this claim, Mrs. Shewbridge testified about her employment during the time her husband studied at NSU; she stated that at one point she worked two jobs. She testified that her work and Mr. Shewbridge's studies took away from their time together and their social life. Mrs. Shewbridge, who was working toward a nursing degree at the time of their marriage, explained that she and her husband reached an agreement whereby she would work while he attended school, and then when they moved to West Virginia he would support her while she enrolled in school to complete her nursing degree. She testified that she expected to benefit from this arrangement in the future when they would have a higher standard of living.

With regard to their financial situation during the marriage, Mrs. Shewbridge testified that they had difficulty making ends meet and that they lived "from paycheck to paycheck." She stated that she was only aware of $500 per month sent by Dr. Shewbridge to supplement their income and denied knowing about other amounts sent by Dr. Shewbridge. Her testimony indicated that payments for rent, groceries, tuition, and books came out of their joint account, that the money sent by Dr. Shewbridge was used on education expenses but that the amount was not sufficient, and that her income was used for all of her husband's living expenses. She also testified that the total cost of Mr. Shewbridge's education was $26,000 and that another $5,000 to $6,000 was spent to purchase tools needed for his training. She stated that the only income reported on their tax returns from 1988 to 1992 was her income. She further testified that Mr. Shewbridge did not work while attending NSU.

Mr. Shewbridge denied that any agreement existed whereby his wife agreed to put him through school. He further denied that she ever paid for his tuition or books, and he testified that she did not pay for all living expenses, such as rent and groceries. He stated that his father sent money for his education and living expenses both prior to and during the marriage. He also maintained that their financial circumstances were sufficiently comfortable to allow the couple to take weekend trips and purchase both a new car and antiques.

Mr. Shewbridge introduced several exhibits into evidence, including a financial compilation of the monies provided by his father and earned by Mrs. Shewbridge. He verified that all income reported on their tax returns for the years 1988 through 1992 was earned by his wife. However, he also testified that he worked thirty to forty hours per week for approximately thirty-two to thirty-six months earning five dollars per hour, paid in cash, as part of his educational program. However, none of this income was reported for tax purposes. With regard to the money provided by Dr. Shewbridge, he testified that his father never asked to be paid back and that his father supported his sister through school in the same way. Mr. Shewbridge further testified that his wife was aware of the money sent by his father on a monthly basis.

Dr. Shewbridge testified that he paid his son money for his education and living expenses while he was in school and that he did the same for his daughter. The payments began in 1985 and ended in August 1992. A copy of a log kept by Dr. Shewbridge of the money he paid to his son was introduced into evidence, along with copies of canceled checks. Dr. Shewbridge testified that he supported his son, as needed, both before and during the marriage. He stated that he gave the money to Mr. Shewbridge to do as he pleased with it and that he had never considered or asked to have the money paid back.

The trial court accepted the facts as recited in Mrs. Shewbridge's post-trial memorandum and ruled in her favor in accordance with the proposal in that memorandum. The proposed amount was determined using the formula set forth in *McConathy v. McConathy*. The amount of contributions attributed to Mrs. Shewbridge was $59,934; the amount of contributions attributed to her husband was $58,305; and the cost of education was set at $29,000. The amount granted by the trial court was $15,314.30. The trial court also awarded Mrs. Shewbridge legal interest from the date of judicial demand. From this judgment, Mr. Shewbridge appeals.

Contributions to Spouse's Education or Training

Mr. Shewbridge generally complains of a lack of evidentiary support for the award. He asserts that there was no evidence — other than Mrs. Shewbridge's own self-serving testimony — of the amount of educational and living expenses she paid, of the sacrifices she made or the detriment she suffered in contributing to his education, and of her failure to realize any benefits from his education.

In *McConathy v. McConathy*, we adopted a formula for calculating an award under La. C.C. art. 121. Under this formula, an equitable award is determined as follows: working spouse's financial contributions to joint living expenses and educational costs of student spouse

> *less* ¹/₂ (working spouse's financial contributions *plus* student spouse's financial contributions *less* cost of education)
> *equals*   equitable award to working spouse. *McConathy v. McConathy*, 632 So. 2d at 1205.

Our review of the record reveals adequate support for the trial court's judgment. The testimony and evidence demonstrated that Mrs. Shewbridge worked during the marriage while her husband attended school. The income earned by Mrs. Shewbridge and at least some of the funds sent to Mr. Shewbridge by his father were placed into a joint account from which living expenses and some educational expenses were paid. It is clear that Mrs. Shewbridge provided support for Mr. Shewbridge while he attended school. While Mr. Shewbridge argues that the evidence does not show what expenses were paid by Mrs. Shewbridge, the evidence also does not show, contrary to his assertion, what particular expenses were paid by funds provided by Dr. Shewbridge. Furthermore, there is no indication in the record that the cash money allegedly made by Mr. Shewbridge was ever used for either educational or living expenses.

Mr. Shewbridge also asserts that there is no showing of any detriment or sacrifice suffered by Mrs. Shewbridge while contributing to his education. He points out that they purchased a car and antiques while married and took weekend trips. However, as previously noted, Mrs. Shewbridge explained in her testimony that most of the antiques were purchased after they moved to West Virginia and while they lived with Mr. Shewbridge's parents; also, most were purchased on layaway plans. She further clarified that the vehicle cost $8,000 and that she paid cash for it after working two jobs and receiving a tax refund. The record indicates that the couple's income during the period Mr. Shewbridge attended school was not substantial and that their income was provided by Mrs. Shewbridge. The fact that Mrs. Shewbridge worked and contributed to expenses while her husband attended school is sufficient to satisfy the requirement of La. C.C. art. 121 in this case.

Mr. Shewbridge also asserts that there is no showing of any benefit lost by Mrs. Shewbridge because his income in 1993, as reported in the financial compilation submitted into evidence, was only $14,338.65. This argument overlooks the purpose of La. C.C. art. 121 which is to compensate the working spouse for contributions which helped to increase the earning power of the other spouse when the working spouse will not benefit from the increased earning power during the marriage. The focus of this article is on increased earning power and not increased earnings. Mr. Shewbridge's earnings will likely rise and Mrs. Shewbridge will not benefit from the increase. Thus, she is entitled to compensation for the contributions she made which enabled him to increase his earning power during their marriage. We therefore find that Mrs. Shewbridge is entitled to a monetary award as provided in La. C.C. art. 121.

Calculating the award using $59,934 as Mrs. Shewbridge's contribution, $57,330 as Mr. Shewbridge's contribution, and $26,000 as the cost of education, we find that amount due to Mrs. Shewbridge for her contributions to her husband's education and training is $14,302.

CONCLUSION

We amend the judgment of the trial court to award Mrs. Shewbridge $14,302 on her claim for contributions to Mr. Shewbridge's education and training. Interest on this award shall run from the date of the judgment. As amended, the judgment is affirmed. Costs are assessed against Mr. Shewbridge.

AMENDED AND, AS AMENDED, AFFIRMED.

Discussion Question

1. What was the main reason why the wife in *Shewbridge* was entitled to compensation, but the wife in *Clemons* was not?

D. REIMBURSEMENT TO THE COMMUNITY: THE CALIFORNIA REMEDY

In California, Family Code §2641 provides the community "reimbursement of community contributions." This reimbursement is limited to "community property contributions to education or training that substantially enhances the earning capacity of the party." Community contributions include payments that come from community or quasi-community property for payment toward education or training, or repayment of a loan incurred for education or training.

CALIFORNIA FAMILY CODE

§2641. Community contributions to education or training

(a) "Community contributions to education or training" as used in this section means payments made with community or quasi-community property for education or training or for the repayment of a loan incurred for education or training, whether the payments were made while the parties were resident in this state or resident outside this state.

(b) Subject to the limitations provided in this section, upon dissolution of marriage or legal separation of the parties:

(1) The community shall be reimbursed for community contributions to education or training of a party that substantially enhances the earning capacity of the party. The amount reimbursed shall be with interest at the legal rate, accruing from the end of the calendar year in which the contributions were made.

(2) A loan incurred during marriage for the education or training of a party shall not be included among the liabilities of the community for the purpose of division pursuant to this division but shall be assigned for payment by the party.

(c) The reimbursement and assignment required by this section shall be reduced or modified to the extent circumstances render such a disposition unjust, including, but not limited to, any of the following:

(1) The community has substantially benefited from the education, training, or loan incurred for the education or training of the party. There is a rebuttable presumption, affecting the burden of proof, that the community has not substantially benefited from community contributions to the education or training made less than 10 years before the commencement of the proceeding, and that the community has substantially benefited from community contributions to the education or training made more than 10 years before the commencement of the proceeding.

(2) The education or training received by the party is offset by the education or training received by the other party for which community contributions have been made.

(3) The education or training enables the party receiving the education or training to engage in gainful employment that substantially reduces the need of the party for support that would otherwise be required.

(d) Reimbursement for community contributions and assignment of loans pursuant to this section is the exclusive remedy of the community or a party for the education or training and any resulting enhancement of the earning capacity of a party. However, nothing in this subdivision limits consideration of the effect of the education, training, or enhancement, or the amount reimbursed pursuant to this section, on the circumstances of the parties for the purpose of an order for support pursuant to Section 4320.

(e) This section is subject to an express written agreement of the parties to the contrary.

Marriage of Graham (California 2003) reveals that California courts must consider reimbursement to the community only for education that "substantially enhances the earning capacity" of the student spouse. The issue in that case was whether the husband's eventual graduation from law school would have substantially enhanced his earning capacity. While in law school, the community contributions to educational expenses were over $12,000. The Court of Appeal affirmed the trial court's decision that the husband's enhancement of earning capacity was too speculative, therefore denying reimbursement to the community and thus to the wife.

MARRIAGE OF GRAHAM

109 Cal. App. 4th 1321, 135 Cal. Rptr. 2d 685 (2003)
California Court of Appeal

MOORE, J.

While Katherine and Jeffrey Graham were married, Jeffrey enrolled in and nearly completed law school. During the marital dissolution proceedings, Katherine requested reimbursement to the community for funds spent on Jeffrey's legal education. In addition, she sought to have child support determined based on her claimed gross monthly income of $3,125. The court denied Katherine's request for reimbursement and determined her gross monthly income to be $5,618.08.

Katherine appeals. We agree with the trial court that whether Jeffrey's eventual graduation from law school might have the effect of substantially enhancing his earning capacity is speculative, making reimbursement for education costs unavailable. In addition, we hold that the trial court did not abuse its discretion in imputing income to Katherine based on a 36-hour workweek, paid at a per diem rate. However, we also hold that the trial court did abuse its discretion in applying an excessive hourly rate to the last four hours of each work shift. Affirmed in part, reversed in part, and remanded with directions.

I.   FACTS

Katherine and Jeffrey were married in 1992. They had two children during the course of their marriage. Jeffrey enrolled as a student at Western State University College of Law (Western State) in 1994. During Jeffrey's enrollment, the couple spent over $12,000 for tuition and related expenses.

In June 1999, Jeffrey filed a petition for dissolution of marriage. At the time of trial in September 2000, Jeffrey had one remaining semester in law school, and did not have plans to take the California bar examination. His cumulative grade point average was approximately 2.2. While in law school, Jeffrey was employed as a police officer by the Costa Mesa Police Department. At the time of trial, he was making over $4,400 per month.

Katherine, a registered nurse, modified her work schedule at the hospital a number of times following the couple's separation. At the time of trial, she was working per diem, rather than full time. The parties disagreed as to the amount of income that should be imputed to her in determining the amount of child support she should receive. As Jeffrey saw it, she should be charged with working 40 hours per week. Katherine, on the other hand, thought her income should be based on a lesser number of hours, approximately 24 to 36 hours per week. The parties also disagreed as to the rate of pay that should be applied to those hours.

The judgment on reserved issues denied Katherine's request for reimbursement with respect to the law school expenses, stating that the court found "no substantive enhanced earning capacity of [Jeffrey] due to said schooling." It also found Katherine's gross monthly income to be $5,618.08, for the purposes of child support.

Katherine now appeals. She contends that the court erred in denying her claim for reimbursement for law school expenses and in imputing a $5,618.08 monthly income to her.

II. Discussion

A. Request for Reimbursement of Law School Expenses

Katherine contends the trial court erred when it denied her claim for reimbursement of the money spent on Jeffrey's law school tuition and related expenses during the marriage. Moreover, she urges this court to rule that legal, medical, dental, and accounting degrees will be presumed to result in a substantially enhanced earning capacity as a matter of law.

Family Code section 2641, subdivision (b), provides in pertinent part, "Subject to the limitations provided in this section, upon dissolution of marriage or legal separation of the parties: [¶] (1) The community shall be reimbursed for community contributions to education or training of a party that substantially enhances the earning capacity of the party." Because both parties argue this appeal based upon the tacit assumption that the tuition was paid from community funds, our sole consideration with respect to the reimbursement issue is whether Jeffrey's legal education substantially enhanced his earning capacity within the meaning of section 2641, subdivision (b)(1).

As Jeffrey mentions in his reply brief, there are very few cases that discuss what is meant by substantial enhancement of the earning capacity of a student spouse. The primary source of guidance regarding the substantial enhancement of earning capacity standard is the Law Revision Commission comment following section 2641. The comment states that "[s]ection 2641 provides authority for reimbursement of educational expenses that have benefited primarily one party to the marriage." (Cal. Law Revision Com. com., 29D West's Ann. Fam. Code (1994 ed.) foll.

§2641, p. 143.) Specifically, the substantial enhancement requirement is a "limitation . . . intended to restrict litigation by requiring that the education or training must demonstrably enhance earning capacity and to implement the policy of the section to redress economic inequity." (*Ibid.*)

In the instant case, Jeffrey attained a grade point average of 2.2 at Western State, and, at the time of trial, had no plans to take the bar examination. Jeffrey testified that he went to law school to further his education, but did not necessarily have any plans to become an attorney. He explained that, when he was in college, he had partied and played football, but had wasted the opportunity to get an education. When he realized that in retrospect, he wanted to make up for the lost opportunity, by furthering his education at that time. He went to law school in pursuit of that objective, not for the purpose of financial gain. Furthermore, Jeffrey was already working at the Costa Mesa Police Department while going to law school, and he argued that his earning potential might well be greater if he remained at that place of employment, rather than pursuing a legal career.

The evidence does not support a conclusion that Jeffrey's legal education had either substantially or demonstrably enhanced his earning capacity. To the contrary, the facts support the trial court's finding that any enhanced earning capacity was questionable. The trial court summed up the situation well by stating: "It's too speculative . . . to try to figure out whether he is going to make more money in the future, and he may or he may not. [¶] He may or may not pass the bar. He may or may not do anything with the law degree. He may decide that he wants to stay in the police department and go for a higher position . . . . [¶] He might find that what he can make there looks pretty good compared with trying to scratch out a living in the legal field. [¶] A law degree is not a ticket to prosperity. Some people are very good at it and make money, and other people become disillusioned and they don't make any money. [¶] So. . . it's all on the come. It may happen, it may not. . . ."

While Katherine requests us to declare that a law degree results in a substantial enhancement of earning capacity as a matter of law, we cannot do so. This is a perfect case to demonstrate the fallacy of the proposed rule.

* * *

III. DISPOSITION

The judgment is affirmed in part, reversed in part, and remanded with directions. We reverse the child support order and remand that matter to the trial court for a determination of the correct amount of child support Jeffrey is to pay Katherine, taking into consideration Katherine's working three shifts a week. In all other respects, the judgment is affirmed. Katherine shall recover her costs on appeal.

SILLS, P.J., and BEDSWORTH, J., concurred.

Discussion Questions

1. The wife urged the court to rule that legal, medical, dental, and accounting degrees all result in substantially enhanced earning capacities as a matter of law.

Why does the court reject this proposition?

2. Would the result have been different if prior to the divorce, the husband had graduated law school and started practicing law?

E. EQUITY FOR THE SUPPORTING SPOUSE: THE ARIZONA REMEDY

Arizona's approach offers a more substantial remedy to the supporting spouse than other community property states. It is equitable in nature. Where a claim is made by a supporting spouse, the court in each case must make specific findings as to whether the education, degree, or license acquired during the marriage involved unjust enrichment of the student spouse, the value of the benefit, and the amount that should be paid to the supporting spouse. This remedy is limited to the financial contributions by the supporting spouse for the student spouse's living expenses and direct educational expenses.

Pyeatte v. Pyeatte (Arizona 1982) illustrates how Arizona's equitable remedy applies. At issue was whether the wife was entitled to restitution for benefits she provided for her husband's educational support. The husband and wife had an agreement that she would put him through law school, and when he finished, he would put her through her master's program. However, after he graduated from law school but before she started her master's program, he divorced her. The court held that the wife was entitled to restitution. She agreed to contribute to her husband's legal education with the expectation that she would be compensated by his reciprocal efforts after graduation. The court realized it would be unjust and inequitable to allow the husband to retain the benefit of his degree without compensating the wife.

PYEATTE v. PYEATTE

135 Ariz. 196, 661 P.2d 196 (1982)
Court of Appeals of Arizona

CORCORAN, Judge.

This is an appeal by the husband from an award of $23,000 in favor of the wife as ordered in a decree of dissolution. Two issues are before us: (1) The validity of an oral agreement entered into by the husband and wife during the marriage, whereby each spouse agreed to provide in turn the sole support for the marriage while the other spouse was obtaining further education; and, (2) whether the wife is entitled to restitution for benefits she provided for her husband's educational support in a dissolution action which follows closely upon the husband's graduation and admission to the Bar. The word "agreement" is used as a term of reference for the stated understanding between the husband and wife and not as a legal conclusion that the agreement is enforceable at law as a contract.

The husband, H. Charles Pyeatte (appellant), and the wife, Margrethe May Pyeatte (appellee), were married in Tucson on December 27, 1972. At the time of the marriage both had received bachelors degrees. Appellee was coordinator of the surgical technical program at Pima College. Appellant was one of her students. In early 1974, the parties had discussions and reached an agreement concerning postgraduate education for both of them.

Appellee testified that they agreed she "would put him through three years of law school without his having to work, and when he finished, he would put [her] through for [her] masters degree without [her] having to work."

Appellant attended law school in Tucson, Arizona, from 1974 until his graduation. He was admitted to the State Bar shortly thereafter.

During appellant's first two years of law school appellee supported herself and appellant on the salary she earned at Pima College. During the last year, appellee lost her job, whereupon savings were used to support the couple. Although each spouse contributed to the savings, a significant amount was furnished by appellee.

After appellant's admission to the Bar, the couple moved to Prescott, Arizona, where appellant was employed by a law firm. Both parties realized that appellant's salary would not be sufficient to support the marriage and pay for appellee's education for a masters degree simultaneously. Appellee then agreed to defer her plans for a year or two until her husband got started in his legal career. In the meantime, she obtained part-time employment as a teacher.

In April, 1978, appellant told appellee that he no longer wanted to be married to her, and in June of 1978, she filed a petition for dissolution. Trial was had in March of 1979, and a decree of dissolution was granted. At the time of the trial, there was little community property and no dispute as to division of any community or separate property. Spousal maintenance was neither sought by nor granted to appellee.

The trial court determined that there was an agreement between the parties, that appellee fully performed her part of that agreement, that appellant had not performed his part of the agreement, and that appellee had been damaged thereby.

Based on appellee's expert testimony on the cost of furthering *her* education, in accordance with the agreement, the trial court awarded judgment of $23,000 against appellant as damages for breach of contract, with additional directions that the judgment be payable through the court clerk on a quarterly basis in a sum of not less than ten percent of appellant's net quarterly income.

The trial court directed appellant to use his best efforts to produce income and to keep accurate records of his income-producing activities, which records would be available to appellee upon request but not more frequently than on a quarterly basis. The court also retained jurisdiction of the case for the purpose of supervising the administration of the payment of the judgment and the keeping of records by the appellant. Appellant filed a timely notice of appeal from the judgment.

On appeal, appellant argues that the agreement did not rise to the level of a binding contract because, among other things, the terms thereof were not definite and could not be legally enforced.

* * *

Having decided that the agreement was not enforceable for the reasons stated above, we need not consider appellant's other arguments regarding that issue.

Statutory Reimbursement Under A.R.S. §25-318

Appellee advances as the first "equitable" basis for sustaining the award the argument that she is entitled to reimbursement of her expenditures for appellant's legal education under A.R.S. §25-318. This section provides in part that the court, in disposing of property in a dissolution, may consider "excessive or abnormal expenditures . . . of community, joint tenancy and other property held in common."

She contends that appellant left the marriage with an asset—his legal education—which was obtained by the exhaustion of the community. Appellee argues that her husband's education was an extraordinary expenditure which inured to his benefit and for which she paid and that she is entitled to equitable reimbursement in the form of a lien upon appellant's separate estate under A.R.S. §25-318. We do not agree. A.R.S. §25-318 concerns disposition of property, and we have already decided that one spouse's education cannot be characterized as property to be divided between the parties. *Wisner v. Wisner*, 129 Ariz. 333, 631 P.2d 115 (App. 1981).

The question of characterizing education and professional degrees or licenses as marital property is one which has been addressed in the context of dissolution in this and a number of other jurisdictions. This court in *Wisner* adopted the view of the majority of those jurisdictions which have considered the issue and rejected the argument that an educational degree, professional license or the increased earning potential each represents is community property subject to valuation and division upon dissolution.

The Restitution Claim

Appellee's last contention is that the trial court's award should be affirmed as an equitable award of restitution on the basis of unjust enrichment. She argues that appellant's education, which she subsidized and which he obtained through the exhaustion of community assets constitutes a benefit for which he must, in equity, make restitution. This narrow equitable issue is one of first impression in this court. We first addressed the broad outlines of the problem in *Wisner*, but in the context of significantly different facts and legal theories. Our recognition of the disparate considerations involved in a case such as the one before us led us to limit our holding in *Wisner* to its facts.

A benefit may be any type of advantage, including that which saves the recipient from any loss or expense. Appellee's support of appellant during his period of schooling clearly constituted a benefit to appellant. Absent appellee's support, appellant may not have attended law school, may have been forced to prolong his education because of intermittent periods of gainful employment, or may have gone deeply into debt. Relieved of the necessity of supporting himself, he was able to devote full time and attention to his education.

The mere fact that one party confers a benefit on another, however, is not of itself sufficient to require the other to make restitution. Retention of the benefit must be unjust.

We see no reason in law or equity why restitution should not be available in an appropriate circumstance to prevent the unjust enrichment of a spouse when a constructive trust is not available, as here, when no property exists. We analogize the two restitutionary devices solely to the extent of illustrating their common essence-prevention of the unjust enrichment of one spouse at the expense of the other.

A number of jurisdictions have addressed the issue of restitution in the context of the marital relationship. The cases which have dealt with the issue involve two factual patterns: (1) The first group consists of those cases in which the couples had accumulated substantial marital assets over a period of time from which assets the wife received large awards of property, maintenance and child support. The courts have refused to apply the theory of restitution on the basis of unjust enrichment in each of these cases. (2) The second group consists of those cases in which the parties are divorced soon after the student spouse receives his degree or license and there is little or no marital property from which to order any award to the working spouse.

In the first group the courts have consistently refused to find a property interest in the husband's education, degree, license or earning capacity or to order restitution in favor of the wife. Because restitution is a matter of equity, the circumstances of these cases preclude at the outset any basis for a finding of inequitable circumstances sufficient to support restitution inasmuch as the wife in each case had received substantial awards of the marital assets and was seeking, in addition to those assets, a property interest in the husband's education, degree, license or earning capacity. Because the property award itself is largely the product of the education, degree, license or earning capacity in which the wife sought a monetary interest, the courts hold that the wife realized her "investment" in the husband's education by having received the benefits of his increased earning capacity during marriage and by receipt of an award of property upon its dissolution.

In *Wisner*, the wife had concededly not made any monetary contribution to her husband's medical education. The parties had married during the husband's final year of medical school and during their 15-year marriage the wife had devoted herself exclusively to homemaking activities. The wife, nevertheless, sought reimbursement "because of her husband's *reduced income* during his education and [his eight-year] training period, and *for her part* in the joint effort of the community in obtaining that education."

We rejected her claim for reimbursement, finding that her contributions to the husband's education; i.e., her homemaking services, were not separately compensable. We stated:

> In each marriage, for example, the couple decides on a certain division of labor, and while there is a value to what each spouse is doing, whether it be labor for monetary compensation or homemaking, that value is consumed by the community in the on-going relationship and forms no basis for a claim of unjust enrichment upon dissolution.

The second group presents the more difficult problem of the "working spouse" claiming entitlement to an equitable recovery where there is little or no marital property to divide and therefore the conventional remedies of property division or spousal maintenance are unavailable. The emerging consensus among those jurisdictions faced with the issue in this factual context is that restitution to the working spouse is appropriate to prevent the unjust enrichment of the student spouse.

Although in *Wisner* we dealt with the first group described above; i.e., a marital community with substantial accumulated assets, we anticipated the second type of case in which (1) the community estate is consumed by the education of the husband which was obtained in substantial measure by the efforts and sacrifices of his wife; (2) the working wife is not entitled to spousal maintenance, having demonstrated an ability to support not only herself but her husband as well; and (3) the divorce follows closely upon the husband's completion of his education before the community realizes any benefit from that education and before the working spouse is able to further her own education and thus increase her own earning capacity. We stated in *Wisner:*

> [A]n important factor to consider in the overall picture is the extent to which the non-license or degree holder has already or otherwise benefitted financially during coverture from his or her spouse's earning capacity. The rather common situation in which one spouse puts the other through professional school, followed closely by a dissolution upon the completion of schooling, is perhaps the clearest picture of the injustice which may evolve. In that situation, the spouse who has devoted much of the product of several years of labor to an "investment" in future family prosperity is barred from any return on his or her investment, while the other spouse has received a windfall of increased earning capacity. However, the acquisition of a considerable estate obviously solves this problem. Such is the situation here. Wife shared in the fruits of husband's education for many years during their marriage, and ultimately realized a value therefrom by a substantial award to her of the community assets, plus spousal maintenance.

The record shows that the appellee conferred benefits on appellant — financial subsidization of appellant's legal education — with the agreement and expectation that she would be compensated therefor by his reciprocal efforts after his graduation and admission to the Bar. Appellant has left the marriage with the only valuable asset acquired during the marriage — his legal education and qualification to practice law. It would be inequitable to allow appellant to retain this benefit without making restitution to appellee.

THE MEASURE OF RECOVERY

Generally, where claims are made by the working spouse against the student spouse, the trial court in each case must make specific findings as to whether the education, degree or license acquired by the student spouse during marriage involved an unjust enrichment of that spouse, the value of the benefit, and the amount that should be paid to the working spouse. A variety of methods of computing the unjust enrichment may be employed in ascertaining the working spouse's compensable interest in the attainment of the student spouse's education, degree or license.

The award to appellee should be limited to the financial contribution by appellee for appellant's living expenses and direct educational expenses.

The nature of equity is individual justice. Since the benefit bestowed upon appellant by appellee was periodic in nature and dependent on her income, we find no abuse of the equity power of the court in awarding appellee periodic payments, especially where she can use them periodically to pursue her own education. By our affirmance of an instalment method of payment in this case, we do not mean to promulgate a rule that will uniformly govern all awards in subsequent cases of that nature. Each will, by virtue of the equitable nature of the claim, require relief tailored to the facts and circumstances of the individuals.

The portion of the judgment in the amount of $23,000 is reversed and remanded for proceedings in accordance with this opinion.

FROEB, Acting P.J., and HATHAWAY, J., concur.

Discussion Questions

1. What must the supporting spouse show in order to receive restitution?
2. Why do courts generally refuse to apply the theory of restitution on the basis of unjust enrichment when the couple is married for a long period of time?

F. EQUITABLE DIVISION OF COMMUNITY PROPERTY ONLY: THE TEXAS REMEDY

Unlike the majority of community property states, Texas denies any recovery to the supporting spouse. In *Frausto v. Frausto* (Texas 1980), the husband sought review of the trial court's divorce decree requiring him to reimburse the wife's share of the community expense for education. The court held that if the trial court awarded future monthly payments to be made by one spouse to the other, such payments must be linked to property in existence at the time of marriage. Since the court held that an educational degree is not property divisible upon divorce, reimbursement was not a permissible remedy. The court did note that the professional educational degree and higher earning capacity could be considered in the division of community property.

FRAUSTO v. FRAUSTO

611 S.W.2d 656 (1980)
Texas Court of Civil Appeals

KLINGEMAN, Justice.

This is a divorce action but the appeal herein pertains to the trial court's division of the properties between the parties. Appellant, Manuel Jesus Frausto, complains only of an order in the divorce decree which requires him to pay to appellee, Maria Lourdes Frausto, the sum of $20,000, payable in the amount of $200 per month, "as a part of the division of the estate of the parties and as reimbursement for petitioner's share of the community expense for respondent's education."

By a number of points of error appellant asserts that the trial court erred in holding that (1) the husband's education preparing him for the practice of medicine was community property and a property right divisible on divorce; and (2) appellee was entitled to such sum as reimbursement for her share of the community expense for appellant's education. We agree.

In addition to a divorce between the parties, the divorce decree appointed the wife managing conservator of the couple's two minor children, and the husband possessory conservator with rights of visitation. The husband was ordered to pay child support of $250 per month for each child. The divorce decree also made a division of the community property, real and personal, between petitioner and respondent. The husband was ordered to pay certain debts, and was also ordered to pay for legal services and expenses in connection with the divorce decree to the wife's attorneys, in the sum of $5,375.

During the early part of the marriage, appellant and appellee were both school teachers. It was agreed by both that the husband would enter medical school. The wife continued to work while the husband was obtaining his medical education, and it is clear that during such period a considerable portion of all expenses of such marriage came from the wife's earnings. After the husband obtained his doctor's license to practice medicine, his earnings at times were substantial, but his work record is spotty, at times he was unemployed, and at other times his earnings were not large by medical standards. The husband testified that he had sustained injuries to both of his legs and that this made it difficult for him to work at times, and that he had quit some jobs because of this problem. There is evidence that at times the husband was a heavy spender. Despite whatever earnings the husband and wife had, no large community estate was accumulated. Both the husband and wife had college degrees, and the wife had taught school for many years and has continued to work as a school teacher. Two children were born of such marriage, one born in 1973 and the other in 1975. This case is somewhat typical of what sometimes happens when one spouse continues to work while the other spouse is obtaining a degree resulting in high potential earnings for the degreed spouse, and a divorce thereafter ensues.

From the plain language of the decree it is apparent that the award of $20,000 to the wife was an attempt by the trial judge to divide the medical education of appellant as a part of the community estate, or to reimburse appellee for expenditures made by the community for appellant's medical education.

There are no Texas cases directly in point. Two community property states, California and Colorado, have passed on the questions here involved. In *Todd v. Todd*, 78 Cal. Rptr. 131, 272 Cal. App. 2d 786 (1969), the California court held that a spouse's education preparing him for the practice of law is not of such a character that a monetary value for division can be placed on it for a division between the spouses in a divorce proceeding.

This rule was reaffirmed in *In re Marriage of Aufmuth*, 152 Cal. Rptr. 668, 89 Cal. App. 3d 446 (1979), wherein it was held that a determination that a legal education is community property would require a division of post-dissolution earnings, even though such earnings are the separate property of the acquiring spouses. A Colorado court in *In re Marriage of Graham*, 38 Colo. App. 130, 555 P.2d 527 (1976), found that education is not a property item capable of division.

We have found only one state which has held that a spouse has a property interest in the other spouse's professional degree. *Inman v. Inman*, 578 S.W.2d 266 (Ky. Ct. App. 1979) (common law state).

We agree with the jurisdictions that have held a professional educational degree is not divisible upon divorce.

In *Nail v. Nail,* 486 S.W.2d 761 (Tex. 1972), it was contended that professional good will was an asset capable of being divided upon dissolution of the marriage. The supreme court rejected this contention and stated that the professional good will of a doctor does not "possess value or constitute an asset separate and apart from his person or from his individual ability to practice his profession. It would be extinguished in the event of his death, or retirement, or disablement, as well as in the event of the sale of his practice or the loss of his patients, whatever the cause." Although Nail does not involve a spouse's education, we regard it as comparable and persuasive.

The trial court, upon divorce, is authorized to divide the "estate of the parties" which has been interpreted to refer to community property alone. Further, the trial court cannot divest spouses of rights to separate property whether real or personal. If the trial court awards monthly payments to be made in the future by one spouse to the other, such payments must be referable to property in existence at the time of marriage.

An award of future monthly payments which is specifically referable to an education received by spouses during marriage, as we have in the case before us, violates the rules and authorities hereinbefore set forth, and an award of monthly payments to be made in the future that is based on future earnings is an award of separate property, property not acquired during the marriage relationship.

We recognize there are inequities which may result from the failure to compensate the spouse who supports the other spouse through college or professional school. However, in an attempt to overcome such difficulties the trial court has wide discretion in dividing the estate of the parties in a divorce decree and may consider many factors including the difference in earning capacity, education and ability of the parties; probable future need for support; fault in breaking up the marriage; and the benefits an innocent spouse may have received from a continuation of the marriage. However, the trial court is limited by our basic community property laws in making a division as hereinbefore outlined.

We hold that a professional education acquired during marriage is not a property right and is not divisible upon divorce.

We must now consider whether the award of $20,000 can be justified on the basis of reimbursement. It is clear from the language of the decree that to whatever extent it is reimbursement, it is reimbursement for appellee's share of community expenses for appellant's education. This is not a typical reimbursement which ordinarily pertains to payments or contributions made by one spouse out of separate property to the community or by the community to one of the spouse's separate property. Reimbursement is ordinarily allowed where money is spent by one estate to pay off a debt of another estate, or where improvements are made from one estate to the other estate. The rule is sometimes stated that on dissolution of the marriage, if one party has contributed separate property, or if community funds have been applied to the enhancement of the property of the other, reimbursement is allowed. We do not have this here. Any reimbursement here is referable only to the education of one of the spouses, which we have held is not a property right, and which was admittedly paid for from community funds. Moreover, there are no pleadings seeking reimbursement. Ordinarily, an award for reimbursement is not allowable in the absence of an allegation of liability of such a nature or anything in the pleading to support such a judgment. Under the pleadings and the record we find no justification for such award on the theory of reimbursement.

The trial court's award of $20,000 to appellee as a part of the division of the estate of the parties and as a reimbursement for appellee's share of community expenses for appellant's education constitutes error and is an abuse of the trial court's discretion.

Where an appellate court finds that the trial court abused its discretion in a divorce suit, ordinarily, the proper order is a reversal and remand. As hereinbefore pointed out, it is not possible for us to determine exactly what portion of the community estate was awarded to the husband, and what portion to the wife. Consequently, it is not possible for us to tell to what extent the trial court considered the professional education and degree and substantially higher earning capacity of the husband, in making a division of the community estate between the parties. The interests of justice will best be served by a remand as to that portion of the divorce decree making a division of the property between the parties.

That portion of the divorce decree pertaining to a division of the property between the parties is reversed and remanded to a trial court for a new trial in a manner not inconsistent with this opinion. The divorce decree in all other things is affirmed.

Discussion Questions

1. What was the court's reasoning in reversing the trial court's decision entitling the wife to reimbursement for her share of the community expenses for the husband's education?

2. How does the court reconcile the obvious inequity in failing to compensate the wife?

3. In general, why do you think courts like this one simply deny recovery to the supporting spouse?

PROBLEM 6.1

Bill and Melinda married right after college. Melinda began working, and Bill enrolled in medical school. Bill's father paid for a portion of Bill's tuition, but community funds were used for the remainder of Bill's tuition, living expenses, and other educational costs. The majority of their community funds came from Melinda's earnings. Bill and Melinda recently filed for divorce. Melinda comes to you for advice, wanting to know whether she will be reimbursed for her community contributions to Bill's education.

PROBLEM 6.2

Same facts as above, but instead of community funds, Melinda's separate property funds were used to pay for Bill's tuition and educational expenses.

PROBLEM 6.3

Sam and Rose are an older, retired couple living in California. They have been married for 40 years, never had children, and are living a comfortable life. However, Sam had always loved philosophy and felt that he had missed out on pursuing an advanced degree. He enrolled in a master's program at the UCLA. He graduated two years later, with the tuition coming to $50,000. The tuition was paid from Sam and Rose's savings from their earnings over the years. Unfortunately, Sam fell in love with his philosophy study partner, and Sam and Rose have separated. Rose wants to know whether she will be entitled to reimbursement for the community contributions of Sam's tuition.

PROBLEM 6.4

Peter and Mary, a married couple who live in Arizona, had an agreement that Mary would put Peter through veterinary school, and when he was finished, he would put her through law school. Peter enrolled in veterinary school and graduated. During that time, Mary's earnings paid for his tuition and other educational and living expenses. Soon after graduation however, Peter divorced Mary. Mary comes to you seeking reimbursement for her contributions to Peter's education.

PROBLEM 6.5

Henry and Wanda live in Louisiana. Shortly after their wedding, Henry decided to go to law school. Wanda obtained a second job in order to keep the community afloat for the three years during Henry's schooling. Henry's tuition and other educational expenses were paid from Wanda's earnings. After graduation, Henry passed the bar and opened up his own law practice. It has been five years, and unfortunately Henry is spending too much time in his office, and they are divorcing. Wanda wants to know what her rights are.

PROBLEM 6.6

Same facts as above, but Henry and Wanda divorce immediately after Henry's graduation from law school and before he begins his practice.

Table 6-1
Educational Degrees in Community Property States

State	Rule	Case/Statute
Arizona	Education is an intangible property right, the value of which, because of its character cannot properly be characterized as property subject to division between the spouses. Education is a factor	*Wisner v. Wisner*, 129 Ariz. 333, 631 P.2d 115 (1981), *Pyeatte v. Pyeatte*, 135 Ariz. 346 (1983)

	to be considered in arriving at an equitable property division. Equitable remedy available if education acquired by student spouse resulted in unjust enrichment. Remedy of restitution includes financial contribution by non-student spouse for student spouse's living expenses and direct educational expenses.	
California	Educational degree not property divisible at divorce. Remedy limited to reimbursement to the community of community contributions to education that substantially enhances the earning capacity of the student spouse. "Substantial enhancement" is a limitation to restrict litigation and implement policy to redress economic inequity.	Family Code §2641 (2009). *Marriage of Graham,* 109 Cal. App. 4th 1321, 135 Cal. Rptr. 2d 1321 (2003)
Idaho	Issue of whether educational degree is property not addressed. Following factors relevant to division of community property: occupation, employability, earning capability of each spouse.	Idaho Code §32-712 (2010)
Louisiana	A professional degree or license is not community property and is not subject to community property distribution. Remedy is to "award a party a sum for his financial contributions made during the marriage to education or training of his spouse that increased the spouse's earning power, to the extent that the claimant did not benefit during the marriage from the increased earning power."	Louisiana Civil Code art. 121 (2010), *Shewbridge v. Shewbridge,* 720 So. 2d 780 (La. App. 1998), *Gill v. Gill,* 895 So. 2d 807 (La. App. 2005), *Clemons v. Clemons,* 960 So. 2d 1068 (La. App. 2007)
Nevada	Issue of whether educational degree is property not addressed. Educational degree may be a factor for a court to depart from equal division if that is a "compelling reason."	Nevada Revised Statutes §125-150 (2010)
New Mexico	A medical license is not community property because it does not possess the attribute of joint ownership. It can be assumed that an educational degree would also not be considered community property.	*Muckleroy v. Muckleroy,* 84 N.M. 14, 498 P.2d 1357 (1972)
Texas	Professional educational degree is not property divisible upon divorce. Education is a factor to be considered when making a "just and right" division of the community estate. No reimbursement of community contributions to the education of the student spouse.	Vernon's Texas Statutes, Family Code §7.001(2010). *Frausto v. Frausto,* 611 S.W.2d 656 (Tex. Civ. App. 1980)
Washington	Refused to address "the somewhat metaphysical question of whether a professional degree is 'property.'"	West's Revised Code of Washington, §§26.09.080 and 26.09.090 (2010),

| | Contribution of supporting spouse to the attainment of a professional degree is a factor to be considered in dividing property or in awarding maintenance. | *Washburn v. Washburn*, 101 Wash. 2d 168, 677 P.2d 152 (1984) |
| Wisconsin | Maintenance and property division statutes provide a flexible means by which the trial court may examine all the relevant circumstances of the particular case and can, in its discretion, award just compensation to a supporting spouse by using either maintenance or property division or both. | *Haugan v. Haugan*, 117 Wis. 2d 200, 343 N.W.2d 796 (1984) |

Chapter 7

Changing the Character of Property During Marriage: Transmutation

During marriage, couples are free to treat their property any way they want, despite the sharing principles of community property law. Some couples, especially those who have been involved in divorce previously, want to have everything spelled out either by an oral or a written agreement. Some will execute a premarital agreement, which in most states has formal written requirements. However, if they marry without a premarital agreement, they may opt for something less formal. Those couples who have few assets and spend all their earnings on family expenses rarely need a formal agreement. Their attitude is, "Why do we need a formal agreement? We share everything anyway."

However, as time goes by and they accumulate assets and receive inheritances from parents, they may feel a need to specify what is separate property and what is community property. After more time goes by, they may realize that they need to do estate planning to avoid probate or to protect the rights of children from a prior marriage. They may also decide to buy an expensive piece of jewelry like the diamond ring that they could not afford at the time they married. If the marriage falters instead of continuing "until death do us part," the community property system will determine whether the formal or informal arrangements that they have made will be respected.

The major issue in this Chapter concerns the requirements for changing property acquired during marriage which is termed "transmutation." The law in many community property states has moved toward requiring married couples to spell out their intentions regarding their property in writing. The reasons are two-fold. First, there is a need to reduce litigation over the issue of the spouses' intentions regarding their property. When divorce is looming, the spouses' memories change as to what they intended at the time they acquired property. If there is a written document, that is considered a better source to determine the spouses' intentions at the time of acquisition. Second, there is a concern that one spouse may take advantage of the other spouse by converting community property into that spouse's separate property. Again a document that reflects the spouses' agreement regarding transmutation of the property is the best source of protection for the disadvantaged spouse.

A fundamental principle is at work here. That principle is that community property remains community property and separate property remains separate property until changed or transmuted. Therefore, a transmutation will possibly change (1) separate property to community property or (2) community property to the separate property of one spouse or (3) the separate property of one spouse to the separate property of the other spouse. Changing separate property to community property is the easiest to document. It is often in the form of taking a title that specifies "to husband and wife, as community property." In that instance, it is possible to ascertain that the spouses agreed in writing to transmute the separate property of one spouse to community property. The separate property owner has actually given one-half of the separate property to the other spouse.

Changing community property to the separate property of one spouse is a scenario that spells danger. In that instance, the concern is that one spouse is taking the other spouse's one-half interest in the community property for his or her own. That scenario justifies a formal requirement that shows that both spouses agree to that transmutation. The requirement can be very strict and the title in one spouse's name would not be sufficient to show that transmutation.

A.   STRICT TRANSMUTATION REQUIREMENTS: THE CALIFORNIA AND IDAHO APPROACHES

1.   *California*

In 1985, the California transmutation statute went into effect. Its purpose was to overturn prior case law that allowed property to be changed by oral or implied agreement. The transmutation statute covers all types of transmutations of separate and community property and has the following requirement:

CALIFORNIA FAMILY CODE

§852(a). Form of transmutation

A transmutation of real or personal property is not valid unless made in writing by an express declaration that is made, joined in, consented to, or accepted by the spouse whose interest in the property is adversely affected.

ESTATE OF MACDONALD

51 Cal. 3d 262, 794 P.2d 911, 272 Cal. Rptr. 153 (1990)
Supreme Court of California,
En Banc

Panelli, Justice.
Civil Code section 852, subdivision (a) [now Family Code §852(a)] provides: "A transmutation of real or personal property is not valid unless made in writing

by an express declaration that is made, joined in, consented to, or accepted by the spouse whose interest in the property is adversely affected."

In this case we are asked to decide what type of writing is necessary to satisfy the statute's requirements. In our view, §852(a) must be construed to preclude reference to extrinsic evidence in the proof of transmutations. Accordingly, we conclude a writing is not an "express declaration" unless it contains language which expressly states that a change in the characterization or ownership of the property is being made. Thus, we affirm the judgment of the Court of Appeal.

FACTS AND PROCEEDINGS BELOW

Decedent Margery M. MacDonald ("Margery" or "decedent") married respondent Robert MacDonald ("Robert") in 1973. Both had been married previously, and each had children by a previous spouse. Robert was president of R.F. MacDonald Company ("the company"), where he participated in a defined benefit pension plan.

In August 1984, Margery learned that she had terminal cancer, and she and Robert made plans to divide their property into separate estates. Wishing to leave her property to her own four children, Margery divided the couple's jointly held stock, sold her half, and placed the proceeds in her separate account. The MacDonalds thereafter consulted with their personal accountant and attorney regarding the division of their jointly held real property. These properties were appraised and divided; Robert paid Margery $33,000 to equalize the division.

Robert was covered by a company defined benefit pension plan which came into existence on January 1, 1977. The designated beneficiary of Robert's interest in the pension plan was a revocable living trust he had established in 1982. The terms of the trust left the bulk of the corpus to Robert's children. In November 1984, Robert turned 65 and his defined pension plan was terminated. On March 21, 1985, Robert received a disbursement of $266,557.90 from the plan. It is undisputed that Margery possessed a community property interest in the plan's benefits. The pension funds were not divided or otherwise accounted for at the time of the couple's previous division of their jointly held assets. These community funds were deposited into IRA accounts at three separate financial institutions.

The IRA accounts were opened solely in Robert's name, the designated beneficiary of each being the revocable living trust which had been designated as beneficiary of the pension plan. The three form documents prepared by the financial institutions for signature by IRA account holders, each entitled "Adoption Agreement and Designation of Beneficiary" ("adoption agreements"), provided space for the signature of a spouse not designated as the sole primary beneficiary to indicate consent to the designation. Robert signed the adoption agreements, indicating his agreement to the terms of the IRA account agreements and designating his trust as beneficiary; Margery signed the consent portions of the adoption agreements ("consent paragraphs").

Margery died on June 17, 1985, bequeathing the residue of her estate to her four children. Executrix Judith Bolton filed a petition to determine title to personal property, seeking to establish decedent's community property interest in the funds held in the IRA accounts. The trial court found that, in signing the consent paragraphs of the adoption agreements, decedent intended to waive any community property interest in the pension funds and to transmute her community property share of those funds into Robert's separate property. The court denied Bolton's petition, ruling that decedent had either waived her community property interest in the pension funds or, alternatively, transmuted it to Robert's separate property.

The Court of Appeal reversed, holding that the adoption agreements did not satisfy section 852(a). A dissenting justice argued that because decedent, in signing the consent paragraphs, had taken "specific, clear and final [action to] accomplish both [a] transfer and a subsequent transmutation, [t]he language and purpose of the statutory requirement were fully satisfied."

We granted review to construe section 852(a).

DISCUSSION

It is undisputed that Margery possessed a community property interest in Robert's pension funds at the time they were disbursed to him. However, in California, married persons may by agreement or transfer, with or without consideration, transmute community property to separate property of either spouse.

In this case, the trial court made a *factual finding* that "[d]ecedent, in executing the Adoption Agreement[s] for the three IRA's, intended to waive any community right she had in those IRA's and in fact to transmute her share of that community property asset to the separate property of Respondent." However, we defer to a trial court's factual findings only when they are supported by substantial evidence.

Our close review of the record reveals that no substantial evidence supported the finding that Margery intended a transmutation. The Court of Appeal incorrectly stated that Robert presented his own testimony and that of decedent's accountant as to decedent's state of mind when she signed the adoption agreements. In fact, there is absolutely no record evidence relating to Margery's intentions or state of mind when she signed the adoption agreements. The only testimony presented as to her state of mind during her estate planning activities relates to when she and her husband arranged an equal division of their jointly held real properties. The couple's accountant testified that she did not assist them in the division of any other assets.

Even if the trial court's findings as to Margery's intent were supported by substantial evidence, however, they would not support a finding of transmutation in this case. The statute providing for transmutation invalidates attempts to transmute real or personal property unless certain conditions are met. We must therefore determine whether Margery's actions, whether or not they were *intended* to transfer her interest in the pension funds, were effective under section 852(a) to transmute those funds from community property to Robert's separate property. We are of the opinion that they were not.

Section 852(a) requires that a valid transmutation be made, not just in writing, but in "writing by an *express declaration* that is made, joined in, consented to, or accepted by the spouse whose interest in the property is adversely affected." There is no dispute that the consent paragraphs in the adoption agreements, and decedent's signatures thereon, are "made in writing." These writings are manifestly "made, joined in, consented to or accepted by the spouse whose interest in the property is adversely affected," viz., decedent. Thus, the sole remaining issue to be decided is whether they constitute "an express declaration" for the purposes of section 852(a).

It is a fundamental rule of statutory construction that a court "should ascertain the intent of the Legislature so as to effectuate the purpose of the law." In determining such intent "[t]he court turns first to the words themselves for the answer."

It is not immediately evident from a reading of section 852(a) what is meant by the phrase "an express declaration." Examination of the words of the statute and their arrangement reveals only that the "express declaration" called for is to be one "by" which "[a] transmutation of real or personal property" is "made." The statute does not state what words such an "express declaration" must include, what information it must convey, or even what topics it should discuss.

Since the words of section 852(a) themselves, including the phrase "an express declaration," are unclear and ambiguous, it is necessary to resort to other indicia of the intent of the Legislature to determine what meaning the statute should be given. In doing so, we consider the historical circumstances of the statute's enactment, as well as its legislative history.

Section 852(a) was adopted in 1984. Both parties refer to a 1983 report of the California Law Revision Commission ("Commission") to ascertain the intent of the Legislature in enacting section 852(a). In recommending that the Legislature enact that statute, the Commission described "[s]ection 852 [as] impos[ing] formalities on interspousal transmutations for the purpose of increasing certainty in the determination whether a transmutation has in fact occurred." The Commission report goes on to state that section 852 overrules existing case law that permitted oral transmutation of personal property.

In its discussion of the law then governing transmutations the Commission observed that "[u]nder California law it is quite easy for spouses to transmute both real and personal property; a transmutation can be found based on oral statements or implications from the conduct of the spouses."

The Commission further observed that "the rule of easy transmutation has also generated extensive litigation in dissolution proceedings. It encourages a spouse, after the marriage has ended, to transform a passing comment into an 'agreement' or even to commit perjury by manufacturing an oral or implied transmutation." The Commission concluded its discussion of transmutation law by saying that "California law should continue to recognize informal transmutations for certain personal property gifts between the spouses, but should require a writing for a transmutation of real property or other personal property." Unfortunately, the Commission did not explicitly expand upon the question of what such a writing should be required to contain, except to warn that "[t]he requirement of a writing should not be satisfied by a statement in a married person's will of the community character of the property, until the person's death." The Commission stated only that its recommendations would be effectuated by the enactment of certain measures, including section 852(a).

It thus appears from an examination of the Commission report that section 852(a) was intended to remedy problems which arose when courts found transmutations on the basis of evidence the Legislature considered unreliable. To remedy these problems the Legislature decided that proof of transmutation should henceforth be in writing, and therefore enacted the writing requirement of section 852(a).

There is no question that the Legislature intended, by enacting section 852(a), to invalidate all solely oral transmutations. (Commission report, *supra*, at pp. 224-225.) By definition, *any* writing requirement would accomplish this limited goal. It is equally clear, however, that the Legislature intended that section 852(a) would invalidate some transmutations which, under then-prevailing case law, would have been upheld on the basis of evidence other than oral statements.

In our view, the Legislature cannot have intended that *any* signed writing whatsoever by the adversely affected spouse would suffice to meet the requirements of section 852(a). First, to so construe that statute would render mere surplusage all the language following the words "unless made in writing," including the phrase "an express declaration." A construction rendering some words surplusage is to be avoided. Second, as respondent acknowledges, some of the "easy transmutation" cases involved non oral conduct or signed writings. Therefore, it seems reasonable to assume that the Legislature intended section 852(a) to invalidate some claimed transmutations even though some form of writing existed.

Thus, to construe section 852(a) so that it does not contain mere surplusage, as well as to effect legislative intent, we must fashion a test by which courts may judge the adequacy of particular writings for section 852(a) purposes.

[W]e conclude that a writing signed by the adversely affected spouse is not an "express declaration" for the purposes of section 852(a) *unless* it contains language which expressly states that the characterization or ownership of the property is being changed.

Our conclusion honors each of the principles of statutory construction we have discussed. First, it interprets "express declaration," so as to give significance to all the words of section 852(a). Second, it effects the intent of the Legislature to create a writing requirement which enables courts to validate transmutations without resort to extrinsic evidence and, thus, without encouraging perjury and the proliferation of litigation.

We must now consider whether the writing involved in this case satisfies section 852(a). Decedent signed paragraphs consenting to the designation of a beneficiary on three standard bank-form adoption agreements. These paragraphs read in full: "If participant's spouse is not designated as the sole primary beneficiary, spouse must sign consent. Consent of spouse: Being the participant's spouse, I hereby consent to the above designation. [Signature.]"

Obviously, the consent paragraphs contain no language which characterizes the property assertedly being transmuted, viz., the pension funds which had been deposited in the account. It is not possible to tell from the face of the consent paragraphs, or even from the face of the adoption agreements as a whole, whether decedent was aware that the legal effect of her signature might be to alter the character or ownership of her interest in the pension funds. There is certainly no language in the consent paragraphs, or the adoption agreements as a whole, expressly stating that decedent was effecting a change in the character or ownership of her interest. Thus, we agree with the Court of Appeal that these writings fail to satisfy the "express declaration" requirement of section 852(a).

We do not hold that section 852(a) requires use of the term "transmutation" or any other particular locution. Although a writing sufficient to satisfy the "express declaration" requirement of section 852(a) might very well contain the words "transmutation," "community property," or "separate property," it need not.

For example, the paragraph signed by decedent here would have been sufficient if it had included an additional sentence reading: "I give to the account holder any interest I have in the funds deposited in this account."

We are aware that section 852(a), construed as we have construed it today, may preclude the finding of a transmutation in some cases, where some extrinsic evidence of an intent to transmute exists. But, as previously discussed, it is just such reliance on extrinsic evidence for the proof of transmutations which the Legislature intended to eliminate in enacting the writing requirement of section 852(a).

Manifestly, there are policy considerations weighing both in favor of and against any type of transmutation proof requirement. On the one hand, honoring the intentions of the parties involved in a purported transmutation may suggest that weight should be given to *any* indication of these intentions. On the other hand, the desirability of assuring that a spouse's community property entitlements are not improperly undermined, as well as concern for judicial economy and efficiency, support somewhat more restrictive proof requirements. The Legislature, in enacting section 852(a), apparently thought it unwise to rely on some kinds of evidence to effect transmutations. It is not for us to question that legislative conclusion. Accordingly, the judgment of the Court of Appeal is affirmed.

Lucas, C.J., and Broussard, Eagleson and Kennard, JJ., concur.

Arabian, Justice, dissenting, to opinion by Panelli, Justice.

INTRODUCTION

If the decedent in extremis had in her last breath uttered the question, "Oh death, where is thy sting?" the majority garbed in grim shrouds would have whispered, "At probate."

It has been said that no good deed goes unpunished. Unhappily, there is a kernel of truth in this otherwise cynical aphorism, perfectly illustrated in the majority opinion, which begins its journey attempting to protect spouses against questionable transmutations of community property, and ends by negating the estate plan of the decedent herein, and of others who, like decedent, can no longer dictate their intentions. Worse, in exalting form over substance, the majority impose unnecessarily rigid requirements on the drafting and interpretation of future transfers between spouses. In the process, they undermine the deference that trial courts deserve and merit on review. Therefore, I must respectfully dissent.

DISCUSSION

The narrow issue presented is whether, in order to satisfy the requirements of section 852(a), a writing must expressly state that the writer is effecting a transmutation of property. Conceding that the statutory language yields no ready answer, the majority turn to legislative history. From their reading of the pertinent sources, they conclude that the statute was intended to foreclose the courts from the use of extrinsic evidence to ascertain the writer's intent. An examination of those same historical sources, however, reveals that the majority's conclusion is fundamentally flawed; the plain evidence shows that the Legislature intended a simple writing requirement akin to the statute of frauds — a formality that would admit the use of collateral evidence to clarify the writer's meaning.

The primary source relied on by the majority is the California Law Revision Commission (Commission) report to the Legislature. The salient portion of the Commission report reads as follows:

> "Under California law it is quite easy for spouses to transmute both real and personal property; a transmutation can be found based on *oral statements or implications from the conduct of the spouses*. [¶] California law permits an oral transmutation or transfer of property between the spouses *notwithstanding the statute of frauds*. [Fn. omitted.] . . . It encourages a spouse, after the marriage has ended, to transform a passing comment into an 'agreement' or even to commit perjury by manufacturing an oral or implied transmutation. [¶] Most people would find an oral transfer of such property, even between spouses, to be suspect and probably fraudulent, either as to creditors or between each other. [¶] California law should continue to recognize informal transmutations for certain personal property gifts between the spouses, but should require *a writing* for the transmutation of real property or other personal property."

Thus, the historical sources — the *very* sources cited and relied on by the majority — demonstrate irrefutably that the underlying purpose of section 852 was to overrule decisions permitting transmutations "based on oral statements or implications from the conduct of the spouses" (Commission report, *supra*, at p. 213), and to create the equivalent of a statute of frauds to govern transmutations of property between spouses.

California's general statute of frauds provides that certain specified contracts are invalid "unless they, or some note or memorandum thereof, are in writing and subscribed by the party to be charged or by the party's agent." To satisfy the statute, it is well settled that a writing must contain only the essential terms of an agreement, and that what is essential depends on the particular agreement and its context.

In light of these settled principles, it is evident that the Legislature could *not* have contemplated the strict test for compliance with section 852 formulated by the majority. As noted, the legislative history reveals an intent to apply the "ordinary rules and formalities" associated with the statute of frauds. The Legislature, therefore, *must* have envisaged the introduction of extrinsic evidence where the writing, "interpreted in accordance with the intentions of the parties" demonstrates at least *an intent to transmute property pursuant to section 852.*

Applying this test to the case at bar, it is clear that such an intention is readily discernible from the face of the IRA agreements. The transfer of the pension disbursement to Robert's IRA accounts involved a transfer of community property funds. The agreements contained an express declaration that the funds were being placed in Robert's name only. Decedent, the spouse whose interest was adversely affected, expressly consented to the designation of Robert's living trust, not herself, as the beneficiary. Thus, as contemplated by section 852, the IRA documents plainly involved a transfer of property and contained an express consent to that transfer by the spouse whose interests were adversely affected.

To be sure, the agreements did not explicitly describe the pension funds as community property or expressly state that decedent intended to transfer her interest to Robert. By requiring her consent, however, the documents clearly alerted decedent to the fact that she had an interest in the funds for which a waiver was required.

The majority, nevertheless, assert that there is *no* substantial evidence to support the trial court's finding that decedent knew she had a community property interest in the pension funds and intended to waive or transmute that interest. This is a patently selective reading of the record, contrary to the fundamental rule that a reviewing court must indulge all reasonable inferences in favor of the judgment. The trial court found, and the undisputed evidence showed, that decedent had worked as a bookkeeper for her husband's business and had managed the family's financial affairs. She was aware of her husband's pension plan. She consented to the designation of Robert's living trust as the beneficiary of the IRA funds. The amount was in excess of $250,000. For what conceivable reason would an intelligent and financially sophisticated woman consent to relinquish so large an interest to which she was not even entitled? It is an insult to the decedent, and a distortion of the appellate review process, to insinuate that decedent was ignorant of her interest in the IRA funds.

In applying the "ordinary rules and formalities" to transfers under section 852, the Legislature intended to preserve the traditional rules that govern the interpretation of writings where the intent of the parties is in dispute and may depend, in part, on the evaluation of extrinsic evidence. The trial court here was in the best position to judge decedent's purpose, construed in light of the documents, the evidence, and the testimony and demeanor of the witnesses. In overruling that court's considered judgment, we not only contravene the legislative intent, but repudiate the necessary deference accorded trial courts in making such difficult determinations.

Worse, however, is the injury that the majority visits upon the decedent and others similarly situated. As her personal accountant testified, Margery's overriding interest, upon learning of her impending death, was to effect a clear allocation of assets in order to avoid any possibility of acrimony between Robert and her children. Her children were well provided for, having received substantial separate property and stock assets. The pension funds, though community property, were essentially the product of Robert's 35 years in business, most of which preceded his marriage to decedent; thus, Margery's election to waive and transfer any interest in those funds was eminently reasonable.

There is no evidence of overreaching here, nor any hint of exploitation. There is only an effort by an obviously intelligent and courageous woman to set her estate in order before her passing, to effectuate a clear and fair allocation of her assets. Her intentions were good, but as Shakespeare observed, "The evil men do lives after them; the good is oft interred with their bones." The majority, sadly, prove the truth of that statement.

Discussion Questions

1. According to the California Supreme Court, what are the requirements of an "expression declaration in writing"?

2. Did the written document signed by Margery MacDonald satisfy the requirements to transmute the IRA account to Robert's separate property?

3. Consider whether the words "I transfer the stock in my account to the account of my wife" are sufficient to transmute the stock to the husband to the wife's separate property?

---

2. *Idaho*

Idaho also has strict requirements for transmuting property, prescribing that "All contracts for marriage settlements must be in writing, and executed and acknowledged or proved in like manner as conveyances of land are required to be executed and acknowledged or proved." Idaho Code §32-917. The burden of proof on the spouse claiming a transmutation is "clear and convincing evidence." When reading the following case, *Hoskinson v. Hoskinson* (2003), consider whether the Idaho Supreme Court's approach is similar or different from the California Supreme Court.

HOSKINSON v. HOSKINSON

139 Idaho 448, 80 P.3d 1049 (2003)
Supreme Court of Idaho

SCHROEDER, Justice.

Reed Hoskinson ("Reed") and Elizabeth Hoskinson ("Elizabeth") were married February 23, 1997, and had a child that year. In 2000 Reed obtained a divorce decree against Elizabeth. Elizabeth appealed to the district court, which affirmed the magistrate judge's decision. Elizabeth argues that the magistrate judge made errors that warrant reversal of the decision, including the magistrate's characterization and division of the community property.

I. BACKGROUND AND PRIOR PROCEEDINGS.

Reed and Elizabeth Hoskinson began living together in May 1995. Elizabeth learned she was pregnant with Reed's child. The couple entered a ceremonial marriage February 23, 1997. Elizabeth gave birth to their child on October 10, 1997.

On December 18, 1998, Reed sued for divorce alleging the marriage date as February 23, 1997, which is the ceremonial marriage date. Reed cited irreconcilable differences as the grounds for divorce. He requested primary physical custody of the child, but he agreed to share legal custody with Elizabeth. The complaint sought to compel Elizabeth to pay child support and to provide medical insurance coverage for the child. The complaint also requested a distribution of community assets and debts.

Elizabeth answered and counterclaimed on January 15, 1999. The answer and counterclaim were amended April 15, 1999. The amended counterclaim sought a divorce based on extreme cruelty and adultery. Both the counterclaim and amended counterclaim stated that Elizabeth and Reed were married on February 23, 1997, the same date alleged by Reed. Elizabeth requested primary physical custody of the child but agreed to share joint legal custody with Reed. Elizabeth sought to compel Reed to pay child support and to provide medical insurance coverage for the child. Elizabeth requested a disproportionate award of community property and debt as well as maintenance and attorney fees.

Reed was granted a divorce on grounds of irreconcilable differences.

In a decision filed August 3, 2001, the district court affirmed the decisions of the magistrate relating to the characterization and division of the parties' property.

On August 22, 2001, Elizabeth sought to appeal to this Court from the memorandum decision, findings and conclusions, judgment and order entered on June 13, 2000.

* * *

V. THE MAGISTRATE DID NOT ERR IN THE CHARACTERIZATION AND DIVISION OF THE PROPERTY.

Elizabeth argues that the magistrate erred by applying the ceremonial marriage date of February 23, 1997, rather than the common law marriage date of May 1, 1995, for purposes of property characterization and division. As a result, she claims the following assets were improperly classified as separate property: (1) the foal crop; (2) hunting and fishing equipment and yard tools; (3) personal property acquired from May 1, 1995, to February 23, 1997; (4) the increase to Reed's retirement and savings from May 1, 1995, to February 23, 1997; and (5) the increase to the value of Reed's home from May 1, 1995, to February 23, 1997.

Elizabeth asserts two other grounds upon which she claims an entitlement to an interest in Reed's home. First, she claims that a 1998 quitclaim deed conveyance from Reed to her and Reed effectively transmuted the property into community property. Second, she argues that she is entitled to an interest in the increased value of the home due to community expenditures, labor and improvements made during marriage.

STANDARD OF REVIEW

The division of community property is subject to the sound discretion of the trial court, whose determination will be upheld on appeal in the absence of a clear showing of an abuse of discretion. . . .

The magistrate's finding that the 1998 quitclaim deed from Reed to himself and Elizabeth did not transmute Reed's home from separate to community property is supported by substantial competent evidence.

Elizabeth argues that the magistrate erred by finding Reed's house was his separate property. In 1998 Reed's home was the subject of two separate quitclaim deeds.

In one deed Elizabeth conveyed her interest in the property to Reed. In the other deed Reed conveyed his interest in the same property to himself and Elizabeth, as "husband and wife." Both deeds were signed and notarized on January 23, 1998. The conveyance from Elizabeth to Reed was recorded the same day. The conveyance from Reed to himself and Elizabeth was recorded on February 9, 1998. Elizabeth claims the second conveyance transmuted Reed's property from separate to community property.

"[A]lthough husband and wife may elect at any time to change their property rights, they must engage in certain formalities." prescribes the requisite formalities as follows: "All contracts for marriage settlements must be in writing, and executed and acknowledged or proved in like manner as conveyances of land are required to be executed and acknowledged or proved." The burden of proof on the party asserting transmutation is a high one, as the Idaho Court of Appeals described in *Ustick v. Ustick,* 104 Idaho 215, 222, 657 P.2d 1083, 1090 (Ct. App. 1983):

> [W]here it is asserted . . . that a spouse intended to transmute property or to make a gift, the burden is on the party urging the assertion to prove the intent in question by clear and convincing evidence. [citations omitted]. Concomitantly, because the question of whether a "clear and convincing" burden of proof has been met is a question for the trier of facts to decide in the first instance, the determination of the trial judge — that a claim was not shown by clear and convincing evidence — is entitled to great weight on appeal. [citations omitted].

In applying Idaho Code §32–917 to the evidence presented at trial, the magistrate made the following findings and conclusion regarding Elizabeth's claim that Reed's quitclaim deed transmuted his separate property into community property:

> Here, the parties offered conflicting evidence of the intent behind the quitclaim deeds. Elizabeth testified that Reed asked her to sign a quitclaim deed to facilitate the financing and that she refused to sign until Reed agreed to sign a deed conveying the property to her and Reed. Reed denied that allegation. He testified he signed the quitclaim deed simply because the lender presented it to him during the loan closing, that he signed it along with many other papers the lender presented to him, and that he had no intent to transmute his property into community property. Reed notes that he alone signed the promissory note for the new loan. Under these circumstances, the court finds that Elizabeth has not proved a transmutation by clear and convincing evidence. The evidence did not establish that Reed intended to make a gift to the community. The evidence did not establish whether the deed to Reed and Elizabeth was signed before or after the deed to Reed. As noted above, Elizabeth damaged her credibility with her lack of candor during her testimony on other issues; therefore, the court is inclined to believe Reed's testimony on the issue.

A trial court's decision will be upheld despite conflicting evidence so long as its findings are supported by substantial competent evidence and are not clearly erroneous. The magistrate found Elizabeth failed to sustain her burden of proving a transmutation. These findings are supported by substantial competent evidence.

Chief Justice TROUT, Justices KIDWELL, EISMANN and BURDICK concur.

Discussion Questions

1. Did the quitclaim deed have any language that indicated a transmutation of husband Reed's separate property to community property?

2. What is the test for whether a written document is a transmutation? And why did Elizabeth fail to prove that there was a transmutation?

B.   ORAL TRANSMUTATIONS PERMITTED: THE WASHINGTON APPROACH

Under Washington law, oral agreements that transmute property from community property to separate property are permitted if "the parties mutually observed the terms of the agreement throughout the marriage." The spouse who is asserting that the property has been transmuted must prove the separate character of the property by clear and convincing evidence. In *Marriage of Mueller* (2007), the Washington Court of Appeals discussed whether the Muellers had an oral agreement to convert John's community property earnings to separate property of each of the spouses. The standard on appeal is whether the trial court's factual findings are supported by substantial evidence. That standard favors the trial court's findings being upheld. In the *Mueller* case, the Court of Appeals stated that the finding was supported by the record but disagreed with the legal conclusion drawn from that finding.

MARRIAGE OF MUELLER

140 Wash. App. 498, 167 P.3d 568 (2007)
Court of Appeals of Washington

Cox, J.

In Washington, all property acquired during marriage is presumptively community property. Spouses may by contractual agreement change their community property into separate property. A spouse seeking to enforce an agreement that purports to convert community property into separate property must establish with clear and convincing evidence both (1) the existence of the agreement and (2) that the parties mutually observed the terms of the agreement throughout their marriage.

Here, John Mueller fails to overcome the presumption that all property acquired during the marriage to Shauna Mueller is community property. We reverse.

Shauna and John Mueller married in 1983 while both were living in Brazil. At the time, they both held full-time jobs. Although John earned more than Shauna, there was not a wide disparity in their incomes.

In 1985, their only child, Mark, was born. Shauna took a leave of absence from her job with Citibank to care for their son. It is undisputed, and the trial court found, that in 1986, following the commencement of Shauna's leave of absence, the parties reached an oral agreement "to divide the remainder of [John's] income after the payment of joint expenses."[8]

The parties dispute the exact circumstances of this discussion. For example, they dispute where the conversation took place, whether Shauna was nursing their son during the conversation, who did what proportion of the talking, and exactly what was said. It is undisputed that they never put the agreement in writing.

Thereafter, the parties abided by the alleged oral agreement to varying degrees of consistency. The trial court noted in its findings specifically how they observed their oral agreement with respect to division of John's income after payment of joint expenses and Shauna's treatment of charitable donations.

After 19 years of marriage, and just after retiring, John commenced this dissolution proceeding. He took the position in this proceeding that the 1986 oral agreement in Brazil converted what was presumptively community property to separate property of each party.[9] Shauna disagreed, arguing that the agreement did not have that effect.

Following a bench trial, the court concluded that the oral agreement changed the character of the property thereafter acquired during marriage to separate property. Based on that characterization, the court divided the property and made other determinations that are at issue on appeal.

Shauna appeals.

CHARACTERIZATION OF PROPERTY

Shauna challenges the division of property. [S]he contends there was no enforceable oral agreement to change the character of the property the parties acquired during marriage from community to separate.

We hold that there was no oral agreement changing the presumptive character of the property as community. Thus, we need not reach her other arguments.

All property acquired during a marriage is presumed to be community property. The law favors characterization of property as community property unless there is no question of its separate character.

A spouse may overcome this heavy presumption with clear and convincing evidence of the property's separate character. Simply placing one's own earnings into a bank account in that spouse's name for management purposes is not sufficient to change the legal character from community to separate property. Likewise, one spouse's control over community funds does not change the character of the property.

Spouses may change the status of their community property to separate property by entering into mutual agreements. These agreements may be oral or written. A spouse seeking to enforce an agreement, whether oral or written, that purports to convert community property into separate property must establish with clear and convincing evidence both (1) the existence of the agreement and (2) that the

---

8. Finding of Fact 2.7(a).

9. At oral argument, the parties agreed that this case was argued below and is argued on appeal on the basis that the community property laws of Washington state applied throughout the marriage of the parties.

parties mutually observed the terms of the agreement throughout their marriage. Because oral agreements are more difficult to prove, courts will overturn an oral property agreement if the parties do not consistently adhere to the agreement during their marriage.

Courts interpret agreements between spouses like they do other types of contracts. In construing contracts, a court's objective is to determine the parties' mutual intent. Extrinsic evidence may be consulted to elucidate the meaning of the contract's terms, but not to contradict the objective manifestations of intent.

In a spousal agreement case such as this one, where the evidentiary standard is clear and convincing, we uphold the trial court's findings of fact if they are supported by "highly probable" substantial evidence. Reviewing a trial court decision under this standard does not permit us to weigh evidence, which is a trial court function. We merely review the factual findings to determine whether they are properly supported by substantial evidence, and whether they in turn support the legal conclusions.

Shauna argues that the trial court erred in concluding that the agreement effectively converted community property into separate property. We agree and hold that John has not met his burden to overcome the community property presumption.

Washington courts have held "on several occasions" that placing one's paycheck into a bank account in that person's own name is insufficient to rebut the presumption that wages earned during a marriage are community property. Likewise, a spouse's physical management and control over community property is allowed by statute and does not change its legal character. More is required.

In contrast, the court in *Dewberry v. George* found clear and convincing evidence of an oral pre-nuptial agreement to convert each spouse's respective income into that spouse's separate property.[28] There, the terms of the agreement were "clear and simple." One spouse testified regarding the terms, and "several witnesses" also testified knowing specifically about the oral pre-nuptial agreement. This evidence supported the existence of four specific terms to which both parties had explicitly, orally agreed, including a provision that each party's income would be the separate property of that party. In addition, the court held that the parties "continually affirmed" the agreement with "painstaking and meticulous effort" over the years through their words and actions. Although the husband later denied the agreement, the trial court specifically found the wife's testimony more credible.

Here, John fails to provide clear and convincing evidence of the first element, the existence of the agreement. He has not proven that the parties agreed to change the legal status of his income from community property to separate property. Rather, he has only shown that they agreed to manage their community income separately.

The trial court made the following finding of fact:

> It is undisputed that in 1986, after [Shauna] stopped working at Citibank, *the parties entered into an oral agreement to divide the remainder of [John's] income after the payment of joint expenses.* ("the Agreement' [sic]) The parties concur that the Agreement was intended to reduce fights between the parties regarding money matters.

---

28. 115 Wash. App. 351, 62 P.3d 525 (2003).

This finding is supported by the record. No one challenges this finding to the extent of what it says.

But the trial court's legal conclusion, that this oral agreement to manage funds changed the legal character of the property, does not follow from this finding of fact. Unlike the wife in *Dewberry*, John offered no evidence that Shauna intended to change the legal ownership of the property. He did not mention the legal status of the property in his conversations with Shauna or explain to her that she would be waiving her community interest in his half of the income. There is simply no evidence in the record that this agreement to manage funds separately was any more than an agreement to manage their community property.

Shauna testified that she understood the agreement was one about management only, as was the case before she took a leave of absence. In contrast, John testified that he thought it effectuated a legal division of the property, although he admitted this term was only "implied." Because the testimony shows that they each objectively manifested different intents, John has not proven a meeting of the minds with regard to the alleged "agreement" he now suggests. Their only objective manifestation of intent was an agreement to divide his income for management purposes.

It is also significant that the alleged agreement to change the character of the parties' property was not reduced to writing. Although a writing is not strictly necessary, some courts have required a writing before finding clear and convincing evidence of an agreement. At one point during the marriage, John's lawyer suggested that he formalize the agreement, but John refused to do so. In any event, the parties' differing recollections of their conversation in forming the alleged agreement undermines John's argument.

Finally, it is undisputed that the management arrangement was originally intended to last only a couple of years, until Shauna returned to work. This fact undercuts the argument that the parties intended to change the legal ownership of John's income for the duration of the marriage.

As to the second element — whether the parties adhered to the agreement — the evidence shows that they somewhat consistently managed their money separately throughout the marriage. As the trial court found, each month John gave Shauna a check for one half of his income after he deducted joint expenses. He inconsistently provided her with written conciliation statements. Each party spent their respective share the way each chose. This behavior is consistent with an agreement to separately manage their community property.

The record also shows that sometimes when Shauna wanted to treat certain expenditures as joint expenses, John disagreed. When that happened, she used her share of the money to make purchases that included things like furnishings for the house and things for their son. These expenses either directly or indirectly benefited the community. So we cannot conclude that the parties consistently adhered to their oral agreement throughout the marriage.

The fact that both spouses made contributions, gifts, and expenditures without consulting one another does not change the fact that John's income presumptively remained community property. Spouses may each control community property.

In his brief, John makes much of the fact that Shauna ended up with less money than he did because she spent more of her share during the marriage. How that changes the proper characterization of the property as community or separate is unclear to this court.

In sum, John has failed to show the existence of an oral agreement to change the presumptive character of the property as community property.

We reverse and remand for further proceedings.

We concur: ELLINGTON and AGID, JJ.

Discussion Questions

1. Why did John fail to rebut the community presumption that his earnings had been transmuted to the separate property of John and Shauna?

2. What is the significance of the determination that John's earnings are considered community property rather than each spouse's separate property?

C.   WRITTEN TRANSMUTATIONS FOR THE PURPOSE OF ESTATE PLANNING: THE WASHINGTON AND CALIFORNIA APPROACHES

As spouses acquire property and they grow older, they often seek the advice of attorneys on estate planning. They anticipate that their marriage will last until "death do us part," and are urged to arrange their affairs for various estate planning purposes. Some of those purposes are to express how they wish their property to be distributed upon death and how to avoid extended probate proceedings and estate taxes. In some cases, they are advised to state in writing whether their property is separate property or community property. When a marriage is stable, they often opt in writing to transmute the separate property of one spouse into community property. They then forget about the agreement that accomplished that transmutation. If divorce occurs, the issue is often whether the transmutation document should be applied when the intention of the spouses at the time was to prepare their affairs in the event of death.

1.   Washington

MARRIAGE OF SCHWEITZER

132 Wash. 2d 318, 937 P.2d 1062 (1997)
Supreme Court of Washington,
En Banc

DOLLIVER, Justice.

In this action for dissolution of marriage, we examine whether a community property agreement is enforceable where extrinsic evidence indicates the parties signed the agreement for estate planning purposes. We also discuss whether the use of community resources for an adult stepchild's college education amounts to a gift of community funds requiring the consent of both spouses.

Fabian and Frances Schweitzer were married in 1973. Mr. Schweitzer came into the marriage with substantial separate assets. During the marriage, Mr. Schweitzer sold all of his separate assets and placed the proceeds in bank accounts containing community funds. Mr. and Mrs. Schweitzer kept separate bank accounts from which they each contributed to community expenses. By the end of the marriage, the Schweitzers had accumulated $1,733,000 in community property.

Mr. and Mrs. Schweitzer signed a standard-form community property agreement in March 1981, just before Mr. Schweitzer was to leave on an international vacation. The couple purchased the agreement at a stationery store and did not consult an attorney. The preamble of the agreement stated it was made "pursuant to the provisions of §26.16.120RCW, permitting agreements between husband and wife fixing the status and disposition of community property to take effect upon the death of either." Ex. 1. Paragraph I of the agreement purported to convert all separate property to community property, and paragraph II stated that all community property would vest in the survivor upon the death of the other spouse. Mr. and Mrs. Schweitzer's signatures were notarized, but the lines for witness signatures were left blank.

When Mrs. Schweitzer filed for dissolution of the marriage in 1992, she sought to enforce the community property agreement. Mr. Schweitzer argued the parties intended the agreement to take effect only upon death and that they did not intend it to transform separate property into community property immediately, as provided by section I of the agreement. Mr. Schweitzer testified he did not remember reading the document.

Mrs. Schweitzer acknowledged at trial that the agreement was intended to provide for her in case anything happened to Mr. Schweitzer while he was on vacation. However, she also claims both she and Mr. Schweitzer intended section I of the agreement to convert any separate property to community property at the time of signing. Mr. and Mrs. Schweitzer did not alter the way they dealt with their property after signing the agreement.

The trial court found the agreement was actually intended as an estate planning document and that neither of the parties intended the agreement to convert separate property to community property at the time of signing. The trial court also found Mr. Schweitzer had adequately traced the proceeds from the sale of his separate property. The court accordingly awarded Mr. Schweitzer $180,231 in cash as his separate property. The court awarded Mrs. Schweitzer $72,027 in cash, inheritances, bonds, and retirement funds as her separate property.

Mrs. Schweitzer appealed. The Court of Appeals held the trial court erred in characterizing any of the property as separate because the community property agreement had converted all separate property to community property at the time of signing. *In re Marriage of Schweitzer*, 81 Wash. App. 589, 594-95, 915 P.2d 575 (1996). The court reasoned the trial court had improperly considered extrinsic evidence of the parties' intent because the evidence contradicted written terms of the agreement. Because the Court of Appeals held the community property agreement was enforceable, it did not rule on whether Mr. Schweitzer had adequately traced his separate property. The court also held the trial court erred in ruling that expenditures and debt incurred for Tony's education were Mrs. Schweitzer's sole responsibility. *Schweitzer*, 81 Wash. App. at 596-98, 915 P.2d 575.

Mr. and Mrs. Schweitzer each petitioned this court for review.

I. WITNESSING REQUIREMENT

Mr. Schweitzer first argues the community property agreement is void because it was not witnessed. RCW 26.16.120 states that property agreements

> may be made at any time by the husband and wife by the execution of an instrument in writing under their hands and seals, and to be witnessed, acknowledged and certified in the same manner as deeds to real estate are required to be. . . .

When the statute was enacted in 1881, deeds were required to be witnessed. However, this requirement was eliminated in 1929. RCW 64.04.020. The reason why a community property agreement was required to be witnessed in the same manner as a deed was because the agreement may have conveyed an interest in real property. Given that the witnessing requirement for deeds was repealed 68 years ago, there is no longer any reason to require community property agreements to be witnessed. When interpreting a statute, this court gives effect to the plain meaning of the statutory language. *Higgins v. Stafford*, 123 Wash. 2d 160, 165, 866 P.2d 31 (1994). The plain meaning of the statute is that community property agreements, like deeds, need not be witnessed.

II. STANDARD-FORM COMMUNITY PROPERTY AGREEMENTS

Next, we examine whether a standard-form community property agreement converts separate property to community property at the time of signing. Although there is no statute specifically authorizing the conversion of separate property to community property prior to death, the court in *Volz v. Zang*, 113 Wash. 378, 194 P. 409 (1920) established that spouses may do so by proper agreement or conveyance. The result of a community property agreement " 'is that neither spouse will have any separate property while both live.' " *Lyon v. Lyon*, 100 Wash. 2d 409, 412, 670 P.2d 272 (1983) (quoting Robert F. Brachtenbach, *Community Property Agreements — Many Questions, Few Answers*, 37 Wash. L. Rev. 469, 479 (1962)).

The standard-form community property agreement signed by the Schweitzers is known in Washington as a "three-pronged" community property agreement. Harry M. Cross, *The Community Property Law in Washington*, 61 Wash. L. Rev. 13, 101 (1985) (hereinafter "Cross"). The first prong converts the separate property of each spouse into community property. The second prong provides that all future-acquired property that would otherwise be separate property shall be community property. The third prong vests title of all community property in the survivor upon the death of the other spouse. The Schweitzer agreement states:

> [P]ursuant to the provisions of §26.16.120 RCW, permitting agreements between husband and wife fixing the status and disposition of community property to take effect

upon the death of either. Witnesseth: That, in consideration of the love and affection that each of us has for each other, and in consideration of the mutual benefits to be derived by each of us, it is hereby agreed, covenanted, and promised as follows:

I.

That all property of whatsoever nature or description whether real, personal or mixed and wheresoever situated now owned or hereafter acquired by us or either of us, including separate property, shall be considered and is hereby declared to be community property, and each of us hereby conveys and quit claims to the other his or her interest in any separate property he or she now owns or hereafter acquires so as to convert the same to community property.

II.

That upon the death of either of us, title to all community property as herein defined shall immediately vest in fee simple in the survivor.

Ex. 1.

Three-pronged community property agreements have been recognized to convert separate property to community property at the time they are signed. In *In re Marriage of Hadley*, 88 Wash. 2d 649, 654, 565 P.2d 790 (1977), we held that an agreement analogous to a community property agreement was binding in dissolution proceedings, even though it was signed in contemplation of death rather than dissolution.

In its oral ruling explaining why it found the agreement was not intended to take effect until death, the trial court reasoned the agreement "was under the statute providing for a disposition of property upon the death of either one of them. . . ." However, the fact that the standard-form three-pronged community property agreement refers in its preamble to RCW 26.16.120, which authorizes agreements between spouses "to take effect upon the death of either," does not mean the first two prongs of the agreement must wait until death to take effect. The first two prongs, which convert present and future separate property to community property, take effect at the time of signing. Indeed, the plain language of section I clearly states, "all property . . . is hereby declared to be community property. . . ."

If Mr. Schweitzer had intended the first two prongs of the agreement to take effect only at death, he could have provided so in the contract. In *In re Estate of Brown*, 29 Wash. 2d 20, 24, 185 P.2d 125 (1947), the parties signed an agreement specifically providing that, "upon the death of either of them such property as they now own or may hereafter acquire . . . shall be considered as community property. . . ." Whereas this type of property transfer takes effect only at death, the three-pronged agreement signed by the Schweitzers converts separate property to community property at the time of execution.

III. Extrinsic Evidence — Generally

We next examine whether the Court of Appeals erred in holding the trial court improperly considered extrinsic evidence of the parties' intent in finding the community property agreement had no effect. *Schweitzer*, 81 Wash. App. at 594-95, 915 P.2d 575. The Court of Appeals reasoned that extrinsic evidence cannot be used to delete or contradict the written terms of an agreement. *Schweitzer*, 81 Wash. App. at 595, 915 P.2d 575. The court concluded the trial court had "used parol evidence impermissibly to subtract an entire paragraph from the agreement and give it no effect whatsoever." *Schweitzer*, 81 Wash. App. at 595, 915 P.2d 575.

The Court of Appeals was correct. In *Berg v. Hudesman*, 115 Wash. 2d 657, 667, 801 P.2d 222 (1990), this court held extrinsic evidence is generally admissible to ascertain the intent of the parties to a contract. However, we made it clear in *Berg* that this rule, known as the "context rule," authorizes the use of extrinsic evidence only to elucidate the meaning of the words of a contract, and "not for the purpose of showing intention independent of the instrument." We emphasized, "[i]t is the duty of the court to declare the meaning of what is written, and not what was intended to be written." We accordingly held in *Berg* that parol evidence cannot be used to "add[ ] to, modify[ ], or contradict[ ] the terms of a written contract, in the absence of fraud, accident, or mistake." The Court of Appeals therefore correctly applied the *Berg* doctrine when it held extrinsic evidence of the parties' intent is generally not admissible to contradict the terms of a written agreement.

IV. Extrinsic Evidence — Mutual Mistake

We next ask whether extrinsic evidence is nonetheless admissible to show the parties made a mutual mistake about the effect of the community property agreement and, if so, whether the evidence shows such a mistake was made by clear, cogent, and convincing evidence.

Although extrinsic evidence is generally not admissible to show intent contrary to the provisions of a written contract, it *is* admissible to show mutual mistake. We stated in *Berg* that parol evidence cannot be used to "add[ ] to, modify[ ], or contradict[ ] the terms of a written contract, *in the absence of fraud, accident, or mistake.*" The parties neither argued this theory to the Court of Appeals, nor did they discuss it in their petitions for review. However, we requested supplemental briefing from the parties on the mutual mistake theory when we granted review.

"Community property agreements are treated as contracts, and the general rules of contract rescission apply." A court can rescind a contract where both parties are mistaken about a basic assumption underlying the agreement. A mistake as to expression is a mistake as to a basic assumption of a contract. Restatement (Second) of Contracts §155 cmt. a (1981); *see also Bergstrom v. Olson*, 39 Wash.2d 536, 542, 236 P.2d 1052 (1951) (mutual mistake found where the intention of the parties was identical at the time of agreement, but the written contract failed to express that intention). However, the party asserting mutual mistake must prove by "clear, cogent, and convincing evidence" that both parties were mistaken.

Mr. Schweitzer argues both he and Mrs. Schweitzer mistakenly assumed the agreement would not take effect until one of them died. Mr. Schweitzer's argument relies almost exclusively upon *In re Marriage of Justus,* an unpublished Court of Appeals decision. 82 Wash. App. 1013, 1996 WL 312526 (No. 14430-5-III June 11, 1996). Unpublished opinions have no precedential value and cannot be cited as authority under RAP 10.4(h). *State v. Sigman,* 118 Wash. 2d 442, 444 n. 1, 826 P.2d 144, 24 A.L.R.5th 856 (1992); *see also* RCW 2.06.040 ("Decisions determined not to have precedential value shall not be published.").

Notwithstanding the fact that he relies upon an unpublished case, Mr. Schweitzer's legal argument is theoretically correct. However, the record does not demonstrate that both parties intended the agreement to operate only at death. If there was any mistake at all, it belonged to Mr. Schweitzer in not reading the community property agreement before signing it. The existence of a unilateral mistake will not void a contract under the theory of mutual mistake. Furthermore, "a party to a contract which he has voluntarily signed will not be heard to declare that he did not read it, or was ignorant of its contents."

Moreover, Mr. Schweitzer testified in his deposition that he had intended all property to be community property if the marriage had continued. Where there is no mutual mistake, but only an expectation that failed to materialize, a court will not rescind a contract.

Mrs. Schweitzer consistently testified that, although both parties intended the agreement to operate at death, she also intended section I of the agreement to transform separate property into community property immediately. Her intention to transfer all community property to the surviving spouse under section II of the agreement does not preclude a coexisting intention to convert any separate property to community property at the time the agreement was signed. Indeed, this is the essence of the three-pronged community property agreement.

Appellate review of a trial court's findings of fact is generally limited to determining whether substantial evidence supports the findings. However, substantial evidence must be "highly probable" where the standard of proof in the trial court is clear, cogent, and convincing evidence. "Courts of equity do not grant the high remedy of reformation upon a probability, nor even upon a *mere* preponderance of evidence, but only upon a certainty of the error."

If the trial court had found clear, cogent, and convincing evidence supported the existence of a mutual mistake, this court would not be able to sustain that finding under the "highly probable" substantial evidence standard. Mr. Schweitzer bears the burden of proving that *both* parties made a mistake; at best, he has proven that *he* made a mistake in not reading the contract. Therefore, the community property agreement will be enforced.

VII. Conclusion

We hold the trial court erred in finding the community property agreement was unenforceable. The agreement converted all separate property to community property at the time it was signed.

We remand this case for a redistribution of property consistent with this opinion.

Durham, C.J., and Smith, Guy, Johnson, Madsen, Alexander, Talmadge and Sanders, JJ., concur.

Discussion Questions

1. In this case, both the husband Fabian and the wife Frances indicated that they intended the agreement to operate at death. Why then was their separate property transmuted to community property at the time it was signed?

2. What should be the role of extrinsic evidence in deciding whether the transmutation agreement should be enforced at divorce?

3. Since Washington has just and equitable division of both separate and community property, why was it necessary to decide the issue of the character of the property?

---

2. California

California's Family Code prescribes strict requirements for transmutations of property during marriage. If done according to those requirements, even a statement in a will can represent a transmutation of property. However, that statement in a will does not control in dissolution proceedings, because that is a "proceeding commenced before the death of the person who made the will."

CALIFORNIA FAMILY CODE

§853. Effect of will

(a) A statement in a will of the character of property is not admissible as evidence of a transmutation of the property in a proceeding commenced before the death of the person who made the will.

Recent litigation in California addressed the issues of whether other estate planning documents effect a transmutation at the time the document is executed and, if so, whether they are admissible in a divorce proceeding. The major estate planning document other than a will is a Trust. A Trust is considered a "will substitute" that is used to transfer property upon death without the necessity of probate proceedings.

MARRIAGE OF HOLTEMANN

166 Cal. App. 4th 1166, 83 Cal. Rptr. 3d 385 (2008)
California Court of Appeal

Perren, J.

In *In re Marriage of Starkman* (2005) 129 Cal. App. 4th 659, 28 Cal. Rptr. 3d 639, we concluded that merely characterizing separate property transferred to a trust established pursuant to an estate plan as "community property" is insufficient to effectuate a transmutation of the property in the absence of "'language which expressly states that the characterization or ownership of the property is being changed.'" (*Id.*, at p. 664, 28 Cal. Rptr. 3d 639, quoting *Estate of MacDonald* (1990) 51 Cal. 3d 262, 272, 272 Cal. Rptr. 153, 794 P.2d 911.) Here we are presented with such a clear expression, in the form of an express agreement to transmute property transferred into a trust established for the same purpose. We conclude that a present transmutation of separate property to community property was thereby effected, notwithstanding language in the transmutation agreement and trust that purports to qualify, limit or condition the transfer upon the death of either spouse.

Frank Gordon Holtemann appeals from a bifurcated order issued in favor of his former wife, Barbara Holtemann, regarding the legal effect of a spousal property transmutation agreement executed during the marriage. Frank contends the family law court erred in finding that the agreement contained an "express declaration" sufficient to transmute his separate property into community property, as contemplated by Family Code section 852, subdivision (a). We conclude otherwise and affirm.

FACTS AND PROCEDURAL HISTORY

Frank and Barbara were married on June 21, 2003, and separated on June 2, 2006. The parties had no children together, although each has adult children from prior marriages.

When the parties were married, Frank had considerable assets while Barbara had few. The parties jointly retained attorney Joseph Look to prepare estate planning documents that would eliminate the need for probate and minimize taxes in the event of either spouse's death. On March 10, 2005, the parties executed a document entitled "Spousal Property Transmutation Agreement" (the Transmutation Agreement) and another entitled "Holtemann Community Property Trust" (the Trust). An introductory provision in the Transmutation Agreement states that "[t]he parties are entering into this agreement in order to specify the character of their property interests pursuant to the applicable provisions of the California Family Code. This agreement is not made in contemplation of a separation or marital dissolution and is made solely for the purpose of interpreting how property shall be disposed of on the deaths of the parties." The parties also acknowledged that Look had explained the "legal consequences" of the agreement, and that they had decided not to retain separate counsel after being advised of the advantages of doing so.

THE TRANSMUTATION AGREEMENT

Article 2.1 of the Transmutation Agreement states as follows: "*Transmutation of Husband's Separate Property to Community Property.* Husband agrees that the character of the property described in Exhibit A (including any future rents, issues, profits, and proceeds of that property) is hereby transmuted from his separate property to the community property of both parties. Exhibit A is attached to and made part of this agreement." Exhibit A, which is identified as both "Husband's Separate Property Being Transmuted to Community Property" and a "List of Community Property," lists a total of eight items of property, including the spouses' residence in Nipomo as well as stock portfolios and land, building, and gas well partnership interests identifying the "Frank G. Holtemann 1996 Trust" as the owner. Article 2.3 further provides that "[c]oncurrently herewith, Husband and Wife have entered into a Declaration of Trust for the Holtemann Community Property Trust; it being the intention of the parties that the property transmuted by Husband hereunder shall be transferred and assigned into such Trust. Wife acknowledges that the transmutation of Husband's separate property into community property herewith was undertaken upon the express condition that the disposition of the trust estate of said Trust, upon the death of Husband and of Wife, as provided for in said Declaration of Trust, dated March 10, 2005, shall remain in effect, and not be amended, modified or changed by Wife, so that upon the death of the parties, the property subject to this Agreement will pass as provided in said Declaration of Trust. The parties further acknowledge that, but for such agreed disposition of the subject property, settlor Frank Holtemann would not have effected the within transmutation of his separate property into community property. Wife agrees not to amend, modify or change the dispositive provisions of any of the trusts established pursuant to said Declaration of Trust without Husband's prior written consent and agreement."

THE TRUST

Article 1.3 of the Trust provides: "*Statement of Intent.* This is a joint trust established by the settlors in order to hold community property of the settlors, which community property was created by the transmutation of separate property of settlor Frank G. Holtemann concurrently with the execution of this trust instrument. The parties each acknowledge that the transmutation of Frank Holtemann's separate property into community property was undertaken upon the condition of and with this trust instrument in mind, in particular with the disposition of the trust estate upon the death of the settlors as provided for herein in mind; and but for such agreed disposition, settlor Frank Holtemann would not have effected the transmutation of his separate property into community property, with which this trust was funded." Article 2.2, entitled "*Character of Trust Assets,*" provides that "[a]ll community property of the settlors transferred to this trust, and the proceeds of all such property, shall continue to be community property under the laws of California, subject to the provisions of this instrument. All separate and quasi-community property shall remain the separate or quasi-community property, respectively, of the contributing settlor."

The Trust further states that "[d]uring the joint lifetimes of the settlors, any trust created by this instrument may be revoked or terminated, in whole or in part, by either settlor as to any separate or quasi-community property of that settlor and any community property of the settlors." The Trust also states that "[u]nless otherwise provided in the revocation or this trust instrument, *any community property so returned shall continue to be the community property of the settlors.*" (Italics added.)

THE PROCEEDINGS

Barbara filed a petition to dissolve the marriage on August 1, 2006. On October 19, 2006, Frank issued notice that he had exercised his right to revoke the Trust. The parties subsequently stipulated to bifurcate the trial to determine the validity of the Transmutation Agreement. The trial court subsequently found that under the express terms of the Transmutation Agreement, Frank had transmuted his separate property identified in exhibit A to community property. In addition, the court ordered Frank to pay $13,000 to Barbara's attorney for the purpose of retaining experts to value the community property identified in exhibit A to the Transmutation Agreement.

The court issued a certificate of probable cause certifying the order for interlocutory review, and we subsequently granted Frank's motion for leave to appeal the order.

DISCUSSION

Frank contends that the Transmutation Agreement and the Trust are insufficient to establish his express intent to transmute his separate property identified in exhibit A to community property, as contemplated by section 852, subdivision (d). According to Frank, his intent in this regard was rendered ambiguous by language in both documents indicating that they were executed solely for estate planning purposes. We disagree.

"Section 850, subdivision (b), provides that married persons may transmute the separate property of either spouse into community property 'by agreement or transfer,' subject to the provisions of sections 851 to 853. Section 852, subdivision (a), provides: 'A transmutation of real or personal property is not valid unless made in writing by an express declaration that is made, joined in, consented to, or accepted by the spouse whose interest in the property is adversely affected.' Our Supreme Court has interpreted 'an express declaration' as language expressly stating that a change in the characterization or ownership of the property is being made. (*Estate of MacDonald, supra,* 51 Cal. 3d at p. 272, 272 Cal. Rptr. 153, 794 P.2d 911.) '[A] writing signed by the adversely affected spouse is not an "express declaration" for the purposes of [Civil Code] section 5110.730(a) [now Fam. Code §852, subd. (a)] *unless* it contains language which expressly states that the characterization or ownership of the property is being changed.' [Citation.]" (*In re Marriage of Starkman, supra,* 129 Cal. App. 4th at pp. 663–664, 28 Cal. Rptr. 3d 639.) "The express declaration must unambiguously indicate a change in character or ownership of property. [Citation.]" (*Id.,* at p. 664, 28 Cal. Rptr. 3d 639.)

"In deciding whether a transmutation has occurred, we interpret the written instruments independently, without resort to extrinsic evidence." (*In re Marriage of Starkman, supra,* 129 Cal. App. 4th at p. 664, 28 Cal. Rptr. 3d 639.) The Transmutation Agreement and Trust at issue in this case establish that Frank intended to, and did, transmute from separate to community property that which was identified in the incorporated exhibit. The Transmutation Agreement unambiguously states that "Husband agrees that the character of the property described in Exhibit A (including any future rents, issues, profits, and proceeds of that property) *is hereby transmuted from his separate property to the community property of both parties.*" (Italics added.) The attached Exhibit A is later expressly identified as "Husband's Separate Property Being Transmuted to Community Property." In referencing the Trust, the Transmutation Agreement states it is "the intention of the parties that *the property transmuted by Husband hereunder* shall be transferred and assigned into such Trust."

(Italics added.) It also states that "Wife acknowledges that *the transmutation of Husband's separate property into community property herewith*" (italics added) is conditioned on her agreement to refrain from amending, modifying or changing the Trust so that "the property subject to this Agreement will pass as provided in said Declaration of Trust. The parties further acknowledge that, but for such agreed disposition of the subject property, *settlor Frank Holtemann would not have effected the within transmutation of his separate property into community property.*" (Italics added.) The Trust similarly provides that it was created "in order to hold community property of the settlors, *which community property was created by the transmutation of separate property of settlor Frank G. Holtemann concurrently with the execution of this trust instrument.*" (Italics added.) As the trial court aptly noted, "[a] clearer statement of a transmutation is difficult to imagine."

An express declaration of transmutation does not necessarily require use of the terms "transmutation," "community property," or "separate property." (*In re Marriage of Starkman, supra,* 129 Cal. App. 4th at p. 664, 28 Cal. Rptr. 3d 639.) Unlike in *Starkman,* in which "transmutation" is never mentioned, here the word is stated repeatedly and pointedly. There can be no doubt that, with the advice of counsel, the parties chose this unique and specific term of art.

Frank nevertheless contends that these repeated, express declarations of transmutation were rendered ambiguous by the statement in the Transmutation Agreement that "[t]his agreement is not made in contemplation of a separation or marital dissolution and is made solely for the purpose of interpreting how property shall be disposed of on the deaths of the parties," as well as statements in both documents reflecting the parties' agreement that Frank would not have transmuted his separate property had Barbara not agreed to refrain from exercising her right to amend, modify or change the trust. According to Frank, "[t]hese provisions negate any legally-mandated conclusion that the [Transmutation] Agreement established the requisite 'unambiguous' proof of a transmutation in this marital dissolution action, prior to the parties' deaths."

We are not persuaded. Regardless of the motivations underlying the documents, they contain the requisite express, unequivocal declarations of a present transmutation. Moreover, the documents reflect that Frank was fully informed of the legal consequences of his actions. Nothing in the record indicates that he was misinformed or misled. On the contrary, counsel sent Frank a letter "reminding" him that "this 'transmutation' of separate into community property has clear and potentially irreversible consequences. . . ."[1] The Trust also expressly provides that if Frank exercised his right of revocation during his lifetime — an event that came to pass — any community property that had been transferred into the Trust would continue to be community property. Under the circumstances, Frank will not be heard to complain that his express declaration of transmutation was unknowing or that he "'slip[ped]' into a transmutation by accident.' [Citation.]" (*In re Marriage of Starkman, supra,* 129 Cal. App. 4th at p. 664, 28 Cal. Rptr. 3d 639.)

Frank also urges us to treat his express declarations of transmutation differently from other express declarations because he did not have his own attorney. He asserts

---

1. While we do not consider extrinsic evidence in deciding whether a transmutation occurred in the first instance (*Estate of MacDonald, supra,* 51 Cal. 3d at pp. 271-272, 272 Cal. Rptr. 153, 794 P.2d 911), counsel's letter is relevant to rebut Frank's claim that his express declaration of transmutation was unknowing or inadvertent.

that "[s]ince Mr. Look represented both parties in the estate plan, he should have added an express disclaimer, to the effect that the transmutation would be inoperative on marital dissolution." As we have already noted, however, Frank was fully advised of the consequences in failing to secure separate counsel, yet chose to proceed.

In any event, we are not aware of any authority for the proposition that a transmutation, once effected, can be limited in purpose or otherwise rendered conditional or temporary. Once the character of the property has been changed, a "retransmutation" can be achieved only by an express agreement to that effect that independently satisfies the requirements of subdivision (a) of section 852. As the trial judge stated: "Husband argues that the transmutation was limited to estate purposes only. In other words, Frank wishes to have his cake and eat it too. He argues that, in the event of either his or Barbara's death, the survivor would be able to use the Transmutation Agreement to claim the property as community property, thus obtaining a full step up in basis to the fair market value of the property at date of death, while at the same time denying the validity of the Transmutation Agreement as an instrument which created community property. Thus, when it would benefit either Frank or his estate, Frank wishes to characterize the property as community. However, when it would be detrimental to Frank, he wishes to ignore the transmutation and call the property separate."

Frank also contends that "[a]s a matter of public policy, . . . Courts should generally exclude revocable estate planning documents like the [Transmutation] Agreement and Trust as evidence of transmutation upon marital dissolution." This contention was not raised below, so it is waived. In any event, the policy he identifies — "to encourage spouses to provide for their surviving spouses in their estate plans" — is not undermined by our conclusion. We conclude, however, that his chosen language speaks to a contrary intent.

For the first time on appeal, Frank also urges us to conclude that the Transmutation Agreement and Trust are governed by section 853, subdivision (a), which provides that "[a] statement in a will of the character of property is not admissible as evidence of a transmutation of property in a proceeding commenced before the death of the person who made the will." Aside from having waived the claim, Frank fails to demonstrate that section 853 is intended to apply to anything other than wills. The only published decision addressing the issue holds otherwise (*In re Cecconi* (Bkrtcy. N.C. Cal. 2007) 366 B.R. 83), and we are persuaded by its reasoning. As we previously recognized in analyzing section 853, wills "are not intended to convey a *present interest* in the property. Further, a will is ambulatory in nature, subject to revocation or modification during the testator's life; it 'speaks' only as of the date of the testator's death." A trust, on the other hand, conveys to the trustee a present interest that passes immediately upon execution. Moreover, "[t]he language of Section 853 says '[a] statement in a will' and does not have any language including will-substitutes." While Frank notes that commentators have deemed it "unclear" why the law distinguishes between wills and trusts in this regard (Hogoboom & King, Cal. Practice Guide: Family Law (The Rutter Group 2007) ¶ 8:846.1), those commentators do not dispute that the distinction exists. Any change in the law is the province of the Legislature.

In his petition for rehearing, Frank warns that our decision will "create havoc" on the "tens of thousands of married couples in California who have executed living trusts." We are confident no such crisis will befall. As the trial court found, the transmutation does not affect Frank's right to seek reimbursement for his contribution of separate property to the community estate pursuant to section 2640, subdivision (b).[2] Neither party has ever disputed this finding.

Because we reject Frank's claim that the assets identified in exhibit A to the Transmutation Agreement and Trust are his separate property, his contention that the court erred in ordering him to pay Barbara's fees incurred in valuing those community property assets is moot.

DISPOSITION

The order is affirmed. Respondent shall recover costs on appeal.

We concur: GILBERT, P.J., and YEGAN, J.

Discussion Questions

1. Compare the facts of *Holtemann* to the facts of *Schweitzer*. What are the similarities? Differences? The results?
2. Did Family Code §853 apply to estate planning documents?

D.   GIFTS OF JEWELRY: THE CALIFORNIA AND LOUISIANA APPROACHES

The strict transmutation requirements enacted by the California Legislature do recognize that in some situations there can be an informal transmutation without an "express declaration in writing." That exception is for certain gifts between spouses, including jewelry and other personal items. But again California prescribes detailed criteria for dispensing with the general written requirements for a transmutation. By contrast, Louisiana uses traditional presumption analysis to determine whether a transmutation was accomplished when one spouse "gives" jewelry to the other spouse.

---

2. Section 2640, subdivision (b) provides: "In the division of the community estate . . . , unless a party has made a written waiver of the right to reimbursement or has signed a writing that has the effect of a waiver, the party shall be reimbursed for the party's contributions to the acquisition of property of the community estate to the extent the party traces the contributions to a separate property source. The amount reimbursed shall be without interest or adjustment for change in monetary values and may not exceed the net value of the property at the time of the division."

CALIFORNIA FAMILY CODE

§852(c). Form of transmutation

This section [express declaration in writing] does not apply to a gift between the spouses of clothing, wearing apparel, jewelry, or other tangible items of a personal nature that is used solely or principally by the spouse to whom the gift is made and that is not substantial in value taking into account the circumstances of the marriage.

MARRIAGE OF STEINBERGER

91 Cal. App. 4th 1449, 111 Cal. Rptr. 2d 521 (2001)
California Court of Appeal

COTTLE, P.J.

After a court trial in a marital dissolution action, the court entered judgment regarding the character and disposition of certain property of the parties. On appeal, the husband contends that the trial court erred with regard to wife's severance pay, certain stock options, and a diamond ring. We find no error by the trial court with regard to wife's severance pay and the stock options, but reverse the judgment with regard to the diamond ring.

I. FACTS

A. PROCEDURAL BACKGROUND

Petitioner Buff Jones and defendant James Mark Steinberger were married on April 30, 1988. They separated on June 14, 1997, after a marriage of 9 years and 1.5 months. The parties have one minor son, born in January of 1996. A status-only dissolution of marriage was filed on December 28, 1998. Later, some of the parties' financial issues were handled by agreements reflected in a stipulated judgment filed on August 13, 1999. Other issues were handled in a court trial, which included the testimony of both parties and other witnesses. The trial was concluded on February 5, 1999, and the resulting judgment was filed on September 2, 1999. The judgment included provisions regarding (1) Buff's severance pay from her employer, Compuware; (2) certain stock options Buff had received from Compuware; and (3) a diamond ring. James has filed a timely appeal focusing on these issues.

* * *

THE DIAMOND RING

A little more than five years after the marriage, the parties bought a loose diamond with community funds. James later set it in a ring and presented it to Buff after their fifth anniversary with a card referring to the five years, and also congratulating Buff on her recent promotion.

Buff testified that she considered it a gift. It was a woman's ring and only she had worn it since receipt. When James was asked at trial whether he presented the ring to Buff as a gift, he stated: "Ah, it was as a gift and as an investment, something that we both could enjoy." James also testified that it was not his intent to give her a fifth year anniversary ring, and that the most expensive gift he had given Buff during the marriage was a Christmas gift that had cost a few hundred dollars.

THE TRIAL

After the trial testimony and briefing and argument by the parties, the trial court found that the diamond ring was unilaterally given to Buff at or about the time of their fifth wedding anniversary as a gift, and that it was therefore Buff's separate property.

II. Discussion

THE DIAMOND RING

The third issue on appeal is the court's ruling regarding the diamond ring. It is undisputed that the diamond was purchased approximately five years after the marriage with community funds. The parties' dispute concerns the application of Family Code section 852 (section 852). That section provides, in pertinent part: "Requirements [¶] (a) A transmutation of real or personal property is not valid unless made in writing by an express declaration that is made, joined in, consented to, or accepted by the spouse whose interest in the property is adversely affected. [¶] ... [¶] (c) This section does not apply to a gift between the spouses of clothing, wearing apparel, jewelry, or other tangible articles of a personal nature that is used solely or principally by the spouse to whom the gift is made and that is not substantial in value taking into account the circumstances of the marriage."

At trial, James argued that the ring was community property, because it was substantial in value taking into account the circumstances of the marriage, and because no valid written transmutation (as required by Family Code section 852) had been made. Buff argued that a written transmutation was not required for gifts of jewelry, and that as a result of the gift, the ring became her separate property.

The trial court found that the ring was Buff's separate property. The trial transcript includes the trial court's finding that the ring was substantial in value taking into account the circumstances of the marriage.[3] In its statement of decision, the trial court stated as follows: "[James] purchased a diamond of substantial value

---

3. The trial transcript includes an exchange in which the attorney for James reads from Buff's prior testimony. He had asked Buff, "Okay, in regards to the ring Mr. Steinberger was testifying to yesterday, did you understand when you received that ring that it had some substantial value to you?" and Buff answered, "Yes, I did." She confirmed that after the bill came, she had the understanding that the ring was worth "a range of at least" $13,000 or $14,000. After this testimony was reread to the trial court, the court stated: "Just a minute. This refreshes my recollection about the value and [Buff's] concession, that even from the amount of money they had, it was substantial, and I think, accordingly, it would be appropriate for me to say that the ring, or the stone, was of substantial value even taking into account the circumstances of the marriage."

using community funds and unilaterally gave it [to Buff] at or about the time of their fifth wedding anniversary as a gift, with a card announcing his congratulations. Prior to the presentation of this gift, [James] had the stone mounted in a gold setting configured in a ring for [Buff] to wear. [Buff] understood the ring and stone to be a gift to her and accepted it as such. [James] never, prior to separation, stated that the ring and stone were purchased as an investment, rather than a gift, as he now contends. On this issue, the court finds the testimony of [Buff] credible and the testimony of [James] not to be credible. Furthermore, there was no evidence that [Buff] was involved in the purchase or setting of the stone and ring. [¶] The credible evidence here was that the stone was put in a women's ring and used exclusively by [Buff], consistent with both the statute and the intent described above. Although the writing accompanying the gift did not satisfy the requirement of Family Code §852(a), the court nevertheless finds that the ring was a 'true gift' and as such, it is the separate property of the recipient, Family Code §770(a)(2) and §850, and 852."

On appeal, James argues that the trial court erred, because "the plain meaning of section 852 is that if the gift between spouses consists of a substantial asset, it is not going to [be] held to be a gift unless there is a written expressed declaration transmuting the property from community to separate. There was not, in this case, such a sufficient writing."

We agree with James's interpretation of the statute. The statute specifically provides that a transmutation is "not valid unless" there is a sufficient writing. (Fam. Code, §852, subd. (a).) The trial court found that the writing here (a card presented to Buff) was not sufficient. The statutory exception for jewelry applies only to a gift that is "not substantial in value taking into account the circumstances of the marriage." In her appellate brief, Buff has not argued that the evidence was insufficient to support the trial court's finding that the ring was substantial in value taking into account the circumstances of the marriage, or that the trial court's factual finding was erroneous. With regard to a substantial gift, the statute simply does not provide for implied or oral transmutations made without a sufficient writing.

We recognize that this statute, with its bright-line test regarding transmutations, may seem harsh in light of the informal, everyday practices of spouses making gifts during a marriage. In enacting section 852, however, the Legislature made a policy decision balancing competing concerns. When the rule now codified in section 852 was being considered, the Law Revision Commission stated as follows: "California law permits an oral transmutation or transfer of property between the spouses notwithstanding the statute of frauds. This rule recognizes the convenience and practical informality of interspousal transfers. However, the rule of easy transmutation has also generated extensive litigation in dissolution proceedings. It encourages a spouse, after the marriage has ended, to transform a passing comment into an 'agreement' or even to commit perjury by manufacturing an oral or implied transmutation. [¶] The convenience and practice of informality recognized by the rule permitting oral transmutations must be balanced against the danger of fraud and increased litigation caused by it. The public expects there to be formality and written documentation of real property transactions, just as it expects there to be formality in dealings with personal property involving documentary evidence of title, such as automobiles, bank accounts, and shares of stock. Most people would find an oral transfer of such property, even between spouses, to be suspect and probably fraudulent, either as to creditors or between each other. [¶] California law should continue to recognize informal transmutations for certain personal property gifts between spouses, but should require a writing for a transmutation of real property or other personal property. In the case of personal property 'gifts' between the spouses, gifts of most items such as household furnishings and appliances should be presumed community and gifts of clothing, wearing apparel, jewelry, and other tangible articles of a personal nature should be presumed separate (unless large or substantial in value). These presumptions most likely correspond to the expectations of the ordinary married couple." (Recommendation Relating to Marital Property Presumptions and Transmutations, 17 Cal. L. Revision Comm'n Reports 205, 213-214 (1984).

Section 852, as enacted, makes it clear that the Legislature chose to balance the various policy concerns (allowance for convenience and informality within marriages, while preventing or minimizing disputes, fraud and perjury) by enacting a clear, bright-line test regarding transmutations of property. In light of the Legislature's decision and the clear language of the statute, it would be inappropriate to hold that a transmutation of jewelry that was substantial in value taking into account the circumstances of the marriage occurred here without the writing required by section 852.

The trial court apparently relied in part on a section in the treatise, Hogoboom & King, California Practice Guide: Family Law (The Rutter Group, 1999). Section 8.510 of that treatise states: "Gifts between spouses: Either spouse can, by making a gift to the other, convert his separate property or interest in community property into the other spouse's separate property. [¶] (1)[8:511] Formalities: If the issue is one of post 1984 transmutation, an 'express written declaration' stating characterization or ownership is being changed will be required [citation]. Presumably, however, true 'gifts' can still be proved by evidence of the ordinary elements of a gift—i.e., *delivery* and *donative intent*.

In light of the clear language of section 852, this comment is only partially correct. The cases cited are not persuasive with regard to gifts of jewelry that are substantial in value, taking into account the circumstances of the marriage, because they precede the enactment of the rule now codified as section 852. Under the clear statutory provision of section 852, gifts of personal property that are substantial in value taking into account the circumstances of the marriage will not be considered converted to separate property without the writing required by section 852.

Because no valid written transmutation was made in this case, the trial court erred in holding that the diamond ring was Buff's separate property. Pursuant to section 852, the ring should be considered community property.

DISPOSITION

In light of our conclusion that the diamond ring should be considered community property, the judgment is reversed, and the matter is remanded for the limited purpose of reconsidering the division of the parties' community property. Each party shall bear his or her costs on appeal.

BAMATTRE-MANOUKIAN and WUNDERLICH, JJ., concur.

STATHAM v. STATHAM

986 So. 2d 894 (2008)
Court of Appeal of Louisiana

GASKINS, J.

In this community property partition, the wife appeals from a judgment classifying property and assessing value. In particular, she objects to the trial court's classification of a diamond ring she received as community property. We affirm the trial court judgment.

FACTS

The parties, Marsha Jo "Jody" Statham and Harry Rufus "Butch" Statham were married in 1970. They divorced in 2005. The community terminated on February 16, 2005, the date of the filing of the divorce petition.

A June 2007 hearing officer conference report made findings and recommendations as to the partition of the community property. Butch filed an objection to the hearing officer's conclusion that a ring valued at about $17,000 and acquired during the marriage was very probably a birthday present to Jody and thus her separate property.

* * *

Jody testified that a ring purchased for more than $15,000 was given to her as a birthday gift and thus was her separate property. According to her, it was purchased two days before her birthday in 2002. She testified that her husband had said they should get her a ring for her birthday when they were joking about their daughter-in-law's engagement ring being larger than hers.[1] She testified that she signed the check for the purchase when she picked the ring up at the jewelry store a few days after they picked it out. Jody admitted that the ring was bought at about the same time they received money back from a cancer policy after Butch's bout with cancer. Butch testified that after they received money back from a cancer policy claim, they each got an expensive item-she got the ring and he got a four-wheeler.[2] He identified a deposit in their joint checking account made on Jody's birthday in 2002 as the insurance proceeds. According to him, his birthday gift to Jody in 2002 was a portrait of their son which was placed on a billboard.

On August 28, 2007, the trial court issued a written ruling. Among the court's determinations was a finding that the ring was community property. It concluded that it was not convinced that the ring was a gift. It found the testimony of Jody and Butch about their "perceptions" as to the ring equally persuasive. Since the ring was presumed to be community and Jody failed to carry her burden of proof on this issue, the court classified the ring as community.

On October 22, 2007, the trial court signed a judgment in conformity with its ruling.

Jody appealed.

---

1. The parties stipulated that Jody's mother and two of her friends would testify that she showed them the ring around the time of her birthday and told them that it was a birthday gift from Butch.
2. A Honda four-wheeler valued at $3,000 is among the community assets allocated to Butch.

CLASSIFICATION OF RING

Jody argues that the trial court erred when it disregarded the hearing officer's finding that, based upon the circumstances and timing of the purchase, it was "very probable" that the ring was intended as a birthday gift to her which should be classified as her separate property. On the other hand, Butch emphasizes the evidence he presented that his birthday gift to Jody in 2002 was a portrait of their son and the display of the portrait on a billboard; this included an invoice from the photographer and corroboration of his own testimony by his friend and former business partner, Mr. Pardue.

Things in the possession of a spouse during the existence of a regime of community of acquets and gains are presumed to be community, but either spouse may prove that they are separate property. La. C.C. art. 2340. The spouse seeking to rebut the presumption bears the burden of proving that the property is separate in nature. *Ross v. Ross*, 2002-2984 (La. 10/21/03), 857 So. 2d 384.

A trial court's findings regarding the nature of the property as community or separate is a factual determination subject to manifest error review. *Ross, supra.*

An appellate court may not set aside a trial court's finding of fact in the absence of manifest error or unless it is clearly wrong, and where two permissible views of the evidence exist, the fact finder's choice between them cannot be manifestly erroneous or clearly wrong. *Cole v. Department of Public Safety & Corrections*, 2001-2123 (La. 9/4/02), 825 So. 2d 1134; *Stobart v. State through Department of Transportation and Development*, 617 So. 2d 880 (La. 1993). Even though an appellate court may feel its own evaluations and inferences are more reasonable than the fact finder's, reasonable evaluations of credibility and reasonable inferences of fact should not be disturbed upon review where conflict exists in the testimony. To reverse a fact finder's determination, the appellate court must find from the record that a reasonable factual basis does not exist for the finding of the trial court and that the record establishes that the finding is clearly wrong.

Where the fact finder's conclusions are based on determinations regarding credibility of the witnesses, the manifest error standard demands great deference to the trier of fact, because only the trier of fact can be aware of the variations in demeanor and tone of voice that bear so heavily on the listener's understanding and belief in what is said.

Jody and Butch diametrically contradicted each other on the subject of the ring. She testified unequivocally that the ring was a birthday gift from Butch to her in 2002. He was equally clear that his birthday gift to her that year was a portrait of their son and its placement on a billboard. He categorically testified that each of them made an expensive purchase after receiving money back on a cancer policy — she bought the disputed ring and he bought a four wheeler, which was included in the community property partition. Each spouse offered testimony of family and/or friends in support of his or her version. The documentation showed that Jody signed the check paying for the ring and that the cancer policy funds were deposited on Jody's birthday.

The trial court found both sides equally credible. As a result, it concluded that Jody had failed to carry her burden of rebutting the presumption that the ring was community property. On the evidence in this record and in light of the credibility determinations made by the trial court, we are unable to find that it was manifestly erroneous or clearly wrong in its ruling.

* * *

Conclusion

The judgment of the trial court is affirmed. Costs of this appeal are assessed to the appellant.

Affirmed.

Discussion Questions

1. In both cases, the Courts of Appeal found that the diamond ring remained community property. Which approach is preferable for determining the character of the diamond ring?

2. In both cases, what happens to the ring on remand in *Steinberger* and upon affirmance of the trial court in *Statham*?

PROBLEM 7.1

Murray and Lana married in 2005. Murray had a dangerous job working on oil rigs all over the world. In 2010, he was dispatched by his company to work on a deep ocean rig. Lana was worried that something might happen to Murray on this job assignment. Murray had recently received a large inheritance from his grandfather and they wanted to assure that Lana would be taken care of if anything happened to Murray on the job. They went on the internet and were able to find a form that stated that "all property whatsoever owned by the spouses shall be considered community property and, in the event of death, shall pass to the surviving spouse." They signed and dated the form. Nothing happened to Murray on that job, but recently their marriage has exploded and they are considering divorce. Murray is claiming that he only signed the form because he did not want Lana to worry. He says that he didn't want to share his inheritance with Lana if they divorced.

Would a court determine that Murray's inheritance was transmuted to community property if they lived in California? Idaho? Washington?

PROBLEM 7.2

Assume the same facts as Problem 7.1, except that Murray and Lana do not sign any form but agree orally that his inheritance belongs to both of them. He says, "Everything I have belongs to us." She says, "I feel that way too." He deposits the check for his inheritance in a checking account in his name. He uses the funds from that account for their expenses.

Would a court determine that Murray's inheritance was transmuted to community property if they lived in California? Idaho? Washington?

PROBLEM 7.3

Karl and Joy married in 2005. They had little money, but Karl had a talent for designing video games. Soon after they married, he landed a job with a start-up company that designed and marketed video games. His first creation was a tremendous success. In 2006, he received a bonus of $30,000 for his design. They invested some of the bonus in stocks but decided to buy a high-quality diamond as an investment. The diamond cost $10,000. In 2010, Karl took the diamond, which had been in a safety deposit box, and had the diamond set in a gold ring. When they went out to dinner for their tenth anniversary, Karl gave the ring to Joy with a note that said "To the Joy in my life, Love always, Karl." Joy wears the ring only on special occasions and keeps it in the safety deposit box. They have recently filed for divorce. Karl is claiming that the ring is community property and Joy is claiming that it is her separate property.

Would a court determine that the ring was Joy's separate property if they lived in California? Louisiana?

Table 7-1
Agreements to Transmute Community/Separate Property in Community Property States

State	Rule	Case/Statute
Arizona	"A husband and wife can, by agreement, transmute separate property to community property." That agreement can be oral or written. An agreement may be implied if the circumstances clearly demonstrate that one spouse intended to effect a change in the status of separate property.	*Moser v. Moser*, 117 Ariz. 313, 572 P.2d 446 (1977)
California	Property may be transmuted if "in writing by an express declaration that is made, joined in, consented to, or accepted by the spouse whose interest in the property is adversely affected." Written document controls not extrinsic evidence of intent. Does not apply to gifts between spouses of clothing, wearing apparel, jewelry, or other tangible articles of a personal nature.	Family Code §852. *Estate of MacDonald*, 51 Cal. 3d 262, 794 P.2d 911, 272 Cal. Rptr. 153 (1990), *Marriage of Benson*, 36 Cal. 4th 1152, 116 P.3d 1152, 32 Cal. Rptr. 3d 471 (2005), *Marriage of Holtemann*, 166 Cal. App. 4th 1166, 83 Cal. Rptr. 385 (2008), *Marriage of Steinberger*, 91 Cal. App. 4th 1449, 111 Cal. Rptr. 2d 521 (2001)

State	Rule	Case/Statute
Idaho	"All contracts for marital settlements must be in writing, and executed and acknowledged or proved in like manner as conveyances of land are required to be executed and acknowledged or proved." Burden of proof on party asserting transmutation to prove the intent to transmute or to make a gift by clear and convincing evidence. Evidence of intent permitted.	Idaho Code §32-917, *Hoskinson v. Hoskinson*, 139 Idaho 448, 80 P.3d 1049 (2003)
Louisiana	Voluntary partition of community property into separate property by oral agreement permitted if supported by objective evidence. Agreement to terminate the "matrimonial regime" (community property system) requires judicial approval.	La. Civ. Code §§2328-2336, *Biondo v. Biondo*, 769 So. 2d 94 (La. App. 2000), *Statham v. Statham*, 986 So. 2d 894 (La. App. 2008)
Nevada	Transmutation from separate to community property and community property to separate property must be shown by clear and convincing evidence.	*Sprenger v. Sprenger*, 110 Nev. 855, 878 P.2d 284 (1994) (separate to community), *Stockgrowers' & Ranchers' Bank v. Milisich*, 52 Nev. 178, 283 P.913 (1930) (community to separate)
New Mexico	"Once the community property presumption is overcome by a preponderance of the evidence, a party must prove the transmutation of the separate property into community property by clear and convincing evidence."	*Nichols v. Nichols*, 98 N.M. 322, 648 P.2d 780 (1982)
Texas	"An agreement to convert separate property to community property: (1) must be in writing and (A) signed by the spouses; (B) identify the property being converted; and (C) specify that the property being converted to the spouses' community property; and (2) is enforceable without consideration. The mere transfer of a spouse's separate property to the name of the other spouse or the name of both spouses is not sufficient to convert the property to community property."	Tex. Const. art. XVI, §15 (effective Jan. 1, 2000), Vernon's Tex. Code §4.203 (effective Jan. 1, 2000). *Welder v. Welder*, 794 S.W. 2d 420 (Tex. Ct. App. 1990.)

State	Rule	Case/Statute
Washington	Community property may be changed to separate property by oral or written agreement. The spouse seeking to enforce the agreement must prove by clear and convincing evidence, the existence of the agreement and that the parties mutually observed the terms of the agreement throughout the marriage. Extrinsic evidence permitted to show intentions of the spouses and mutual mistake.	*Marriage of Mueller*, 140 Wash. App. 498, 167 P.3d 568 (2000) (community to separate), *Marriage of Schweitzer*, 132 Wash. 2d 318, 937 P.2d 1062 (1997) (separate to community)
Wisconsin	Transfer of separately owned property into joint tenancy transmutes the character of ownership in the entire property into marital property that is subject to division at divorce.	Wis. Stat. §§767.255(2), 766.58-766.60, *Steinmann v. Steinmann*, 309 Wis. 2d 29, 749 N.W.2d 145 (2008)

Chapter 8

Management and Control of Community Property: One Spouse or Both?

Spousal equality is the paradigm of management and control of community property. For instance, the Arizona statute states that "The spouses have equal management, control and disposition rights over community property and have equal power to bind the community."[1] Beyond that broad statement, management and control of community property is sometimes called "either/or" management and control. There are different formulations of "either/or" management and control in the various community property states. Examples include: "Either spouse has the management and control of the community property personal property"[2] or "Each spouse may act alone to manage, control, or dispose of community property"[3] or "Either spouse alone has full power to manage, control, dispose of and encumber the entire community personal property."[4] To understand the import of "either/or" management and control, let us return to one of our hypothetical couples, Michael and Lisa. Lisa receives a $10,000 bonus at work and deposits it in their joint checking account. The bonus is community personal property. Under "either/or" management and control, Michael and Lisa each have the right to manage and control that money. If Lisa wants to spend the bonus on a new wardrobe, she has the right to do so. If Michael wants to spend the bonus on a fishing trip, he has the right to do so. Of course, it is easy to imagine that if both Michael and Lisa exercise their right to manage and control the community property bonus without consulting the other, the bonus would be gone and they may be in debt for an additional $10,000. That leads to the question of whether there are any restrictions in the equal management and control statutes that exist in all the community property states.

The most important limitation on equal management and control is the condition of joinder of both spouses in some transactions. For community real property, both spouses must join in the transactions. For instance, in Arizona, "joinder of both spouses is required in . . . any transaction for the acquisition, disposition or encumbrance of an interest in real property other than an unpatented mining

1. Ariz. Rev. Stat. §25-214.
2. Cal. Fam. Code §1100.
3. La. Civ. Code art. 2346.
4. New Mex. Stat. §40-3-13.

claim or a lease of less than one year."[5] Let's say that Michael and Lisa want to move out of their apartment in Phoenix because Lisa is expecting their first child. Lisa finds an apartment near where her parents live. The location is terrific, the apartment is new and spacious, and the price is right. She wants to sign the lease for one year. Because she is acquiring an interest in real property, Michael must also sign the lease. It is most likely that the landlord is aware of the community property law and the standard lease form most probably requires the signatures of both spouses.

Another common limitation on equal management and control is the requirement that a spouse consent to gifts to third parties. In New Mexico and Washington, their statutes state that "Neither spouse may make a gift of community property without the express or implied or consent of the other."[6] Let's say that Michael and Lisa moved to Seattle rather than staying in Phoenix. After their baby was born, Lisa wanted to make a charitable donation of part of her $10,000 community bonus to the hospital where she delivered the baby. She surely has the right to do so under equal management and control principles, but Michael's express or implied consent is necessary. Again, the hospital would be aware of community property law. For donations, they most probably have set up a mechanism to assure that when a married person wants to make a donation their spouse is aware and has consented to the donation.

It is clear that if a spouse exercises his or her right to manage and control the community personal property, that spouse must have the other spouse's interests in mind. That requirement is called a duty of act in "good faith" toward the other spouse or a "fiduciary duty" owed toward the other spouse. This is particularly important when one spouse alone manages and controls a community property business. The next section of this Chapter will examine both issues: management and control of a community property business and the duty the managing spouse owes to the other spouse.

A. MANAGEMENT AND CONTROL OF A COMMUNITY PROPERTY BUSINESS AND FIDUCIARY DUTY

1. Specific Requirements in California, Nevada, and Washington

California, Nevada, and Washington have specific statutes dealing with management and control of a community property business. Beyond the "either/or" provisions, there is a specific reason for giving a spouse who manages a community business additional powers: the smooth operation of that business. Let us return to Michael and Lisa who now live in Seattle. After saving for several years from his job designing logos for an advertising company, Michael thinks it is time to start his own

5. Ariz. Rev. Stat. §25-214(C)(1).
6. New Mex. Rev. Stat. §123.230(2), Wash. Rev. Code §16.16.030(2), see also Cal. Fam. Code §1100(b).

logo-designing business. He uses community funds to start his business. He rents an office on a monthly basis, buys an updated computer system with advance graphics capabilities, buys advertising space in several publications, and sends letters to his contacts in the advertising business. He clearly has the power to use community property funds to set up the business and expend community funds for all those transactions. There is no requirement to obtain Lisa's consent nor does she have to join in those transactions. The optimal situation is that Michael has discussed his plans with her and sought her advice and counsel, but that is not required under Washington community property law.

From one of the letters he sent to a contact in the advertising business, he finds out that another very lucrative logo-designing business is for sale. There are several other companies interested in buying that business. He must act quickly if he wants to acquire the business. Under Washington community property law, the question is whether he must receive Lisa's consent before he makes this major outlay of money to acquire this other business. If both spouses participate in the management of the business, he must obtain Lisa's consent. If only one spouse participates in management of the business,

> "the participating spouse . . . may, in the ordinary course of such business, acquire, purchase, sell, convey or encumber the assets, including real estate, or the goodwill of the business without the consent of the nonparticipating spouse. . . ."[7]

So it would seem that Michael would be able to acquire the other logo-designing business without Lisa's consent. On one hand, that ability to act without obtaining the nonparticipating spouse's would facilitate business dealings, but, on the other hand, the nonparticipating spouse may find that the participating spouse made a very poor business decision. In that case, the question is whether the nonparticipating spouse would be responsible for that poor decision. That exact question was explored in the following case, *Consumers Insurance Co. v. Cimoch*, 69 Wash. App. 313, 848 P.2d 763 (1993).

CONSUMERS INSURANCE CO. v. CIMOCH

69 Wash. App. 313, 848 P.2d 763 (1993)
Court of Appeals of Washington

SCHOLFIELD, Judge.

Consumers Insurance Company appeals the trial court's judgment in favor of Mary Ann Cimoch, claiming the trial court erred in dismissing its claim against the marital community of Norman Cimoch and Mary Ann Cimoch, dismissing its claim against Mary Ann Cimoch individually, and awarding Mary Ann Cimoch attorney's fees. We affirm.

The issues presented in this case are whether Norman Cimoch's agreement to purchase the stock of a corporation subjected his marital community to liability where his wife, Mary Ann Cimoch, did not join in the transaction, and whether

---

7. Wash. Rev. Code §26.16.030(6). Similar language in New. Mex. Rev. Stat. §123.230(6)

Mary Ann Cimoch ratified the transaction so as to incur separate liability for the obligation.

Appellant Consumers Insurance Company (Consumers) is engaged in the business of buying real estate receivables, contracts, mortgages, and deeds of trust, and is also engaged in life insurance and real estate transactions.

Both Western United Life and its sister company, Consumers Indemnity Company (CIC), were subsidiaries of Consumers. CIC was formed in 1981 from a "reciprocal"[1] insurance company known as Consumers Insurance Exchange (CIE).

Respondents Norman and Mary Ann Cimoch were married in 1957 and divorced in 1989. . . .

In early 1984, Norman Cimoch began negotiating with the parent company of CIC, appellant Consumers, for the purchase of CIC. As of this time, Norman Cimoch had acquired a substantial amount of stock (worth approximately $1.5 million) through the compensation agreement. Cimoch advised his then wife, Mary Ann Cimoch, that he was interested in acquiring CIC, and that the acquisition would take place by an exchange of the stock he had acquired for the capital stock of CIC. . . .

Norman Cimoch was the only person involved from the purchaser's end of the transaction. He initially believed he could transfer . . . stock, valued at between $1.3 and $1.6 million dollars, for the CIC stock.

The negotiations culminated in the execution of a "Stock Sale Agreement," dated June 10, 1984. The agreement was drafted by appellant Consumers, and called for Norman Cimoch to purchase the capital stock of CIC for a total price of $2,952,000, to be paid in monthly installments of approximately $14,137 per month. These installments later were temporarily adjusted to over $16,800 per month. This agreement made no reference to the exchange of Norman Cimoch's . . . stock as part of the purchase price; however, an exchange of this stock was later arranged as a partial payment of the total purchase price.

Although Mary Ann Cimoch was informed that the transaction had been completed, she was not advised that it involved anything other than a stock transfer, and she was not aware that the transaction involved any cash outlay or debt. The agreement was not prepared for Mary Ann Cimoch's signature, nor was she invited to review the agreement, approve or disapprove it, or sign it. Norman Cimoch did not tell his wife that the terms of the transaction had changed, and did not inform her of his obligation to pay installments of over $14,000 per month under the agreement. Norman did not tell Mary due to his concerns about her scrutinizing the transaction. . . .

CIC continued to issue mechanical breakdown policies until 1988, when the State Insurance Commissioner obtained an order appointing a receiver for CIC. Norman Cimoch did not pay the monthly installment due under the purchase and sale agreement due on September 1, 1988, nor did he make any payments under the agreement thereafter.

Before and after the execution of the agreement, the Cimochs received salaries and other benefits from CIC. Mary Ann Cimoch did not learn, until the current action was commenced in October 1988, that Norman Cimoch had consummated

---

1. A "reciprocal" insurance company is a less than fully capitalized insurance company.

the transaction by any means other than the exchange of his previously acquired stock.

In October 1988, Consumers Insurance Company brought this action against Norman Cimoch, Mary Ann Cimoch, and Cimoch, Inc., a Washington corporation, seeking damages for breach of contract. Consumers later filed an amended complaint seeking damages against Norman Cimoch individually, Mary Ann Cimoch individually, and the marital community of Norman and Mary Ann Cimoch. Norman Cimoch and Mary Ann Cimoch filed separate answers denying Consumers' claims.

Prior to trial in this case, the trial court entered partial summary judgment in favor of respondents, ruling that Mary Ann Cimoch had not consented to the execution of the agreement by Norman Cimoch. Consumers does not assign error to this finding.

The case was tried to the court in July 1991. The court concluded that Norman Cimoch breached the purchase and sale agreement and that judgment should be entered against him individually for installment payments currently due and those to become due. The court ruled the agreement did not bind the marital community of Mary Ann and Norman Cimoch under RCW 26.16.030(6) because Mary Ann Cimoch did not join in the transaction, consent to the agreement, or ratify Norman Cimoch's execution of the agreement. For the same reasons, the court ruled the agreement did not bind Mary Ann Cimoch individually. Therefore, the court dismissed with prejudice Consumers' action against Mary Ann Cimoch individually and against the community of Mary Ann Cimoch and Norman Cimoch. This appeal followed.

Consumers contends a contractual agreement to purchase the stock of a business creates a marital community obligation and is not excepted from the rule of community liability by RCW 26.16.030(6).

The Cimochs (respondents) contend that an agreement to purchase the assets of a business through the purchase of all the capital stock of the corporation requires the participation of both spouses.

The dispute centers on the proper interpretation to be given to RCW 26.16.030(6). That statute states as follows, in part:

> Property not acquired or owned, as prescribed in RCW 26.16.010 and 26.16.020, acquired after marriage by either husband or wife or both, is community property. Either spouse, acting alone, may manage and control community property, with a like power of disposition as the acting spouse has over his or her separate property, except:
>
> . . .
>
> (6) Neither spouse shall acquire, purchase, sell, convey, or encumber the assets, including real estate, or the good will of a business where both spouses participate in its management without the consent of the other: PROVIDED, That where only one spouse participates in such management the participating spouse may, in the ordinary course of such business, acquire, purchase, sell, convey or encumber the assets, including real estate, or the good will of the business without the consent of the nonparticipating spouse.

Assuming for the moment that the statute governs the acquisition of an incorporated business, it can be seen that the present transaction does not bind the marital community under subsection (6). If Mary Ann Cimoch is regarded as having participated in the management of the couple's business operations, it is not a transaction of the marital community given the trial court's uncontested finding that she did not consent to the acquisition.[2] If she is treated as having been a nonparticipant, the transaction fails to bind the marital community due to the trial court's uncontested finding that the acquisition was not in the ordinary course of [the] business or the business of the Cimoch marital community.

Consumers contends that RCW 26.16.030(6) applies only to existing businesses, and is not applicable to the purchase of a new business. There is some support for this claim in the wording of the statute itself. The statute seems to refer to existing community businesses, not those to be acquired. However, the statute has not been construed in the fashion urged by Consumers.

In *Pixton v. Silva*, 13 Wash. App. 205, 534 P.2d 135 (1975), the court addressed whether the acquisition of a dairy farm by a dairy operator, Manuel Silva, could legally bind the Silva community under the ordinary course of business exception of RCW 26.16.030(6), where Mrs. Silva had not been joined in the transaction. The court ruled that even if Mr. Silva was the sole manager of the couple's present dairy business, "the sale of a community dairy in one area and the purchase of a . . . community dairy in another area is not 'in the ordinary course of *such* business.'" *Pixton*, at 210, 534 P.2d 135. The court ruled that, under RCW 26.16.030(6), Mr. Silva could not alone bind the community to the purchase of plaintiffs' dairy.

[A]lthough the section does not explicitly address itself to the purchase of a community business, it does state, in part, "Neither spouse shall *acquire, purchase* . . . the assets, including real estate, and goodwill of the business without the consent of the other. . . ." This language along with the policy of protecting the community "blue chip" assets suggests that *both spouses always will need to consent to an acquisition of a community business.*

Pixton, at 210, 534 P.2d 135 (quoting Cross, *Management and Disposition of Community Property*,[3] 48 Wash. L. Rev. 527, 541 (1973)).

Consumers contends the wording of subsection (6) is ambiguous, whereas the wording of the general provision (RCW 26.16.030) is clear. Relying on *State v. Wright*, 84 Wash. 2d 645, 652, 529 P.2d 453 (1974), Consumers claims that statutory provisions excepting or limiting the general statute to which they are appended should be strictly construed with any doubt to be resolved in favor of the general provisions, rather than the exceptions. While there is some force to this argument, we do not believe a strict or literal construction of RCW 26.16.030(6) would be consistent with the purposes of the provision.[4] We are in accord with Professor Cross' belief that, although not explicitly stated in the statute, the language and policy of RCW 26.16.030(6) indicate that both spouses must consent to the acquisition of a community business. *See* Cross, *supra* at 541.

* * *

2. The effect of any possible ratification by Mary Ann Cimoch will be discussed later.

3. The Pixton court stated the incorrect title for the Cross article. The proper title is Equality for Spouses in Washington Community Property Law — 1972 Statutory Changes.

4. Professor Cross has stated as follows regarding the purpose of RCW 26.16.030(6):

> [T]he purpose of requiring consent in transactions involving the community business is to protect the nonacting spouse (and thus the community) from imprudent and arbitrary decisions involving "blue chip" community assets. . . .
>
> Requiring the consent of both spouses in community business transactions predominates in the new paragraph (6), reflecting a policy judgment that community business transactions should be subject to joint consent. . . .

(Italics ours.) Cross, supra, at 538-39.

Consumers next contends that a wife ratifies her husband's contract to purchase stock when she has general knowledge of the transaction and accepts the benefits of the transaction. It claims that a wife's ratification of the transaction creates separate liability in the wife as well as marital community liability for the obligation. Consumers claims that in this case, the trial court erred in finding that Mary Ann Cimoch did not ratify the transaction entered into by her husband.

The consent requirement of RCW 26.16.030(6) can be met by ratification by the nonparticipating spouse. *See Reid v. Cramer,* 24 Wash. App. 742, 747, 603 P.2d 851 (1979) (joinder requirement of RCW 26.16.030(4) is satisfied if there is sufficient evidence of authorization or ratification of the transaction by nonacting spouse).

> Since the requirement of "participation" in real property transactions can be met by ratification, estoppel or authorization, it certainly follows that the "consent" requirement of R.C.W. §26.16.030(6) should be satisfied if the nonacting spouse authorizes or ratifies the transactions or is estopped to disaffirm the contract.

Cross, 48 Wash. L. Rev. at 538-39. Ratification in community property law rests on principles of agency. *Smith v. Dalton,* 58 Wash. App. 876, 881, 795 P.2d 706 (1990). "Ratification is the affirmance by a person 'of a prior act which did not bind him but which was done or professedly done on his account.'" *Smith,* at 881, 795 P.2d 706 (quoting *Nichols Hills Bank v. McCool,* 104 Wash. 2d 78, 85, 701 P.2d 1114 (1985)).

In *Geoghegan v. Dever,* 30 Wash. 2d 877, 194 P.2d 397 (1948), the court adopted the following rule regarding ratification:

> "In order that her conduct or acts may operate as a ratification, it is essential that the wife should have full knowledge of all the facts and a reasonable opportunity to repudiate the transaction; and the retention of benefits after acquiring knowledge of the facts does not amount to a ratification if at that time conditions are such, without the fault of the wife, that she cannot be placed in statu[s] quo or cannot repudiate the entire transaction without loss."

Geoghegan, at 898, 194 P.2d 397. Relying on a case cited by the *Geoghegan* court, *Heinzerling v. Agen,* 46 Wash. 390, 393, 90 P. 262 (1907), Consumers contends that a ratification can occur where the principal accepts the benefits of the contract.[7] *Heinzerling* and other cases have stated the rule in this fashion. *See Stroud v. Beck,* 49 Wash. App. 279, 286, 742 P.2d 735 (1987) (for principal to be charged with unauthorized act of agent by ratification, it must act with full knowledge of the facts or accept benefits of act or intentionally assume the obligation imposed without inquiry). *See also Swiss Baco Skyline Logging, Inc. v. Haliewicz,* 18 Wash. App. 21, 32, 567 P.2d 1141 (1977).

To the extent the above rule is construed as imposing liability based solely on a principal's acceptance of benefits, it does not accurately reflect the law. "The acceptance or retention of benefits derived from an agent's unauthorized act does not amount to a ratification of such act if the principal, in accepting such proceeds or benefits, does not have knowledge of all the material facts surrounding the

---

7. Mary Ann and Norman Cimoch received benefits from CIC in the form of salaries from 1984 to 1988. Their combined salaries from CIC during those years are as follows: 1984: $144,000; 1985: $237,295; 1986: $231,000; 1987: $21,540; 1988: $0.

transaction." (Footnote omitted.) 3 Am. Jur. 2d *Agency* §195, at 698 (1986). *See also Smith v. Hansen, Hansen & Johnson, Inc.,* 63 Wash. App. 355, 369, 818 P.2d 1127 (1991) (ratification occurs where corporate principal, *with full knowledge of the material facts,* receives, accepts, and retains benefits from a transaction), *review denied,* 118 Wash. 2d 1023, 827 P.2d 1392 (1992); *Barnes v. Treece,* 15 Wash. App. 437, 443, 549 P.2d 1152 (1976). In a series of uncontested findings, the trial court in this case found that Mary Ann Cimoch had no knowledge of the details of the transaction entered into by her husband. The court also found that there was no reason for Mary Ann Cimoch to know

> by virtue of the operation of either Northwest Underwriters or Consumers Indemnity after the execution of the agreement in June, 1984, that the Agreement had been completed in any manner other than that which had been represented to her, that is, a straight exchange of stock previously acquired by Norman Cimoch.

Finding of fact 19. Mary Ann Cimoch testified she would never have agreed to the actual terms of the agreement. Because she did not know or have reason to know of the terms of the transaction, she could not ratify it simply by accepting salary benefits from CIC. The trial court's finding that Mary Ann Cimoch did not ratify the transaction must be upheld.

There is no basis for individual liability because Mary Ann Cimoch did not ratify the transaction. Pursuant to the contractual attorney's fee clause in the purchase and sale agreement, and RCW 4.84.330, respondents Mary Ann Cimoch and the marital community are entitled to attorney's fees at trial and on appeal.

Judgment affirmed.

Pekelis, Acting C.J., and Kennedy, J., concur.

Discussion Questions

1. What were Consumers' arguments that wife Mary Ann and the marital community were responsible for husband Norman's agreement to purchase CIC? Why did the arguments fail?

2. What is the purpose of the consent provisions regarding management and control of a community business?

California's management and control statutes give a spouse who operates a community business "primary management and control" of that business. Family Code §1100(d) explains that:

> Primary management and control means that the managing spouse may act alone in all transactions but shall give prior written notice to the other spouse of any sale, lease, exchange, encumbrance or other disposition of all or substantially all of the personal property used in the operation of the business . . . whether or not title to that property is held in the name of only one spouse. . . . Remedies for the failure to give prior written

notice as required by this subdivision are only as specified in Section 1101 [Remedies for breach of fiduciary duty]. A failure to give prior written notice shall not adversely affect the validity of a transaction nor of any interest transferred.

Discussion Questions

1. How does the California statute differ from the Washington statute? What is the purpose of the California statute?

2. How would the *Consumers* case have been argued and decided if the same facts had occurred in California?

---

2.   Fiduciary Duty

The "either/or" nature of the management and control statutes relies on the trust that spouses place in each other, that each will exercise their right to act alone by taking into consideration the best interests of each other. Trust is difficult to legislate. It is easier to state the duty owed to the other spouse when a spouse manages community property than it is to understand its meaning and its enforcement. The California Family Code §721 describes the "fiduciary relationship of husband and wife" as being "subject to the general rules governing fiduciary relationships which control the actions of persons occupying confidential relations with each other." That is rather vague, so the §721 continues: "This confidential relationship imposes a duty of the highest good faith and fair dealing on each spouse, and neither shall take any unfair advantage of the other." "Highest good faith and fair dealing" sound like a worthy goal — be fair to the other spouse, something most couples would hope would be the case. Then comes the prohibition — not to take unfair advantage of the other. Again hopefully that would be the case.

More specifically, in management and control of community personal property, §721 is incorporated by reference and specifies that the fiduciary duty includes "the obligation to make full disclosure to the other spouse of all material facts and information regarding the existence, characterization, and valuation of all assets in which the community has or may have an interest. . . ." Cal. Fam. Code §1100(e). Finally, there is a specific duty — full disclosure of community assets.[*] Thus, in management and control of community property, the California statutes have the laudatory goals of fostering communication between the spouses as to the financial affairs and of treating each other fairly in financial transactions. When marriages start out on that footing and continue sharing information with each other about their community property, there seems to be little need for interference with the private structuring of the spouses' handling of their community property. It is when marriages deteriorate and spouses lose the sharing spirit of community property law, that often community assets are hidden and spouses no longer feel

---

[*] Section (e) also includes full disclosure of "debts for which the community is or may be liable, and to provide equal access to all information, records, and books that pertain to the value and character of those assets and debts, upon request."

compelled to honor the duty to disclose and act fairly. Once the inevitable divorce looms, that is when courts must be available to enforce the fiduciary duty. This is especially true since under California law, the fiduciary duty extends "until such time as the assets and liabilities have been divided by the parties or the court." Cal. Fam. Code §1100(e). In California, because there is bifurcation of the dissolution of the marriage and division of the assets, the fiduciary duty regarding the community property may last for several years after the actual divorce is final.

The following case from Arizona, *Gerow v. Covill*, 192 Ariz. 9, 960 P.2d 55 (Ct. App. 1998), illustrates how the husband Bruce, soon after his wife Ann filed a petition for dissolution of their marriage, attempted to arrange the community business in a way that did not manifest the "highest good faith and fair dealing."

GEROW v. COVILL

192 Ariz. 9, 960 P.2d 55 (1998)
Court of Appeals of Arizona

LANKFORD, Presiding Judge.

¶1 Bruce E. Covill ("Husband") appeals from that part of a domestic relations judgment pertaining to Cyber Publishing, Inc. ("Cyber"). The trial court found that Husband had fraudulently conveyed his consulting business. The court accordingly awarded Ann L. Gerow ("Wife") a fifty percent ownership of that business, Cyber.

¶2 The facts are as follows. Husband and Wife married in 1974. Twenty years later, in May 1994, Wife filed a petition for dissolution.

¶3 At the time of filing, Husband was self-employed as an independent consultant working with information systems and information delivery, with a focus on electronic media. He worked primarily with the travel industry. By August 1994, Husband was involved in a new business entity, Cyber.

¶4 Cyber began as the result of conversations among Husband and his brother and sister-in-law, Jeff and Ann Covill. Cyber was to produce electronic brochures for businesses interested in having a presence on the Internet. Husband was named the president and a director of the company and was responsible for the day-to-day management of company affairs. Incorporation occurred in August 1994, with Ann Covill listed as the sole shareholder. She had contributed $2500 for start-up costs. No shareholder, officer, director or employee of Cyber has ever contributed any further capital.

¶5 Shortly after incorporation, Wife learned of Cyber when she found the incorporation papers in Husband's office in their shared home. Husband disclosed information about Cyber to Wife in a letter sent a few weeks later.

¶6 Two of the four clients Husband had worked with in his independent consulting business in recent years became Cyber's major clients. Cyber provided Internet services for both companies, The Hotel Industry Switch Company ("THISCO") and Best Western International.

¶7 Though he had maintained his sole proprietorship through the first few months of Cyber's existence, Husband had ceased his business completely and worked solely for Cyber by February 1995. His salary was increased from $2500 per month to $10,000 per month and he received a $30,000 bonus in 1994. Husband received no designated payment for any intangible assets he brought to Cyber from his sole proprietorship, such as goodwill or a client list.

¶8 In the joint pretrial statement, Wife raised the issue of the true ownership of Cyber. She claimed that instead of merely being an employee of the company, Husband actually was an owner. She sought equitable distribution of Cyber as a community asset. The joint pretrial statement was filed June 7, 1995. Though the trial had originally been set to begin in July 1995, it was continued and began September 21, 1995, and concluded on January 17, 1996, after a total of nine trial days.

¶9 The parties submitted their proposed findings of fact and conclusions of law. Husband objected to Wife's proposed findings and conclusions. The court adopted substantially all of Wife's proposals. . . .

¶10 The court made extensive findings of fact. It stated that it disbelieved Husband's statement that he was financially unable to start Cyber himself in light of his historical six-figure income and the expenditure of "tens of thousands of dollars" in gifts and loans to a female friend. The court saw the incorporation of Cyber as an attempt to "remove the business and its asset from the marital community." The court also found that all of Cyber's revenue-producing clients were either prior clients of Husband's or derived from his prior business contacts, which had developed during the marriage. The court noted that Cyber had been "remarkably successful and highly lucrative for a start-up business." The court also found that Husband had breached a fiduciary duty owed to Wife by "permitting his sole proprietorship to be incorporated and wholly owned by his sister-in-law."

¶11 As a result of these findings, the court ordered in its judgment and decree that:

[A]s between petitioner and respondent, petitioner is and shall be the owner of one-half of the capital stock in Cyber Publishing, Inc. Upon resolution, whether by consent or by adjudication, as against Ann Covill that the stock ostensibly in her name is in fact owned by husband or the marital community of husband and wife, the ownership of the stock on the books and records of Cyber Publishing, Inc. shall also be changed to reflect wife's one-half ownership interest as provided hereon.

The court denied Husband's motion for new trial.

¶12 Husband advances several contentions on appeal. They are as follows:

* * *

3. The evidence does not support the trial court's finding that Husband transferred community property to Cyber. . . .

6. The court erred in finding that Husband owed Wife a fiduciary duty and that Husband breached that duty.

* * *

¶24 The third issue raised by Husband is that the evidence does not support the trial court's finding that Husband transferred community property to Cyber. Reviewing the sufficiency of evidence, we will not reweigh the evidence; we determine only if substantial evidence supported the court's action. Absent clear error, we are bound by the trial court's findings. In this case, we look to see if the evidence supports the existence and transfer of a community asset.

¶25 Husband argues that though the trial court found that his "contacts," "expertise," and "knowledge" were the assets transferred to the corporation, these are not community assets. Actually, the court never stated specifically that these were the community assets removed by Husband, and indeed the court was never precise in its description. However, the court recognized that intangible assets were involved. Because Husband received a substantial salary and bonuses, he was compensated for his labor and the expertise and knowledge he employed in his work. Wife has not attempted to take any portion of Husband's income. As long as he is compensated for those intangibles, the corporation does not retain them as its own assets.

¶ 26 Other intangible assets may constitute community property. For example, the "goodwill" developed in connection with Husband's sole proprietorship during the marriage is considered a community asset. *See Mitchell v. Mitchell*, 152 Ariz. 317, 320, 732 P.2d 208, 211 (1987). Goodwill is defined as an intangible asset that is "an element responsible for profits in a business." *Wisner v. Wisner*, 129 Ariz. 333, 337, 631 P.2d 115, 119 (App. 1981) (citation omitted). Goodwill may also be defined as one's reputation. *Id.* A spouse has a claim for a share of goodwill as a community asset:

> Under the principles of community property law, the wife, by virtue of her position as wife, made to that value [goodwill] the same contribution as does a wife to any of the husband's earnings and accumulations during marriage. She is as much entitled to be recompensed for that contribution as if it were represented by the increased value of stock in a family business.

152 Ariz. at 320, 732 P.2d at 211 (citation omitted).

¶ 27 Husband cannot change the community nature of the goodwill asset by merely changing the form of its ownership through incorporation. The goodwill created was due to Husband's labors expended during marriage and the community is entitled to the asset he created.

¶ 28 Wife has asked for and received only a portion of those community assets developed during the marriage and transferred to Cyber for no consideration.[6] Because Husband concedes that Cyber well compensated him for his labor, the award of Cyber stock necessarily represents a division of the capital of Cyber and not an award based on the value of Husband's labor.[7]

¶ 29 The evidence supports the court's decision. All of the revenue-producing clients of Cyber were developed through Husband's previous clientele and associations acquired during the marriage. Cyber was conceived of and developed by Husband during the marriage. Negotiations for one of the Cyber contracts were undertaken by Husband during his sole proprietorship before Cyber's incorporation. If Husband had incorporated Cyber, instead of allowing Ann Covill to do so, Cyber would have been a community asset and subject to asset distribution pursuant to the dissolution.

---

6. During oral argument on appeal, Husband argued that the trial court could not distribute property on which no value had been placed. This argument fails to recognize the court's broad discretion in apportioning community assets as the court sees fit. *Neal v. Neal*, 116 Ariz. 590, 594, 570 P.2d 758, 762 (1977). We see no absolute need to value an asset if it may otherwise be distributed proportionately between spouses.

Husband advanced a related contention during oral argument for the first time. Husband contended that the court did not have the power to award Wife any portion of the stock. Instead, he argued the court was limited to awarding monetary compensation for that portion of the stock determined to be Wife's. Again, this ignores the well-established discretionary power of the court. Id.

7. The capital of Cyber may include not only the goodwill contributed by Husband, but also the cash contributed by Covill and the goodwill developed by Cyber. However, Husband does not contend that these considerations render the award of one-half of the stock excessive.

¶ 30 Husband cites a number of cases in support of his contention that no community asset was created or transferred. While the cases he cites find no community property in professional licenses or degrees, in post-dissolution separate earnings, or in contingent fees paid after dissolution, Husband overlooks that the cases do recognize goodwill as a community asset. *See, e.g., Wisner,* 129 Ariz. 333, 631 P.2d 115 (holding that a professional degree or license is separate property but professional goodwill of a business earned during marriage is community property); *Koelsch v. Koelsch,* 148 Ariz. 176, 181, 713 P.2d 1234, 1239 (1986) (holding that post-dissolution earnings or benefits are separate property, but those earnings and/or retirement benefits earned during marriage are community property). We hold that the trial court properly found and distributed a community asset.

¶ 37 Husband contends, as his sixth issue, that the court erred when it found that Husband owed Wife a fiduciary duty and that the duty was breached. Whether a duty exists is a question of law, so we review it *de novo.*

¶ 38 Husband concedes that a fiduciary duty exists between spouses, but he contends that duty ceases upon notice of intent to dissolve the marriage. He cites *Applebaum v. Applebaum,* 93 Nev. 382, 566 P.2d 85, 87 (1977), in which the court, confronted with the settlement negotiations between divorcing spouses, found that continued shared residence or the absence of animosity did not create a fiduciary duty between the parties. Unlike the present action, the court addressed only the existence of a fiduciary duty in settlement negotiations between the spouses who continue to reside together amicably during dissolution proceedings. This narrow holding may not be extended to cover the question of a continuing fiduciary duty between spouses regarding the transfer of community assets to outside parties before termination of the marriage.

¶ 39 More on point, though, are the cases Wife cites. In *Smith v. Smith,* 124 Idaho 431, 860 P.2d 634, 643 (1993), the Idaho Supreme Court held that the fiduciary duty of spouses does not cease until termination of the marriage. In *Smith,* the husband had earned approximately $94,000 in fees during the marriage but settled for considerably less than half that amount, thereby depriving the community of an asset. In *In re Marriage of Modnick,* 33 Cal. 3d 897, 191 Cal. Rptr. 629, 663 P.2d 187, 191 (1983), the California Supreme Court recognized the confidential and fiduciary relationship between spouses and found that the duty continues until dissolution and property distribution are complete. In that case, the court found a breach of fiduciary duty where the husband had concealed bank accounts to which he had contributed during the marriage. Though Husband here asserts that no assets were concealed, the effect of removal or concealment of marital assets is the same.

¶ 40 Agreeing with the Idaho and California courts, we hold that a fiduciary relationship between spouses does exist with respect to community assets until the marriage is terminated. Removal of community assets without spousal notice and/or approval can constitute a breach of that duty. Here, Husband removed a community asset, the goodwill of the sole proprietorship, from the marital community without notice to Wife. He gifted that community property asset to an outside party, though the marital community was never compensated for its loss. The trial court had evidence from which it could conclude that Husband breached his fiduciary duty to Wife.

¶ 47 For these reasons, the judgment of the superior court is affirmed.

GARBARINO and GRANT, JJ., concur.

Discussion Questions

1. Which community asset did the husband Bruce transfer to his sister-in-law Ann Covill?

2. How did the Court of Appeals define the fiduciary duty? How long does it last?

It is clear that the fiduciary duty a spouse managing a business owes to the other spouse extends beyond the time a married couple separates. In the California case, *Marriage of Czapar*, 232 Cal. App. 3d 1308, 285 Cal. Rptr. 479 (1991), the Court of Appeal supported the trial court's finding that the community should be reimbursed for improper expenditures from the community business during the period of the separation.

MARRIAGE OF CZAPAR

232 Cal. App. 3d 1308, 285 Cal. Rptr. 479 (1991)
California Court of Appeal

WALLIN, Associate Justice.

William and Phyllis Czapar each appeal from the judgment in this marital dissolution. Phyllis contends the trial court erred in deducting the value of a future covenant not to compete from the value of the family business awarded to William. William contends the trial court erred in reclassifying certain amounts paid to Phyllis during separation as spousal support, finding he had wasted community assets by his mismanagement of the family business during separation and awarding Phyllis attorneys' fees. We conclude the future covenant not to compete was improperly considered and remand for further proceedings. In all other respects the judgment is affirmed.

William filed a petition for marital dissolution in September 1984 to end his 22-year marriage to Phyllis. A major asset of the parties was a business called Anaheim Custom Extruders, Inc., (ACE), a plastic extruding company, which was started by them in 1977. William and Phyllis agree the business is community property.

The parties separated in January 1983. Before separation, William managed, and Phyllis had been employed by, ACE. After separation, William continued to manage ACE. Phyllis also continued to work for ACE until she was fired by William in December 1984. The trial court, after rejecting both parties' testimony regarding the value of ACE, ordered ACE sold in June 1987. However, on Phyllis's motion the court subsequently appointed its own expert to value ACE in April 1988. In July and August 1988, the court held a trial on the value of ACE and other reserved issues. The final judgment was entered on May 9, 1989.

The trial court awarded ACE to William and ruled it had a cash value to the community of $494,058. ACE's actual market value was $644,058, but the court concluded that should William sell ACE he would be required to give a covenant not to compete which diminished the value of the asset to the community. The court valued a covenant not to compete at $150,000 based upon William's prospective loss of earnings and reduced the value of ACE accordingly.

I

Phyllis contends the trial court erred in reducing the community property value of ACE by the value of a covenant not to compete because the existence of such a covenant is entirely speculative and, in any event, it is community property.

* * *

Establishing a value for a future covenant not to compete, separate from the value of the business goodwill itself is entirely too speculative. "[O]nce having made [an] equal division [of community property], the court is not required to speculate about what either or both of the spouses may possibly do with his or her equal share and therefore to engraft on the division further adjustments reflecting situations based on theory rather than fact." If ACE is ever sold it will be William's decision affecting his separate property. The true value of a possible covenant not to compete can only be determined with reference to his circumstances at that time. Reducing the community value of ACE by the covenant's speculative value was error.

* * *

III

William contends the trial court erred in ordering him to reimburse the community for amounts spent by ACE during the parties' separation which the court ruled were not proper business expenses. During the period of separation ACE paid for many of William's personal expenses including meals, vacations, a video cassette recorder, personal estate planning and accounting services, personal insurance premiums and other entertainment items. The trial court ordered William to pay Phyllis $27,494.50 which was one-half of the total amount which the court found ACE had improperly spent on these items.

William challenges the trial court's finding with respect to three specific expenditures. First, ACE purchased a 1984 Porsche automobile for William at a cost of $5,699. The company already provided him with a 1982 Porsche. ACE paid the insurance, maintenance, and principal and interest payments on the new car. While it owned the 1984 Porsche, ACE was unable to resell the 1982 Porsche. The court found the acquisition of the 1984 Porsche cost ACE a total of $7,499. Secondly, ACE made a charitable contribution of $8,500 to William's alma mater. Finally, ACE hired William's girlfriend and paid her $22,500 as a marketing director, although she had no experience in marketing, to develop new markets for an airless tire inner tube. She was on the company payroll at a time when William asserted ACE was experiencing cash flow problems causing him to reduce his salary from $100,000 to $35,000. Her college degree was in home economics and she had worked for 22 years as a high school counselor. She proposed creating a campus student sales force to sell the inner tube. Her efforts produced virtually no sales. The court found that a manager would not have hired and paid for such an employee in a "non-amorous relationship."

A spouse who has the management and control of a business which is community property has a duty to act in good faith towards the other spouse in the management and control of the business. (Civ. Code, §5125, subd. (e).) The standard of care imposed is the same duty owed by persons having relationships of personal confidence specified in Civil Code section 5103. The trial court found William was guilty of wasting community assets by his actions in managing ACE and of violating the standard of care owed to Phyllis. William argues the purchase of the car, the charitable contribution and the hiring of his **girlfriend** were all for legitimate corporate purposes although, in retrospect, they **were not** good choices from a business standpoint.

Reimbursement of the community is allowed when the managing spouse abuses his right of management and control. (*In re Marriage of Smaltz* (1978), 82 Cal. App. 3d 568, 571, 147 Cal. Rptr. 154.) The trial court found William abused his management right by using ACE for personal expenditures. There is substantial evidence in the record to support its finding. The charitable contribution to William's alma mater was a gift of community personal property without Phyllis's consent. The court could also conclude that payment of a salary to William's girlfriend was an improper use of community assets. Finally, the court could conclude that ACE's purchase of the 1984 Porsche when William already had a company car was an improper expense.

* * *

Disposition

The judgment is reversed with respect to the valuation of ACE. In all other respects the judgment is affirmed. The matter is remanded to the trial court for further proceedings in accordance with the opinion. Phyllis is entitled to her costs of appeal.

Crosby, Acting P.J., and Moore, J., concurred.

Discussion Question

1. How did William violate his fiduciary duty to Phyllis?

B. GOODWILL

Let us return to Michael and Lisa. Michael's logo-design business has been highly successful, largely due to Michael's creativity. He has been sought after by businesses large and small to update their company logos. Unfortunately because of Michael spending so much time at his computer, their marriage has suffered. In the event of divorce, one issue would be the value of Michael's company. It was started during their marriage, so it would most likely be considered community property. Even so, it has little tangible value beyond some items like the computer and office equipment that Michael uses. The major value is the intangible quality that involves Michael's talent and creativity that has earned the company the reputation of being a leader in the field of logo-design. That intangible quality can be designated as "goodwill." Although often difficult, business goodwill can be valued and divided at divorce.

When a professional like an accountant, medical doctor or veterinarian runs a business, most community property states find that a professional practice can have goodwill. If generated during marriage, that goodwill would be community property. It is designated as "professional goodwill." However, it is more complicated. Two states, Louisiana and Texas, and the trend in other community property states, is to differentiate between what is called professional goodwill and personal goodwill. Simply stated, the professional goodwill attaches to the *business* of the professional and can be community property, but personal goodwill attaches to the *person* who is the professional and cannot be community property.

One can ask why there is any controversy at all about a professional practice. If a professional is operating a business and businesses have goodwill, surely that should end the controversy. Part of the controversy is about how to value the goodwill when that valuation depends on the past and possibly future success of the individual professional. Future success of the business would occur after a divorce and thus is separate property. The other aspect of the controversy is that most community property states have found that an advanced educational degree is not property divisible at divorce and is owned solely by the spouse who earned the degree. If that spouse subsequently uses that degree to have a professional practice, logic may dictate that the goodwill of the practice is also owned solely by the professional.

One part of the controversy is not usually addressed directly. That results from the divorce scenario where one spouse, usually the husband, is the professional and the other spouse, the wife, has not worked outside the home. After a lengthy marriage, the professional will walk away with continuing earning capacity while the wife will have little or none. Finding that a professional practice has goodwill that is community property is a way of equalizing this economic disparity.

In most community property states, Michael's logo-designing business would be considered community property. Beyond the tangible items in the business, courts would include goodwill as part of the value of the business. Accountants for both Michael and Lisa would use various formulas to ascertain the value of the goodwill. That value would be split between Michael and Lisa — meaning ordinarily that Lisa would gain a greater share of community property than if the tangible items only were valued. In Louisiana and Texas, the courts carve out from the professional's practice goodwill that which is attributed to the professional's "personal quality"[*] or the "professional's skills."[†]

---

[*] La. Rev. Stat. art. 9:2801.2.

[†] *Nail v. Nail*, 486 S.W.2d 761 (Tex. Sup. Ct. 1972); *Guzman v. Guzman*, 827 S.W.2d 445 (Tex. Ct. App. 1992).

1.   Is Professional Goodwill Community Property? Arizona and Idaho Approaches

In the following two cases, *Mitchell v. Mitchell*, 152 Ariz. 317, 732 P.2d 208 (1987), and *Stewart v. Stewart*, 143 Idaho 673, 152 P.3d 544 (2007), the Supreme Courts of Arizona and Idaho both concluded that a professional practice has goodwill that can be divided as community property at divorce. It did not matter that the professional practiced in a partnership or in a corporation. When reading the cases, note how the Courts dealt with the educational/professional/personal controversy.

MITCHELL v. MITCHELL

152 Ariz. 317, 733 P.2d 208 (1987)
Supreme Court of Arizona

HOLOHAN, Justice.

Carole Anne Mitchell, appellant, sought review by this court of the decision of the Court of Appeals in *Mitchell v. Mitchell*, 152 Ariz. 312, 732 P.2d 203 (App. 1985). We granted review to clarify the proper treatment to be accorded goodwill in a professional partnership under Arizona community property laws. The issues on review are:

1. In a marital dissolution proceeding is there a community property interest in the goodwill of a professional practice conducted as a partnership?
2. If so, did the wife forfeit her claim to the goodwill asset of the husband's ongoing CPA practice as a result of signing a partnership agreement that specified that no value be placed on the firm's goodwill?

We have jurisdiction under Arizona Const. art. 6, §5(3) and A.R.S. §12-120.24.

The parties were married in 1954 and have two adult children. The appellee husband received his degree in accounting in 1958. Appellant was not employed outside the home for most of the marriage. The couple moved to Arizona in 1958 where the appellee joined a national accounting firm. He was licensed as a Certified Public Accountant (CPA) in 1960. Several years later, appellee and two associates formed a partnership which lasted until 1968. From 1968 until 1975, appellee practiced as a sole practitioner. In 1975 he entered into an accounting partnership with Earl Hardy under the firm name of Mitchell & Hardy. A third person joined the partnership in 1978, but he withdrew before the end of 1979.

Since 1979 Mitchell & Hardy has operated under a written partnership agreement that was admitted in evidence. The agreement, signed by both appellee and appellant, provides in pertinent part:

17. GOODWILL. The parties to this partnership agreement specifically intend that no value be placed upon any Goodwill of the firm that may exist, and therefore, specify that no valuation shall be attempted in eventual determination of a partner's interest in the net assets of the partnership, its capital or for any other purpose.

Although the 1979 agreement specified no valuation for goodwill, it did contain special provisions providing for payments of money to a partner upon retirement or death. The provisions for such payments were not limited to the firm's tangible assets and accounts receivable but also included a share of the net profits for a limited period.

The trial court in granting a dissolution found *inter alia* that the community interest in the partnership was valued at $150,000. This sum included an amount for the partnership capital assets and goodwill. The Court of Appeals, Division II, reversed the judgment of the trial court and remanded the case for a redetermination of the value of the partnership interest without placing any value on goodwill. The Court of Appeals ruled that appellant was bound by the terms of the partnership agreement which placed a zero valuation on goodwill. The Court of Appeals also held that the goodwill of a professional partnership is not a divisible community asset. In doing so the court distinguished *Wisner v. Wisner*, 129 Ariz. 333, 631 P.2d 115 (App. 1981), which held that the goodwill of a professional corporation was property subject to equitable distribution under A.R.S. §25-318. The court analogized the goodwill of a partnership to a personal achievement such as an educational degree which cannot be exchanged on the open market, citing *Pyeatte v. Pyeatte*, 135 Ariz. 346, 661 P.2d 196 (App. 1982); *Holbrook v. Holbrook*, 103 Wis. 2d 327, 309 N.W.2d 343 (App. 1981).

I. IS GOODWILL OF A PROFESSIONAL PARTNERSHIP A COMMUNITY PROPERTY ASSET?

The concept of "goodwill" is elusive, leading over the years to a variety of judicial definitions. *Wisner v. Wisner*, 129 Ariz. at 337, 631 P.2d at 119, *citing* Vol. 38 C.J.S. *Good Will*, §1; 38 Am. Jur. 2d *Good Will* §1, and cases cited therein. The definitions range from the narrow view of goodwill as a probability of repeat customers, Annot., *Accountability for Good Will of Professional Practice in Actions Arising from Divorce or Separation*, 52 A.L.R.3d at 1344 n. 1, to its broadest sense as reputation, *Spheeris v. Spheeris*, 37 Wis. 2d 497, 155 N.W.2d 130, 135 (1967). In Arizona, it has been defined as "that asset, intangible in form, which is an element responsible for profits in a business." *Jacob v. Miner*, 67 Ariz. 109, 120, 191 P.2d 734, 741 (1948).

In *Wisner*, the Court of Appeals held that the goodwill of a professional corporation is based on numerous factors, including: "the practitioner's age, health, past earning power, reputation in the community for judgment, skill and knowledge, and his or her comparative professional success." 129 Ariz. at 337-38, 631 P.2d at 119-20. *Wisner* relied upon a case from California and a case from Washington, both of which discussed goodwill within the context of marital dissolution proceedings. Both cases surmounted the difficulty of valuing professional goodwill while holding that indeed there *was* goodwill in the professional partnership and sole proprietorship at issue. *In re Marriage of Lukens*, 16 Wash. App. 481, 558 P.2d 279 (1976) (goodwill of sole medical practice a divisible marital asset regardless of asset's marketability); *In re Marriage of Lopez*, 38 Cal. App. 3d 93, 113 Cal. Rptr. 58 (1974) (whenever the issue is raised, trial court must make specific finding of the existence and value of the goodwill of a professional practice whether in the form of sole practice, partnership or professional corporation). *Wisner* dealt with a professional corporation with one shareholder, but it is instructive in its description of the factors to be considered in establishing the value of goodwill in a professional practice. We believe that the *Wisner* principles are equally applicable to a professional partnership. *Wisner* does not support appellee's argument that a partner's goodwill is a personal, non-divisible asset because it is not readily marketable.

It would be inequitable to hold that the form of the business enterprise can defeat the community's interest in the professional goodwill. Such a result ignores the contribution made by the non-professional spouse to the success of the professional, especially when the marriage spans as many years as in the present case. Under community property principles the wife made the same contribution to the community asset of the professional partnership as she would have made had the business been a professional corporation. As one court has stated:

> Under the principles of community property law, the wife, by virtue of her position as wife, made to that value [goodwill] the same contribution as does a wife to any of the husband's earnings and accumulations during marriage. She is as much entitled to be recompensed for that contribution as if it were represented by the increased value of stock in a family business.

Golden v. Golden, 270 Cal. App. 2d 401 at 405, 75 Cal. Rptr. 735 at 738 (1969). The confusion in this area of the law exists partially because many of the cases concerning the existence and evaluation of goodwill involve partnership dissolution, and not marital dissolution. Often the valuation of partnership assets, including goodwill, is controlled by the partnership agreement. In this case we are dealing with a marital dissolution which does not affect the continuation of the business partnership. The current situation is aptly described as follows:

> A professional practice goes automatically to the spouse licensed to practice it. He is not selling out or liquidating, but continuing in business. Effectively, it is the case of the silent partner withdrawing from a going business. And, if such partner is to receive fair compensation for her share, or her enforced retirement, it should be so evaluated.

Brawman v. Brawman, 199 Cal. App. 2d 876, 882, 19 Cal. Rptr. 106, 109-10 (1962). Finally, a professional practice's intangible goodwill is not the same as a professional license or degree, neither of which have been treated as community property within the meaning of A.R.S. §25-211. *Wisner v. Wisner, supra.* The better analogy is to pension rights which are marital property. Goodwill and pension rights acquired during the marriage are community assets, although in a form where the enjoyment is deferred. *See Koelsch v. Koelsch,* 148 Ariz. 176, 713 P.2d 1234 (1986); *In re Marriage of Slater,* 100 Cal. App. 3d 241, 160 Cal. Rptr. 686 (1979); *In re Marriage of Fonstein,* 17 Cal. 3d 738, 552 P.2d 1169, 131 Cal. Rptr. 873 (1976). The partnership agreement in this case recognizes the firm's intangible value above tangible assets by providing special compensation in the event of retirement, death or disability of a partner. The agreement implicitly recognizes that there is an intangible value to the partnership above the tangible assets that should be paid for by the partners who continue the practice.

We note that some jurisdictions hold that the goodwill of a professional partnership or proprietorship is not a divisible marital asset. *Powell v. Powell,* 231 Kan. 456, 648 P.2d 218, 223-24 (1982); *Nail v. Nail,* 486 S.W.2d 761 (Tex. 1972); *Austin v. Austin,* 619 S.W.2d 290 (Tex. Civ. App. 1981). However, because the professional practice of the sole practitioner or partner will continue after dissolution of the marriage, with the same goodwill as it had during the marriage, we find that a refusal to consider goodwill as a community asset does not comport with Arizona's statutory equitable distribution scheme. We prefer to accept the economic reality that the goodwill of a professional practice has value, and it should be treated as property upon dissolution of the community, regardless of the form of business. *Wisner v. Wisner, supra* (corporation); *In re Marriage of Fonstein, supra* (partnership); *In re Marriage of Watts,* 171 Cal. App. 3d 366, 217 Cal. Rptr. 301 (1985) (partnership); *In re Marriage of Fenton,* 134 Cal. App. 3d 451, 184 Cal. Rptr. 597 (1982) (corporation); *In re Marriage of Slater, supra* (partnership); *In re Marriage of Foster,* 42 Cal. App. 3d 577, 117 Cal. Rptr. 49 (1974) (sole practice); *In re Marriage of Lopez, supra* (partnership); *Golden v. Golden, supra* (sole practice); *In re Marriage of Hull,* 712 P.2d 1317 (Mont. 1986) (professional corporation); *Lockwood v. Lockwood,* 205 Neb. 818, 290 N.W.2d 636 (1980) (partnership); *Dugan v. Dugan,* 92 N.J. 423, 457 A.2d 1 (1983) (solely owned professional corporation); *In re Marriage of Hall,* 103 Wash. 2d 236, 692 P.2d 175 (1984) (professional corporation); *Matter of Marriage of Fleege,* 91 Wash. 2d 324, 588 P.2d 1136 (1979) (sole practice); *Marriage of Lukens, supra* (sole practice).

The trial court did not err in treating the goodwill of a professional partnership as a community asset.

III. Valuation

Because we hold that there is goodwill in appellee's professional practice and that appellant did not forfeit her interest by signing the partnership agreement, we must address appellee's contention that the trial court erred in valuing the goodwill. In reviewing the findings below, we will view the evidence in the light most favorable to support the decision. *Johnson v. Johnson,* 131 Ariz. 38, 44, 638 P.2d 705, 711 (1981). The finding will be upheld if there is any reasonable evidence to support it. *Id.*

It is a difficult task at best to arrive at a value for the intangible component of a professional practice attributable to goodwill. "No rigid and unvarying rule for the determination of the value of goodwill has been laid down by prior case law and each case must be determined on its own facts and circumstances." *Wisner v. Wisner, supra; see also,* Annot. *Accountability for Good Will of Professional Practice in Actions Arising from Divorce or Separation,* 52 A.L.R.3d at 1344.

In the instant case, the trial court heard testimony from four CPAs, including appellee. The partnership's estimated goodwill value ranged from zero according to appellee, to $160,000 according to appellant's experts. Based upon testimony of appellee's own expert that (1) accounting practices are bought and sold in Arizona and (2) the gross fees approach is preferable to the excess earnings method advocated by appellant, the trial court arrived at a total value of $150,000 for the practice, including its tangible assets. The record indicates the latter to be no more than $35,000. The trial court's final figure also included an offset for a one time "windfall" of approximately $12,000 in fees to prevent an inflated valuation. Although the court did not separately value the firm's goodwill, tangible assets or the "windfall" offset, we cannot say as a matter of law that the trial court erred in its valuation. An adequate basis exists in the record in the form of expert testimony which reasonably supports the valuation of the partnership. Nevertheless, more precise findings are preferable. As a general rule, "the court should clearly state whether it finds the practice to have any goodwill, and if so, its value, and how it arrived at that value." *Poore v. Poore*, 75 N.C. App. 414, 331 S.E.2d 266 (1985). However, because the trial court stated that it utilized the gross fees approach advocated by appellee's own expert, and the valuation was reasonably supported in the record by expert testimony, we find no error.

We vacate that portion of the Court of Appeals' decision relating to goodwill in a professional practice. The case is remanded to the superior court for further proceedings.

GORDON, C.J., FELDMAN, V.C.J., and CAMERON, J., concur.

HAYS, J., Retired, did not participate in the determination of this matter.

Discussion Questions

1. What reasons did the *Mitchell* Court give for rejecting the husband's argument that a partner's goodwill in a professional practice is a "personal, non-divisible asset that is not readily marketable"?
2. How does the *Mitchell* Court deal with the professional degree/professional goodwill issue?

STEWART v. STEWART

143 Idaho 673, 152 P.3d 544 (2007)
Supreme Court of Idaho

TROUT, Justice.

Dr. James Stewart (James) appeals from a magistrate court's division of community property and award of spousal support to his wife, Sarah Stewart (Sally). The case addresses the characterization of goodwill in a professional services corporation as community property in a divorce proceeding, together with an award of maintenance.

I.   FACTUAL AND PROCEDURAL BACKGROUND

James and Sally Stewart married in 1981. Two children were born into the marriage, both of whom are now of majority age. Sally helped put James through medical school and throughout the marriage cared for the children and worked as a teacher. The family moved several times before settling in Boise in 1995, where James joined Dr. Gerald Overly in a dermatology practice. In 1996, James and Dr. Overly formed the Dermatology Clinic of Idaho, P.A. (DCI). James is a forty-five percent shareholder in DCI and his practice includes general dermatological services and surgical procedures as well as a subspecialty in "MOHS" micrographic surgery, a method of removing certain skin cancers. Sally has continued to work as an elementary school teacher but, at the time of the divorce, reduced her schedule due her degenerative illness, post-polio syndrome.[1] The Stewarts own a residence with a stipulated value of $360,000. The personal property accumulated during the marriage includes the interest in DCI, retirement accounts, stock, automobiles, and furniture.

On April 23, 2003, James filed a complaint for divorce, and the matter proceeded to trial before a magistrate judge. The judge found James' dermatology practice to be valued at $130,554.00 in tangible assets. In addition, he found there to be $210,747.00 in professional goodwill associated with DCI separate and apart from James' skill. To the extent that this goodwill exceeded James' personal skill and knowledge, the magistrate judge concluded, this goodwill constituted community property subject to distribution.

The trial court awarded Sally an unequal division of the community property valued at $788,372.11, including the Stewart residence and various bank and retirement accounts. In light of the community property award, the magistrate judge calculated the level of spousal support necessary to support Sally to be $5,166 per month for twelve years. The judge noted that Sally would not be eligible to receive Social Security until approximately twelve years from the date of the order, the same time she would become eligible to draw on her retirement accounts without penalty. The magistrate judge also considered Sally's post-polio condition, which at the time of the divorce had caused Sally to reduce her work schedule to 80% of full time.

James appealed the award, challenging the community property characterization of his businesses' professional goodwill; the amount of interest found in his medical practice; and the amount and duration of spousal support. The district court affirmed the valuation of the community interest in the medical practice, but vacated and remanded for further proceedings the award of spousal support because of a mathematical error in calculating the length of time maintenance should be paid. James appealed the district court's ruling to this Court; meanwhile, the magistrate court continued to hold proceedings on remand. The magistrate judge issued an order on remand noting the mathematical error in the spousal support calculation but concluding that the error made no difference in his determination of the overall spousal support award. After James appealed the magistrate judge's order on remand to the district court, this Court stayed all district court proceedings pending resolution of this appeal.

. . .

---

1. According to the magistrate's findings, Sally suffers from post-polio syndrome and a mild depression secondary to the disease. Post-polio syndrome emerges years after polio infection and its symptoms include muscle fatigue or atrophy causing pain and/or weakness. Post-polio syndrome is a progressive, degenerative disease for which there is currently no cure. In the future, Sally can expect to rely on a cane, brace, crutch, or wheelchair.

III.   DISCUSSION

A.   PROFESSIONAL GOODWILL

1. Characterization of Professional Goodwill

James disputes the magistrate judge's characterization of his portion of the professional goodwill in DCI as community property to be divided in a divorce. This Court has held that good will is an appropriate factor in determining the value of a business. *Olsen v. Olsen*, 125 Idaho 603, 606, 873 P.2d 857, 860 (1994). The goodwill of a business is "the custom which it attracts, and the benefits or advantage it receives from constant or habitual customers, and the probability that the old customers will continue to come to the place." *Harshbarger v. Eby*, 28 Idaho 753, 761, 156 P. 619, 621 (1916); *see also McAffee v. McAffee*, 132 Idaho 281, 286, 971 P.2d 734, 739 (1999).

The question presented by this case is whether goodwill is an appropriate factor to consider in determining the community property value of a professional services corporation, an issue of first impression. Any division of property in a divorce proceeding begins with the presumption that all property acquired after marriage is community property. *Reed*, 137 Idaho at 58, 44 P.3d at 1113. The trial court reasoned that James acquired all of his interest in DCI during marriage and that the value of his interest in DCI, including goodwill, was community property.

There seems to be no principled reason to treat the goodwill of a business differently when it is a professional services corporation. The property rights of individuals with professional educations and licenses do not differ from the rights of people engaged in other types of business. Determining the value of goodwill in small professional services corporations may indeed be difficult, since Idaho law treats personal skill and reputation as separate assets rather than community property. *See Wolford v. Wolford*, 117 Idaho 61, 67, 785 P.2d 625, 631 (1990) (holding that personal attributes, including knowledge, skill, and reputation, were not property, either separate or community); *Olsen*, 125 Idaho at 606, 873 P.2d at 860 (stating that knowledge, background, and talent are personal assets rather than community property). Where a professional business is an independent entity, however, goodwill is calculable and divisible in divorce just as goodwill in any other business. DCI was such an independent entity, and it was possible for the magistrate judge to distinguish between James' identity and the separate identity of DCI. A practitioner's knowledge, skill, and background are personal attributes. To the extent a professional services corporation has goodwill value beyond these personal assets, however, that goodwill is community property.

2. Valuation of Professional Goodwill

* * *

The record reflects that the magistrate judge considered testimony from both parties' experts that DCI had goodwill and that James had an interest in that goodwill. In estimating James' interest in the goodwill of DCI, Sally's expert first calculated James' average income, weighted more heavily towards his most recent annual salary. The expert then compared James' average income with the average compensation of a doctor with the same specialty and in the same geographic region as James. In determining the average income of a local dermatologist, the expert consulted the 2001 Physician Compensation and Production Survey, published by the Medical Group Management Association and also relied on his own familiarity with the local market. Concluding that the appropriate income to compare to James' was $423,023.00 — the average compensation for dermatologists in the nine- tieth percentile of earnings nationwide — the expert then subtracted this number from James' average income to reach excess earnings. He then applied a capitalization rate of 22.1% to reach a goodwill value of $210,747.00. Importantly, in evaluating the accuracy of this number as a reflection of James' interest in DCI's goodwill, the magistrate judge made the factual findings that DCI's name, location, and reputation had value separate and apart from James' skill, and was designed to attract new patients not familiar with either James or Dr. Overly. The magistrate judge did not err in concluding that James' interest in DCI's goodwill totaled $210,747.00 and the record is sufficient to support the magistrate judge's findings.

IV.   CONCLUSION

The magistrate judge's order calculating the value of the community's interest in DCI and awarding Sally an unequal division of the community property is affirmed, together with the award of spousal maintenance. We award costs but not attorney fees to Sally on appeal.

Chief Justice SCHROEDER and Judge SCHILLING, Pro Tem, Concur.

Justice EISMANN, Dissenting with respect to Part II.A and Concurring in Parts II.B and III.

Because the majority fails to distinguish between business good will, which is community property, and personal good will, which is not, I respectfully dissent.

The central error made by the CPA and the court was the failure to distinguish between personal goodwill and business goodwill. James's income derives from per- sonally providing services to his patients. As a result, he has personal goodwill and possibly business goodwill. His personal goodwill comes from his personal attributes that attract patients or referrals and repeat business, including his training, experience, reputation, and patient satisfaction. The business itself, Dermatology Clinic of Idaho, may also have business goodwill, based upon factors such as its location and reputation. The CPA's testimony upon which the magistrate relied did not distinguish between personal goodwill and business goodwill. In fact, he testified that he did not know of any way to separate out James's personal goodwill. James's personal goodwill is not community property. His personal attributes are not community property, *Olsen v. Olsen*, 125 Idaho 603, 873 P.2d 857 (1994); *Wolford v. Wolford*, 117 Idaho 61, 785 P.2d 625 (1990), and so his post-divorce ability to earn above-average income because of his personal attributes is not community property.

In a divorce action, a trial court must determine the value of community assets, including a community business. Value is "what a willing buyer would pay a willing seller for the business." *Chandler v. Chandler*, 136 Idaho 246, 250, 32 P.3d 140, 144 (2001). A willing buyer cannot purchase James's personal attributes. A willing buyer cannot purchase the relationship James has with his patients or their confidence in him.

The business where James works is Dermatology Clinic of Idaho. The goodwill at issue is the goodwill of that entity. It is "'the general public patronage and encouragement which it receives from constant or habitual customers, on account of its local position, or common celebrity, or reputation for skill or affluence. . . .'" *Chandler v. Chandler*, 136 Idaho 246, 250, 32 P.3d 140, 144 (2001) (quoting *Newark Morning Ledger Co. v. United States*, 507 U.S. 546, 555, 113 S. Ct. 1670, 1675, 123 L. Ed. 2d 288, 299 (1993)). The relevant common celebrity and reputation for skill or affluence is that of Dermatology Clinic of Idaho, not James. Certainly, business entities providing professional services to patients or clients can have goodwill that is independent of the professionals who actually provide those services. The longer the entity has been in business and the higher the number of professionals working in it, the greater the likelihood it will have business goodwill. In this case, however, there is no evidence showing the value, if any, of the business goodwill of Dermatology Clinic of Idaho.

I would vacate the magistrate judge's valuation of the community's interest in Dermatology Clinic of Idaho and remand for further proceedings consistent with the above. If such revaluation results in a significant reduction in the value of the community property awarded to Sally, I would also permit the magistrate to reevaluate the amount of spousal support.

Justice JIM JONES Concurring in Parts IIIA, IIIC, and IV, and Concurring in the result of Part IIIB.

The Court's treatment of the issue of professional goodwill is right on point. James had urged that the Court make a distinction between the personal goodwill of his professional practice and the "enterprise" or professional goodwill of the business. In my view, the goodwill of a business, whether professional or otherwise, if it exists and is properly characterized as community property, is subject to division upon divorce. With regard to the maintenance award, I would not disturb the result reached by the trial court but do think two matters raised on appeal by James should be addressed.

With regard to the goodwill issue, the Court was correct in declining James' invitation to draw a distinction between enterprise goodwill and personal goodwill when considering the value of his business. In urging the adoption of this distinction, James called our attention to *May v. May*, 214 W. Va. 394, 589 S.E.2d 536 (2003), wherein the West Virginia Supreme Court asserted "there are two types of goodwill recognized by courts in divorce litigation: enterprise goodwill (also called commercial or professional goodwill) and personal goodwill (also called professional goodwill)." *Id.* at 541. Before one jumps to the conclusion that both types of goodwill are one and the same, i.e. professional goodwill, the West Virginia Supreme Court went on to say:

> "Enterprise goodwill attaches to a business entity and is associated separately from the reputation of the owners. Product names, business locations, and skilled labor forces are common examples of enterprise goodwill. The asset has a determinable value because the enterprise goodwill of an ongoing business will transfer upon sale of the business to a willing buyer."

* * *

"[P]ersonal goodwill is associated with the individuals. It is that part of increased earning capacity that results from the reputation, knowledge and skills of individual people. Accordingly, the goodwill of a service business, such as a professional practice, consists largely of personal goodwill."

Id. at 541-2. James would have the Court enter the morass of trying to draw a distinction between the value attributable to a professional practice by virtue of the individual attributes of the professional and the value of goodwill not attributable to those personal assets, valuing each separately, and then dividing the latter but not the former. Quite frankly, such an approach does not make a good deal of sense.

Some businesses, regardless of whether they are professional practices, retail businesses, or manufacturing operations, will have more value than a competitive business because of the energy, good sense, and other personal attributes of the person or persons operating them, as compared to the competitor. When valuing service businesses, such as restaurants, retail sales operations, and the like, an income approach is often employed. A business that provides exceptional service will often produce a greater income, and larger income approach valuation, than one which does not. The value created by extra effort, skill, and attention to detail is comparable to the value created by the personal attributes that a successful professional adds as goodwill in his or her professional practice. We have held that special attributes of a proprietor, adding to the value of a restaurant business, can be goodwill to be considered in establishing the business value for purposes of division of community property. *Chandler v. Chandler*, 136 Idaho 246, 32 P.3d 140 (2001). There is no reason why value added to a professional practice by virtue of the personal attributes of the professional practitioner cannot also be treated in such fashion.

While the professional attributes and skills of the marital partners are not community property, the employment of those attributes and skills during the course of the marriage can produce value in a business, whether professional or otherwise, that becomes community property. *Wolford v. Wolford*, 117 Idaho 61, 785 P.2d 625 (1990), tells us that personal attributes, including knowledge, background and talent, are not in themselves community property. *Id.* at 67, 785 P.2d at 631. However, *Wolford* also says that "Personal attributes can enhance income which . . . is community property. . . ." *Id.* Personal attributes can also enhance the value of a business, including a professional practice, thus creating value that is community property. We don't shrink back from considering a spouse's earning capacity, based upon knowledge, background and talent, in determining the amount of future spousal maintenance, where such an award is appropriate, nor in considering how much that spouse must contribute to the support of minor children. Neither should we ignore the value of goodwill built up by a spouse in a business or professional practice during the course of the marriage because that value is a present value that can be allocated between the parties. It is not an allocation of future earnings. Rather, it is a calculation of what the business or professional practice might be worth on the market, based upon expert evidence presented by one knowledgeable in calculating such value.

In this case, Sally's expert presented credible testimony regarding valuation of the goodwill built up in James' professional practice during the course of the marriage. James' expert sought to call the methodology into question but did not offer any testimony regarding a different calculation of the value. The trial court, although identifying the methodology concern noted in the Court's opinion, wrote that the result produced by Sally's expert was "nevertheless reasonable because it was consistent with other resources and . . . the best evidence in the record from which the court can fix the value of James' interest in DCI's goodwill." The Court properly affirms that result.

* * *

Discussion Questions

1. How did the *Stewart* majority define professional goodwill?
2. What were the reasons that Justice Eismann dissented? Justice Jones concurred? Who do you agree with?
3. How would Michael's logo-design business be treated by the *Mitchell* Court and by the three *Stewart* opinions?

---

2. Separating Personal and Business Goodwill: The Louisiana Approach

The Louisiana legislature in 2004 tried to clarify the law regarding goodwill, by specifying that personal attributes should not be part of the valuation of a business.

LOUISIANA REVISED STATUTES
Art. 9:2801.2 (2004)

In a proceeding to partition the community, the court may include, in the valuation of any community owned corporate, commercial, or professional business, the goodwill of the business. However, that portion of the goodwill attributable to any personal quality of the spouse awarded the business shall not be included in the valuation of a business.

In the following case, *Statham v. Statham*, 986 So. 2d 894 (Ct. App. 2008), the court discussed the application of Art. 9:2801.2.

STATHAM v. STATHAM
986 So. 2d 894 (2008)
Court of Appeal of Louisiana

GASKINS, J.

In this community property partition, the wife appeals from a judgment classifying property and assessing value. In particular, she objects to the trial court's classification of a diamond ring she received as community property. Additionally, she complains of the trial court's classification of post-termination distributions to the husband from the community business as his separate property, and the court's assessment of a value of $34,000 to the community business. We affirm the trial court judgment.

FACTS

The parties, Marsha Jo "Jody" Statham and Harry Rufus "Butch" Statham were married in 1970. They divorced in 2005. The community terminated on February 16, 2005, the date of the filing of the divorce petition.

A June 2007 hearing officer conference report made findings and recommendations as to the partition of the community property. Butch filed an objection to the hearing officer's conclusion that a ring valued at about $17,000 and acquired during the marriage was very probably a birthday present to Jody and thus her separate property. Jody objected to several findings, including the hearing officer's acceptance of Butch's evidence that the community business was valued at $33,000 and his denial of Jody's assertion that part of Butch's post-termination income should be classified as community property.

A bench trial on the community property partition was held on July 27, 2007. Six witnesses testified. In addition to the parties, Jody presented the testimony of Richard W. Guillot, a business valuation expert, and Gary L. Booth, a certified public accountant (CPA) who performed work for Butch's insurance brokerage company, P & S Benefits Consultants, Inc. (P & S). Butch presented the testimony of Albert Carlton Clark, III, a business valuation expert, and Troy Pardue, an insurance agent who was Butch's business partner for 11 years.

According to Mr. Guillot's analysis, the fair market value of P & S as of February 2005 was $310,766. When he compiled his report in June 2006, he based his opinions on fair market value, a willing buyer and a willing seller. However, Mr. Clark — who was hired two months before trial — estimated the value at $34,000 for purposes of the community property partition. In reaching this figure, he estimated that P & S had a total value of $220,008, but a total goodwill value of $207,094. He then assessed 90 percent of the total goodwill value of the company to personal goodwill, as opposed to enterprise goodwill.

[Discussion of classification of the ring is found in Chapter 7, Transmutation.]

As to the value assessment of P & S, the court found the testimony of Mr. Clark more convincing than that of Mr. Guillot. Specifically, it concluded that the basis of Mr. Clark's opinion was more valid since Mr. Guillot's report used 2005 data and failed to assess goodwill. Thus, the court assigned a value of $34,000 to the company. On the issue of post-termination distributions from P & S to Butch, the court found that this income resulted from effort, skill and industry exercised by Butch after the termination of the community; thus, it was classified as his separate property.

On October 22, 2007, the trial court signed a judgment in conformity with its ruling. Jody appealed.

VALUATION OF COMPANY

As to the valuation of P & S, Jody contends that the trial court erred in concluding that Mr. Clark's opinion was more valid because it used more recent financial information; according to Jody, the evidence shows that P & S's cash flow has remained consistent through 2007. She claims that the 90 percent figure used for personal goodwill by Mr. Clark cannot be sustained and it ignores the fact that much of the company's stability came from selling policies from major companies like Blue Cross/Blue Shield.

Butch argues that his expert, Mr. Clark, properly applied La. R.S. 9:2801.2, which provides for the exclusion of "goodwill attributable to any personal quality of the spouse awarded the business" from the business' valuation. On the other hand, he asserts that Jody's expert failed to apply the statute in his analysis. Butch also maintains that the testimony of his former business partner, Mr. Pardue, corroborated his own testimony about the nature of the business and his personal relationship with his clients.

La. R.S. 9:2801.2 states:

> In a proceeding to partition the community, the court may include, in the valuation of any community-owned corporate, commercial, or professional business, the goodwill of the business. However, that portion of the goodwill attributable to any personal quality of the spouse awarded the business shall not be included in the valuation of a business.

Where one spouse holds a professional degree or license and the goodwill results solely from that professional's personal relationship with clients, that goodwill is not included in the community. *Clemons v. Clemons*, 42,129 (La. App. 2d Cir. 5/9/07), 960 So. 2d 1068, *writ denied*, 2007-1652 (La. 10/26/07), 966 So. 2d 583.

The rule that questions of credibility are for the trier of fact applies to the evaluation of expert testimony, unless the stated reasons of the expert are patently unsound. Credibility determinations, including the evaluation of and resolution of conflicts in expert testimony, are factual issues to be resolved by the trier of fact, which should not be disturbed on appeal in the absence of manifest error. *Hanks v. Entergy Corporation*, 2006-477 (La. 12/18/06), 944 So. 2d 564.

The two experts used similar methodologies to value P & S. However, they differed substantially on the methods used to determine goodwill. To make this assessment, Mr. Clark began with his fair market calculation of $220,008 and subtracted $12,914 for business assets (like accounts receivable, furniture, and fixtures). Mr. Clark found the remaining value of $207,094 was goodwill. In determining the percentage of goodwill attributable to personal goodwill and to enterprise goodwill, Mr. Clark considered Butch's personality, his relationship with his customers, the amount of his business coming from referrals, the loyalty of his customers who would follow him regardless of his company name, and the good service Butch provides to his customers. Mr. Clark assigned little value to the product because other insurance agents sell the same group health lines. Pursuant to La. R.S. 9:2801.2, for purposes of the community property partition, Mr. Clark concluded that 90 percent of the value was attributable to Butch's personal attributes and only 10 percent to the enterprise or business itself. Thus, he found that the company's value, for partition purposes, was $34,000.

Mr. Guillot testified that Mr. Clark's assignment of 90 percent to personal goodwill was unreasonable and that any methodology to assign personal goodwill was, at best, subjective. His analysis does not appear to assess goodwill under La. R.S. 9:2801.2. Instead, to compensate for goodwill, he merely increased the salary for Butch in the analysis by which he determined the value of P & S.

Our review of the testimony of the experts reveals that the trial court made a credibility determination in favor of Butch's expert, Mr. Clark. As we do not find any indication that Mr. Clark's reasons are "patently unsound," we are obliged to defer to the trier of fact. The trial court's findings on this issue are not manifestly erroneous or clearly wrong. Therefore, the trial court did not err in accepting Mr. Clark's valuation of the company.

CONCLUSION

The judgment of the trial court is affirmed. Costs of this appeal are assessed to the appellant.

Affirmed.

Discussion Questions

1. What factors led the trial court to conclude that 90 percent of Butch's P & S business was personal goodwill? What was Jody's argument against that 90 percent figure?

2. How would Michael's logo-design business be treated by a Louisiana court?

---

3. Can an Individual Have Goodwill? The California Answer

The short answer is "No," based on the same considerations of personal and business attributes. The answer is not without controversy, as there was a vigorous dissent in *Marriage of McTiernan and Dubrow*, 133 Cal. App. 4th 1090, 35 Cal. Rptr. 3d 287 (2005). The case involved a famous movie director, John McTiernan, with movie credits of "Die Hard" and "The Hunt for Red October." His wife, Donna Dubrow, was also in the motion picture production business. The Court of Appeal noted that in their eight and three-quarter years of marriage, John had earned approximately $15 million while Donna had earned about $1 million. The trial court found that there was goodwill in his business as a motion picture director and that all of the $1.5 million goodwill was community property. John appealed. While reading the case, note how personal/business goodwill issue was resolved.

MARRIAGE OF McTIERNAN AND DUBROW

133 Cal. App. 4th 1090, 35 Cal. Rptr. 3d 287 (2005)
California Court of Appeal

FLIER, J.

John McTiernan (husband) and Donna Dubrow (wife) both appeal from a judgment in the dissolution of their marriage. Their appeals raise distinct issues. Husband primarily challenges the trial court's determination that there existed goodwill in his business as a motion picture director, and that all of the $1.5 million of goodwill constituted community property.

We find merit in husband's contention that there is no goodwill in his career as a motion picture director. We reverse the judgment as to those elements, and affirm it in all other respects.

FACTS

The parties were married in November 1988. They separated in July 1997, and husband commenced this proceeding the following month. The matter was extensively litigated, including 21 days of trial, conducted between June 1999 and June 28, 2000. The court's 34-page statement of decision was filed August 23, 2000, and the judgment under review was entered on August 28, 2002. At that time, husband was 51 years old and wife was 59.

The evidence showed that, during and after the marriage and to some extent before, husband was a very successful motion picture director, commanding six- to high seven-figure compensation per film, and having to his credit such blockbusters as Die Hard (20th Century Fox 1988), The Hunt for Red October (Paramount Pictures 1990), and The Thomas Crown Affair (Metro-Goldwyn-Mayer 1999). Wife also pursued a career in motion picture production, and before the marriage she was earning $195,000 a year as a production company executive. She produced several films during the marriage, while accompanying husband in his directorial pursuits. The trial court found that during the eight and three-quarter years of marriage before separation, husband had earned approximately $15 million, and wife had earned about $1 million. Predictably, the parties' community estate was substantial, as was the scale of their lifestyle.

Because the issues raised on these appeals largely involve distinct factual and legal bases, we will state the facts relevant to each issue in conjunction with its discussion. We proceed to consideration of the issues.

I.   HUSBAND'S APPEAL

A.   PROFESSIONAL GOODWILL

1. The Trial Court's Ruling and Husband's Contention on Appeal

The trial court found that husband "is a motion picture director who has achieved exceptional success in that field. His success is dependent upon his personal skill, experience and knowledge, and the Court finds that, in that respect, the profession which he practices is similar to that of an attorney, physician, dentist, accountant, editor, architect, or any other professional who has established a successful professional practice, with quantifiable expectation of future patronage, based upon his or her personal skill, experience and knowledge."

The finding that husband has achieved exceptional success as a motion picture director is based for the most part on testimony presented by Arthur De Vany, Ph.D., an economist who is a professor in the Department of Economics of the Institute of

Mathematics and Behavioral Sciences at the University of California, Irvine. The trial court found that the "evidence presented by Dr. De Vany was persuasive . . . that Petitioner [husband] has developed an earning capacity and reputation in his profession as a motion picture director which greatly exceeds that of most persons involved in that profession and that Petitioner commands a premium for his services. [¶] In addition, the evidence established that Petitioner can reasonably expect to continue to enjoy said premium. In other words, he has expectation of continued patronage at his prior level of compensation."

The trial court detailed the facts upon which these conclusions were based. Among these facts are that husband is ranked No. 13 among 1,058 motion picture directors in cumulative box office revenues during 1985-1996, No. 8 in terms of gross domestic revenues produced by movies he directed, and No. 1 in terms of production budgets entrusted to his control. Husband does not contest the trial court's conclusion that all of this boils down to the fact that he has, in the trial court's words, "elite professional standing."

The trial court determined the value of husband's goodwill by means of the "excess earnings" approach. It has been noted that the "excess earnings" method is a method that is commonly used to determine the value of the goodwill in a professional practice. (Hogoboom & King, Cal. Practice Guide: Family Law (The Rutter Group 2005) ¶ 8:1445, p. 8–350.) Broadly put, the excess earnings approach is predicated on a comparison of the earnings of the professional in question with that of a peer whose performance is "average."[1] Using this method with some modifications, the trial court determined that husband's goodwill at the time of separation was $1.5 million.

Husband contends that he does not possess an asset that can be properly classified as goodwill. Relying on *In re Marriage of Rives* (1982) 130 Cal. App. 3d 138, 153, 181 Cal. Rptr. 572, and *In re Marriage of Aufmuth* (1979) 89 Cal. App. 3d 446, 460-462, 152 Cal. Rptr. 668, among other cases, husband points out that skill, reputation and experience are not community property. Husband contends that the goodwill found to exist in this case is in reality nothing other than his skill, reputation and experience.

2. The Issue Defined

The trial court found that husband has a "quantifiable expectation of future patronage." Future, or continued, public patronage is one essential aspect of

1. "Pursuant to this method, one first determines a practitioner's average annual net earnings (before income taxes) by reference to any period that seems reasonably illustrative of the current rate of earnings. One then determines the annual salary of a typical salaried employee who has had experience commensurate with the spouse who is the sole practitioner or sole owner/employee. Next, one deducts from the average net pretax earnings of the business or practice a 'fair return' on the net tangible assets used by the business. Then, one determines the 'excess earnings' by subtracting the annual salary of the average salaried person from the average net pretax earning of the business or practice remaining after deducting a fair return on tangible assets. Finally, one capitalizes the excess earnings over a period of years by multiplying it by a factor equal to a specific period of years, discounted to reflect present value of the excess earnings over that period. The period varies according to factors such as the type of business, its stability, and its earnings trend." (*In re Marriage of Garrity and Bishton* (1986) 181 Cal. App. 3d 675, 688, fn. 14, 226 Cal. Rptr. 485.) As noted (Hogoboom & King, Cal. Practice Guide: Family Law, *supra*, ¶ 8:1445, p. 8-350), this description may be flawed, especially in subtracting the annual salary of the average *salaried* person, when the comparison should be with a peer who, in the usual setting, will not be salaried. (See *In re Marriage of Iredale & Cates* (2004) 121 Cal. App. 4th 321, 329-330, 16 Cal. Rptr. 3d 505.)

goodwill. "The 'good will' of a business is the expectation of continued public patronage." (Bus. & Prof. Code, §14100.) However, there is more to goodwill than expectation of continued patronage. "The good will *of a business* is property and is transferable." (Bus. & Prof. Code, §14102, italics added.)

Since the goodwill *of a business* is property (Bus. & Prof. Code, §14102), the question is: What is the meaning of "a business" in the definition of goodwill?

There are two possible answers.

One answer is that the term "a business" also includes "a person doing business." This is the interpretation that the trial court adopted in this case.

The other answer is that "a business" refers to a professional, commercial or industrial enterprise with assets, i.e., an entity other than a natural person.

There are three reasons why the second answer is the better one. First, it conforms to the historical understanding of goodwill. Second, the plain text of Business and Professions Code sections 14100 and 14102, which, in this respect, have not been amended since their enactment in 1872, speaks of "a business," and not of natural persons. Third, interpreting the term "a business" as it appears in Business and Professions Code sections 14100 and 14102 to refer to a professional, commercial or industrial enterprise with assets ensures that the interest that is divided as goodwill is "property," as "property" is defined by law.

3. The Historical Understanding of "a Business"

The precursors of Business and Professions Code sections 14100 and 14102 were Civil Code sections 992 and 993, which were enacted in 1872 as part of the Civil Code. Contemporaneously with the enactment of the California Civil Code in 1872, and as of the closing decades of the 19th century, the courts spoke of goodwill as an incident of an existing business; goodwill did not exist in the abstract, apart from a business.

One of the classic definitions of goodwill in our case law appears in *In re Lyons* (1938) 27 Cal. App. 2d 293, 297-298, 81 P.2d 190.[6] This definition, ... predicates the existence of goodwill on the operations of a business entity with assets separate and distinct from the person or persons who operate, own or manage the business.

In this respect, nothing had changed since these early cases were decided. No California case has held that a natural person, apart and distinct from a "business," can create or generate goodwill. In the instance of professionals, the courts have spoken of "the nature and duration of his business as a sole practitioner" (*In re Marriage of Lopez* (1974) 38 Cal. App. 3d 93, 109-110, 113 Cal. Rptr. 58) and of the value of a "professional practice" (*Golden v. Golden* (1969) 270 Cal. App. 2d 401,

---

6. "Good will has been defined 'to be the advantage or benefit which is acquired by an establishment beyond the mere value of the capital stock, funds, or property employed therein, in consequence of the general public patronage and encouragement which it receives from constant or habitual customers, on account of its local position, or common celebrity, or reputation for skill or affluence, or punctuality, or from other accidental circumstances, or necessities, or even from ancient partialities or prejudices. (Story on Part., Sec. 99.) ... According to Lord Eldon it is the probability that the old customers will resort to the old place. It is the probability that the business will continue in the future as in the past, adding to the profits of the concern and contributing to the means of meeting its engagements as they come in.'" (*In re Lyons, supra,* 27 Cal. App. 2d at pp. 297-298, 81 P.2d 190, cited in 11 Witkin, Summary of Cal. Law, *supra,* Community Property, §69.)

405, 75 Cal. Rptr. 735; see also *Todd v. Todd* (1969) 272 Cal. App. 2d 786, 792, 78 Cal. Rptr. 131). It is the business, i.e., the practice, that generates goodwill, even if the practice is conducted by a sole practitioner, as was the case in *Golden* and *Todd.*

4. Business and Professions Code Sections 14100 and 14102 Endow a Business, and Not a Person, with the Capacity to Generate Goodwill

"There is order in the most fundamental rules of statutory interpretation if we want to find it. The key is applying those rules in proper *sequence.* [¶] First, a court should examine the actual language of the statute. . . . [¶] In examining the language, the courts should give to the words of the statute their ordinary, everyday meaning. . . . [¶] If the meaning is without ambiguity, doubt, or uncertainty, then the language controls."

There is no doubt about the "ordinary, everyday meaning" of the term "a business," nor is the term ambiguous or uncertain. In the term "a business," the word "business" is a noun, and means a professional, commercial or industrial enterprise with assets. It is also clear that "a business" is not a natural person.

It may be asked whether the term "a business" should be read to include "a person doing business," in which event Business and Professions Code section 14102 would effectively read: "The good will of a business *or of a person doing business* is property and is transferable."

It is not within the powers of a court to amend the statute in such a fashion. And there is no doubt that this would be an amendment of the statute. It would enlarge the scope of the statute beyond the traditional understanding of goodwill, which anchors goodwill to a business establishment with assets. Nor can it be said that "a person doing business" is logically included in the term "a business." In the ordinary, everyday sense, "a business" refers to an establishment, a thing, and not a person. With deference to our dissenting colleague, expanding Business and Professions Code section 14102 to state "[t]he good will of a business *or of a person doing business* is property and is transferable" should be left to the Legislature, especially since such an expansion involves considerations of social policy, as appears in the following paragraph.

Endowing "a person doing business" with the capacity to create goodwill, as opposed to limiting goodwill to "a business," has wide ramifications. "A person doing business" includes much of the working population. Notably, there would be no principled distinction between husband in this case, who is a director, and actors, artists and musicians, all of whom could be said to be "persons doing business." Thus, all such persons who would have the "expectation of continued public patronage" would possess goodwill. This would create a substantial liability, as in this case, without a guaranty that the liability would be funded. It is clear that, from an economic perspective, the "goodwill" in this case is based on earnings, and that "goodwill" is an expression of husband's earning capacity.[7] However, there is no guaranty, especially in the arts, that earnings will not decline or even dry up, even

7. While we acknowledge that the "excess earning" method of valuing goodwill in a professional corporation is generally accepted, it is true that this method is not far removed from a prediction about future earnings. For good and sufficient reasons, the *expectancy of future earnings* may not be considered in determining goodwill. (See generally 11 Witkin, Summary of Cal. Law, *supra,* Community Property, §71.)

though expectations were to the contrary. In such an event, a person would find him- or herself saddled with a massive liability without the means of satisfying it. Putting it another way, endowing directly persons with the ability to create goodwill would create an "asset" predicated on nothing other than predictions about earning capacity.

5. Interpreting the Term "a Business" as It Appears in Business and Professions Code Sections 14100 and 14102 To Refer to a Professional, Commercial or Industrial Enterprise with Assets Ensures That the Interest That Is Divided As Goodwill Is "Property."

The trial court found that husband "has developed an earning capacity and reputation in his profession as a motion picture director which greatly exceeds that of most persons involved in that profession and that [husband] commands a premium for his services." In order for this to be divisible as community property, it must be, in the first place, property, and, in the second place, it must have been acquired during marriage. "Except as otherwise provided by statute, all property, real or personal, wherever situated, acquired by a married person during the marriage while domiciled in this state is community property." (Fam. Code, §760.)

Since every kind of property that is not real is personal, the property interest in this case, if it exists, must be personal. Personal property may be incorporeal, i.e., without tangible substance, and it may be intangible in the sense that it is a right rather than a physical object. But, even if incorporeal or intangible, property must be capable of being transferred. "[I]t is a fundamental principle of law that one of the chief incidents of ownership in property is the right to transfer it." "A common characteristic of a property right, is that it may be disposed of, transferred to another."

Husband's "earning capacity and reputation in his profession as a motion picture director which greatly exceeds that of most persons involved in that profession" or, in the trial court's shorthand, his "elite professional standing," cannot be sold or transferred. His high standing among other motion picture directors is entirely personal to him. He cannot confer on another director his standing as No. 13 in cumulative box office revenues during 1985-1996. He cannot sell this standing to another, because a buyer would not be John McTiernan, no matter how much the buyer was willing to pay. For the same reason, and unlike a law or medical practice, husband cannot transfer his "elite professional standing." That standing is his, and his alone, and he cannot bestow it on someone else. Thus, an essential aspect of a property interest is absent.

Whether categorized as "excess earnings" or "future earnings," the point is that this type of goodwill is an expression of earnings that have not yet been paid. Thus, when, as here, a person "doing business" is found to have goodwill, and the goodwill is measured by the excess earnings approach, the "asset" that is created is a prediction, not a fact. This is quite a distance from an established business enterprise with assets, and a clientele, that has generated goodwill in the traditional sense.

The fact that husband's "elite professional standing" is not transferable effectively refutes the trial court's conclusion that husband's "practice" as a motion picture director is like the "practice" of an attorney or physician. The practice of an attorney, physician, dentist, or accountant is transferable, but husband's "elite professional standing" is his alone, and not susceptible to being transferred or sold.

That husband's "elite professional standing" is not a property interest is also reflected by the trial court's calculation of husband's "goodwill." Under the excess earnings method, the court must deduct from the average net pretax earnings of the business being valued the "fair return" on the "net tangible assets used by the business." (Fn. 1, *ante.*) No such deduction was made in this case, and the comparison was between husband's pretax net income, and that of a motion picture director who is compensated at minimum levels. Thus, the trial court's calculation of "goodwill" demonstrates that there was no business — there were no assets — that would qualify as property.

Were we to construe the goodwill *of a business* as the trial court did in this case, we would be faced with a conflict between Business and Professions Code section 14102 (the goodwill of a business is property) and the fundamental concept that property is transferable. Under section 14102, we would call "property" something that is not transferable, and therefore is not property. Instead, we anchor goodwill to "a business," as the statute requires. This ensures that goodwill is attached to property that is transferable, as a professional, commercial or industrial enterprise is transferable.

In sum, adhering to the rule that property, in order to qualify as property, must be transferable is not a theoretical exercise. Something that cannot be transferred or sold has no value on the market. Dividing such a nontransferable quantity as community property therefore creates an obligation without ensuring that that obligation can be funded. However, when "a business" with assets is divided, there is some assurance that the obligation created by the division can and will be met.

6. Respondent's Arguments in Support of the Trial Court's Finding of Goodwill Are Without Merit

Respondent contends that the "existence of a business in the traditional sense is not a prerequisite to finding professional goodwill." The contrary is true. As we have seen, the plain text of Business and Professions Code sections 14100 and 14102, as well as its predecessors, refers to the "good will of a business." As we have shown, this is a reference to a professional, commercial or industrial enterprise with assets.

Respondent contends that since there is substantial evidence that husband has an expectation of continued public patronage, husband has goodwill. This begs the question. It is true that "[t]he 'good will' of a business is the expectation of continued public patronage." (Bus. & Prof. Code, §14100.) However, the "expectation of continued public patronage" must be generated by "a business." A business is a professional, commercial or industrial enterprise with assets; "a business" is not earning capacity or professional reputation.

Finally, the fact that the trial court was able to, and did, apply the "excess earnings" method to calculate goodwill does not mean that there is goodwill in this case. Boiled down to its essentials, the excess earnings method is a comparison of husband's earnings with that of an "average" peer. The fact that this calculation can be performed, as it was performed, does not convert husband's skill and reputation into "a business," and does not transmute unique and idiosyncratic talents into property that can be transferred or sold.

We conclude that the trial court erred in finding that there was goodwill in husband's practice or career as a motion picture director. Accordingly, the judgment must be modified to eliminate $1.5 million in assets that are subject to division. As noted in the text, *post*, this affects the calculation of attorney's fees under the formula crafted by the trial court.

DISPOSITION

The judgment is to be modified by deleting $1.5 million in assets, denominated as goodwill, from property that is subject to division. In all other respects, the judgment is affirmed. Wife shall recover costs on both appeals.

BOLAND, J., Concurring.

I concur in the judgment and write separately to state the rationale I believe justifies the conclusion that, as a matter of law, John McTiernan's work as a movie director is not a business or professional practice to which goodwill may attach.

Let me begin with several points on which there is no dispute.

First, goodwill may exist in a professional practice or in a business which is founded upon personal skill or reputation. (*In re Marriage of Foster* (1974) 42 Cal. App. 3d 577, 582, fn. 2, 117 Cal. Rptr. 49.)

Second, the goodwill of a business is property and is transferable. (Bus. & Prof. Code, §14102.) Otherwise stated, goodwill is an asset of a business or professional practice, and where the business or professional practice is community property, it is a community asset. (*Golden v. Golden* (1969) 270 Cal. App. 2d 401, 405, 75 Cal. Rptr. 735.)

Third, "[a]lthough the goodwill of a business may be the result of the personal skill, talent, experience, or reputation of an individual connected with the business, it may attach to and continue with the business even after the separation of the individual on whom it was founded." (*Smith v. Bull* (1958) 50 Cal. 2d 294, 302, 325 P.2d 463.)

Fourth, "[w]hen goodwill attaches to a business, its value is a question of fact." (*In re Marriage of King* (1983) 150 Cal. App. 3d 304, 309, 197 Cal. Rptr. 716.)

From these well-settled points, two other principles seem clear:

- Goodwill, as a divisible asset, does not exist apart from the business or professional practice to which it attaches.
- Because it is property, any business or professional practice (along with any goodwill attached to it) is and must be, at least in legal theory, transferable from one person or entity to another.

Accordingly, in the first instance, the question is whether McTiernan — or, more properly, the marital community — owned a business or a professional practice to which goodwill could attach. In my view, the answer is no, because McTiernan cannot — even in theory — sell or otherwise transfer his "professional practice" or "business" to a third party. This is not because there is no market for the business, but for the more fundamental reason that nothing exists to sell. McTiernan has only his talent as a director, and he cannot transfer it to anyone else. In this, he is no different from any other artist, entertainer or athlete with a talent that commands high compensation. While the occupations of these individuals, like most other occupations, are in common parlance denominated "professions," they are neither businesses nor professional practices that can be expanded beyond the individual in whom the talent resides. Unlike a doctor, lawyer, accountant or other business person, McTiernan cannot hire someone else to direct a movie he has been hired to direct. He cannot expand his "practice" or "business" because he has only his own artistic talent to offer. Whatever we may call it — talent, occupation, livelihood or profession — the creative processes of a movie director, like that of any other artist, cannot be bought, sold or given away, and therefore do not fit within any recognized definition of property. Consequently, no business or professional practice constituting property exists in McTiernan's case, within the meaning of current statutory or case law. Goodwill as statutorily defined, as merely an intangible asset of a business or professional practice, necessarily cannot exist in the absence of a business or professional practice.

In short, the Legislature has defined goodwill as property only in connection with a business, and it has specified that the goodwill of a business is transferable. Where there is no transferable business, there is no property to divide, and there is necessarily no goodwill. The Legislature, of course, is at liberty to define goodwill in a more expansive manner, so that it would include the ability of an artist or entertainer to generate excess earnings by virtue of his or her talent and the resulting encomium of a receptive public. It has not yet done so, and it was therefore error for the trial court to conclude that McTiernan possessed professional goodwill that was a divisible community asset.

Cooper, P.J., Concurring and Dissenting.

I concur in the lead opinion and in the judgment with respect to all issues but one. I respectfully dissent from my colleagues' conclusion that husband has no divisible goodwill. The facts found by the trial court establish that husband possesses valuable goodwill, as traditionally recognized by California case law. In holding otherwise as a matter of law, the majority apply restrictive concepts that disregard established family law precedent. Moreover, even under this legal revision, substantial evidence still supports the trial court's findings that husband possessed goodwill in his professional business, in which wife was entitled to share.

Business and Professions Code section 14102 declares the goodwill of a business to be property, albeit intangible. Section 14100 of the same code compactly defines goodwill as "the expectation of continued public patronage." The United States Supreme Court has similarly stated, "Although the definition of goodwill has taken different forms over the years, the shorthand description of goodwill as 'the expectancy of continued patronage' [citation] provides a useful label with which to identify the total of all the imponderable qualities that attract customers to the business." (*Newark Morning Ledger Co. v. United States* (1993) 507 U.S. 546, 555-556, 113 S. Ct. 1670, 123 L. Ed. 2d 288.)

In California, spousal goodwill is uniformly recognized as subject to assessment and award in proceedings for division of community property. (See 11 Witkin,

Summary of Cal. Law (9th ed. 1990) Community Property, §69, pp. 461-462.) "Although community goodwill is usually associated with a professional practice, it may exist in any business which is founded upon personal skill or reputation." (*Id.* at p. 461.) Both the existence and the value of goodwill in a particular case are questions of fact, and their determination is reviewed on appeal under the substantial evidence test.

Previous decisions have attributed goodwill to a variety of professional individuals and situations, including an attorney who worked at home on appointed criminal appeals (*In re Marriage of Rosen* (2002) 105 Cal. App. 4th 808, 130 Cal. Rptr. 2d 1), a computer consultant who worked at home or at his clients' facilities, with "no plant, no commercial location, no employees and [no] office" (*In re Marriage of King* (1983) 150 Cal. App. 3d 304, 310, 197 Cal. Rptr. 716), and a law firm partner who was found to possess professional goodwill as an individual (*In re Marriage of Iredale & Cates* (2004) 121 Cal. App. 4th 321, 16 Cal. Rptr. 3d 505; accord, *In re Marriage of Fenton* (1982) 134 Cal. App. 3d 451, 463, 184 Cal. Rptr. 597; see *In re Marriage of Nichols* (1994) 27 Cal. App. 4th 661, 673, fn. 4, 33 Cal. Rptr. 2d 13).

In the present case, husband's business and profession were that of a motion picture director. The trial court found, after assessing extensive evidence, that husband possessed professional goodwill of a value of $1.5 million. Because all of this value had developed during the parties' marriage, wife was entitled to a compensatory payment of $750,000.

The majority now set aside these findings by superimposing on the concept of marital goodwill a novel set of elements. In brief, the majority opine that a professional individual such as husband may not possess goodwill without having a "business" (which husband supposedly did not have), and that there can be no goodwill unless it, or the accompanying business, can be sold (which husband's allegedly cannot). These artificial restrictions are legally unfounded and factually inaccurate; moreover, even were they correct, they would provide no cause for reversing the award of goodwill in this case as a matter of law.

The lead opinion's effort to limit goodwill to a "business" as opposed to an individual is semantic. Any professional who independently practices his or her profession, for profit — be it lawyer, doctor, computer consultant, or film director — thereby conducts a business, within the lead opinion's own unattributed definition, as well as more traditional ones.[1] It is therefore neither factually nor legally correct to say that only a business, and not a natural person, may generate or possess goodwill. When the consultant in *In re Marriage of King, supra,* 150 Cal. App. 3d 304, 197 Cal. Rptr. 716, and the lawyers in *In re Marriage of Rosen, supra,* 105 Cal. App. 4th 808, 130 Cal. Rptr. 2d 1, and *In re Marriage of Iredale and Cates, supra,* 121 Cal. App. 4th 321, 16 Cal. Rptr. 3d 505, generated goodwill while practicing their professions, they did so as individuals.[2]

---

1. Thus, Webster's Third New International Dictionary (1993), page 301, defines "business" as "a commercial or industrial enterprise," and then immediately offers as an example, "he's in [business] for himself. . . ." The denotation does not include the lead opinion's element of "with assets."

2. The notion that compensating for an individual's goodwill would create liabilities that might not be recoverable is also unrealistic. Assessments and valuations of goodwill, as in this case, take into account the individual or other business's apparent prospects, negative as well as positive. Any such assessment, whether for a doctor or a delicatessen, is a "predictio[n] about earning capacity" (lead opn., p. 294), based on prior experience.

But whichever view one takes of this issue, it cannot properly oust husband and wife of the palpable, valuable goodwill that the trial court found husband had developed. By any realistic understanding, husband earned his professional compensation, and developed an expectation of continued patronage, while practicing a business, of directing motion pictures. This business comprised not just husband's talent, but a series of corporations, one of which owned an airplane, which husband used to travel to and scout film locations. Husband had as much a "business" as the professionals in the cases last cited.

The second disqualifying element, in the majority's view, is the notion that husband's goodwill was not transferable. This too is not a valid ground for reversing the present findings and award for goodwill.

The lead opinion's treatment of this subject rests substantially on the incorrect perception that husband's goodwill, as found below, consisted of the "elite professional standing" the trial court found he enjoyed. But the finding of "elite standing" was only prefatory to the ultimate finding that husband possessed goodwill, in the court's words, "an expectation of continued patronage at his prior level of compensation." (Cf. Bus. & Prof. Code, §14100.)

As for whether this goodwill is transferable and therefore qualifies as property, the short answer is that the law has determined both questions. Business and Professions Code section 14102 establishes, as a matter of law, that "The good will of a business is property and is transferable." That includes the goodwill of husband's business as a director. Whether or not a third party is willing to buy it is not material. (Accord, *In re Marriage of Watts* (1985) 171 Cal. App. 3d 366, 372, 217 Cal. Rptr. 301.)

There is a reason why the existence of goodwill in a marital context does not depend upon the practical transferability of the professional spouse's practice. Insofar as it is assessed and disposed of in a judicial proceeding upon dissolution of the marriage, goodwill is not a commodity in the marketplace, but rather "a portion of the professional practice as a going concern on the date of the dissolution of the marriage." (*In re Marriage of Foster* (1974) 42 Cal. App. 3d 577, 584, 117 Cal. Rptr. 49 (*Foster*).)

Foster further explained, "As observed in *Golden* [*v. Golden* (1969) 270 Cal. App. 2d 401, 405, 75 Cal. Rptr. 735], '. . . in a matrimonial matter, the practice of the sole practitioner husband will continue, with the same intangible value as it had during the marriage. Under the principles of community property law, the wife, by virtue of her position of wife, made to that value the same contribution as does a wife to any of the husband's earnings and accumulations during marriage. She is as much entitled to be recompensed for that contribution as if it were represented by the increased value of stock in a family business.'" (*Foster, supra,* 42 Cal. App. 3d at p. 584, 117 Cal. Rptr. 49.) Accordingly, *In re Marriage of Watts, supra,* 171 Cal. App. 3d 366, 217 Cal. Rptr. 301, disposed of the notion that transferability as a practical matter is a prerequisite of a business with goodwill: "In the dissolution of marriage context, the mere fact that a professional practice cannot be sold, standing alone, will not justify a finding that the practice has no goodwill nor that the community goodwill has no value." (*Id.* at p. 372, 217 Cal. Rptr. 301.)

Acknowledging that goodwill is transferable by law, the concurring opinion yet pursues the question of transferability, by asserting that husband cannot sell or transfer his professional business, because "nothing exists to sell." (Conc. opn., p. 304.) As just explained, this would not be dispositive, even if correct. But the concurrence's assertion that husband's business is not amenable to sale or transfer is a supposition, grounded not in the record of this case but in speculation, about a business and craft that we appellate jurists know very little about.[3] This is not a proper basis for reversal.

In this case the trial court properly determined the existence and extent of husband's goodwill, in accord with substantial evidence and with California law, as consistently expounded for half a century. Even under the majority's refashioning of that law, those determinations remain sustainable. I respectfully dissent.

Discussion Questions

1. What was Judge Flier's definition of a "business" and how did that affect whether John McTiernan's career as a motion picture director had goodwill?
2. What was the main point made in Judge Boland's concurrence?
3. Why did Presiding Judge Cooper dissent?

PROBLEM 8.1

Barbara and Carl were married several years, when Barbara decided to open a mobile pet grooming business. Barbara had worked at a veterinarian's office, washing and grooming dogs. She had saved much of her salary and used that to buy a van and equip it with supplies. The total investment was $50,000. She was able to purchase the van for $25,000 with an auto loan. She advertised in pet shops and veterinarian's offices and soon had a booming business which she called Pet Spot. Many of the customers were thrilled with Barbara's expertise in grooming dogs and particularly liked her ability to calm them down. One of her clients sold dog accessories and toys. Barbara purchased about $10,000 of those accessories and toys to stock in her van. All along she had discussed her business venture with Carl in general terms, but the decision to pursue the auto loan and the purchase of the accessories and toys were made on her own. If Barbara and Carl live in Washington, would Carl's consent be required for the loan and the purchase? What is required of Barbara if they live in California?

---

3. Thus, although irrelevant, it is by no means certain that husband could not procure someone else to direct one of his films. For example, John Frankenheimer replaced Arthur Penn as director of The Train (United Artists 1964), Otto Preminger replaced Rouben Mamoulian as director of Laura (20th Century Fox 1944), and Victor Fleming succeeded George Cukor as director of Gone With the Wind (Metro-Goldwyn-Mayer 1939). (See, respectively, http://imdb.com/title/tt0059825/ fullcredits# directors [as of Oct. 26, 2005], http://imdb.com/title/tt0037008/fullcredits # directors [as of Oct. 26, 2005], http://imdb.com/title/tt0031381/fullcredits# directors [as of Oct. 26, 2005].)

PROBLEM 8.2

Barbara has learned that a competitor's grooming business, Pets R Us, is for sale. Pets R Us has a fleet of five mobile grooming vans. Barbara purchases Pet R Us for $150,000. She borrows the money to finance the deal. She completes the purchase without discussing it with Carl. When Carl finds out, he is quite upset and feels that it was a foolish decision. Under Washington law, would Carl be responsible if Barbara is unable to pay off the loan? What are the requirements of California law regarding the purchase of Pets R Us?

PROBLEM 8.3

Assume that Barbara's businesses Pet Spot and Pets R Us are very successful. With six vans, she has employed several other groomers and she has trained them all in her special methods to calm dogs. However, many clients prefer to have Barbara to personally do the grooming because of her expertise and special touch. She is very much in demand. She has worked so many hours that it has taken a toll on her marriage and Carl has filed for divorce. Carl is demanding one-half of Barbara's businesses including goodwill. What arguments will Carl and Barbara make regarding goodwill?

PROBLEM 8.4

Arthur has been married to Beverly for many years. They live in California. Arthur is an artist who paints murals on city buildings, depicting the culture of the particular city. He is very much in demand and has painted murals in many cities and towns in California and all over the United States. He commands at least $500,000 for each mural. Over the last year, he has been away on so many trips that their marriage is on the verge of divorce. Beverly consults an attorney to find out if she has any right to the success Arthur has achieved as a famous artist. Discuss if Arthur has goodwill that would be considered community property.

Table 8-1
Management and Control in Community Property States

State	Rule	Case/Statute
Arizona	The spouses have equal management, control, and disposition rights over their community property and have equal power to bind the community. Either spouse may bind the community except joinder of both spouses required for real property transactions.	Ariz. Rev. Stat. §25-214. *Mezey v. Fioramonti*, 204 Ariz. 599, 08, 65 P.3d 980, 989 (Ct. App. 2003), disapproved on other grounds by *Bilke v. State*, 206 Ariz. 462, 80. P.3d 269 (2003)

State	Rule	Case/Statute
	A gift of substantial community property ot a third person without the other spouse's consent may be revoked and set aside for the benefit of the aggrieved spouse.	
California	Either spouse has the management and control of the community personal property with like absolute power of disposition as the spouse has of the separate estate of the spouse. Spouse who operates a community business has primary management of a community business and can act alone in all transactions but must give written notice to disposition of all or substantially all of the business personal property. Spouses owe each other a fiduciary duty.	California Family Code §1100, *Spreckels v. Spreckels*, 172 Cal. 775, 158 P. 537 (1916)
	Gifts to third parties require written consent of the other spouse. Nonconsenting spouse may void the gift up to one-half the value of the gift.	
Idaho	Either the husband or the wife shall have the right to manage and control the community property and either may bind the community property by contract. Exception for community real property which requires consent of the other spouse. Express power of attorney may be given to the other spouse to sell, convey, or encumber real or personal community property.	Idaho Code §32-912, *Anderson v. Idaho Mut. Ben. Ass'n*, 77 Idaho 373, 292 P.2d 760, (1956)
	A gift of community property, if substantial in amount and done without one spouse's consent, is voidable by that spouse.	
Louisiana	Each spouse may act alone to manage, control, or dispose of community property. Concurrence required for community immovables, enterprises, gifts. But "a spouse acting alone may make a usual or customary gift of a value commensurate with the economic position of the spouses at the time of donation."	Louisiana Civil Code arts. 2346, 2347, 2349

State	Rule	Case/Statute
Nevada	Either spouse, acting alone, may manage and control community property with the same power of disposition as the acting spouse has over his or her separate property. Written power of attorney may be given to the other spouse to sell, convey or encumber any property held as community property. Exceptions for gifts, sale of real property. If only one spouse participates in management of community business, that spouse may acquire, sell, or encumber the assets without the consent of the nonparticipating spouse.	Nevada Revised Statutes §123-230
New Mexico	Either spouse alone has full power to manage, control, dispose of, and encumber the entire community personal property. Real property transactions require joinder of both spouses. A gift of substantial community property to a third person without the other spouse's consent may be revoked and set aside for the benefit of the aggrieved spouse.	New Mexico Stat. §§40-3-13, 40-3-14, *Roselli v. Rio Communities Serv. Station, Inc.*, 109 N.M. 509, 787 P.2d 428 (1990)
Texas	Each spouse has the sole management, control, and disposition of the community property that the spouse would have owned if single. Community property is subject to joint management unless the spouses provide otherwise by power of attorney in writing or other agreement. Courts will set aside any unilateral gift of community funds if the gift is capricious, excessive or arbitrary.	Vernon's Texas Statutes, Family Code §3.102, *Carnes v. Meador*, 533 S.W.2d 365 (Tex. Civ. App. 1975)
Washington	Either spouse (or either domestic partner), acting alone, may manage and control community property, with a like power of disposition as the acting spouse or domestic partner has over his or her separate property. Exceptions for gifts, real property. Gifts require consent. Real property requires joinder.	West's Revised Code of Washington, §26.16.030

State	Rule	Case/Statute
Wisconsin	A spouse, acting alone, may manage and control marital property held in that spouse's name alone or not held in the name of either spouse. Spouses may manage and control marital property held in the names of both spouses only if they act together.	Wis. Stat. §§766.51, 766.53

Table 8-2
Professional Goodwill in Community Property States

State	Rule	Case/Statute
Arizona	Goodwill of a professional practice has value and that value is divisible upon dissolution of the marital community, regardless of the form of business.	*Mitchell v. Mitchell,* 152 Ariz. 317, 732 P.2d 208 (1987); *Wisner v. Wisner,* 129 Ariz. 333, 631 P.2d 115 (Ct. App. 1981)
California	Professional goodwill is intangible property that is taken into consideration in dividing community property. The practice of an attorney, physician, dentist, or accountant is transferable, but celebrity goodwill cannot be sold or transferred.	*Marriage of Foster,* 42 Cal. App. 3d 577, 582, 117 Cal. Rptr. 49, 52 (1974), *Marriage of McTiernan & Dubrow,* 133 Cal. App. 4th 1090, 35 Cal. Rptr. 3d 287 (2005)
Idaho	"Where a professional business is an independent entity, however, goodwill is calculable and divisible in divorce just as goodwill in any other business. . . . A practitioner's knowledge, skill, and background are personal attributes. To the extent a professional services corporation has goodwill value beyond these personal assets, however, that goodwill is community property."	*Stewart v. Stewart,* 143 Idaho 673, 152 P.3d 544 (2007)
Louisiana	"If the underlying business is community, the goodwill will be considered as community property for purposes of partition. . . . In addition, where one spouse holds a professional degree or license and the goodwill results solely from that professional's personal relationship with clients, that goodwill is not included in the community." (*Gill*)	*Clemons v. Clemons,* 960 So. 2d 1068 (La. App. Ct.), writ denied, 966 So. 2d 583 (2007) La. Rev. Stat. Ann. §9:2801.2 *Gill v. Gill,* 895 So. 2d 807 (La. App. Ct. 2005)

State	Rule	Case/Statute
Nevada	"The goodwill developed in a professional practice during marriage is also included in the community property estate and the value thereof is subject to division at divorce."	*Williams v. Waldman*, 108 Nev. 466, 836 P.2d 614 (1992)
New Mexico	"[A]lthough the individual right to practice is a property right which cannot be classed as community property, the value of the practice as a business at the time of dissolution of the community is community property."	*Hurley v. Hurley*, 615 P.2d 256 (N.M. 1980), overruled on other grounds by *Ellsworth v. Ellsworth*, 637 P.2d 564 (N.M. 1981)
Texas	Under *Nail*, the Texas Supreme Court held that goodwill was not subject to division because the goodwill in that case didn't exist independently of the professional's skills. However, in *Guzman*, the court noted that subsequent decisions have refined *Nail* and the court called into question the fairness of the *Nail* decision. The court stated the "goodwill in a professional business is not considered part of the marital estate unless it exists independently of the professional's skills, and the estate is otherwise entitled to share in the asset." Professional goodwill that exists independently of the professional's skills may be subject to division. In *Guzman*, the Texas Supreme Court withdrew the application for writ of error on procedural grounds, not on the merits of the case.	Tex. Fam. Code Ann. §7.001, *Nail v. Nail*, 486 S.W.2d 761 (Tex. 1972); *Guzman v. Guzman*, 827 S.W.2d 445 (Tex. 1992)
Washington	Professional goodwill is recognized as intangible property that is subject to disposition in marriage dissolution.	Wash. Rev. Code Ann. §26.09.080, *Marriage of Luckey*, 73 Wash. App. 201, 868 P.2d 189 (1994); *Matter of Marriage of Crosetto*, 82 Wash. App. 545, 553, 918 P.2d 954, 958 (1996)
Wisconsin	A spouse acting alone may give a third person marital property greater than $1,000 if the gift is reasonable in amount considering the economic position of the spouses. Salable professional goodwill may be included as divisible property at divorce	*McReath v. McReath*, 329 Wis. 2d 155, 789 N.W.2d 89 (Ct. App. 2010)

Chapter 9

Separate Property Business: Ownership of Profits?

If a spouse owns a business prior to marriage or starts a business during marriage using separate property funds, that business is characterized as separate property and would not be considered as part of the community estate. Consider the example of our hypothetical couple, Harry and Wilma. Harry had a business before he married Wilma. He worked hard during their marriage expending his efforts to increase the profits and value of the business. He did not take a regular salary, but instead took a "draw" that the couple lived on. If they divorce, it is clear that the business belongs to Harry. However, Wilma would certainly feel that she deserves a portion of the wealth or increase in value that accumulated from the separate property business. It seems inequitable that Harry would walk away from the marriage with the business and all the wealth generated by the business, leaving Wilma without any property. The principle that spousal effort during marriage is considered community property would support Wilma's claim that any increase in the value attributed to that effort should be shared by the community. Harry would argue that he came into the marriage with the business and the increase in value should follow the characterization of the business as separate property. The issue of how to treat the increase in value of a separate property business has been considered in all the community property states.

There is a split in how to treat that increase in value. The split is caused by a difference in a basic principle of community property law — the characterization of the rents, issues and profits generated by a separate property business. A minority of states, Idaho, Louisiana and Texas, follow the Civil Rule. A majority of states, Arizona, California, Nevada, New Mexico, and Washington, follow the American Rule. Under the Civil Rule, income from separate property due to the labor of a spouse is community property. In the case of Harry and Wilma, the Civil Rule clearly favors Wilma. Based on the Civil Rule, the community automatically has a claim to the increased value of Harry's business because all the profits of Harry's separate property business are characterized as community property. The only argument supporting Harry is that the community has already been adequately compensated by the profits that have been taken out of the business during the marriage. Under the American Rule, the rents, issues, and profits of separate property are separate property. In the case of Harry and Wilma, the American Rule seems to favor Harry. However, the states following the American Rule, have long recognized that the community is entitled to a portion of the increase in value of a separate property business where that increase can be attributed to spousal effort. Based on the American Rule, the main debate concerns the reason for the increase in value. If the increase in value can be attributed to Harry's efforts, then the majority of that increase will go to the community. Harry would be given a portion of the increase that can be attributed to the capital or investment in the business. If the increase in value is attributed to economic conditions rather than spousal labor, a court would determine if the community was adequately compensated by Harry's actual salary or the reasonable value of his services. These two approaches were developed from the early California cases of *Pereira v. Pereira*, 156 Cal. 1, 103 P. 488 (1909), and *Van Camp v. Van Camp*, 53 Cal. App. 17, 199 P. 885 (1921).

The outcome of the Harry and Wilma scenario depends initially on whether the state follows the Civil Rule or the American Rule. The Civil Rule describes the remedy as "reimbursement" to the community. The American Rule describes the remedy as "apportionment" of the separate and community interests.

A. THE CIVIL RULE STATES: THE TEXAS, IDAHO, AND LOUISIANA EXPERIENCE

Under the Civil Rule, income from separate property is defined as community property. Therefore, there would seem to be no need to determine whether the increase in value of a separate property business was due to spousal effort or economic conditions. However, the community is only compensated during marriage for community effort. Therefore, one factor in deciding whether compensation is due is whether there was community effort in the separate property business. Then the major issue is whether the community was adequately compensated during the marriage. If not, then the community is entitled to reimbursement for being uncompensated or under-compensated. The most recent cases have dealt with (1) who bears the burden of proof on the community effort issue and (2) how to deal with a separate property business that is not a sole proprietorship but is instead in the form of a corporation.

1. *Reimbursement or Community Interest? The Texas and Idaho Answers*

(a) Texas

The Texas Supreme Court, in *Jensen v. Jensen*, 662 S.W.2d 107 (Tex. 1984), dealt with the issue of which remedy is appropriate when a separate property business in the form of a corporation appreciates in value. In that case, the corporation's stock was owned before marriage and appreciated in value due to the efforts of the separate property owner. The court considered what is the best way to balance the interests of the community and the interests of the separate property owner.

JENSEN v. JENSEN

665 S.W.2d 107 (1984)
Supreme Court of Texas

WALLACE, Justice.

This court's opinion and judgment of November 9, 1983, are withdrawn and the following opinion is substituted therefor.

Petitioner, Robert Lee Jensen, and Respondent, Burlene Parks Jensen, were divorced on May 21, 1980. The decree of divorce provided that 48,455 shares of stock in RLJ Printing Co., Inc., acquired by Mr. Jensen four months prior to marriage, together with any increase in value in such stock which occurred during marriage, were the separate property of Mr. Jensen, and denied Mrs. Jensen any interest in the stock or its increased value. The court of appeals reversed and remanded, holding that the community should be compensated for an enhancement in value of the stock because such appreciated value had been due primarily to the time, toil and effort of Mr. Jensen. 629 S.W.2d 222. We remand to the trial court for determination of the amount, if any, of reimbursement to the community.

On March 21, 1975, Mr. Jensen formed the RLJ Printing Company, Inc. (RLJ) and for $1.56 per share acquired 48,455 of the 100,000 shares outstanding. On May 16, 1975, RLJ acquired Newspaper Enterprises, Inc., in what the trial court found to be a "unique business opportunity." The Jensens were married on July 21, 1975, separated on June 3, 1979, and divorced on May 21, 1980. At all pertinent times, Mr. Jensen was the key man in the operation of RLJ, which was a holding company whose sole assets consisted of all of the stock of Newspaper Enterprises, Inc. Mr. Jensen's compensation from RLJ, consisting of salary, bonuses and dividends, was $64,065.97 in 1976, $95,426.00 in 1977, $106,143.00 in 1978 and $115,000.00 in 1979.

The record does not reflect that any evaluation of the RLJ stock was made as of the date of the marriage. At trial, the per share value of the stock was $13.48 according to Mr. Jensen's expert and $25.77 according to Mrs. Jensen's expert.

The findings of fact and conclusions of law made by the trial court are as follows:

FINDINGS OF FACT

1. The RLJ Printing Company, Inc. was created by Respondent before the marriage of the parties.
2. RLJ Printing Company, Inc. acquired the stock of Newspaper Enterprises, Inc., 64 days before the marriage of the parties in a unique business opportunity.
3. RLJ Printing Company, Inc. is not an alter ego of the Respondent.
4. RLJ Printing Company, Inc. was not created in fraud of the rights of the community estate.
5. The salary paid Respondent has been adequate and reasonable.
6. The dividends paid Respondent have been adequate and reasonable.
7. The bonuses paid Respondent have been adequate and reasonable.
8. Respondent was the key man in the operation of RLJ Printing Company, Inc.
9. The successful operations of RLJ Printing Company, Inc. were primarily due to the time, toil and effort of Respondent.

CONCLUSIONS OF LAW

1. The community was not the equitable owner of any shares of RLJ Printing Company, Inc.
2. The community was not entitled to receive the value of the appreciation in shares of RLJ Printing Company, Inc. that was due to the successful operations of the company.
3. The community was not entitled to receive the value of the appreciation in shares of RLJ Printing Company, Inc., that was due to the time, toil and effort of Respondent.

The point of first impression squarely before us is how to treat, upon divorce, corporate stock owned by a spouse before marriage but which has increased in value during marriage due, at least in part, to the time and effort of either or both spouses.

The community property states have adopted variations of either "reimbursement" or "community ownership" theories. Common to both theories is the general concept that the community should receive whatever remuneration is paid to a spouse for his or her time and effort because the time and effort of each spouse belongs to the community. Though sharing a common conceptual basis, the two theories diverge when it comes to the valuation of the community's claim against separately owned stock that has appreciated by virtue of a spouse's time and effort. The "reimbursement" theory provides that the stock, as it appreciates, remains the separate property of the owner spouse. Under this theory, the community is entitled to reimbursement for the reasonable value of the time and effort of both or either of the spouses which contributed to the increase in value of the stock. The "community ownership" theory, on the other hand, holds that any increase in the value of the stock as a result of the time and effort of the owner spouse becomes community property.

A consideration of the writings of various scholars in this field, the treatment of the issue by our sister community property states, and the constitutional, statutory and case law of Texas leads to the conclusion that the reimbursement theory more nearly affords justice to both the community and separate estates. This theory requires adoption of the rule that the community will be reimbursed for the value of time and effort expended by either or both spouses to enhance the separate estate of either, other than that reasonably necessary to manage and preserve the separate estate, less the remuneration received for that time and effort in the form of salary, bonus, dividends and other fringe benefits, those items being community property when received.

This rule is a reasonable means of assuring that the community will be fully reimbursed for the value of community assets, i.e., time and effort expended, while at the same time providing that the property interest of the separate estate is also protected and preserved. As a practical matter, this rule will obviate the need for the trial court to undertake the onerous and quite often impossible burden that would be placed on it under the community ownership theory of attempting to determine just what factors actually contributed to the increase in value of the stock and in what proportion. The reimbursement theory of compensation is also consistent with the laws of Texas as found in the Texas Constitution, statutes and Supreme Court opinions set out below.

The Texas Constitution, Art. XVI, §15, provides that property owned by a spouse before marriage remains the separate property of that spouse during marriage. In *Welder v. Lambert*, 91 Tex. 510, 44 S.W. 281 (1898), this Court decided that all property held by either a husband or a wife before marriage remains the separate property of such spouse and the status of the property is to be determined by the origin of the title to the property, and not by the acquisition of the final title. This Court has consistently adhered to the rule expressed in *Welder*. The shares of RLJ stock thus remain the separate property of Mr. Jensen, subject only to the right of reimbursement, if any, proven by Mrs. Jensen.

The trial court found that Mr. Jensen was adequately and reasonably compensated for his time and effort expended in enhancing the value of the RLJ shares. This finding, if sustained, precludes Mrs. Jensen's right to reimbursement because that compensation was community property.

The only evidence offered at trial to establish the reasonableness of Mr. Jensen's compensation was the testimony of Mr. T. Wesley Hickman. Mr. Hickman was an expert in the field of corporate evaluation. It was his opinion that Mr. Jensen was reasonably compensated, but he based that opinion "primarily upon Mr. Jensen's percentage of the stock ownership." He further stated that without the stock ownership he seriously doubted that Mr. Jensen would have stayed with RLJ. His opinion as to reasonable compensation was primarily based upon Mr. Jensen's stock ownership and not upon the salary, bonuses and dividends received by the community due to the time, toil and effort of Mr. Jensen. Therefore the trial court's finding that Mr. Jensen's compensation was reasonable is without adequate support. Without that finding of fact there is no basis for the trial court's finding that "the community was not entitled to receive the value of the appreciation in shares of RLJ Printing Company, Inc. that was due to the time, toil and effort of respondent."

Upon retrial of this case the burden of proving a charge upon the shares of RLJ owned by Mr. Jensen will be upon the claimant, Mrs. Jensen. The right to reimbursement is only for the value of the time, toil and effort expended to enhance the separate estate other than that reasonably necessary to manage and preserve the separate estate, for which the community did not receive adequate compensation. However, if the right to reimbursement is proved, a lien shall not attach to Mr. Jensen's separate property shares. Rather, a money judgment may be awarded.

It has long been the rule of this court to remand to the trial court rather than to render judgment when the ends of justice will be better served thereby. Such remanding has often been ordered to supply additional testimony or to amend pleadings.

Therefore, pursuant to TEX. R. CIV. P. 505, we remand this cause to the trial court for the limited purpose of determining the amount of reimbursement, if any, due to the community as a result of the time, toil and talent expended by Mr. Jensen toward enhancement of the stock of RLJ. From the value of the time, toil and talent expended is to be subtracted the compensation paid to Mr. Jensen for such time, toil and talent in the form of salary, bonuses, dividends and other fringe benefits. Any remainder is the reimbursement due the community. This reimbursement, if any, shall be distributed by the trial court in addition to the property division heretofore made to the parties.

Discussion Question

1. Who really won this case? Mr. Jensen or Mrs. Jensen?

(b)   Idaho

In *Neibaur v. Neibaur*, 142 Idaho 196, 125 P.2d 1072 (2005), the husband Steve's corporation, Steve Neibaur Farms, Inc., had dramatically increased in value during his marriage to Penny. The Farm was a corporation and all the shares were in Steve's name. Penny argued that the court should look beyond the corporate form and characterize the corporate assets as community property. The Idaho Supreme Court rejected her argument and instead held fast to the reimbursement remedy to compensate the community.

NEIBAUR v. NEIBAUR

142 Idaho 196, 125 P.2d 1072 (2005)
Supreme Court of Idaho

SCHROEDER, Chief Justice.

This is a dispute regarding the value of Penny Neibaur's community property interest, if any, in Steve Neibaur Farms, Inc., upon the divorce of Steve and Penny Neibaur. The magistrate court held that the community was entitled to reimbursement in the amount of $750,000 for community efforts that enhanced the value of the corporation, and the district court affirmed. Steve appealed to the Court of Appeals, which reversed the decision of the magistrate court. This Court granted a Petition for Review filed by Penny.

I.   FACTUAL AND PROCEDURAL BACKGROUND

The Court of Appeals stated the facts as follows:

> Steve and Penny Neibaur married in 1982. At that time, Steve was the sole shareholder in Steve Neibaur Farms, Inc., which was formed by Steve approximately one year before the marriage. All shares of stock have always been held in Steve's name. To the date of divorce, Steve had directed all of the farming operations and management of the corporation, and all corporate decisions were made solely by him. Penny, who had outside employment (primarily as a school teacher), provided virtually no services to the corporate farming operation. Under Steve's direction, the corporation farmed about 2,100 acres of land and had one full-time employee and several seasonal employees. The value of the corporation increased from approximately $146,466 at the time of incorporation to $1,050,000 at the time of divorce.

In 2001, Steve filed a petition for divorce from Penny. At trial, Penny argued that the corporation was the alter ego of Steve and therefore the court should "pierce the corporate veil" and recharacterize the corporate assets as community property. In findings and conclusions rendered after a trial, the magistrate concluded that the corporation was Steve's separate property but also found that $750,000 of the increase in the value of the corporation during the marriage was due to community effort, namely Steve's services, expended for the benefit of the corporation. The magistrate further found that evidence presented at trial did not establish that the community was adequately compensated for Steve's work. As a result, the magistrate held that the community was entitled to reimbursement in the amount of $750,000 for community efforts that enhanced the value of the corporation, and the magistrate granted the community a lien in that amount against Steve's shares of stock.

Steve appealed to the district court, which affirmed the magistrate's order with regard to the corporation. *Neibaur v. Neibaur*, 2004 WL 1699023 *1 (Ct. App. 2004).

The Court of Appeals reversed the decision of the magistrate court and held that the portion of the divorce decree awarding the community $750,000 and a lien in that amount against the stock of Steve's corporation be vacated. Penny filed a Petition for Review, which was granted by this Court.

. . .

III.   THE TRIAL COURT ERRED IN UTILIZING THE CONCEPT OF PIERCING THE CORPORATE VEIL TO DETERMINE THE COMMUNITY INTEREST

Property owned by either spouse prior to marriage remains the separate property of that spouse under Idaho's community property laws. Generally, if separate property has been improved by the community effort, the community is entitled to reimbursement from the separate estate unless the community contribution was intended as a gift. However, when the separate property is a spouse's corporation, the right of reimbursement does not follow this general rule. Instead, this Court has recognized two methods by which the community may be reimbursed from the separate property corporation. The community may be reimbursed if the community was not adequately compensated for a spouse's labor devoted to the separate property corporation. The community may also be reimbursed if the separate property corporation unreasonably or fraudulently retained earnings instead of distributing profits as dividends.

The magistrate and district courts ruled in favor of Penny regarding her argument that there is a third method by which the community may obtain a right of reimbursement from a separate property corporation. She relied upon *Sherry v. Sherry*, 108 Idaho 645, 649, 701 P.2d 265, 269 (Ct. App. 1985), to support her claim that the court may pierce the corporate veil of a separate property corporation and award a share of the corporation as community property. While there is some support for utilization of the concept of piercing the corporate veil in the division of a community property estate, it is not the majority rule.

The Court declines to adopt the remedy of piercing the corporate veil in the context of a divorce division of community property. Idaho law provides two circumstances under which the community has a right to reimbursement for labor devoted to a separate property corporation. The community may be reimbursed if the community was not adequately compensated for a spouse's labor devoted to the separate property corporation. The community may also be reimbursed if the separate property corporation unreasonably or fraudulently retained earnings instead of distributing profits as dividends.

If community efforts have been expended in the conduct of a separate property business, the proper inquiry in a divorce proceeding is whether the community has received fair and adequate compensation for its labor. The trial court should take the following factors into consideration: "the nature of the business, the size of the business, the number of employees, the nature and extent of community involvement in the conduct of the business, the growth pattern of the business," and then decide whether the over-all compensation received by the community is equivalent to the compensation which a business would have had to pay to secure a non-owner employee to perform the same services. In this case the magistrate court found the evidence did not establish whether Steve was adequately compensated or the amount of any deficiency. The burden is on the spouse asserting the claim for reimbursement, and Penny failed to produce evidence to show what would be adequate compensation. In fact, she successfully objected when Steve offered such evidence, so the particular issue was not appealed.

The community may also be reimbursed if the separate property corporation unreasonably or fraudulently retained earnings instead of distributing profits as dividends. The Court of Appeals correctly stated that the earnings and profits of a corporation remain the property of the corporation, and shareholders do not have property rights in a corporation's retained earnings until those earnings are distributed to shareholders as dividends. The income to the shareholder is community property once distributed as dividends. The Court has recognized that a shareholder spouse with sufficient control of a separately held corporation can cause earnings to be inappropriately retained rather than distributed as dividends, to the detriment of the community. To the extent that the retention of the net earnings of the corporation is unreasonable from a business point of view or was done to defraud the community, the community is entitled to reimbursement.

In the present case, Steve was in a position to control the retention of corporate earnings and his compensation. The magistrate court found that Steve had not defrauded the community in his operation of the corporation, but it did not address whether any retention of earnings or his compensation was unreasonable from a business standpoint. While a case of this nature would normally be decided on Penny's failure of proof, it appears that counsel for Penny and the magistrate court relied upon an approach they thought to be approved by the Court of Appeals. Consequently, the Court remands the case for a determination of the division of property pursuant to the principles set forth in this case.

V.   CONCLUSION

The magistrate court's order awarding $750,000 to the community and the lien against Steve's shares of stock in that amount is vacated. The case is remanded for distribution of property in accordance with this decision. The magistrate court may, in its discretion, take additional evidence. Costs are awarded to Steve Neibaur. No attorney fees are allowed.

Justices TROUT and JONES and Justices Pro Tem KIDWELL and DENNARD concur.

Discussion Questions

1. Why do you think that the Court rejected Penny's argument?
2. How does a trial court determine the amount of reimbursement to the community? Do you think Penny will succeed on remand?

---

2. Who Has the Burden of Proof? The Louisiana Answer

The Louisiana Legislature has codified how to treat a separate property business that increases in value. Louisiana Civil Code art. 2368 states:

> If the separate property of a spouse has increased in value as a result of the uncompensated labor or industry of the spouses, the other spouse is entitled to be reimbursed from the spouse whose property has increased in value one-half of the increase attributed to the common labor.

Despite Louisiana following the Civil Rule that the income from separate property is community property, the Louisiana Civil Code requires proof that the separate property of a spouse increased in value because of the uncompensated labor or industry of the spouses. The question is who carries the burden of proving whether the increase was due to spousal labor or to other factors. The issue was addressed by the Louisiana Supreme Court in *Krielow v. Krielow*, 635 So. 2d 180 (La. 1994). The context was the increase in value of the husband's stock in a family-owned corporation. An example of how to determine under-compensation is found in *Craft v. Craft*, 914 So. 2d 648 (La. 2005).

KRIELOW v. KRIELOW

635 So. 2d 180 (1994)
Supreme Court of Louisiana

Rehearing Denied June 17, 1994.

Husband filed for partition of community property following divorce. The 31st Judicial District Court, Parish of Jefferson Davis, William N. Knight, J., partitioned community property, and wife appealed. The Court of Appeal, Knoll, J., affirmed, 622 So. 2d 732, and wife was granted writ of certiorari. The Supreme Court, Charles A. Marvin, J. Ad Hoc, held that: (1) once former wife established that former husband was undercompensated by separately-owned corporation of which he was part owner, burden of proof shifted to husband to prove enhancements in separate property's value occurred because of factors other than husband's labor, and (2) debt incurred by husband for business enterprise was community liability.

Reversed and remanded.

Watson, J., dissented, with statement, and would grant rehearing.

Charles A. Marvin, Justice Ad Hoc.

In this action to partition community property, we granted writs to determine whether the lower courts applied the wrong burden of proof on a spouse who sought to show that uncompensated or undercompensated community labor performed by the other spouse on his separate property during the course of the marriage enhanced, or increased the value of, his separate property.

We reverse and remand. C.C. Art. 2368; *Abraham v. Abraham*, 87 So. 2d 735 (La. 1956); *Deliberto v. Deliberto*, 400 So. 2d 1096 (La. App. 1st Cir. 1981).

Factual Summary

Lynn Naebers and Carl Krielow married on June 20, 1980, about six years after he and his brothers created a family owned corporation, Krielow Brothers, Inc., hereafter KBI. The community terminated in November of 1988 with the filing of a motion for a legal separation. A judgment of divorce was rendered a year later. Carl Krielow filed a petition for partition of the community property on August 1, 1989. The judgment partitioning the community property was signed on March 18, 1992.

Carl Krielow and his two brothers each owned one-third of the corporate stock of KBI, 1980 to 1984. In 1984, the mother of the three acquired 90 percent of the KBI stock, who, in turn, granted KBI an irrevocable option to repurchase the shares. By action of its board of directors, including Carl Krielow, before the community was terminated in 1988, KBI exercised its option, acquiring the mother's shares as treasury stock and thereafter sold some of the shares to Carl, increasing his stock to his original one-third of the shares. The appellate court noted in its opinion that Carl's one-third shares in KBI "increased from $32,000 [in 1984] to $320,000 [in 1988]," but attributed the increase to the mother's "causing the corporation to repurchase [her] stock. 622 So. 2d 732." The record does not allow the conclusion that the mother "caused" this to occur, but compels the contrary conclusion because her share ownership was subject to the irrevocable option of KBI to repurchase her shares, which KBI exercised.

Burden of Proof

If the separate property of a spouse has increased in value as a result of the uncompensated common labor or industry of the spouses, the other spouse is entitled to be reimbursed from the spouse whose property has increased in value one-half of the increase attributed to the common labor.

C.C. Art. 2368.

After finding that the stock increased in value during the marriage, the trial court concluded that Lynn failed to prove by "a preponderance of the evidence that the increase in value was a result of Carl's labor and industry, *and not as a result of other factors.*" Our emphasis. The trial court stated:

> Probably the most tell-tale evidence came from Mr. Ellis, Lynn's CPA and expert witness who candidly admitted on cross-examination that he did not know what caused the increase in value. Certainly, after analyzing the corporation and, in particular, with his expertise, he would be in a better position than the court to conclude that the increase in value was as a result of Carl's labor and industry, and not as a result of other factors, if this were the case. However, even after his analysis, he could not so conclude and neither can this court.

The appellate court said:

> [T]he trial court applied the proper standard: Lynn, the claimant spouse, has the initial burden of proving that the increase in value of Carl's separate property is the result of the uncompensated common labor and industry of the spouses; then, if Lynn meets her burden of proof, the burden shifts to Carl to prove that any increase in the value of his separate property is due to the ordinary course of things, rise in value, or chances of trade.

The trial court did not impose the "proper" burden, but misapplied Art. 2368 by declaring that Mrs. Krielow was required to show that the increase in value of Carl's stock was "not a result of other factors."

The claimant spouse must first prove that common or community labor of the spouses was expended on separate property. A spouse should not be permitted to deprive the community of a spouse's earnings that would be community property when that community labor enhances or increases the value of the laboring spouse's separately owned property. If a claim exists because the laboring spouse was either uncompensated or undercompensated, the measure of reimbursement is one-half of the increase attributable proportionately to the uncompensated labor of the spouse. Katherine S. Spaht and W. Lee Hargrave, in *Matrimonial Regimes*, §7.17, 16 *Louisiana Civil Law Treatise* (1989), carefully explain and discuss the controlling authorities derived from *Abraham v. Abraham*, 230 La. 78, 87 So. 2d 735 (La. 1956).

Under former Art. 2408, the jurisprudence required proof of 1) the condition of the property at the time of the marriage; 2) the value of the property at dissolution in the state it was at the time of the marriage; 3) the real value of said property with all of the improvements in the condition it was at the time of dissolution of the community; and 4) the difference between the two estimates. The present Art. 2368 does not impose a greater burden.

Regarding former Art. 2408, this court has stated:

> [W]hen it is shown that community labor, expenses or industry has provided an increase to the separate property, the burden shifts to the owner of the separate property to rebut this proof and *affirmatively establish* that the increase is due *only* to the ordinary course of things, rise in values or chances of trade.

Abraham v. Abraham, 87 So. 2d at 739.

Compare *Guarisco v. Guarisco*, 526 So. 2d 1126 (La. App. 1st Cir. 1988); *Fontenot v. Fontenot*, 339 So. 2d 897 (La. App. 3d Cir. 1976), writ denied, 342 So. 2d 217 (1977);

and *Mohr v. Mohr*, 374 So. 2d 203 (La. App. 4th Cir. 1979), which failed to adhere to the *Abraham* standard and required the claimant to show that the enhancement did not result in the ordinary course of events.

Hartfield v. Hartfield, 602 So. 2d 179 (La. App. 3d Cir. 1992); *Deliberto v. Deliberto*, supra; and *Downs v. Downs*, 410 So. 2d 793 (La. App. 3d Cir.), writ denied, 414 So. 2d 375 (1982), rejected *Fontenot* as inconsistent with *Abraham* because it placed the burden of persuasion on the claimant to prove that the increase was not due to the ordinary course of things.

Regarding the appellate jurisprudential inconsistency, Spaht and Hargrave commented:

> If it is proved that separate property has increased in value due to the uncompensated labor of a spouse, then arguably there is proof that the property did not increase due to the ordinary course of things. Furthermore, shifting the burden of persuasion to the spouse whose separate property has increased in value to prove that the increase was due to the ordinary course of things seems eminently fair. Many times the separate property alleged to have increased in value is a separate partnership interest or separate stock in a closely held corporation. Under such circumstances the spouse in a position to know whether an increase in value is the result of a rise in property values or inflation is the spouse whose separate property has benefited.

By enacting Art. 2368, the legislature did not intend to overrule the jurisprudence interpreting Art. 2408. We shall continue to follow the standard pronounced by this court in *Abraham*, supra.

Mrs. Krielow established a prima facie case that her husband's separately owned stock increased in value during the marriage. Carl Krielow contends that Lynn failed in her burden because her CPA, Ellis, could not distinctly fix the value of KBI, the separately owned corporation, on the date of marriage in 1980 or on the date the community terminated in 1988.

The trial court found that the value of the separate property increased during the marriage. The court of appeal did not refute or upset this finding. We make no specific finding about value, but note that the testimony *indicates* that KBI may have been worth $12,000 at the time of the marriage in 1980, $0 in 1984, and at $960,000 in 1988 when the community was terminated. In 1988, Carl Krielow owned one-third of the shares of KBI.

The trial court did not reach the question of whether Carl was uncompensated or undercompensated. The court of appeal stated:

> We find that Mr. Ellis' testimony and other record evidence is not sufficient to meet Lynn's burden of proving that the value of Carl's separate property was increased by his uncompensated labor.

While Carl Krielow concedes that the appellate court erroneously stated that the trial court applied the "proper" standard, he asserts the appellate court found the trial court properly followed the jurisprudence and placed the initial burden of proof upon his ex-wife. Carl Krielow contends that notwithstanding the trial court's applying the wrong standard, the record demonstrates that Lynn Krielow failed to meet her burden of proof even under the correct standard.

Carl Krielow claims that Lynn Krielow failed to prove that he was undercompensated for the work he performed for KBI. Citing *Pellerin v. Pellerin*, 550 So. 2d 1250 (La. App. 4th Cir. 1989); and *Phillips v. Wagner*, 470 So. 2d 262 (La. App. 5th Cir.), writ denied, he argues that Lynn may satisfy this burden by proving that the amount of compensation received by him from KBI was less than that which he could have received in the open market. Carl asserts that CPA Ellis was unable to testify as to the amount of compensation that he could have obtained in the open market. Noting that the growth of the corporation occurred when he owned only 3.33 percent of the shares, Carl asserts that he had no practical power to fix his own compensation. CPA Ellis explained that competent people, officers and management make a business entity such as KBI grow and increase in value.

Noting his ex-wife's contention that the corporation only paid or allowed him to "draw" money that was absolutely necessary for the subsistence of the community, Carl Krielow asserts that the record is not only devoid of such evidence, but establishes otherwise. Carl points to testimony showing that KBI provided him and Lynn with a full-time house-keeper/sitter, the unrestricted use of a new Volvo automobile equipped with a cellular phone, and the funds sufficient to make political contributions.

The record shows that Carl Krielow began working full-time for KBI in mid-1984, bidding and overseeing KBI jobs in various locations. He worked without any salary his first year, and thereafter remained active as an employee and director of KBI. Lynn Krielow emphasizes a KBI promotional brochure showing Carl Krielow as vice-president, director, and one of the two operating officers of KBI. Prior to Carl Krielow's being solely employed by KBI, KBI had no revenue, no income, and no increase in assets. During the community, Carl was not paid a salary by KBI, but was paid or allowed "draws" from corporate accounts, which income he reported on a Federal Tax 1099 form rather than the usual W-2 forms used by salaried employees.

Carl and his brother, Bill Krielow, ran and managed KBI. The other brother-stockholder, Chris, had no interest in the day-to-day operations of KBI. Carl Krielow, on the other hand, worked solely for and devoted all of his time to KBI. We must conclude through Carl's competency, KBI flourished. Carl has been a director and an employee of KBI since it was first formed in 1974. Regardless of his ownership percent, Carl Krielow and his brother, Bill, are, and have been, the primary managerial officers of KBI.

Carl's draws were relatively low, according to this record. KBI also paid Carl's telephone and utility bills and furnished him with vehicles. The CPA, Ellis, concluded that the community should have received an additional $177,332 between 1984 and 1988, and that Carl Krielow's low income from KBI was not the result of lack of profitability. We must conclude on this record that Carl Krielow was undercompensated to some degree which the trial court shall determine on remand.

Because Lynn Krielow has established on this record that Carl's undercompensated community labor for KBI enhanced or increased Carl's separately owned stock, the burden shifts to Carl, as the owner of the separate property, to prove that some or all of the enhancement occurred because of other factors. It is Carl who has failed to meet his burden of proof.

Once a claimant has established that the increase in separate property of the other spouse is entirely or partially due to the under- or uncompensated community labor of the other spouse, the claimant is entitled to one-half of the enhanced value of the separate property. Even if that value exceeds the value of the uncompensated labor, the claimant is nevertheless entitled to recover the greater amount. Art. 2368 does not impose a limitation on the amount recoverable.

We shall reverse the judgment in this respect and remand to the trial court to allow the proper measure of reimbursement to be determined and judgment entered in favor of Lynn Krielow consistent with this opinion.

DECREE

The judgment of the court of appeal is reversed and the case is remanded to the trial court to resolve, in accord with this opinion, the issues remaining.

WATSON, J., dissents, believing that the trial court and the Court of Appeal were correct.

CRAFT v. CRAFT

914 So. 2d 648 (2005)
Louisiana Court of Appeal

CARAWAY, J.

Following their 27-month marriage and divorce, the parties brought this community property partition action pursuant to La. R.S. 9:2801 in which they disputed certain reimbursement claims regarding the husband's business which was his separate property and the assets and liabilities of the community. The trial court awarded reimbursement on certain claims in favor of the wife and the husband appeals. With an amendment to the amount of one reimbursement award, we affirm the trial court's ruling.

FACTS

Alfred M. Craft ("Alfred") and Connie Faye Cantrell Craft ("Connie") were married on January 29, 1999, and separated on March 5, 2001. On May 15, 2001, Connie filed a petition seeking a divorce on the basis of La. C.C. art. 102. The resulting divorce judgment in January 2002 terminated the community property regime as of May 15, 2001.

In this suit initiated by Alfred, the pre-trial pleadings indicated that the parties acquired very few assets during their short marriage. The suit therefore involves certain reimbursement claims asserted by the parties arising out of their matrimonial regime.

At trial, the primary issues raised by the parties which now are the subject of Alfred's appeal were: (1) one-half of the increased value of Alfred's separate business, Bo Construction and Dirt Co., Inc.; (2) one-half of the payments made with community funds towards Alfred's separate obligations; (3) one-half of the value of a 1990 Ford Taurus which was purchased during the marriage and retained by Connie; and (4) one-half of the Discover credit card debt of $5,538.93. The trial court entered judgment in Connie's favor awarding her a total reimbursement amount of $10,795.31, which relates primarily to the above disputed items.

DISCUSSION

ALFRED'S BUSINESS

Alfred argues that the trial court erred in granting Connie reimbursement in the amount of $3,526.84 (one-half of $7,053.67) for an increase in the value of his construction and dirt work business. Prior to the marriage and throughout its existence, Alfred was the sole proprietor of the business which owned and operated excavators and dirt moving/hauling equipment.

At trial, Alfred presented the testimony of his accountant, Judy Garrett ("Garrett"), who was familiar with his business. Garrett prepared the corporate and individual tax returns throughout the time of the marriage, and those returns were filed into evidence. Garrett also prepared a comparative balance sheet for the business, showing its assets, liabilities and equity at the beginning of the marriage and at the time of termination of the community. Garrett testified that the major assets of the business were its heavy equipment, all of which was bought in 1996 and 1997 before the marriage. The balance sheet reflects that during the community, the value of the equipment was reduced by $113,995.74 to a total of $326,623.45 due to the accounting for depreciation placed on the equipment. During the same time period, the principal of the business indebtedness was reduced $98,919.31 and the cash assets increased $22,130.10. Without taking into account whether the accelerated depreciation allowances employed in the accounting reflect the actual value of the business equipment, the above accounting data produced a $7,053.67 gain in the retained earnings and total equity of Alfred's business. That was the precise amount utilized by the trial court in making the reimbursement award to Connie.

Additionally, the evidence shows that the business only paid Alfred an annual salary of approximately $12,000. The evidence also indicated that he received from his business an additional amount for rental income relating to his home office. Nevertheless, his total income from the business was always under $20,000 annually. The other labor costs of the business as reflected on its tax returns were very low, indicating that Alfred primarily performed the work for conducting the business. Thus, Alfred's income attributable to the community regime was low when compared to the $550,000 (approx.) in gross receipts for the business as shown on the two corporate tax returns for the time during the marriage.

If the separate property of a spouse has increased in value as a result of the uncompensated common labor or industry of the spouses, the other spouse is entitled to be reimbursed from the spouse whose property has increased in value one-half of the increase attributed to the common labor. La. C.C. art. 2368.

* * *

Based upon the above, the trial court concluded that Alfred had paid himself only a nominal salary and that the unpaid income was retained in the business and used to decrease the business's considerable debt and increase Alfred's equity. This focus by the trial court was clearly the appropriate analysis mandated by the above law. The conclusions are reasonably supported by Alfred's own financial data. In particular, the substantial reduction in the principal balances for the various loans shown on the company balance sheet represents the satisfaction of Alfred's separate obligations that came about during the community by the fruits of his labor and industry as the sole proprietor of the business. Instead of Alfred receiving a higher salary for his labor or dividends from the corporate earnings, those fruits of his business labors, which would have fallen into the community, were used instead to reduce the corporate debt and increase the retained earnings in Alfred's separate property business. Nevertheless, pursuant to Civil Code Article 2368, a reimbursement claim is appropriate for what Alfred could have received in compensation as it increased the value of his separate property.

Alfred's assignment of error regarding this reimbursement to Connie is therefore without merit.

CONCLUSION

For the foregoing reasons, the trial court's adjudication of the reimbursement claims was correctly decided. We amend the award concerning the amount paid to Alfred's brother, and as amended, the judgment in favor of Connie in the amount of $9,535.31 is affirmed. Costs of appeal are assessed to appellant.

Judgment amended, and as amended, affirmed.

Discussions Questions

1. How does the Court's decision in *Krielow* regarding the burden of proof favor the wife in this case? Is it fair to assign the burden of proof as determined by the Court?

2. Why did the Court of Appeal in *Craft* uphold the trial court's reimbursement award to Connie?

B.   THE AMERICAN RULE STATES: BALANCING THE SEPARATE AND COMMUNITY INTERESTS

1.   Introduction: The California Approaches

The primary issue in the American Rule States is what causes the increase in value of the separate property business. Once that is determined, the states that follow the lead of California, apply two different formulas based on the cases of *Pereira* and *Van Camp*. If the increase in value can be attributed to community effort, the *Pereira* approach is used. Under the *Pereira* approach, which usually favors the community, the increase in value of a separate property business is apportioned by allocating a fair return on the separate property investment to the separate property owner. The balance of the increase is allocated to the community and split 50/50 between the spouses. If the increase in value can be attributed to economic conditions, the *Van Camp* approach is used. Under the *Van Camp* approach which usually favors the separate property owner, the court determines the owner's salary or the reasonable value of the owner's services and deducts the couple's family expenses from that amount. That remaining amount (if any) is allocated to the community and the rest of the increase in value belongs to the separate property owner. The following California cases illustrate how these approaches work.

BEAM v. BANK OF AMERICA

6 Cal. 3d 12, 490 P.2d 257, 98 Cal. Rptr. 137 (1971)
Supreme Court of California, En Banc

TOBRINER, Associate Justice.

Mrs. Mary Beam, defendant in this divorce action, appeals from an interlocutory judgment awarding a divorce to both husband and wife on grounds of extreme cruelty. The trial court determined that the only community property existing at the time of trial was a promissory note for $38,000, and, upon the husband's stipulation, awarded this note to the wife; the court found all other property to be the separate property of the party possessing it. The court additionally awarded Mrs. Beam $1,500 per month as alimony and granted custody of the Beam's two minor children to both parents, instructing the husband to pay $250 per month for the support of each child so long as the child remained within the wife's care.

On this appeal, Mrs. Beam attacks the judgment primarily on the grounds that the trial court (1) failed adequately to compensate the community for income attributable to the husband's skill, efforts and labors expended in the handling of his sizable separate estate during the marriage, and (2) erred in suggesting that community living expenses, paid from the income of the husband's separate estate, should be charged against community income in determining the balance of community funds. In addition, the wife challenges the court's categorization of several specific assets as separate property of her husband. For the reasons discussed below, we have concluded that substantial precedent and evidence support the various conclusions under attack; thus we conclude that the judgment must be affirmed.

1.   THE FACTS.

Mr. and Mrs. Beam were married on January 31, 1939; the instant divorce was granted in 1968, after 29 years of marriage. Prior to and during the early years of the marriage, Mr. Beam inherited a total of $1,629,129 in cash and securities, and, except for brief and insignificant intervals in the early 1940's, he was not employed at all during the marriage but instead devoted his time to handling his separate estate and engaging in private ventures with his own capital. Mr. Beam spent the major part of his time studying the stock market and actively trading in stocks and bonds; he also undertook several real estate ventures, including the construction of two hotel resorts, Cabana Holiday I at Piercy, California, and Cabana Holiday II at Prunedale, California. Apparently, Mr. Beam was not particularly successful in these efforts, however, for, according to Mrs. Beam's own calculations, over the lengthy marriage her husband's total estate enjoyed only a very modest increase to $1,850,507.33.

Evidence introduced at trial clearly demonstrated that the only moneys received and spent by the parties during their marriage were derived from the husband's separate estate; throughout the 29 years of marriage Mrs. Beam's sole occupation was that of housewife and mother (the Beams have four children). According to the testimony of both parties, the ordinary living expenses of the family throughout the marriage amounted to $2,000 per month and, in addition, after 1960, the family incurred extraordinary expenses (for travel, weddings, gifts) of $22,000 per year. Since the family's income derived solely from Mr. Beam's separate estate, all of these household and extraordinary expenses were naturally paid from that source.

On this appeal, Mrs. Beam of course does not question the disposition of the promissory note, but does attack the trial court's conclusion that this asset was the only community property existing at the time of the divorce. Initially, and most importantly, the wife contends that the trial court erred in failing to find any community property resulting from the industry, efforts and skill expended by her husband over the 29 years of marriage. We address this issue first.

2.   The Trial Court Did Not Err in Concluding that There Was No Net Community Property Accumulated During the Marriage from the Earnings of Mr. Beam's Separate Property.

Section 5108 of the Civil Code provides generally that the profits accruing from a husband's separate property are also separate property. Nevertheless, long ago our courts recognized that, since income arising from the husband's skill, efforts and industry is community property, the community should receive a fair share of the profits which derive from the husband's devotion of more than minimal time and effort to the handling of his separate property. Furthermore, while this principle first took root in cases involving a husband's efforts expended in connection with a separately owned farm or business (e.g., Pereira v. Pereira (1909) 156 Cal. 1, 103 P. 488; Huber v. Huber (1946) 27 Cal. 2d 784, 792, 167 P.2d 708; Van Camp v. Van Camp (1921) 53 Cal. App. 17, 29, 199 P. 885; Stice v. Stice (1947) 81 Cal. App. 2d 792, 796, 185 P.2d 402) our courts now uniformly hold that "(a)n apportionment of profits is required not only when the husband conducts a commercial enterprise but also when he invests separate funds in real estate or securities." Without question, Mr. Beam's efforts in managing his separate property throughout the marriage were more than minimal, and thus the trial court was compelled to determine what proportion of the total profits should properly be apportioned as community income.

Over the years our courts have evolved two quite distinct, alternative approaches to allocating earnings between separate and community income in such cases. One method of apportionment, first applied in Pereira v. Pereira (1909) 156 Cal. 1, 7, 103 P. 488 and commonly referred to as the Pereira approach, "is to allocate a fair return on the (husband's separate property) investment (as separate income) and to allocate any excess to the community property as arising from the husband's efforts." The alternative apportionment approach, which traces its derivation to Van Camp v. Van Camp (1921) 53 Cal. App. 17, 27-28, 199 P.2d 885, is "to determine the reasonable value of the husband's services . . . , allocate that amount as community property, and treat the balance as separate property attributable to the normal earnings of the (separate estate)."

In making such apportionment between separate and community property our courts have developed no precise criterion or fixed standard, but have endeavored to adopt a yardstick which is most appropriate and equitable in a particular situation . . . depending on whether the character of the capital investment in the separate property or the personal activity, ability, and capacity of the spouse is the chief contributing factor in the realization of income and profits (citations). . . . (Par.) In applying this principle of apportionment the court is not bound either to adopt a predetermined percentage as a fair return on business capital which is separate property (the Pereira approach) nor need it limit the community interest only to (a) salary fixed as the reward for a spouse's service (the Van Camp method) but may select (whichever) formula will achieve substantial justice between the parties.

The trial court in the instant case was well aware of these apportionment formulas and concluded from all the circumstances that the Pereira approach should be utilized. As stated above, under the Pereira test, community income is defined as the amount by which the actual income of the separate estate exceeds the return which the initial capital investment could have been expected to earn absent the spouse's personal management. In applying the Pereira formula the trial court adopted the legal interest rate of 7 percent simple interest as the "reasonable rate of return" on Mr. Beam's separate property; although the wife now attacks this 7 percent simple interest figure as unrealistically high, at trial she introduced no evidence in support of any other more "realistic" rate of return and, in the absence of such evidence "the trial court correctly adopted the rate of legal interest."

Testimony at trial indicated that, based upon this 7 percent simple interest growth factor, Mr. Beam's separate property would have been worth approximately 4.2 million dollars at the time of trial if no expenditures had been made during the marriage. Since Mrs. Beam's own calculations indicate that the present estate, plus all expenditures during marriage, would not amount to even 4 million dollars, it appears that, under Pereira, the entire increase in the estate's value over the 29-year period would be attributable to the normal growth factor of the property itself, and, thus, using this formula, all income would be designated as separate property. In other words, under the Pereira analysis, none of the increased valuation of the husband's separate property during the marriage would be attributable to Mr. Beam's efforts, time or skill and, as a result, no community income would have been received and, consequently, no community property could presently be in existence.

The wife concedes that the use of the Pereira formula does sustain the trial court's conclusion that the present remainder of the husband's estate is entirely his separate property, but she contends that, under the circumstances, the Pereira test cannot be said to "achieve substantial justice between the parties" and thus that the trial court erred in not utilizing the Van Camp approach. Although the trial judge did not explicitly articulate his reasons for employing the Pereira rather than the Van Camp analysis, we cannot under the facts before us condemn as unreasonable the judge's implicit decision that the modest increment of Mr. Beam's estate was more probably attributable to the "character of the capital investment" than to the "personal activity, ability, and capacity of the spouse." In any event, however, we need not decide whether the court erred in applying the Pereira test because we conclude, as did the trial court, that even under the Van Camp approach, the evidence sufficiently demonstrates that all the remaining assets in the estate constitute separate property.

Under the Van Camp test community income is determined by designating a reasonable value to the services performed by the husband in connection with his separate property. At trial Mrs. Beam introduced evidence that a professional investment manager, performing similar functions as those undertaken by Mr. Beam during the marriage, would have charged an annual fee of 1 percent of the corpus of the funds he was managing; Mrs. Beam contends that such a fee would amount to $17,000 per year (1 percent of the 1.7 million dollar corpus) and that, computed over the full term of their marriage, this annual "salary" would amount to $357,000 of community income. Mrs. Beam asserts that under the Van Camp approach she is now entitled to one-half of this $357,000.

Mrs. Beam's contention, however, overlooks the fundamental distinction between the total community Income of the marriage, i.e., the figure derived from the Van Camp formula, and the community Estate existing at the dissolution of the marriage. The resulting community estate is not equivalent to total community income so long as there are any community Expenditures to be charged against the community income. A long line of California decisions has established that "it is presumed that the expenses of the family are paid from community rather than separate funds (citations) (and) thus, in the absence of any evidence showing a different practice the community earnings are chargeable with these expenses. [O]nce a court ascertains the amount of community income, through the Van Camp approach, it deducts the community's living expenses from community income to determine the balance of the community property."

If the "family expense" presumption is applied in the present case, clearly no part of the remaining estate can be considered to be community property. Both parties testified at trial that the family's Normal living expenses were $2,000 per month, or $24,000 per year, and if those expenditures are charged against the annual community income, $17,000 under the Van Camp accounting approach, quite obviously there was never any positive balance of community property which could have been built up throughout the marriage. "When a husband devotes his services to and invests his separate property in an economic enterprise, the part of the profits or increment in value attributable to the husband's services must be apportioned to the community. If the amount apportioned to the community is less than the amount expended for family purposes and if the presumption that family expenses are paid from community funds applies, all assets traceable to the investment are deemed to be the husband's separate property."

In sum, even if the trial court had utilized the Van Camp approach in determining community income, as the wife suggests, the court would still have properly concluded that there was no resulting community property from the earnings of her husband's separate property. We therefore conclude that the wife's initial contention is without merit.

* * *

The judgment is affirmed.

WRIGHT, C.J., and McCOMB, PETERS, BURKE, and SULLIVAN, JJ., concur.
MOSK, J., concurs in the judgment.

GILMORE v. GILMORE

45 Cal. 2d 142, 287 P.2d 769 (1955)
Supreme Court of California

TRAYNOR, Justice.

Plaintiff and defendant were married in 1946 and lived together for approximately six years before this action for divorce was filed in 1952. There were no children of the marriage. The trial court awarded defendant an interlocutory decree of divorce based on findings of extreme cruelty. It also found that defendant had not been guilty of cruelty or desertion, that there was no community property, that specified real and personal property belonged to the parties as joint tenants, and that the remainder of the property claimed to be community was the separate property of defendant or a corporation owned by him.

* * *

Plaintiff contends that the trial court erred in finding that there was no community property. She bases this contention on the fact that during the marriage defendant's net worth representing his interests in three incorporated automobile dealerships increased from $182,010.46 to $786,045.52. During this period defendant received salaries from his dealerships ranging from a total of $22,250 in 1946 to a total of $66,799.92 in 1952. The trial court found that the salaries paid defendant by the corporations for his services "rendered to and on behalf of said corporations during the married life of the parties hereto, were and are sufficient to fully compensate said defendant and the community for all of the services rendered to and on behalf of said corporations by defendant during said period of marriage, all of which said salaries have been used and expended for community purposes during said marriage." "In regard to earnings, the rule is that where the husband is operating a business which is his separate property, income from such business is allocated to community or separate property in accordance with the extent to which it is allocable to the husband's efforts or his capital investment." It has frequenty been held that a proper method of making such allocation is to deduct from the total earnings of the business the value of the husband's services to it. The remainder, if any, represents the earnings attributable to the separate property invested in the business. This method was followed by the trial court in this case, and the evidence sustains its finding. Defendant's corporations were staffed by well trained personnel who were capable of carrying on the businesses unassisted. Defendant worked relatively short hours and took many extended vacations. There was expert testimony that the salaries he received, which were found to constitute community income, were more than ample compensation for the services he rendered. Moreover, during the period involved there was a tremendous increase in automobile business that was accompanied by an increase in the value of dealer franchises.

Plaintiff contends, however, that the proper method for determining what part of the increase in value of the business was community property is to subtract from the total increase a reasonable return on the value at the time of the marriage and treat the remainder as community property. She relies on Pereira v. Pereira, 156 Cal. 1, 7, 103 P. 488, 491, 23 L.R.A., N.S., 880, in which the court stated: "In the absence of circumstances showing a different result, it is to be presumed that some of the profits were justly due to the capital invested. There is nothing to show that all of it was due to defendant's efforts alone. The probable contribution of the capital to the income should have been determined from all the circumstances of the case, and, as the business was profitable, it would amount at least to the usual interest on a long investment well secured." If this method were followed in the present case it would be necessary to allocate to the community a large part of the increase in defendant's net worth during the marriage. The rule of the Pereira case is not, however, in conflict with the rule followed by the trial court in this case. It is to be applied only "In the absence of circumstances showing a different result," and the court clearly recognized that if the husband could prove that a larger return on his capital had in fact been realized the allocation should be made differently. In the present case defendant introduced substantial evidence that the salaries he received were a proper measure of the community interest in the earnings of the businesses, and the trial court's finding based thereon cannot be disturbed on appeal.

The judgment is affirmed.

GIBSON, C. J., and CARTER and SCHAUER, JJ., concur.
SHENK, EDMONDS and SPENCE, JJ., concur in the judgment.

Discussion Questions

1. In *Beam*, why didn't the wife succeed in showing that the community had an interest in the husband's stock? Was it fair?

2. In *Gilmore*, why did the Court of Appeal use the *Van Camp* approach? What would the husband argue? The wife?

---

2. Applying the California Approaches: The Nevada and New Mexico Variations

The Nevada Supreme Court explicitly adopted the *Pereira/Van Camp* approaches to assessing the separate property and community interests in a separate property business. The Nevada case of *Schulman v. Schulman* decided in 1976 clearly illustrates the different results when applying the two approaches. The New Mexico case of

Gillespie v. Gillespie decided in 1973 does not mention the *Pereira/Van Camp* approaches but explains both the return on capital and value of the separate property owner's contribution must be taken into account. Both cases favored the separate property owner.

SCHULMAN v. SCHULMAN

92 Nev. 707, 558 P.2d 525 (1976)
Supreme Court of Nevada

MOWBRAY, Justice.

Mary Ann Schulman commenced this action by filing for divorce against Albert S. Schulman. She won a decree of divorce, but has appealed from that portion of the decree settling the property rights of the parties.

1. Mary Ann and Albert were married in 1968. The divorce proceedings were filed in 1973. At the time of the marriage, Albert, who for approximately 40 years had been in the retail and wholesale business as a market manager, meat market owner, and processor of meats, was the sole owner and proprietor of Schulman Meats and Provisions (Schulman Meats), a wholesale and retail meat business operating in Las Vegas, Nevada. The business continued as a sole proprietorship until 1972, when it was incorporated, Albert receiving all 1,000 shares of the corporation's no-par stock. A loan from the Small Business Administration (SBA) — originally in the amount of $300,000, but later increased to $440,000 — was obtained to finance expansion. Mary Ann was required by the FDA to sign a guaranty.

2. During their marriage, the parties acquired a personal residence, title taken in joint tenancy. The parties also had the use of several cars, title being held by the business. Mary Ann testified that at the time of incorporation Albert had promised orally to give her one-half of the stock in the corporation. She further testified that she had contributed her services to the business by designing advertisements.

3. In his report, the master estimated Albert's business to have been worth $28,212 at the time of the marriage. The master arrived at this figure by subtracting the difference between the business's 1968 net profit and Albert's draw for that year from the book value of the business:

Net book value of business		$63,196
Net profit	$54,984	
Albert's draw	-20,000	
		-34,984
Net worth of business		$28,212

The master estimated the present value of the business to be $600,000. He arrived at this figure by multiplying the estimated value of the corporation's assets in February 1974 by 50.4%, a formula taken from a report published by the American Meat Institute (AMI), and extrapolating to allow for normal growth to the time of valuation.

In allocating the increased value of Schulman Meats between the separate and community property, the master used the approach established in Pereira v. Pereira,

156 Cal. 1, 103 P. 488 (1909), finding that Albert's personal efforts were principally responsible for the growth and continuity of the business. Under this approach, a fair return is allocated to the separate property, and the remainder of the increased value is allocated to the community. Here, the master determined 8.27% to be a fair return, a percentage taken from the AMI report. The return on the separate property investment at this rate over the 7 years of the marriage was calculated to be $16,000, making Albert's separate property share of the business $44,547. The master had valued the business at $600,000; so the community share was $555,453.

4. The district judge granted Mary Ann a decree. However, he rejected as "clearly erroneous" certain portions of the master's report. NRCP 53(e)(2). Specifically found erroneous was the master's determination that Albert's efforts were primarily responsible for the increase in value of Schulman Meats. Instead, the district judge attributed the increase in value to the population growth in Las Vegas during the time of the marriage, and the business's expansion made possible by the SBA loan. He rejected the Pereira approach used by the master and adopted the formula announced in Van Camp v. Van Camp, 53 Cal. App. 17, 199 P. 885 (1921), wherein the community is allocated a share of the increased value equal to the fair value of the community services less amounts withdrawn to meet family expenses. The district judge found Albert's services for the period of the marriage to be worth $318,777, predicated on a study by Robert Morris Associates reporting officers' salaries in similar businesses.

The district judge computed the business income used to meet family expenses to be Albert's actual draw, estimated to be $245,507, plus $2,500 worth of meat and groceries and $15,000 in the use of cars purchased by the business. Thus, the district judge found that the family expenses exhausted a total of $263,007 of the $318,777 due for Albert's services. The remaining community interest in the business was found to be $55,770, of which Mary Ann's share was $27,885. Albert was ordered to pay this amount over a period not to exceed 30 months.

Mary Ann contends that the district judge abused his discretion in applying the Van Camp formula of apportionment, because that formula did not render substantial justice in the instant case. We do not agree. Two distinct alternative nounced in Pereira v. Pereira, supra, is to allocate a fair return on the husband's separate property investment as separate income and to allocate any excess to the community property as arising from the husband's efforts. The alternative apportionment approach, which traces its derivation to Van Camp v. Van Camp, supra, is to determine the reasonable value of the husband's services, allocate that amount as community property, and treat the balance as separate property attributable to the normal earnings of the separate estate.

In Beam v. Bank of America, 6 Cal. 3d 12, 98 Cal. Rptr. 137, 141, 490 P.2d 257, 261 (1971), the court said:

> In making such apportionment between separate and community property our courts have developed no precise criterion or fixed standard, but have endeavored to adopt a yardstick which is most appropriate and equitable in a particular situation . . . depending on whether the character of the capital investment in the separate property or the personal activity, ability, and capacity of the spouse is the chief contributing factor in the realization of income and profits (citations). . . . (Par.) In applying this principle of apportionment the court is not bound either to adopt a predetermined percentage as a fair return on

business capital which is separate property (the Pereira approach) nor need it limit the community interest only to (a) salary fixed as the reward for a spouse's service (the Van Camp method) but may select (whichever) formula will achieve substantial justice between the parties. (Citations.)

The reasoning of Beam was adopted by this court in Johnson v. Johnson, 89 Nev. 244, 247, 510 P.2d 625, 626-627 (1973), overruling Lake v. Bender, 18 Nev. 361, 7 P. 74 (1884), where the court ruled:

> We now depart from the all-or-nothing approach of Lake v. Bender, supra, and announce the rule that the increase in the value of separate property during marriage should be apportioned between the separate property of the owner and the community property of the spouses. . . .
> Both approaches (Pereira and Van Camp) have vitality and may be applied as circumstances warrant. Courts of this state are not bound by either the Pereira or the Van Camp approach, but may select whichever will achieve substantial justice between the parties. . . .

In Van Camp, the defendant husband was president and manager of the Van Camp Sea Food Company, to which he devoted his exclusive attention. In rejecting the Pereira approach, the California court held, 199 P. at 889:

> In our opinion, the circumstances attending the Pereira Case are not applicable to the facts involved herein. While it may be true that the success of the corporation of which defendant was president and manager was to a larger extent due to his capacity and ability, nevertheless without the investment of his and other capital in the corporation he could not have conducted the business; and while he devoted his energies and personal efforts to making it a success, he was by the corporation paid what the evidence shows has an adequate salary, and for which another than himself with equal capacity could have been secured. . . .

In the instant case, the district judge determined that Schulman Meats could not have been conducted without the separate property investment of capital specifically without the SBA loan secured by the business assets. This determination was supported by the evidence.

Mary Ann's remaining objections to the use of the Van Camp formula are meritless. She contends that the district judge erred in finding that the increased value of the business was also the result of the general increase in population in the Las Vegas area, on the ground that no direct evidence was presented of such growth or its effect on the Schulman business. Albert contends that the district judge was entitled to take judicial notice of this fact, pursuant to NRS 47.130. It is not necessary to reach this issue, since the district judge's choice of approach was alternatively based on an adequate ground—the importance of the capital investment as security for the SBA loan. Nothing in Johnson or in the Pereira-Van Camp line of decisions suggests that a court must identify the economic factors which caused the return on the capital investment. We find that the application by the district judge of the Van Camp method was inherently fair and that it did not contravene substantial justice.

The judgment of the court below is affirmed.

GUNDERSON, C.J., and BATJER, ZENOFF and THOMPSON, JJ., concur.

GILLESPIE v. GILLESPIE

84 N.M. 618, 506 P.2d 775 (1973)
Supreme Court of New Mexico

STEPHENSON, Justice.

Defendant-Appellant ("wife") appeals from the judgment of the Bernalillo County District Court in this divorce proceeding.

The parties were married on December 23, 1952 and the trial court's decision and judgment were entered in November, 1971. The trial court was confronted with the array of controverted issues normal to divorce actions. In this appeal we are asked to review only the decision in respect to a separately owned business of husband and its value.

Prior to the marriage husband, by purchase, became an equal partner in a business which sold tile at wholesale and retail and contracted tile jobs. Husband's initial investment was five thousand dollars, portions of which were borrowed.

As to the business, the trial court found that the purchase money used in husband's acquisition of an interest had been borrowed and repaid prior to marriage; that at the time of marriage, husband's investment was $13,768.52; and that no community property was invested in the business except in respect to a car. As to the car, the court found that husband had a car prior to marriage and that after successive trades its descendent was contributed to the capital of the tile company. The court found that the value of the contributed car was $1,359.40 "in which the community had a minimal interest, if any."

Further as to the business, the court found that during the marriage husband's withdrawals from it equaled the value of his services and personal efforts in its conduct; that the value of the business was $52,470.75 of which $48,344.20 represented husband's separate interest and $4,126.55 was the community interest in undistributed profits.

The court then made disposition of the asset in a manner consistent with its findings.

The correctness of the trial court's decision must be gauged by §57-3-5, N.M.S.A. 1953 providing, inter alia, that property owned by a husband before marriage, with the rents, issues and profits thereof is his separate property; §57-4-1, N.M.S.A. 1953 providing that all other property acquired during marriage is community, and our root cases on the subject, notably Katson v. Katson, 43 N.M. 214, 89 P.2d 524 (1939), and Laughlin v. Laughlin, 49 N.M. 20, 155 P.2d 1010 (1944).

A good deal is said in the briefs of the need to see to it that in situations such as this the community and the wife be fairly and equitably treated. We are aware of this. We are however no less concerned with according the same sort of treatment to the husband's rights and his separate property which are just as sacred as is the right of the parties in their community property.

The trial court found that husband's investment in the tile company amounted to $13,768.52 at the time of the marriage. The parties were married on December 23, 1952 and the source of the figure mentioned was a financial statement kept in the ordinary course of business as of January 31, 1953.

* * *

The trial court found that the value of husband's investment had increased to $48,344.20 representing the rents, issues and profit of his separate estate together with his original investment. This figure was determined upon a computation predicated upon a rate of return equal to the prime rate prevailing during the marriage plus two percentage points. The theory of the testimony was that had the business capital been borrowed, such would have been the rate required to be paid. Use of the formula was based upon expert testimony. The "prime rate" is the minimum interest rate charged by banks on business loans made to the most credit worthy entities.

Wife argues that the one issue is whether the community interest in husband's business was properly evaluated as a matter of law. She does not seem to claim an absence of substantial evidence.

Wife refers to the trial court's determination of the value of husband's separate estate as being "an enormous award." She states that during the marriage the average yield on government bonds was 4.07% whereas the average rate during that period applied by the court was 6.84%. Presumably this is intended to shock us. It doesn't. It only indicates that the government's credit is better than husband's, notwithstanding that the latter operated at a profit and the former seems to encounter some difficulty in breaking even. It does not seem inherently unreasonable for the court to have determined that husband would have had to pay two percentage points more on borrowings than, for example, General Motors Corporation. Tying the rate of return to the prime rate also has the virtue of taking into account the fact that the cost of money fluctuates as does the cost of other commodities. It is basically unrealistic to apply a flat rate of interest over a long period of time such as nineteen years, the duration of the marriage here, if the reasonable return is to be tied to an interest rate at all.

This is an "if" of some consequence. The trial court here was guided by the measure announced in some of our cases such as Jones v. Jones, 67 N.M. 415, 356 P.2d 231 (1960) of "usual interest on a long investment well secured." This standard is certainly conservative. Why a capital investment in a small business should be deemed "well secured" is not readily apparent. The mortality rates of small businesses indicates they are risky ventures. An equity investment is not secured in any case. We doubt that a prudent investor would have invested in the tile company for an anticipated return on equity of no more than 6.84%. In view of the disposition we make of this case, we need not consider this standard further.

It is impossible to lay down hard and fast guidelines in apportioning assets between the separate estate of a conjugal partner and the community. The surrounding circumstances must be carefully considered and the ultimate answer calls into play the nicest and most profound judgment of the trial court. As was said in Laughlin:

> Each case will depend upon its own facts; a situation often encountered by trial courts. Mathematical exactness is not expected or required, but substantial justice can be accomplished by the exercise of reason and judgment in all such cases.

By what we have said, we do not wish to be understood as approving use of the prime rate, or in fact any interest rate, as a rule of thumb in all cases. It is easy to conceive of a separate business in which all of the profits and increase stemmed from a prudent investment or business arrangement made prior to coverture so that the community would have no interest in it at all. It is equally easy to visualize the converse situation in which all of the profits and increase stem from the labor and skill of a conjugal partner and hence belong to the community. We are considering a fact situation in which there were substantial withdrawals and increases in the value of the business, and taking into account all of the circumstances, we see no error in the manner in which the apportionment was made by the trial court.

We approve the statement by de Funiak in his Principles of Community Property, Section 72, quoted with approval in Laughlin to the effect that:

> . . . each case must be determined with reference to its surrounding facts and circumstances and that therefrom must be determined what amount of the income is due to personal efforts of the spouses and what is attributable to the separate property employed. Dependent upon the nature of the business and the risks involved, it must be reckoned what would be a fair return on the capital investment as well as determined what would be a fair allowance for the personal services rendered.

In the words of Mr. Justice McGhee, speaking for the court in Campbell v. Campbell, 62 N.M. 330, 310 P.2d 266 (1957), a proper apportionment "depends on what is best under all the proof."

We reach the same result by another route which we will mention because of its significance in respect to other limbs of the case. Katson and Laughlin deal with the classification and apportionment of property as separate or community in situations where labor, industry and skill of the husband (community property) is expended on separate property or in a separate business. It is clear from the construction placed on §§57-3-5 and 57-4-1 by those cases that there must be a fair apportionment between the return on the separate property or on capital invested in a separate business, which goes to the owner of it, and the value of the labor, industry and skill of the husband which belongs to the community. The entire income, here partly in the form of withdrawals and partly in the form of increased value of the business, must be taken into account. In order to have proper appellate review the trial court should make findings as to both the value of the separate property and the value of the community property as was done here. However issues in the same case may well be formulated differently upon trial than on appeal. In this case the trial court found:

> During the period of the marriage, plaintiff's withdrawals from Crest Tile Company amounted to $250,750.09, which amount represents the reasonable value of the services and personal efforts in the conduct of the business during the marriage.

In Katson on this subject we said:

> In the absence of other definite proof of the value of appellant's services to the partnership and corporation, the salary he was paid is assumed to be their value.

It was there held that the amount of the withdrawals was substantial evidence of the value of the services, absent evidence on the subject. The same would probably be true here but we are spared the necessity of deciding this because the last quoted finding is not attacked. We must therefore accept it as true and established.

If the value of the husband's services and personal efforts is in an established amount, what more could the community be entitled to? Wife attacks the court's findings as to the value of the business which were predicated upon the books of account, claiming that no going concern value was taken into account. This argument relies heavily on accounting texts and the like cited as precedent, but the query arises as to what difference it could make, so long as the correct amount was taken into account for the reasonable value of the husband's services and efforts. Suppose the business was worth twice as much. We have already established that the business was husband's separate property.

Similarly wife argues that unreasonable amounts of cash were retained in the business, thereby depriving her of some interest in them because they didn't come out of the business. If the cash was separate property in the business, it would have remained so had it been withdrawn, so long as the value of his services and personal effort was established and properly taken into account.

There is certain minor confusion in the trial court's findings in that after finding the value of the husband's services and personal efforts and the accumulated value of his separate and community interests in the tile company, it then found that of the latter amount $4,126.55 was the community interest in the undistributed profits of the business. With the value of the services and efforts being established and not challenged, and all of those monies having been withdrawn from the business, it is difficult to see how there could have been a community interest still in the business. Wife, with admirable grace says "the inconsistency, if there be any, should be ignored." Husband does not cross-appeal. Wife points out that the evidence indicates that the business earned money between the date of the balance sheet from which the figures were determined, July 31, 1971, and the date of the hearing September 15, 1971. Doubtless the court had this in mind in determining that $4,126.55 of community interest remained in undistributed profits.

Discussion Questions

1. Do you agree that the *Van Camp* approach achieved "substantial justice" in the *Schulman* case?

2. How does the *Gillespie* Court apportion the separate property owner's interest and the community interest?

---

3.   Favoring the Community: The Arizona Approach

Arizona has adopted the California approaches to dividing the increase in value of a separate property business. In *Cockrill v. Cockrill*, 124 Ariz. 50, 601 P.2d 1334 (1979), the Arizona Supreme Court recognized that an increase in separately owned property will usually be caused by a combination of community efforts and the inherent rise in the property. At issue in *Cockrill* was the husband Robert's separate property Cockrill Farms. During the marriage, the business had a net worth increase of $79,000. Prior Arizona case law held that the profits of separate property are either community or separate, depending on what contributed to the increase. Because the increase was due to both community labor and inherent increase in the business, the court abandoned the "all or none" approach and instead gave the trial court discretion to select a method of apportionment that would achieve substantial justice.

Rueschenberg v. Rueschenberg, 219 Ariz. 249, 196 P.3d 853 (2008), is a recent example of the application of how Arizona courts apportion the increase in value and profits of a separate property business. In that case, labor of the wife in the husband's separate property business was responsible for two-thirds of the increase in value, while external factors contributed to the other one-third of the increase. The Court of Appeals affirmed the trial court's judgment that gave the husband a fair return on his original investment and divided the remainder of the increase between the husband and wife — clearly a *Pereira* analysis.

COCKRILL v. COCKRILL

124 Ariz. 50, 601 P.2d 1334 (1979)
Supreme Court of Arizona

GORDON, Justice.

Robert E. Cockrill, Sr., and Rose Cockrill were divorced on April 5, 1977. Robert Cockrill appeals from the trial court's finding that the increase in value of his separate property, during the marriage, was community property. [W]e reverse the judgment of the Superior Court.

Appellant Robert Cockrill and Rose Cockrill, appellee, were married on June 15, 1974. At the time of the marriage, appellant owned, as his separate property, a farming operation known as Cockrill Farms. There seems to be no dispute that the net worth increase of the farm, during the two year and ten month marriage, after some credits, was $79,000. The trial court found that this increase was attributable primarily to the efforts of Mr. Cockrill and was, therefore, community property. Appellant contends that the net worth increase was primarily due to the inherent nature of his separate property, the farm, and was, therefore, also his separate property.

The profits of separate property are either community or separate in accordance with whether they are the result of the individual toil and application of a spouse or the inherent qualities of the business itself. . . . It is unclear, however, where the burden of proof lies in this type of situation. That is to say, using the facts of this case as an illustration, is the burden upon Mr. Cockrill to prove that the increase in value of his separate property is due to the inherent nature of the property, or is the burden upon Mrs. Cockrill to show that the increase in value of her husband's separate property is, in reality, the result of his work efforts during the marriage?

Several presumptions fundamental to Arizona community property law come into conflict when one spouse brings separate property into a marriage, and one or both of the spouses work to improve the property during the marriage. Property acquired by either spouse during marriage is presumed to be community property, and the spouse seeking to overcome the presumption has the burden of establishing the separate character of the property by clear and convincing evidence. Moreover, there is a strong presumption, rebuttable only by clear and convincing evidence, that all earnings during coverture are community in nature.

On the other hand, the Court of Appeals, Division Two, held in Percy v. Percy, 115 Ariz. 230, 564 P.2d 919 (App. 1977), that where separately owned property has increased in value there is a presumption that the increase is also separately owned. Percy places a burden upon the spouse who contends that the increase is community property to prove that the increase in value of separate property is due to the labor and efforts of the community and is not the product of the inherent qualities of the separate property. Prior Arizona case law, however, placed the burden upon the spouse who contends that the increase in value of separate property is also separate property. [T]his Court stated:

> (W)here doubts exist as to whether the proceeds represent the product of skill, labor, or management, as opposed to inherent return on investment, they are generally resolved in favor of finding the former, there being a strong presumption, rebuttable only by clear and convincing evidence, that all earnings during coverture are community in nature.

We are persuaded by the above language in Barr, supra, and hold that when the value of separate property is increased the burden is upon the spouse who contends that the increase is also separate property to prove that the increase is the result of the inherent value of the property itself and is not the product of the work effort of the community. Language to the contrary in Percy, is overruled. We emphasize, however, that the separate property of the spouse remains separate. It is merely the profits or the increase in value of that property during marriage which may become community property as a result of the work effort of the community.

Seldom will the profits or increase in value of separate property during marriage be exclusively the product of the community's effort or exclusively the product of the inherent nature of the separate property. Instead, as in the instant case, there will be evidence that both factors have contributed to the increased value or profits. In Arizona, these "hybrid profits" have been governed by what can be labeled the "all or none rule." Pursuant to this rule, the profits or increase in value will be either all community property or all separate property depending on whether the increase is primarily due to the toil of the community or primarily the result of the inherent nature of the separate property. *[handwritten: all or nothing rule]*

If there is insufficient evidence for the trial court to determine what the primary cause of the increased value is, the entire increase in value will be found to be community property, because, as stated previously, the burden of proof is upon the spouse who seeks to establish that the increase is separate property.

Seemingly, none of the other community property law states follow the "all or none" approach. Instead, each recognizes some method of apportioning profits that result from a combination of separate property and community labor.

Arizona embraced the all or none doctrine in In re Torrey's Estate, supra, quoting from the Nevada Supreme Court opinion in Lake v. Lake, (Bender), 18 Nev. 361, 4 P. 711 (1894). (Nevada, however, departed from the all or none approach in 1973.) Johnson v. Johnson, 89 Nev. 244, 510 P.2d 625 (1973).

> We now depart from the all-or-nothing approach of Lake v. Bender, supra, and announce the rule that the increase in the value of separate property during marriage should be apportioned between the separate property of the owner and the community property of the spouses. Profit or increase in value of property may result either from the capital investment itself, or from the labor, skill and industry of one or both spouses or from both the investment of separate property and the labor and skill of the parties. Where both factors contribute to the increase in value of a business, that increase should be apportioned between separate and community property. The rule we announce today is necessary in order to prevent the inherent injustice of denying the owner of separate property a reasonable return on the investment merely because the increase in value results 'mainly' from the labor, skill or industry of one or both spouses.

This Court has also become disenchanted with the all or none rule. To implement the all or none rule and determine the Primary source of the profits, the portion of the profits that resulted from each source must be calculated. Once this has been done, it is only logical to apportion the profits, or increased value, accordingly. To do otherwise will either deprive the property owner of a reasonable return on the investment or will deprive the community of just compensation for its labor.

We, therefore, also depart from the all or none rule and hold that profits, which result from a combination of separate property and community labor, must be apportioned accordingly.

There are several approaches to the problem of apportionment:

> In making such apportionment between separate and community property our courts have developed no precise criterion or fixed standard, but have endeavored to adopt a yardstick which is most appropriate and equitable in a particular situation. . . .

In the case of real estate, the owner of the real property can be awarded its rental value, with the community being entitled to the balance of the income produced from the lands by the labor, skill and management of the parties. Another approach is to determine the reasonable value of the community's services and allocate that amount to the community, and treat the balance as separate property attributable to the inherent nature of the separate estate. Finally, the trial court may simply allocate to the separate property a reasonable rate of return on the original capital investment. Any increase above this amount is community property.

All of these approaches have merit, with different circumstances, requiring the application of a different method of apportionment. We, therefore, hold that the trial court is not bound by any one method, but may select whichever will achieve substantial justice between the parties.

The judgment of the Superior Court is reversed and the case remanded for the trial court to apportion the profits or increase in value of appellant's separate property between separate and community property.

Discussion Questions

1. How did the Arizona Supreme Court in *Cockrill* reconcile the strong presumption that earnings during marriage are community property with the ownership of a separate property business that increases in value?

2. Why did the Arizona Supreme Court in *Cockrill* abandon the "all or none" rule?

RUESCHENBERG v. RUESCHENBERG

219 Ariz. 249, 196 P.3d 852 (2008)
Arizona Court of Appeals

BARKER, P.J.

Scott Rueschenberg ("Husband") appeals from the trial court's award of $296,667 to Jubie Rueschenberg ("Wife") as one-half of the community's share in the value of Husband's separate property. For the reasons that follow, we agree with the trial court and affirm.

FACTS AND PROCEDURAL HISTORY

Wife and Husband were married May 15, 1998. Prior to and at the time of marriage, Husband owned a business called Desert Mountain Medical ("DMM"). DMM sells medical hardware, for the repair of human joints, to surgeons and hospitals. It is undisputed that DMM is Husband's separate property.

The parties resolved all issues regarding the dissolution of marriage through mediation except for the issue of any community interest in the increase in value of DMM over the life of the marriage. On December 14, 2005, the trial court appointed a special master at the request of the parties. On December 22, 2006, the special master filed a report with the trial court.

The special master's report . . . awarded Husband a sole and separate property interest of $550,000. It arrived at this figure by giving what it considered to be a fair rate of return on the original investment of $163,166. The report then subtracted that $550,000 from the value at the dissolution of marriage, $1,440,000, and found that the community was responsible for two-thirds of the resulting increase (i.e. two-thirds of $890,000), which amounts to $593,333. It then awarded Wife half of this amount, or $296,667.

The report found that the community's labor was only responsible for two-thirds of the increase in the value of the company because external factors were responsible for one-third of the increase. Husband had presented evidence that the company's increase in value was due to an increase in manufacturer marketing and sales assistance, increased customer acceptance of the products, increased research and development by manufacturers, natural population growth in the market area, and other DMM sales personnel expanding the market.

The special master's report also found that the community had received virtually 100% of the net distributable earnings during the marriage, but did not include a finding as to what that amount was. Wife's expert believed the *total* amount of monies distributed to the community during marriage to be $2,875,000 while Husband's expert believed it to be $3,122,521.

The trial court incorporated the special master's findings verbatim into its decree of dissolution. Husband filed a timely notice of appeal.

DISCUSSION

Husband makes several arguments on appeal: 1) that the court erred in giving the community an interest in DMM's increased value (here, goodwill) when the community had already received the company's profits (net distributable earnings) generated during the course of the marriage, 2) that the trial court erred in awarding the community a further interest in DMM when a fair salary had already been paid to the community, 3) that the trial court abused its discretion in finding that two-thirds of DMM's growth was due to community labor and efforts, and 4) that the trial court abused its discretion in apportioning the increase in value when the community had already received more than its pro rata share of the total increase in net profits and value.

* * *

He argues that *Cockrill* tried to balance the underlying tension between §25-213(A) (attributing increase in separate property to the separate property) and §25-211 (providing that all property acquired during marriage is community property). In view of that balance, he argues, *Cockrill* permits an award to the community only for profits (net distributable earnings) *or* increase in value (here, goodwill), but not both. We reject this interpretation of *Cockrill.*

Therefore, we hold that when apportioning the increase in value and/or profits from a separately held business, it is not error to apportion both profits (net earnings) and increase in value (whether that is goodwill or a measurable increase in value of some other asset) if the community labor was responsible for a portion of both and if such an apportionment "will achieve substantial justice between the parties." Rather, as we describe more fully below, we hold that the trial court must equitably apportion the combined total of the profits (net distributable earnings) and increase in value (whether goodwill or otherwise) of the separate business if the efforts of the community caused a portion of that increase and substantial justice requires it.

2.   A FINDING OF REASONABLE COMPENSATION DOES NOT NECESSARILY PRECLUDE AN AWARD BASED ON INCREASED VALUE AND/OR PROFITS.

Husband next argues that when the community has received a fair salary for the community's labor contributed to the separately held business, the *Cockrill* inquiry ends and no further apportionment is permitted. We disagree.

* * *

It is instructive to consider, . . . that a different analysis would apply in a typical business setting than one involving both separate and community property. For example, in a typical business, A (the business owner) hires B (the employee) to work for A's company. A is the sole owner of the company. A agrees to pay B a reasonable salary. Assume that over the course of five years A's business increases substantially in value and that 50% of the increase in value can be attributed to B's efforts. The law does not entitle B to 50% of any increase in value or profits because his contractual arrangement was only for the fair salary, which had been paid and received. To grant B a share of the profits and/or of the company's increased value would essentially make B an equity partner with A. This, however, was not the contractual arrangement.

Now, if we change the facts to reflect a community property scenario, the result is different. Assume that all facts in the hypothetical are the same except that the business is A's separate property and when A hires B, they are married to each other and remain married during the relevant time period. The reason for the different result is the community nature of the property that results from the labor of B. In short, B's labor on behalf of the community makes the community a form of equity partner (to the extent of the community's toil) in A's sole and separate business. The Arizona Supreme Court put it this way:

> Where either spouse is engaged in a business whose capital is the separate property of such spouse, the profits of the business are either community or separate in accordance with whether they are the result of the individual toil and application of the spouse, or the inherent qualities of the business itself.

Thus, the company's profits, and as set forth above we construe that to also include its increase in value, become a community asset to the extent "they are the result of the individual toil and application of the spouse." *Id.* In essence, our community property laws transform the community into an equity partner with the sole and separate property-owning spouse to the extent the community's efforts have generated net earnings, increased the value, or otherwise increased the net worth and/or market value of the company. Under our hypothetical, the community is apportioned 50% of the total increase (however denominated) of A's company, as that is the amount attributable to B's efforts. The community's share is not eliminated just because the laboring spouse has been paid a fair salary along the way.[7]

Thus, to the extent that receipt of a fair salary deprives the community of an interest in value and/or profits in a separate business, otherwise due the community, it is contrary to *Cockrill* and we decline to follow it.

3. THE FACTS SUPPORT THE FINDING THAT TWO-THIRDS OF DMM'S GROWTH WAS ATTRIBUTABLE TO THE COMMUNITY'S LABOR.

Husband argues that the trial court abused its discretion in finding that the community was responsible for two-thirds of DMM's growth. He argues that no evidence was presented that anything other than external factors contributed to DMM's growth after 1999.

Husband misperceives the burden of proof. It was not the responsibility of Wife to present evidence that DMM's growth was due to the community labor; rather, it was Husband's burden to show that it remained separate property.

Here, it was within the trial court's discretion to start with the presumption that all of the growth in DMM was community property and then look to the evidence presented by Husband to see if he had managed to overcome that presumption. Husband did present evidence that DMM's growth was influenced by external factors, including an increase in manufacturer marketing and sales assistance, increased customer acceptance of the products, increased research and development by manufacturers, natural population growth in market area, and other DMM sales personnel expanding the market. However, Wife testified that she served as the manager of operations of DMM from 1999 until the couple separated. Wife's expert testified that the primary factor responsible for DMM's growth was the "work effort of the community." Because there was reasonable evidence supporting the trial

---

7. In the event A did more than simply own the separate property, a court tasked with determining the community's fair share would also have to determine the company's increase and profits attributable to A's toil during the marriage. Our hypothetical assumes that only B provided effort or contributed to the company's profits and/or increase in value.

court's finding that two-thirds of the growth in DMM was primarily due to community labor, there was no error.

Discussion Questions

1. In *Rueschenberg*, the husband argued that the community was sufficiently compensated if the spouse working in a separate property business received a fair salary. Do you agree?

2. In *Rueschenberg*, it was the wife who worked as a manager of the husband's separate property business. Does it matter which spouse puts in the efforts in the business?

---

4. Application to Unmarried Cohabitants: The Washington Approach

Unmarried cohabitants in Washington State may be treated as married couples if they have a marital-like relationship. In that scenario, the courts may distribute that property that would have been community property if they had actually married. In the Washington case, *Lindemann v. Lindemann*, 92 Wash. App. 64, 960 P.2d 966 (Wash. App. 1998), discussed how to treat the increase in the value of separate property of one on the cohabitants. The remedy for the community is couched in the terms of "reimbursement" as an equitable remedy to make sure that the separate owner is not unjustly enriched at the expense of the community. Consider as you read this case whether the Washington courts favor a *Pereira* or *Van Camp* approach to separate property businesses.

LINDEMANN v. LINDEMANN
92 Wash. App. 64, 960 P.2d 966 (1998)
Washington Court of Appeals

BECKER, Judge.

The trial court distributed the property of David and Kimi Lindemann, an unmarried cohabiting couple, by applying community property principles to the extent allowed by *Connell v. Francisco*. Finding that the net value of David's separately-owned auto body business had increased solely as the result of David's labor during the relationship, the court required him to reimburse Kimi for half of the increased value. Because a quasi-marital community is entitled to the fruits of each party's labor, and David has not shown that any part of the increase in value was inherent in the nature of his business, we hold the reimbursement ruling was a proper exercise of the court's discretion.

David and Kimi Lindemann married in 1978, separated in 1981, and obtained a decree of dissolution in 1982. In October 1982, David started an auto body repair business, working out of his garage. He got a business license and opened a checking account for the business in 1984. David and Kimi began living together again in 1985, without remarrying. They stayed together for 10 years, raised their two children, held themselves out as a marital community, and expended little if any effort to keep their income or property separated. During those 10 years, David worked at his auto body business, which he incorporated in 1993, while Kimi worked for a newspaper. Kimi did not do any work for David's business. In 1995 David and Kimi separated again, and Kimi petitioned the court to make an equitable division of their property and liabilities.

There is no dispute that David and Kimi lived in a stable, quasi-marital relationship in which they cohabited knowing a lawful marriage between them did not exist (sometimes archaically referred to as a meretricious relationship). The Washington Supreme Court held in *Connell v. Francisco* that upon the demise of such a relationship, the characterization of property as separate and community will apply by analogy even though in the absence of a marriage there is by definition no true community property. At issue in this appeal is how a trial court should characterize and distribute the property interests in a business begun as a separate, unincorporated enterprise, but transformed into a successful corporation by the owner's labor during the quasi-marital relationship.

Upon dissolution of a marriage, all separate and community property is before the court for distribution. A different rule applies upon the break-up of a quasi-marital relationship. To avoid equating cohabitation with marriage, the Supreme Court held in *Connell* that a court may distribute only the property that the cohabiting couple has acquired through efforts extended during the relationship. Separate property is not before the court for distribution.

Because David started his business after his marriage to Kimi ended, but before they began living together again, the trial court determined on summary judgment that David's Auto Body, Inc., was David's separate property, not before the court for distribution. But while the pretrial order of partial summary judgment precluded Kimi from obtaining an ownership interest in the business, it did not prevent her from seeking an equitable share of the value added to the business during the quasi-marital relationship. The court properly reserved that issue for trial.

There is a presumption that any increase in the value of separate property is likewise separate in nature. Thus, at the end of a marriage each spouse is entitled to "the increase in value during the marriage of his or her separately owned property, except to the extent to which the other spouse can show that the increase was attributable to community contributions." The spouse with the separate ownership interest may defend against the other spouse's claim of an equitable interest by showing that the increase in value is attributable not to community contributions of labor or funds, but rather to rents, issues and profits or other qualities inherent in the business. But if the court is persuaded by direct and positive evidence that the increase in value of separate property is attributable to community labor or funds, the community may be equitably entitled to reimbursement for the contributions that caused the increase in value. And in situations where income from the separate property has been commingled with income from community labor to produce an increase in value of the property, the community claimant may invoke a presumption that unless there has been a segregation at the time the income arises, the increase in value belongs to the community.

Applying these principles in the present case, the trial court found after a trial that David's Auto Body, Inc., had increased in value during the 10 years David and Kimi lived together. Efforts at contemporaneous segregation had been negligible. Evidence that David's labor on behalf of the community was the sole source of the increased value overcame the presumption that the increased value of the business was separate in nature. The court awarded one half of that increase, or $109,362.75, to Kimi as her share of the reimbursement.

INCREASE IN VALUE OF SEPARATE PROPERTY

David first claims that Kimi did not prove either that the business increased in value, or the amount of the increase. We conclude the findings of fact on which the trial court based those determinations are supported by substantial evidence. Kimi testified that when David moved in with her in 1985, he had only his clothes and a motorcycle, and he was just in the process of starting the auto body business. The trial court found the business at that point had a net value of no more than $10,000. That finding is supported by evidence that David could not afford tools for his shop, owed back taxes, had a small balance in his checking account, and relied on his parents' home as security for a loan of $11,000.

The trial court found the net increase in the value of the business as a going concern was $218,725.51 at the time of separation. That finding is adequately supported by a business evaluation. David assigns error to the court's reliance on an evaluation instead of an appraisal, but he offered no appraisal himself, and has not presented authority or argument to show why the court's reliance on an evaluation was unjustified.

David claims Kimi failed to prove that the increase in value of his business was due to community effort. But again, there is adequate support for the court's finding that the increase in value of the business was entirely attributable to David's labor. The business initially was marginal and did not prosper until 1991, when David overcame a drug addiction and was able to be more effective and productive. David testified that he worked about 65 hours a week and that the business would fail without his presence and his personal efforts. There was no evidence that the business would have survived, appreciated or earned any income due to its inherent qualities. David made no showing that the increase in value of his business was due to rents, issues, or profits.

Ordinarily, a marital community is entitled to the fruits of all labor performed by either party to the relationship because each spouse is the servant of the community. David argues that this rule should not apply to a quasi-marital relationship because the parties have decided not to commit themselves formally to the mutual obligations of a marital community. But if the labor of each party during a quasi-marital relationship were to be presumptively regarded as separate in character, little would remain of the Supreme Court's holding in *Connell*. The court's intention in *Connell* was to "allow the trial court to justly divide property the couple has earned during the relationship through their efforts." The "community" in that case was held entitled to reimbursement for the value of one member's labor. We similarly conclude that David owed his efforts to his quasi-marital community to the same extent as if they had been married.

David next contends that his obligation to devote his labor to the community was adequately fulfilled by the work he did on the jointly-owned real property. He testified that he pulled up stumps, built a three-car garage with a mother-in-law apartment, and frequently helped with the cooking, cleaning and vacuuming. Given these labors on behalf of the community, he argues, the court should have viewed the labor he contributed to his separate business as "separate" efforts.

David is unable to cite any authority recognizing the concept of "separate" efforts. He supports his argument by analogizing labor to money in an account. Community property law allows the apportionment of money in a single bank account to separate and community sources, and recognizes a presumption that improvements to separate property have been paid for by separate funds if there are enough funds in the account originating from a separate source. David argues that he should similarly be able to apportion his labor so that labor devoted to his business would be presumptively regarded as originating from a separate source, and labor devoted to household chores regarded as originating from a community source.

The Supreme Court rejected a similar argument in *In re Estate of Witte*. The husband came into the marriage with separate property but failed to maintain a segregation between what he earned from his labor and what he realized as rent, issue or profit of his separate property. The trial court characterized as the husband's separate property the land he acquired during the marriage with his commingled income. The Supreme Court, reversing, declared itself unwilling to let the characterization of property turn on how much each spouse helped around the house. Whether the wife did or did not contribute significantly to housekeeping or child-raising was immaterial "for, even if she did not, the personal earnings of the husband nevertheless belonged to the community." David's industry in home improvement projects is similarly irrelevant; his earnings, like Kimi's, belonged to the community.

Unlike money, which can be separate in character when it is acquired before the relationship, labor performed during a marital or quasi-marital relationship has a community character from its inception. In our community property system, there is no basis for allocating one party's labor to a separate property account.

The trial court did not err in concluding that Kimi carried her burden of proving that the increase in value of David's business was the product of community labor.

REIMBURSEMENT AND OFFSET

The right to reimbursement is an equitable remedy, intended to assure that the separate owner is not unjustly enriched at the expense of the community. Therefore, the right of reimbursement may not arise if the court finds that the community realized a "reciprocal benefit" for "its use and enjoyment of the individually owned property."

At trial David introduced evidence of draws and checks he wrote from his business account to pay for family expenses. These contributions, he claims, were a benefit provided by his business to the community offsetting any community contribution of his labor to the business. According to David, the right of reimbursement runs in the opposite direction. The community, he argues, should reimburse his business for expenditures from his business account on behalf of the community, over and above the salary he received after incorporation. Such expenditures include the lease payments on a vehicle and cellular telephone, and payments on Kimi's health insurance and term life insurance.

Washington courts have in some cases denied reimbursement to the community if one spouse's labor in a separate business has been adequately compensated by a salary. *Hamlin v. Merlino* is one such case, and David relies on it for the proposition that Kimi had the burden of proving that his salary (or in the early years, the total of his draws and checks for community purchases) did not fairly and adequately compensate the community for the value of his labor.

In *Hamlin*, the husband owned the stock of an incorporated grocery business before marrying. The couple made a prenuptial agreement providing that their separate property would remain separate. During their marriage, the husband paid himself a salary of $1,858 per year. The salary was consumed by the community's living expenses. After the wife died, the administrator of her estate brought suit, claiming that the increased value of the husband's business was community property because it accrued as a result of the husband's labor during the marriage.

Cautioning that each case turns on its own facts, the Supreme Court in *Hamlin* rejected the administrator's claim. The court first acknowledged that such an increase presumptively belonged to the community absent "a contemporaneous segregation of the income between the community and the separate estates." But Mr. Merlino's consistent segregation of his separate estate overcame the presumption. The court reasoned that Mr. Merlino's corporate salary adequately compensated the community for its contribution of his labor. Any dividends paid or any enhanced value of the stock resulting from profits reinvested in the corporation remained separate in character as the issues and profits of his separate property.

Hamlin, as well as *In re Hebert's Estate*[26] on which *Hamlin* relies, involved a consistently profitable incorporated business which the husband at all times carefully preserved as a separate legal entity apart from his personal affairs. The circumstances of the present case stand in marked contrast.[27] David did not come into the relationship with an incorporated, thriving business and a salary. Instead, he came into the relationship virtually broke and addicted to drugs. His business, as described by the trial court, had little if any market value: "In October of 1985, soon after cohabitation, David's parents had to co-sign and offer their home as security so David could get a business loan of $10,979.13 with small monthly payments of $295.85. . . . That shows that the bank did not consider the business to have sufficient assets to secure a relatively small loan." David did not receive a salary until he incorporated the business eight years into the 10 year period of their quasi-marital relationship. He pledged the business against loans for the community's needs, and pledged the community home against loans for the business. He made no

---

26. *In re Hebert's Estate*, 169 Wash. 402, 14 P.2d 6 (1932).

27. The facts of the present case are closer to *In re Buchanan's Estate*, 89 Wash. 172, 177-80, 154 P. 129 (1916), in which a woman's initial capital investment in a business, which was separate in character as it was given shortly before marriage, was later mixed with her husband's considerable labor, resulting over ten years in a valuable business. Although the business in *Buchanan's Estate* was organized as a corporation, "it might be said to have been operated much as a partnership." *Buchanan's Estate*, 89 Wash. at 177, 154 P. 129. The court in *Buchanan's Estate* held the business to be entirely community in character because the value of the labor so dramatically outweighed the value of the wife's capital investment in causing the business to succeed.

discernible effort to segregate the income attributable to his community labor from any "rents, issues, and profits" inherently arising from his unincorporated business.[29] Under these circumstances, it was appropriate for the court to conclude that David's Auto Body, Inc., was not in the same category as the business in *Hamlin*, and that the increased value of David's business was community in character because it had been achieved by community labor.

By showing that the increase was due to community labor, Kimi satisfied her burden of proving that the community was entitled to reimbursement. Contrary to David's assertion, it was not necessary for Kimi to further prove the absence of an offset. There could be an offset only if the community received some beneficial use of David's separate business. David's contributions to the community in the form of draws on his business account were not an amenity or benefit provided to the community courtesy of David's Auto Body. Rather, the community was entitled to these contributions as the fruits of David's labor. The trial court properly characterized them as earned income to David.

In summary, the trial court reasonably found the community entitled to reimbursement for the increased value David's labor added to his business.

The judgment is affirmed. Both parties' requests for fees on appeal are denied.

Affirmed.

AGID and ELLINGTON, JJ., concur.

Discussion Questions

1. Under Washington's doctrine regarding separate property businesses, why was Kimi able to succeed in receiving one-half of the increase in David's auto body business?

2. Can you identify David's misconceptions about community property law?

PROBLEM 9.1

Frank inherited his farm from his father before he married Fannie. During their marriage, Frank read about the growing demand for "heirloom tomatoes." He decided that he would take part of the farm acreage and plant those tomatoes. Fannie investigated the types of tomatoes that would grow in their climate and how to take care of them. She ordered the seed and fertilizer that was necessary

---

29. *See Marriage of Johnson*, 28 Wash. App. 574, 578, n. 1, 625 P.2d 720 (1981) ("The rule of contemporaneous segregation was devised to cope with problems of identification arising from the hopeless commingling or confusion of income from separate property, usually an unincorporated business, with income from community labor. In such cases the difficulty lies in ascertaining the extent or proportion to which these sources have produced the resulting income . . . the presumption in favor of the community prevails unless there has been a segregation at the time the income arises.").

to grow the tomatoes. Frank worked on the farming aspect and Fannie helped market the tomatoes to upscale markets. The weather cooperated and their first crop was a success. The next year they increased the acreage devoted to the tomatoes and the farm has had excellent profits and has increased in value. During that time, most of the profits from the tomato crops were plowed back into the farm. They lived very frugally and they had a small income from Fannie's online bookkeeping service. Unfortunately, Fannie no longer wants to live down on the farm and is filing for divorce. She comes to you for advice about whether she has a share in the farm. How will the courts in Civil Rule states determine Fannie's rights? American Rule states?

Table 9-1
Separate Property Businesses in Community Property States

State	Rule	Case/Statute
Arizona	Follows American Rule: rents, issues, and profits of SP are SP. Strong presumption that increase during marriage through efforts of a spouse is CP, spouse claiming increase was due to SP has burden of proof that the increase is the result of inherent value of SP and not product of the effort of the community. Equitable division of CP	*Cockrill v. Cockrill*, 124 Ariz. 50, 601 P.2d 1334 (1979), *Rueschenberg v. Rueschenberg*, 219 Ariz. 249, 196 P.3 852 (Ariz. App. 2008) (equitable apportionment of profits and increase in value)
California	Follows American Rule: rents, issues, and profits of SP are SP. Uses *Pereira/Van Camp* to apportion increase in value between SP owner and community. Mandatory 50/50 division of CP	*Pereira v. Pereira*, 156 Cal. 1, 103 P. 488 (1909), *Van Camp v. Van Camp*, 53 Cal. App. 17, 199 P. 885 (1921), *Gilmore v. Gilmore*, 45 Cal. 2d 142, 287 P.2d 769 (1955), *Beam v. Bank of America*, 6 Cal. 3d, 490 P.2d 257, 98 Cal. Rptr. 137 (1971)
Idaho	Follows Civil Rule: rents, issues, and profits of SP are CP. Community may be reimbursed if the community was not adequately compensated for a spouse's labor devoted to a SP corporation or if the SP corporation unreasonably or fraudulently retained earnings instead of distributing profits as dividends. Equitable division of CP	*Neibaur v. Neibaur*, 142 Idaho 196, 125 P.2d 1072 (2005)
Louisiana	Follows Civil Rule: rents, issues, and profits of SP are CP. Claimant spouse must first prove that community labor of the spouses was expended on SP. If laboring spouse was either	*Louisiana Civil Code* art. 2368, *Krielow v. Krielow*, 635 So. 2d 180 (1994), *Craft v. Craft*, 914 So. 2d 648 (2005)

State	Rule	Case/Statute
	uncompensated or undercompensated, the measure of reimbursement is 1/2 of enhanced value of the separate property. Even if that value exceeds the value of the uncompensated labor, the claimant is entitled to recover the greater amount.	
	If community labor shown, SP owner has burden of showing increase due to ordinary course of things	
	Mandatory 50/50 division of CP	
Nevada	Follows American Rule: rents, issues, and profits of SP are SP	*Johnson v. Johnson*, 510 P.2d 625 (Nev. 1973), *Schulman v. Schulman*, 558 P.2d 525 (Nev. 1976)
	Uses *Pereira/Van Camp* to apportion increase in value between SP and community	
	Equitable division of CP	
New Mexico	Follows American Rule: rents, issues, and profits of SP are SP	*Gillespie v. Gillespie*, 84 N.M. 618, 506 P.2d 775 (1973), *Zemke v. Zemke*, 116 N.M. 114, 860 P.2d 756 (1993)
	Requires a fair apportionment between the return on the separate property that goes to the SP owner and the value of the labor, industry and skill of the spouse which belongs to the community	
	Any increase in SP is presumed to be also separate unless rebutted by direct and positive evidence that the increase was due to community labor	
	Mandatory 50/50 division of CP	
Texas	Follows Civil Rule: rents, issues, and profits of SP are CP	*Vallone v. Vallone*, 644 S.W.2d 455 (Tex. 1983), *Jensen v. Jensen*, 665 S.W.2d 107 (Tex. 1984)
	Right of reimbursement arises when community time, talent and labor are utilized to benefit and enhance a spouse's separate estate without the community receiving adequate compensation	
	Equitable division of CP	
Washington	Follows American Rule: rents, issues, and profits of SP are SP	*Hamlin v. Merlino*, 272 P.2d 125 (1954), *Marriage of Elam*, 97 Wash. 2d 811, 650 P.2d 213 (1982), *Lindemann v. Lindemann*, 92 Wash. App. 64, 960 P.2d 966 (1998)
	If SP is real estate or an unincorporated business where there is community labor, the rule is that all income or increase will be considered as CP in the	

State	*Rule*	*Case/Statute*
	absence of contemporaneous segregation of the income between community and separate estates	
	If stock in a corporation is owned before marriage, salary paid to SP owner is compensation to the community and dividends/increased value are SP	
	Equitable division of property	
Wisconsin	Application of one spouse of substantial labor, effort, inventiveness, physical or intellectual skill, creativity or managerial activity of either spouse's property other than marital property creates marital property attributable to that application if both of the following apply: (1) reasonable compensation is not received and (2) substantial appreciation of the property results from the application.	Wis. Stat. §766.63(2), *Haldemann v. Haldemann*, 145 Wis. 2d 296, 426 N.W.2d 107 (Ct. App. 1988)

Chapter 10

Borrowing Money: Creditors' Rights

This Chapter covers married couples who incur debt before and during marriage. The overriding policy regarding debt in all community property states is that creditors should be paid. There are two different approaches to determining liability for debts incurred by married couples. One approach, followed in Arizona, New Mexico, and Washington, is called the "community debt system." In that system, it is first necessary to determine if a debt is a community debt or a debt is a separate debt of one spouse. That seems logical because then community property is liable only for community debts and separate property of the spouse who incurred the debt would be liable for his or her separate debt. The most common definition of a "community debt" is a debt that is incurred for the benefit of the community. A separate one is a debt that is not incurred for the benefit of the community. Those categories present significant difficulties when trying to determine if a tort committed by one spouse can be for the benefit of the community. It is counterintuitive to think that a spouse who commits a tort would ever do that "for the benefit of the community." However, the tort victim who tries to collect a judgment should be able to reach the community property especially if the tortfeasor has no separate property.

The "managerial system" with some modifications is followed in the other community property states. In those states, liability for debts follows management and control of the community property and does not depend on the purpose of the debt. If a spouse incurs a debt during marriage, the general rule is that the community property is liable for the debt. There are exceptions, for instance for tort liability, where the tortfeasor's separate property may be liable before the community property can be reached.

One important topic is whether the community will be liable for the debt a spouse brings into a marriage. For instance, let us return to our hypothetical couple Michael and Lisa. They are a young couple engaged to be married. Michael accumulated debt when he pursued an advanced degree. Lisa accumulated debt while setting up an interior design business. They know that they will be paying off these debts after they marry. They believe that each should be responsible for paying his or her own debt. They want to check to see if their understanding matches community property law where they live. The answer depends on the approaches of various states. In New Mexico, the community is not liable. In California, the community is liable, but earnings of the other spouse may be shielded from liability. The differing approaches to liability for debts will be considered in detail in this chapter.

A.   THE COMMUNITY DEBT SYSTEM: EXAMPLES FROM ARIZONA AND WASHINGTON

For those entering the legal profession, it soon becomes clear that collecting attorneys' fees is of utmost importance. The following case, *Cardinal & Stachel, P.C. v. Curtiss*, 225 Ariz. 381, 238 P.3d 649 (Ct. App. 2010), illustrates how courts will protect creditors under the community debt system and how the issue of characterizing debt is accomplished in that system.

CARDINAL & STACHEL, P.C. v. CURTISS

225 Ariz. 381, 238 P.3d 649 (2010)
Arizona Court of Appeals

KELLY, Judge.

Appellant Cardinal & Stachel, P.C., ("the law firm") appeals from the trial court's dismissal of its claim against Kieran Curtiss for attorney fees incurred by his wife Leela, who died while their marriage dissolution proceedings were pending. The law firm maintains the court erred in determining the fees were not community debts for which Kieran was liable after his wife's death. We agree and therefore reverse the trial court's judgment.

BACKGROUND

"On review of a trial court's decision granting a motion to dismiss, we assume the truth of the allegations set forth in the complaint. . . ." In May 2008, Leela Curtiss entered into a fee agreement with the law firm "for Representation and Advice Related to: Dissolution of Marriage/Legal Separation; Temporary Orders." Leela died in May 2009 and the dissolution case was dismissed that month.

The law firm brought this action in June 2009, seeking to recover its fees from Kieran, as Leela's widower, and from Leela's estate.[1] Kieran, "in his individual capacity," moved to dismiss the complaint, arguing the law firm had failed to state a claim upon which relief could be granted. *See* Ariz. R. Civ. P. 12(b)(6). Stating it would consider "only the issues of whether the attorney's fees are considered Community Debt and . . . 'necessaries,'" the trial court reasoned the fees were not community debts because they were incurred to destroy the community, granted Kieran's motion, and dismissed the case. This appeal followed.

DISCUSSION

The law firm contends the trial court erred in granting Kieran's motion to dismiss. It maintains that because debts incurred during a marriage are presumed to be

---

1. There is nothing in the record before us pertaining to Leela's estate.

community debts and because the Curtiss's marriage was never dissolved, it is entitled to collect from Kieran the legal fees Leela incurred during the dissolution proceeding. "Generally, we review a trial court's grant of a motion to dismiss for abuse of discretion, but we review issues of statutory interpretation de novo." And, we will "uphold dismissal only if the plaintiffs would not be entitled to relief under any facts susceptible of proof in the statement of the claim."

The transcripts of the proceedings have not been made part of the record on appeal. Generally, in the absence of transcripts, we presume they support the trial court's factual findings and rulings. But, in this case, the trial court made clear in its ruling that it was addressing solely the legal issue of whether attorney fees incurred in a divorce proceeding can be community debt. And, because Kieran moved to dismiss the petition pursuant to Rule 12(b)(6), the trial court could not have considered evidence outside the pleadings without converting the motion to one for summary judgment, which it did not do. *See* Ariz. R. Civ. P. 12. Thus we address this legal question of first impression in this state on its merits.

"Generally, all debts incurred during marriage are presumed to be community obligations unless there is clear and convincing evidence to the contrary." *Schlaefer v. Fin. Mgmt. Serv., Inc.*, 196 Ariz. 336, ¶ 10, 996 P.2d 745, 748 (App. 2000). As exceptions to this general rule, the legislature has set forth several instances in which "joinder of both spouses is required" in order to bind the community. A.R.S. §25-214. Section 25-214 requires such joinder after service of a petition for dissolution of marriage when that petition ends in dissolution, but it does not require joinder for fees incurred before the petition is filed, or for fees incurred when no dissolution ultimately occurs.

Outside of the specific exceptions set forth in §25-214, "[t]he test of whether an obligation is a community debt" is whether the obligation is "'intended to benefit the community.'" A.R.S. §25-215(D) ("Except as prohibited in [A.R.S.] §25-214, either spouse may contract debts and otherwise act for the benefit of the community."). We disagree with the trial court's conclusion that attorney fees incurred during a dissolution proceeding can never be incurred for the benefit of the community and we cannot say these fees are debts in "no way connected with the community and from which the community receives no benefit." *Hamada v. Valley Nat'l Bank*, 27 Ariz. App. 433, 436, 555 P.2d 1121, 1124 (1976). Indeed, although initially counterintuitive in the context of dissolution proceedings, in some cases the community may benefit from the orderly and lawful division of assets, including temporary orders which protect community assets. And, in certain circumstances, the advice of counsel and the entry of temporary orders providing for a spouse's necessary living expenses may, when coupled with mediation or counseling, actually preserve the marriage.

Our legislature has viewed legal representation as sufficiently important to the dissolution process to include it, along with "necessities of life" in the expenditures either party may make from community assets after [the] filing of a petition for dissolution. A.R.S. §25–315(A)(1)(a). Likewise, in discussing whether attorney fees could be awarded to a spouse who was not destitute under A.R.S. §25-324, this court recognized the principle that "*every* spouse . . . owes a duty of support to his or her marital partner," and that duty extends to the payment of dissolution-incurred attorney fees under certain circumstances. *Magee v. Magee*, 206 Ariz. 589, ¶ 14, 81 P.3d 1048, 1051 (App. 2004).

Additionally, we note that in a community where children are present, child custody will be determined in the dissolution proceeding and the best interests of the child must be served in that determination. A.R.S. §25-403. Thus, attorneys for the spouses also play a role in benefiting the children of the community in dissolution. *Cf. Bustos v. Gilroy,* 106 N.M. 808, 751 P.2d 188, 190-91 (N.M. Ct. App. 1988) (although concluding attorney fees not presumptively community debt, finding fees relating to child custody issues community debt in light of statute providing that debts are community unless, inter alia, they do not benefit "spouses or their dependents").

In order to constitute community debt, a debt need not be incurred with the primary intent of benefiting the community. *Hofmann Co. v. Meisner,* 17 Ariz. App. 263, 268, 497 P.2d 83, 88 (App. 1972). Rather "[a]ll that is required is that some benefit was intended for the community." *Id.* Furthermore, no actual pecuniary benefit need be received by the community. *Lorenz-Auxier Fin. Group, Inc. v. Bidewell,* 160 Ariz. 218, 220, 772 P.2d 41, 43 (App. 1989). Thus, the fact that attorney fees may benefit the client spouse more than the community as a whole is not determinative; rather, there need only be some intent to benefit the community. If such intent exists, the attorney fees can be a community debt, despite the fact the proceeding in which they are incurred ultimately will divide the community assets and terminate the community.

As the law firm points out, Kieran has not cited, nor has our review found, "any cases in other community property jurisdictions that *disallow* attorney's fees incurred in dissolution of marriage actions." Although the cases the law firm cites in support of its argument are distinguishable based upon differences in state law, they generally support the proposition that attorney fees incurred in a dissolution action can, under some circumstances, be community debt. As noted above, even though New Mexico courts have rejected the argument that such fees are presumptively community debt, they have characterized fees incurred in relation to child custody matters as community debt. *See Bustos,* 751 P.2d at 190–91. Louisiana provides by statute that these fees are community debt. La. Civ. Code Ann. art. 2362.1 (2009) ("An obligation incurred before the date of a judgment of divorce for attorney fees and costs in an action for divorce and in incidental actions is deemed to be a community obligation."); *Carroll v. Carroll,* 753 So. 2d 395, 395-96 (La. Ct. App. 2000).[5] And, although it was not the primary issue before the court, in *Wileman v. Wade,* the Texas Court of Appeals accepted a trial court's finding that attorney fees incurred by a wife during a dissolution action were community debt. 665 S.W.2d 519, 520 (Tex. App. 1983); *see also Sandone v. Miller-Sandone,* 116 S.W.3d 204, 205, 208 (Tex. App. 2003) (stating "attorney's fees incurred in connection with the divorce are presumptively a community debt" and court "may apportion [them] . . . as part of a just and right division of property."). In sum, other community property states have identified circumstances in which attorney fees incurred in dissolution are community debt.

We agree that attorney fees incurred in dissolution may, in some circumstances, be community debt. But here, the trial court concluded that attorney fees incurred in a dissolution proceeding could never be community debts, as a matter of law.

---

5. Idaho also had such a statutory provision, but it since has been eliminated. *See Bell v. Bell,* 122 Idaho 520, 835 P.2d 1331, 1338 (Idaho Ct. App. 1992).

Thus, on the record before us, the court did not address whether Leela had evinced any intent to benefit the community. Accordingly, on remand the trial court should consider whether Leela intended a benefit to the community and if, therefore, the attorney fees at issue here were community debt. In so doing, the court should disregard Leela's "subjective intent" and consider "only the surrounding circumstances at the time of the transaction . . . in ascertaining h[er] objective intent." *Hofmann*, 17 Ariz. App. at 267, 497 P.2d at 87.

Finally, we note Kieran moved to dismiss "in his individual capacity, and not as the Personal Representative of the Estate of Leela Curtiss." As mentioned earlier, the trial court stated in its ruling that it would address only the legal issue whether the attorney fees were community debt. But, it dismissed the complaint entirely, not just against Kieran in his individual capacity. The law firm does not specifically challenge the dismissal of the complaint against any such estate.[7] *See* Ariz. R. Civ. App. P. 13(a)(6).

<h2 style="text-align:center">DISPOSITION</h2>

The judgment of the trial court, including its award of attorney fees, is reversed as to Kieran Curtiss and the matter is remanded for further proceedings consistent with this decision. The law firm requests an award of its attorney fees and costs incurred in prosecuting this matter on appeal and in the trial court, pursuant to A.R.S. §§12-341 and 12-341.01. "Because the award of fees incurred at trial lies within the discretion of the trial court, we remand for that determination [as well]." On appeal, the law firm is entitled to its costs as the prevailing party, *see* §12–341, and that request is granted upon its compliance with Rule 21, Ariz. R. Civ. App. P. In our discretion, however, we deny its request for attorney fees on appeal.

Concurring: GARYE L. VÁSQUEZ, Presiding Judge and PETER J. ECKERSTROM, Judge.

Discussion Questions

1. What is the definition of a community debt? How can attorneys' fees incurred by one spouse in a dissolution action be considered a community debt?
2. What do you think will be the outcome of this case on remand?

When there is a judgment against one spouse who has committed a tort, the question is whether the community property is liable to pay the judgment. The policy of the creditors being paid is most acute when there is an injured victim who is trying to collect on a judgment. Against that backdrop are the feelings of the spouse who did not commit the tort who may feel that I (as one-half of the community) should not be responsible for paying for the misdeeds of my spouse.

To resolve the question of community liability, courts in a community debt system must find that the debt is "for the benefit of the community." That is a difficulty since it is hard to say that a tort committed by one spouse is ever for the benefit of the community as it seems that a tort committed by one spouse is a detriment to the community. The following case of *Clayton v. Wilson*, 168 Wash. 2d 57, 227 P.3d 278 (2010), addressed that issue in a particularly painful scenario involving sexual abuse of a young boy.

CLAYTON v. WILSON

168 Wash. 2d 57, 227 P.3d 278 (2010)
Supreme Court of Washington

SANDERS, J.

For a number of years Douglas Wilson sexually abused Andrew Clayton, a young boy hired to help with yard work on properties owned by the Wilsons' marital community. Clayton eventually notified police of the abuse, which led to Mr. Wilson's arrest. When Mr. Wilson was released from jail but still awaiting trial, the Wilsons executed a property agreement giving Mary Kay Wilson more than 90 percent of the community assets.

Clayton filed a tort action against the Wilsons. After a bench trial the King County Superior Court found the marital community liable and awarded damages against Mr. Wilson separately, as well as jointly and severally against Ms. Wilson. The court also voided the property transfer after finding it fraudulent. Ms. Wilson appealed and the Court of Appeals affirmed. *Clayton v. Wilson*, 145 Wash. App. 86, 186 P.3d 348 (2008), *review granted*, 165 Wash.2d 1019, 203 P.3d 378 (2009).

We likewise affirm.

FACTS

When Andrew Clayton was eight or nine years old, his family rented a house owned by Douglas and Mary Kay Wilson. The Wilsons hired Clayton to perform yard work around the rental property and other properties owned by the Wilsons. Almost immediately Mr. Wilson began sexually abusing Clayton when he completed the day's work. From the beginning Mr. Wilson linked the abuse to the yard work. Mr. Wilson started giving Clayton clothed back massages under the pretense of relieving sore muscles. Those massages gradually progressed into shirtless back massages, nude full-body massages, genital fondling, masturbation, and oral sex. All told, Mr. Wilson abused Clayton more than 40 times between Clayton's 9th and 15th or 16th year of age. Mr. Wilson did not pay Clayton until that day's sexual abuse was finished. Mr. Wilson used community assets to pay Clayton, his employee and tenant.

When he turned 18, Clayton described the sexual abuse to his mother, who notified police. Police arrested Mr. Wilson on December 5, 2002. Ms. Wilson visited him in jail on December 7, 2002, at which point Mr. Wilson told her he had victimized other boys. On December 11 — two days after Mr. Wilson was released from jail and awaiting charges — the Wilsons met with an attorney to seek marital dissolution and property distribution. The Wilsons knew Clayton and other victims could file lawsuits against them. On December 19 and 20 the Wilsons executed a property settlement agreement transferring $1,639,501, which totaled 90.5 percent of community assets, to Ms. Wilson. The property agreement went into effect upon execution, not upon dissolution of the marriage. Ms. Wilson permitted Mr. Wilson to live at the couple's Seabeck property rent free while awaiting sentencing. The Wilsons dissolved their marriage on March 31, 2003.

In June 2004 Clayton filed suit against the Wilsons. After a bench trial the King County Superior Court awarded Clayton approximately $1.4 million ($1.2 million for emotional distress, $200,000 for future lost wages, $4,024.50 for past medical expenses, and $14,200 for future medical costs). The trial court also found the marital community liable and entered judgment against Mr. Wilson separately and against Ms. Wilson as a jointly and severally liable judgment debtor. The court also enjoined the Wilsons from disposing of any former community property without court approval until an accounting was complete as to Mr. Wilson's separate property.

Additionally the trial court found the Wilsons' property agreement fraudulent on four separate grounds, and voided it. Ms. Wilson appealed to the Court of Appeals, which unanimously affirmed.[1] We granted review to decide (1) whether the Wilsons' marital community is liable for Mr. Wilson's intentional torts, (2) whether the property transfer between the Wilsons is void as fraudulent, and (3) whether Clayton proved future lost wages.

ANALYSIS

Whether a marital community is liable for the intentional tort of one of its members and whether a property transfer is fraudulent are mixed questions of law and fact. We review mixed questions of law and fact de novo. We review conclusions of law under the same de novo standard. The trial court determined Clayton's future lost wages in findings of fact 18-22 (Clerk's Papers (CP) at 848-50). We review findings of fact under a substantial evidence standard, defined as a quantum of evidence sufficient to persuade a rational fair-minded person the premise is true.

MARITAL COMMUNITY LIABILITY

Whether the Wilsons' marital community is liable for Mr. Wilson's intentional torts hinges on whether the sexual abuse occurred in the course of managing community business. In *LaFramboise v. Schmidt*, 42 Wash. 2d 198, 254 P.2d 485 (1953), we held a marital community liable for indecent liberties committed by the husband against a young girl entrusted to the community's care. The parents of six-year-old Beverly LaFramboise left her in the care of Louis and Blanche Schmidt while her parents toured Alaska. The parents paid the Schmidts $35 per week to care for

---

1. The Court of Appeals ordered the trial court to amend conclusion of law 8 to clarify Ms. Wilson "is liable to Andrew [Clayton] to the extent of the former community property," not her separate property. *Clayton*, 145 Wash. App. at 100, 186 P.3d 348.

Beverly. At trial, a jury rendered a verdict against the marital community based on a jury instruction that stated the marital community would be liable if the jury found the indecent liberties occurred "'during the period while said child was in the care and custody of said defendant and of the said community.'" *Id.* at 199, 254 P.2d 485 (quoting jury instructions).

The Schmidts claimed the community could not be liable because Louis committed the act individually and because Louis acted outside the scope of his employment (i.e., no respondeat superior). *Id.* We rejected defendants' claims holding, "the community is not liable for the torts of the husband, *unless* the act constituting the wrong *either* (1) results or is intended to result in a benefit to the community *or* (2) is committed in the prosecution of the business of the community." *Id.* at 200, 254 P.2d 485 (emphasis added). We reasoned because Louis committed the intentional tort while conducting community business, the community bore responsibility. *Id.*

Ms. Wilson claims *deElche v. Jacobsen*, 95 Wash. 2d 237, 622 P.2d 835 (1980), modified our *LaFramboise* two-pronged approach to community liability. In *deElche* a married man raped a woman who was sleeping on a sailboat. The victim sued the husband-rapist and won damages, but the husband-rapist had no separate assets with which to satisfy the judgment. We held where a plaintiff wins a judgment against an insolvent tortfeasor spouse for a separate tort (i.e., not committed during community business), the plaintiff may recover from the tortfeasor's one-half interest in the marital community's personal property. *Id.* at 246, 622 P.2d 835.[2] We embraced the rule in *deElche* to provide courts a clean, reasonable, and fair means of giving plaintiffs relief against insolvent *separate* tortfeasors, instead of condoning the pre-existing practice among lower courts of stretching community liability to apply to situations where it was questionable. *See deElche*, 95 Wash. 2d at 242, 622 P.2d 835. For torts involving management of *community* business, however, we left our *LaFramboise* approach undisturbed. "Torts which can properly be said to be done in the management of community business, or for the benefit of the community, will remain community torts with the community *and* the tortfeasor separately liable." *Id.* at 245, 622 P.2d 835 (emphasis added). As Professor Cross pointed out in his influential article, "the reasoning that there was a community enterprise being conducted [in *LaFramboise*] during which the tort occurred probably leaves the community liability intact." Harry M. Cross, *The Community Property Law (Revised 1985)*, 61 Wash. L. Rev. 13, 139 (1986).

Unfortunately we generated confusion by criticizing *LaFramboise* as a case that found community liability "upon tenuous contacts with the community" and based on "'emotional factors or overtones.'" *deElche*, 95 Wash. 2d at 242, 245, 622 P.2d 835 (quoting *Smith v. Retallick*, 48 Wash. 2d 360, 365, 293 P.2d 745 (1956)). Ms. Wilson claims these criticisms led to "misguided reliance" on *LaFramboise* by the Court of Appeals. Pet. for Review at 10 (emphasis removed).

Even though we decided *LaFramboise* more than a half-century ago — not to mention that we cast stones at it in *deElche* — *LaFramboise*'s approach to community liability remains good law. The *deElche* case altered our approach to liability only for separate torts, not community torts. As Professor Cross stated:

---

2. We later extended *deElche*, 95 Wash. 2d 237, 622 P.2d 835, to include real property. *See Keene v. Edie*, 131 Wash. 2d 822, 935 P.2d 588 (1997).

It appears probable then, that *deElche* stands only for the proposition that a separate tort creditor can reach the tortfeasor spouse's half interest in community personal property and perhaps in community real property, in those situations involving purely personal wrongs having *no conceivable connection* with community property or affairs.

Cross, *supra*, 61 Wash. L. Rev. at 140 (emphasis added). Of the cases in our jurisprudence, *LaFramboise* most closely parallels the facts in the instant matter. It controls here.

The Wilsons' marital community is liable for Mr. Wilson's intentional torts under *LaFramboise*'s second prong. From the beginning Mr. Wilson linked Clayton's sexual abuse with management of community business. We broadly construe *LaFramboise*'s second prong. According to Professor Cross:

> There obviously would be some difficulty in saying that the husband was managing community property at the time or that [child molestation] was intended to benefit the marital community, although the employment to care for the child was so intended. *In this area the concept of "business" is not narrow and the looseness of the test which the cases developed is better identified as requiring that the spouse be engaged in some community errand, affair, or business at the time of the tort to establish community liability.*

Id. at 137 (emphasis added).

Mr. Wilson used yard work as a means to groom the young boy. The abuse always occurred within the context of yard work, which consisted of community business. Mr. Wilson sexually abused Clayton while overseeing him as an employer, supervisor, landlord, and caretaker. The marital community benefited from Clayton's labor. Mr. Wilson paid Clayton for his work with community funds,[3] and only after he finished abusing Clayton on each occasion. Given the breadth of *LaFramboise*'s second prong, these facts point confidently toward community liability because Mr. Wilson's torts occurred while he was on "some community errand, affair, or business at the time of the tort." *Id.* The facts here closely parallel those of *LaFramboise*, in which we assigned liability to the marital community. 42 Wash. 2d at 199-200, 254 P.2d 485.

Ms. Wilson cites opinions that apply respondeat superior to determine whether a marital community bears liability for a spouse's individual tort. Her reference to these cases (including *LaFramboise*) is confounding because their underlying current counsels when an agent or member of a marital community commits an intentional tort connected to the community, the community bears liability.[4] Ms. Wilson even cites one case that finds community liability for an intentional tort arguably less connected to the marital community than the instant facts. *See McHenry v. Short*, 29 Wash. 2d 263, 186 P.2d 900 (1947) (assault committed by husband due to personal grudge, but while evicting victim from community rental property, deemed community liability). The cases cited by Ms. Wilson merely

---

3. Ms. Wilson claims, without any support, that *LaFramboise* is distinguishable because the marital community in that case *received* payment and, here, the marital community *paid* Clayton. There is no reason to make a distinction; both instances clearly involve managing community business.

4. "The basis of the community liability is said to lie in the principle of respondeat superior, even though there is no principal or master in the ordinary sense. While there is greater difficulty in finding an intentional tort than a negligent tort within the ambit of the principle, the tort committed while managing or protecting a community property asset will result in community liability whether the act is negligent or intentional." Cross, *supra*, at 137 (footnote omitted).

examine different facts under the same standard.[5] Other factually divergent cases come to the opposite conclusion and, instead, impose community liability. *See, e.g., Blais v. Phillips*, 7 Wash. App. 815, 502 P.2d 1245 (1972) (community liability for fight that arose in parking lot following a trial concerning management of community property); *Benson v. Bush*, 3 Wash. App. 777, 477 P.2d 929 (1970) (assault committed during dispute involving community dog deemed community liability).

In the end *LaFramboise* presents the closest facts to the instant matter. We applied our reasoning in *LaFramboise* with respondeat superior in mind and found community liability. 42 Wash. 2d at 200, 254 P.2d 485. The aforementioned cases, at best, show inconsistent application of our law and, at worst, undermine Ms. Wilson's position.

Ms. Wilson further contends her former husband's intentional sexual tort brought him outside the scope of community business while sexually abusing Clayton, thus excusing liability of the marital community. She cites numerous cases involving the employer-employee (or master-servant) relationship. *See, e.g., Niece v. Elmview Group Home*, 131 Wash. 2d 39, 929 P.2d 420 (1997) (employer not liable for sexual assault committed by employee); *C.J.C. v. Corp. of Catholic Bishop of Yakima*, 138 Wash. 2d 699, 985 P.2d 262 (1999) (diocese held not liable for actions of pedophile priest); *Bratton v. Calkins*, 73 Wash. App. 492, 870 P.2d 981 (1994) (school district not liable for sexual relationship between teacher-employee and student); *Thompson v. Everett Clinic*, 71 Wash. App. 548, 860 P.2d 1054 (1993) (hospital not liable for molestation committed by doctor-employee); *S.H.C. v. Lu*, 113 Wash. App. 511, 54 P.3d 174 (2002) (religious organization not liable for molestation committed by nonmanagerial guru). However, all are distinguishable because they do not address liability of a marital community. The cases upon which Ms. Wilson erroneously relies stand for the proposition that an *employer* is not liable for the intentional torts of its *employees*—an irrelevant issue here. Ms. Wilson also relies heavily on *Francom v. Costco Wholesale Corp.*, 98 Wash. App. 845, 991 P.2d 1182 (2000). *Francom* held the victim of a nonmanagerial co-worker's sexual harassment could not recover from the harasser's marital community because the tort occurred outside the employee's scope of employment. *Id.* at 869. *Francom*, like the cases above, involved a nonmanagerial employee, not an owner or manager.

A husband or wife would be more properly considered an owner, employer, agent, or member of a marital community, not an employee. As the Court of Appeals noted, a more apt analogy is found in *Glasgow v. Georgia-Pacific Corp.*, 103 Wash. 2d 401, 693 P.2d 708 (1985). In *Glasgow* we found employer liability when an owner, manager, partner, or corporate officer personally participates in workplace harassment. *Id.* at 407, 693 P.2d 708. As a member of his marital community, Mr. Wilson's actions fit *Glasgow* better than the cases cited by Ms. Wilson.

We hold the Wilsons' marital community is liable for Mr. Wilson's intentional torts because he committed them while conducting community business.

---

5. *See, e.g., Bergman v. State*, 187 Wash. 622, 60 P.2d 699 (1936) (community liability not imposed when husband self-destructively burned down community real estate for insurance money. But note, "[a]lthough the court refused community liability because the crime was outside the scope of management, the respondeat superior principle may not be that restrictive anymore, as later cases seem to establish." Cross, *supra*, at 143 n.730); *Smith v. Retallick*, 48 Wash. 2d 360, 293 P.2d 745 (1956) (marital community not liable when husband ceased community activity to begin fistfight with another man for purely personal reasons); *Aichlmayr v. Lynch*, 6 Wash. App. 434, 493 P.2d 1026 (1972) (marital community not liable when husband engaged in criminal conversation and alienation of affection with another man's wife).

PROPERTY TRANSFER

The trial court found four distinct bases for voiding the Wilsons' property transfer: (1) actual fraud under RCW 19.40.041(a)(1), (2) conclusive common law fraud, (3) constructive fraud as to present creditors under RCW 19.40.051(a), and (4) constructive fraud as to present and future creditors under RCW 19.40.041(a)(2).

Ms. Wilson challenges only two of the trial court's four findings of fraud. "If the Supreme Court accepts review of a Court of Appeals decision, the Supreme Court will review only the questions raised in the motion for discretionary review. . . ." RAP 13.7(b); *see also State v. Radcliffe*, 164 Wash. 2d 900, 907, 194 P.3d 250 (2008). In this case the two grounds not raised by Ms. Wilson each independently applies — and independently voids the transfer — even if we were to reverse on the two claimed grounds.

In any event the two grounds claimed by Ms. Wilson do not merit reversal. The trial court properly applied the law to the facts to void the property transfer.

* * *

CONCLUSION

We affirm the Court of Appeals because (1) under *LaFramboise* the Wilsons' marital community is liable for Mr. Wilson's intentional torts, which he committed while managing community business; (2) the property transfer between the Wilsons was void as fraudulent; and (3) Clayton proved future lost wages.

We concur: Chief Justice BARBARA A. MADSEN, Justice SUSAN OWENS, Justice CHARLES W. JOHNSON, Justice MARY E. FAIRHURST, Justice GERRY L. ALEXANDER, Justice JAMES M. JOHNSON, Justice DEBRA L. STEPHENS, and Justice TOM CHAMBERS.

Discussion Questions

1. Why was the community liable for the tort judgment when only Mr. Wilson committed the tort?

2. Why wasn't the Supreme Court more sympathetic to Ms. Wilson's arguments that the community should not be liable?

B.   THE MANAGERIAL SYSTEM: LIABILITY FOR DEBTS PRIOR TO AND DURING MARRIAGE

An example of a community property state that follows the "managerial system" is California. It allows creditors to reach community property without first classifying the debt as community or separate. For instance, in California, Family Code §910(a) states that "the community estate is liable for a debt incurred by either spouse before or during marriage, regardless of which spouse has the management and control of the property and regardless of whether one or both spouses are parties to the debt or to a judgment for the debt." The scope of this statute and its protection of creditors are breathtaking. Either spouse can subject the community property to debt. A spouse can subject the community property to liability for a debt without the other spouse even being a party to the debt. It applies to debts incurred by one spouse before marriage. However, there are exceptions. For instance, it is possible for a spouse to shield his or her earnings from the premarital debt of the other spouse. For instance, in our case of Michael and Lisa, each would not be liable for a premarital debt of the other if their earnings "are held in a deposit account in which the person's spouse has no right of withdrawal and are uncommingled with other property in the community estate, except property insignificant in amount." Cal. Fam. Code §911(a). Similarly, a child or spousal support order from a prior marriage will be treated as a premarital debt and can be shielded as well. Cal. Fam. Code §915(a).

1. Community Property Liability Not Community Debt

Even those states classified as following the "managerial system" sometimes use the terminology of "community debt" but that does not accurately reflect the rights of creditors to reach the community property. The following case, *Twin Falls Bank & Trust Co. v. Holley*, 111 Idaho 349, 723 P.2d 893 (1986), illustrates how the community property might be liable for a debt incurred by one spouse alone.

TWIN FALLS BANK & TRUST CO. v. HOLLEY

111 Idaho 349, 723 P.2d 893 (1986)
Supreme Court of Idaho

BAKES, Justice.

Twin Falls Bank & Trust Company (bank) appeals a decision of the district court granting summary judgment in favor of defendant Joan F. Holley in the bank's action to collect on a debt arising from a promissory note executed by Mrs. Holley's husband prior to their divorce. The bank also appeals the district court's decision awarding attorney fees to defendant Joan Holley. Appellant bank contends that the debt arising from the promissory note is a community obligation and collectable from the community assets which Mrs. Holley received in the divorce settlement.

Respondent Joan F. Holley and her husband John E. Holley were married for a period of 23 years, terminating in divorce on August 28, 1981, in Twin Falls. John Holley operated a construction business (J. Holley Construction) both during the time of marriage and thereafter. During the period of their marriage the construction company was a community asset.

John Holley began borrowing money for his construction business from the bank in December, 1980. He borrowed $25,000 to pay off loans from other banks and for operating expenses of the construction business. In March, 1981, Mr. Holley was granted a general line of credit for the operation of the construction company. By April, 1981, Mr. Holley had borrowed $65,000 on that line of credit. Mr. Holley failed to timely repay the loans on the line of credit; nevertheless, the bank "renewed" the obligations on June 26, 1981. At that time, Mr. Holley signed an *unsecured* promissory note for $125,000. The note consisted of a renewal of the $65,000 previously owed plus an advancement of an additional $60,000. The note called for payment of the principal plus interest on September 28, 1981. The bank issued the note in reliance on a financial statement submitted by Mr. Holley on December 30, 1980. That financial statement showed that Mr. Holley was married to respondent Joan F. Holley, but other than her name and Social Security number the statement provided no information about Joan. Questions regarding Joan's finances were left unanswered, based on the following specific language found on the statement, "Information regarding your spouse need not be revealed unless such spouse will be contractually liable upon the loan or you are relying upon such spouse's income as a basis for the credit request." Mr. Holley alone signed the financial statement.

At the time the $125,000 promissory note was signed, Mr. Holley and his wife were separated and living apart. Like the financial statement, the promissory note was signed by Mr. Holley alone. Following the signing of the June 26, 1981, promissory note, the bank maintained close contact with Mr. Holley and ultimately became aware of his marital problems and that a divorce had been filed.

As part of the divorce decree entered on August 28, 1981, Mr. Holley was awarded the construction business and certain other real and personal property, and he assumed the June 26, 1981, promissory note obligation. Mr. Holley subsequently failed to repay the note when it came due on September 28, 1981. The bank, however, chose not to proceed to collect from Mr. Holley's assets or from any other community assets divided as a result of the divorce decree. Instead, the bank and Holley renegotiated the terms of the note and executed an "extension agreement" on October 9, 1981. The bank agreed to extend the due date on the June 26th promissory note to November 22, 1981, in exchange for a security interest in all of Mr. Holley's real and personal property, including a mortgage on Mr. Holley's commercial property. The deed of trust executed in favor of the bank by Mr. Holley specifically indicated that Mr. Holley was "a divorced man, d/b/a J. Holley Construction Co." Joan Holley was neither informed nor consulted about the extension agreement, nor did she sign the agreement. Additionally, the renegotiated or "renewed" note was based on a financial statement dated October 6, 1981, under the name of John E. Holley. The financial statement specifically lists Mr. Holley as unmarried and the statement recites that the reduction in value of the real estate previously listed in the 1980 financial statement was the result of a property settlement made with Mrs. Holley.

Though solvent at the time the extension agreement was entered into, Mr. Holley eventually defaulted on the renegotiated promissory note. On February 19, 1982, he filed for bankruptcy and was discharged the following year. The bank failed or neglected to either promptly or properly record its deed of trust on Holley's real property and, as a result, the real property securing the promissory note was lost to the trustee in bankruptcy. The bank was, however, successful in taking possession of various equipment prior to the filing of bankruptcy and received some payments from Mr. Holley as a result of the bankruptcy proceedings. However, the bank was left substantially unsatisfied on the $125,000 note with a principal balance still owing of $65,000 and interest due in excess of $50,000. Unable to collect from Mr. Holley, the bank commenced the present action against Joan Holley on January 26, 1984. Apparently, this was the first time Mrs. Holley had any contact with the bank regarding the loan.

The district court found that while normally the bank could look to community property distributed pursuant to a divorce decree to satisfy community obligations, the bank's action in executing the "extension agreement" effectively removed the obligation from any community assets distributed to Joan pursuant to the divorce decree. The district court found that the "extension agreement" was a new agreement between the bank and Mr. Holley and, as such, extinguished the June 26, 1981, promissory note. The court specifically found that the intent of the bank and Mr. Holley in executing the extension agreement was "to rely solely on the assets of John E. Holley and his construction business in satisfaction of the debt." The district court granted summary judgment in favor of Joan, as well as awarding her costs plus $4,500 in attorney fees, based on its finding that the bank's action was without foundation and frivolous (I.R.C.P. 54(e)). We affirm the district court, albeit on different grounds.

I

This case can be resolved based on fundamental principles governing the debtor-creditor relationship. Generally speaking, a creditor must obtain a judgment to collect on a debt whether it is based on contract, tort or other obligations. The exception would be if the obligation was secured by a mortgage or some other form of security interest. Once a creditor obtains a judgment he is able to collect on his debt by execution on the debtor's assets. "These judicial procedures do not change whether dealing with a single or married debtor. The difference is the type of property that is subject to execution or attachment for the debt involved." J. Henderson, Creditors Rights under a Community Property System, Idaho Law Foundation, *Idaho Community Property Law*, §9.4 (1983). Under the facts of this case, a debtor-creditor relationship existed only between the bank and respondent's ex-husband John Holley. The debt evidenced by the June 26, 1981, promissory note was incurred by John Holley for the benefit of the marital community. However, respondent Joan Holley, not having signed the note, was not contractually liable for the debt evidenced by the promissory note; only John Holley signed and is liable for the note.

The bank contends that since the debt incurred by John Holley was for the benefit of the community it is properly characterized as a "community debt." The phrase "community debt" is correct terminology insofar as it is used to signify a debt incurred for the benefit of the marital community. However, to the extent the phrase is used to imply the existence of a "community debtor," the phrase is imprecise and misleading. The marital community is not a legal entity such as a business partnership or corporation. *de Elche v. Jacobsen*, 95 Wash. 2d 237, 622 P.2d 835, 838 (1980); *Bortle v. Osborne*, 155 Wash. 2d 585, 285 P. 425 (1930); 15A Am. Jur. 2d, *Community Property*, §5 (1976). While one may properly speak of a "corporate debtor," there is no such entity as a "community debtor." *See Williams v. Paxton*,

98 Idaho 155, 559 P.2d 1123 (1977); J. Henderson, Creditors Rights under a Community Property System, *supra*. To the extent a lending institution enters into a creditor-debtor relationship with either member of the marital community or with both members, it does so on a purely individual basis. Thus, the lending institution may have a creditor-debtor relationship with either spouse separately or with both jointly. As stated earlier, the community property system does not affect the fundamental principles governing such a relationship and the procedures required of a creditor in order to collect upon his debt. Rather, the community property system merely affects the type or kinds of property to which the creditor may look for satisfaction of his unpaid debt. J. Henderson, Creditors Rights Under a Community Property System, *supra*. Essentially, the community property system merely makes additional resources (community property) available to a creditor from which to seek satisfaction of unpaid debt. Thus, under the community property system in Idaho and I.C. §32-912,[1] which has established a rule of co-equal management of community assets or property, when either member of the community incurs a debt for the benefit of the community, the property held by the marital community becomes liable for such a debt and the creditor may seek satisfaction of his unpaid debt from such property. *Simplot v. Simplot*, 96 Idaho 239, 526 P.2d 844 (1974); W. deFuniak & M. Vaughn, Principles of Community Property, §159 (2d ed. 1971).

The debt upon which the bank is asserting this claim against Mrs. Holley was evidenced by the promissory note executed solely by Mr. Holley on June 26, 1981, which had renewed an earlier note. At that time the bank had a claim against Mr. Holley which it could satisfy by judgment and execution against either Mr. Holley and any separate property which he may have had, or against the community property of Mr. and Mrs. Holley. Mr. and Mrs. Holley were subsequently divorced and the community property was equitably divided between them and became the separate property of each. When the June 26, 1981, note became due in September of 1981, the bank could have immediately proceeded to judgment against John Holley and levied against the property of John Holley, including any community property which was distributed to John Holley. If that community property distributed to John Holley was insufficient to satisfy the obligation, the bank could have proceeded by execution against the community property which had been awarded to Mrs. Holley and which was now her separate property, as hereinafter discussed. However, the bank chose not to do this. Rather, when the note became due in September, 1981, the bank extended the note and additionally took a security interest in property held by John Holley. Mr. Holley subsequently defaulted on the extension agreement and later filed for bankruptcy. The bank was successful in taking possession of several pieces of property under its security

---

1. "32-912. Control of community property. Either the husband or the wife shall have the right to manage and control the community property, and either may bind the community property by contract, except that neither the husband nor wife may sell, convey or encumber the community real estate unless the other joins in executing and acknowledging the deed or other instrument of conveyance, by which the real estate is sold, conveyed or encumbered, and any community obligation incurred by either the husband or the wife without the consent in writing of the other shall not obligate the separate property of the spouse who did not so consent; provided, however, that the husband or wife may by express power of attorney give to the other the complete power to sell, convey or encumber community property, either real or personal. All deeds, conveyances, bills of sale, or evidences of debt heretofore made in conformity herewith are hereby validated."

agreement with Mr. Holley. However, the bank failed to perfect its security interest in real property held by Mr. Holley, losing it to the bankruptcy trustee. In short, the bank's inability to obtain satisfaction for its unpaid obligation was in large part attributable to the bank's failure to perfect its security interest in real property held by John Holley. After bankruptcy and Mr. Holley's discharge from the obligation to the bank, when the bank had not received sufficient satisfaction from Mr. Holley's assets to satisfy his obligation to the bank, this proceeding was brought against Mrs. Holley. However, Mrs. Holley had not signed the June 26, 1981, note and thus was not personally liable for that obligation. *See Williams v. Paxton*, 98 Idaho 155, 559 P.2d 1123 (1977).

Absent allegations of such contractual liability, a creditor may not, with one exception, proceed against community assets distributed to Mrs. Holley pursuant to a divorce decree. The sole exception to this rule was set forth in our case of *Spokane Merchants Ass'n v. Olmstead*, 80 Idaho 166, 327 P.2d 385 (1958). In that case we held that where, pursuant to divorce proceedings, one member of the marital community is responsible for a community obligation but is not awarded sufficient community assets to satisfy such a debt, a creditor may properly seek satisfaction for the debt from community property distributed to the other spouse. Essentially, the holding of *Spokane Merchants Ass'n v. Olmstead, supra,* is that members of the marital community may not utilize divorce proceedings to perpetrate a fraud on creditors of the community. In order for the bank in the present case to avail itself of the exception set forth by the *Olmstead* case, it must allege and prove that Mr. Holley was not awarded sufficient community assets which would enable him to satisfy the community debt which he assumed pursuant to the property settlement agreement. This the bank has failed to do in the present case. Indeed, the bank does not even allege facts to bring it within the *Olmstead* exception. Instead, the record indicates that sufficient assets were distributed to Mr. Holley as part of the divorce proceedings which would have enabled him to satisfy the community obligation which he assumed pursuant to the property settlement agreement.

We conclude that the bank was without any basis in law or fact to sue Joan Holley or otherwise execute on former community property now in her possession. Because of our disposition of this issue, we need not reach the issue upon which the district court relied in awarding summary judgment to respondent, namely, that the extension agreement constituted a new agreement between the bank and John Holley, effectively extinguishing the June 26, 1981, promissory note.

II

On appeal, the bank additionally contends that it was error for the district court to award attorney fees to respondent Joan Holley. We disagree. In its order awarding attorney fees, the district court specifically found that the bank's actions were without foundation and, as we have discussed in the preceding section, we agree. The award of attorney fees is a matter committed to the sound discretion of the trial court and will not be overturned on appeal absent a showing of abuse of discretion. We find no such abuse of discretion in the present case and affirm the district court's order awarding attorney fees.

The order of the district court awarding summary judgment and attorney fees to respondent is affirmed. On appeal, costs and attorney fees to respondent.

DONALDSON, C.J., and BISTLINE and HUNTLEY, JJ., concur.
SHEPARD, J., concurs in result.

Discussion Questions

1. According to the Supreme Court, what is "imprecise and misleading" about the phrase "community debt?"
2. Why did the Bank fail in its attempt to reach the Holleys' community property?

2.   Liability for Premarital Debts

In California's statutory scheme, community property is liable for premarital debts. The following two cases, one from Idaho which is a managerial state, and one from New Mexico which is a community debt state, illustrate differing views toward premarital debt.

ACTION COLLECTION SERVICE, INC. v. SEELE

138 Idaho 753, 69 P.3d 173 (2003)
Court of Appeals of Idaho

PERRY, Judge.

Shelly L. Seele appeals from the district court's intermediate appellate decision affirming the magistrate's denial of her motion to vacate and set aside a judgment and to quash a continuing garnishment of her wages. We affirm.

I.   FACTS AND PROCEDURE

On March 12, 1992, Action Collection Service, Inc. filed a complaint against Seele and her former husband seeking monetary judgment on a number of uncollected debts that had been incurred by Seele and her husband during their marriage and which were assigned to Action by various creditors.[1] On May 5, an answer was filed bearing the typewritten signature of Shelly L. Calkins. Action thereafter moved for and was granted summary judgment after a hearing at which Seele failed to appear. A judgment was entered in favor of Action in the amount of $1,957.46. Action subsequently attempted to locate Seele in order to collect on the judgment but was unsuccessful. Five years later, on June 18, 1997, Action filed a motion to renew the judgment, which was granted. After the judgment had been renewed,

---

1. Seele's former husband was not a party to the underlying proceedings and is not a party to the present appeal.

Action located Seele and sent her several notices in an attempt to collect on the judgment to no avail.

In the early part of 2000, Action sought to enforce its judgment by garnishing Seele's wages. Seele, who had remarried since entry of the judgment, presented a claim of exemption. Action thereafter filed a motion to contest Seele's claim of exemption, and Seele filed a motion to vacate and set aside the judgment and to quash the continuing garnishment of her wages. On June 8, the magistrate denied Seele's motion and granted Action's motion to contest Seele's claim of exemption. Seele appealed and the district court affirmed. The district court also awarded costs and attorney fees to Action. Seele now appeals to this Court, asserting that: (1) the original judgment is void because the magistrate did not have personal jurisdiction over her; (2) her motion to vacate and set aside the judgment was timely; (3) the magistrate erred by concluding that her wages could be garnished to satisfy Action's judgment, which consisted of her separate, antenuptial debt; (4) Action unlawfully brought the underlying action against her; (5) her right to due process has been violated; and (5) the award of attorney fees to Action on the intermediate appeal was improper.

. . .

III.   Analysis

A.   Motion for Relief from Judgment Under I.R.C.P. 60(b)

1. *Validity of the judgment*

* * *

Accordingly, we conclude that the magistrate had personal jurisdiction over Seele at the time the judgment was entered and, therefore, Seele has failed to establish that the judgment is void. We further conclude that no violation of Seele's right to due process has been shown. Because of our resolution of this issue, it becomes unnecessary for us to address Seele's alternative contention that she did not voluntarily appear before the magistrate by virtue of the answer filed bearing only her typewritten signature. We also need not address Seele's second contention on appeal concerning the timeliness of her motion to set aside the judgment pursuant to Rule 60(b)(4).

* * *

B.   Motion to Quash Garnishment of Wages

In its order denying Seele's motion to vacate and set aside the judgment and quash the continuing garnishment of her wages, the magistrate found that although Seele's wages were community property relative to her remarriage, they were not exempt from execution upon Action's judgment. On appeal, Seele argues that the magistrate erred by concluding that her wages could be used to satisfy Action's judgment because the judgment constituted her separate antenuptial debt.

All property of either a husband or a wife owned before marriage, and that acquired afterward either by gift, bequest, devise or descent, or that which either acquires with the proceeds of his or her separate property, remains his or her sole and separate property. I.C. §32–903. All other property acquired after marriage by either the husband or the wife, including his or her salary, is community property. I.C. §32-906; *see Martsch v. Martsch,* 103 Idaho 142, 147, 645 P.2d 882, 887 (1982). The statutes dealing with Idaho's community property system do not directly address the question we are asked to decide. Idaho Code Section 32–910 provides that the separate property of the husband is not liable for the debts of the wife contracted before the marriage. Section 32-911 provides that the separate property of the wife is not liable for the debts of her husband, but is liable for her own debts contracted before or after marriage. However, these statutes provide minimal guidance for the issue presented by Seele because they concern the liability of the separate property of the spouses for debts incurred by the husband or the wife. Conversely, the issue we face here concerns the liability of one spouse's community property upon remarriage for the separate antenuptial debts of that spouse.

Likewise, few Idaho cases have dealt with this particular issue. In *Holt v. Empey,* 32 Idaho 106, 178 P. 703 (1919), the real property of Empey's husband was attached by Holt to satisfy a debt that the husband had incurred as a surety for a third party. Empey intervened in the action, alleging that the property attached was community property and not subject to levy for the separate debt of her husband. The Idaho Supreme Court disagreed, holding that the community property was liable for the separate debts, obligations, and liabilities of the husband and that the community real estate was liable to attachment and execution for the debts of the husband, whether incurred for his own use or for the benefit of the community. It is unclear from the Court's opinion whether the husband's debt was incurred before or during the marriage but, presumably, the community property was liable regardless of whether the debt was antenuptial or postnuptial. *See* JOANN HENDERSON, IDAHO LAW FOUNDATION, COMMUNITY PROPERTY LAW OF IDAHO ch. 9, at 15 (1982).

In *Gustin v. Byam,* 31 Idaho 538, 240 P. 600 (1925), Gustin and her husband lived on land owned by Gustin's father under an arrangement whereby the husband was to farm the land during the year and give one-half of the crops to the father for use of the land. During the marriage, the husband gave a note to his brother secured by a chattel mortgage covering the whole of the crops, including the share of Gustin's father. At the father's insistence, the mortgage was subsequently released by the brother. At around the same time, the brother indorsed the note to a hardware company, which then brought suit to collect on the note. A default judgment was obtained, and the husband's share of the crops was levied upon and sold in order to satisfy the judgment. Gustin filed an action seeking to set aside the judgment and to recover the value of the crops, claiming that the crops were community property and exempt from execution. On appeal from a judgment entered in favor of the defendants, the Idaho Supreme Court noted that at that time, I.C. §32-912 gave the husband the management and control of the community property, with full power of alienation except as provided in the statute. Among the powers the husband could exercise alone was the sale of community personal property, whether it was exempt from execution or not. Relying on the holding in *Holt,* the Court held that the community property was liable for the separate debts of the husband as well as for community debts. The Court held that in order to defeat the threatened alienation of the community personal property, Gustin was required to prove that her husband's alienation of the community property was done for the sole purpose of depriving her of her rights in the community property, which she failed to do. Consequently, Gustin was unable to recover the property sold.

Both *Holt* and *Gustin* were decided at a time when the husband was given sole power to manage and control the community property by statute. In 1974, the legislature amended I.C. §32-912, giving the husband and the wife equal management and control of the community property. *See* 1974 Idaho Sess. Laws ch. 194, §2. Despite the change in the management and control of the community property and in spite of any doubt concerning the continued vitality of *Holt* and *Gustin*, those cases were cited with approval by our Supreme Court in *Bliss v. Bliss*, 127 Idaho 170, 898 P.2d 1081 (1995). In that case, the Court recognized that parties often marry with separate antenuptial debts. Citing *Holt* and *Gustin*, the Court observed in dicta that the separate antenuptial debts of a husband or wife are payable from community property.

Although the Court in *Bliss* was not presented with the situation facing us in this case, where a judgment creditor is attempting to garnish one spouse's community property wages to satisfy that spouse's separate antenuptial debt, the Court's holding was not limited to the facts of that case and we perceive no reason to do so. To prevent Action from levying against Seele's wages to collect on its judgment and allow Seele to avoid her responsibility for the debts encompassed by Action's judgment would result in marital bankruptcy, particularly if Seele has insufficient separate property to satisfy the judgment. Hence, although Seele argues to the contrary, she remains responsible for the unpaid debts constituting Action's judgment and her community property wages should not be placed beyond Action's reach to satisfy its judgment.

Further, we must assume that when I.C. §32-912 was amended in 1974, the legislature had full knowledge of the existing judicial decisions construing that statute's meaning. *See Ultrawall, Inc., v. Washington Mutual Bank,* 135 Idaho 832, 836, 25 P.3d 855, 859 (2001). The elevation of the status of wives to equal managers of the community property by virtue of the amendment, without a specific exemption of the liability of the community property for each spouse's separate debts, suggests that the legislature intended for the rules of law enunciated in *Holt* and *Gustin* to apply equally to the husband and the wife after amendment of the statute. Therefore, just as the community property in those cases was liable for the separate debts of the husband, whether antenuptial or postnuptial, so are Seele's community property wages liable to satisfy Action's judgment. For these reasons, we conclude that Action was entitled to garnish Seele's community property wages in order to collect on its judgment against her and that the magistrate did not err by denying Seele's motion to quash continuing garnishment of her wages.[3]

* * *

3. Seele relies on *Twin Falls Bank & Trust Co. v. Holley*, 111 Idaho 349, 723 P.2d 893 (1986), to support her argument that Action cannot garnish her community property wages. That case is inapposite to the case at bar, however. In that case, the promissory note to the bank was signed only by the husband and, therefore, the husband alone was contractually liable for the debt. Here, Seele does not dispute that she was contractually liable for the debts encompassed by Action's judgment. In addition, the issue in *Holley* was whether the bank could reach former community property awarded to the wife during the parties'

IV. CONCLUSION

We conclude that Seele was served with the summons and complaint in the proceedings brought by Action against her. Therefore, we hold that the magistrate had personal jurisdiction over Seele at the time the judgment against her was entered and that Seele has failed to demonstrate that Action's judgment is void. Due to our resolution of this issue, we need not address Seele's alternative contention that she did not voluntarily appear before the magistrate by virtue of the answer filed bearing only her typewritten signature. It is also unnecessary to consider Seele's second contention on appeal concerning the timeliness of her motion to vacate and set aside the judgment pursuant to I.R.C.P. 60(b)(4). We also do not address the merits of Seele's defense to Action's motion for summary judgment and the ensuing entry of the judgment against her because that issue is not properly before us. We further conclude that Action is entitled to garnish Seele's community property wages in order to satisfy its judgment against her. Therefore, we hold that the magistrate did not err by denying Seele's motion to quash continuing garnishment of her wages.

Because there was no determination of Action's entitlement to attorney fees in the district court's intermediate appellate decision, it was not until Action petitioned for rehearing on the issue of attorney fees and the district court issued its order awarding attorney fees to Action that the fourteen-day time limit contained in I.A.R. 40 became applicable. Seele has not claimed that Action failed to timely file a memorandum of costs and attorney fees after entry of that order. Accordingly, there was no error in the district court's award of costs and attorney fees to Action on the intermediate appeal.

Finally, we award costs and attorney fees to Action on the present appeal pursuant to I.C. §12-120(1) and (5). The order of the district court affirming the magistrate's order denying Seele's motion to set aside the judgment and quash the continuing garnishment of her wages is affirmed.

Chief Judge LANSING and Judge GUTIERREZ concur.

Discussion Questions

1. What does the Court of Appeals mean when it refers to Seele's "separate antenuptial debt"?
2. How did Action get Seele's attention? Did she succeed in fighting the creditor?

garnishing her wages   no

---

divorce to satisfy the husband's unsecured debt. In this case, Action is not seeking to collect on former community property awarded to Seele. Rather, Action is attempting to garnish Seele's wages which are the community property of Seele and her new husband.

WIGGINS v. RUSH

83 N.M. 133, 489 P.2d 641 (1971)
Supreme Court of New Mexico

MONTOYA, Justice.

This is a suit wherein the plaintiff-appellee Walt Wiggins, hereinafter called "Mr. Wiggins," in an action for a declaratory judgment, filed a complaint against his wife Roynel F. Wiggins, hereinafter called "Mrs. Wiggins," Wilfred E. Rush, hereinafter called "Mr. Rush," and others, the latter being the grantors of three deeds to certain property wherein Mr. and Mrs. Wiggins were the grantees. Mr. Wiggins alleged the property was his sole and separate property. Appellant Mr. Rush was the only answering defendant in the case and he contends that the property in question was held either in joint tenancy or as community property, and that the transcript of the judgment filed by him, which had been obtained in a case for an antenuptial debt of Mrs. Wiggins, was a valid lien against the property described in the complaint.

In summary, the following are the pertinent findings made by the trial court. Prior to her marriage to Mr. Wiggins in April 1963, Mrs. Wiggins had signed and delivered to Mr. Rush her promissory note for $35,000 dated September 1, 1962. At the time of her marriage, Mrs. Wiggins owned separate property in Texas and Arizona.

* * *

The deed from Stephens conveyed that land to Mr. and Mrs. Wiggins as joint tenants. During their marriage, Mr. and Mrs. Wiggins acquired title to two other tracts of land in Lincoln County, New Mexico, and title was conveyed to them as joint tenants. When the properties in Kansas and Texas were purchased, both Mr. and Mrs. Wiggins executed notes and mortgages to secure the purchase price. In acquiring the Arkansas property, both Mr. and Mrs. Wiggins assumed the encumbrances on the property.

During their marriage, Mr. and Mrs. Wiggins had joint bank accounts, or other accounts on which Mrs. Wiggins was authorized to sign checks. No effort was made by them to separate their properties or moneys during their marriage. They commingled their property and income and no effort was made to segregate income acquired from separate property. Substantial mortgage payments from joint accounts were made by Mr. Wiggins from his earnings upon the property acquired during the marriage. The court also found that they never intended to take title to their properties in joint tenancy, and that Mr. Wiggins never intended to give his wife an undivided one-half interest in the properties. The court further found that the properties involved in this action were acquired through the joint efforts of both Mr. and Mrs. Wiggins and were community property.

Mr. Rush obtained a judgment against Mrs. Wiggins in the Sierra County District Court, based upon the $35,000 promissory note, and filed a transcript of said judgment in Chaves County. In another case filed in Chaves County, a decree was obtained foreclosing the Sierra County judgment lien against the undividual interest of property conveyed to Mr. and Mrs. Wiggins by Stephens et ux., but no adjudication was made as to the character and extent of such interest because Mr. Wiggins was not a party to such action.

The trial court concluded that Mr. and Mrs. Wiggins did not intend to take the properties as joint tenants; that the evidence was clear and convincing the properties in question were acquired through their joint efforts; and that the properties in question were community property.

The trial court also concluded that the community property of Mr. and Mrs. Wiggins was not liable for the antenuptial debts of Mrs. Wiggins. Therefore, the judgments in cause No. 35085 of the District Court of Chaves County, and cause No. 7076 in Sierra County and recorded also in Chaves County, did not constitute effective liens to the properties described in Mr. Wiggins' complaint.

Appellant Mr. Rush relies upon two points in seeking reversal of the trial court's decision. One contention is that there was no evidence to overcome the statutory presumption of joint tenancy, and the trial court's finding, that the property of Mr. and Mrs. Wiggins was community property, was not supported by substantial evidence. The other contention advanced by appellant is that, even if the property is community property, it would be liable for the antenuptial debts of Mrs. Wiggins.

* * *

Because it was not the intention of Mr. and Mrs. Wiggins to hold the property as joint tenants, and because community funds were used to purchase the property, the trial court concluded that a joint tenancy was not created. This conclusion, being supported by evidence of a clear and convincing nature, should be upheld.

* * *

Having held that the property in question was community property, the next question is whether the interest of Mrs. Wiggins in the community property is liable for her antenuptial debts.

There are several statutory provisions governing the community estate. See, §§57-3-8, 57-3-9, 57-4-2, 57-4-3, 29-1-8, N.M.S.A., 1953 Comp., and §29-1-9, N.M.S.A., 1953 Comp. (1969 Pocket Supp.), but none of these sections deal with the precise question of whether the community is liable for antenuptial debts of either spouse. This court has held the wife's separate property was not liable for community debts, *E. Rosenwald & Son v. Baca et al.,* 28 N.M. 276, 210 P. 1068 (1922), but we have not decided whether the community would be liable for a spouse's antenuptial debt.

There is no unanimity among the courts as to how this question should be resolved. The California court has held that the separate property of the wife and the community estate were equally liable for the debts of the wife contracted before marriage. *Van Maren v. Johnson,* 15 Cal. 308 (1860). Texas also reached the same result, however the holding in the Texas case may be modified by reason of subsequently enacted statutes. *Dunlap v. Squires,* 186 S.W. 843 (Tex. Civ. App. 1916).

In Washington, the court held that community property would not be liable for the antenuptial debt of one of the spouses. *Escrow Service Co. v. Cressler,* 59 Wash. 2d 38, 365 P.2d 760 (1961). That decision apparently was based upon a statute lending itself to that interpretation. See, R.C.W. 26.16.200. The Arizona court also has determined that the community estate would not be liable for the antenuptial debts of one spouse. *Forsythe v. Paschal,* 34 Ariz. 380, 271 P. 865 (1928), see discussion of case infra.

This being a question of first impression in this jurisdiction, counsel for appellant urges this court to apply common law principles to the instant case, because of the 1876 statute declaring the common law shall be the rule of practice and decision in New Mexico. Counsel argues that the application of common law principles would result in a finding that the husband is liable for the debts of his wife contracted dum sola. See, *Van Maren v. Johnson*, supra.

Appellant further contends that New Mexico's community property statutes were, in large part, adopted from the California statutes then in effect. He cites the general rule to-wit: The adoption of the statutes from another state includes prior construction of those statutes by the courts of that state. Appellant, therefore, urges us to follow the California decision holding that the community property of the wife is liable for her antenuptial debts. That argument was disposed of by this court in *McDonald v. Senn*, 53 N.M. 198 at 205, 204 P.2d 990 at 993-994, 10 A.L.R.2d 966 at 971 (1949), as follows:

> It is true, the New Mexico community property laws were largely an adoption of the California statutes. But this court has never followed the decisions of the California courts with respect to the interests of the spouses in community property; nor have the courts of any other state done so. This conflict of decisions goes back to an early date.

This court has held that common law principles, which are applicable to our conditions and circumstances, are the rule of practice and decision in New Mexico. *Browning v. Estate of Browning*, 3 N.M. (Gild), 659, 9 P. 677 (1886). We have also held that, when dealing with community property concepts, it is necessary to look to the Spanish-Mexican law for definitions and interpretations concerning the community estate. *Beals v. Ares*, 25 N.M. 459, 185 P. 780 (1919). In addition, this court stated in *McDonald v. Senn*, 53 N.M. at 213, 204 P.2d at 999, 10 A.L.R.2d at 977:

> The state's public policy on the subject of community property is expressed in the statutes, interpreted in the light of the Spanish-Mexican law. . . .

It appears the community property concept is unique and not part of the common law of New Mexico. We must, therefore, reject appellant's contention that common law principles apply and look instead to the Spanish-Mexican law.

The Supreme Court of Louisiana, in *Fazzio v. Krieger*, 226 La. 511 at 516-517, 76 So. 2d 713 at 715 (1954), pointed out:

> . . . Research into the Spanish law of community property reveals that since the year 1255 A.D. the Spanish law has contained the provision that an antenuptial debt of one spouse is the liability of his separate property alone. . . .

We are in complete accord with the Louisiana court in the interpretation of the Spanish law on this subject.

Mr. William Q. deFuniak, in his authoritative treatise, Principles of Community Property, Vol. I, §158 at 442, is critical of court decisions holding the community estate liable for the antenuptial debts of one of the spouses, and states:

> The conclusion regrettably reached from the foregoing is that in none of the states discussed is there any clear understanding of the true principles applicable so far as community property is concerned. But another view exists in some of the community property states which seems to represent a more correct understanding and proper application of the law. This view denies any liability of the community property for antenuptial debts and

obligations of the spouses. In justification of this view it is pointed out that the proper maintenance and protection of the family would be endangered if the community estate and earnings could be diverted from its purpose of insuring such maintenance and protection, in order to satisfy debts in no way connected with the family. . . .

We believe the view expressed by Mr. deFuniak is the better rule.

A close examination of *Forsythe v. Paschal*, supra, is warranted because the facts of that case closely parallel the instant case and call for an application of the above cited rule. In Forsythe, the Arizona court faced the question of whether the community property was liable for the separate debts of either spouse contracted before marriage. As in New Mexico, Arizona had statutes governing community property, but those statutes were silent on the question of liability of the community for the antenuptial debts of either spouse. See, R.S.A.1913, Civil Code, 3853 and 3854. Like New Mexico, Arizona also and a statute adopting the common law as the rule of decision in all courts of that state. Laws of Arizona 1907, Ch. 10, §8; see also, *Hageman v. Vanderdoes*, 15 Ariz. 312, 138 P. 1053 (1914).

Two contentions raised in Forsythe v. Paschal, supra, were argued in the instant case. First, that it was the rule in certain other community property states, notably California and Texas, that the community property was liable for the antenuptial debts of either spouse. Secondly, that the maxim of "expressio unius est exclusio alterius" should be applied to the statutes governing community property. It was argued that, since the legislature expressly stated the separate property of either spouse should not be liable for the antenuptial debts of the other and did not expressly exempt the community estate from liability for such debts, the maxim of "expressio unius" implied that the community would be liable for antenuptial debts.

The Arizona court disposed of the first contention by citing its former decisions holding that the nature of the community property estate was based upon a different theory than Texas and California. Consequently, decisions of those states were not controlling in Arizona. In dealing with the contention that the maxim of "expressio unius" applied, the court reasoned that, though the maxim was true as a general principle, when the public policy of the state was vitally affected the maxim would not be applied to contradict it.

The State of New Mexico has a vital interest in the marital status. This interest is clearly expressed in our statutory framework concerning the marital status, including its creation, dissolution, and the methods by which the parties to the marriage can hold property. It is this vital state interest in the marital status that distinguishes the marriage relationship from other contractual relationships. For a creditor of one of the spouses to be allowed to collect his debt from the community estate would materially affect the property of the family unit, and could ultimately undermine the marital relationship. As the Arizona court stated in *Forsythe v. Paschal*, 34 Ariz. at 386, 271 P. at 867:

> . . . There are few things which would do more to destroy the solidarity of family life and the proper maintenance of the children of the marriage than the possibility that the community estate and earnings primarily intended by the state for this protection could be diverted from that purpose to satisfy debts in no way connected with the family. . . .

This court is in full accord with the Arizona court on this point. New Mexico's interest in the protection of the family relationship, as expressed in our statutes, indicates that the state deems itself an interested party when the community estate and the marriage itself are affected. If the legislature had intended that the community property of the marriage should be subjected to the antenuptial debts of either spouse, it would so state. This it has not done.

For this court to hold that the community estate of Mr. and Mrs. Wiggins is liable for the antenuptial debt of Mrs. Wiggins would be against the public policy of New Mexico.

The decision of the trial court is affirmed.

It is so ordered.

COMPTON, C.J., and McMANUS, J., concur.

Discussion Questions

1. Why did the Supreme Court hold that community property is not liable for the antenuptial debts of Mrs. Wiggins?
2. Most of the cases relied on in *Wiggins* date back to the early part of the 19th and 20th century. Does the reasoning of *Wiggins* and those cases still hold today?

C.   CONTRACTING OUT OF DEBT BY PREMARITAL AGREEMENT

A premarital agreement can specify that the spouses' earnings are separate property and also that debts incurred by each spouse prior to and during marriage are the sole responsibility of the spouse who incurs the debt. The question raised by the following case, *Schlaefer v. Financial Management Service, Inc.*, 196 Ariz. 336, 996 P.2d 745 (2000), is whether that type of premarital agreement will bind a creditor of one of the spouses.

SCHLAEFER v. FINANCIAL MANAGEMENT SERVICE, INC.
196 Ariz. 336, 996 P.2d 745 (2000)
Arizona Court of Appeals

GERBER, Judge.

The trial court found Christopher M. Schlaefer ("Schlaefer") liable for a debt incurred by his former wife during their marriage. It entered summary judgment in favor of the creditor, Financial Management Service, Inc. ("FMS"). Schlaefer now appeals from the judgment and the award of attorneys' fees to FMS. For the reasons stated below, we must reverse and remand.

Factual and Procedural Background

Schlaefer and his former wife, Shelley, were married in 1994. They entered into a premarital agreement prior to their marriage, which provided, in part, that each spouse's earnings during marriage would remain the separate property[1] of each spouse and that any interest in any property would also remain the separate property of the acquiring spouse. The agreement also provided:

> Any debts of Bride incurred prior to or during marriage, except debts for joint obligations incurred after the effective date of this Agreement, shall be the sole responsibility of Bride and her separate property, including debts for separate property secured by loans requiring signatures of both parties.

During the marriage, Shelley incurred a debt for medical care at Columbia Paradise Valley Hospital. Schlaefer did not sign any of the paperwork regarding Shelley's medical care nor did he ever sign any agreement for payment. After Schlaefer and Shelley divorced, FMS sought to collect from him the debt for Shelley's medical care.

Schlaefer filed a motion for summary judgment in which he argued that he was not liable for Shelley's medical debt under the premarital agreement. FMS filed a cross motion for summary judgment in which it claimed that the debt was community and, further, that it was bound neither by the premarital agreement nor by the divorce decree's designation of the debt as separate. The trial court found the premarital agreement unconscionable because, in its view, the agreement purported to "sign away each other's debts." It concluded that "there is no question" but that the debt was community and that FMS was entitled to judgment against Schlaefer. It subsequently granted FMS's request for attorneys' fees and costs in the amount of $1331.

Schlaefer timely appeals from the judgment and award of attorneys' fees. We have jurisdiction pursuant to Arizona Revised Statutes Annotated ("A.R.S.") section 12-2101(B) (1994).

Discussion

* * *

---

1. The agreement also contained the following provision:

> Each party shall be obligated to contribute an equal amount to a community bank account or accounts in the names of the parties in order to maintain the community residence, joint costs of living and any joint obligations which may be acquired. Contributions of earnings or other funds to a joint account, jointly held asset or joint enterprise will be deemed a gift to the community unless memorialized to the contrary in writing, signed by the parties.

III. COMMUNITY OR SEPARATE NATURE OF THE DEBT AND SCHLAEFER'S LIABILITY

Generally, all debts incurred during marriage are presumed to be community obligations unless there is clear and convincing evidence to the contrary. *See Hofmann Co. v. Meisner,* 17 Ariz. App. 263, 267, 497 P.2d 83, 87 (1972). "The necessary medical care of a spouse would normally be 'intended to benefit the community,' which is the test of whether an obligation is a community debt." FMS correctly argues that the medical debt is presumed to be a community obligation. This presumption may be overcome by clear and convincing evidence that the debt is intended as the separate debt of one of the spouses rather than both. *See MacCollum v. Perkinson,* 185 Ariz. 179, 183, 913 P.2d 1097, 1101 (App. 1996).

Schlaefer claims that he rebutted this presumption with evidence of the premarital agreement coupled with the fact that he did not sign any documents authorizing Shelley's medical debt. He is correct in both respects. In Arizona, spouses may enter into a premarital agreement prospectively abrogating their respective claims on what would ordinarily be community property. Indeed, under the same premarital agreement statute, parties may contract with respect to "the rights *and obligations* of each of the parties in any of the property of either or both of them whenever and wherever acquired," and to "[a]ny other matter, *including their personal rights and obligations,* not in violation of public policy. . . ." A.R.S. §25-203(A)(1), (8) (emphasis added). Nothing in the statute prohibits such parties from agreeing to keep their property *and their debts* separate during marriage. The emphasized language of the statute expressly allows agreements such as the one at issue here.

Under the terms of this agreement, neither Schlaefer nor his ex-wife acquired any community property during the marriage. All the debts incurred during their marriage, "except joint obligations," remained the separate debt of the spouse incurring the debt. Although the term "joint obligations" is undefined, a reader of the agreement must conclude that only obligations signed or authorized by both spouses are "joint." The agreement clearly shows that the spouses intended to hold their present and future property and obligations separately and that no community property would exist except to pay the expenses of a marital residence, the joint costs of living, or similar "joint" obligations. If "joint" obligations is read to include what otherwise would be community obligations apart from the agreement, such a reading defeats the spouses' clear intent to the contrary. Thus, "joint" obligations must be those that, consistent with the contract's language, reveal that both spouses authorized them.

Because Schlaefer did not authorize or sign any of the documents authorizing Shelley's medical care or assume liability for her resulting debt, that debt never became a joint obligation but remained at all times Shelley's separate obligation. The premarital agreement and lack of Schlaefer's consent to the debt constitute clear and convincing evidence rebutting the ordinary presumption that the debt was community. Moreover, the trial court in the underlying divorce action expressly found in its dissolution order that Schlaefer and Shelley had no community debts. Both spouses agreed to this finding by signing the consent decree, which also states that there are no community debts.

FMS argues that Schlaefer was required to show that Shelley intended the debt to be her separate obligation. It cites no authority for this proposition. Moreover, nothing suggests that Shelley executed the agreement involuntarily or without fair and reasonable disclosure of the property and obligations of each spouse. Her voluntary and knowing execution of the agreement is undisputed. The agreement's express terms show that she intended that all debts she incurred during the marriage would remain her sole and separate obligation. As further evidence, Shelley had listed this same hospital debt as her sole and separate responsibility in her *proper* petition for dissolution in the trial court.

FMS also argues that as a third party creditor, it cannot be bound by the spouses' premarital agreement. It draws an analogy to *Community Guardian Bank v. Hamlin,* 182 Ariz. 627, 898 P.2d 1005 (App. 1995), which held that third-party creditors are not bound by the allocation of community debts in a divorce decree. *See id.* at 631, 898 P.2d at 1009. Such general statements do exist: "'The allocation of community liabilities determines the rights and obligations of the parties before the court only with respect to each other.' *Lee v. Lee,* 133 Ariz. 118, 124, 649 P.2d 997, 1003 (App. 1982). A creditor is not bound by the allocation." *Id.*

However, in a scenario closer to the present one, in *Elia v. Pifer* this court held that "[a] valid premarital agreement abrogating community property rights precludes a creditor of one spouse from proceeding against the separate property of the other spouse on a claim arising during marriage." *Elia,* 194 Ariz. at 84, ¶ 51, 977 P.2d at 806. *Elia* did not specifically address *Hamlin* or the argument FMS raises here. *Elia* cites a California case, *Leasefirst v. Borrelli,* 13 Cal. App. 4th Supp. 28, 17 Cal. Rptr. 2d 114, 116-17 (1993), which also held that a premarital agreement that transmutes otherwise community property into separate property prevents creditors from collecting from the non-debtor spouse. *Leasefirst* expressly rejected the creditor's claim that premarital agreements fail to protect third-party creditors. To the contrary, it held that

> third party creditors can easily avoid the risk of unknown interspousal transfers (and the embarrassment or burden of inquiring about them) by obtaining both spouses' signatures on notes. . . . Obtaining both spouses' signatures is a reasonable burden to place on creditors who later attempt to recover against former community assets.

Id. (quoting *Kennedy v. Taylor,* 201 Cal. Rptr. 779, 781 (App. 1984)).

This reasoning answers FMS's concerns. Although *Hamlin* addressed third-party creditors' rights, it involved a community debt. 182 Ariz. at 631, 898 P.2d at 1009. The court's allocation of a community debt does not change its nature or limit the right of a creditor to seek satisfaction from either spouse; it only determines the rights and obligations of the spouses "with respect to each other." *Id.* Here FMS seeks payment for a separate debt. The trial court did not and can not transmute the nature of the debt; it was always separate because of the premarital agreement and the lack of both spousal signatures. Obtaining both signatures is a reasonable means of protecting the creditor's interests in pursuing both spouses for satisfaction of a debt.

Moreover, third-party creditors like FMS are afforded protection under laws that presume generally that obligations incurred during marriage are community. *See Gutierrez v. Gutierrez,* 193 Ariz. 343, 346, ¶ 6, 972 P.2d 676, 679 (App. 1998) (presumption that debts incurred during marriage are presumed to be community absent clear and convincing evidence to the contrary is primarily intended for the benefit of creditors). The spouse seeking to avoid liability bears the burden of rebutting that presumption by clear and convincing evidence. *Id.* Schlaefer has done so here. To hold that creditors can avoid valid premarital agreements allows one spouse to defeat the terms of the premarital agreement by incurring debts for which the non-debtor spouse would be liable in the face of express contrary language in the agreement. *See Kennedy,* 201 Cal. Rptr. at 781.

Accordingly, FMS is bound by the terms of this valid premarital agreement. The agreement is not unconscionable; no evidence or judicial findings exist to suggest that it is. Under the agreement, the debt was not a joint obligation but Shelley's separate debt. Therefore, we reverse the grant of judgment in favor of FMS and remand for entry of summary judgment in favor of Schlaefer.[2] As the successful party on appeal, we award him his attorneys' fees incurred on appeal pursuant to A.R.S. §12-341.01(A) (1992), upon compliance with Rule 21, Arizona Rules of Civil Appellate Procedure. We remand for entry of judgment in his favor and reconsideration of the award of attorneys' fees incurred in the trial court.

Concurring: EDWARD C. VOSS, Presiding Judge, and JEFFERSON L. LANKFORD, Judge.

Discussion Question

1. Why didn't the creditor succeed in collecting the debt for medical care of Schlaefer's former wife?

PROBLEM 10.1

Elmer and Leslie were long-time residents of a community property state. Elmer borrowed $100,000 from Big Bank to purchase stock in a company. He pledged those shares as security for the loan. Elmer sustained losses from this investment when the stock depreciated in value. He defaulted on the loan and Big Bank received a judgment against Elmer for $100,000 plus interest. Big Bank wants to execute the judgment against Elmer and Leslie's community property. How will a community debt state approach the liability of the community property? A managerial state?

PROBLEM 10.2

Assume the same facts as Problem 10.1, except that Elmer borrowed the $100,000 before he married Leslie and that Big Bank had received the judgment against Elmer before he married Leslie. What rights would the creditor have in California? In Idaho? In New Mexico?

---

2. Having reversed the judgment in favor of FMS, we need not address Schlaefer's claims that FMS lacked standing to challenge the premarital agreement and the attorneys' fees issue.

PROBLEM 10.3

Claudia and David, who were married in 1990, hoped to buy a house. They saved money from their salaries and were able to buy a "fixer-upper." Since David was in the construction business, he thought it would be a great opportunity to make the home their dream home. While working on the roof with several workers, one fell off the roof and was seriously injured. The worker sued David and obtained a judgment against David for negligent supervision of this worker. David had incurred attorneys' fees in the amount of $50,000 defending the lawsuit. How would an Arizona and Washington court treat the judgment and the attorney's fees?

Table 10-1
Creditors' Rights in Community Property States

State	*Rule*	*Case/Statute*
Arizona	Community/Separate Debt State Debts incurred by either spouse during marriage, intended to benefit the community, are presumed to be community debts. Rebuttal by clear and convincing evidence that the spouses intended separate debt. Spouses shall be sued jointly and the debt shall be satisfied, first, from the community property, and second, from the separate property of the spouse contracting the debt.	Ariz. Rev. Stat. §25-215, *Schlaefer v. Financial Management Services, Inc.*, 196 Ariz. 336, 996 P.2d 745 (Ct. App. 2000) (although the wife's medical debt was for the benefit of the community, the spouses premarital agreement rebutted the presumption and the community was not liable)
California	"Modified" Management State The community estate is liable for a debt incurred by either spouse before or during marriage, regardless of which spouse has the management and control of the property regardless of whether one or both spouses are parties to the debt. Earnings of a spouse can be sheltered from liability for premarital debt of the other spouse if in a separate account and uncommingled with other community property. Satisfaction of tort liability may be first from community and second from separate property, depending on whether liability based on an act that occurred while performing an activity for the benefit of the community.	Cal. Fam. Code §910-911, 1000

Idaho	Managerial State When either member of the community incurs a debt for the benefit of the community, the property held by the marital community becomes liable for that debt and the creditor may seek satisfaction of the unpaid debt from that property. Liability does not extend to the separate property of the spouse who did not contract for the debt. Community property is liable for premarital debt.	*Twin Falls Bank & Trust Co. v. Holley,* 111 Idaho 349, 723 P.2d 893 (1986), *Williams v. Paxton,* 98 Idaho 155, 556 P.2d 1123 (1976), *Action Collection Service, Inc. v. Seele,* 138 Idaho 753, 69 P.3d 173 (2003)
Louisiana	"Modified" Managerial State A separate or community obligation may be satisfied during the community property regime from community property and from the separate property of the spouse who incurred the obligation. An obligation incurred by a spouse before or during the community property regime may be satisfied after termination of the regime from the property of the former community and from the separate property of the spouse who incurred the obligation.	La. Civ. Code §§2345,2357, *Lawson v. Lawson,* 535 So. 2d 851 (1988) (a spouse's creditor has the same property available to satisfy the debt after the community regime has ended as during the existence of the community: all assets of the community and the separate property of the spouse who incurred the debt)
Nevada	Managerial State Neither the separate property of a spouse nor the spouse's share of the community property is liable for the debts of the other spouse contracted before the marriage. Community property is subject to debts of a spouse during the marriage?	Nev. Rev. Stat. Ann. §123.050, *Randono v. Turk,* 86 Nev. 123, 466 P.2d 218 (1970)
New Mexico	Community/Separate Debt State Presumption is that a debt created during marriage is a community debt, rebuttal by demonstrating that the debt is in the category of a separate debt pursuant to N.M 40-3-9(A)(1)–(6).	N.M. Stat. Ann. §§40-3-9 (A)(B), 40-3-10, 140-3-11, *Huntington Nat. Bank v. Sproul,* 116 N.M. 254, 861 P.2d 935 (1993) (both spouses not required to join in execution of a note creating community debt), *Beneficial Finance Co. of New Mexico v. Alarcon,* 112 N.M. 420, 816 P.2d 489 (1991) (a spouse that commits a separate tort is individually liable for damages arising out of the tort)

Texas	Managerial State Either spouse can incur contractual liability that will bind the share of the noncontracting spouse's community property, but not the noncontracting spouse's separate property. A spouse is personally liable only for a debt for necessaries or if the spouse acts as the other spouse's agent when incurring debt. Community property subject to a spouse's sole management and control is not subject to liabilities incurred by the other spouse before marriage or any nontortious liabilities that the other spouse incurs during marriage.	Tex. Fam. Code Ann. §§4.031, 5.61, *Nelson v. Citizen's Bank & Trust Co. of Bayton*, 881 S.W.2d 128 (Tex. Ct. App. 1994) (wife's separate property and sole management and control property were not subject to the debt executed by husband)
Washington	Community/Separate Debt State Presumption that contractual debt incurred by a spouse during marriage is for the benefit of the community and therefore is a community debt. Rebuttal that it is a separate debt by clear and convincing evidence. Definition of community benefit stretched to cover tort liability obligation of one spouse. If tort liability is not for the benefit of the community, the tortfeasor's separate property will be liable, but the tortfeasor's half of community property will be liable if separate property is insufficient. Community is not liable for premarital debts of a spouse, but the earnings of that spouse shall be available to the legal process of creditors.	Wash. Rev. Code Ann. §26.16.200, *deElche v. Jacobsen*, 95 Wash. 2d 237, 622 P.2d 835 (1980), *Keene v. Edie*, 131 Wash. 2d 822, 935 P.2d 588 (1997), *Haley v. Highland*, 142 Wash. 2d 135, 12 P.3d 119 (2000)
Wisconsin	An obligation incurred by a spouse in the interest of the marriage or the family may be satisfied only from all marital property and all other property of the incurring spouse.	Wis. Stat. §766.55, *Curda-Derickson v. Derickson*, 266 Wis. 2d 453, 668 N.W.2d 736 (Ct. App. 2003) (restitution order for husband's criminal conviction not a marital debt), *St. Mary's Hosp. Medical Center v. Brody*, 186 Wis. 2d 100, 519 N.W.2d 707 (Ct. App. 1994) (husband's medical expenses could be recovered from marital property)

Chapter 11

Disability Strikes: Character of Disability Insurance Proceeds

Let us imagine our hypothetical couple George and Martha. Martha is a pediatric dentist who has an excellent reputation for her expertise and her ability to engage with children. Most of their income comes from Martha's practice. Martha is also very cautious about financial matters. She has set up a large account with a brokerage to make sure that when she retires she and George can continue their life style they have had throughout their marriage. Knowing that their livelihood relies primarily on Martha's skill as a dentist, Martha has taken out a disability insurance policy. That policy provides that in the event Martha becomes disabled and is not able to continue practicing dentistry, she will be paid a monthly amount equal to approximately her monthly income.

If George and Martha's marriage continues until Martha retires from dental practice, they will be able to draw from her brokerage account. If Martha becomes disabled before she planned to retire, the disability insurance policy will provide financial security since Martha's capacity to work is impaired. Both the brokerage account and the disability insurance replace earnings, which by definition are community property. In addition, if both the brokerage account and the disability insurance were acquired during marriage with community funds, it would be logical to conclude that both would be community property. However, disability insurance has an additional aspect: it not only replaces actual earnings but replaces the earning capacity of the disabled spouse. That fact complicates the characterization of disability insurance in the event of divorce.

Let's imagine that Martha does become disabled during marriage and cannot practice dentistry. Under the disability insurance paid with community property funds, she begins receiving a monthly payment that according to the policy will continue for life. George and Martha's marriage deteriorates after she stops working and they divorce. Since the insurance was paid with community funds, George would argue that the post-dissolution payments are also community property and they should be shared with George. Martha would argue that since she has lost her earning capacity due to her disability and George retains his earning capacity, the disability payments should be considered her separate property.

Another aspect of disability insurance is consideration of its purpose because in some cases the spouses may intend it to replace retirement funds. Let us return to George and Martha, Martha has not been able to set aside any of her earnings for retirement. However, knowing that a disability could render her unable to work, she makes it a priority to purchase disability insurance which would substitute for retirement funds if she can no longer practice dentistry. Thus there is a dual purpose — provide retirement funds and loss of earning ability due to disability. This dual purpose has led to controversy particularly in California where the case of *Marriage of Elfmont*, 9 Cal. 4th 1026, 291 P.2d 136, 39 Cal. Rptr. 2d 290 (1995), produced concurring and dissenting opinions in a 4-3 split decision.

A. COMMUNITY: THE IDAHO, NEW MEXICO, AND TEXAS APPROACH

In *Guy v. Guy*, 98 Idaho 205, 560 P.2d 876 (1977), the Supreme Court of Idaho discusses the approaches to characterizing disability insurance proceeds from a policy from husband Walter's employer. It is a poignant fact scenario since both Walter and his wife Elizabeth are totally disabled. Focus on the reasons why the Court rejected Walter's argument that the disability payments were his separate property. The New Mexico Court of Appeals adopted the Idaho approach in *Douglas v. Douglas*, 101 N.M. 570, 686 P.2d 260 (1984). Texas courts have also followed this reasoning, as in *Andrle v. Andrle*, 751 S.W.2d 955 (Ct. App. 1988).

GUY v. GUY

98 Idaho 205, 560 P.2d 876 (1977)
Supreme Court of Idaho

SHEPARD, Justice.

This is an appeal from a judgment by the district court which in turn affirmed a judgment and decree of the magistrate court in a divorce action which distributed property determined to be community. We affirm the decisions of the lower courts.

In 1964 the plaintiff-appellant Walter Guy, while employed by Litton Industries, became insured under the provisions of a group term disability insurance policy. That policy acquired no cash or loan value and the premiums were paid solely by the employer. During 1971 the insurance carrier was changed, however, the terms remained substantially the same and the employer continued to pay the premiums.

The relationship between appellant and respondent Elizabeth Guy dates to at least 1965 during which they participated in a void marriage ceremony. Thereafter the relationship continued until a valid marriage of October 30, 1970. At that time appellant was approximately 49 years of age and respondent was 28 years of age. On June 30, 1973, appellant was determined to be totally disabled due to advanced arteriosclerosis and other complications. Five days later his employment with Litton was terminated. Under the provisions of the disability insurance policy appellant began to receive payments of $1,313.00 per month in January, 1974. Those payments are reduced by appellant's Social Security benefits ($297.00 per month) and retirement benefits from previous employment ($24.00 per month). So long as his disability exists, those payments will continue until he reaches the age of 65.

Respondent has education and experience skills in the field of biological computer systems and is a laboratory technician. She also is totally disabled due to a hip separation and back problem. She receives monthly disability benefits from Social Security in the amount of $264.00.

Following hearing, a painstaking and well reasoned memorandum decision was rendered by the magistrate court, much of which is the basis for this opinion. Thereafter judgment was rendered and upon appeal to the district court it was affirmed. Although other issues may appear present, we emphasize that the sole error urged upon appeal is the determination that the future benefits to be paid under the terms of the disability insurance policy are community property and the allocation of those net monthly benefits equally between the parties. Hence, while the problem presented is broad in scope and of first impression in this jurisdiction, the issue is narrow and quickly stated.

Our legislative frame of reference is likewise narrow and easily stated. I.C. §32-903 provides:

> All property of either the husband or the wife owned by him or her before marriage, and that acquired afterward by either by gift, bequest, devise or descent, or that which either he or she shall acquire with the proceeds of his or her separate property, by way of moneys or other property, shall remain his or her sole and separate property.

I.C. §32-906 provides:

> All other property acquired after marriage by either husband or wife, including the rents and profits of the separate property of the husband and wife, is community property, unless by the instrument by which any such property is acquired by the wife it is provided that the rents and profits thereof be applied to her sole and separate use. . . .

Any asset acquired during marriage is rebuttably presumed to be community property and the burden of proof rests with the party asserting a separate property interest. If these benefits were acquired during the marriage, we must uphold the presumption that they were community property since the record is devoid of any contrary evidence. It is not disputed that they were fringe benefits or emoluments of appellant's employment and therefore they derive from the community labors of the appellant.

A group term disability policy, like a similar life insurance policy, is a unique form of property interest. It has no cash surrender value, no loan value and interest does not accumulate thereon. Here over the course of appellant's employment it actually constituted a series of unilateral contracts, each beginning with the payment of a premium for a specified period (presumably annual) and terminated at the expiration of that annual period.

'Protection for the coming year depends exclusively upon payment of an advance premium. The length of time the insured has had the policy and the number of premiums previously paid are irrelevant. If the term passes without the insured's death, the protection purchased expires without loss. The insured has had the benefit of protection for the year and it has been "used up." He must pay another premium to enjoy further protection.

'The risk payment doctrine correctly treats term insurance as a series of unilateral contracts rather than as one bilateral contract. . . . (E)ach premium payment is both a condition precedent to and a consideration necessary for the insurance company's promise to pay a benefit upon the death of the insured.' Comment, Community and Separate Property Interests in Life Insurance Proceeds: A Fresh Look, 51 Wash. L. Rev. 351, 353, 374 (1976) (emphasis supplied).

Here appellant initially began his employment and the disability insurance policy was initiated prior to the marriage. Nevertheless, during the course of the marriage at the end of each term period a new contract of insurance arose and thus for the nearly three years between the marriage and the determination of disability new policies of term length originated.

This Court has found a community property interest to exist in two similar fringe benefits or emoluments of employment in the form of life insurance and military retirement benefits. As stated by the court in Stephen v. Gallion, 5 Wash. App. 747, 491 P.2d 238 (1971):

> A retirement pension under a noncontributory, employer-financed plan is not a gratuity, but is pay withheld, and constitutes delayed compensation for services rendered. (citations). Just as the pension benefits do not constitute a gratuity, so also the premiums paid or payable by the employer are not gratuities. They are paid by the employer as an essential part of employment based upon the continuing employment of each and every employee covered under the plan during any given monthly period. Although no portion of any given premium passes through the pockets of any given employee, and thus he receives some tax advantage, nevertheless, it does constitute something produced by such employee by his toil or talent. The benefit to the employee is part of the consideration for his services. To that extent, if he is married, it is earned by and belongs to the community.
>
> For purposes of determining the legal status of policy proceeds, we see no logical reason to distinguish between an insurance plan which provides for a retirement or pension benefit and one which provides for a death or disability benefit.

At 240.

We deem it clear that in the case at bar the disability benefits are to be paid as partial consideration for past employment. It has been held such benefits are community property, not only where the premiums are paid with community funds, but also where the funds are paid by the employer.

Appellant argues for adoption of the apparent California approach to disability payments as mandating the conclusion that the disability insurance proceeds in the instant case are separate property. In re Marriage of Jones, 13 Cal. 3d 457, 119 Cal. Rptr. 108, 531 P.2d 420 (1975); In re Marriage of Loehr, 13 Cal. 3d 465, 119 Cal. Rptr. 113, 531 P.2d 425 (1975); In re Marriage of Olhausen, 48 Cal. App. 3d 190, 121 Cal. Rptr. 444 (1975). Both Jones and Loehr are distinguishable in that there the California court concluded that federal military disability benefits do not primarily serve as a form of deferred compensation for a serviceman's past employment. We do not read those cases that all disability payments assume that separate property character. Here we reiterate that in the case at bar the disability benefits do not constitute a gratuity, but rather compensation for appellant's labors. Further, we think that portion of the analysis of Jones dealing with a pain and suffering component is inapplicable since disability insurance benefits derived from employment are designed to compensate for loss of earnings and do not consider or compensate for the pain and suffering.

In the case at bar, the benefits vested during the time of the marriage. Clearly community labor was the source of the benefits. Hence, we continue to look in

Idaho to the source of the benefit rather than the purpose of payment analysis rationale of the California court in Olhausen. See, Note, In re Marriage of Olhausen: The Characterization of State Disability Retirement Benefits After Dissolution, 3 Pepperdine L. Rev. 205 (1975). *reasoning*

Appellant next contends that the disability benefits should be his separate property in that such is analogous to personal injury damages and tort under the authority of Rogers v. Yellowstone Park Co., 97 Idaho 14, 539 P.2d 566 (1974). Appellant's assertion is correct that Rogers held that the pain and suffering component of a tort recovery for personal injuries is the separate property of the injured spouse. Rogers it will be remembered involved the liability between husband and wife resulting from the tortious act of the husband. Here no portions of these disability proceeds are shown to compensate the pain and suffering aspect of disability. As to loss of earnings, it was held in Rogers that the rule was tailored to compensate the injured without rewarding the guilty spouse. In the usual third-party tort situation, however, the rule remains unchanged, i.e., an award for future earnings is community property at least to the extent the award compensates for earnings to be lost during the marriage. See, Doggett v. Boiler Engineering & Supply Co., 93 Idaho 888, 477 P.2d 511 (1970). *reasoning*

The California cases . . . may be explained as a practical accommodation to the rigid rule in that jurisdiction that all community property must be equally divided, California Civil Code §4800. By contrast, in Idaho, our courts have the equitable power and discretion to divide community property toward the end of achieving a just and equitable result. I.C. §32-712(1). Here we find no abuse of the lower courts' discretion in dividing the community property of the parties. While the focus of asserted error is solely upon the distribution of the disability insurance benefits, we have examined other aspects of the lower courts' judgment. We find the lower court well considered a complex property situation involving the separate property of each of the parties accumulated before the marriage, property accumulated as community during the marriage and property which was considered as mixed separate and community. The lower courts considered the personal situations and abilities and disabilities of both parties. In the ordinary and normal situation and in the absence of factors which in the discretion of the trial court require otherwise, we would expect community property assets to be divided equally between the parties. The burden of persuading the trial court of the existence of factors to require other than a one-half to each party distribution must be upon the party asserting the need therefor. We find nothing in the record presented here to demonstrate that the appellant so carried that burden of persuasion.

The judgments of the lower courts are affirmed. Costs to respondent.

McFADDEN C.J., and DONALDSON, BAKES and BISTLINE, JJ., concur.

Discussion Questions

1. Why did the Supreme Court conclude that the disability insurance proceeds were community property?

2. Why did the Supreme Court reject Walter's argument that the disability insurance proceeds were his separate property?

B.   PART COMMUNITY/PART SEPARATE: THE ARIZONA AND WASHINGTON APPROACH

In Arizona, the accepted position is that disability benefits are separate property of the disabled spouse in the event of divorce. The question in *Hatcher v. Hatcher*, 188 Ariz. 154, 933 P.2d 122 (1996) was whether any part of an employee's lump sum disability insurance settlement received during marriage was community property. The trial court had held that it was husband Marvin's separate property and wife Julia appealed. Similarly, in the Washington case of *Marriage of Brewer*, 137 Wash. 2d 756, 976 P.2d 102 (1999), the Supreme Court considered the following issue:

> The question presented in this case is whether monthly payments to a permanently disabled spouse under a private disability insurance policy after dissolution of a marriage constitutes separate property and not community property, even though the policy was acquired during marriage and premiums were paid from community funds before premiums were waived by the issuing companies.

Id. at 759, 976 P.2d at 103.

The Supreme Court clarified the law, emphasizing that disability benefits received after dissolution of the marriage should be characterized as separate property even though premium payments were made from community funds during the marriage. As you read the cases, examine how disability benefits are similar to and different from personal injury tort recoveries.

HATCHER v. HATCHER

188 Ariz. 154, 933 P.2d 1222 (1996)
Arizona Court of Appeals

THOMPSON, Judge.

Appellant Julia M. Hatcher (wife) seeks review of a dissolution decree awarding jointly-held real property to Appellee Marvin L. Hatcher (husband). Wife contends that the trial court erred in finding that the proceeds from a disability insurance settlement awarded to husband, and the family residence and an apartment complex purchased with the insurance proceeds and held in joint tenancy, were husband's separate property. We agree that the insurance proceeds were, in part, community property, and reverse.

FACTS AND PROCEDURAL HISTORY

The parties were married in Arizona on December 6, 1980. They had four children during the marriage. Husband worked for Ralston Purina Company, and voluntarily agreed to participate in an insurance program offered by his employer in April 1982. The "Voluntary Personal Accident Plan" (VPA) provided for benefits to the employee's family or to the employee in the event of accidental death, dismemberment or disability. Husband initially designated his wife and son as beneficiaries of the insurance policy, subsequently amending the policy to include coverage for his three after-born children. Premiums for the VPA program were automatically deducted from husband's paycheck.

In November 1984, husband suffered the loss of his right hand and the partial loss of his right arm in a work-related accident. Husband missed work for three months because of his injuries. During this time, husband received a small worker's compensation award which went toward household expenses. Under the VPA policy, he received a lump sum settlement of $120,000 and monthly structured payments for a period of fifty-four months.

A portion of the VPA proceeds was placed in a joint account which the husband and wife maintained at a local credit union, and later used as a down payment on the purchase of the family residence in Flagstaff, Arizona. The parties subsequently used payments from the monthly structured disability settlement to pay the remaining balance owed on the house. Title to the residence was taken by husband and wife as joint tenants with right of survivorship.

The parties also used some of the insurance settlement proceeds to construct an apartment complex on a parcel of land owned by husband prior to marriage. Two different lenders provided construction and permanent financing for the apartments. Both husband and wife signed the promissory note and held title to the property as joint tenants with right of survivorship. The rental income produced by the apartments fully satisfied each month's mortgage payments owed on the property.

Wife filed for divorce in February 1991. At trial, the court found that the insurance settlement proceeds were husband's separate property. The court held that, although the residence and apartment complex were held in joint tenancy, husband had "shown by clear and convincing evidence that it was not his intent to make a gift of the real property to the community." The court therefore ordered that the real property was the separate property of husband. Wife appeals from these determinations.

DISCUSSION

On appeal, wife argues that the VPA insurance proceeds constituted community property because the premiums were paid with community funds and because the settlement monies were received during the course of the parties' marriage. Alternatively, wife contends that even if the insurance proceeds were in fact husband's separate property, he failed to rebut the presumption created by the joint tenancy deeds for the residence and apartment complex that husband intended to make a gift of these properties to her.

We first consider the character of husband's VPA insurance benefits. Husband relies on *Jurek v. Jurek*, 124 Ariz. 596, 606 P.2d 812 (1980), for his assertion that the disability benefits received for his personal injuries were separate property. In *Jurek*, our supreme court held that a recovery for personal injuries is comprised of various component parts which may be either community or separate in nature. *Id.* at 597-98, 606 P.2d at 813-14. Compensation for any expenses incurred by the community for medical treatment and any loss of wages resulting from the personal injury are deemed community property. *Id.* at 598, 606 P.2d at 814. Any portion of the recovery intended to provide compensation for injury to a spouse's personal well-being is considered that spouse's separate property. *Id.* Husband contends that the VPA proceeds were wholly intended to compensate him for his personal injuries and, therefore, were his separate property under *Jurek.*

Two Arizona cases subsequent to the *Jurek* decision are cited by husband to support his position. In *In re Marriage of Kosko*, 125 Ariz. 517, 611 P.2d 104 (App. 1980), we held that disability benefits are the separate property of the disabled spouse after dissolution. In characterizing the nature of disability benefits, we noted:

> Whether paid for by the employer or the employee, the amount expended [for disability insurance] is to protect against a risk of disability which may, but usually does not, occur. The amount paid to protect against this risk does not accumulate in a fund, nor does it build into an equity having an ascertainable value. Although the entitlement to this benefit may be attributed to employment and thus have a community origin, the money so expended does not produce a community asset subject to division at dissolution. What it produces is coverage for the *individual spouse* against the risk of disability and loss of future earning ability. . . . While disability income protection may arise during marriage, it is for the protection of community earnings during the existence of the marriage and for the protection of separate earnings of the disabled spouse in the event of dissolution.

125 Ariz. at 518-19, 611 P.2d at 105-06.

Thus, consistent with *Jurek*, this court concluded that disability benefits are the separate property of the disabled spouse after dissolution. *Id.* Division Two of this court adopted the same view of disability benefits in *McNeel v. McNeel*, 169 Ariz. 213, 818 P.2d 198 (App. 1991).[1]

Neither of these cases is dispositive here. While *Kosko* and *McNeel* establish that any portion of disability proceeds which represent compensation for post-dissolution earnings of the injured spouse is the separate property of that spouse, neither case clearly addresses the proper characterization of disability benefits received *during* marriage. Whether a non-disabled spouse may claim a community interest in disability benefits received by an injured spouse during marriage has not been directly decided in Arizona.

We conclude that the proceeds from a disability insurance policy for an accident occurring during marriage may be subject to division at dissolution. Contrary to wife's assertion, the determination that a disability insurance policy was acquired with community funds does not necessarily lead to the conclusion that the disability benefits are community property. *Lachney v. Lachney*, 529 So. 2d 59, 64 (La. Ct. App. 1988). Rather, like personal injury recoveries, disability benefits have various component parts. *See Villasenor v. Villasenor*, 134 Ariz. 476, 657 P.2d 889 (App. 1982) (disability retirement benefits divided into community and separate property). The primary intent of a disability policy is to insure against the risk of loss of the insured's future earning capacity. *In re Marriage of Leland*, 69 Wash. App. 57, 847 P.2d 518, 526 (1993). Indeed, by purchasing disability insurance, a married couple

---

1. Other community property states consider disability benefits to be community property. *See, e.g., Guy v. Guy*, 98 Idaho 205, 560 P.2d 876 (1977) (group term disability policy); *Hughes v. Hughes*, 96 N.M. 719, 634 P.2d 1271 (1981) (civil service disability policy); *Busby v. Busby*, 457 S.W.2d 551 (Tex. 1970) (disability retirement benefits).

protects against the possibility of economic loss caused by injury to either spouse's earning ability. *See Kosko,* 125 Ariz. at 518, 611 P.2d at 105 (disability insurance provides coverage "against the risk of disability and loss of future earning ability"). While the marital community exists, a disabled spouse's reduced earning capacity results in a loss to the community. *Luna v. Luna,* 125 Ariz. 120, 125, 608 P.2d 57, 62 (App. 1979); *In re Marriage of Jones,* 13 Cal. 3d 457, 119 Cal. Rptr. 108, 111, 531 P.2d 420, 423 (1975). At dissolution, however, the loss to the community ceases and any reduced earning capacity becomes the separate loss of the disabled spouse. 119 Cal. Rptr. at 111-12, 531 P.2d at 423-24.

Here, the loss of husband's arm and hand resulted in both a loss of earnings and a permanent impairment to his future earning ability.[2] Workers' compensation insurance provided compensation, at least in part, for any lost earnings.[3] The disability policy protected the community against the risk of loss or reduction of the insured's future earning capacity. Because husband received a lump sum disability policy settlement for a disability that extended through the remainder of marriage and beyond, at least part of the insurance proceeds compensated the community for husband's reduced earning capacity during marriage. We conclude that the portion of the disability proceeds which represented compensation for husband's loss of earning ability during marriage was community property. *Queen v. Queen,* 308 Md. 574, 521 A.2d 320, 327 (1987); *cf. In re Marriage of Cupp,* 152 Ariz. 161, 163, 730 P.2d 870, 872 (App. 1986) (portion of lump sum workers' compensation award for lost wages during marriage is a community asset). The remainder of the lump sum payment, although paid during marriage, was in lieu of future (post-dissolution) lost earning capacity due to husband's personal injuries. This portion is husband's separate property.

By treating the portion of disability benefits received during marriage as community property, we extend by analogy the distinction between personal injury recoveries and disability insurance proceeds articulated in *Kosko.* In a personal injury action, recovery may be had for any diminution in earning ability as distinct from loss of earnings. *Mandelbaum v. Knutson,* 11 Ariz. App. 148, 149, 462 P.2d 841, 842 (1969). Just as recovery for loss of earning capacity must be proven by such factors as plaintiff's age, health, life expectancy, habits, occupation, experience, and training in personal injury cases, the trial court in dissolution proceedings should similarly consider this type of evidence in equitably dividing disability proceeds received during marriage. *Id.* at 149-50, 462 P.2d at 842-43. The trial court in this case erred in determining that all of the disability proceeds constituted the husband's separate property. A portion of the proceeds was community property

---

2. It is clear from the record that husband's injuries resulted in an impairment to his earning capacity. At trial, he testified that "because of the loss of my arm, I can't just go out and get a job anyplace else anymore. I couldn't go out anyplace else and get a job. I'm not trained or educated in any other way to go out and make a living."

3. Workers' compensation is awarded to an injured employee in lieu of lost wages and is based on lost earning capacity during the period of disability. *Bugh v. Bugh,* 125 Ariz. 190, 192, 608 P.2d 329, 331 (App. 1980). In this case, husband received a workers' compensation award for only three months. Accordingly, the disability policy payments, which extended over a period of fifty-four months, did not provide significant, if any, overlapping compensation for husband's diminution in earning ability. Further, the disability proceeds were intended, in part, to provide compensation for any loss of husband's power to earn in the future, whereas the three-month workers' compensation award clearly did not contemplate any future economic harm.

because it represented compensation for husband's lost earning ability while married.

The trial court's award of the real properties to husband as his separate property was based on the erroneous determination that the insurance proceeds were exclusively the property of husband. Indeed, in order to award the real properties to husband as his separate property, the court had to find that the insurance proceeds with which the residence and the apartment complex were purchased belonged solely to husband. *Blaine v. Blaine*, 63 Ariz. 100, 108-09, 159 P.2d 786, 790 (1945) (where claim is made that property purchased during marriage is the separate property of one of the spouses, fund with which property was acquired must be clearly shown to have been separate property of such spouse). Because the trial court erred in this finding, the award to husband cannot stand, and we must remand this case to the trial court for additional fact-finding and disposition. Because the funds used to purchase the real properties were part community funds and part husband's separate property, the trial court must revisit wife's claim that, in placing title in joint tenancy with wife, husband made a gift of his separate property to her. *See, e.g., Cely v. DeConcini, McDonald, Brammer, Yetwin & Lacy, P.C.*, 166 Ariz. 500, 506, 803 P.2d 911, 917 (App. 1990) (where further fact-finding is required after reversal on appeal, reviewing court will remand to trial court for resolution of unresolved issues).

Where separate funds of one spouse have been used to purchase real property and title has been taken in joint tenancy, a presumption arises that a gift to the non-contributing spouse was intended. *Battiste v. Battiste*, 135 Ariz. 470, 472, 662 P.2d 145, 147 (App. 1983). The spouse seeking to overcome that presumption has the burden of establishing the separate character of the property by clear and convincing evidence. *Cupp*, 152 Ariz. at 164, 730 P.2d at 873. The presumption of gift cannot be overcome simply by husband's after-the-fact testimony that the property was placed in joint tenancy for some other reason than as an intended gift. *Valladee v. Valladee*, 149 Ariz. 304, 307, 718 P.2d 206, 209 (App. 1986). If, after considering the evidence in light of these principles, the trial court sustains the presumption of gift, the community and joint property must be equitably divided between the parties; if wife's claim of gift is again rejected, the trial court must assign each spouse's separate property and then equitably divide community and joint property. A.R.S. §25-318(A).

CONCLUSION

We find that the portion of the VPA disability proceeds which represented compensation for husband's loss of earning ability during marriage should have been classified as community property. The part of the disability benefits representing post-dissolution diminution in earning capacity was his separate property. The trial court must determine whether husband's use of some of these disability proceeds classified as separate property to purchase the residence and apartment complex in joint tenancy with right of survivorship constituted a gift to his wife. We reverse the trial court's classification of the VPA disability proceeds and the residence and apartment complex as husband's separate property, and remand with an order directing additional fact-finding and disposition, including an equitable division of the properties between the parties, in accordance with this opinion and pursuant to A.R.S. §25-318(A).

GERBER, P.J., and VOSS, J., concur.

MARRIAGE OF BREWER

137 Wash. 2d 756, 976 P.2d 102 (1999)
Supreme Court of Washington

SMITH, J.

Petitioner Michael A. Brewer seeks review of a decision of the Court of Appeals, Division II, which reversed and remanded to the Clark County Superior Court a ruling characterizing monthly payments to a permanently disabled spouse under a private disability insurance policy after dissolution of a marriage as separate property and not community property. We granted review. We affirm the Court of Appeals in part and reverse it in part.

QUESTION PRESENTED

The question presented in this case is whether monthly payments to a permanently disabled spouse under a private disability insurance policy after dissolution of a marriage constitutes separate property and not community property, even though the policy was acquired during the marriage and premiums were paid from community funds before premiums were waived by the issuing companies.

STATEMENT OF FACTS

Petitioner Michael A. Brewer and Respondent Deborah Q. Brewer were married on May 20, 1988 in King County, Washington. No children were born of the marriage, although Respondent has two children from a prior marriage. Respondent has been a full-time elementary school teacher since 1977 with net income between $2,200.00 and $2,300.00 per month. At the time of the marriage Petitioner was a dentist who practiced his profession at the Kaiser Company until December 1991 when he was diagnosed with a progressively deteriorating disease, multiple sclerosis. Petitioner was unable to continue the practice of dentistry. The Social Security Administration determined him to be permanently disabled. A similar determination was made by the companies issuing his disability insurance policies, Mutual of New York (MONY) and New York Life Insurance Company (NYLIC). Petitioner receives a monthly non-taxable income of $6,193.00 from the disability insurance policies and $1,212.00 from Social Security, totaling approximately $7,400.00. This is his sole source of income.

On March 3, 1995 Petitioner served Respondent with a summons and petition for dissolution of marriage which he filed in the Clark County Superior Court. On March 1, 1996 the Honorable Robert L. Harris signed a decree of dissolution.

The following statements concerning the disability insurance policies were made by the trial court in the findings of fact and conclusions of law:

> A. The *Petitioner's New York Life and Mutual of New York disability insurance benefits are not assets subject to division in this case.* Such benefits should be awarded to the Petitioner Michael Brewer free of any claims of the Respondent Deborah Q. Brewer. The court notes that the community paid about $12,000 in premiums for such disability pay; however the court also notes that the community received about $6,000 on a monthly basis from these private disability policies, from the time of the Petitioner's disability until the parties separation, as well as during the period of parties separation under court order which also benefited the parties.
>
> B. Furthermore, the *property division in this case is fair and equitable in that it has also taken into account and recognized the disability benefits received and to be received by the Petitioner. The court notes that the Respondent* has a *substantial separate property estate that the Petitioner does not have.* Furthermore, *the court has made disproportionate award of community property in favor of the Respondent. The total property award received by Respondent is in excess of that to be received by Petitioner. Such award takes into consideration the fact of the disability payments that Petitioner has and will receive.* (emphasis added).

Each party was awarded all policies insuring their own lives. The parties were to equally divide cassette tapes valued at $1,500.00, family photographs, and share reproduction costs for the photographs. No maintenance was ordered. Child support was not an issue. In the findings of fact and conclusions of law the trial court indicated awards to Petitioner of approximately $56,521.00 net value in community assets, plus a marital lien of $10,000.00, and community debts of $11,500.00 for a total of $55,021.00; and to Respondent approximately $94,057.00 in community assets less the marital lien of $10,000.00, and community debts of $11,800.00 for a total of $72,257.00. Judge Harris determined that, based on this distribution of property, Respondent had a disproportionate award of community property in her favor in addition to approximately $350,000.00 in separate assets, for a total of $422,257.00. The value of assets awarded Respondent far exceeded the value of assets awarded to Petitioner.

In addressing the MONY and NYLIC disability insurance policies, the trial court concluded that the community paid the last actual premiums on all policies immediately prior to the onset of Petitioner's disability in December 1991, after which no further premiums were paid under waiver provisions in the policies. The trial court concluded that Respondent Deborah Q. Brewer had no claims to the disability policies because (1) the policies were intended to replace future income for Petitioner at income levels he attained before his disability and at levels for a dentist which were expected to increase; (2) the policies were not intended for retirement purposes because they terminate when Petitioner reaches age 65; and (3) the community paid approximately $12,000.00 in premiums on the policies and received from them approximately $300,000.00 in monthly disability payments prior to the dissolution.

The Court of Appeals, the Honorable Karen G. Seinfeld writing, reversed the trial court, holding that the court "erred in ruling that [Dr. Brewer's] postdissolution disability payments [are] . . . separate property." The case was remanded to allow the trial court to "exercise its discretion to either reaffirm its distribution [of property] or redistribute the property" according to the Court of Appeals' decision. Petitioner then sought review by this Court, which was granted on July 8, 1998.

DISCUSSION

Petitioner Michael A. Brewer contends the Court of Appeals erred in ruling that private disability insurance benefits are a divisible asset in a dissolution proceeding. He claims that court's decision is in conflict with Supreme Court decisions in *In re Marriage of Brown*[34] and *In re Marriage of Hall*[35] and in conflict with prior Court of Appeals decisions in *In re Marriage of Huteson*[36] and *In re Marriage of Anglin*.[37]

Respondent Deborah Q. Brewer answers to the contrary that the Court of Appeals was correct. She asserts that the decision is based on *Chase v. Chase*[38] which has not been overruled by *Brown*, nor is it in conflict with *Brown* because the cases have different facts and address different issues. Neither party disputes the trial court's findings of fact. They are thus verities on this appeal.[39]

The principal issue addressed by the Court of Appeals was whether the "trial court err[ed] in characterizing postdissolution disability payments as [Petitioner Michael A. Brewer's] separate property." Despite questioning the continued viability of *Chase*, the Court of Appeals relied upon it in concluding that the trial court mischaracterized as Petitioner's separate property monthly payments under the disability insurance policies privately purchased with community funds.

Characterization of property as community or separate is not controlling in division of property between the parties in a dissolution proceeding, but "the court must have in mind the correct character and status of the property . . . before any theory of division is ordered." All property, both separate and community, is before the court. Under RCW 26.16.010 and RCW 26.16.020 *separate property* is "[p]roperty and pecuniary rights" owned by each spouse before marriage or acquired afterwards by gift, bequest, devise, descent or inheritance." Under RCW 26.16.030 *community property* is property that is not defined as separate property under RCW 26.16.010 or RCW 26.16.020 and is "acquired after marriage by either husband or wife or both. . . ." In prior decisions this Court has favored characterizing property as community instead of as separate property unless there is clearly no question of its character. The decision in *Chase* is consistent with that approach.

In *Chase* this Court announced the rule that "if . . . premiums are paid with community funds, the insurance proceeds are community property." Respondent asserts "[t]here has been no . . . change or inconsistency in Washington law that mandates essentially rethinking [*Chase*]." This assertion is not correct. *Chase* does not accurately reflect the current law for characterizing proceeds of insurance policies in dissolution proceedings. Professor Harry M. Cross, an acknowledged authority on community property in Washington, suggests that the rule announced in *Chase* that "if the community pays premiums, insurance proceeds are community property" should not apply to disability policies. He suggests that disability insurance payments should be characterized in the same manner as tort damages were characterized in *Brown*.

---

34. 100 Wash. 2d 729, 675 P.2d 1207 (1984).
35. 103 Wash. 2d 236, 692 P.2d 175 (1984).
36. 27 Wash. App. 539, 619 P.2d 991 (1980).
37. 52 Wash. App. 317, 759 P.2d 1224 (1988).
38. 74 Wash. 2d 253, 444 P.2d 145 (1968).
39. *Moreman v. Butcher*, 126 Wash. 2d 36, 39, 891 P.2d 725 (1995).

Brown, in defining community property, limited it to acquisitions "through the toil, talent or other productive faculty of either spouse, but not compensation for personal injury." Under that definition, the case held tort damages which compensate for services or earnings lost by the community, or for expenses incurred by the community during the injury, would be community property; but tort damages which compensate for pain and suffering to the injured party and injury-related expenses after dissolution of the marriage would be separate property. The Court reached this conclusion in order to eliminate the inequity of an uninjured spouse sharing in reimbursement of expenses for which that person has no liability.

A logical application of *Brown* to privately purchased disability insurance policies suggests that after dissolution of a marriage payment of monthly benefits which constitute future income, or compensation for pain and suffering, should be characterized as separate property even though premium payments were made from community funds during the marriage. Insurance compensating for expenses incurred during a marriage or for earnings lost during the marriage or proceeds that in fact constitute deferred compensation should be characterized as community property in proportion to the community's contribution to those expenses or deferred compensation. This Court has previously recognized disability payments which are in fact deferred compensation in *Arnold v. Department of Retirement Sys.*[59] Thus, as in *Brown*, a former spouse not responsible for an injured ex-spouse's future expenses would not "share in reimbursement for expenses which [that person] . . . is not obligated to, and does not, pay."

Petitioner asserts that proceeds from privately purchased disability insurance policies should not be a divisible asset in marital dissolution proceedings regardless whether they are characterized as separate property or community property.

Under RCW 26.09.080 trial courts have broad discretion in the distribution of property and liabilities in marriage dissolution proceedings.[62] This discretion applies to distribution of monthly payments under privately purchased disability insurance policies acquired during the marriage. Distribution of property by the trial court should be disturbed only if there has been a manifest abuse of discretion. The trial court is in the best position to assess the assets and liabilities of the parties and determine what is "fair, just and equitable under all the circumstances."

Under the facts of this case, the trial court did not abuse its discretion in distributing future monthly disability payments to Petitioner Michael A. Brewer under the private disability insurance policies purchased during the marriage with premiums paid from community funds. The community paid $12,000.00 in premiums on the

---

59. 128 Wash. 2d 765, 778, 912 P.2d 463 (1996) ("Despite the general community property presumption under RCW 26.16.030, Washington courts have refused to treat disability income, including disability pensions, as community assets subject to allocation in a dissolution proceeding in the absence of substantial elements of either deferred compensation or retirement. Such payments are for lost future income and are not 'earned' as are retirement benefits."). *See also In re Marriage of Kollmer*, 73 Wash. App. 373, 870 P.2d 978 (1994).

62. *In re Marriage of Konzen*, 103 Wash. 2d 470, 477-78, 693 P.2d 97 (1985) (former RCW 26.09.080 provides "[T]he court shall, without regard to marital misconduct, make such disposition of the property and liabilities of the parties, *either community or separate*, as shall appear *just and equitable after considering all relevant factors* including, but not limited to: (1)[t]he nature and extent of the community property; (2) [t]he nature and extent of the separate property; (3)[t]he duration of the marriage; and (4)[t]he economic circumstances of each spouse at the time the division of property is to become effective, including the desirability of awarding the family home or the right to live [in it] . . . for reasonable periods to a spouse having custody of any children." (emphasis added)).

policies and received disability payments totaling $300,000.00 prior to the dissolution. In making distribution to the parties, the trial court properly determined what was fair, just and equitable under all of the circumstances.

SUMMARY AND CONCLUSIONS

The Court of Appeals agreed with the trial court only in its distribution of property in this dissolution, but disagreed with its comments that it felt bound to award future disability payments under the disability insurance policies to Petitioner Michael A. Brewer as his separate property. The Court of Appeals, relying upon *Chase v. Chase*, concluded that disability insurance payments were community property. But this Court in *Marriage of Brown*, has moved away from such an absolute conclusion.

Under *Brown*, monthly payments under a disability insurance policy intended to compensate the insured for future income or pain and suffering should be characterized as separate property. Monthly payments under the policy which compensate for expenses incurred during the marriage, or earnings lost during the marriage or payments which are in fact deferred compensation, should be characterized as community property in proportion to the community's contribution to those expenses or to the deferred compensation plan.

Although under RCW 26.09.080 the trial court in a dissolution proceeding must consider the character and status of property before distribution, the actual characterization of property as community or separate is not essential to the exercise of discretion by the trial court in distributing assets and liabilities. The trial court under the facts of this case, in the exercise of its discretion, could award future disability payments to Petitioner Michael A. Brewer, regardless whether those payments are characterized as community property or separate property. The fact the trial court characterized the disability policies as separate property, even if in error, would not affect the discretionary disposition to Petitioner Michael A. Brewer. The trial court, under *Brown*, could properly characterize the monthly disability payments after the dissolution as the separate property of Petitioner Michael A. Brewer.

We therefore disagree with the Court of Appeals only in its determination that remand to the trial court was necessary. Any error committed by the trial court in concluding the disability insurance benefits were not assets subject to division was cured by the authority given courts under RCW 26.09.080 to divide both community property and separate property between the parties in a marriage dissolution, keeping in mind the correct character and status of the property and determining what is "fair, just and equitable under all the circumstances."

We conclude instead that the privately purchased disability insurance policies (Mutual of New York and New York Life Insurance Company) for Petitioner Michael A. Brewer acquired during the marriage with premiums paid from community funds retained their character as *community property* until the dissolution; but after the dissolution monthly payments to Petitioner Michael A. Brewer changed in character to his *separate property*. The trial court incorrectly concluded the disability insurance benefits were "not assets subject to division in this case."

We agree with the Court of Appeals on its conclusion that property distribution in this case was proper, but disagree only with that portion of its decision which remanded the case to the Clark County Superior Court. In so doing, we affirm the decision of the trial court which awarded to Petitioner Michael A. Brewer as his separate property future monthly disability payments under the private disability insurance policies purchased during his marriage to Respondent Deborah Q. Brewer with premiums paid from community funds during the marriage until the premiums were waived by the companies issuing the policies.

JOHNSON, TALMADGE, SANDERS and IRELAND, JJ., concur.

GUY, C.J. (concurring).

I agree with the majority that the rule enunciated in *In re Marriage of Brown,* 100 Wash. 2d 729, 675 P.2d 1207 (1984), applies to wage-replacement disability insurance benefits. I write separately because (1) I would specifically overrule *Chase v. Chase,* 74 Wash. 2d 253, 444 P.2d 145 (1968), and (2) I would clarify that post-dissolution wage-replacement benefits are not "assets" that are before the trial court in a dissolution proceeding.

In my view, we should clarify the law by overruling *Chase* and hold: Disability payments which are in the nature of earnings replacement are treated the same as the earnings of a healthy spouse. Therefore, when the parties are married and not separated, the replacement earnings would be community property; assets purchased with or generated by community funds are assets belonging to the community. RCW 26.16.030. When the parties are separated, their earnings — whether a result of wage replacement disability benefits or of personal labor — are separate property. RCW 26.16.140. Future, post-dissolution earnings, whether received from employment, business ventures, investment, or disability benefits, are not "assets" which are before the court for disposition in a dissolution action. *See Brown,* 100 Wash. 2d at 738, 675 P.2d 1207; *In re Marriage of Hall,* 103 Wash. 2d 236, 247, 692 P.2d 175 (1984) (future earning capacity is not a marital asset). However, the trial court may consider such earnings when determining what constitutes a fair and equitable distribution of the assets and debts which are before the court. RCW 26.09.080 (economic circumstances of each spouse is a relevant factor in making a property disposition); *Hall,* 103 Wash. 2d at 247, 692 P.2d 175; *In re Marriage of Leland,* Wash. App. 57, 72, 847 P.2d 518 (1993). The trial court also may consider such earnings when determining the propriety and amount of any maintenance award. RCW 26.09.090.

ALEXANDER, MADSEN and DURHAM, JJ., concur.

Discussion Questions

1. In *Hatcher,* the disability insurance was a voluntary program at husband Marvin's employment. In *Brewer,* the disability was a private disability insurance policy purchased by husband Michael. Did that difference change the character of the disability benefits?

2. What reasoning do the courts in *Hatcher* and *Brewer* use to support the conclusion that disability benefits are community property during marriage and separate property of the disabled spouse after divorce?

C. IT DEPENDS ON THE PURPOSE: THE LOUISIANA AND CALIFORNIA APPROACH

Louisiana and California courts have struggled with the scenario that disability benefits may possibly be a substitute for retirement benefits. In *Bordes v. Bordes*, 730 So. 2d 443 (La. 1999), the Louisiana Supreme Court addressed how to classify disability benefits when provided by an employee's retirement system. In *Marriage of Elfmont*, 9 Cal. 4th 1026, 891 P.2d 136, 29 Cal. Rptr. 2d 590 (1995), the California Supreme Court considered if private disability insurance coverage should be classified as community property if the spouses' intended it to substitute for retirement income.

BORDES v. BORDES

730 So. 2d 443 (1999)
Supreme Court of Louisiana

JOHNSON, Justice.

We granted certiorari in this case to review the court of appeal's ruling that the disability retirement benefits paid by the Parochial Employees' Retirement System of Louisiana are community property. For reasons discussed below, we reverse the judgment finding the benefits paid by the Parochial Employees' Retirement System of Louisiana are community property.

FACTS AND PROCEDURAL HISTORY

Mr. Gary Bordes and Ms. Roselyn Zito Bordes were married on December 5, 1981. The parties were divorced after ten years of marriage by a petition filed on May 8, 1991. One son was born to this union and he lives with Mr. Bordes. Prior to their marriage, Mr. Bordes was employed with the Water Department of Jefferson Parish. This employment, which began May 1, 1974, continued until November 17, 1994 when Mr. Bordes was declared totally disabled due to aplastic anemia and avascular necrosis of his hips. As a result of his total disability, Mr. Bordes began receiving disability retirement benefits from the Parochial Employees' Retirement System of Louisiana ("Parochial System") and the Employees' Retirement System of Jefferson Parish ("Jefferson System"). He receives $1,310.24 from the Parochial System and $503.69 from the Jefferson System, for a total of $1,813.93 per month.

On October 5, 1995, Ms. Bordes filed a petition to partition the community of acquets and gains along with a sworn detailed descriptive list. A trial on the merits of the petition was held on December 17, 1996. Before the trial began, the parties entered into a consent judgment stipulating to the following matters:

(1) That there will be a judgment rendered in favor of Ms. Bordes and against Mr. Bordes for one-half of the amount received from cashing in any

community U.S. Savings Bonds from May 8, 1991 through December 17, 1996, the trial date of the partition.

(2) That there would be judgment in favor of Mr. Bordes and against Ms. Bordes for one-half of the principal reduction of the mortgage on her separate property residence paid during the marriage.

(3) That the parties would enter into a Qualified Domestic Relations Order ("Q.U.A.D.R.O.") reflecting Ms. Bordes' 23% interest in the retirement plan of Mr. Bordes from both the Parochial System and the Jefferson System, to be effective May 17, 2012.

(4) That the parties have settled a claim regarding the patio and roof in favor of Mr. Bordes and against Ms. Bordes in the amount of $500.00 and agreed to divide the furniture and fixtures in kind.

The parties also stipulated to the following dates:

(1) The date of employment of Mr. Bordes with Jefferson Parish is May 1, 1974.

(2) The date of marriage is December 5, 1981

(3) The date of termination of the community is May 8, 1991.

(4) The date of Mr. Bordes' disability and termination of employment is November 17, 1994.

(5) The date Mr. Bordes would be eligible for normal retirement is May 17, 2012.

After the stipulations, the only issue remaining for trial was the classification of the disability retirement benefits received by Mr. Bordes since November 17, 1994. The trial court determined that the disability retirement benefits are based on the total years of service and the maximum salary earned during the highest three years of payment. Therefore, the benefits are deferred compensation which Mr. Bordes has elected to receive via early retirement and as such they are community assets. The court also ordered that the community interest of Ms. Bordes in the disability retirement benefits be determined using the formula established in *Sims v. Sims*, 358 So. 2d 919 (La. 1978).

On appeal, the Fifth Circuit Court of Appeal determined that there was sufficient evidence to support the trial court's conclusion that Ms. Bordes was entitled to share in the benefits received from the Parochial Employees' Retirement System. The court found the benefits from the Parochial System were deferred compensation within the meaning of *T.L. James & Company, Inc. v. Montgomery*, 332 So. 2d 834 (La. 1975); *Sims v. Sims*, 358 So. 2d 919 (La. 1978); and *Hare v. Hodgins*, 586 So. 2d 118 (La. 1991). However, the Jefferson Parish benefits were distinguished from the Parochial benefits. The court found the Jefferson benefits were not based on the actual years employed, but on a formula which allows additional years to be added; the benefits were only available upon disability; and Ms. Bordes would not receive any portion of the benefits remaining after Mr. Bordes' death because she would not be a surviving spouse. The portion of the trial court judgment finding the Jefferson System benefits to be community funds was reversed. In all other respects, the trial court judgment was affirmed. *Bordes v. Bordes*, 97-967 (La. App. 5th Cir. 1/27/98), 707 So. 2d 471. Mr. Bordes' writ to review the correctness of this ruling that the benefits paid by the Parochial Employees' Retirement System are community assets. *Bordes v. Bordes*, 98-1004 (La. 7/2/98), 721 So. 2d 897.

DISCUSSION

It is well settled in Louisiana that a former spouse is entitled to a pro rata share of the retirement benefits of a member spouse to the extent the retirement benefits were attributable to the former community. *Frazier v. Harper*, 600 So. 2d 59 (La. 1992); *Sims v. Sims*, 358 So. 2d 919 (La. 1978). The issue presented by this case is whether disability retirement benefits constitute deferred compensation in the nature of retirement or pension income so as to be classified as community property.

The courts of appeal have addressed the classification of disability benefits on numerous occasions. *See Hyde v. Hyde*, 96 1725 (La. App. 1st Cir. 6/26/97); 697 So. 2d 1061, *writ denied*, 97-1987 (La. 11/7/97); 703 So. 2d 1274; *Mercer v. Mercer*, 95–1257 (La. App. 3rd Cir. 4/3/96); 671 So. 2d 937; *Brant v. Brant*, 26,508 (La. App. 2d Cir. 1/25/95); 649 So. 2d 111; *Arnaud v. United Brotherhood of Carpenters and Joiners of America*, 577 So. 2d 184 (La. App. 1st Cir.), *writ not considered*, 580 So. 2d 369 (La. 1991); *Johnson v. Johnson*, 532 So. 2d 503 (La. App. 1st Cir. 1988); *Lachney v. Lachney*, 529 So. 2d 59 (La. App. 3rd Cir.), *writ denied*, 532 So. 2d 764 (La. 1988).

In *Lachney v. Lachney*, 529 So. 2d 59, the Third Circuit Court of Appeal considered a disability insurance policy available through the employee-spouse's employer. The employee spouse had not paid for the disability insurance coverage and the policy had no cash surrender value. Further, if the employee reached the age of sixty-five (65) without suffering a disability, the employee would never receive any benefits under the policy. The court held that the disability payments made under the policy were not deferred compensation, but were in the nature of tort damage awards and worker's compensation benefits. Accordingly, the court determined that the employee's spouse had no interest in the employee's monthly disability benefits received after dissolution of the community.

When presented with another opportunity to determine the appropriate classification of disability benefits, the Third Circuit again held that disability payments under a policy purchased with community funds were the separate property of the claimant spouse. *Mercer v. Mercer*, 671 So. 2d 937, 939–940. The court reasoned that since the disability policy had no cash surrender value, required periodic medical examinations for continuation of the benefits, and provided for termination of the disability benefits upon the claimant's death or the attainment of the age of sixty-five (65); the disability payments made pursuant to the policy were substitutions for wage losses and did not constitute deferred compensation in the nature of retirement or pension income to which his spouse had a legally recognizable claim.

The Second Circuit Court of Appeal followed the same line of reasoning as the Third Circuit when it decided *Brant v. Brant*, 649 So. 2d 111. The court determined that disability payments, which represented compensation a claimant would have earned if not for his illness, were not deferred income and required classification of those benefits in accordance with the approach used by the courts in allocating tort damage awards and worker's compensation benefits.

In *Johnson v. Johnson*, 532 So. 2d 503, the First Circuit held that disability benefits received by an employee spouse pursuant to La. Rev. Stat. Ann. 33:2113.1 were community assets. The disability benefits were paid from a fund comprised, in part, of employee contributions; the payment was a percentage of the employee's average compensation; and the actual percentage was based on the number of years of service of the injured employee. Upon retirement, the accumulated contributions of the employee, together with an amount taken from the pension account, were placed in a reserve account for the payment of future retirement benefits. The court explained that the employee's right to receive compensation for his disability was based entirely on his contributions to the fund from community earnings and his years of service. Accordingly, the court determined that the disability benefits were community property.

More recently, the First Circuit concluded that disability benefits received by an employee-spouse until he reaches age sixty-five (65) are not deferred compensation and are not in the nature of retirement benefits. *Hyde v. Hyde*, 697 So. 2d 1061. The court found that the employee-spouse did not make any contribution to the disability plan whatsoever. If he had continued to work without suffering from a disabling condition, he would not have been entitled to receive any disability benefits and if he was able to return to work, his monthly disability benefits would be discontinued. Further, at retirement age (65 years old), the employee-spouse would receive unreduced retirement benefits, a proportionate interest of which would belong to his spouse. Therefore, the court found that the disability benefits received by the employee-spouse as a result of his disability were more representative of compensation for lost earnings due to an inability to work and, as such, were his separate property. *Hyde*, 697 So. 2d at 1065.

The case sub judice involves disability retirement benefits from two separate retirement systems, the Parochial Employees' Retirement System of Louisiana and the Employees' Retirement System of Jefferson Parish. The Court of Appeal determined that benefits paid by the Employees' Retirement System of Jefferson Parish are the separate property of Mr. Bordes. Ms. Bordes did not seek review of the correctness of this determination, therefore, the only issue before this Court is the proper classification of the benefits paid by the Parochial Employees' Retirement System of Louisiana.

Parochial Employees' Retirement System of Louisiana

Mr. Bordes applied for disability retirement with the Parochial System on November 17, 1994. A member of the Parochial System is eligible to retire and receive a disability benefit if he has at least five years of creditable service, is not eligible for normal retirement, and suffers disability. La. Rev. Stat. Ann. 11:1943. Mr. Bordes has 20.46575 years of creditable service with Jefferson Parish, he has been disabled by aplastic anemia with avascular necrosis of both hips, and he is not eligible for normal retirement.[1] Having met the conditions for disability retirement benefits, Mr. Bordes is required to undergo a medical examination every year for the first five years of disability and once every three years thereafter until he attains

---

1. Pursuant to La. Rev. Stat. Ann. 11:1941, a member of the Parochial System is eligible to retire if he has at least:

    (1) Thirty years of creditable service, regardless of age.
    (2) Twenty-five years of creditable service, and is at least age fifty-five.
    (3) Ten years of creditable service, and is at least age sixty.

Mr. Bordes was 42 years old when he applied for disability retirement benefits, failing to meet the eligibility requirements for normal retirement.

normal retirement age. La. Rev. Stat. Ann. 11:1934(A). If he engages in or is able to engage in gainful occupation, his disability retirement benefits will be terminated. La. Rev. Stat. Ann. 11:1934(B). In order to insure that he is not able to engage in gainful employment, Mr. Bordes is required to submit an annual income statement to the Parochial System.

As an employee of the Water Department, Mr. Bordes was eligible to participate in the Jefferson Parish and the Parochial Retirement Systems. Membership in the two retirement systems was a benefit of employment with the Water Department. He made contributions to both retirement systems and the Water Department made contributions as well. Mr. Bordes' contributions went into an annuity savings account and his employer's contributions went into the general fund of the pension plan. According to Mr. A.C. Tynes, Secretary-Manager of the Jefferson System, the annuity savings account accumulates until the employee starts receiving a monthly benefit. The funds in the annuity savings account are exhausted first, then payments are made from the general fund.

Mr. Bordes elected to receive the maximum allowance from the Parochial System. This election gives Mr. Bordes the maximum disability retirement allowance payable for life, with no provisions for a survivor benefit. If Mr. Bordes should die before having received in retirement benefits the amount he contributed to the system, the balance will be refunded in a lump-sum payment to his designated beneficiary. The disability payment is determined by multiplying the years of creditable service by three percent and then multiplying that number by the employee's highest total earnings for any 36 successive months. This calculation gave Mr. Bordes a total monthly benefit of $1,813.93, of which $1,310.24 is paid by the Parochial System. The remaining $503.69 is paid by the Employees' Retirement System of Jefferson Parish.

The normal retirement age for Mr. Bordes is age sixty. When he reaches this age, his disability retirement benefit will automatically become a normal retirement benefit. Unlike the disability insurance policies reviewed by the Courts of Appeal in *Mercer*, 671 So. 2d 937; *Brant*, 649 So. 2d 111; and *Lachney*, 529 So. 2d 59, the benefits payable under this plan are not really disability benefits. Rather the significance of disability under this retirement plan is that disability triggers the early entitlement to retirement benefits which, but for the disability, would not be payable until normal retirement age. Further, the Parochial System plan does not provide for termination of monthly disability retirement benefits when the employee reaches normal retirement age. To the contrary, when Mr. Bordes reaches normal retirement age the amount of payment does not change, nor does the source of payment. The only changes are the discontinuance of the income statement requirement and the periodic medical examination. However, like the aforementioned plans, Mr. Bordes' monthly disability retirement benefits will be terminated if he is able to return to work.

The purpose of paying benefits under a retirement plan is different when the benefits are payable because the employee spouse becomes disabled than when the benefits are payable because the employee spouse reaches normal retirement age. When the divorced employee spouse receives benefits because of disability, the benefits are paid in lieu of income that would otherwise be the employee spouse's separate property. Basing the classification of benefits upon the purpose of the payment of the benefits is fair and equitable, and provides ease of administration.

When the employee spouse becomes disabled, the benefits replace the working wages he or she can no longer earn. On the other hand, the non-employee spouse can continue to earn (and keep) one hundred percent of the wages he or she was earning when the employee spouse became disabled. Awarding a share of disability retirement benefits to the non-employee spouse who does not need to replace wages lost because of inability to work, while reducing the amount of benefits payable to the disabled spouse who has such a need, is contrary to the purpose of a disability feature in a retirement plan.

While the source of Mr. Bordes' disability retirement benefits is the same as his normal retirement benefits, this alone does not make the payments more representative of retirement income. Other factors support classifying the benefits as compensation for lost earnings. They include the fact that the payments are conditioned on Mr. Bordes' continuing disability, that he is required to undergo periodic medical examinations and submit annual income statements while receiving the benefits, and the benefits automatically convert to a normal retirement benefit upon his reaching retirement age. If the disability retirement benefits were normal retirement benefits, there would be no changes when the employee reaches normal retirement age. It is clear that Mr. Bordes' disability retirement benefits are more akin to compensation for lost earnings due to serious injury or illness. Under La. Civ. Code Ann. art. 2344, damages due to personal injuries, including the portion of the award designed to compensate for loss of earnings, are separate property. Accordingly, Mr. Bordes' disability retirement benefits are his separate property and Ms. Bordes is not entitled to share in these benefits.

As previously stated, Mr. Bordes' disability retirement benefits will automatically convert into a normal retirement benefit when he reaches age sixty. A spouse's right to receive benefits payable by a retirement plan is an asset of the community. *Sims*, 358 So. 2d 919, 922 (La. 1978). At the time of partition, the non-employee spouse is entitled to a declaration of the interest attributable to the community in retirement benefits, if and when they become due. When they do become due, the non-employee spouse is entitled to receive the proportion of them recognized as attributable to the other spouse's employment during the existence of the community. *Sims*, 358 So. 2d 919, 923-924. The parties entered into a consent judgment which recognized Ms. Bordes' 23% interest in the retirement plan from both the Parochial System and the Jefferson System to be effective May 17, 2012. Therefore, Ms. Bordes is entitled to receive the proportion of Mr. Bordes' retirement benefits attributable to his employment during the community on May 17, 2012.

Decree

For the foregoing reasons, we reverse the portion of the court of appeal judgment finding the benefits received from the Parochial Employees' Retirement System of Louisiana are community property. It is ordered that there be judgment in favor of Mr. Bordes, and against Ms. Bordes, that the disability retirement benefits received from the Parochial Employees' Retirement System of Louisiana are his separate property. Further, it is ordered that there be judgment in favor of Ms. Bordes recognizing her 23% interest in the retirement benefits to be paid by the Parochial Employees' Retirement System of Louisiana and the Employees' Retirement System of Jefferson Parish effective May 17, 2012. The matter is remanded to the trial court for further proceedings in accordance with this order.

Reversed and remanded.

Discussion Question

1. What are the main features of a disability/retirement plan that determine whether the disability benefits are community or separate property?

MARRIAGE OF ELFMONT

9 Cal. 4th 1026, 891 P.2d 136, 29 Cal. Rptr. 2d 590 (1995)
Supreme Court of California

WERDEGAR, Associate Justice.

Under what circumstances should disability insurance benefits received by a husband after dissolution of the marriage be divided as community property? In *In re Marriage of Saslow* (1985) 40 Cal. 3d 848, 221 Cal. Rptr. 546, 710 P.2d 346 (hereafter *Saslow*), where the insurance was purchased wholly out of community funds and payment of the benefits commenced during the marriage, we held benefits received after separation were community property, insofar as they were intended to provide retirement income, and separate property, insofar as they were intended to replace the disabled spouse's postdissolution earnings.

Here, although disability term insurance for the husband was purchased out of community funds during the marriage, payment of the benefits did not commence until 32 months after the parties' separation, during which time the husband had paid renewal premiums out of his separate property to keep the insurance in effect. As in *Saslow*, there was evidence the premium payments during the marriage were made with an intent to provide retirement income. It also appears the husband's physical condition at the time of separation might have precluded his continuing to enjoy comparable disability coverage without the automatic policy renewal rights that had been purchased by the community.

Under *Saslow*, however, we look to "the spouses' intent" not only "at the time the disability insurance was originally purchased," but also "at the times that decisions were made to continue the insurance in force rather than let it lapse" (40 Cal. 3d at p. 861, 221 Cal. Rptr. 546, 710 P.2d 346). In the present case, no evidence indicates the husband's decision to renew the insurance after the parties' separation, by paying premiums out of his separate property, was accompanied by any intent to provide community retirement income. Accordingly, proof that continuation of his disability coverage was dependent upon policy renewal rights purchased with premiums paid out of community funds would not establish any community property interest in the insurance proceeds. Decisions basing community property interests in term *life* insurance proceeds upon the community's purchase of policy renewal rights (e.g., *Biltoft v. Wootten* (1979) 96 Cal. App. 3d 58, 157 Cal. Rptr. 581) are distinguishable, because of differences between the respective purposes of life and disability insurance, and because interests in term life insurance do not depend upon the *Saslow* requirement that an intent to provide community retirement income accompany the premium payment for the term in which the proceeds become payable.

Here, the husband appealed from a judgment characterizing disability insurance proceeds as community property. The Court of Appeal reversed. We shall affirm the judgment of the Court of Appeal.

I.   Facts and Procedural Background

John H. Elfmont (husband) and Edie M. Elfmont (wife) were married in 1975 and separated on May 1, 1987. They have a daughter born in 1978 and a son born in 1979. The present dissolution proceeding was commenced in August 1987.

Husband was born in February 1939. During the marriage he practiced medicine as an obstetrician and gynecologist. In 1977, he incorporated his medical practice, established a corporate pension and profit-sharing plan, and took out disability insurance that would pay $3,500 per month. The coverage under that policy was increased to $4,000 per month in 1980 and to $5,000 per month in 1983. In 1982 and 1984 he purchased two more policies, each for $2,000 per month, bringing the total benefits payable upon his disability to $9,000 per month. All of this disability coverage was in the form of three-month term insurance. Each policy guaranteed renewal upon timely payment of the renewal premium, but provided that, if the premium were not paid within the 31-day grace period following the expiration of any 3-month term, the policy would lapse. Before the parties' separation, all the premiums were paid out of community earnings.

At the time of separation, husband's medical practice was grossing about $450,000 per year and contributing almost $60,000 per year to the corporate retirement plan, which had a total value of approximately $600,000. After separation, husband kept the disability insurance in effect by paying the premiums out of his separate property.

In 1989 husband became disabled from a disorder of the lower back. He thereafter made arrangements to sell his medical practice, with a covenant not to compete, for $265,000. As of January 1, 1990, he applied for disability insurance benefits of $9,000 per month. The benefits became payable, after policy waiting periods, on February 1, 1990, under the larger ($5,000 per month) policy and on April 1, 1990, under the two smaller policies. Payment of the benefits is expected to continue indefinitely, so long as he remains unable to resume the practice of medicine.

At the trial to determine issues of property division and support, husband explained how his lower back disorder, for which he receives the benefits, interfered with his obstetrics practice. He described his disability as consisting of multi-level degenerative disc disease in the lower back, a compression fracture of the first lumbar vertebra, and osteoarthritis in the neck. He thereby related the disability to two separate incidents, one before, and the other after, the parties' separation.

Husband testified the first incident was brought to light, in 1985 or 1986, by CAT-scan (computerized axial tomography) findings showing a large herniated disc between the fifth lumbar and first sacral vertebrae on the left side.

In hindsight, he traced the source of those findings to an occasion in 1980 or 1981 when he lifted his then two-year-old daughter off a coffee table. He knew at the time he had hurt his back, but did not then think the injury was significant. In written applications for increased disability insurance in 1982, 1983 and 1984, he denied having any back disorder or other physical impairment.

The second incident occurred in the summer of 1989, when he was injured on a ride at a water slide park. An examination showed he had incurred a compression fracture of the body of the first lumbar vertebra and a slipped disc between the fourth and fifth lumbar vertebrae on the right side.

Wife testified as follows: When husband lifted their daughter from the coffee table in 1980 or 1981, he had significant pain "a good part of the week" and, after that, intermittent pain that "never went away." One day he told her of hearing about a physician in his 50's who hated his practice and wanted to quit. The physician had a slipped disc that he deliberately neglected, letting it degenerate, with the result he ultimately was able to claim disability. Someone had suggested to husband that he "do that." He told wife, "I'm going to retire by the time I'm fifty no matter what happens." Wife's testimony was corroborated by a family friend, who testified to hearing repeated expressions by husband of a desire to retire by the age of 50.

After considering arguments on the applicability of *Saslow, supra,* 40 Cal. 3d 848, 221 Cal. Rptr. 546, 710 P.2d 346, the trial court made oral findings to the following effect: The benefits husband receives from the disability coverage as originally purchased in 1977 and increased in 1980 to $4,000 per month are his separate property, because that coverage was intended to replace his earnings. But the remaining benefits of $5,000 per month, derived from the addition of $1,000 per month to the original policy and the acquisition of two more policies for $2,000 per month each, are community property, because husband acquired the additional insurance for a different purpose. As the court explained: "Circumstances had changed. He [husband] knew he had a problem with the back. I don't think there was anything fraudulent about [insurance] applications, because there was no specific proof that he had a herniated disc.... But I think in the back of his head he knew he was going to have a problem, and that consequently that whole program was geared toward that." Since the court was speaking in the context of our *Saslow* decision, we infer that, in the court's view, the purpose for which husband acquired the additional insurance was to provide retirement income.

The judgment, dated June 14, 1990, describes the three disability insurance policies and provides that (1) $1,000 out of the $5,000 to be paid monthly under the first policy is community property; (2) all of the $4,000 per month to be paid under the other two policies is community property; and (3) the total monthly community property benefits of $5,000 are to be paid $2,500 to husband and $2,500 to wife. The judgment also requires that husband be reimbursed $7,850 from the community for "payments from his separate property of premium payments on the community portion of the Provident disability policy." Husband appealed, challenging only the provisions of the judgment finding $5,000 per month of his disability benefits to be community property. Wife did not appeal.

The Court of Appeal, one justice dissenting, reversed with directions to find all the disability insurance benefits to be husband's separate property and to adjust spousal and child support accordingly. The majority declined on two grounds to apply the requirement of *Saslow, supra,* 40 Cal. 3d 848, 221 Cal. Rptr. 546, 710 P.2d

346, that postseparation disability benefits be classified as community property inso-far as they are intended to replace retirement income. First, husband here not only purchased disability insurance, but also invested community funds in a substantial retirement plan, whereas the husband in *Saslow* did not have a retirement or pension plan and could reasonably be found to have procured disability insurance as a substitute for any such plan (40 Cal. 3d at pp. 855, 862, 221 Cal. Rptr. 546, 710 P.2d 346). Second, unlike the husband in *Saslow*, who began drawing disability benefits before the parties separated, husband here used his separate property to pay renewal premiums on the insurance after separation, and his disability giving rise to the benefits occurred only thereafter, during a policy term for which the premium had not been paid with community funds.

The dissent in the Court of Appeal, on the other hand, would have allowed the community a reduced amount of the $5,000 per month benefits the trial court found to be community property, calculating the reduction as follows: First, those benefits would be divided between community and separate property shares proportionately to the relative amounts of community and separate funds used to pay the premiums on the underlying insurance before and after separation. Second, the community property share would be further restricted to benefits received by husband before he reaches $59\frac{1}{2}$, the age at which his fully funded pension plan becomes available as a retirement resource. All subsequently received disability benefits would be husband's separate property, on the theory those benefits were intended to provide for retirement only until he begins to receive pension benefits.

II.   INTENT TO PROVIDE RETIREMENT INCOME

In *Saslow, supra*, 40 Cal. 3d 848, 221 Cal. Rptr. 546, 710 P.2d 346, we recognized that "[t]he primary purpose of disability benefits is to compensate the disabled spouse for lost earnings — earnings which would normally be separate property" (*id.* at p. 860, 221 Cal. Rptr. 546, 710 P.2d 346). The benefits, if acquired with community funds, become community property only "insofar as they are intended to provide retirement income." (*Id.* at p. 861, 221 Cal. Rptr. 546, 710 P.2d 346, fn. omitted.)

The Court of Appeal concluded any finding of an intent during the marriage to use the disability benefits as retirement income was precluded by the fact that here, unlike in *Saslow*, husband had invested up to $60,000 a year in his professional corporation's tax-qualified pension plan, a plan that was worth approximately $600,000 at the time of separation and was to become available for distribution when he reached the age of $59\frac{1}{2}$. We disagree. Husband's investment in the pension plan did not preclude the trial court from finding the parties intended to supplement the retirement income produced by the plan with benefits from the disability insurance. The court could reasonably infer income from both sources would be required to maintain the standard of living the parties were deriving from husband's lucrative solo medical practice, particularly since further contributions to the pension plan would be cut off if he fulfilled his wish to retire at age 50.

Other evidence tends to support the trial court's view, expressed in oral findings, that, prior to the parties' separation, the disability insurance in dispute was acquired and maintained out of community funds for the purpose of providing retirement income. Husband testified he hated medical practice, and wife gave testimony of husband's determination to retire by the time he was 50, no matter what happened, and of his tale of a physician who also hated medical practice and had deliberately let his back deteriorate in order to claim disability benefits. Husband's experience of hurting his back in lifting his small daughter, while it did not produce an injury significant enough to require disclosure on disability insurance applications, may have raised in his mind the possibility of following the other physician's example.

Saslow, however, indicates that in apportioning disability insurance benefits between community and separate property, the court should consider the spouses' intent not only "at the time the disability insurance was originally purchased," but also "at the times that decisions were made to continue the insurance in force rather than let it lapse" (40 Cal. 3d at p. 861, 221 Cal. Rptr. 546, 710 P.2d 346). Spousal intent at the latter time is especially important when a basic change of circumstances, such as the parties' separation, has intervened since the insurance was originally purchased. Here, of course, there is no indication or suggestion that husband had any intent of providing *community* retirement income when, after the parties' separation, he used his separate funds to renew the disability policies for additional terms.

III. PURCHASE OF INSURANCE WITH COMMUNITY FUNDS

Postseparation disability benefits, even if intended to provide retirement income, may be treated as community property only to the extent they were "purchased during marriage with community funds" (*Saslow, supra*, 40 Cal. 3d at p. 854, 221 Cal. Rptr. 546, 710 P.2d 346). During the parties' marriage and up to the time of separation, community funds were used to purchase each of the insurance policies underlying husband's disability benefits and to renew each policy for additional three-month terms. After separation, however, husband paid further renewal premiums out of his separate property, thereby keeping the insurance in force until he qualified for disability benefits 32 months later.

Term disability insurance is similar in some, but not in all, respects to term life insurance. "Term life insurance policies typically contain two elements, dollar coverage payable in the event of death and a right to renewal for future terms without proof of current medical eligibility. [¶] . . . [A]s to dollar coverage, term life insurance upon which premiums were paid from community funds has no value after the term has ended without the insured having become deceased." (*Estate of Logan* (1987) 191 Cal. App. 3d 319, 324, 236 Cal. Rptr. 368.) "If the insured remains insurable, the right to renew the policy has no value since the insured could obtain comparable term insurance for a comparable price in the open market." (*Id.* at p. 325, 236 Cal. Rptr. 368; accord, *In re Marriage of Spengler* (1992) 5 Cal. App. 4th 288, 6 Cal. Rptr. 2d 764; see *In re Marriage of Lorenz* (1983) 146 Cal. App. 3d 464, 194 Cal. Rptr. 237 [term life policy insuring a still living spouse not a community asset because it lacks present cash surrender value].)

An insured who is not medically "insurable," however, may be unable after separation to continue life insurance coverage except by exercising the policy's renewal right, previously purchased with community funds, and paying renewal premiums for one or more additional terms out of his or her separate property. If the insured then dies during an additional term thus purchased, it has been held that the community has an interest in the life insurance proceeds commensurate with its contributions to the right of renewal. (See *Bowman v. Bowman* (1985) 171 Cal. App. 3d 148, 159, 217 Cal. Rptr. 174; *In re Marriage of Gonzalez* (1985) 168 Cal. App. 3d 1021, 214 Cal. Rptr. 634; *Biltoft v. Wootten, supra,* 96 Cal. App. 3d 58, 157 Cal. Rptr. 581.)

That the community's purchase of renewal rights in term *disability* insurance gives rise to an analogous community property interest in disability benefits does not, however, follow. Term life insurance and term disability insurance have dissimilar purposes. The proceeds of a term life policy are payable not to the insured, but to survivors, offsetting the economic consequences of the insured's death. To provide for a former spouse's participation in those proceeds, when premium payments from community funds have purchased policy renewal rights necessary to keep the insurance in force, may well be appropriate.

The purpose of term disability insurance, by contrast, is to replace lost earnings. If during the marriage an insured spouse becomes disabled, the benefits received are community property because they replace community earnings. (*In re Marriage of Jones* (1975) 13 Cal. 3d 457, 462, 119 Cal. Rptr. 108, 531 P.2d 420.) If the benefits continue after the spouses have separated, they are the separate property of the insured spouse whose earnings they replace, unless during the marriage the premiums were paid out of community funds with the intent that the benefits provide retirement income. (*Saslow, supra,* 40 Cal. 3d at pp. 860-861, 221 Cal. Rptr. 546, 710 P.2d 346.) If, however, the insured spouse has not become disabled during the last policy term for which a premium was paid before the parties' separation, the community will have no interest in benefits produced by renewals of the policy for subsequent terms, because the renewal premium will not have been paid "during the marriage with community funds" and with the intent of providing community retirement income (*id.* at pp. 854, 861, 221 Cal. Rptr. 546, 710 P.2d 346).

A contractual renewal right that is included in a term disability policy purchased and renewed during the marriage with community funds may afford an insured spouse, who is medically ineligible for new insurance when the parties separate, an opportunity to obtain further disability coverage that would otherwise be unavailable. But unlike a right to renew term life insurance, which keeps alive a possibility of benefits in which the community will have an interest, the right to renew the insured spouse's term disability insurance after separation does not give rise to any community property interest in the insured's disability benefits. (See *Saslow, supra,* 40 Cal. 3d at p. 861, fn. 5, 221 Cal. Rptr. 546, 710 P.2d 346.)

IV.   Conclusion

None of husband's disability insurance benefits became payable during terms of policy coverage for which the premiums had been paid out of community funds during the marriage with the intent of providing community retirement income. Instead, husband became entitled to draw the benefits only after he had renewed all three term policies, following the parties' separation, with premiums paid out of his separate property and with no such intent. Accordingly, all the benefits are his separate property.

The judgment of the Court of Appeal is affirmed.

LUCAS, C.J., and MOSK, ARABIAN and BAXTER, JJ., concur.

BAXTER, Associate Justice, concurring.

I have signed the majority opinion because I concur in the majority's judgment that the disability insurance proceeds are the husband's separate property. I also agree with the majority's reasoning that the present case is distinguishable from *In re Marriage of Saslow* (1985) 40 Cal. 3d 848, 221 Cal. Rptr. 546, 710 P.2d 346 (*Saslow*) because the husband in the present case renewed the insurance policies after the parties' marital separation, with premiums paid with his separate property, i.e., his postseparation income, and with no intent to provide retirement income to the marital community. I write separately, however, because I believe that instead of merely distinguishing *Saslow* we should overrule it. *Saslow* was poorly reasoned and incorrect in result and may continue to cause future problems that, unlike this case, cannot be distinguished.

As the majority correctly explains, *Saslow* held that disability insurance proceeds received after marital separation are community property if three conditions are met: (1) the insurance was purchased wholly with community funds; (2) payment of the benefits began before the separation; and (3) the benefits were intended to provide community retirement income. My principal objection to *Saslow* is the third element. In the private disability insurance context, I see no apparent logic in the notion that disability benefits can be a replacement for retirement income.

Saslow, supra, 40 Cal. 3d 848, 221 Cal. Rptr. 546, 710 P.2d 346, must first be put in context. It was preceded by a number of decisions dealing with government pensions and disability payments. For example, in the case on which *Saslow* relied most heavily, the husband was entitled to choose between military disability and retirement pay. (*In re Marriage of Stenquist* (1978) 21 Cal. 3d 779, 148 Cal. Rptr. 9, 582 P.2d 96 (*Stenquist*).) He chose the disability alternative because its payments were higher — 75 percent of his salary rather than 65 percent if he chose the retirement alternative. (Like his retirement, the disability payments were based on length of service and rank.) No one disputed that his retirement pension was a community asset. He contended, however, that the disability payments were his separate property. The court disagreed, finding that he should not be allowed to defeat the community interest in the retirement pension by electing the disability alternative. Specifically, the holding was that military retirement pay for disability contains two components, compensation for lost earnings (separate property) and retirement support (community property).

In *Saslow, supra,* 40 Cal. 3d 848, 221 Cal. Rptr. 546, 710 P.2d 346, as in the present case, the husband was not a government worker. The disability payments were purchased from a private insurer. *Saslow* acknowledged this difference and acknowledged the difficulty of applying the *Stenquist, supra,* 21 Cal. 3d 779, 148 Cal. Rptr. 9, 582 P.2d 96, reasoning, but nevertheless held that private disability benefits are separate property if they are intended by the parties to replace postdissolution earnings that would have been the spouse's separate property, but are community property to the extent they are intended to replace retirement income. *Saslow, supra,* 40 Cal. 3d 848, 221 Cal. Rptr. 546, 710 P.2d 346, misinterpreted *Stenquist, supra,* 21 Cal. 3d 779, 148 Cal. Rptr. 9, 582 P.2d 96. As a later Court of Appeal observed,

"The case [*Stenquist*] holds only that the portion of a disability pension which is attributable to employment longevity rather than to the disability is akin to a retirement pension and thus is community property." (*In re Marriage of Fisk* (1992) 2 Cal. App. 4th 1698, 1705, 4 Cal. Rptr. 2d 95.) In *Saslow, supra,* 40 Cal. 3d 848, 221 Cal. Rptr. 546, 710 P.2d 346, as in the present case, no portion of the disability benefits were attributable to longevity of employment and thus bore no attribute of a retirement pension. *Saslow* extended *Stenquist, supra,* 21 Cal. 3d 779, 148 Cal. Rptr. 9, 582 P.2d 96, beyond its logical limits.

Aside from a lack of precedent, the threshold problem with *Saslow, supra,* 40 Cal. 3d 848, 221 Cal. Rptr. 546, 710 P.2d 346, is that it does not comport with commercial insurance reality. A disability insurer does not pay its insured to retire; rather, the whole purpose of coverage is to replace lost earnings. Imagine the response if a person called his or her insurer and said, "I'm tired of working, sell me a lot of disability coverage, so I can claim a disability and retire early." Preposterous as that is, it is the cornerstone of *Saslow.* One simply cannot, however, purchase disability insurance to retire.

The point in *Stenquist, supra,* 21 Cal. 3d 779, 148 Cal. Rptr. 9, 582 P.2d 96, and the other government-worker cases was that the bureaucrat had a fund from which to draw based on his years of service, salary, and the like. He could take it either as a retirement pension or as disability. The courts believed the worker should not be allowed to defeat a spouse's interest in this fund that had been acquired with community labor during the marriage merely by labeling the payments as being for disability rather than for retirement. In that limited context, the reasoning perhaps makes some sense. But, in the private disability insurance context, the principle is not only difficult to apply, as acknowledged in *Saslow, supra,* 40 Cal. 3d 848, 221 Cal. Rptr. 546, 710 P.2d 346, the principle also simply makes no sense. If the person is able to work, he will not be paid the benefits, i.e., as a practical matter insurance companies are not charitable institutions. They are not going to pay an insured to take an early retirement under the ruse of a disability.

Implicit in *Saslow, supra,* 40 Cal. 3d 848, 221 Cal. Rptr. 546, 710 P.2d 346, was the view that the insurance company had been "scammed." Perhaps the facts in a given case may suggest a spouse has manipulated his or her circumstances so as to quit work early in life. But we should not be second-guessing the carrier's determination that its insured is disabled. If it believed he or she was not disabled, it surely would not have honored the claim for benefits. To suggest that disability insurance is a form of retirement planning will greatly surprise the insurance industry.

Moreover, the *Saslow* holding, *supra,* 40 Cal. 3d 848, 221 Cal. Rptr. 546, 710 P.2d 346, seems to require a court to second-guess every insurer's determination to pay benefits. If the insurer refuses to pay, the question of characterization of payments never arises. Thus, the question can arise only when the insurer concludes the insured is legitimately disabled. To characterize the payments as community property, however, the court will have to conclude that the carrier was duped and that the payments are really for retirement rather than for disability. This seems a curious result.

In light of all the flaws in *Saslow, supra,* 40 Cal. 3d 848, 221 Cal. Rptr. 546, 710 P.2d 346, and the problems it causes, I would overrule that decision. Otherwise, I concur in the present majority opinion.

ARABIAN, J., concurs.

GEORGE, Associate Justice, concurring and dissenting. (omitted)

KENNARD, Associate Justice, dissenting.

In a unanimous decision rendered in 1985, this court held that when a married couple buys a disability insurance policy with community funds, and the disabled spouse begins receiving benefits on the policy *during the marriage*, policy benefits paid after the couple has separated are the disabled spouse's separate property if such benefits were intended to replace that spouse's postdissolution earnings, but are community property if the couple purchased the policy with the intent to provide retirement income. (*In re Marriage of Saslow* (1985) 40 Cal. 3d 848, 221 Cal. Rptr. 546, 710 P.2d 346 (hereafter *Saslow*).) In this case, noncancelable term disability insurance1 was purchased with community funds, but benefit payments did not commence until *after the couple's separation*, during which time the insured spouse had used separate property to pay for renewal of the policy. Concluding that *Saslow* is inapplicable here, the majority holds that the disability benefits are entirely the property of the insured spouse.

I disagree. Although disability insurance is rarely purchased for the purpose of providing retirement income, when a couple *has* bought a disability insurance policy with this goal in mind we should recognize the community's interest in the policy, just as we recognize the community's interest in retirement pensions paid for with community funds. Here, in awarding all of the disability insurance benefits to the insured spouse, the majority disregards the substantial sums the community paid to purchase the policy. Not only is this an inequitable result, it is also an erosion of this court's decision in *Saslow, supra*, 40 Cal. 3d 848, 221 Cal. Rptr. 546, 710 P.2d 346. Unlike the majority, I would apply the *Saslow* rule to this case and hold that to the extent the marital couple intended the disability policy to provide for retirement income, the policy proceeds are community property, in an amount proportional to the percentage of the policy premiums paid for with community funds.

I

. . .

The trial court found that during their marriage the Elfmonts had bought 80 percent of their first disability insurance policy (providing $4,000 a month in benefits) as a replacement for husband's income if he became disabled, and that these benefits were thus his separate property. With regard to the remaining 20 percent of that policy (providing benefits of $1,000 per month) and the couple's other two disability insurance policies (each providing benefits of $2,000 per month) — all bought after husband had injured his back in 1980 or 1981 — the court found that the parties purchased the disability insurance to provide retirement income, rather than to replace earnings, and that therefore the benefits were community property. Consequently, the court awarded the wife half of these benefits, amounting to $2,500 per month. The court ordered the community to reimburse husband for the separate funds he expended to renew the "community portion" of the policies. The Court of Appeal reversed the judgment, holding that all of the disability benefits were husband's separate property.

II

In *In re Marriage of Stenquist* (1978) 21 Cal. 3d 779, 148 Cal. Rptr. 9, 582 P.2d 96 (hereafter *Stenquist*), we addressed the issue of whether the military disability pension of a husband should be treated as community or as separate property. The husband married six years after joining the army. Three years after the marriage, he suffered an injury that resulted in amputation of his left arm, but he chose to stay in the service and did not retire until 17 years later. At that time, he elected to receive a disability pension at 75 percent of his basic pay, in lieu of a retirement pension at 65 percent of basic pay.

In a subsequent court proceeding for dissolution of the marriage, the husband contended that the disability pension was his separate property. In support, he cited this court's decisions in *In re Marriage of Jones* (1975) 13 Cal. 3d 457, 119 Cal. Rptr. 108, 531 P.2d 420 and *In re Marriage of Brown* (1976) 15 Cal. 3d 838, 126 Cal. Rptr. 633, 544 P.2d 561. *Jones* held that a military person's right to disability benefits, acquired before earning a "vested" right to ordinary retirement benefits, was separate property. The next year, in *Brown*, we held that retirement benefits earned during the marriage, irrespective of whether they were "vested" or "nonvested" at the time of separation, were valuable community assets deserving of judicial protection.

We concluded in *Stenquist* that neither *Jones* nor *Brown* lent support to the husband's claim in *Stenquist* that the disability pension was his separate property. We said: "Looking beneath the label of a 'disability' pension, . . . the trial court found that only the excess of the 'disability' pension rights over the alternative 'retirement' pension represented additional compensation attributable to husband's disability; the balance of the pension rights acquired during the marriage, it ruled, served to replace ordinary 'retirement' pay and thus must be classed as a community asset. [¶] We agree with the reasoning of the trial court; to permit the husband, by unilateral election of a 'disability' pension, to 'transmute community property into his own separate property' (*In re Marriage of Fithian* [(1974)] 10 Cal. 3d 592, 602, 111 Cal. Rptr. 369, 517 P.2d 449), is to negate the protective philosophy of the community property law as set out in previous decisions of this court. We therefore affirm the judgment of the trial court apportioning husband's pension rights between separate and community assets and dividing the community interest equally between the spouses." (*Stenquist, supra*, 21 Cal. 3d at pp. 782-783, 148 Cal. Rptr. 9, 582 P.2d 96, fn. omitted.)

As we later explained in *Saslow, supra*, 40 Cal. 3d at pages 858-859, 221 Cal. Rptr. 546, 710 P.2d 346, our decision in *Stenquist, supra*, 21 Cal. 3d 779, 148 Cal. Rptr. 9, 582 P.2d 96, articulated two rationales in affirming the trial court's disposition: "First, [*Stenquist*] held that it could not 'permit the serviceman's election of a" disability "pension to defeat the community interest in his right to a pension based on longevity.' (*Stenquist, supra*, 21 Cal. 3d at p. 786, 148 Cal. Rptr. 9, 582 P.2d 96.) Such a result would 'violate the settled principle that one spouse cannot, by invoking a condition wholly within his control, defeat the community interest of the other spouse.' (*Ibid.*) It would unjustly deprive the wife of a valuable property right "simply because a misleading label has been affixed to [the] husband's pension fund benefits." (*Id.*, at pp. 786-787 [148 Cal. Rptr. 9, 582 P.2d 96.]) [¶] "Second, the *Stenquist* court discussed the purposes of a military disability pension. Such pensions were said to function in part to compensate the veteran for lost earnings and personal suffering caused by the disability. To that extent they were held to constitute separate property. (*Stenquist, supra,* 21 Cal. 3d at pp. 787-788, [148 Cal. Rptr. 9, 582 P.2d 96.]) [¶] However, the court recognized that a 'disability' pension received later in life might function principally as a retirement pension. (*Ibid.*) Indeed, the court found that the 'primary objective' of the disability pension in *Stenquist* was to provide retirement support. Therefore, it held that the portion of the disability pension that was equivalent to the regular retirement pension was community property. (*Id.*, at pp. 788-789 [148 Cal. Rptr. 9, 582 P.2d 96.])"

Applying to the facts of *Saslow* the rationale of *Stenquist, supra,* 21 Cal. 3d 779, 148 Cal. Rptr. 9, 582 P.2d 96, we concluded that when disability insurance is purchased to replace a disabled spouse's lost earnings, any postseparation disability benefits are the disabled spouse's separate property. (*Saslow, supra,* 40 Cal. 3d at pp. 860-861, 221 Cal. Rptr. 546, 710 P.2d 346.) Benefits under the disability insurance policy, if acquired with community funds, become community property only if the benefits were intended to provide the marital couple with retirement income. (*Ibid.*) Pointing out that under California law a retirement pension is community property to the extent that it was paid for with community funds, *Saslow* held that disability benefits intended to take the place of retirement benefits should be treated the same way. To do otherwise, we observed, would deprive the nondisabled spouse of a valuable property right simply because the benefits received were given the "misleading label" of disability rather than retirement benefits. (*Saslow, supra,* 40 Cal. 3d at p. 860, 221 Cal. Rptr. 546, 710 P.2d 346.)

We acknowledged in *Saslow* that the "purpose" analysis articulated in *Stenquist, supra,* 21 Cal. 3d 779, 148 Cal. Rptr. 9, 582 P.2d 96, would in some cases be difficult to apply, citing the factual scenario in *Saslow* itself as a prime example. But, expressing faith in the ability of experienced trial judges to make difficult factual determinations, we concluded in *Saslow* that *Stenquist*'s "purpose" or "primary objective" analysis would lead to "the most equitable distribution of disability insurance benefits." (*Saslow, supra,* 40 Cal. 3d at pp. 860-861, 221 Cal. Rptr. 546, 710 P.2d 346.)

The facts of this case are almost identical to those of *Saslow, supra,* 40 Cal. 3d 848, 221 Cal. Rptr. 546, 710 P.2d 346. The only difference is that in *Saslow* the disabled husband retired and began receiving benefits under the disability policy before he and his wife separated, while here the disabled husband started drawing disability benefits three years after he and his wife had separated. The majority regards this difference as significant. I do not.

As I have pointed out previously, the marital community retains a postseparation interest in a spouse's retirement pension that has not vested at the time of separation. (*In re Marriage of Brown, supra,* 15 Cal. 3d 838, 126 Cal. Rptr. 633, 544 P.2d 561.) In my view, there is a similar community interest in a noncancelable term disability insurance policy which was purchased by the marital community for the primary purpose of providing retirement income, from which no benefits are being drawn at the time of separation. In either case, the marital community looks to the pension or the insurance as a source for retirement funds. In each situation, the community's interest is contingent: at the time of dissolution there is no assurance that any insurance or pension benefits will ever be paid to either spouse. In each case, accrual of benefits depends on the actions of one spouse: unless the spouse bcarrying the disability insurance continues to pay the premiums on the policy, no benefits on the policy will be paid, and unless the spouse eligible for the pension continues employment at the job until the pension vests, no pension benefits will be paid (*In re Marriage of Foster* (1986) 180 Cal. App. 3d 1068, 1072-1074, 227 Cal. Rptr. 446).

Because, as just explained, disability insurance purchased as a substitute for retirement benefits shares the same purpose and essential characteristics of a pension, it should be treated the same as a pension under our community property system, regardless of when the benefits on the pension or the disability insurance policy are first paid. Thus, the rule this court enunciated in *In re Marriage of Brown, supra,* 15 Cal. 3d 838, 126 Cal. Rptr. 633, 544 P.2d 561 — that postseparation retirement benefits are community property to the extent those benefits are attributable to the community — should apply with equal force to postseparation disability benefits that the parties intended as retirement income, even when no disability benefits are paid until after the spouses have separated. For the reasons set forth above, I conclude that this case is governed by this court's decision in *Saslow, supra,* 40 Cal. 3d 848, 221 Cal. Rptr. 546, 710 P.2d 346.

For the reasons set forth above, I conclude that the trial court properly found that $5,000 per month in disability benefits that were intended to provide retirement income should not be treated as husband's separate property. The trial court, however, erred when it concluded that *all* of those benefits were community property. Those benefits are in part attributable to husband's postseparation renewal of the insurance with his separate funds, and the trial court's order that the community pay husband the amount of the premiums paid with his separate property does not adequately compensate husband for his separate interest in the insurance benefits. A retirement pension paid for partly with community and partly with separate funds would be subject to apportionment. Similarly, in this case the trial court should have apportioned the benefits based on the contributions of the community and of husband's separate property from the time the community first purchased the policies. The majority of the premiums were paid with community funds; accordingly, a corresponding percentage of the benefits should be community property.

I would reverse the judgment of the Court of Appeal.

Discussion Question

1. Why did the majority conclude that the husband John's disability insurance benefits were his separate property? Why did concurring Justice Baxter think that the *Saslow* case should be overruled? Why did dissenting Justice Kennard think that the *Saslow* case applied here?

PROBLEM 11.1

Richard and Susan were married in 2010. Before they married, Susan had worked as a doctor until 2000 when she stopped practicing medicine because of mental health problems. In 2001, she began receiving monthly benefits from a private disability insurance policy that she had purchased in 1995. No premiums on the policy were due once it was determined that she was disabled. Susan worked part-time as a music teacher during their marriage but received only very minimal income. She has not returned to the practice of medicine.

They have recently separated and Richard is claiming that the monthly disability benefits are community property because they were received during marriage. Susan claims that the benefits are her separate property because they were purchased before marriage. One issue is whether Richard has any rights to the monthly disability benefits Susan received during marriage and she will continue to receive after divorce.

How would an Idaho court characterize Susan's disability benefits? An Arizona court? A California court?

PROBLEM 11.2

Ron and Cynthia were married in Louisiana in 1990. Soon after their marriage, Ron began work as a firefighter for the New Orleans Fire Department. The Fire Department had a Pension and Relief Fund that included employer and employee contributions. When Ron lost vision in one eye in 2010, he opted to take retirement benefits for disability. The benefits he received were based on a percentage of his average pay. That percentage was calculated based on the number of years he had served as a firefighter. The benefits will continue for Ron's life. Recently, Ron and Cynthia have separated. Cynthia claims that the benefits are community property and she is entitled to a share of those benefits after dissolution. Ron claims that the benefits are his separate property because they substitute for his lost wages.

How would a Louisiana court characterize Ron's benefits? An Idaho court? A Washington court?

Table 11-1
Disability Insurance Benefits in Community Property States

State	Rule	Case/Statute
Arizona	Disability proceeds that are compensation for loss of earning ability during marriage are classified as community property. Disability proceeds that represent post-dissolution dim-inution of earning capacity are separate property of the disabled spouse.	*Hatcher v. Hatcher*, 188 Ariz. 154, 933 P.2d 1222 (1996)
California	Classification of disability insurance purchased during marriage determined by the spouses' intent and/or funds used to purchase the policy. If intended to replace lost earnings resulting from disability, benefits are separate	*Marriage of Saslow*, 40 Cal. 3d 848, 710 P.2d 346, 221 Cal. Rptr. 546 (1985) (intent controls) *Marriage of Elfmont*, 9

	property. If intended to replace retirement income, benefits are community property. If disability insurance purchased with separate property funds after separation or before marriage, benefits are separate property.	Cal. 4th 1026, 891 P.2d 136, 39 Cal. Rptr. 2d 590 (1995) (funds and intent control), *Marriage of Rossin*, 172 Cal. App. 4th 725, 91 Cal. Rptr. 3d 427 (2009)
Idaho	Where payments for disability insurance is paid with community funds or paid by the employer, the benefits are characterized as community property.	*Guy v. Guy*, 98 Idaho 205, 80 P.2d 876 (1977)
Louisiana	Disability insurance benefits purchased with community funds are separate property of the disabled spouse if the policy substitutes for wage losses from the disability. If classified as deferred compensation like retirement or pension income then benefits would be community property.	*Bordes v. Bordes*, 730 So. 2d 443 (La. 1999)
Nevada	Disability benefits with a retirement component may be consider community property	*Powers v. Powers*, 105 Nev. 514, 779 P.2d 91 (1989), *Shelton v. Shelton*, 119 Nev. 492, 78 P.3d 507 (2003)
New Mexico	Time and manner of acquisition controls character of disability insurance benefits. If acquired during marriage with community funds, the benefits are community property.	*Douglas v. Douglas*, 101 N.M. 570, 686 P.2d 260 (Ct. App. 1984)
Texas	Disability insurance benefits are community property if the right to them was part of the disabled spouse's compensation for services during marriage.	*Simmons v. Simmons*, 568 S.W.2d 169 (Tex. Ct. App. 1978), *Andrle v. Andrle*, 751 S.W.2d 955 (Tex. Ct. App. 1988)
Washington	Disability insurance benefits acquired with community funds are community property until dissolution, but after dissolution the benefit payments are separate property. Benefits intended to compensate the insured for future income or pain and suffering should be characterized as separate property. Benefits which compensate for expenses incurred during marriage or earnings lost during marriage should be characterized as community property. Benefits which are in fact deferred compensation should be characterized as community property in proportion to the community's contributions to the deferred compensation plan. Trial courts have discretion to divide both community and separate property as is "fair, just, and equitable."	*Marriage of Brown*, 100 Wash. 2d 729, 675 P.2d 1207 (1984), *Marriage of Brewer*, 137 Wash. 2d 756, 976 P.2d 102 (1999)
Wisconsin	When insurance proceeds compensate for the loss of a gifted asset, they are non-divisible. When insurance proceeds compensate for loss of income, they are divisible at divorce.	*Wright v. Wright*, 307 Wis. 2d 156, 747 N.W.2d 690 (Ct. App. 2007)

Chapter 12

Discovery That the Marriage Is Not Valid: Putative Spouse Doctrine

Let us return to our hypothetical couple Harry and Wilma. Imagine that during the 25 years of their marriage, Wilma believed that she was divorced from her high school sweetheart Mark. That marriage was very short and Mark supposedly took care of their divorce. When Wilma returned many years later for a high school reunion, Mark professed his undying love for Wilma and revealed to her that he had never filed for divorce. She was horrified, because she knew that it meant that she was never legally married to Harry. When Harry found out, he was upset and he insisted that they consult an attorney.

This is what they learn. Harry and Wilma's marriage is void because Wilma was still married to Mark at the time she married Harry. Rights to community property arise only through the creation of a valid marriage. Therefore, because Harry was the wage earner in their family and Wilma was a stay-at-home Mom, all Harry's earnings would belong to him as an unmarried man. In the event that they divorce or Harry dies, Wilma would have no community property rights. Of course, Wilma would feel that is exceedingly unfair that she would not share in the wealth created during their 25 years together when they both thought they were married. The attorney would assure them that the "putative spouse doctrine" protects those who have a "good faith" belief that the marriage was valid. The doctrine, which is based in equity, has been adopted in all community property states that have considered the problem. It has been adopted either by legislation or by court decision.

Establishing putative spouse status is dependent on a "good faith" belief that the marriage was valid. California, Idaho, and Louisiana have adopted the doctrine via statute. In 2004, the Nevada Supreme Court adopted the doctrine in a case of first impression, *Williams v. Williams*, 120 Nev. 559, 97 P.3d 1124 (2004). The case establishes the criteria for establishing putative spouse status and the rights that flow from that status.

WILLIAMS v. WILLIAMS

120 Nev. 559, 97 P.3d 1124 (2004)
Supreme Court of Nevada

PER CURIAM.

This is a case of first impression involving the application of the putative spouse doctrine in an annulment proceeding. Under the doctrine, an individual whose marriage is void due to a prior legal impediment is treated as a spouse so long as the party seeking equitable relief participated in the marriage ceremony with the good-faith belief that the ceremony was legally valid. A majority of states recognize the doctrine when dividing property acquired during the marriage, applying equitable principles, based on community property law, to the division. However, absent fraud, the doctrine does not apply to awards of spousal support. While some states have extended the doctrine to permit spousal support awards, they have done so under the authority of state statutes.

We agree with the majority view. Consequently, we adopt the putative spouse doctrine in annulment proceedings for purposes of property division and affirm the district court's division of the property. However, we reject the doctrine as a basis of awarding equitable spousal support. Because Nevada's annulment statutes do not provide for an award of support upon annulment, we reverse the district court's award of spousal support.

FACTS

On August 26, 1973, appellant Richard E. Williams underwent a marriage ceremony with respondent Marcie C. Williams. At that time, Marcie believed that she was divorced from John Allmaras. However, neither Marcie nor Allmaras had obtained a divorce. Richard and Marcie believed they were legally married and lived together, as husband and wife, for 27 years. In March 2000, Richard discovered that Marcie was not divorced from Allmaras at the time of their marriage ceremony.

In August 2000, Richard and Marcie permanently separated. In February 2001, Richard filed a complaint for an annulment. Marcie answered and counterclaimed for one-half of the property and spousal support as a putative spouse. In April 2002, the parties engaged in a one-day bench trial to resolve the matter.

At trial, Richard testified that had he known Marcie was still married, he would not have married her. He claimed that Marcie knew she was not divorced when she married him or had knowledge that would put a reasonable person on notice to check if the prior marriage had been dissolved. Specifically, Richard stated that Marcie should not have relied on statements from Allmaras that he had obtained a divorce because Marcie never received any legal notice of divorce proceedings. In addition, Richard claimed that in March 2000, when Marcie received a social security check in the name of Marcie Allmaras, Marcie told him that she had never been divorced from Allmaras. Marcie denied making the statement.

Marcie testified that she believed she was not married to her former husband, John Allmaras, and was able to marry again because Allmaras told her they were divorced. Marcie further testified that in 1971, she ran into Allmaras at a Reno bus station, where he specifically told her that they were divorced and he was living with another woman. According to Marcie, she discovered she was still married to Allmaras during the course of the annulment proceedings with Richard. Marcie testified that if she had known at any time that she was still married to Allmaras, she would have obtained a divorce from him.

During the 27 years that the parties believed themselves to be married, Marcie was a homemaker and a mother. From 1981 to 1999, Marcie was a licensed child-care provider for six children. During that time, she earned $460 a week. At trial, Marcie had a certificate of General Educational Development (G.E.D.) and earned $8.50 an hour at a retirement home. She was 63 years old and lived with her daughter because she could not afford to live on her own.

Both parties stipulated to the value of most of their jointly-owned property. At the time of the annulment proceeding, the parties held various items in their joint names, including bank accounts, vehicles, life insurance policies, a Sparks home, a radiator business, and a motorcycle.

The district court found that Marcie had limited ability to support herself. The district court also concluded that both parties believed they were legally married, acted as husband and wife, and conceived and raised two children. Marcie stayed home to care for and raise their children. Based upon these facts, the district court granted the annulment and awarded Marcie one-half of all the jointly-held property and spousal support. The district court did not indicate whether its award was based on the putative spouse doctrine or an implied contract and quantum meruit theory. The final judgment divided the parties' property so that each received assets of approximately the same value. It also ordered Richard to pay Marcie the sum of $500 per month for a period of four years as "reimbursement and compensation for the benefit received by [Richard] by way of [Marcie's] forgoing a career outside the home in order to care for [Richard] and their children." Richard timely appealed the district court's judgment.

Discussion

ANNULMENT

A marriage is void if either of the parties to the marriage has a former husband or wife then living. Richard and Marcie's marriage was void because Marcie was still married to another man when she married Richard. Although their marriage was void, an annulment proceeding was necessary to legally sever their relationship. An annulment proceeding is the proper manner to dissolve a void marriage and resolve other issues arising from the dissolution of the relationship.

ASSERTIONS OF ERROR

First, Richard contends that Marcie is not entitled to one-half of their joint property because their marriage was void. Richard asserts that application of the putative spouse doctrine and quasi-community property principles was improper. Alternatively, Richard argues that if the district court relied on implied contract and quantum meruit theories, the district court should have divided the parties' residence according to this court's decision in *Sack v. Tomlin*, which would provide Richard with 67 percent of the assets instead of 50 percent.

Second, Richard argues that the district court erred in awarding spousal support. Richard contends support is not permitted, absent statutory authority, under the putative spouse doctrine and that there is no basis in Nevada law for awarding compensation for services rendered during the marriage under a theory of quantum meruit.

Because the record does not reflect the basis for the district court's decision, resolution of Richard's contentions requires us to address the putative spouse doctrine.

PUTATIVE SPOUSE DOCTRINE

Under the putative spouse doctrine, when a marriage is legally void, the civil effects of a legal marriage flow to the parties who contracted to marry in good faith. That is, a putative spouse is entitled to many of the rights of an actual spouse. A majority of states have recognized some form of the doctrine through case law or statute. States differ, however, on what exactly constitutes a "civil effect." The doctrine was developed to avoid depriving innocent parties who believe in good faith that they are married from being denied the economic and status-related benefits of marriage, such as property division, pension, and health benefits.

The doctrine has two elements: (1) a proper marriage ceremony was performed, and (2) one or both of the parties had a good-faith belief that there was no impediment to the marriage and the marriage was valid and proper. "Good faith" has been defined as an "honest and reasonable belief that the marriage was valid at the time of the ceremony." Good faith is presumed. The party asserting lack of good faith has the burden of proving bad faith. Whether the party acted in good faith is a question of fact. Unconfirmed rumors or mere suspicions of a legal impediment do not vitiate good faith "'so long as no certain or authoritative knowledge of some legal impediment comes to him or her.'" However, when a person receives reliable information that an impediment exists, the individual cannot ignore the information, but instead has a duty to investigate further. Persons cannot act "'blindly or without reasonable precaution.'" Finally, once a spouse learns of the impediment, the putative marriage ends.

We have not previously considered the putative spouse doctrine, but we are persuaded by the rationale of our sister states that public policy supports adopting the doctrine in Nevada. Fairness and equity favor recognizing putative spouses when parties enter into a marriage ceremony in good faith and without knowledge that there is a factual or legal impediment to their marriage. Nor does the doctrine conflict with Nevada's policy in refusing to recognize common-law marriages or palimony suits. In the putative spouse doctrine, the parties have actually attempted to enter into a formal relationship with the solemnization of a marriage ceremony, a missing element in common-law marriages and palimony suits. As a majority of our sister states have recognized, the sanctity of marriage is not undermined, but rather enhanced, by the recognition of the putative spouse doctrine. We therefore adopt the doctrine in Nevada.

We now apply the doctrine to the instant case. The district court found that the parties obtained a license and participated in a marriage ceremony on August 26, 1973, in Verdi, Nevada. The district court also found that Marcie erroneously believed that her prior husband, Allmaras, had terminated their marriage by divorce and that she was legally able to marry Richard. In so finding, the district court also necessarily rejected Richard's argument that Marcie acted unreasonably in relying on Allmaras' statements because she had never been served with divorce papers and that she had a duty to inquire about the validity of her former marriage before marrying Richard.

Although Richard's and Marcie's testimony conflicted on this issue, judging the credibility of the witnesses and the weight to be given to their testimony are matters within the discretion of the district court. "This court reviews district court decisions concerning divorce proceedings for an abuse of discretion. Rulings supported by substantial evidence will not be disturbed on appeal." Substantial evidence is that which a sensible person may accept as adequate to sustain a judgment. We apply the same standard in annulment proceedings. The district court was free to disregard Richard's testimony, and substantial evidence supports the district court's finding that Marcie did not act unreasonably in relying upon Allmaras' representations. The record reflects no reason for Marcie to have disbelieved him and, thus, no reason to have investigated the truth of his representations. Although older case law suggests that a party cannot rely on a former spouse's representation of divorce, more recent cases indicate this is just a factor for the judge to consider in determining good faith. We conclude that the district court did not err in finding that Marcie entered into the marriage in good faith. She therefore qualifies as a putative spouse. We now turn to the effect of the doctrine on the issues of property division and alimony.

PROPERTY DIVISION

Community property states that recognize the putative spouse doctrine apply community property principles to the division of property, including determinations of what constitutes community and separate property. Since putative spouses believe themselves to be married, they are already under the assumption that community property laws would apply to a termination of their relationship. There is no point, therefore, in devising a completely separate set of rules for dividing property differently in a putative spouse scenario. We agree with this reasoning.

In some states, courts apply community property principles to divide property acquired during the purported marriage. In other states, the property is considered to be held under joint tenancy principles and is divided equally between the parties. Regardless of the approach, all states that recognize the putative spouse doctrine divide assets acquired during the marriage in an equitable fashion. We conclude that the application of community property principles to a putative marriage, as indicated in *Sanguinetti v. Sanguinetti*, is the better approach to the division of property in such cases.[25] In this case, the district court treated the parties' property as quasi-community property and equally divided the joint property between the parties. Substantial evidence supports the district court's division, and we affirm the district court's distribution of the property.

25. Different rules may apply when one of the parties qualifies as a putative spouse and the other does not. When a person enters into the relationship with knowledge of an impediment and knowledge the marriage is not valid, some states have found the person who acted in bad faith is not entitled to benefit from the marriage. We do not reach this issue because the facts of this case involve two innocent putative spouses.

SPOUSAL SUPPORT

States are divided on whether spousal support is a benefit or civil effect that may be awarded under the putative spouse doctrine.[26] Although some states permit the award of alimony, they do so because their annulment statutes permit an award of rehabilitative or permanent alimony.[27] At least one state, however, has found alimony to be a civil effect under the putative spouse doctrine even in the absence of a specific statute permitting an award of alimony.[28]

We can find no case, and Marcie has cited to none, in which spousal support was awarded to a putative spouse absent statutory authority, fraud, bad faith or bad conduct. Although one commentator favors such awards on the theory that the purpose of the putative spouse doctrine is to fulfill the reasonable expectations of the parties, we are unaware of any court adopting such a standard.

The putative spouse doctrine did not traditionally provide for an award of spousal support. Extensions of the doctrine have come through statute or findings of fraud and bad faith. As neither is present in this case, we decline to extend the doctrine to permit an award of spousal support when both parties act in good faith. Richard and Marcie's marriage was void, and there was no showing of bad faith or fraud by either party. Absent an equitable basis of bad faith or fraud or a statutory basis, the district court had no authority to grant the spousal support award, and we reverse that part of the judgment awarding spousal support.

CONCLUSION

We conclude that an annulment proceeding is the proper method for documenting the existence of a void marriage and resolving the rights of the parties arising out of the void relationship. We adopt the putative spouse doctrine and conclude that common-law community property principles apply by analogy to the division of property acquired during a putative marriage. However, the putative spouse doctrine does not permit an award of spousal support in the absence of bad faith, fraud or statutory authority. Therefore, we affirm that portion of the district court's order equally dividing the parties' property and reverse that portion of the order awarding spousal support.

---

26. Blakesley, *supra* note 7, at 41.

27. *Matter of Marriage of Denis*, 153 Or. App. 655, 958 P.2d 199 (1998); *Jones v. Jones*, 48 Wash. 2d 862, 296 P.2d 1010 (1956); Cal. Fam. Code §2254 (West 1994); Colo. Rev. Stat. Ann. §14-2-111 (West 2003); 750 Ill. Comp. Stat. Ann. 5/305 (West 1999); Minn. Stat. Ann. §518.055 (West 1990); Mont. Code Ann. §40-1-404 (2003).

28. *Cortes v. Fleming*, 307 So. 2d 611 (La. 1973). While the Louisiana Supreme Court did not rely on a statute specifically granting a putative spouse the right to alimony in its decision, the court did use an annulment statute as a basis of the award. The court indicated the term "civil effect" in the annulment statute was broad enough to include alimony. Nevada does not have similar language in its annulment statutes.

Discussion Questions

1. What are the main requirements of attaining putative spouse status? Who is favored by the doctrine?

2. What are the limits on the putative spouse doctrine in Nevada?

If we apply the *Williams* requirements to Harry and Wilma's situation, both Harry and Wilma are putative spouses. It can be assumed that Harry and Wilma had a proper marriage ceremony, including a marriage license. They both had a good faith belief that there was no impediment to the marriage and the marriage was valid and proper. Even if Harry would want to contest Wilma's putative spouse status, it is doubtful that he would succeed. He would have the burden of proof and Wilma's surprise and horror at Mark's revelation supports her position that she had an honest and reasonable belief that her marriage to Harry was valid at the time of the ceremony. Harry and Wilma's assets accumulated during their purported marriage will be treated as community property.

A.   WHAT CONSTITUTES A GOOD FAITH BELIEF IN A VALID MARRIAGE? EXAMPLES FROM LOUISIANA, TEXAS, AND CALIFORNIA

As noted in the *Williams* case, the determination of whether there is a good faith belief is a question of fact. When reading the following cases, consider whether the criteria outlined in *Williams* are adopted in these other states. Also pay particular attention to whether the test for good faith is objective, subjective, or a combination of both. Note which "wife" was able to succeed in attaining putative spouse status and why she did or did not succeed.

1.   Louisiana

THOMASON v. THOMASON

776 So. 2d 553 (2000)
Court of Appeal of Louisiana

Doucet, Chief Judge.

The Defendant, Roger Randolph Thomason, appeals the trial court's determination that, although the marriage was invalid, Barbara Ann Hughes Thomason was in good faith and entitled to the civil effects of marriage as a putative spouse.

Barbara Thomason filed for a divorce in December 1998. In his answer to the petition for divorce, Mr. Thomason stated that no marriage had taken place. A hearing was held on December 6, 1999, at which the following facts were brought to light. The parties met in a sanitarium where both were being treated for tuberculosis. After being released they continued to see each other and on April 5, 1958, Roger asked Barbara to go to Mississippi with him to get married. They went to the courthouse in Port Gibson, Mississippi and obtained a marriage license. At this point the parties' version of events diverge. Barbara testified that they then went to a house and spoke to a man. Although no ceremony was held, she thought this was the justice of the peace and that she was married to Roger. They left the house and checked into a hotel together. She testified that Roger gave her a wedding ring. The next day they returned to Louisiana.

Roger disagreed with this account. At the hearing, he testified that after getting the license they were unable to find a justice of the peace; that they never went to anyone's house but simply checked into a hotel. He testified that he knew no marriage had taken place. It is undisputed that from that time until Barbara left the matrimonial domicile, the two held themselves out as married.

On December 6, 1999, the court held a hearing to determine the issues of marriage and putative spouse status. After hearing the evidence of both parties. The trial court made the following findings:

> From the testimony of both parties, the Court has determined that even though Barbara Hughes Thomason "believed" that they were married on April 5, 1958, in reality, they were not. It is this Court's opinion that Roger Randolph Thomason took advantage of Barbara's ignorance about marriage and deliberately did not say that they were not married after leaving the home of the justice of the peace and never told Barbara. Although Roger testified that one time during the marriage, he told Barbara that they were not legally married, this Court does not find his testimony to be credible.
>
> . . . .
>
> This Court has determined that Barbara Ann Hughes Thomason did not know during all the years she was together with Roger that her marriage was defective in the eyes of the law. This does not mean that she is to blame for the marriage not being valid, only that she trusted and loved someone so completely that she never thought they would be deceitful to her.

The court rendered judgment finding that the two were never validly married but that Barbara was in good faith until Roger filed his answer to her petition for divorce and was, therefore, "entitled to the civil effects of the marriage as a putative spouse." Roger appeals.

GOOD FAITH

Roger's first two assignments of error address the existence of good faith on the part of Barbara and the date on which her good faith, if any, ended.

> "Good faith" is defined as an honest and reasonable belief that the marriage was valid and that no legal impediment to it existed. "Good faith" consists of being ignorant of the cause which prevents the formation of the marriage, or being ignorant of the defects in the celebration which caused the nullity. The question of whether a party is in good faith is subjective, and depends on all the circumstances present in a given case. Although the good faith analysis test incorporates the objective elements of reasonableness, the inquiry is essentially a subjective one.

Roger testified that because they never found a justice of the peace and never went through a marriage ceremony, Barbara had to know that they were not married. Barbara testified that she thought they were married when they signed the license and saw the man she thought was a justice of the peace. Roger further argues that any good faith belief Barbara had in the validity of the marriage ended when he told her they were not really married shortly before their first child was born. He testified that he told her because he thought they should get married to legitimate the child, but that she did not want to hear it. Barbara testified that the validity of the marriage was never brought into question until Roger filed his answer to the petition.

> The determination of whether good faith is present is a factual question and the finding of the trial judge is entitled to great weight on appeal. That factual determination will not be overturned unless it is shown to be clearly wrong. Any doubt as to the existence of good faith is to be resolved in favor of a finding of good faith.

Id. at p. 5; 739 So. 2d at 949.

In this case, the trial court apparently based its determination on a credibility evaluation, accepting Barbara's testimony over that of Roger.

> When findings are based on determinations regarding the credibility of witnesses, the manifest error-clearly wrong standard demands great deference to the trier of fact's findings; for only the factfinder can be aware of the variations in demeanor and tone of voice that bear so heavily on the listener's understanding and belief in what is said. Where documents or objective evidence so contradict the witness's story, or the story itself is so internally inconsistent or implausible on its face, that a reasonable factfinder would not credit the witness's story, the court of appeal may well find manifest error or clear wrongness even in a finding purportedly based upon a credibility determination. But where such factors are not present, and a factfinder's finding is based on its decision to credit the testimony of one of two or more witnesses, that finding can virtually never be manifestly erroneous or clearly wrong.

Rosell v. ESCO, 549 So. 2d 840, 844-45 (La. 1989) (citations omitted).

In this case, it was not Barbara's testimony which was inconsistent, but Roger's. Throughout his testimony instances of obvious inconsistencies with his deposition testimony were pointed out. Under the circumstances, his credibility is far more questionable than that of Barbara. Therefore, we find no error in the trial court's decision to credit Barbara's testimony. We further find no manifest error in his decision to find that Barbara was in good faith and entitled to the civil benefits of marriage as a putative spouse.

END DATE OF THE COMMUNITY REGIME

La. Civ. Code art. 96 provides in pertinent part that: "An absolutely null marriage nevertheless produces civil effects in favor of a party who contracted it in good faith for as long as that party remains in good faith." We agree with the trial court that Barbara remained in good faith until Roger filed his answer to her petition on April 20, 1999. Therefore, the court correctly found that Barbara continued to be entitled to the civil effects of marriage until that date.

PUTATIVE SPOUSE STATUS FOR ROGER THOMASON

Finally, Roger contends that the court found him also to be in good faith and that, as a result, the civil effects of marriage should be extended to him as well. The Defendant misreads the court's judgment. The court, both in its reasons for judgment and in the judgment itself stated that "the actions of both parties constituted good faith." However, a full reading of the reasons makes it clear that the trial court considered that the actions of both parties showed that Barbara was in good faith. The trial judge made no finding that Roger was in good faith. In fact, his findings of fact make it clear that Roger was not in good faith and knew from the beginning that the marriage was not valid. He states, in his written reasons, that: "Roger Randolph Thomason took advantage of Barbara's ignorance about marriage and deliberately did not say that they were not married after leaving the home of the justice of the peace. Roger knew when leaving, that the marriage license was not filed (sic) out by the justice of the peace and never told Barbara." Accordingly, the trial court correctly declined to extend the civil effects of marriage to Roger.

CONCLUSION

For these reasons, the judgment of the trial court is affirmed. Costs of this appeal are to be paid by Roger Thomason.

Affirmed.

Discussion Question

1. According to *Williams*, the first element of the putative spouse doctrine is "a proper marriage ceremony was performed." Why did the Court of Appeal in Louisiana dispense with that requirement in this case?

---

2.   Texas

CARDWELL v. CARDWELL

195 S.W.3d 856 (2006)
Court of Appeals of Texas

Opinion by Justice FITZGERALD.

This is an appeal, by both parties, from a divorce judgment. Appellant Donald Lee Cardwell ("Husband") challenges two specific trial court rulings concerning the property division ordered in that judgment. Cross–Appellant Sharon Ann Cardwell ("Wife") challenges the trial court's refusal to find the existence of a putative marriage between the parties. For the reasons that follow, we affirm the judgment of the trial court.

BACKGROUND

Sometime in 1984 or 1985, Wife married a man named Bruce Gay. She left Gay in 1986. In 1988, Wife married Virgil Hill; she divorced Hill in 1992. Then, in 1995, Wife married Husband. Sometime during 1999, Wife learned that she had never been divorced from Gay and informed Husband of that fact. With Husband's assistance, Wife initiated divorce proceedings against Gay at that time; that divorce was final on December 7, 1999. Husband and Wife separated in 2003. Husband initiated this proceeding seeking a divorce, and Wife filed a counter-petition.

In the trial court, Wife argued that she and Husband had a putative marriage from the time of their ceremonial marriage until she was divorced from Gay. The trial court rejected this theory, but concluded the parties did have a common law marriage as of December 7, 1999, when the divorce from Gay was final. The trial court also made a detailed identification and division of the couple's separate and community property.

On appeal, Wife challenges the trial court's rulings concerning the putative marriage. Husband challenges two particular aspects of the property division. A trial court is charged with dividing the estate of the parties in a just and right manner, considering the rights of both parties. We review a trial court's division of property under an abuse of discretion standard.

EXISTENCE OF A PUTATIVE MARRIAGE

In deciding the putative marriage issue, the trial court found:

> there was not a putative marriage because the Respondent did not enter into the marriage in good faith, having been still married to a former husband and making no effort to determine the legal status of that marriage before entering into another marriage.

A putative marriage is one entered into in good faith by at least one party, but invalid because of an existing impediment on the part of one or both parties. *Garduno v. Garduno*, 760 S.W.2d 735, 738 (Tex. App.-Corpus Christi 1988, no writ). If a court determines a putative marriage exists, then the putative spouse who acted in good faith receives the same rights in property that she would have received were she a lawful spouse. *See id.* at 739. The key to the putative-marriage argument is good faith. In her first cross-point, Wife argues there was no evidence that she was actually aware, when she entered into the ceremonial marriage with Husband in 1995, that an impediment existed which prevented her ceremonial marriage to Husband from becoming a valid marriage relationship. In her second cross-point, Wife argues that no evidence was offered at trial to "rebut the presumption of good faith" surrounding her belief that her marriage to Gay had been dissolved. For these reasons, she argues, she has established that she entered the ceremonial marriage in good faith.

Wife did testify that she was not aware she was still legally married to Gay when she entered into the ceremonial marriage. However, the trial court, as fact-finder, was charged with evaluating Wife's credibility. *See Griffin Indus., Inc. v. Honorable*

Thirteenth Court of Appeals, 934 S.W.2d 349, 355 (Tex. 1996) ("In a nonjury trial or hearing, the trial court is the sole judge of the witness' credibility and the testimony's weight."). The court was free to disbelieve any or all of Wife's testimony. *See id.* ("The trial court, as the fact-finder, has the right to accept or reject all or any part of any witness' testimony."). Thus, the trial court could have concluded Wife knew she was still legally married to Gay in 1995 and rejected Wife's good-faith argument on that basis alone.

Moreover, we disagree with Wife's premise that only actual knowledge of the impediment would defeat the purported putative marriage. When the party arguing for a putative marriage is aware that there was a former marriage, "the question becomes one of the reasonableness of that party's belief that the former marriage has been dissolved." *Garduno,* 760 S.W.2d at 740. In this case, Wife testified that after she left Gay in 1986, she did nothing to initiate divorce proceedings. She testified further that Gay told her he was taking care of the divorce, but she admitted she did nothing to determine whether Gay had done so. Even after going through divorce proceedings following her second marriage, Wife did nothing to determine whether or not she was still married to Gay when she married Husband. We will not disturb the trial court's finding on this matter when Wife's own testimony establishes that she made no reasonable inquiry into her marital status before she purported to enter into another marriage.

We need not address the existence or extent of the presumption Wife depends upon to support her good faith in this case. The same evidence — that is, Wife's own testimony — that allowed the trial court to question the reasonableness of Wife's belief would suffice to rebut any such presumption in this case.

We find no abuse of discretion in the trial court's findings on putative marriage. We overrule Wife's cross-points.

RIGHT TO REIMBURSEMENT OR ECONOMIC CONTRIBUTION

Husband's first appellate issue relates to a ranch of approximately 120 acres in Melissa, Texas.[2] The trial court concluded the ranch was Husband's separate property, but the court also concluded the community estate had a right to reimbursement for improvements made to the ranch during the course of the common-law marriage.[3] Thus, included in Wife's recovery was a judgment in the amount of $234,000, "in part for improvements to the separate property of [Husband], and to arrive at a just and right division of community property." The judgment was secured by an equitable lien on the ranch.

Ample evidence supports the trial court's decision here: we find no abuse of discretion in the trial court's award to the community estate or in Wife's money judgment generally. We decide Husband's first issue against him.

2. The record indicates the ranch included 120.4 acres in all. The trial court's award to Husband as separate property was 118 of the approximately 120 acres. However, evidence of the market value of the property was taken in light of the total acreage. We use the figure of 120 acres for purposes of calculations under the family code.

3. The trial court's specific finding was that:

the community estate has a right of reimbursement for improvements made to the 118 acre tract found to be the separate property of [Husband] in an amount which exceeds the principal amount of the judgment awarded to Wife.

CHARACTERIZATION OF KANSAS OIL AND GAS VENTURE

In his second issue, Husband argues the trial court erroneously characterized a Kansas oil and gas venture as community property rather than as Husband's separate property. Property possessed by either spouse during or on the dissolution of marriage is presumed to be community property; a party claiming such property is his separate property must offer clear and convincing evidence to that effect. Husband did not meet his burden of proving the venture was his separate property by clear and convincing evidence. The trial court did not abuse its discretion in its characterization of the oil and gas venture. Husband's second issue lacks merit.

CONCLUSION

We have denied both parties' issues on appeal. Accordingly, we affirm the judgment of the trial court.

Discussion Question

1. What were Wife Sharon Ann's arguments? Husband Donald's arguments? Who won? Who lost? Why?

---

3. *California*

The major issue in *Ceja v. Rudolph & Sletten, Inc.*, 194 Cal. App. 4th 584, 125 Cal. Rptr. 3d 98 (2011), is whether the test for "good faith" belief is a subjective or objective test. Please note that the California Supreme Court recently affirmed the Court of Appeals, *see* _Cal. 4th_, 302 P.3d 211 (June 20, 2013). At the time of publication of this book, it is still on appeal. Whatever is decided by the Supreme Court, the Court of Appeal's decision provides insight into the legal analysis for determining what is a "good faith" belief.

CEJA v. RUDOLPH & SLETTEN, INC.

194 Cal. App. 4th 584, 125 Cal. Rptr. 3d 98 (2011)
Court of Appeal

RUSHING, P.J.

I. INTRODUCTION

Nancy and Robert Ceja were married by the pastor of a Pentecostal church in a big wedding ceremony attended by many guests. Four years later, Robert Ceja was killed in an accident at work. Nancy Ceja sued his employer for wrongful death. However, before filing the action, she learned that her marriage was void because the wedding had taken place a few months before Robert Ceja's divorce from his first wife became final. Consequently, to establish her standing to sue, Nancy Ceja alleged that she was a "putative spouse" under Code of Civil Procedure section 377.60, which defines a putative spouse as party to a void or voidable marriage who is found by the court to have "believed in good faith that the marriage . . . was valid."[1] (§377.60, subd. (b).)

The employer moved for summary judgment claiming that Nancy Ceja did not qualify as a putative spouse. The trial court agreed and granted summary judgment. Applying an objective test for putative status, the court found that it was not objectively reasonable for Nancy Ceja to have believed that her marriage was valid.

We conclude that the court applied the wrong test. Section 377.69 requires only that an alleged putative spouse "believed in good faith" that the marriage was valid. We hold that this language does not establish an objective standard; rather it refers to the alleged putative spouse's state of mind and asks whether that person actually believed the marriage was valid and whether he or she held that belief honestly, genuinely, and sincerely, without collusion or fraud. In so holding, we disagree with *In re Marriage of Vryonis* (1988) 202 Cal. App. 3d 712, 248 Cal. Rptr. 807 (*Vryonis*), which held that the statutory language incorporates an objective test.

It follows from our holding that the issue before the trial court on summary judgment was *not* whether there were triable issues of fact concerning whether Nancy Ceja's belief was objectively reasonable. The issue was whether there were triable issues concerning whether Nancy Ceja harbored a good faith belief. Because the record before us reveals a number of disputed facts necessary to resolve that issue, we reverse.

II. Statement of the Case

Plaintiff Nancy Ceja appeals from a judgment entered after the trial court granted defendant Rudolph & Sletten, Inc.'s motion for summary judgment.[2] She claims the trial court erred in granting the motion on the ground that she lacked standing to sue as a putative spouse. We agree that the court erred and reverse the judgment.

---

1. Section 377.60 provides, in relevant part, as follows. "A cause of action for the death of a person caused by the wrongful act or neglect of another may be asserted by any of the following persons or by the decedent's personal representative on their behalf: [¶] (a) The decedent's surviving spouse. . . . [¶] (b) Whether or not qualified under subdivision (a), if they were dependent on the decedent, the putative spouse. . . . As used in this subdivision, 'putative spouse' means the surviving spouse of a void or voidable marriage who is found by the court to have believed in good faith that the marriage to the decedent was valid."

All further unspecified statutory references are to the Code of Civil Procedure.

2. In a second amended complaint, Nancy Ceja added Jose Delgadillo as a plaintiff. He too worked for defendant and was injured in the same accident. The trial court denied defendant's motion for summary judgment against Delgadillo.

We further note that Christine Ceja, Robert Ceja's first wife, filed a separate wrongful death action against defendant on behalf of their children.

III. Factual Background[3]

In 1995, Robert married Christine. During their marriage, they had two children. Robert and Christine separated, but they shared custody of the children. In 1999, Robert met Nancy. He told her he was married but separated. In 2001, they started living together, and Robert filed for divorce. During this time, Nancy and Christine saw each other at events involving the children.

On September 24, 2003, Robert and Nancy obtained a marriage license. The form contained areas for personal information, including whether the parties had been married before; how many times; when the marriages ended; and how they ended. Robert and Nancy each put zero for the number of prior marriages. Robert and Nancy signed the form, which included a preprinted declaration that they were "an unmarried man and unmarried woman" and that the information provided was "true to the best of [their] knowledge."

On September 27, 2003, Nancy and Robert were married in a ceremony in San Juan Bautista performed by Andy Salinas, the pastor of a Pentecostal church. According to Nancy, over 250 people attended. Thereafter, Nancy and Robert lived together as husband and wife until his death in 2007.

On November 23, 2003, Robert signed a declaration in support of his petition for dissolution, asserting, among other things, that he and Christine had entered a stipulated judgment concerning property rights. On December 26, 2003, a judgment of dissolution of marriage was entered, and notice was sent to him. The notice warned against marrying before the judgment of dissolution was filed. In 2004, Nancy forwarded copies of Robert's divorce papers to his union so that she could be added to his insurance.

On September 19, 2007, Robert was killed in an accident at work.

IV. The Motion for Summary Judgment and Court's Ruling

In moving for summary judgment, defendant claimed that the evidence conclusively negated Nancy's alleged putative status. Defendant noted that (1) they were married before his divorce became final, and therefore, the marriage was bigamous and void (Fam. Code, §2201, subd. (b) [a bigamous marriage is void or voidable]); (2) before their marriage, Nancy knew that Robert had been married to Christine; (3) both of them signed a marriage license in which Robert falsely represented that he had not been married before; and (4) after the marriage, Nancy sent Robert's divorce papers to the union. Defendant argued that it was not objectively reasonable for Nancy to believe her marriage was valid, that is, a reasonable person, knowing these facts, could not believe in good faith in the validity of the marriage.

In opposition, Nancy declared that she knew Robert had been married to Christine. However, they had separated, and in 2001, she understood that Robert had filed for divorce. She did not know what happened after that because he refused to discuss the subject. Nancy further declared that she did not read the marriage

---

3. Because Robert Ceja, Christine Ceja, and Nancy Ceja share the same surname, we use their first names for convenience and clarity and intend no disrespect. (See, e.g., *Blache v. Blache* (1945) 69 Cal. App. 2d 616, 618, 160 P.2d 136 (*Blache*); *In re Marriage of Schaffer* (1999) 69 Cal. App. 4th 801, 803, fn. 2, 81 Cal. Rptr. 2d 797.).

license closely before signing it. Nor did she read Robert's divorce papers closely before forwarding them to his union.

In addition, Nancy declared that after their marriage, she and Robert wore wedding rings, they lived together as husband and wife, they told people they were married, they filed taxes as a married couple, and they shared a bank account. She also adopted Robert's surname. Nancy stated that she always believed their marriage was valid. She averred that if she had doubted its validity before the wedding, she would have postponed it; and after the wedding, if she had discovered the problem, they would have simply gotten remarried.

As noted, the court granted defendant's motion. Relying on *Welch v. State of California* (2000) 83 Cal. App. 4th 1374, 100 Cal. Rptr. 2d 430 (*Welch*) and *Vryonis, supra,* 202 Cal. App. 3d 712, 248 Cal. Rptr. 807, the court found that Nancy could not qualify as a putative spouse because a belief in the validity of her marriage was not objectively reasonable. Thus, since Nancy lacked standing to sue as a putative spouse, defendant was entitled to judgment.

* * *

VI. THE PUTATIVE SPOUSE DOCTRINE

To explain our analysis and conclusion concerning the standard for determining putative status, we consider it helpful to review the origin and development of the putative spouse doctrine (the doctrine).

In California, the doctrine first arose as a judicially recognized equitable corollary of the community property system, which California inherited from Spanish civil law and formally adopted by statute in 1850.

The community property system rests on the concept that marriage is a partnership, and the property and earnings acquired during a valid marriage are the property of both partners in equal shares. The putative spouse doctrine extends this partnership concept to innocent parties of an invalid marriage. Thus, in *Vallera v. Vallera* (1943) 21 Cal. 2d 681, 134 P.2d 761 (*Vallera*), the Supreme Court considered it "well settled that a woman who lives with a man as his wife in the belief that a valid marriage exists, is entitled upon termination of their relationship to share in the property acquired by them during its existence." The purpose of the doctrine is to protect the expectations of innocent parties and achieve results that are equitable, fair, and just.[4]

The doctrine is typically applied to distribute quasi-marital property at the end of a putative marriage. The doctrine has also been recognized in a number of related contexts, for example, in determining (1) the interest of a putative spouse in a

---

4. In *Coats v. Coats, supra,* 160 Cal. 671, 118 P. 441, the court opined, "To say that the woman in such case, even though she may be penniless and unable to earn a living, is to receive nothing, while the man with whom she lived and labored in the belief that she was his wife shall take and hold whatever he and she have acquired, would be contrary to the most elementary conceptions of fairness and justice." (*Id.* at p. 675, 118 P. 441; see *Jackson v. Jackson* (1892) 94 Cal. 446, 463-464, 29 P. 957 (conc. opn. Harrison, J.) [recognizing "equitable grounds" to divide property between spouses upon annulment of marriage].) In contrast, common law jurisdictions apply the rule that a party to a void or voidable marriage gains no rights to property acquired during the "marriage." (See Schneider, *supra,* 183 Cal. at pp. 337-339, 191 P. 533 [discussing difference between common law and community property jurisdictions]; *DeFrance v. Johnson* (1886) 26 F. 891, 894 [applying common law rule].)

decedent's property (*Feig v. Bank of Italy etc. Ass'n* (1933) 218 Cal. 54, 21 P.2d 421);
(2) the right to statutory benefits upon the death of a police officer (*Adduddell v. Board of Administration* (1970) 8 Cal. App. 3d 243, 87 Cal. Rptr. 268); and (3) the applicability of the rule of imputed contributory negligence applied (*Caldwell v. Odisio, supra,* 142 Cal. App. 2d 732, 299 P.2d 14). The doctrine has also expanded beyond putative spouses to putative domestic partners. (*In re Domestic Partnership of Ellis* (2008) 162 Cal. App. 4th 1000, 76 Cal. Rptr. 3d 401; but see *Velez v. Smith* (2006) 142 Cal. App. 4th 1154, 1172-1174, 48 Cal. Rptr. 3d 642 [doctrine not applicable to domestic partnership law].)

CODIFICATION OF THE JUDICIAL DOCTRINE

In 1969, the Legislature codified the doctrine in former Civil Code section 4452, which was then part of the new, now former, Family Law Act. That section provided, in relevant part, "Whenever a determination is made that a marriage is void or voidable and the court finds that either party or both parties believed in good faith that the marriage was valid, the court shall declare such party or parties to have the status of a putative spouse. . . ." This particular provision authorized the equal distribution of property acquired during the putative marriage. In codifying the doctrine, the Legislature simply adopted existing case law and did not intend to change the definition of a putative spouse or restrict application of the doctrine.

In 1992, the Legislature repealed the former Family Law Act and enacted the Family Code, in which section 2251 reiterates the former Family Law Act provision concerning putative spouses.

In 1975, the Legislature codified the doctrine again when it amended the wrongful death statute, former section 377. Among other things, the amendment added the previously codified definition of putative spouse and added putative spouses to the list of those with standing to sue. Here too, the amendment did not change the doctrine or even the scope of the statute; it merely conformed the statute to existing case law holding that a putative spouse had standing to sue.

THE STATE OF THE DOCTRINE WHEN CODIFIED

We now turn to a number of cases that show how the doctrine was applied at the time it was codified, that is, cases that reveal what was required to establish putative status and how courts determined it.

[I]n *Flanagan v. Capital Nat. Bank of Sacramento* (1931) 213 Cal. 664, 3 P.2d 307, the court denied a woman putative status. It found that she had not genuinely believed her marriage was valid. The record revealed that the couple had not obtained a license or had a ceremony. Moreover, the woman testified that her putative husband had told her they did not need a license because they could get along "'as good as any couple that is married and better.'" The court opined, "It would be difficult to believe that even an inexperienced foreigner, unacquainted with the laws and customs of this country, would consider that by this arrangement she had contracted a valid marriage. But plaintiff was not inexperienced. She had lived all her life in California, and had been previously legally married and divorced.

Everything in the record suggests that she viewed the relationship not as a marriage, but as a satisfactory substitute for a marriage." (*Ibid.;* see *Miller v. Johnson* (1963) 214 Cal. App. 2d 123, 29 Cal. Rptr. 251 [no honest belief where parties obtained no license, they secured Mexican divorce and fake divorce decree under suspicious circumstances, they gave inconsistent testimony about the decree, and they had a perfunctory marriage ceremony].)

In *In re Goldberg's Estate* (1962) 203 Cal. App. 2d 402, 21 Cal. Rptr. 626 (*Goldberg's Estate*), around 1943, a man told a woman he had separated from his first wife and was getting divorced. This was in 1943. They never discussed the subject again. The woman had been married twice before and divorced once, and she thought her second marriage had been annulled, although there was no documentary evidence of it. In March 1944, the two were married in Mexico in a ceremony performed in Spanish. Thereafter, they lived as husband and wife. In July 1944, there was an interlocutory divorce decree, and the man's divorce became final in July 1945. The woman testified that all the documents concerning marriages and divorces had been stolen during a trip to Alaska. The trial court found that the woman had married the man believing in good faith that both were eligible to marry.

On appeal, the reviewing court observed that there was substantial evidence undermining the woman's claim that she thought her marriage was valid. The court noted, however, that the trial court had observed her testify and believed her testimony that she thought her marriage had been annulled and his marriage had been dissolved. The court opined, "If [the woman] believed in good faith that a valid marriage existed, then in law she was a putative spouse. [Citation.] The belief held at the time of the alleged marriage is the determining factor. . . ." The court further explained that although the woman's testimony was pretty "weak," "the testimony of a party to the action, if believed, is sufficient to support the judgment of a trial court even though contradicted by a great deal of contrary evidence. [Citation.] Whether or not the required belief was held in good faith by [the woman] *was a question of fact* to be resolved by the trial court. [Citation.]" (*Id.* at p. 412, 21 Cal. Rptr. 626, italics added.) In this regard, the court opined that the conduct of their parties after their marriage and for the next 16 years supported the trial court's finding of a good faith belief.

As these cases reveal, when the putative spouse doctrine was codified, courts treated putative status as a factual question concerning a party's state of mind: did he or she honestly and genuinely believe that the marriage was valid. The answer hinged in large part on the credibility of the alleged putative spouse. And in determining credibility, courts also considered the circumstances surrounding the putative marriage and the person's level of education, marital experience, intelligence, and even the conduct after the putative marriage. If the trial court found that a party harbored a good faith belief, and if there was substantial evidence to support it, the reviewing court upheld the finding of putative status.

For many years after codification, courts understood and applied the doctrine in this way.

In *Wagner v. County of Imperial* (1983) 145 Cal. App. 3d 980, 193 Cal. Rptr. 820 (*Wagner*), a particularly pertinent case, a couple, Sharon and Clifton, exchanged personal marriage vows, Sharon used Clifton's name, they held themselves out as husband and wife, and they had a child. When Clifton was killed in a car accident, Sharon sued for wrongful death under former section 377, alleging that she was a putative spouse. Although the trial court found that she harbored a good faith belief in the validity of her common law marriage, it denied her standing because her putative marriage had not been solemnized.

On appeal, the court reversed. The court noted that solemnization had never been a prerequisite for putative status. It further observed that the statutory definition of a putative spouse did not require solemnization. Rather, to qualify as a putative spouse, "Sharon must only prove she had a good faith belief her marriage to Clifton was valid; solemnization would be at most evidence of such good faith belief. . . . '[T]he essence of a putative spouse is a good faith belief in the existence of a valid marriage.' Here the superior court specifically found Sharon believed in good faith she was validly married to Clifton. The court's legal conclusion Sharon was not Clifton's putative spouse is contrary to such express finding of good faith. The court should have held Sharon was Clifton's putative spouse."

VRYONIS AND THE REQUIREMENT OF AN OBJECTIVE STANDARD

With this understanding of how courts applied the doctrine before and after codification, we turn to *Vryonis, supra*, 202 Cal. App. 3d 712, 248 Cal. Rptr. 807, which added a further requirement for putative status: a party's good faith belief must also be objectively reasonable.[8]

The pertinent facts in *Vryonis* are as follows. A visiting Iranian professor at UCLA named Fereshteh alleged that she was the putative spouse of a resident professor named Speros. She was a Shia Muslim, and he was a nonpracticing member of the Greek Orthodox Church. They went out together, but her religion prohibited dating without a marriage or formal commitment. At Fereshteh's request, Speros agreed to a marriage authorized by her religion. Fereshteh performed the private ceremony in accordance with religious liturgical requirements. Later, she sought to solemnize the marriage in a mosque, but Speros refused. Nevertheless, he assured her that they were married. A couple of years later, however, he announced that he was going to marry another woman. Fereshteh publicly revealed their marriage, but he married the other woman anyway. Fereshteh then sought a determination of her rights as a putative spouse.

The trial court found that Fereshteh had believed in good faith that she was validly married. It noted that Speros had agreed to be married, and they had a proper, albeit private, marriage ceremony authorized by her religion. Speros had also assured Fereshteh that they were married, although he did not think the marriage was valid under California law. Fereshteh was unaware of his views or California's requirements for marriage.

---

8. Years before Vryonis, the Fifth Circuit in *Spearman v. Spearman* (5th Cir. 1973) 482 F.2d 1203 upheld the trial court, which had applied an objective test. In finding no error, the Fifth Circuit concluded that an objective test was "perfectly consonant with the California decisions that have developed and applied the 'putative spouse' doctrine." (*Id.* at p. 1207.) The court acknowledged that no court had ever applied such a test but opined that no court that had discussed good faith had rejected or precluded such a test. (*Ibid.*)

Spearman is not binding on us, and we do not consider its seems-all-right analysis to be persuasive support for an objective test. (See *People v. Williams* (1997) 16 Cal. 4th 153, 190, 66 Cal. Rptr. 2d 123, 940 P.2d 710 [decisions of lower federal courts are not binding authority].)

On appeal, the *Vryonis* court rejected the trial court's factual finding of putative status. It held that Fereshteh's good faith belief, no matter credible and sincere, was simply not enough. Her belief had to be tested against an objective standard. It had to be objectively reasonable, that is, it had to rest on facts that would cause a reasonable person to believe the marriage was valid under California law. Noting that Fereshteh had made no effort to comply with California's statutory marriage requirements, the court concluded that a reasonable person would not have believed he or she was validly married after some private religious ceremony. Thus, because Fereshteh's belief was not objectively reasonable, she could not have held it in good faith and was not entitled to putative status.

We first observe that in imposing an objective test for putative status, the *Vryonis* court, in effect, gave appellate courts the opportunity to determine putative status de novo. As noted, putative status had always rested on the trial court's factual finding concerning good faith belief, and that finding was upheld if supported by substantial evidence. Whether a good faith belief is objectively reasonable added a purely legal question to the determination of putative status, a question subject to independent review.

Next we observe that appellate courts, including this court, have adopted *Vryonis*, accepting its objective test without critical analysis of its rationale. Indeed, its objective test has become firmly lodged in the judicial boilerplate describing the putative spouse doctrine. (See, e.g., *Centinela Hospital Medical Center v. Superior Court* (1989) 215 Cal. App. 3d 971, 975, 263 Cal. Rptr. 672 (*Centinela Hospital*); *Welch*, (2000) 83 Cal. App. 4th 1374, 1378, 100 Cal. Rptr. 2d 430; *Estate of DePasse* (2002) 97 Cal. App. 4th 92, 107-108, 118 Cal. Rptr. 2d 143; *In re Marriage of Xia Guo and Xiao Hua Sun* (2010) 186 Cal. App. 4th 1491, 1497, 112 Cal. Rptr. 3d 906.)

However, the time has come, belatedly, to review the analysis in *Vryonis*, and because we reject it, we shall do so in detail.[9]

In adding an objective test, the *Vryonis* court did not rely on the long history of putative spouse cases or cite cases suggesting that a good faith belief, by itself, was not enough to qualify for putative status. Nor did the court find a legislative intent to establish an objective test in the history of codification of the doctrine. Rather, the source of the test was the court's simple declaration that a "'[g]ood faith belief' is a legal term of art, and in both the civil and criminal law a determination of good faith is tested by an objective standard." In other words, the phrase "good faith belief" necessarily and automatically incorporates an objective standard of reasonableness.

In support, the court quoted excerpts from [several cases].

These excerpts share two qualities. None suggests that "good faith belief" inherently means a belief that is also objectively reasonable; and they are irrelevant in determining what the requirements for putative status are or arguably should be.

[T]he definition of putative spouse has never required a *reasonable* good faith belief or even used the word "reasonable."

In sum, the *Vryonis* court's declaration that "good faith belief" necessarily incorporates an objective standard of reasonableness lacks any supportive authority. Moreover, even cursory research refutes that notion and reveals that long before

---

9. We are not alone in rejecting *Vryonis*. (See Bassett, *California Community Property Law* (2011 ed.) §2:8, pp. 71-78 [criticizing *Vryonis* and its progeny].)

Vryonis, courts have understood the concepts of good faith and reasonableness to be separate and distinct and, as a consequence, used different tests to evaluate them.

In *People v. Nunn* (1956) 46 Cal. 2d 460, 296 P.2d 813, the court explained that "[t]he phrase 'good faith' in common usage has a well-defined and generally understood meaning, being ordinarily used to describe that *state of mind* denoting honesty of purpose, freedom from intention to defraud, and, generally speaking, means being faithful to one's duty or obligation."

Reasonableness, on the other hand, refers to an objective quality determined with reference to common experience and generally refers to something that is arrived at logically, enjoys factual support, and is not arbitrary or capricious.

Thus, when the question is whether a party acted in good faith, the inquiry concerns the party's subjective state of mind and whether it is genuine and sincere or tainted by fraud, dishonesty, collusion, deceit, and unfaithfulness. Whether a reasonable person would have acted similarly under the same conditions is not relevant to that inquiry. On the other hand, when the question is whether a party acted reasonably, the inquiry *is* whether a reasonable person under the similar circumstances would have acted in the same way. In this context, whether the party acted in good faith is not relevant. Both civil and criminal cases reflect the distinction between good faith and reasonableness and the difference in how each is determined.

Corbett v. Hayward Dodge, Inc. (2004) 119 Cal. App. 4th 915, 14 Cal. Rptr. 3d 741 (*Corbett*) is particularly pertinent here. It involved Civil Code section 1780, subdivision (e), which authorizes an award of reasonable attorney fees to a prevailing defendant if the trial court finds that "the plaintiff's prosecution of the action was not in good faith." The issue there was whether a subjective or objective test governed the determination of good faith. In holding that a subjective test applied, the court pointed out that this subjective test also applied in determining whether to award expenses under section 128.5 that a party incurred because of an opposing party's "bad-faith actions or tactics that are frivolous or solely intended to cause unnecessary delay." The court further observed that "good faith" had uniformly been construed to require a subjective test involving a factual inquiry into the actor's actual state of mind.

Similarly, a good faith but mistaken belief in the need to defend oneself or another against imminent danger of great bodily injury will negate the malice element required for a murder conviction and thus can limit a defendant's culpability for an unlawful homicide to voluntary manslaughter. Again, if the mistaken belief is held in good faith, it need not be objectively reasonable to have an exculpatory effect. On the other hand, if one reasonably believes in the need to defend oneself or another against imminent peril, one's conduct is justified and criminal.

Last, we observe that courts and the Legislature consistently demonstrate their understanding that good faith is distinct from reasonableness and does not incorporate an objective standard. For example, when courts intend to require conduct that is both in good faith and objectively reasonable, they do so expressly and unequivocally. (See, e.g., *United States v. Leon* (1984) 468 U.S. 897, 104 S. Ct. 3405, 82 L. Ed. 2d 677 [creating exception to the exclusionary rule based on good faith *and* objectively reasonable reliance on warrant]; *People v. Salas* (2006) 37 Cal. 4th 967, 38 Cal. Rptr. 3d 624, 127 P.3d 40 [recognizing defense to sale of unregistered securities based on reasonable good faith belief that securities were exempt]; *People v. Mayberry, supra*, 15 Cal. 3d 143, 125 Cal. Rptr. 745, 542 P.2d 1337 [recognizing defense to rape based on reasonable and good faith belief that victim consented]; *People v. Hernandez* (1964) 61 Cal. 2d 529, 39 Cal. Rptr. 361, 393 P.2d 673 [same re statutory rape based on good faith and objectively reasonable belief that victim was not underage]; *People v. Vogel* (1956) 46 Cal. 2d 798, 299 P.2d 850 [same re defense to bigamy based on reasonable good faith belief in divorce]; *Baker v. American Horticulture Supply, Inc.* (2010) 186 Cal. App. 4th 1059, 111 Cal. Rptr. 3d 695 [recognizing defense to willful failure to pay commission based on reasonable good faith belief that claim for commission is invalid].)

Likewise the Legislature uses express, unequivocal language when it intends to require conduct or belief that is both held in good faith and objectively reasonable. (See, e.g., §1985.3, subd. (g) ["a reasonable and good faith attempt"]; Pen. Code, §278.7 ["with a good faith and reasonable belief"]; Pub. Util. Code, §588, subd. (b)(1) ["reasonable, good faith belief"]; compare with Fin. Code, §5204, subd. (b) [requiring only good faith belief].)

In this case, we have found no evidence suggesting that when the Legislature codified the doctrine, it intended to require that an alleged putative spouse's belief in the validity of a marriage be both held in good faith and objectively reasonable. This is understandable because, as noted, the Legislature intended only to continue the judicial doctrine as it had been understood and applied.

At this point, it is helpful to recap our analysis and discussion. The original judicial definition of a putative spouse required only a good faith belief in the validity of a marriage. The Legislature codified that definition without intending to change it. The *Vryonis* court engrafted an objective test to the statutory definition based on the legally unsupported view that "good faith belief" necessarily incorporates an objective standard. However, good faith and objective reasonableness are separate and distinct concepts, and each is evaluated differently. The determination of good faith belief focuses on a party's subjective state of mind and evidence of honesty, sincerity, faithfulness, fraud, or collusion and not on whether the belief is objectively reasonable. And when courts and Legislature intend to require conduct or belief that is both held in good faith and objectively reasonable, they do so clearly.

In light of our discussion, we hold that the statutory definition of putative spouse in section 377.60 is clear and unambiguous. It requires a good faith belief in the validity of a marriage. Giving the statutory language its ordinary meaning, we hold that the phrase "believed in good faith" refers to a state of mind and a belief that is held honestly, genuinely, and sincerely, without collusion or fraud. It does not require that the belief also be objectively reasonable.

As noted, *Vryonis* created a conflict with prior cases holding that putative status required only a good faith belief and not a good faith *and reasonable* belief. When there is an unresolved conflict in the judicial holdings concerning the application of a statute, its reenactment cannot reasonably be deemed legislative acquiescence in either side of the conflict.[15]

ERROR IN GRANTING SUMMARY JUDGMENT

Given our rejection of *Vryonis*, we conclude that the trial court erred in applying an objective standard to determine Nancy's putative status and granting summary judgment on the ground that a belief in the validity of her four-year marriage to Robert was not objectively reasonable. That error, however, does not necessarily require reversal. On appeal "[w]e need not defer to the trial court and are not bound by the reasons in its summary judgment ruling; we review the ruling of the trial court, not its rationale. [Citation.]"

Again, the issue before the trial court was not whether there were triable issues concerning whether Nancy's belief was objectively reasonable. The determinative question was whether there were triable issues concerning whether Nancy believed in good faith that her marriage was valid. We conclude that there were.

Whether Nancy harbored a good faith belief involves a factual inquiry into her subjective state of mind: what did she know and believe; and was her belief honest, sincere, and genuine or tainted by fraud or collusion. The determination of putative status also involves an inquiry into the circumstances before, during, and after the marriage.

15. Although our discussion focuses solely on the addition of an objective test, the *Vryonis* court added another requirement. The court opined that it was not enough to believe in the validity of *a* marriage. Rather, to qualify for putative status, one had to believe in good faith that the marriage complied with California's statutory requirements for a lawful marriage. Turning to the facts before it, the court reasoned that because Fereshteh had made no attempt to comply with the statutory prerequisites for lawful marriage, she could not have actually believed that her private religious ceremony had resulted in a lawful California marriage. (*Vryonis, supra*, 202 Cal. App. 3d at pp. 722-723, 248 Cal. Rptr. 807.)

> We need not analyze the court's reasoning because here, the record establishes that Nancy and Robert attempted to comply with the statutory requirements. We note, however, that at least one commentator — Professor Bassett — finds this aspect of *Vryonis* particularly troubling. He questions the equation of a belief that a marriage is valid, as required by statute, with the belief that a marriage is *lawful* in that it complied with the California's statutory requirements. He opines that this equation considerably narrows the traditional scope of the putative spouse doctrine and suggests that ignorance of the statutory requirements and the inevitable failure to comply with them preclude a good faith belief. According to Professor Bassett, this approach to determining putative status is overly formalistic and inconsistent with the equitable origin and purpose of the doctrine. (Bassett, *California Community Property Law, supra*, §2:8, pp. 74-79.) Professor Bassett's critique raises legitimate concerns about the propriety of this additional requirement.
>
> We note that while the circumstances surrounding a marriage are relevant in determining good faith belief, ignorance of the law and failure to comply with statutory prerequisites have not invariably precluded a finding of good faith belief and putative status. (See, e.g., *Vallera, supra*, 21 Cal. 2d at pp. 682-684, 134 P.2d 761 [no effort to get married in California]; *Wagner, supra*, 145 Cal. App. 3d 980, 193 Cal. Rptr. 820 [solemnization not a prerequisite to putative status]; *Monti, supra*, 135 Cal. App. 3d at pp. 52-54, 56, 185 Cal. Rptr. 72 [no effort to comply with California law]; *Sancha v. Arnold* (1952) 114 Cal. App. 2d 772, 251 P.2d 67 [putative status based on common law marriage]; *Santos v. Santos, supra*, 32 Cal. App. 2d 62, 89 P.2d 164 [putative status despite inability to speak English and ignorance of marriage laws].)

For example, suppose in *Vryonis* that Fereshteh had lived with Speros for many years after their religious marriage, raised a family, and accumulated a substantial amount of property, and he then decided to lawfully marry one of his students. In our view, denying Fereshteh a share of the property as a putative spouse because she was unaware of and thus made no attempt to comply with California's marriage laws would seem inconsistent with the fundamental equitable purpose of the doctrine: to protect the expectations of innocent parties to a marriage that later proves to be invalid.

In her declaration, Nancy said she believed her marriage was valid. She stated that Robert told her he was getting a divorce from Christine and then refused to discuss it any further. She said she did not read the marriage license closely, implying that she did not know that Robert had falsely represented his marital history. She stated that she did not read the final divorce papers that he received and she then forwarded to his union. Nancy also asserted, in essence, that if she had known that there was a problem before her wedding she would have postponed it; and if she had later learned that the wedding took place a few months too soon, they would have gotten remarried after the divorce became final.

If true, these statements could support a finding of good faith belief and establish putative status. However, the truth of Nancy's statements depends on her credibility. The credibility of a declarant, in general, cannot be assessed adequately in a motion for summary judgment; it is more appropriately determined through actual examination and cross-examination, during which the trier of fact can hear her testimony, observe the witness's demeanor, and decide whether the witness is being truthful.

Defendant's argument below and the trial court's reasoning were that given the misrepresentation in the marriage license that Robert had no prior marriages, a reasonable person could not believe in good faith that the marriage was valid. As we have explained, whether a reasonable person would harbor a belief is irrelevant. Therefore, that theory does not support denial of putative status on summary judgment.

In sum, having independently reviewed the pleadings in support of and opposition to the motion for summary judgment, we find triable issues of fact that preclude summary judgment on the issue of Nancy's putative status.

VII.   Disposition

The judgment is reversed. Plaintiff is entitled to her costs on appeal. (Cal. Rules of Court, rule 8.278(a)(1).)

We concur: Premo and Elia, JJ.

Discussion Questions

1. Why would Nancy succeed under a subjective test but fail under an objective test?

2. Why did the Court of Appeal opt for a subjective test?

B. CAN A "BAD FAITH" SPOUSE CLAIM PROPERTY RIGHTS?

In *Williams*, the Nevada Supreme Court mentioned but did not address the situation where one party qualifies as a putative spouse and the other does not: "When a person enters into the relationship with knowledge of an impediment and knowledge the marriage is not valid, some states have found the person who acted in bad faith is not entitled to benefit from the marriage."[1] When reading the following California cases, *Marriage of Tejeda* and *Marriage of Xia Guo and Xia Hua Sun*, consider which has the most compelling reasoning and fair result. Discussion questions will follow both cases.

MARRIAGE OF TEJEDA

179 Cal. App. 4th 973, 102 Cal. Rptr. 3d 361 (2009)
Court of Appeal

McADAMS, J.

This case requires us to construe Family Code section 2251.[1] Subject to the requirements of that provision, a marriage that is invalid due to a legal infirmity may be recognized as a putative marriage. Property acquired during a putative marriage (quasi-marital property) is divided as if it were community property.

In this case, the parties' marriage was invalid because respondent already had a wife when he married appellant. The trial court declared appellant a putative spouse. She appeals the judgment of nullity, challenging the determination that property acquired in her name during the union is quasi-marital property.

Applying the unambiguous language of section 2251, we conclude that the parties' union is a putative marriage and that the property acquired during that union is quasi-marital property subject to division as community property. We therefore affirm the judgment.

FACTUAL BACKGROUND

In 1973, appellant Petra Tejeda (Petra) and respondent Pablo Tejeda (Pablo) were married in Las Vegas. At the time of the marriage ceremony, and unbeknownst to Petra, Pablo was married to Margarita Rivera Tejeda (Margarita). In 1975, Pablo petitioned to dissolve his marriage to Margarita, and a judgment of dissolution was

1. *Williams v. Williams*, 120 Nev. 559, 97 P.3d 1124 n.15 (2004).
1. Unspecified statutory references are to the Family Code.
Section 2251 provides in pertinent part as follows: "If a determination is made that a marriage is void or voidable and the court finds that either party or both parties believed in good faith that the marriage was valid, the court shall: [¶] (1) Declare the party or parties to have the status of a putative spouse. [¶] (2) If the division of property is in issue, divide, in accordance with Division 7 (commencing with Section 2500), that property acquired during the union which would have been community property or quasi-community property if the union had not been void or voidable. This property is known as 'quasi-marital property.'" (§2251, subd. (a).)

entered the following year. In 1988, Pablo and Petra participated in a marriage ceremony in a Mexican church, unaccompanied by any civil formalities.

The parties' union lasted more than thirty years. During this time, Petra and Pablo had five children together. Petra began acquiring real property in 1994, taking title in her name, together with other relatives, but not with Pablo.

PROCEDURAL HISTORY

In March 2006, Pablo filed an action to end his union with Petra, petitioning for dissolution in San Benito County. In a response filed in May 2006, Petra likewise requested dissolution of marriage. Thereafter, she amended her response to seek a judgment of nullity of marriage. In October 2007, after the action had been transferred to Santa Cruz County, Petra filed another amended response. As before, Petra requested a judgment of nullity. Petra also requested that all property in her possession be confirmed as her separate property.

In January 2008, the court conducted an evidentiary hearing to determine the validity of the marriage.

Prior to the hearing, the attorneys for both parties submitted written briefing, which included both exhibits and arguments. Petra argued that the union was bigamous and thus void under section 2201. She asserted that Pablo could not demonstrate the requisite reasonable good faith belief in the validity of the marriage required for putative spouse status under section 2251. Petra clarified that she was not seeking putative spouse status for herself. In his trial brief, Pablo asserted his belief that he and Petra were married. In any event, Pablo maintained, "fault" is irrelevant in a putative marriage.

At the hearing, only Petra testified. At the time of her 1972 Las Vegas wedding, Petra stated, she did not know that Pablo was still married to Margarita. Pablo told Petra that he was divorced. Petra did not discover the truth until 2006. Up until then, Petra testified, "I thought I was married."

Following Petra's testimony, the trial court made an oral finding "that the marriage is either void or voidable because Mr. Tejeda was already married." The court also found that "at all times, Mrs. Tejeda believe[d] that she was married to someone who at the time of their marriage ceremony was single." That belief, the court said, was reaffirmed "by her actions over some period of time" such as filing joint tax returns, confirming her marital status for immigration purposes, taking Pablo's name, and using "medical benefits under his insurance, social security benefits under his name."

Given these factual findings, the court concluded, the matter was governed by section 2251, which required the court to "declare the party or parties to have the status of a putative spouse." The property thus was quasi-marital property. The court did not divide the property, observing that there might be defenses to the presumption of equal division, or tracing issues, or other questions concerning characterization.

In June 2008, the court entered a judgment of nullity, which incorporated its earlier determinations. The court found that since "either party (here, specifically Petra Tejeda) or both parties believed in good faith that the marriage was valid," the court was statutorily required to "declare the party or parties to have a status of putative spouse." Under "the mandatory language" of section 2251, the court stated, it was "obligated to find that the property of the parties is quasi-marital . . . property."

This appeal ensued.

CONTENTIONS

Petra asserts that the "plain language" of section 2251 "is ambiguous, to the extent it is susceptible to the interpretation applied by the Trial Court." As a matter of legislative intent, she argues, the statute should "only be applied at the request of the putative (innocent) spouse."

Pablo disagrees, arguing that the statutory language "is clear: if either party or both parties have the status of a putative spouse, community property principles apply to the division of any quasi-marital property at issue."

DISCUSSION

As a framework for our discussion, we begin by setting forth the legal principles that govern our analysis. We then apply them to this case.

I. LEGAL PRINCIPLES

A. PUTATIVE MARRIAGES

"Where a marriage is invalid due to some legal infirmity, an innocent party may be entitled to relief under the putative spouse doctrine." (*Estate of DePasse* (2002) 97 Cal. App. 4th 92, 107, 118 Cal. Rptr. 2d 143; accord, *In re Marriage of Ramirez* (2008) 165 Cal. App. 4th 751, 756, 81 Cal. Rptr. 3d 180.)

1. Legal Infirmity

Invalid marriages include those that are void or voidable. Bigamy renders the later marriage either void or voidable, depending on the circumstances. (§2201, subd. (a).) One "may *never* legally remarry prior to dissolution of his or her existing marriage."

2. Putative Spouse Doctrine

"Under the equitable putative spouse doctrine, a person's reasonable, good faith belief that his or her marriage is valid entitles that person to the benefits of marriage, even if the marriage is not, in fact, valid."

The putative spouse doctrine is "an equitable doctrine first recognized by the judiciary, and later codified by the Legislature." "In 1969, the Legislature codified the putative spouse doctrine in former Civil Code section 4452" as part of the Family Law Act. "Prior to the enactment of the Family Law Act, no statute granted rights to a putative spouse. The courts accordingly fashioned a variety of remedies by judicial decision." Some "decisions affirmed the power of a court to employ equitable principles to achieve a fair division of property acquired during putative marriage."

Codification "was not intended to narrow the application of the doctrine only to parties to a void or voidable marriage. Instead, the Legislature contemplated the continued protection of innocent parties who believe they were validly married."

The current version of the putative spouse doctrine is contained in section 2251, subdivision (a), which provides in relevant part: "If a determination is made that a marriage is void or voidable and the court finds that either party or both parties believed in good faith that the marriage was valid, the court shall: [¶] (1) Declare the party or parties to have the status of a putative spouse." The language of this provision is "almost identical" to that of its predecessor, former Civil Code section 4452, the original provision in the Family Law Act.

B.   QUASI-MARITAL PROPERTY

Quasi-marital property is "property acquired during the union which would have been community property or quasi-community property if the union had not been void or voidable." "The theory of 'quasi-marital property' equates property rights acquired during a putative marriage with community property rights acquired during a legal marriage."

Upon declaration of putative spouse status, the court is required to divide the quasi-marital property as if it were community property. Thus, "the share to which the putative spouse is entitled is the same share of the quasi-marital property as the spouse would receive as an actual and legal spouse if there had been a valid marriage, i.e., it shall be divided equally between the parties." "These principles were established by numerous judicial decisions, and were made a part of our positive law by the enactment, in 1969, of Civil Code section 4452, a part of the Family Law Act, effective January 1, 1970."

C.   APPELLATE REVIEW

As both parties acknowledge, the issue presented here "is one of statutory construction that is subject to our independent review."

"In construing a statute, our fundamental task is to ascertain the Legislature's intent so as to effectuate the purpose of the statute." "We begin with the language of the statute, giving the words their usual and ordinary meaning." "The words of the statute must be construed in context, keeping in mind the statutory purpose, and statutes or statutory sections relating to the same subject must be harmonized, both internally and with each other, to the extent possible." Thus, "every statute should be construed with reference to the whole system of law of which it is a part, so that all may be harmonized and have effect."

"If the terms of the statute are unambiguous, we presume the lawmakers meant what they said, and the plain meaning of the language governs." As the California Supreme Court recently reaffirmed, "judicial construction of unambiguous statutes is appropriate only when literal interpretation would yield absurd results." Where the statutory language is clear, resort to extrinsic aids is neither necessary nor proper.

II. ANALYSIS

As we now explain, our analysis begins and ends with an examination of the statutory language, construed in context and in light of the statutory purposes.

A. THE STATUTORY LANGUAGE

The language of the governing statute is clear and unambiguous.

Section 2251 requires two predicate findings: that the "marriage is void or voidable" and "that either party or both parties believed in good faith that the marriage was valid. . . ." (§2251, subd. (a).) If the predicate findings are made, "the court shall" do these two things: "(1) Declare the party or parties to have the status of a putative spouse" and (2) divide any quasi-marital property as if it were community property.

For purposes of this provision, "shall" is mandatory.

1. *Putative Spouse Determination*

Upon a finding that the marriage is invalid, the statute requires the court to declare any party with the requisite good faith belief to be a putative spouse.

As Petra observes, "the status is not automatically applied to both parties, only those with a good faith belief in the validity of the marriage." In the words of one court: "The status of 'putative spouse' requires innocence or good faith belief."

What Petra fails to acknowledge, however, is that once either party is a putative spouse, the union is a *putative marriage*. "By definition, a putative marriage is a union in which at least one partner believes in good faith that a valid marriage exists. As in this case, the couple conducts themselves as husband and wife throughout the period of their union." Thus, even where only one party has the requisite good faith belief in the validity of the marriage, thereby qualifying as the sole putative spouse, the court's declaration of his or her status operates as a declaration that the union itself is a putative marriage.

2. *Property Division*

The statute commands the court to divide the quasi-marital property as if it were community property, using these words: "If the division of property is in issue," the court shall "divide, in accordance with Division 7 (commencing with Section 2500), that property acquired during the union which would have been community property or quasi-community property if the union had not been void or voidable." (§2251, subd. (a)(2).) Division 7 governs the division of property; section 2550 generally requires the court to "divide the community estate of the parties equally."

Nothing in the language of section 2251's property division mandate suggests that it is limited to cases where both parties are putative spouses. To the contrary, read in combination with the preceding sentence — the grant of putative spouse status to "the party or parties" — it plainly compels division of the quasi-marital property regardless of whether both parties have been declared putative spouses. (§2251, subd. (a)(1).)

This reading is consistent with long-standing decisional law, which holds that "property acquired during the void or voidable union . . . is divided as community property would be divided upon the dissolution of a valid marriage." "There is no reason to believe that the Legislature . . . intended to change those principles." (*Ibid.*)

B.   THE STATUTORY CONTEXT

We do not consider the words of the statute in isolation. Rather, we examine the statutory language "in context, keeping in mind the statutory purpose," and harmonizing the statute with related provisions. (*Dyna-Med, Inc. v. Fair Employment & Housing Com., supra*, 43 Cal. 3d at p. 1387, 241 Cal. Rptr. 67, 743 P.2d 1323.) Petra urges us to do so here, claiming that related statutory law "supports the conclusion that the equity-based putative spouse doctrine codified in . . . §2251 may only be applied to the benefit (and at the request) of the innocent spouse."

1.   *Related Provisions*

Two relevant provisions are sections 2254 and 2255. Section 2254 permits an order for support, "if the party for whose benefit the order is made is found to be a putative spouse." Section 2255 provides that fees and costs in a nullity proceeding may be granted only to a party "found to be innocent of fraud or wrongdoing in inducing or entering into" a putative marriage.

These provisions support an inference that the Legislature intended to treat "guilty" and "innocent" parties to a putative marriage differently. In the words of one commentator, "the fact that the Legislature limited *support* and *attorney fee* rights to the 'good faith' (innocent) spouse . . . may be some indication it also intended only the putative spouse to be entitled to quasi-marital property rights." (Hogoboom & King, Cal. Practice Guide: Family Law (The Rutter Group 2009), ¶ 19:62, pp. 19-20, discussing §§2254, 2255.)

On the other hand, the opposite inference might be drawn by applying the maxim *expressio unius est exclusio alterius:* "The expression of some things in a statute necessarily means the exclusion of other things not expressed." Here, the Legislature singled out the "innocent" party in providing for fees, and it likewise singled out the "putative spouse" in providing for support, but it did not limit quasi-marital property division to an innocent putative spouse, either explicitly or implicitly. In making this choice, we assume that the Legislature was aware of the substantial body of decisional law providing for equal division of quasi-marital property.

2.   *Statutory Purpose*

Disregarding guilt and innocence in property division also serves to support the purposes of the Family Law Act. "The main focus of the act was to eliminate the artificial fault standard." "The basic substantive change in the law" engendered by the act was "the elimination of fault or guilt as grounds for granting or denying divorce and for refusing alimony and making unequal division of community property." "The equal division of community property was one of the ways 'of advancing [the act's] primary no-fault philosophy.'" The equal division of quasi-marital property likewise serves those purposes.

This reading of the statute, without regard to guilt or innocence, is bolstered by dicta from the California Supreme Court decision in *Marvin*, which states: "In a putative marriage the parties will arrange their economic affairs with the expectation that upon dissolution the property will be divided equally. If a 'guilty' putative spouse receives one-half of the property under [the statute], no expectation of the 'innocent' spouse has been frustrated."

c. Conclusion

Based on the plain language of the statute, read in context and with due regard for the purposes of the broader law of which it is a part, we conclude that the mandate of section 2251 must be applied, without regard to guilt or innocence, when the court makes the predicate findings that (1) the marriage is void or voidable, and (2) at least one party to the union maintained a good faith belief in the validity of the marriage.

Disposition

The June 2008 judgment of nullity is affirmed.

We concur: Bamattre-Manoukian, Acting P.J., and Duffy, J.

MARRIAGE OF XIA GUO AND XIAO HUA SUN

186 Cal. App. 4th 1491, 112 Cal. Rptr. 3d 906 (2010)
Court of Appeal of California

Kitching, J.

Introduction

The superior court entered a judgment nullifying the marriage of appellant Xiao Hua Sun and respondent Xia Guo on the ground that Sun was married to another woman when he purportedly married Guo. The court also denied Sun's claim that he was Guo's putative spouse pursuant to Family Code section 2251. Sun appeals the order denying his putative spouse claim.

A party claiming to be a putative spouse must show, among other things, that he or she believed in good faith that the marriage was valid. A determination of good faith is tested by an objective standard. In this case, the superior court found that Sun did not have an objectively reasonable belief that he was married to Guo, and thus was not Guo's putative spouse.

There are two main issues on appeal. The first is whether there was substantial evidence supporting the superior court's finding that Sun did not have a good faith belief that the marriage was valid. We shall conclude that there was substantial evidence to support that finding.

The second issue is whether Sun can claim putative spouse status based on Guo's alleged good faith belief in the validity of the marriage, even though Sun did not have such a good faith belief. We hold that Sun is not a putative spouse under these circumstances. In so holding, we respectfully disagree with the holding in *In re Marriage of Tejeda* (2009) 179 Cal. App. 4th 973, 102 Cal. Rptr. 3d 361 (*Tejeda*).

The order denying Sun's claim for putative spouse status is affirmed.

FACTUAL AND PROCEDURAL BACKGROUND

Sun and Guo met in North Korea in 1997 or 1998, began a romantic relationship, and shortly thereafter moved together to Los Angeles. Prior to the purported marriage between Sun and Guo, Guo knew that Sun was married to another woman in Italy.

In approximately January 2001, Sun met with his lawyer, Tonnie Cheng, and advised Cheng that he wanted to divorce his wife in Italy. Sun testified that although Guo was not present at his initial meeting with Cheng, shortly thereafter Guo met Cheng and worked with Cheng to arrange for Sun's divorce from his first wife. Guo testified that she did not meet Cheng until one or two years after Guo purportedly married Sun.

On February 14, 2001 — Valentine's Day — Sun and Guo decided to marry, went to Las Vegas, and were married that day. Both Sun and Guo claim that at the time, they believed that Sun was already divorced from his Italian wife and that Sun and Guo were legally married. Guo's belief that Sun divorced his first wife prior to February 14, 2001, was based solely on Sun's representation to her that he had done so. Although both Sun and Guo knew that Sun was previously married, their marriage license stated that this was Sun's first marriage.

On February 15, 2001, Cheng filed on behalf of Sun a petition to dissolve Sun's marriage with his Italian wife. On August 21, 2001, the superior court entered a judgment dissolving Sun's first marriage.

On August 24, 2007, Guo filed a petition for dissolution of marriage. Guo filed an amended petition on January 7, 2008. In her amended petition, Guo sought to nullify her marriage with Sun on the ground that Sun entered into a bigamous marriage.

On August 15, 2008, the superior court entered a judgment of nullity. The court found that the marriage of Sun and Guo was illegal and void pursuant to section 2201 because Sun was married at the time he purportedly married Guo. This judgment determined the status of the marriage only, and did not adjudicate the division of the couple's assets.

After the judgment, Sun sought to be declared a putative spouse. The court held a two-day bench trial on the issue. On December 22, 2008, the court entered a memorandum of decision. In its memorandum, the court found that Sun did not have an objectively reasonable good faith belief that his prior marriage was dissolved prior to his purported marriage with Guo.

On February 17, 2009, the court entered an order denying Sun's request for a finding of putative spouse status. This appeal followed.

CONTENTIONS

Sun does not challenge the judgment of annulment on appeal. Rather, he contends that the superior court erroneously denied his request to be declared a putative spouse. In particular, Sun contends that the superior court erroneously found that he did not have an objective good faith belief that a valid marriage existed.

Sun further contends that the superior court failed to consider Guo's good faith belief in the validity of the marriage in determining whether Sun was Guo's putative spouse. According to Sun, under Family Code section 2251, he is entitled to putative spouse status even if he did not have a good faith belief in the validity of the marriage, if Guo had such a belief.

DISCUSSION

1.   THE PUTATIVE SPOUSE DOCTRINE

The putative spouse doctrine is "an equitable doctrine first recognized by the judiciary, and later codified by the Legislature." In 1943, our Supreme Court stated that "[i]t is well settled that a woman who lives with a man as his wife in the belief that a valid marriage exists, is entitled upon termination of their relationship to share in the property acquired by them during its existence."

The doctrine, however, cannot be invoked unless the putative spouse had a *good faith* belief in the existence of a valid marriage. "[I]n the majority of cases, the de facto wife attempted to meet the requisites of a valid marriage, and the marriage proved invalid only because of some essential fact of which she was unaware, such as the earlier undissolved marriage of one of the parties [citations], a consanguineous relation between the parties [citations], or the failure to meet the requirement of solemnization. [Citations.]"

The purpose of the doctrine is to protect the "innocent" party or parties of an invalid marriage from losing community property rights. (See *Schneider v. Schneider* (1920) 183 Cal. 335, 337, 340, 191 P. 533.) As our Supreme Court explained in *Schneider v. Schneider,* "the common-law rule as to the consequences of a void marriage upon the mutual property rights of the parties to it is inapplicable where the community property régime prevails. This conclusion is dictated by simple justice, for where persons domiciled in such a jurisdiction, believing themselves to be lawfully married to each other, acquire property as the result of their joint efforts, they have impliedly adopted . . . the rule of an equal division of their acquisitions, and the expectation of such a division should not be defeated in the case of innocent persons." (*Id.* at pp. 339–340, 191 P. 533.)

In 1969, the Legislature codified the putative spouse doctrine in former Civil Code section 4452 as part of the Family Law Act. Former Civil Code section 4452 "used language almost identical to that in Family Code section 2251, subdivision (a), which contains the current version of the putative spouse doctrine and provides in relevant part: 'If a determination is made that a marriage is void or voidable and the court finds that either party or both parties believed in good faith that the marriage was valid, the court shall: [¶] (1) Declare the party or parties to have the status of a putative spouse.'"

"Prior to the enactment of the Family Law Act, no statute granted rights to a putative spouse. The courts accordingly fashioned a variety of remedies by judicial decision." Some decisions, as we explained in our discussion *ante,* "affirmed the power of a court to employ equitable principles to achieve a fair division of property acquired during putative marriage."

The codification of the putative spouse doctrine was not intended to make substantive changes to the case law before the enactment of the Family Law Act in 1969. "Instead, the Legislature contemplated the continued protection of *innocent* parties who believe they were validly married."

After the codification of the doctrine, this court held that the term "good faith" in the putative spouse statute meant an objective good faith, and not merely a subjective good faith. Other courts which have considered the issue have come to the same conclusion.

2.   THERE WAS SUBSTANTIAL EVIDENCE SUPPORTING THE SUPERIOR COURT'S FINDING THAT SUN WAS NOT GUO'S PUTATIVE SPOUSE

We review a finding that a party is a putative spouse under the substantial evidence standard of review. """When a finding of fact is attacked on the ground that there is no substantial evidence to sustain it, the power of an appellate court *begins* and *ends* with the determination as to whether there is any substantial evidence, contradicted or uncontradicted, which will support the finding of fact. [Citations.] [¶] When two or more inferences can reasonably be deduced from the facts, a reviewing court is without power to substitute its deductions for those of the trial court."""

In its memorandum of decision, the superior court gave three reasons why it found that Sun did not have an objectively reasonable good faith belief that his prior marriage was dissolved before marrying Guo. First, Sun "signed the marriage license which required him to note how many prior marriages he had, and he said his impending marriage to [Guo] was his first marriage[.]" The trial court was entitled to make a reasonable inference that, because he knew that his marriage with his Italian wife was not dissolved, Sun falsely stated he did not have any prior marriages.

Second, the trial court noted that Sun's petition to dissolve his marriage with his Italian wife was filed the day after he purportedly married Guo, not one month earlier, when he visited attorney Cheng's office. This fact undermines Sun's position because the superior court could reasonably infer that Sun was aware of his attorney's actions on his behalf. In light of the timing of the petition to divorce his Italian wife, it was obvious to a reasonable person in Sun's shoes that he was still married to his Italian wife on the date of his purported marriage to Guo.

Finally, the court stated that even if Sun's petition to divorce his Italian wife had been filed one month earlier, Sun "presented no evidence to show that he had a good faith belief that the finalization of that dissolution would occur within one month." A reasonable person would know that an attorney cannot by herself grant her client a divorce decree, that obtaining a divorce decree requires filing papers in court, and that the client will be notified if the attorney obtains such a decree from a court. At a bare minimum, a reasonable person in Sun's shoes would have inquired on or before February 14, 2001, whether his divorce to his Italian wife was final.

When Sun purportedly married Guo, either (1) he was willfully ignorant of the status of the proceedings to divorce his Italian wife or (2) he actually contacted his attorney about the matter, in which case he would have been informed that a petition for dissolution had not yet been filed. The fact that the petition was filed *the day after* he ostensibly married Guo suggests that he had a conversation with attorney Cheng immediately before or after the Las Vegas marriage. In either case — whether Sun was willfully ignorant of his marital status or he was actually informed that he was still married to his Italian wife — there was substantial evidence to support the trial court's conclusion that Sun did not have an objectively reasonable good faith belief that he was single when he purportedly married Guo.

3.   WHETHER GUO IN GOOD FAITH BELIEVED IN THE VALIDITY OF THE MARRIAGE IS IRRELEVANT TO SUN'S CLAIM FOR PUTATIVE SPOUSE STATUS

Sun contends that the superior court erroneously failed to consider whether Guo had a good faith belief that the marriage was valid. As stated, section 2251, subdivision (a) provides that "[i]f a determination is made that a marriage is void or voidable and the court finds that *either* party or both parties believed in good faith that the marriage was valid, the court shall: [¶] (1) Declare the party or parties to have the status of a putative spouse." (Italics added.) Sun argues that the word "either" indicates that he is entitled to putative spouse status if either he or Guo had a good faith belief in the validity of the marriage. In other words, according to Sun, if either party has a good faith belief in the marriage, there is a "putative marriage," and thus a party who does not have a good faith belief in the marriage can claim to be a putative spouse even where, as here, the other party does not claim to be a putative spouse. We reject this argument.

"In construing a statute, our fundamental task is to ascertain the Legislature's intent so as to effectuate the purpose of the statute. [Citation.] We begin with the language of the statute, giving the words their usual and ordinary meaning. [Citation.] The language must be construed 'in the context of the statute as a whole and the overall statutory scheme, and we give "significance to every word, phrase, sentence, and part of an act in pursuance of the legislative purpose."'"

Here, the language of section 2251, subdivision (a)(1), undermines Sun's position. The statute permits the court to declare that "the party or parties" have the status of a putative spouse. Under Sun's interpretation of the statute, the word "party" is superfluous because both spouses are putative spouses in a putative marriage if either party has, or both parties have, a good faith belief in the marriage. Conversely, the words "the party or parties" have meaning if they refer to the party or parties *who believed in good faith the marriage was valid.* By giving the court the option of declaring one or both parties to be a putative spouse, the Legislature retained the common law rule that only an innocent party can seek to be a putative spouse.

In addition, Sun's interpretation of section 2251 would not further the purpose of the statute. As stated, the statute is based on equitable principles and is meant to protect an *innocent* party who in good faith believed a marriage was valid. Hence, if Guo in good faith believed that the marriage was valid — as Sun contends — then the statute is meant to protect her. But she does not seek the statute's protection. Thus whether Guo had a good faith belief in the validity of the marriage is irrelevant to Sun's putative spouse claim.

In *Tejeda*, the court interpreted section 2251 differently. It concluded that section 2251 must be applied "without regard to guilt or innocence, when the court makes the predicate findings that (1) the marriage is void or voidable, and (2) at least one party to the union maintained a good faith belief in the validity of the marriage." In reaching this conclusion, the court correctly noted that section 2251's predecessor statute, former Civil Code section 4452, was part of the Family Law Act. The court further correctly noted that "'[t]he main focus of the act was to eliminate the artificial fault standard.'"

The Family Law Act, however, was a comprehensive revision of California marital laws (*In re Marriage of Banks* (1974) 42 Cal. App. 3d 631, 635, 117 Cal. Rptr. 37), which included diverse areas of family law. Many sections of the act, most notably those sections pertaining to the dissolution of marriage included substantial, fundamental changes to the law. Other parts of the act, however, did not. Of relevance here, the sections relating to void marriage, including the predecessor to section 2251 — former Civil Code section 4452 — were largely declaratory of existing law and were "*not intended to work significant substantive changes.*"

Hence, contrary to the view expressed in *Tejeda*, the purpose of the putative spouse statute was *not* different than the equitable purpose of the putative spouse doctrine created by the courts. (See Luther & Luther, *Support and Property Rights of the Putative Spouse* (1973) 24 Hastings L.J. 311, 327 [Former Civil Code sections 4452 and 4455 appear to have accomplished the intent of the Governor's Commission on the Family — "'to award support of an innocent spouse who has lived with another person in good faith for a number of years, only to find that the marriage was void'"].) The courts thus have continued to refer to "innocent" parties when discussing putative spouses *after* enactment of the Family Law Act. (*In re Marriage of Ramirez, supra*, 165 Cal. App. 4th at p. 756, 81 Cal. Rptr. 3d 180; *Estate of DePasse, supra*, 97 Cal. App. 4th at p. 107, 118 Cal. Rptr. 2d 143; *Velez v. Smith* (2006) 142 Cal. App. 4th 1154, 1172, 48 Cal. Rptr. 3d 642; *Elden v. Sheldon* (1988) 46 Cal. 3d 267, 275, 250 Cal. Rptr. 254, 758 P.2d 582; *Estate of Hafner* (1986) 184 Cal. App. 3d 1371, 1376-1377, 229 Cal. Rptr. 676; *In re Marriage of Recknor* (1982) 138 Cal. App. 3d 539, 544, 187 Cal. Rptr. 887; *Nieto v. City of Los Angeles* (1982) 138 Cal. App. 3d 464, 471, 188 Cal. Rptr. 31; *Estate of Vargas* (1974) 36 Cal. App. 3d 714, 717, 111 Cal. Rptr. 779.)

The *Tejeda* court's reliance on *Estate of Leslie* (1984) 37 Cal. 3d 186, 207 Cal. Rptr. 561, 689 P.2d 133 is unpersuasive. In *Estate of Leslie*, the court held that a man who had a good faith belief in the validity of a marriage was a putative spouse, and thus was entitled to succeed to a share of his putative wife's separate property under the Probate Code. (*Id.* at pp. 190, 197, 207 Cal. Rptr. 561, 689 P.2d 133.) In other words, the court permitted an *innocent* spouse to assert a putative spouse claim. Here, by contrast, Sun is not an innocent party. *Estate of Leslie* is thus distinguishable from this case.

The *Estate of Leslie* court did *not* hold that a party lacking a good faith belief in the validity of the marriage can assert a putative spouse claim. Indeed, apart from *Tejeda,* Sun does not cite, and we are unable to find, any case in California that so holds.[6]

Having determined that the purpose of section 2251 is to protect innocent parties of an invalid marriage from losing community property rights, we disagree with the holding in *Tejeda.* If *Tejeda* were correct, then a party who fraudulently and in bad faith conceals his or her bigamy can reap the benefits of putative spouse status even when his or her innocent spouse does not contend that there was a putative marriage. This result is inconsistent with the equitable principles underlying section 2251. We thus hold that a party who seeks to be a putative spouse must have an objective good faith belief in the validity of the marriage.

DISPOSITION

The superior court order dated February 17, 2009, denying appellant Sun's request to be declared a putative spouse is affirmed. Respondent Guo is awarded costs on appeal.

We concur: KLEIN, P.J., and ALDRICH, J.

Discussion Questions

1. What are the reasons for the *Tejeda* court's holding that a "bad faith" spouse could receive the benefits of the putative spouse doctrine? What are the reasons for the *Guo & Sun* court's holding that only a "good faith" spouse could receive the benefits of the putative spouse doctrine?

2. Why didn't the "wives" both cases who had a "good faith" belief seek putative spouse status?

---

6. In addition to the purported change in the purpose of section 2251, the *Tejeda* court gave other reasons to support its holding. For example, the court opined that two related statutes, sections 2254 and 2255, included provisions that differentiated between "guilty" and "innocent" parties. (*Tejeda, supra,* 179 Cal. App. 4th at p. 984, 102 Cal. Rptr. 3d 361.) The absence of such a provision in section 2251, the court reasoned, leads to the inference that the statute allows a party to become a putative spouse even though he or she did *not* have a good faith belief in the validity of the marriage. (*Ibid. contra* Hogoboom & King, Cal. Practice Guide: Family Law (The Rutter Group 2009) ¶ 19:62, p. 19-20 [discussing §§2254 and 2255].) In light of the language and purpose of section 2251, we find the *Tejeda* court's analysis unpersuasive.

C. HOW DO COURTS RESOLVE DISPUTES BETWEEN A LEGAL AND POSSIBLY PUTATIVE SPOUSE? EXAMPLES FROM CALIFORNIA, TEXAS, AND LOUISIANA

These cases usually arise at death of the "guilty" spouse. Most reported cases deal with the death of a husband whose was never divorced from his wife, but has "married" to another who claims putative spouse status. The courts have had to deal with the issues of (1) whether the putative spouse has a good faith belief in her marriage to the decedent and (2) how to split the decedent's estate when there are two "spouses" with legitimate claims to the community property accumulated during the "marriages." As you read the following cases, examine how the courts determined that the putative spouse had a good faith belief and how the courts divided the property between the legal and putative spouses.

1.   California

ESTATE OF VARGAS

36 Cal. App. 3d 714, 111 Cal. Rptr. 779 (1974)
Court of Appeal

FLEMING, J.

For 24 years Juan Vargas lived a double life as husband and father to two separate families, neither of which knew of the other's existence. This terrestial paradise came to an end in 1969 when Juan died intestate in an automobile accident. In subsequent heirship proceedings the probate court divided his estate equally between the two wives. Juan's first wife Mildred appeals, contending that the evidence did not establish Juan's second wife Josephine as a putative spouse, and that even if Josephine were considered a putative spouse an equal division of the estate was erroneous.

Mildred presented evidence that she and Juan married in 1929, raised three children, and lived together continuously in Los Angeles until Juan's death in 1969. From 1945 until his death Juan never spent more than a week or 10 days away from home. They acquired no substantial assets until after 1945.

Josephine countered with evidence that she met Juan in 1942 while employed in his exporting business. They married in Las Vegas in February 1945 and went through a second marriage ceremony in Santa Ana in May 1945. Josephine knew Juan had been previously married, but Juan assured her he had acquired a divorce. In July 1945 they moved into a home in West Los Angeles and there raised a family of four children. After 1949 Juan no longer spent his nights at home, explaining to Josephine that he spent the nights in Long Beach in order to be close to his business, but he and Josephine continued to engage in sexual relations until his death in 1969. He visited Josephine and their children every weekday for dinner, spent time with them weekends, supported the family, and exercised control over its affairs as husband and father. Throughout the years Josephine continued to perform secretarial work for Juan's business at home without pay.

The foregoing evidence amply supports the court's finding that Josephine was a putative spouse. (2) An innocent participant who has duly solemnized a matrimonial union which is void because of some legal infirmity acquires the status of putative spouse. Although Josephine's marriage was void because Juan was still married to Mildred, Josephine, according to her testimony, married Juan in the good-faith belief he was divorced from his first wife. Her testimony was not inherently improbable; her credibility was a question for determination by the trial court and court acceptance of her testimony established her status as a putative spouse.

The more difficult question involves the equal division of Juan's estate between Mildred and Josephine.

California courts have relied on at least two legal theories to justify the award of an interest in a decedent's estate to a putative spouse. (Luther & Luther, *Support and Property Rights of the Putative Spouse*, 24 Hastings L.J. 311, 313-317; see also Annot., 31 A.L.R.2d 1255, 1271-1277.) The theory of "quasi-marital property" equates property rights acquired during a putative marriage with community property rights acquired during a legal marriage. (*Blache v. Blache*, 69 Cal. App. 2d 616, 624 [160 P.2d 136].) Subsequent to the time of Juan's death this theory was codified in Civil Code section 4452: "Whenever a determination is made that a marriage is void or voidable and the court finds that either party or both parties believed in good faith that the marriage was valid, the court shall declare such party or parties to have the status of a putative spouse, and, if the division of property is in issue, shall divide, in accordance with Section 4800, that property acquired during the union which would have been community property or quasi-community property if the union had not been void or voidable. Such property shall be termed 'quasi-marital property.'"

A second legal theory treats the putative marriage as a partnership: "In effect, the innocent putative spouse was in partnership or a joint enterprise with her spouse, contributing her services - and in this case, her earnings — to the common enterprise. Thus, their accumulated property was held in effect in tenancy-in-common in equal shares. Upon death of the husband, only his half interest is considered as community property, to which the rights of the lawful spouse attach." (*Sousa v. Freitas*, 10 Cal. App. 3d 660, 666 [89 Cal. Rptr. 485].)

In practice, these sometimes-conflicting theories have proved no more than convenient explanations to justify reasonable results, for when the theories do not fit the facts, courts have customarily resorted to general principles of equity to effect a just disposition of property rights. (*Coats v. Coats*, 160 Cal. 671, 678 [118 P. 441].) For example, in *Brown v. Brown*, 274 Cal. App. 2d 178 [79 Cal. Rptr. 257], the court found that a legal wife's acquiescence in a putative wife's 28-year marriage equitably estopped the legal wife from claiming any interest in the community property.

The present case is complicated by the fact that the laws regulating succession and the disposition of marital property are not designed to cope with the extraordinary circumstance of purposeful bigamy at the expense of two innocent parties.[2] The laws of marital succession assume compliance with basic law and do not provide for contingencies arising during the course of felonious activity. For this reason resort to equitable principles becomes particularly appropriate here. "Equity or

---

2. "[I]n most, if not all, of the reported decisions involving a putative spouse, the supposed husband did in fact separate from his lawful wife." (Luther & Luther, *supra*, at p. 318.)

chancery law has its origin in the necessity for exceptions to the application of rules of law in those cases where the law, by reason of its universality, would create injustice in the affairs of men." Equity acts "in order to meet the requirements of every case, and to satisfy the needs of progressive social condition, in which new primary rights and duties are constantly arising, and new kinds of wrongs are constantly committed." Equity need not wait upon precedent "but will assert itself in those situations where right and justice would be defeated but for its intervention." For example, in *Estate of Krone*, 83 Cal. App. 2d 766, 769-770 [189 P.2d 741], where the putative husband died intestate and there was no legal wife, the court awarded the entire quasi-marital estate to the putative wife, even though the putative wife had no legal claim to the husband's share of the quasi-marital estate.

(3b) In the present case, depending on which statute or legal theory is applied, both Mildred, as legal spouse, and Josephine, as putative spouse, have valid or plausible claims to at least half, perhaps three-quarters, possibly all, of Juan's estate. The court found that both wives contributed in indeterminable amounts and proportions to the accumulations of the community. (*Vallera v. Vallera*, 21 Cal. 2d 681, 683 [134 P.2d 761].) Since statutes and judicial decisions provide no sure guidance for the resolution of the controversy, the probate court cut the Gordian knot of competing claims and divided the estate equally between the two wives, presumably on the theory that innocent wives of practicing bigamists are entitled to equal shares of property accumulated during the active phase of the bigamy. No injury has been visited upon third parties, and the wisdom of Solomon is not required to perceive the justice of the result.

The judgment is affirmed.

Discussion Questions

1. Why did the Court of Appeal support the finding that Josephine was a putative spouse?

2. The Court of Appeal stated that "both Mildred, as legal spouse, and Josephine, as putative spouse, have valid or plausible claims to at least half, perhaps three-quarters, possibly all, of Juan's estate." Try to figure out on what basis they would have these claims.

---

2.   Texas

DAVIS v. DAVIS

521 S.W.2d 603 (1975)
Supreme Court of Texas

REAVLEY, Justice.

Charles Davis was killed by shipwreck in the Sea of Java on December 24, 1970, at the age of 36 years. The Probate Court of Chambers County, where the administration of his estate is pending, is in possession of the small amount of his personal property, together with wages due from his employer, Reading & Bates Offshore Drilling Company, and the proceeds of a group accidental death insurance policy which was purchased by that employer and issued a few days prior to the death of Charles. The insurer has paid $51,031.38 into the registry of the Chambers County Court. This litigation will determine the heirship of Charles Davis and the manner of division of this property.

Charles married Mary Nell in Liberty County in 1966, and in 1967 he departed for Australia without her on an assignment with Reading & Bates. After a year or so in Australia he was in Iran briefly, and then in August of 1968 he was assigned to Singapore. On October 2, 1968, a Buddhist wedding ceremony was performed to unite Charles and Nancy, and they lived together as man and wife in Singapore from that time until his death. Approximately one month after his death, both Mary Nell and Nancy gave birth to daughters.

This controversy ensues over the status and rights of Mary Nell and Nancy, and of the daughter of each. The County Probate Court held that Nancy was the lawful widow of Charles and that both of these daughters were entitled to inherit as children of Charles. The District Court, after an appeal and de novo trial without a jury, decided that Mary Nell was the widow, that Nancy was the putative wife, but that the daughter born to Mary Nell after the death of Charles was not his child and was not entitled to inherit any portion of his estate. The Court of Civil Appeals agreed that Mary Nell was the lawful widow and that her daughter was not the child of Charles, but it held that Nancy was not the putative wife at the time of the death of Charles. 507 S.W.2d 841. The only difference between the District Court and the Court of Civil Appeals in the division of the property was in the allotment to Nancy. What did not go to Nancy, under either judgment, went one-half to Mary Nell and the remaining one-half in equal parts to the children of Charles. The District Court awarded Nancy one-half of the wages due and the insurance proceeds; the Court of Civil Appeals judgment gave her nothing. Both Courts ruled that Mary Nell's daughter was not the child of Charles, and both ruled that Nancy's daughter inherited as a child of Charles. Even though the Court of Civil Appeals held that Nancy's putative status was terminated prior to the death of Charles, that holding would not prevent the daughter from being a legitimate child of their marriage. V.A.T.S. Probate Code, §42.

Nancy is here contending that she is the lawful widow or, at least, that she was the putative wife. Mary Nell's daughter contends that she is the legitimate child of Charles.

We hold, first, that Nancy was not the lawful widow of Charles. While it is initially presumed that Charles and Mary Nell were divorced prior to the wedding ceremony between Charles and Nancy (*Texas Employers' Insurance Ass'n v. Elder*, 155 Tex. 27, 282 S.W.2d 371, 1955; Vernon's Tex. Family Code Ann. §2.01, 1973), the evidence presented by Mary Nell was legally adequate to rebut that presumption. It is shown that the records in Chambers and Liberty Counties reflect no divorce between them, that the records of the State of Queensland, Australia, show no divorce during the period from September 1, 1967 to December 31, 1970, and that the records in Singapore show no divorce between them during that same period. It is not necessary in order to rebut the presumption that Mary Nell prove the nonexistence of divorce in every jurisdiction where proceedings could have been possible; it is only necessary to rule out those proceedings where Charles might reasonably have been expected to have pursued them. *Caruso v. Lucius*,

448 S.W.2d 711 (Tex. Civ. App. 1969, writ ref'd n.r.e.). The trial court was entitled to find that there had been no divorce between Charles and Mary Nell and that Mary Nell was therefore his lawful widow.

We next hold that Nancy was the putative wife of Charles. A written contract of marriage (the Chinese document and the English translation), signed by Charles and Nancy, together with her father and another witness, certifying the marriage as being solemnized on October 2, 1968, was placed in evidence. Nancy and two other witnesses testified to the full formality of the ceremony, which was held in the home of her parents with all of her family participating and with twenty persons in attendance. For more than two years thereafter, and until the date of his death, Charles and Nancy lived together as man and wife. Nancy testified that Charles told her of his previous marriage but also assured her that he was divorced and free to marry her. The evidence clearly warrants the finding that Nancy entered this relationship in good faith.

The Court of Civil Appeals has held that even though Nancy may have become the putative wife of Charles at the outset and continued in that relationship for two years thereafter, at a time prior to his death she was put on notice that he was not divorced from Mary Nell — whereupon her putative standing terminated. The evidence on this point turns on the following testimony by Nancy:

> *Q:* Now, during — well — subsequent to April 2, 1968 and before December 23, 1970, you learned, did you not, that Mary Nell Davis was trying to get a divorce from Charles Davis?
> *A:* I didn't learn nothing of that.
> *Q:* Well, you remember you (sic) asking that question on your deposition?
> *A:* You asking me whether I received —
> *Q:* No ma'am, I didn't ask you if you received it. I asked you if you learned that Mary Nell Davis was trying to get a divorce from Charles?
> *A:* I learned it.
> *Q:* Yes.
> *A:* I know it.

The interrogation on the occasion of Nancy's deposition, which was introduced at the trial by the lawyer for Nancy to show a waiver of the dead man's statute, does not throw much light on this matter except for her statements that she knew that Charles was asked to sign a paper which came in the mail at a time when she was pregnant with the child born after the death of Charles. This testimony does not establish conclusively her lack of good faith. In the first place, it is not clear when Nancy understood that Mary Nell was "trying to get a divorce." She appreciated the facts as of the time of the trial, but it is not clear that she did so prior to the death of Charles. And even if she knew that these were divorce papers, it does not necessarily follow that Nancy had any reason to believe that Charles had been dishonest with her and had not obtained a prior divorce from Mary Nell. Before we charge Nancy with bad faith or impose upon her a duty to investigate matters, we must take into account that she was in Singapore and not in Texas, that she knew nothing of Texas law, and that she was a 20 year old Chinese woman who had always lived in Singapore and was then expecting a child by a husband who had given her no reason to believe that he had another wife. The trial court was entitled to find in her favor; we hold that the record does not conclusively establish her lack of good faith.

As a putative wife Nancy is entitled to the same right in the property acquired during her marital relationship with Charles as if she were a lawful wife. *Lee v. Lee*, 112 Tex. 392, 247 S.W. 828 (1923); Speer's Marital Rights in Texas §56 (4th ed. 1961). In her case it will be half of the wages owed by the employer at the date of his death as well as half of the proceeds from the insurance policy which was furnished by the employer as an incident of the employment.

The judgment of the Court of Civil Appeals is reversed; the judgment of the District Court is affirmed.

Discussion Questions

1. According to the Texas Supreme Court, what factors were important in finding that Nancy was a putative spouse?
2. How did the Texas Supreme Court divide Charles' estate?

3. Louisiana

SUCCESSION OF DAVID JONES

6 So. 3d 331 (2009)
Court of Appeal of Louisiana

PETERS, J.

This litigation involves, in part, the determination of the marital status of David Jones, Jr., who is now deceased. Two women, Harriett Boyer Jones (Harriett) and Ethel LeDuff Jones (Ethel), both claim to have been his legal spouse and entitled to all legal rights arising from that status. The trial court declared Ethel to be the sole surviving spouse, and Harriett has appealed that determination. For the following reasons, we reverse the trial court judgment, designate Harriett as David Jones, Jr.'s legal surviving spouse, but recognize Ethel as his putative spouse. We remand the matter to the trial court for it to determine the proper disposition of the assets of the estate of David Jones, Jr. in accordance with law.

DISCUSSION OF THE RECORD

Certain facts are not in dispute. David Jones, Jr. (David) and Harriett were married in Bexar County, Texas on October 8, 1956, and three children were born of that marriage: Carol Ann, David Allen, and June René. All of these children are now competent majors. David and Harriett were divorced on February 24, 1976. David had made a career of the military and was stationed in Missouri at the time of the divorce.

After the divorce, Harriett returned to her family in Houston, Harris County, Texas. Thereafter, David retired from the military and returned with his son to live on family property in Alexandria, Rapides Parish, Louisiana. Still, he maintained communications with his former wife. In fact, on April 12, 1978, David and Harriett remarried in Houston.

The second marriage did not last. Four months later, on September 12, 1978, David filed a petition against Harriett seeking to be awarded a separation from bed and board.

David filed a supplemental and amending petition on February 2, 1979, wherein he acknowledged that the marriage took place in Houston, and not Rapides Parish, but argued that because he and Harriett never lived together thereafter, he should be awarded an annulment of that marriage. In the alternative, he maintained his request for a separation from bed and board.

Because of the physical incapacity of the attorney appointed to represent Harriett, a second attorney was appointed to represent her as an absentee. This appointment was made by the trial court on April 18, 1979. On May 1, 1979, that attorney filed an answer to the supplemental and amending petition wherein he reiterated the previously filed answer. A subsequent pleading filed by the appointed attorney on September 21, 1979, reflected that he had forwarded a copy of the supplemental and amending petition to Harriett, but that it was returned as not deliverable. This pleading represents the last filing in the suit record.

David and Ethel were married in Mansura, Avoyelles Parish, Louisiana, on April 8, 1983, and lived together as husband and wife in Rapides Parish until David's death on March 31, 2005. After David's death, Ethel filed a petition to probate his statutory testament and to be named executrix of his succession. On April 25, 2006, Harriett filed a petition seeking to have Ethel's marriage to David declared absolutely null and to be placed in possession of her share of the community property belonging to her as David's surviving spouse. The trial of this issue resulted in a trial court judgment declaring Ethel to be David's legal wife and surviving spouse and recognizing her as the individual entitled to all legal rights associated with that status. This judgment gave rise to the appeal now before us.

OPINION

Harriett's five assignments of error can be reduced to two arguments: (1) the trial court erred in finding that Ethel was David's legal wife, and (2) the trial court erred in failing to admit into evidence search certificates from Harris County, Texas and Avoyelles Parish and Rapides Parish, Louisiana. We will address the evidentiary issue first.

* * *

After reviewing the evidence, we find that Harriett has satisfactorily proven that her 1978 marriage to David had not been dissolved prior to his 1983 marriage to Ethel. Thus, we find that the trial court erred in concluding that Ethel's marriage to David was not null and void.

PUTATIVE SPOUSE ISSUE

Our inquiry does not end with our conclusion that the trial court erred in rendering judgment in Ethel's favor. Having found that the marriage between David and Ethel was absolutely null, we must next determine whether Ethel was in good faith in contracting the marriage such that she acquired putative spouse status.

Louisiana Civil Code Article 96 provides:

> An absolutely null marriage nevertheless produces civil effects in favor of a party who contracted it in good faith for as long as that party remains in good faith.
>
> When the cause of the nullity is one party's prior undissolved marriage, the civil effects continue in favor of the other party, regardless of whether the latter remains in good faith, until the marriage is pronounced null or the latter party contracts a valid marriage.
>
> A marriage contracted by a party in good faith produces civil effects in favor of a child of the parties.
>
> A purported marriage between parties of the same sex does not produce any civil effects.

The "good faith" necessitated by La. Civ. Code art. 96 was discussed in *Alfonso v. Alfonso*, 99-261, p. 5 (La. App. 5 Cir. 7/27/99), 739 So. 2d 946, 948-49:

> "Good faith" is defined as an honest and reasonable belief that the marriage was valid and that no legal impediment to it existed. *Saacks v. Saacks*, 96-736 (La. App. 5 Cir. 1/28/97), 688 So. 2d 673. "Good faith" consists of being ignorant of the cause which prevents the formation of the marriage, or being ignorant of the defects in the celebration which caused the nullity. The question of whether a party is in good faith is subjective, and depends on all the circumstances present in a given case. Although the good faith analysis test incorporates the objective elements of reasonableness, the inquiry is essentially a subjective one.

Whether good faith exists is a factual question, and subject to the manifest error/clearly wrong standard of review. In this matter, we find no manifest error in the trial court's factual determination that Ethel was in good faith in entering into, and maintaining, the marriage with David.

The evidence establishes that Ethel is a Rapides Parish native and was thrice married and divorced before her marriage to David. She and David began dating shortly after her return from Alaska in 1978. They began cohabiting in 1979, and were married in Avoyelles Parish on April 8, 1983. Ethel testified that she knew David had been previously married and divorced, but first learned of his second marriage to Harriett following his death in 2005, when she was informed of Harriett's challenge to her receipt of surviving spousal benefits by the military. She claimed to have no knowledge of the specifics or timing of David's first divorce, but was aware that he had three children. She had met the children but had never met or spoken with Harriett.

Ethel explained that she and David were married in Avoyelles Parish because they did not want to draw any attention to the ceremony, given the fact that they had been living together for such a long period. Ethel and David bought, sold, and mortgaged property as husband and wife. Additionally, David enrolled her as his spouse for benefits through his employment with the Rapides Parish School Board, as the beneficiary of his life insurance policy, and as the beneficiary of his Army pension.

David Allen and June René both testified that they told Ethel their parents were still married. David Allen stated that he met Ethel in Alexandria prior to his father retiring from the military, and after he moved to Alexandria, he babysat her children approximately once a month while she and his father went out. Sometime thereafter, he moved to Houston, and he and his sister met Ethel while visiting their father in Rapides Parish in 1981. According to David Allen, Ethel hugged both of them and told them that she was going to be their step-mother. He testified that he became angry and informed Ethel that he already had a mother. According to David Allen, when he made this statement, David became upset and professed to not know what he was talking about. Thereafter, David Allen claimed, he never again spoke to Ethel until after his father's death.

June René's testimony concerning the 1981 incident paralleled her brother's. She also responded to Ethel's comment by stating that she already had a mother and that her father already had a wife.

The trial court found that Ethel was in good faith in entering into and throughout her marriage to David. With regard to the statements of David Allen and June René that they already had a mother, the trial court concluded that these statements failed to contain "any certain or authoritative knowledge of some legal impediment that would have prompted further investigation."

After reviewing the record, we cannot say that the trial court was clearly wrong in finding that Ethel was in good faith when she entered into and throughout her marriage to David. Accordingly, we find no error in its finding that she is entitled to putative spouse status.

As David's putative wife, Ethel is entitled to share in the civil effects of the putative community of acquets and gains which existed between them. La. Civ. Code art. 96. Furthermore, as the marriage between Harriett and David was valid, a legal community of acquets and gains still existed between them. Thus, both communities co-existed between April 8, 1983 and March 31, 2005. In a similar scenario, the court in *In re Succession of Gordon*, 461 So. 2d 357 (La. App. 2 Cir. 1984), *writ denied*, 464 So. 2d 319 (La. 1985), citing the supreme court's opinion in *Prince v. Hopson*, 230 La. 575, 89 So. 2d 128 (1956), divided the community property so that the legal and putative spouses each received a one-fourth interest and the decedent's heirs received a one-half interest. We agree that this manner of division would be most equitable. Accordingly, we remand the matter so that the trial court can continue with the division of community property in accordance with our determination.

CONCLUSION

For the foregoing reasons, we reverse the judgment of the trial court. We now render judgment declaring that Harriett Boyer Jones is the sole surviving spouse of David Jones, Jr. and declaring the marriage of David Jones, Jr. and Ethel LeDuff Jones null and void. We further render judgment declaring that Ethel LeDuff Jones was the putative spouse of David Jones, Jr. and is entitled to the civil effects arising from their marriage as that status allows. We remand the matter to the trial court for further proceedings consistent with this opinion. We assess the costs of these proceedings equally between Harriett Boyer Jones and Ethel LeDuff Jones.

Reversed, rendered, and remanded.

Discussion Question

1. How did the Court of Appeal divide the community property?

PROBLEM 12.1

Hal and Wendy met at a New Year's party in Las Vegas. They married on Valentine's Day at a wedding chapel. The romance did not last and they separated on the Fourth of July. They petitioned for a divorce right after Thanksgiving Day. Hal met Pat at a New Year's party. He told all his friends of his hopes that the New Year was going to be better than the last because of his disastrous marriage to Wendy. He found that Pat was a good listener and he appreciated her interest in him. Pat was originally from Chile where she was an attorney. She had been in the United States for several years and had also received a law degree from an American school. She was working for a law firm that represented many clients with business in South America. When Hal proposed marriage to Pat, she asked if his divorce from Wendy was final. He assured her that it was, but never showed her the papers. He said that he was trying to forget that mistake. It was clear that he didn't want to talk about it. Pat respected his wishes and they never discussed the subject.

Hal and Pat had a quiet marriage ceremony attended only by close friends. They both worked long hours and accumulated many assets. About ten years later, their long work hours took a toll on their marriage. They separated. After Pat filed a petition for dissolution of their marriage, Hal filed a petition to nullify their marriage. He revealed that at the time they married, his divorce from Wendy was not final.

Pat is claiming that she is a putative spouse and is entitled to division of the community property accumulated during their "marriage." Discuss whether she would be considered in good faith under Nevada law or California law.

PROBLEM 12.2

Assume the same facts as in Problem 12.1, but change the facts and assume that during their marriage Pat was the primary wage-earner in their marriage. Could Hal claim rights as a putative spouse in Nevada or California?

PROBLEM 12.3

Sam and Paula did not believe that a piece of paper was necessary for them to show their commitment to each other. They exchanged personal marriage vows to live together until death parted them. They lived together, held themselves out as husband and wife, and had a child together. Paula took Sam's name. After three years of their "marriage," Sam unfortunately was killed in an auto accident. Since the accident was due to the negligence of County highway workers, Paula sued the

County for wrongful death. The wrongful death statute permits a claim by a "putative spouse." The County responded to Paula's claim by pointing out that she is not a "putative spouse" even though she alleged that she had a "good faith belief that she was validly married to Sam." How will a court decide?

PROBLEM 12.4

Manuel was married to Maria in Portugal in 1970. Three years later, Manuel left and never returned to Portugal. He came to California and in 1975, filed for divorce from Maria; however, the divorce papers had several defects. Therefore, he was never properly divorced from Maria. In 1980, he married Pamela. During the time of their "marriage," Manuel accumulated a large estate. Recently Manuel died. Maria found out about his death and his attempt to divorce her. She filed a complaint against his estate, claiming that as the legal surviving spouse, she was entitled to his entire estate. Pamela responded by claiming his entire estate, as the putative spouse, because all the property was acquired during the time they were "married." How would a California court resolve the claims of Maria and Pamela?

Table 12-1
Putative Spouse Doctrine in Community Property States

State	Rule	Case/Statute
Arizona	Recognizes putative spouse doctrine–uses authority from other states (*Stevens v. Anderson*).	*In re Marriage of Fong*, 121 Ariz. 298, 589 P.2d 1330 (1978), holding that husband is entitled all community property acquired after the date that he had good-faith belief that first wife died *Stevens v. Anderson*, 75 Ariz. 331, 256 P.2d 712 (1953)
California	California Family Code §2251 provides that if a determination is made that a marriage is void or voidable and the court finds that either party or both parties believed in good faith that the marriage was valid, the court shall declare the party or parties to have the status of a putative spouse.	*Marriage of Vryonis*, 202 Cal. App. 3d 712, 248 Cal. Rptr. 208 (1988), holding that good faith belief must be objectively reasonable, but see *Ceja v. Rudolph & Sletten, Inc.*, 194 Cal. App. 4th 584, 125 Cal. Rptr. 3d 98 (2011), good faith test is subjective, affirmed by Cal. Supreme Court(2013) *Marriage of Tejeda*, 179 Cal. App. 4th 973, 102 Cal. Rptr. 3d 361 (2009), holding that "bad faith" spouse can receive benefits of the putative spouse doctrine, but see *Marriage of Xia Guo and Xia Hua Sun*, 186 Cal. App. 4th 1491, 112, holding that only a "good faith" spouse can receive the benefits of the putative spouse doctrine

Idaho	Idaho Code §5-311 defines "putative spouse" as the surviving spouse of a void or voidable marriage who is found by the court to have believed in good faith that the marriage to the decedent was valid.	
Louisiana	Louisiana Civil Code Art. 96 provides that an absolutely null marriage nevertheless produces civil effects in favor of a party who contracted it in good faith for as long as that party remains in good faith. When the cause of the nullity is one party's prior undissolved marriage, the civil effects continue in favor of the other party, regardless of whether the latter remains in good faith, until the marriage is pronounced null or the latter party contracts a valid marriage.	*Succession of Chavis,* 211 La. 313, 29 So. 2d 860 (1947), *Succession of Jones,* 6 So. 3d 331 (2009), *Funderburk v. Funderburk,* 214 La. 717, 38 So. 2d 502 (1949), *Thomason v. Thomason,* 776 So. 2d 553 (2000)
Nevada	The putative spouse doctrine has two elements: (1) a proper marriage ceremony was performed; and (2) one or both of the parties had a good-faith belief that there was no impediment to the marriage and the marriage was valid and proper.	*Williams v. Williams,* 97 P.3d 1124, 120 Nev. 559 (2004)
New Mexico	Putative spouse doctrine has not been addressed.	
Texas	A putative marriage is a marriage that is null and void due to an existing defect or impediment. Customarily, the impediment consists of the fact that one spouse is already married and not divorced.	*Cardwell v. Cardwell,* 195 S.W.3d 856 (2006), holding that a wife who failed to make a reasonable effort to determine whether an earlier marriage had ended in divorce prevented her from establishing a subsequent marriage as being putative
Washington	Where woman entered into marriage in good faith without knowledge that marriage was void because husband had been divorced within less than six months previously, and they lived together in good faith as man and wife and accumulated property by their joint efforts, she was awarded one-half of property, as just and equitable distribution of their joint accumulations. *In re Benchley's Estate,* 96 Wash. 223, 164 P. 913 (1917).	*Marriage of Himes,* 136 Wash. 2d 707, 965 P.2d 1087 (1998)
Wisconsin	A putative marriage is a marriage which has been solemnized in proper form and celebrated in good faith by one or both parties, but which, by reason of some legal infirmity, is either void or voidable.	*Xiong v. Xiong,* 255 Wis. 2d 693, 648 N.W.2d 900 (Ct. App. 2002) (for wrongful death action, the term spouse can include putative spouse)

Chapter 13

Character of Property During Separation

It is common that married couples physically separate before deciding to actually go through with divorce. They may seek counseling and reconcile. If counseling does not work, they will then file for divorce. In that case, there will be a period of time, loosely called "separation," when their earnings could be considered either separate property of the earning spouse or community property of the couple. For instance, take our hypothetical couple Michael and Lisa. Their marriage unfortunately has deteriorated and Lisa moves out of their home. Counseling does not help save their marriage. Lisa files for divorce two years after she has moved out. During the time they were not living together, Lisa presented a cost-cutting idea to her company and received a large bonus for that idea. The question is whether the bonus she received is community property because Lisa earned it while still married to Michael or whether the bonus is separate property because it was earned after they separated. The answer will depend on when the economic community ends and earnings become the property of the earning spouse. The answer to the question varies depending on the law in the community property state where the couple lives.

In this scenario, California and Washington treat earnings during "separation" as separate property of the earning spouse. In Arizona, there is a bright-line test for when separation begins. Separation is dated from "service of a petition of dissolution of marriage . . . if the petition results in a decree of dissolution." A.R.S §25-211(A)(2). If Michael and Lisa actually go through with the divorce in Arizona, the question would depend on whether Lisa earned the bonus after her petition of dissolution was filed. If earned before, the bonus would be community property; if earned after, the bonus would be Lisa's separate property. In Washington and California, courts must determine when the couple is "living separate and apart." Wash. Rev. Code §26.16.140, Cal. Fam. Code §771. The actual determination is made on a case-by-case examination of the particular facts. In those cases, the courts of Washington and California have developed particular tests for determining the exact date of separation. In those states, there is often litigation concerning the exact date, particularly when the period of physical separation has been long and much property accumulated during that period.

In the other five community property states, property acquired during separation would likely be considered community property. The community ends when there is a decree of dissolving the marriage. Those states include Idaho, Louisiana, Nevada,

New Mexico, and Texas. Therefore, Lisa's bonus would be considered community property. However, because of "equitable division" of community property at divorce, in some of those states, one spouse may be awarded more than one-half of community property. Depending on the factors the courts use to determine what is equitable, Lisa could be awarded more than one-half of the bonus.

A.   FACTS DETERMINING SEPARATION DATE

1.   *Washington*

In Washington, "When spouses or domestic partners are living separate and apart, their respective earnings and accumulations shall be the separate property of each." Wash. Rev. Code §26.16.140. "Living separate and apart" means "permanent separation of the parties — a defunct marriage." *Seizer v. Sessions*, 132 Wash. 2d 642, 649, 940 P.2d 261, 264 (1997). A marriage is "defunct," when "the facts involved situations where both parties demonstrated that the marriage was over." *Id.* at 657, 940 P.2d at 268. This, according to the Washington Supreme Court, requires "*some* conduct on the part of *both* spouses." *Id.* at 658, 940 P.2d at 268. (Italics in the original). That means that "both parties to the marriage no longer have the will to continue the marital relationship" or "when the deserted spouse accepts the futility of hope for restoration of a normal marital relationship, or just acquiesces in the separation." *Id.* at 658, 940 P.2d at 269. The Court of Appeal in *Marriage of Johnson*, 1998 WL 898810 (Ct. App.),[1] discussed the facts that determine whether a marriage is defunct. The wife Marcy moved out of the family home in 1985. She filed a petition for dissolution in 1996. The question on appeal was which was the correct date for determining when they actually were living separate and apart.

MARRIAGE OF JOHNSON

93 Wash. App. 1043 (1998)
Court of Appeals of Washington

UNPUBLISHED OPINION

AGID.

Marcy Johnson appeals the trial court's property distribution in the dissolution of her marriage from Lance Johnson. She contends that the trial court erred in concluding that she and Lance were legally separated in 1996 and not in 1985, and that it improperly characterized and valued certain assets. Because the evidence establishes that the parties separated in 1985, we reverse and remand for reconsideration of the property distribution.

---

1. Unpublished opinion.

FACTS

Lance and Marcy Johnson were married in 1969 and have one daughter, Tera, born in 1980. After graduating from the University of Washington in 1972, Lance started working as an architect and Marcy began a small weaving business known as The Weaving Works. They lived in a house in Montlake which they bought with no money down in 1969 and also owned a vacant lot near the Hyak Ski Resort which they bought in 1967. In 1972, they bought a building in the University District that consisted of a small commercial space with two residential units ("the store/duplex"). In 1974, after Marcy and Lance remodeled the commercial space, Marcy moved The Weaving Works into it. The Weaving Works paid rent for the use of that space, and the mortgage was paid off within a few years. In 1978, Lance and Marcy bought a 9-unit apartment building in Eastlake called Roanoke Court. Marcy handled the books and dealt with tenants, while Lance handled most of the repairs. In 1981, they sold the Montlake home and bought a large house on Capital Hill. On August 1, 1985, Marcy and Tera moved out of the family home into one of the units in the store/duplex. Lance visited approximately twice a week during the school year to help Tera with her homework, often staying for supper, but Marcy and Lance have maintained completely separate households since 1985.

In 1986, Lance transferred his 50 percent shareholder interest in The Weaving Works to Marcy. In 1988, Lance and Marcy bought the Johnson Building in the University District which The Weaving Works had committed to occupy. Marcy contributed $15,000 in earnest money and together they borrowed $400,000 to complete the purchase, securing it by the Roanoke Court and duplex/store properties. After spending $63,000 to remodel the building, The Weaving Works moved in. It has made all the mortgage payments on the building and, since 1994, has paid $2,000 per month more to the lender than required under the mortgage.

Marcy filed a petition for dissolution in 1996. In his response, Lance admitted that he and Marcy been separated since August 1, 1985. Lance also agreed that the recital in a document he signed in 1986 transferring his interest in The Weaving Works to Marcy declaring that they were then "separated and contemplating dissolution of their marriage" was a true statement. But at trial, he took the position that he and Marcy did not separate until 1996 when Marcy filed the petition to dissolve the marriage. The trial court agreed with Lance and distributed the parties' assets accordingly.

DISCUSSION

I.   DATE OF SEPARATION

While assets acquired during marriage are presumed to be community property, this presumption may be rebutted by evidence that the acquisition fits within a separate property provision. Separate property is defined as property acquired before marriage or acquired after marriage by gift, bequest, devise or descent. Separate property also includes the earnings and accumulations of a husband or a wife while living separate and apart. A marriage is "defunct" for purposes of RCW 26.16.140, the "living separate and apart" statute, "when both parties to the marriage no longer have the will to continue the marital relationship" or "when the deserted spouse accepts the futility of hope for restoration of a normal marital relationship, or just acquiesces in the separation."

Whether a husband and wife are living separate and apart depends on the peculiar facts of each case. "[M]ere physical separation of the parties does not establish that they are living separate and apart sufficiently to negate the existence of a community." "The test is whether the parties by their conduct have exhibited a decision to renounce the community, with no intention of ever resuming the marital relationship." As the Washington Supreme Court recently explained in *Seizer v. Sessions*, Washington's community property laws are based on the existence of a viable marital community. A community encompasses more than mere satisfaction of the legal requirements of marriage. The theory underlying community property is that it is obtained by the efforts of either the husband or wife, or both, for the benefit of the community. Therefore, when a marital community no longer exists, there can be no community property because there is no longer any common enterprise to which each spouse is contributing.

The statute distinguishes between a "marital" and a "community" relationship. Mere physical separation does not dissolve the community, but it is not necessary for purposes of RCW 26.16.140 that a dissolution action be final or even pending.

Courts have considered various other factors in determining that a marriage is defunct, including whether a petition for dissolution or a separation or property division agreement has been filed; the parties participated in marital and individual counseling in an attempt to save their marriage; they continued to share the same bed and have sexual relations; they maintained separate bank accounts or left some of their personal possessions in the other's separate living space; and the extent to which they continued to go to movies, parties, work-related social events or on vacations together. All cases in which a marriage has been found to be defunct have required "some conduct on the part of both spouses" indicating that they no longer had the will to continue the marriage or, at least, "an acquiescence in the separation."

Here, Lance conceded that he and Marcy have not shared the same bed and have lived in separate homes since August 1, 1985. He explained that they talked about getting a divorce when they first separated but that both of them then ignored the issue. He admitted that Marcy rejected his suggestion they participate in counseling shortly after their separation and that they never again discussed counseling or reconciliation during the 10 years that followed. Lance agreed that he and Marcy have attended no social occasions together as a couple since 1985. They have gone on occasional trips and participated in social events because they involved Tera, including customary Easter get-togethers with other members of their families. Lance occasionally joined Marcy on her walks around Green Lake but admitted he invited himself along. Marcy explained that he knew it was her habit to walk around Green Lake after she dropped Tera off at school in the mornings, and she assumed that his purpose in joining her was to catch up on matters related to Tera.

Lance's comment when asked to explain the nature of the parties' relationship after Marcy moved out, and whether it had changed, is telling:

> Well, she was the mother of my child, so we kept a very close relationship because of Tera and working visitation which has worked out very well. I was able to have, you know,

share a lot in Tera's, you know, upbringing and activities and taking her out all the time and visiting. Our personal side with Tera.

On our business side, with all the properties and things with all that, it didn't change virtually.

Lance's response to the question makes clear that the parties' relationship did change after their separation. They maintained a personal relationship not because Marcy was Lance's wife but because she was the "mother of [his] child." Although the parties continued to participate in joint business enterprises after Marcy moved out of the family home, Lance's own description reveals that the personal side of their relationship was confined to parenting. His use of the term "visitation" to describe the time he was able to spend with Tera is a strong indication that he, like Marcy, understood that the parties were indeed separated and their marriage was defunct.

The trial court nevertheless concluded that the parties' marriage was not defunct, citing as its primary reasons its belief that there needed to exist "some writing supporting that intent" and the fact that the parties continued to cooperate in an amicable way in raising their daughter. The trial court was able to conclude that there was no writing to support the parties' intent, however, only because it chose to discount the documents Lance signed in 1986 transferring his 50 percent shareholder interest in The Weaving Works to Marcy. Those documents recited that the parties to the agreement were then separated and contemplating dissolution of their marriage:

> Lance H. Johnson and Marcy R. Johnson are husband and wife currently separated and contemplating dissolution of their marriage and are residents of the State of Washington. . . .
> Lance H. Johnson hereby assigns, transfers, and conveys to Marcy R. Johnson all of his community interest in and to The Weaving Works, Inc., a Washington corporation. . . . The parties agree that the stock in The Weaving Works, Inc. has always been intended to be the sole separate property of Marcy R. Johnson.

The Assignment of Stock Agreement similarly provides that Lance's shares of common capital stock of The Weaving Works, Inc., were transferred to Marcy "in consideration of our current marital separation and our contemplated marital dissolution." While Lance admitted that the first recital was true, when asked about the remaining recitals, he stated that it was not really his intention to transfer his interest to Marcy and that he only meant to help her to qualify as a minority-owned business. Lance also testified that he had not read the document carefully before he signed it.

Based on Lance's testimony, the trial court concluded that it could not rely on the document to establish that the parties were separated at the time they executed it in 1986. But it did decide that Lance was bound by the agreement to the extent that it purported to transfer his share in the Weaving Works to Marcy. While the trial court correctly found that the agreement was binding, it erred in deciding that it did not constitute evidence that the parties were separated in 1986. First, the statement that the parties separated in 1986 is the one assertion which Lance admitted unequivocally was true. Second, that statement is consistent with Marcy's testimony that they separated on August 1, 1985. The only contemporaneous writing in evidence, in other words, which clearly states that the parties had separated, is uncontradicted.

Nor does the mere fact that the parties amicably parented their daughter and attended family events with her on occasion provide a basis for finding that there was no separation. This is especially true in light of Lance's admission that the only social activities in which the parties participated together were activities involving Tera. We will not impose on parents who are separated some implied requirement that they behave in an uncooperative or hostile manner with regard to parenting their children before we will recognize that their marriage is defunct.

Other factors not considered in prior cases also militate in favor of finding that the parties have been separated since 1985. Especially significant is Marcy's undisputed testimony that Tera understood her parents to be separated but that, unlike many of her school friends who were "stressed about their parents getting back together again," Tera had always told her she was really glad her parents made no attempt to get back together. The court found both Lance and Marcy were exemplary parents. Neither, surely, would have led the daughter they both loved to believe that they were separated when in fact they were not.

All these reasons lead us to conclude that the parties separated in 1985. The trial court itself recognized that the parties' circumstances were "unusual." What it does not appear to have considered is that it is precisely those circumstances that made their relationship a technical "marriage" and not a "community" after August 1, 1985. As noted in Seizer, a community is comprised of "more than mere satisfaction of the legal requirements of marriage." While the "the legal requirements of marriage" remained in place until 1996, the marital "community" ceased to exist in 1985 when Marcy moved permanently out of the family home.

Neither the fact that the parties filed joint tax returns nor their continued participation in joint business ventures changes this result. While those are certainly factors to be considered, they do not, in our view, outweigh the other evidence in this case. As counsel pointed out during oral argument, the complexity of the business relationship above simply made it easier for both parties to file joint tax returns.

Discussion Questions

1. What reasons did the trial court give for why the Johnson's marriage was not defunct?

2. Do you agree with the trial court or the appellate court's analysis for the date of separation for purposes of marital characterization? Why did the Court of Appeals conclude that the trial court erred in its reasoning that the marriage was not defunct until 1996?

---

2. California

Similarly in California, Family Code §771 states that "The earnings and accumulations of a spouse . . . while living separate and apart from the other spouse, are the separate property of the spouse." Although "living separate and apart" is not defined in the statute, the courts have long interpreted its meaning through case law.

MARRIAGE OF HARDIN

38 Cal. App. 4th 448, 45 Cal. Rptr. 2d 308 (1995)
Court of Appeal

SONENSHINE, Acting P. J.

Doris and Victor Hardin married in 1961. On June 28, 1969, Victor walked out of their apartment and although he and Doris continued their economic relationship, saw each other often, and communicated regularly, they eventually dissolved their marriage.

None of the above is so unusual. Many couples experiencing marital problems stop living in the same residence but nevertheless maintain financial ties and a cordial relationship until they finally go forward with the dissolution. What makes this situation unique is the time frames of these events. Specifically, 14 years transpired between Victor's exiting the family residence and dissolution of the marriage. And even then the matter was not entirely concluded. Although the parties dissolved their marriage in 1983, they neither divided their property nor established support obligations. Indeed, those matters are *still* pending. However, progress is being made. In 1991, Doris and Victor, wishing to finally resolve the remaining issues, agreed the court should determine their date of separation.

At the hearing, Doris contended they separated in 1983 when Victor, wishing to remarry, went forward with the dissolution. The trial court, however, agreed with Victor who argued the date of separation occurred on June 28, 1969, when he moved out of their residence. Doris appeals.

. . .

II

Doris makes several arguments but the thrust of her appeal is the trial judge, by relying on an objective test, misconstrued the standard for determining the date of separation. Specifically, Doris refers to the judge's statement he was disregarding his own finding that Victor had "not made up [his mind] regarding a divorce until 1982 or 1983" because he concluded the appropriate standard was: "'Would society at large deem the couple to be separated based upon the facts and based upon the evidence [presented]?'" For reasons we now explain, the trial court erred.

III

In many dissolution proceedings, the date of separation is a critical fact affecting the parties' rights to property and income. Nevertheless, the Legislature has neither defined "date of separation" nor specified a standard for determining it. The only statutory reference to this term is found in Family Code section 771 which provides:

> The earnings and accumulations of a spouse . . . while living separate and apart from the other spouse, are the separate property of the spouse.

Since the Legislature has failed to provide guidance, we look to case law defining the date of separation. In *Makeig v. United Security Bk. & T. Co.* (1931) 112 Cal. App. 138, 143 [296 P. 673], the court held living separate and apart is a "condition where the spouses have come *to a parting of the ways and have no present intention of resuming the marital relations and taking up life together under the same roof.*" (italics added.) This definition was further amplified in *In re Marriage of Baragry* (1977) 73 Cal. App. 3d 444, 448 [140 Cal. Rptr. 779]: "The question is whether the *parties' conduct evidences a complete and final break in the marital relationship.*" (italics added.)

In *In re Marriage of von der Nuell* (1994) 23 Cal. App. 4th 730 [28 Cal. Rptr. 2d 447], the court combined the *Makeig* and *Baragry* definitions. "[B]ecause rifts between spouses may be followed by long periods of reconciliation, and the intentions of the parties may change from one day to the next, we construe *Baragry* to hold *legal separation requires not only a parting of the ways with no present intention of resuming marital relations, but also, more importantly, conduct evidencing a complete and final break in the marital relationship.*"

Simply stated, the date of separation occurs when either of the parties *does not* intend to resume the marriage *and* his or her actions bespeak the finality of the marital relationship. There must be problems that have so impaired the marriage relationship that the legitimate objects of matrimony have been destroyed and there is no reasonable possibility of eliminating, correcting or resolving these problems.

IV

The courts have neither defined the standard to be employed nor the factors to be considered in determining the date of separation. Nevertheless, the answers are implicitly contained within the cases. All factors bearing on either party's intentions "to return or not to return to the other spouse" are to be considered. No particular facts are per se determinative. The ultimate test is the parties' subjective intent and all evidence relating to it is to be objectively considered by the court.

Several cases illustrate this concept. In *Makeig v. United Security Bk. & T. Co.*, the parties told only a few of husband's friends they had married, resided in the same home for just six weeks and then maintained separate residences for fourteen years until husband's death. Nevertheless, the court concluded they had never separated because there was no evidence they considered dissolving the marriage.

Also instructive is *In re Marriage of Baragry*, which reversed a trial court finding the parties separated when husband moved out of the family home to live with his girlfriend on his boat. The court looked to the parties' continuous and frequent contacts and the husband's intentions as expressed in cards sent to his wife. Moreover, the filing of joint tax returns, and husband's other written acknowledgements that he resided at the family residence convinced the court a complete and final break in the marital relationship did not occur until husband filed the petition to dissolve four years after he moved out. The court discounted the significance of the absence of a sexual relationship between the parties and husband's cohabitation with his girlfriend as "evidence [which is not] tantamount to legal separation."

Courts have concluded the filing of a dissolution petition or recitations in a marital settlement agreement do not by themselves compel a finding the parties were thereafter living separate and apart. As the court observed in *Umphrey*, "Our conclusion that there is nothing sacrosanct about a separation date recited in a settlement agreement recognizes not only the equitable nature of the proceedings, but the idiosyncrasies of human relationships. As this case illustrates, *it is not uncommon for parties to a marriage gone sour to live their lives separate and apart while maintaining some vestiges of the marital relation. Many marriages are 'on the rocks' for protracted periods of time and it may be many years before the spouses decide to formally dissolve their legal relationship.* In such situations, separation dates can often be 'guesstimates' or approximations selected at random or without careful consideration." (italics added.)

Finally as noted in *In re Marriage of von der Nuell*, the date of separation is determined by more than when a party leaves the family residence or files a dissolution petition. The length of time voluntary support is paid and the "ongoing economic, emotional, sexual and social ties between the parties and their attempts at reconciliation [also indicates when] a complete and final break . . . occur[s]. . . ."

Applying the above principles here the trial court's error is clear. The *ultimate question to be decided in determining the date of separation is whether either or both of the parties perceived the rift in their relationship as final.* The best evidence of this is *their words and actions.* The husband's and the wife's subjective intents are to be objectively determined from all of the evidence reflecting the parties' words and actions during the disputed time in order to ascertain when during that period the rift in the parties' relationship was final.

V

The effect of the trial court's error in relying only on certain evidence in making its determination is pervasive, resulting in its exclusion of what it considered to be subjective evidence. As indicated by the court's statement of decision and its response to Victor's objections, the court failed to make factual findings necessary to a resolution of disputed material issues. The court also did not consider certain undisputed evidence. The result is a statement of decision which is inadequate as a matter of law.

Because the matter must be remanded for further consideration of the date of separation, we review the evidence the trial court did and did not consider.

The court relied on the following facts in determining the date of separation: (1) the date Victor moved out of the family residence; (2) he never moved back; (3) the move followed a heated argument; (4) the parties previously had a number of other arguments; (5) Victor never again slept at the house; (6) the parties thereafter dated other people; (7) the parties thereafter did not attend business, social or family events together; and (8) Doris filed three different petitions for dissolution of marriage, always specifying June 28, 1969, as the date of separation.

These are relevant considerations but, as discussed, they are not in and of themselves determinative and the court failed to consider extremely relevant undisputed evidence, including the parties' close personal ties from June 28, 1969, through February 1983. They saw each other regularly, their economic relationship remained unchanged and they acquired real property together. Victor continued to receive mail at Doris's residence and on various forms he indicated he resided at her home. Doris remained a corporate officer in the family business and signed, at Victor's request, all documents presented to her in connection with this business. Bank documents executed in 1982 indicated they were married and not separated and all of their property was community.

The court failed to consider other significant evidence indicating Victor's intentions. He testified he did not make a decision to end his marriage until between early 1982 and early 1983. In his February 16, 1983, declaration in support of his motion to bifurcate, he stated it was his desire to "restructure his own life and enable Petitioner to do the same" and he wished a dissolution of marriage at that time "so that all parties *may begin* to develop as soon as possible a new life . . . ." Moreover, Victor never disclosed to any person, including Doris, that he intended to end the marriage by divorce until January of 1983 and he sent her many cards in which he wrote: "Love," "All my love," "Your loving husband," "I'll straighten out some day," and "You deserve lots of sympathy for putting up with me."

The court also failed to make findings on significant disputed facts, including the extent of their social relationship. Doris continued to appear at various business functions from 1969 to 1983 including picnics and the annual Christmas party. She contended she was a hostess at such events. "[Victor's] son, Dennis Hardin, testified that while [Doris] mingled with and greeted employees she was not designated in any official capacity as a hostess or greeter. [Doris] sent Christmas cards to the employees from she [*sic*] and [Victor] on an annual basis through 1982."

The judgment is reversed and the matter is remanded for a new trial to determine the date of separation guided by the principles set forth in this opinion. Doris shall recover her costs on appeal.

Wallin, J., and Rylaarsdam, J., concurred.

Discussion Questions

1. How does the California test for living separate and apart differ from Washington's test for a defunct marriage?

2. Why did the Court of Appeal decide that the later date was when Victor and Doris were living separate and apart?

B.   BRIGHT-LINE TESTS — COMMUNITY PROPERTY UNTIL DIVORCE? FILING THE PETITION?

Some states treat earnings during separation as community property until the actual divorce decree is filed. Arizona originally took this approach. Clearly that prevents litigation over determining when the moment of separation occurs. However, it can sometimes lead to inequities.

1. Arizona

LYNCH v. LYNCH

164 Ariz. 127, 791 P.2d 653 (1990)
Court of Appeals of Arizona

A man who won the lottery before the pending dissolution of his marriage seeks to reverse the trial court's grant of half his winnings to his wife. We hold that the winnings were community property and affirm.

FACTS

Michael Lynch (husband) and Bonnie Lynch (wife) were married in 1968. Their only child was born in 1971. The couple separated in 1985, and within a year husband began living with a woman named Donna Williams. Wife filed for dissolution shortly after.

Wife's petition was uncontested, and at a default hearing on February 10, 1987, wife testified that the marriage was irretrievably broken. *See* A.R.S. §25-312(3). A decree of dissolution is ordinarily entered at the conclusion of a default hearing. However, on February 10, the trial court took the matter under advisement and, on February 19, vacated the hearing because husband had received untimely notice.

On February 21, husband and Donna Williams won a $ 2.2 million jackpot in the Arizona State Lottery. Each owned half a share of the winning ticket. Wife then filed an amended petition in the unconcluded dissolution seeking half of husband's share. This time husband answered, the case went on to trial, and in the ultimate decree of dissolution the trial court awarded wife half of husband's lottery share.

Husband has appealed the trial court's ruling. [H]e attempts to establish that the parties acquired no community property after February 10, 1987, when the invalid default hearing was held.

COMMUNITY DURATION

When an Arizona spouse acquires an asset before marital dissolution, Arizona law treats the asset as community property unless it falls within one of several statutory exceptions. This "bright line" rule is established by A.R.S. §25-211, which provides: "All property acquired by either husband or wife *during the marriage*, except that which is acquired by gift, devise or descent, is the community property of the husband and wife." (Emphasis added.) A marriage endures in Arizona — and thus the acquisition of community property continues — "until the final dissolution is ordered by the court."

In some jurisdictions, acquisition of community property ceases when spouses begin to live "separate and apart." In Arizona, however, demarcation by decree "avoids the factual issue of when the couple began living apart, and provides appropriate treatment for the on-again-off-again manner in which some couples try to resolve their differences and patch up their marriages."

An Arizona couple that wishes to end the acquisition of community property before (or without) dissolution has a statutory means to do so. A.R.S. §25-313(B) provides for entry of a decree of legal separation that terminates "community property rights and liabilities . . . as to all property, income and liabilities received or incurred after [its] entry." In the absence of a decree of legal separation, however, acquisition of community property continues in Arizona until the decree of dissolution is filed.

Discussion Questions

1. In *Lynch*, would the outcome have been different had this couple lived in California or Washington? Which is the preferable way to determine when the economic community ends?

2. Do you agree with the court in *Lynch* that Arizona community property law such as Ariz. Rev. Stat. §25-211 encourages couples to reconcile as opposed to that of Washington and California?

The Arizona Legislature changed the bright-line rule and now it provides a different bright-line rule that "All property acquired by either husband or wife during the marriage is the community property of the husband and wife except for property that is acquired after service of a petition for dissolution of marriage . . . if the petition results in a decree of dissolution of marriage." Ariz. Rev. Stat. §25-211(A)(2). Discuss whether this bright-line rule encourages couples to reconcile.

2.   New Mexico

In New Mexico, the general rule is that "Until spouses obtain a final, judicial order dissolving their marriage or ordering a legal separation, they retain all the legal benefits and obligations of the marital status, including the presumption that all property acquired during the marriage is community property." *Medina v. Medina,* 139 N.M. 309, 312, 131 P.3d 696, 699 (App. Ct. 2006). In *Medina,* the Court of Appeals considered whether a wife could share in her husband's retirement benefits for the period in which the wife engaged in bigamy. The Court concluded that engaging in bigamy does not terminate a spouse's community property rights.

MEDINA v. MEDINA
139 N.M. 309, 131 P.3d 696 (2006)
Court of Appeals of New Mexico

PICKARD, Judge.
This divorce case requires us to decide whether the trial court erred in refusing to award Wife any portion of Husband's retirement benefits for the period following

her bigamous marriage to another man. We hold that the mere fact of bigamy is insufficient to deprive Wife of her share of community property. We determine that a bigamous spouse should be deprived of his or her community property rights only when the circumstances of the case shock the conscience of the court, and we remand for the trial court to make additional factual findings and reconsider the issue.

FACTS

Jose Medina (Husband) and Rachael Medina (Wife) were married on May 14, 1993. They lived together for some period of time, although the parties dispute their date of separation. Husband alleges that they separated in 1997, while Wife alleges that they separated in 2003. The trial court specifically declined to make a factual finding regarding the date of the parties' separation. In 2003, Husband filed for divorce.

At trial, Wife testified that she married a man named Paul Orozco at a ceremony in Colorado on September 22, 1999, while she was still legally married to Husband. Before marrying Orozco, Wife applied for a marriage license. On the application, she used a fictitious name, birth date, and social security number. Wife also checked the box on the application marked "widowed" and indicated that her previous husband had died in New Mexico in 1992. Orozco was ill at the time of the marriage, and he died on October 21, 2002.

The trial court did not enter findings regarding whether Wife ever lived with Orozco. The trial court's findings also do not indicate when Husband and Wife lived together between Wife's marriage to Orozco in 1999 and Husband's filing for divorce in 2003. However, it appears that the parties may have lived together at least sporadically during this time. There is also an ongoing factual dispute regarding when Husband became aware of Wife's marriage to Orozco. Wife argues that Husband found out about the marriage two weeks after it occurred, and she states that at the very least, he was aware of it by 2000. Husband alleges that he had some suspicions regarding the marriage in 2000, but that he "was not able to absolutely confirm the fact of a bigamous marriage" until Orozco's sister testified regarding the marriage at trial. The trial court did not make any findings with respect to Husband's knowledge of the marriage to Orozco.

At trial, Husband argued that Wife should not receive a share of his retirement benefits for the period during which she was married to Orozco. The trial court ruled that Wife's entitlement to the benefits would be terminated as of the date of her marriage to Orozco, and Wife appeals only that ruling.

STANDARD OF REVIEW

We review de novo whether there should be any circumstances, beside the fact of bigamy, relevant to the determination of whether a bigamous spouse should lose his or her share of community property.

DISCUSSION

1. GENERAL RULES CONCERNING BIGAMY

Many states have statutes characterizing bigamous marriages as void ab initio. New Mexico does not appear to have such a statute, although our state does make bigamy a criminal offense. Colorado, however, has a statute mandating that a court shall declare a bigamous marriage invalid from its inception. Colo. Rev. Stat. Ann. §14-10-111(1)(g)(I), (5) (1998). In New Mexico, the validity of a marriage is governed by the law of the jurisdiction in which the marriage was celebrated. Thus, because Wife's marriage to Orozco is invalid under Colorado law, it is also invalid in New Mexico and does not operate to nullify her marriage to Husband.

However, the fact that a bigamous marriage does not technically nullify a prior marriage does not necessarily mean that the second marriage has no legal effect on the first marriage and its incidents. Many courts, under circumstances which we will discuss below, have applied a theory of estoppel or unclean hands to similar cases involving bigamy. We agree that under some circumstances, a bigamous spouse should be precluded from reaping the benefits of his or her first marriage. Before examining this issue, we address the proposition that a second, bigamous marriage should automatically deprive a spouse of his or her share of the community's assets.

2. THE MERE FACT OF BIGAMY DOES NOT DEPRIVE A SPOUSE OF COMMUNITY PROPERTY RIGHTS

In support of her argument that bigamy alone is not sufficient to deprive a spouse of community property rights, Wife relies on *Beals v. Ares*, 25 N.M. 459, 185 P. 780 (1919), which we find helpful. In *Beals*, our Supreme Court considered whether a wife "forfeited her interest in the community property by the commission of adultery." The Court first stated that under the civil laws of Spain and Mexico, a wife did forfeit her "matrimonial gains" when she committed adultery. The Court then noted that when New Mexico passed a statute adopting the common law, the civil law was completely supplanted and the common law became "the rule of decision." After examining the common law involving a wife's property rights, the Court stated as follows:

> There being no applicable provisions of the common law, or any statute of this state barring the wife of her interest in the community property by reason of the commission of adultery, we conclude that her rights and interests in the community property are not affected by any wrongs which she may have committed, however grievous they may have been. As the legislature has not seen fit to deprive her of the interest which it conferred upon her, in the property earned by the parties to the union, because she may have violated her marital vows, the courts can not legislate upon the subject and by judicial fiat correct that which many think is a serious defect in our laws. The remedy is with the legislature and not the courts.

The most logical rationale for a holding that bigamy automatically deprives a spouse of community property rights would be that the spouse forfeits those rights as a result of his or her misconduct. We note that some jurisdictions appear to have distinguished cases like *Beals* from cases involving bigamy. However, we agree with Wife that *Beals* stands for the proposition that a spouse does not forfeit community property rights merely by engaging in misconduct relative to the marriage.

Marriage is a civil contract that confers a certain status upon the parties. New Mexico does not recognize common law marriage. Thus, a marriage is valid only if it is "formally entered into by contract and solemnized before an appropriate official." Similarly, if parties want to alter their marital status, they must initiate and complete legal proceedings. We note that even in jurisdictions that do recognize or have recognized common law marriage, the concept of "common law divorce" has been consistently rejected, and courts have required legal proceedings to alter the marital status. Thus, the general rule is that until spouses obtain a final, judicial order dissolving their marriage or ordering a legal separation, *see* NMSA 1978, §40-3-8(A)(2) (1990) (defining separate property to include property acquired after a legal separation), they retain all the legal benefits and obligations of the marital status, including the presumption that all property acquired during the marriage is community property. *See* NMSA 1978, §40-3-12(A) (1973) (stating that property acquired by either spouse during marriage is presumed to be community property). For these reasons, we cannot agree with Husband that the mere fact of bigamy causes a de facto divorce, thereby depriving the parties of the benefits of their marriage.

At oral argument, Husband argued that *Beals* is inapplicable because bigamy, unlike adultery, is a criminal offense. We do not find this argument persuasive. Other criminal acts that adversely affect the marital relationship, such as domestic violence, do not result in a forfeiture of community property rights. Rather, the general rule is that such property rights are affected only when one spouse has taken some unilateral action to improperly dissipate or otherwise damage the community's property. In such cases, that spouse can be required to compensate the other spouse for the improperly used resources.

We also agree with Wife that to inject an element of moral fault into the rules governing the distribution of community property on divorce might be inconsistent with New Mexico's system of no-fault divorce.

Finally, we recognize that when our Legislature has wanted to make fault relevant to the disposition of community property, it has done so. Thus, if bigamy is to automatically deprive a spouse of community property rights, that is a decision best made by the Legislature.

In accordance with *Beals* and New Mexico's preference for removing the element of moral fault from issues involving marital property division, we hold that a spouse does not automatically forfeit his or her community property rights upon the commission of bigamy. Thus, we remand this case for further consideration because the trial court's written ruling and oral comments indicate that the court did make its ruling based on the mere fact of bigamy. We now turn to our examination of when a spouse's bigamy might preclude him or her from claiming the benefits of a prior marriage.

* * *

Having surveyed the case law in this area and addressed the parties' arguments, we believe it prudent to provide some guidelines on the issue of when a bigamous spouse should be deprived of his or her share of the community property. As we have detailed above, established law in New Mexico dictates that marriage establishes a contractual relationship that generally cannot be repudiated except through formal divorce or separation proceedings. Moreover, moral fault is irrelevant in divorce actions. In accordance with these principles, we hold that a spouse should only be deprived of community property due to bigamy if the circumstances of the case shock the conscience of the court. Equal division of community property should be the norm even where bigamy is involved, and the burden falls on the spouse seeking an unequal division to prove circumstances that shock the conscience.

While this case does not require us to set forth exhaustive guidelines regarding hypothetical situations that might rise to the appropriate level, we do note that the trial court should consider when the non-bigamous spouse became aware of the bigamy. If the non-bigamous spouse knows or should know that the other spouse is committing bigamy, then he or she has the option of taking steps, such as getting a divorce, to protect his or her assets. If the non-bigamous spouse chooses not to take any such steps, community property should likely be divided equally. Conversely, if the non-bigamous spouse has no actual or constructive knowledge of the bigamous marriage, then perhaps he or she should not be required to divorce in order to protect his or her assets. This would be particularly true if there was evidence that the bigamous spouse took affirmative steps to hide the second marriage.

In sum, we emphasize that the trial court should consider the overall equities of the situation, and it should only order an unequal distribution of community property in those rare cases in which it would be a violation of equity and good conscience to allow the bigamous spouse who has also demonstrated aggravated conduct to enjoy an equal share of the community.

CONCLUSION

We remand for the trial court to reconsider its decision with regard to the proper distribution of Husband's retirement benefits and to make findings regarding the factors that it finds to be controlling. In its discretion, it may take additional evidence. If the trial court does not choose to allow further evidence to be taken or if the evidence adduced does not vary materially from the evidence presented below, then the trial court should enter an order equally dividing the retirement benefits earned for the entire duration of the parties' marriage.

Discussion Questions

1. Do you agree with the Court of Appeals' decision to analogize bigamy to adultery as proposed by the wife's reliance on *Beals v. Ares*, 25 N.M. 459 (1919)?

2. Do you think that bigamy is similar misconduct as adultery *or* do you believe that bigamy constitutes a break in a marriage that should entail an end of community property rights?

3. If the same facts of *Medina* had taken place in Washington or California, would a court treat the husband's retirement benefits as community or separate property?

3. Texas

Texas Family Code §3.003 states that "Property possessed by either spouse during or on dissolution of marriage is presumed to be community property." There are several assets that are presumptively community, one being *property acquired after the spouses separate but before they divorce*, unless the property is defined as separate under Texas Family Code §3.001. Either spouse can establish that property is separate property by overcoming the presumption with clear and convincing evidence. Tex. Fam. Code §3.003 (2010). This general rule and its application is discussed in *Wilson v. Wilson*, 44 S.W.3d 597 (Tex. App.-2d 2001). In *Wilson*, the husband complained that the trial court failed to distribute the property in a fair and just manner and argued that the trial court should have distributed the property according to the date of the couple's separation, not the date of divorce. Nevertheless, the court held that the trial court did not err in considering property acquired after separation as community property. Although in Texas community property continues to exist even after separation, a court at its discretion may order "[A]n unequal division of marital property when a reasonable basis exists for doing so."

WILSON v. WILSON

44 S.W.3d 597 (2001)
Court of Appeals of Texas

On February 18, 2000, following a bench trial, the trial court signed its final decree of divorce and judgment, dissolving the 32-year marriage of Appellant John H. Wilson and Appellee Shirley L. Wilson and dividing their community estate. This appeal arises from the trial court's distribution of the marital property. On appeal, Appellant raises three issues challenging the fairness of the trial court's distribution of property and the trial court's order that Appellant pay Shirley's attorney's fees. We affirm.

I. BACKGROUND

Appellant and Shirley L. Wilson were married on March 26, 1968. They separated in 1990, and Shirley filed for divorce on October 21, 1998. At the time of separation, Shirley moved out of the family home. The couple's sixteen year old son continued to live with Appellant for four years after the separation. Shirley did not pay Appellant child support, and Appellant did not pay Shirley spousal support.

The trial court finalized the divorce on February 18, 2000. As part of the property distribution, Appellant was ordered to pay Shirley $ 10,000 for her share in the family home. Shirley also received fifty percent of Appellant's investment plan with General Dynamic's; fifty percent of Appellant's saving's and stock plan with Lockheed Martin; fifty percent of Appellant's retirement plan with Lockheed Martin; and attorney's fees of $7,129. Appellant had been in the military for twenty years, eight of which were during his marriage to Shirley; therefore, Shirley also received a portion of Appellant's military retirement.

. . .

III.   Distribution of Property

Appellant complains that (1) the trial court should have distributed the property as of the date of the Wilsons' separation instead of the date of their divorce, and (2) the trial court ignored several facts that should have affected the property distribution.

The trial judge has wide discretion in dividing the parties' community estate. The party attacking the property division bears the heavy burden of showing that the trial court's property division was not just and right. We must indulge every reasonable presumption in favor of the trial court's proper exercise of its discretion.

One who complains of the trial court's division of property must be able to demonstrate from evidence in the record that the division was so unjust and unfair as to constitute an abuse of discretion. A trial court's division will not be disturbed on appeal unless it appears from the record that the division was clearly the result of an abuse of discretion. The test for whether the trial court abused its discretion is whether the court acted arbitrarily or unreasonably.

Section 7.001 of the family code provides that a divorce decree "shall order a division of the estate of the parties in a manner that the court deems just and right." Tex. Fam. Code Ann. §7.001. The "estate of the parties" has been construed to mean only the parties' community property. Property possessed by either spouse during or on dissolution of marriage is presumed to be community property. Tex. Fam. Code Ann. §3.003. The family code provides only three instances in which property may be classified as separate property: (1) property owned or claimed by either spouse before marriage; (2) property acquired during marriage by gift, devise, or descent; and (3) recovery for personal injuries, except for loss of earning capacity. Tex. Fam. Code Ann. §3.001.

Because the Wilsons were still married even after their separation in 1990, the property they continued to acquire between the date of separation and divorce was still considered community property, unless either spouse could establish that the property was separate property under section 3.001. Appellant provided no evidence that any of the property acquired between the date of the Wilsons' separation and their divorce fulfilled any of the requirements in section 3.001. Therefore, the trial court did not abuse its discretion in distributing the property acquired after the Wilsons separated in 1990.

Appellant also alleges that the trial court ignored three relevant facts in distributing the community property: (1) Appellant cared for the couple's minor son after Shirley left the family home; (2) Appellant paid the mortgage on the home during the separation; and (3) Shirley's testimony that she had told Appellant when they separated that he could have the house. The trial court may consider a variety of factors when dividing an estate, such as: (1) relative earning capacities and business experience of the parties; (2) educational background of the parties; (3) size of separate estate; (4) the age, health, and physical condition of the parties; (5) fault in the dissolution of the marriage; (6) the benefits the innocent spouse would have received had the marriage continued; and (7) probable need for future support.

Appellant does not complain about the trial court's division of any particular property; instead he argues that the trial court's overall distribution failed to take into account the facts of the case. However, we find nothing in the record, nor has

Appellant pointed us to anything in the record, that suggests the trial court ignored the facts when it distributed the property. The essence of Appellant's complaint is that he should have received a larger portion of the property because he cared for the couple's son, he paid the mortgage on the house, and Shirley told him he could have the house when they were separating ten years earlier. We cannot say that the trial court's awarding the community property and debts equally to each spouse was manifestly unjust. Therefore, we overrule Appellant's third issue.

IV. Conclusion

Having overruled Appellant's three issues on appeal, we affirm the trial court's judgment.

Sam J. Day, Justice.

Discussion Questions

1. How did the *Wilson* court arrive at its conclusion that the trial court did not err in its property distribution?

2. Do you agree with the *Wilson* court that the trial court's equal award of community property to each spouse was not unjust?

PROBLEM 13.1

Harry and Wilma married in 2005. Harry worked hard as a hedge fund manager, while Wilma was primarily a homemaker with occasional freelance writing work. During this time, after their son was born in 2007, they grew apart. After six years of marriage, the couple decided to separate as Wilma was unable to cope with Harry's increasingly long hours at work. Wilma and their son moved out of the family home and she moved in with her parents who lived nearby. She took up a new job as a junior editor at a publishing company, where she met and started dating a managing editor. In the meantime, Harry attempted to reconcile with Wilma by calling her and writing her emails. Harry and Wilma were able to agree to arrangements for their son that allowed each of them to have equal time with him. Harry wants to reconcile with Wilma for the sake of their son, but he realizes that Wilma wants to move on with her life. After Wilma moved out of their home, Harry received a large bonus from the hedge fund where he worked. Recently, Wilma and her new boyfriend have decided that they want to marry and Wilma filed a petition to dissolve her marriage from Harry.

How would Harry's bonus be treated in Washington and California? In Arizona, New Mexico, and Texas? What other facts would be important in determining whether Harry's bonus was community or separate property?

Table 13-1
Character of Property During Separation in Community Property States

State	Rule	Case/Statute
Arizona	Property acquired after service of a petition for dissolution of marriage if the petition results in a decree of dissolution is not community property. A.R.S. §25-211(A)(2). (Equitable division of community property)	*Lynch v. Lynch*, 164 Ariz. 127, 791 P.2d 653 (1990) (trial court held husband's lottery winnings were community property because marriage was not finally dissolved even though husband and wife were living separate and apart) Legislature amended statute to overrule *Lynch*. Community ends upon filing petition of dissolution.
California	Family Code §771 states that "The earnings and accumulations of a spouse . . . while living separate and apart from the other spouse, are the separate property of the spouse." The term "living separate and apart" is defined by case law. (Mandatory 50/50 division of community property)	*Marriage of Baragry*, 73 Cal. App. 3d 444, 140 Cal. Rptr. 779 (1977), *Marriage of Hardin*, 38 Cal. App. 4th 448, 45 Cal. Rptr. 2d 308 (1995) Courts must look at all the conduct of the spouses to determine the actual date of living separate and apart
Idaho	Idaho Code §32-903 Separate property of husband and wife Idaho Code §32-906 Community property-Earnings of spouse following separation and up to the date of divorce must be included as community property. (Equitable division of community property)	*Suter v. Suter*, 97 Idaho 461, 546 P.2d 1169 (1976), *Desfosses v. Desfosses*, 120 Idaho 354, 815 P.2d 1094 (1991) Earnings following separation up to the date of divorce must be included as separate property
Louisiana	La. Civil Code Art. 159: A judgment of divorce terminates a community property regime retroactively to the date of filing the petition in the action in which the judgment of divorce is rendered. (Mandatory 50/50 division of community property)	*Brar v. Brar*, 796 So. 2d 810 (La. App. 2001) (separation of property regime is retroactive to date original divorce petition was filed) La. Civil Code Art. 2375 (A) (C): a judgment decreeing separation of property terminates the community property regime retroactively to the date the original petition for divorce was filed
Nevada	Nev. Rev. Stat. Ann. §123.220 Community property defined: all property acquired after marriage by either husband or wife or both is community property unless	*Forrest v. Forrest*, 99 Nev. 602, 668 P.2d 275 (1983) (all property acquired by the parties until the formal

Table 13-1
Character of Property During Separation in Community Property States

State	Rule	Case/Statute
	otherwise provided. Courts read this statute to extend until formal dissolution of the marriage. (Equitable division of community property)	dissolution of the marriage is community property), *Hybarger v. Hybarger*, 103 Nev. 255, 737 P.2d 889 (1987) (separation of the parties does not dissolve the community and does not alter the character of the parties' income during the period of separation)
New Mexico	N.M. Stat. Ann. §40-3-12 Presumption of community property; presumption of separate property where property acquired by married woman prior to July 1, 1973 N.M. Stat. Ann. §40-3-8 Classes of property "The general rule is that until spouses obtain a final, judicial order dissolving their marriage or ordering a legal separation, they retain all the legal benefits and obligations of the marital status, including the presumption that all property acquired during the marriage is community property." (Mandatory 50/50 division of community property)	*Medina v. Medina*, 139 N.M. 309, 131 P.3d 696 (2006) (a spouse does not forfeit community property rights merely by engaging in misconduct relative to the marriage, the mere fact of bigamy does not automatically deprive a spouse of the benefits of marriage)
Texas	Family Code §3.003 Property possessed by either spouse during or on dissolution of marriage is presumed to by community property, unless either spouse could establish the property was separate property. (Equitable division of community property)	*Wilson v. Wilson*, 44 S.W.3d 597 (2001) (because husband could not provide evidence that property acquired during separation was separate property, court could divide that property equally)
Washington	Wash. Rev. Code §26.16.140 When spouses or domestic partners are living separate and apart, their respective earnings and accumulations shall be the separate property of each. (Equitable division of community property)	*Seizer v. Sessions*, 132 Was. 2d 642, 940 P.2d 261 (1997) (living separate and apart means "permanent separation of the parties—a defunct marriage. A marriage is defunct when there is some conduct on the part of both spouses that demonstrate that the marriage is over.) *Marriage of Johnson*, 1998 WL 898810 (discussing factors that determine whether marriage is defunct)

Chapter 14

Division of Community
Property at Divorce

One of the most significant issues at divorce in community property states is how to divide the couple's property at divorce. In three community property states, California, Louisiana, and New Mexico, there is mandatory 50/50 division of community property at divorce. For instance, California Family Code §2550 states that "the court shall . . . divide the community estate equally." La. Civ. Code art. 2336, *Bustos v. Bustos*, 100 N.M. 556, 558 P.2d 1289 (1983). In those states, litigation regarding what would be equitable division is curtailed. Once the community estate, including property and debt, is assessed, the question of division is simplified. The options are to split each item of property equally, award each spouse an asset of equal value, or have one spouse buy out the other spouse's interest.

Let's take an example. Our hypothetical couple, George and Martha, has been married many years. George has been an employee at a manufacturing company in a management position and has a pension that is worth $1 million. Martha has not worked outside the home but raised their four children who have all reached maturity. Their home is also worth $1 million. They have always lived frugally and have no debt. After their children left home, their marriage deteriorated and they are considering divorce. In the mandatory 50/50 states, the solution to property division is straightforward. George will want his pension; Martha will want the home. They could easily reach an agreement that would divide their property as they wish. However, the question is whether equal is always equitable. Here George leaves the marriage with the capacity to earn more money. Martha leaves the marriage with a significant asset but it cannot easily be tapped for income. She would have to encumber the home or sell it to have funds to live on. Her contribution to the community was in raising the children and caring for the home. She leaves with few skills that would allow her to pursue the lifestyle that she had enjoyed during the marriage. Often the way to equalize the differences in spousal earning capacity after a lengthy traditional marriage is to award spousal support. But it is clear that even though community property is divided equally, that equal division may not be equitable when looking at the broader view of the spouses' situation.

In the other five community property states, the division of the spouses' property could be very different. In these states, the courts are empowered to "equitably" divide community property. For instance, in Arizona and Idaho, "equitable" or "just" division of community property means "substantially equal" unless "sound reason" or "compelling reasons" dictate otherwise. Ariz. Rev. Stat. §24-318(A),

Idaho Code §32-712. Nevada courts are instructed to make an "equal disposition" of community property except that "unequal disposition" is permitted as the court "deems just if the court finds a compelling reason to do so." The reasons must be explained in writing. Nev. Rev. Stat. §125.150(1)(b). Thus, in Nevada, the starting point is equal division and a court would have to be convinced to deviate from equal division. Texas and Washington give the courts discretion to divide the couple's property as "just and right" or "just and equitable." In Texas, the statute has the vague words "having due regard for the rights of each party and any children of the marriage." Vernon's Tex. Stat. §7.001. Washington courts are given the power to divide community property and the separate property of the spouses to attain an equitable division of the couple's assets. West's Rev. Code of Wash. §26.09.080.

Therefore, returning to the situation of George and Martha, it would seem that the equitable division states would start with equal division of the property with George receiving his pension and Martha receiving the home. The length of the marriage and the lack of Martha's earning capacity might lead to Martha receiving a portion of George's pension. That could justify an unequal division of their assets. The Idaho Code specifically mentions the following factors to consider when deviating from the equal division: "the duration of the marriage," "the age, health, occupation, amount and source of income, vocational skills," "needs of each spouse," and "the present and potential earning capacity of each spouse." Thus, a court could justify awarding Martha more than one-half of the community property. If a Nevada court faced the same scenario, unequal division is the exception and if the court deviated from 50/50 division by giving Martha a share of George's pension, its reasons would have to be stated in writing in its opinion.

Although Texas' formulation is vague — having due regard for the rights of each party, Texas allows the consideration of fault in the determination of division of community property. For instance, if there were fault grounds for the divorce against George, a Texas court could potentially award all of the community property to Martha. The use of fault as a basis for dividing property is controversial especially since most jurisdictions have abolished fault as a basis for divorce and for division of community property. In Arizona, the legislature prohibited the consideration of fault in the division of community property, by specifying equitable division "without regard to marital misconduct." Ariz. Rev. Stat. §25-318(A). Accord, West's Wash. Rev. Code §26.09.080 ("without regard to misconduct").

Washington's division of a divorcing couple's property is the most far-reaching of all the community property states. It not only takes into consideration the separate property of the spouses, but it authorizes the division of that property: "the court shall . . . make such disposition of the property and liabilities of the parties, *either community or separate*, as shall appear just and equitable. . . ." West's Rev. Code Wash. §16.09.080.

In the case of George and Martha, if George has substantial separate property, like an inheritance, that will be included in the consideration of how to divide the couple's community property. The Washington court may not give Martha a portion of that inheritance, but may use that to substantiate an award of part of George's pension to Martha. Or George might agree to a lump-sum to be paid from that inheritance to substitute for the part of his pension going to Martha. In essence, the Washington courts have the broadest discretion to decide what is fair and equitable.

A. FACTORS IN DETERMINING UNEQUAL DIVISION: ARIZONA AND IDAHO

1. Arizona: Length of Marriage/Fault

In *Toth v. Toth* (1997), the Supreme Court of Arizona broadly interpreted the concept of "equitable division." According to the Court, "'Equitable' means just that-it is a concept of fairness dependent on upon the facts of particular cases." When reading the *Toth* decision, consider what role the length of the marriage and fault in the breakup of a marriage should play in the division of community property.

TOTH v. TOTH

190 Ariz. 218, 946 P.2d 900 (1997)
Supreme Court of Arizona,
En Banc

MARTONE, Justice.

We granted review to decide whether an equitable distribution of marital joint property upon dissolution under A.R.S. §25-318(A) requires an equal distribution of the assets in this case. We conclude that it does not. We also hold that joint tenancy property and community property should be treated alike under A.R.S. §25-318(A).

I. INTRODUCTION

Anthony Toth and Gloria Snyder Toth met at a senior citizens dance in Mesa in 1992. Anthony was 87 and Gloria was 66. They married a year later on December 13, 1993. The following day, Anthony used $140,000 of his sole and separate funds to buy a house for the couple. They took title as joint tenants with the right of survivorship. About two weeks later, Anthony moved out of the marital bedroom, and on January 10, 1994, he filed for an annulment. The court ultimately entered a final decree of dissolution on September 19, 1995. The house was the only property to be divided. The court awarded Gloria $15,000 as her share. She appealed.

The court of appeals decided that A.R.S. §25-318(A)[1] requires a substantially equal division of joint property, absent sound reason to the contrary. The court indicated that sound reason is limited to the statutory factors of fraud, excessive or abnormal expenditures, destruction, or concealment. It then held that the trial

---

1. Section 25-318(A) provides that:

In a proceeding for dissolution of the marriage, or for legal separation . . . the court shall assign each spouse's sole and separate property to such spouse. It shall also divide the community, joint tenancy and other property held in common equitably, though not necessarily in kind, without regard to marital misconduct. . . . Nothing in this section shall prevent the court from considering excessive or abnormal expenditures, destruction, concealment or fraudulent disposition of community, joint tenancy and other property held in common.

court had abused its discretion in ordering a substantially unequal division of the property and reversed. Judge Kleinschmidt dissented, believing that "equitable" had a broader meaning than the majority gave it. Believing that an important issue of law had been decided incorrectly, we granted Anthony's petition for review.

II.   ANALYSIS

A.   TREATMENT OF JOINT TENANCY PROPERTY UNDER A.R.S. §25-318

Gloria argues that the gifted portion of the property is her sole and separate property and, therefore, the court must award her half its value under A.R.S. §25-318(A).

Section 25-318(A) provides that "the court shall assign each spouse's sole and separate property to such spouse." It then provides that the court shall "divide the community, joint tenancy and other property held in common equitably, though not necessarily in kind, without regard to marital misconduct."

B.   MEANING OF EQUITABLE DIVISION UNDER A.R.S. §25-318

Although A.R.S. §25-318(A) requires an equitable division of joint property, it also provides that nothing shall prevent the court from considering "excessive or abnormal expenditures, destruction, concealment or fraudulent disposition" of the property in making that equitable division. Gloria argues that the statute requires an equal division of joint property absent exceptional circumstances. She contends that those circumstances are limited to the parties' relationship to the property, rather than to each other. She characterizes other factors, such as the duration of the marriage, as inquiring into fault, which the statute prohibits.

We disagree for two reasons. First, the legislature's intent that the division be equitable, not equal, is clearly evidenced by the legislative history of the dissolution statute. In 1973, a proposed version of the statute required an equal division of all common assets. Senator O'Connor then moved to replace "equally" with "equitably," to be defined as "equally absent compelling reasons to the contrary." The version eventually adopted states only that the court shall make an "equitable" division. The legislature clearly contemplated that the trial court should not be bound by any per se rule of equality, but rather intended the court to have discretion to decide what is equitable in each case.

Second, the statute does not limit the inquiry to conduct regarding the property. Instead, it expressly instructs the court to divide the marital property equitably. Although the statute forecloses an argument that the listed factors are not relevant, it does not purport to define the universe of relevance. "Equitable" means just that — it is a concept of fairness dependent upon the facts of particular cases.

This is not a departure from the general principle that all marital joint property should be divided substantially equally unless sound reason exists to divide the property otherwise. That approach simply reflects the principle that community property implies equal ownership. In most cases, therefore, an equal distribution of joint property will be the most equitable.

However, there may be sound reason to divide the property otherwise. The trial court has discretion in this decision. *Wayt*, 123 Ariz. at 446, 600 P.2d at 750; *Hatch*, 113 Ariz. at 133, 547 P.2d at 1047. The trial judge in this case found sound reason to divide the Toths' property unequally, and we agree.

In this case, equal is not equitable. Community property rests on the assumption that the two spouses worked together to accumulate property for the community, each contributing in pecuniary or other ways. Anthony paid for this property entirely from his separate funds. Gloria made no contribution — pecuniary or otherwise — to the purchase of the house. The marriage lasted two weeks, allowing no time for a marital relationship to develop, or for other equities to come into play. This is not a determination of fault; why the marriage dissolved is irrelevant. This unusual case is one of those "rare occasions when the circumstances and facts are such that, in all fairness to the parties, the property should not be characterized as community and should, instead, be awarded [in large measure] to one spouse accordingly."

The court of appeals found that the trial judge's division in this case was contrary to *Whitmore v. Mitchell*, 152 Ariz. 425, 733 P.2d 310 (App. 1987) and *Valladee v. Valladee*, 149 Ariz. 304, 718 P.2d 206 (App. 1986). In those cases, the court of appeals found that the trial judge had abused his discretion by ordering an unequal division of joint tenancy property solely to reimburse the purchasing spouse. But in *Valladee*, the parties had been married for sixteen years and had four children. And in *Whitmore*, the parties had been married over a year, and had a prenuptial agreement regarding their property, which the trial judge ignored. In both cases, as is likely in any real marriage of any significant duration, other equities made a division based solely on reimbursement clearly inappropriate. The facts here, of course, are vastly different. This is not a case in which an equitable division is based "solely" on reimbursement. Source of funds can be a factor in determining what is equitable. *Wayt*, 123 Ariz. at 446, 600 P.2d at 750. The "marriage" lasted two weeks. Every judge who has reviewed this case saw that equal was not equitable. The trial judge so found. The majority of the court of appeals said it seemed "somewhat unfair" for Gloria to receive half the value of the house in these circumstances, but thought the law required that result. Mem. Decision at 3-4. The dissenting judge thought equitable was broader than equal. We agree that an equal distribution here is not equitable. Indeed, if this is not a case in which "equitable" means something other than "equal," we would be hard pressed to imagine one.

C.   CONSIDERATION OF MARITAL MISCONDUCT

Gloria argues that the trial court made a finding of fault when it stated that she had not made a "good faith effort to create a viable marriage." While the statement does connote fault, it is unclear whether the trial court relied on it in dividing the property. The statement is part of the court's description of the facts of the case. But in its findings, the court noted only that the marriage was of extremely short duration, and that the husband had paid the entire purchase price of the house, as well as subsequent maintenance costs, solely from his separate property. We note that the court received evidence on the parties' ages, needs, health, income and personal situations. It heard evidence that Gloria sold her house, that Anthony continued to pay household expenses after he moved out and that Gloria lived in the house for 1¹/₂ years thereafter. The court found that Gloria should not receive an equal portion of the residence, and allocated $15,000 as her equitable share. Thus, it may be that the court did not use the "good faith" finding in dividing the property. But we cannot be sure.

III.   Conclusion

We vacate the memorandum decision of the court of appeals and remand to the superior court for further consideration of the evidence in light of today's opinion. The court may allocate equitably rather than equally and the court may consider source of funds. The court may consider other equitable factors as they may bear on the outcome, but the court may not consider fault. It may be, that after reconsideration, the court will conclude that it did not consider fault and affirm its prior allocation. We remand only to ensure that fault played no role in the court's determination.

JONES, V.C.J., and FELDMAN, J., concur.

MOELLER, Justice, dissenting.

I respectfully dissent. I do so because I believe the trial court's unequal division of the home is contrary to Arizona case law, to Arizona statutory law, and to basic principles of fairness and equity. In my view, the court of appeals correctly held that the case should be remanded with instructions for a substantially equal distribution. Mr. Toth chose to make a gift of one-half of the house to Mrs. Toth. Having chosen to make a gift, Mr. Toth seeks the help of the domestic relations court to compel Mrs. Toth to give it back. The majority opinion permits the trial court to order her to give it back despite established Arizona law prohibiting an unequal division for any of the reasons relied upon by the trial court.

A.R.S. §25-318(A) ("the statute") does permit the trial court to divide joint tenancy property "equitably" rather than "equally." If the legislature intended by this statute to permit courts to order the disgorgement of gifts, it did not say so. Doubtless, the 1973 enactment of the statute permitting equitable division of jointly held property was in recognition of the fact that married couples commonly use community funds to acquire joint tenancy property. In dissolution actions prior to enactment of the statute in 1973, courts could not order the parties to divest themselves of title to their separate property, and their interest in joint tenancy property was separate property. The statute was intended to alleviate some practical problems by permitting joint tenancy property to be divided equitably, but not necessarily in kind. As the *Valladee* case makes clear, the statute was never intended to convert property held in joint tenancy into community property. The statute only contemplates a significantly unequal distribution in cases of "excessive or abnormal expenditures, destruction, concealment or fraudulent disposition" of the property. A.R.S. §25-318(A). None of the statutory elements permitting an unequal division are present here. What then justifies an unequal division? The trial court supported its unequal division of the property with the following findings:

All the money used to purchase the residence located at 2303 North 76th Street was the sole and separate property of the Petitioner/Husband, Anthony Toth. The Respondent/Wife, Gloria Toth, did not contribute any money toward the purchase of the residence. The Respondent/Wife, Gloria Toth, did sell her former residence and is now receiving monthly payments from said sale.

* * *

The parties lived together as husband and wife for only two weeks. For one additional week, Petitioner/Husband, Anthony Toth, lived in a separate room in the marital residence. After approximately three weeks, Petitioner/Husband moved out of the marital residence and has lived in a separate residence since that time.

* * *

Petitioner/Husband, Anthony Toth, expected that the parties would each make a good faith effort to live together as husband and wife for the rest of their lives. No evidence has been presented that Respondent/Wife, Gloria Toth, made a good faith effort to create a viable marriage.

THE COURT FINDS that the facts and circumstances of this case indicate that this was a marriage of extremely short duration. Respondent/Wife contributed nothing economically either toward the purchase of the marital residence or toward the necessary expenses of utilities and taxes on the residence since its purchase, even though she has remained in the residence since January of 1994. . . .

THE COURT FURTHER FINDS it would be unjust enrichment and a windfall to Respondent/Wife to award her an equal disposition of the value of the marital residence. While this Court may not set aside a transaction merely because one of the parties to a marriage contract may have been imprudent or made a poor bargain, nonetheless, the Court must make an equitable disposition pursuant to A.R.S. sec. 25-318(A).

Any reasonable reading of these findings compels the conclusion that the trial judge made the unequal division because of some perceived fault on Mrs. Toth's part and to reimburse Mr. Toth because he paid for the house out of his separate funds. Under Arizona law, neither reason authorizes an unequal division of the joint tenancy property.

It is also clear from the trial court's findings that the unequal division was based, in part, on the trial court's perception that Mrs. Toth was more at fault than Mr. Toth for the failure of the marriage. I find nothing in the record that supports that view, but even if it is well-founded, it is not a permissible reason for an unequal division. The statute upon which the majority relies to support the unequal division expressly precludes consideration of fault. Similarly, Arizona case law precludes consideration of fault in making a property allocation.

The majority readily acknowledges that fault, even if it exists, cannot support an unequal division. The majority also acknowledges that the trial court used language indicating fault, but the majority concludes that it is "unclear" whether the trial court relied upon its finding of fault in dividing the property and concludes that "it may be that the [trial] court did not use" the finding. The majority refers to other evidence before the trial court that it believes might justify the trial court's disparate distribution. I fail to find the trial court's comments concerning Mrs. Toth's fault to be as antiseptic as does the majority. Since the only issue being addressed was division of the property, I rely on the language used by the trial court in dividing the property. I find no justification to speculate, as does the majority, that the trial court might have intended to rely on other unreferred-to evidence.

The trial court also found and relied upon the obvious: that this was a short marriage. The trial court obviously blamed Mrs. Toth for the brevity of the marriage. I find no authority for the proposition that a spouse must remain married for a certain number of years before her right to retain a gift vests, nor has the majority or Mr. Toth cited any. The marriage was as short for Mrs. Toth as it was for Mr. Toth. Because fault cannot be considered, I find no relevance to the length of the marriage.

Under Arizona case law, equitable division has been interpreted to mean a substantially equal division "unless some sound reason exists for a contrary result." Length of marriage has never been held to constitute a "sound reason" to divide joint tenancy property other than substantially equally. Cases in which our courts have upheld unequal distributions have dealt with the factors given in A.R.S. §25-318 that the court may legitimately consider. *See Martin v. Martin,* 156 Ariz. 452, 454-55, 457-58, 752 P.2d 1038, 1040-41, 1043-44 (1988) (court upheld giving wife sum of money to reimburse her for improper dissipation of community assets by husband); *Hrudka v. Hrudka,* 186 Ariz. 84, 93-94, 919 P.2d 179, 188-89 (App. 1995) (court upheld husband receiving more assets than wife because trial court found waste on wife's part where wife transferred, concealed, and sold substantial assets in violation of a trial court order); *Kosidlo v. Kosidlo,* 125 Ariz. 32, 607 P.2d 15 (App. 1979), *disapproved on other grounds,* 125 Ariz. 18, 607 P.2d 1 (trial court justified in concluding that equity favored distributing greater share of community assets to wife where husband refused to use checking account, insisted on cash transactions, secreted large amounts of cash, and evaded questions about community assets); *Lindsay v. Lindsay,* 115 Ariz. 322, 565 P.2d 199 (App. 1977) (court directed trial court to award sum of money to wife representing her share of community's interest in an aircraft where her husband secretly sold aircraft during dissolution proceedings and lost the proceeds in gambling).

Factors permitting unequal distribution of joint tenancy property should be limited to those enumerated in A.R.S. §25-318(A), which should not be expanded to include perceptions of fault or evaluations of the length of the marriage. No §25-318 factor exists here. Under the majority's length-of-marriage test, how long is long enough? The majority opinion states that gifts of joint tenancy property "are made in expectation of a permanent relationship, but if cut short, fully subject to equitable divestment under the statute." Maj. op. at 220, 946 P.2d at 902. Under this approach, joint tenancy property can always be divided unequally in any dissolution because the relationship, by definition, turned out not to be permanent. Such a result is totally at variance with Arizona law as it has existed to date. There are very few valid reasons to divide joint tenancy property unequally, because each spouse has a vested separate property interest in one-half of the property and A.R.S. §25-318 does not change that well-established tenet.

In summary, no proper reason supports an order requiring Mrs. Toth to return the gift Mr. Toth chose to make. The court of appeals correctly concluded that a substantially equal division should have been ordered. The remand should be limited to ordering an equal division.

ZLAKET, C.J., concurs.

Discussion Questions

1. Why does the majority in *Toth* think the length of the marriage is significant in determining equitable division of community property?

2. The dissent in *Toth* criticizes the majority for considering factors such as the length of the marriage and fault in the breakup of the marriage. The dissent cites several cases that "dealt with factors . . . that the court may legitimately consider to support unequal division." How do those cases differ from the facts of *Toth*?

FLOWER v. FLOWER

223 Ariz. 531, 225 P.3d 588 (2010)
Court of Appeals of Arizona

BROWN, Judge.

The question we address here is whether the family court abused its discretion in ordering a substantially unequal distribution of marital assets and debts under the equitable principles explained in *Toth v. Toth*, 190 Ariz. 218, 946 P.2d 900 (1997). For the following reasons, we affirm.

BACKGROUND

Judy D. Flower ("Wife") married Norman L. Flower ("Husband") on January 26, 2006. She was 55 years old and he was 76. Entering into the marriage, both Husband and Wife owned separate real property. Husband owned the "Sugar Creek" house, and Wife, together with her son, owned the "Queen Valley" house. Shortly after the wedding, Husband signed a deed to the Sugar Creek residence which transferred title to both parties as community property with right of survivorship. Ownership of the Queen Valley house was not changed.

Husband and Wife lived in the Sugar Creek house for approximately the first six months of the marriage. During that time, they made improvements to the Queen Valley house and then moved into it.[1] They also incurred over $61,000[2] of debt during the marriage. Although the exact amount of debt the community incurred to improve the Queen Valley residence is disputed, Wife concedes that at least $32,000 was spent for this purpose. A significant portion of the funds used to pay for the improvements came from a home equity loan on the Sugar Creek house. Most of the remainder came from credit cards and a line of credit used to purchase flooring and other materials for the Queen Valley house.

1. Wife's son moved into the Sugar Creek house when Husband and Wife moved to the Queen Valley house. The son lived in the Sugar Creek house for about four months and paid rent of $600 per month for two of those four months; he ceased paying rent when Husband gave him notice to vacate the property.

2. The record indicates that the community incurred the following debts: (1) a home equity loan on the Sugar Creek house for $30,000; (2) Home Depot credit card for $3,180; (3) Visa credit card for $9,157; (4) Mohawk flooring line of credit for $15,490; and (5) JCPenney credit card for bedroom furniture for $3,887.

In January 2007, Husband filed a petition for annulment, alleging Wife never had a romantic interest in him and her decision to enter into the marriage was financially motivated. Wife denied the allegations and counter-petitioned for dissolution of the marriage. At trial, the parties presented evidence regarding the annulment and dissolution petitions. The primary disputes, however, involved the division of the Sugar Creek house and the allocation of debts incurred to improve the Queen Valley house.

Husband had purchased the Sugar Creek house in 1989 for $123,000. At the time of trial, the parties stipulated that the value of the house was $350,352. The property was encumbered by a first mortgage of approximately $71,000 and the $30,000 home equity line of credit used to improve Wife's residence. Husband acknowledged that in executing the deed to the Sugar Creek property, he gave Wife a one-half interest in the property. He took the position that transfer of the house was "procured by misunderstanding, fraud, or coercion." Alternatively, Husband asserted that if he did gift one-half of the property to Wife, equitable principles favored awarding him the entire property.

Conversely, Wife argued that both the transfer of an interest in the Sugar Creek house and the expenditures made on the Queen Valley house were gifts from Husband to her; therefore, she claimed entitlement to an equal portion of the value of the Sugar Creek house and asserted that Husband should be solely liable for the debts incurred to improve her sole and separate property. Alternatively, Wife argued that if the improvements to her separate property were not gifts, then the debts should be divided equally between the parties.

The court denied Husband's petition for annulment, reasoning that later-in-life marriages are often entered into for reasons other than a sexual relationship, such as companionship, and even if Wife married Husband for financial reasons, she still demonstrated genuine affection towards him as both parties had suffered significant personal losses that may have brought them together. The court thus determined that a valid marriage existed.

As to the division of property and debts, the court did not expressly determine whether Husband's transfer of title to the Sugar Creek house constituted a gift to the community; however, based on the assumption it was a "gift without legal or factual impediment," the court recognized it was obligated to consider the "overall issue of fairness and equity" in allocating the value of the house. The court also noted that with respect to the debts incurred to improve the Queen Valley house, "technically, the community contributed the funds"; not Husband.

Applying the concepts of equity discussed in *Toth v. Toth*, the family court determined the circumstances presented here fell within the rare exception to the general rule that an equitable property division should be substantially equal. 190 Ariz. at 221, 946 P.2d at 903. Accordingly, the court awarded all right, title, and interest in the Sugar Creek house to Husband, recognizing that (1) no community funds were used to improve the residence; (2) there was no effort, toil, or contribution from the community to increase the property's value; and (3) Husband's pre-marital equity in the property decreased as a result of funds drawn against the line of credit loan used to fund improvements to Wife's residence. The court concluded that "to the extent Wife can assert she was due any greater sums for her share of the Sugar Creek residence pursuant to [Arizona Revised

Statutes ("A.R.S.") section] 25-318(A), such 'equitable claims' are more than compensated by the improvements made to her sole and separate property, the denial of any equitable lien thereon[,] and the assignment of debt (including the line of credit)" to Husband.

The court also determined that the Queen Valley house was Wife's sole and separate property free from any claims of Husband, including any equitable liens arising from community debt incurred to fund improvements to it. Additionally, the court ordered that Husband be responsible for payment of approximately $42,000 in debts incurred for the improvement of the Queen Valley house and that Wife be responsible for the remaining debts incurred to improve her house, approximately $16,000. Wife timely appealed and we have jurisdiction pursuant to A.R.S. §12-2101(B) (2003).

DISCUSSION

I. THE SUGAR CREEK RESIDENCE

Wife argues the family court "erred as a matter of law by expanding the findings of *Toth* . . . beyond the very rare facts of that case."

As recognized by our supreme court, the general principle is that "all marital joint property should be divided substantially equally unless sound reason exists to divide the property otherwise." "That approach simply reflects the principle that community property implies equal ownership." Thus, in most cases, dividing jointly held property equally will be the most equitable. *Id.*

In determining an equitable division, the family court has broad discretion in the specific allocation of individual assets and liabilities. Under A.R.S. §25-318(C), consideration may be given to (1) excessive or abnormal expenditures and (2) the destruction, concealment, or fraudulent disposition of property. But the family court's attempt to achieve an equitable division is not limited by these statutory factors; instead, the court may consider other factors that bear on the equities of a particular case. In balancing such equities, courts might reach different conclusions in similar cases without abusing their discretion. Thus, we will not disturb a court's ruling absent a clear abuse of discretion.

B. EQUITABLE PROPERTY DIVISION UNDER *TOTH*

Although the family court must divide community and jointly held property equitably upon dissolution of the marriage, a substantially equal division is not required if a sound reason exists to divide the property otherwise. The touchstone of determining what is "equitable" is a "concept of fairness dependent upon the facts of particular cases."

In *Toth*, our supreme court analyzed the meaning of "equitable" as used in A.R.S. §25-318(A), and concluded that in addition to the statutorily enumerated factors, a court may consider the source of the funds used to purchase or improve the property in question and any "other equitable factors that bear on the outcome" of an equitable division, such as, but not limited to, the duration of the marriage. The husband in *Toth* used $140,000 of his separate funds to buy a house that the couple took title to as joint tenants with right of survivorship. In doing so, he made a presumptive gift to his wife of a one-half interest in the house. The marriage, however, lasted only two weeks.

3. Length of the Marriage

Wife asserts that an equitable division in the case before us demands a substantially equal division based on the length of her marriage to Husband. She attempts to distinguish her thirteen-month marriage with Husband from the marital relationship in *Toth*, which effectively lasted two weeks, solely on the basis of overall duration. She vigorously argues that expanding *Toth*'s scope beyond a two-week marriage increases the uncertainty parties face during a dissolution proceeding and threatens to undermine community property concepts.

But nowhere in *Toth* does the length of the marriage play such a singularly significant factor in the final assessment of what is determined to be equitable under the circumstances. Under *Toth*, the family court is free to consider any factor that has bearing on the equitable division of the marital property; how long a marriage lasts is but one factor, albeit an important one, in the assessment of what constitutes an equitable property division. In the final analysis, *Toth*'s essential holding is that when the legislature enacted §25-318, it intended courts to consider "fairness" on a case-by-case basis, rather than being bound by *per se* rules.

The court's order here fits within *Toth*'s limited emphasis on the length of marriage. Although the family court did not expressly rely on the length of marriage as a basis for its final order, the court did acknowledge the relatively short duration of the marriage. In addition, as noted, the court focused on the pre-marriage character of the assets in question, the allocation of community debt in relation to the retention of assets associated therewith, and the legal consequence of interspousal gifts upon dissolution. It was within the court's discretion to consider such factors when determining an equitable division of the marital property.

Nonetheless, Wife argues that *Toth* suggests a "length-of-marriage" test by characterizing any marriage that survives more than one year as one of "significant duration" (distinguishing *Whitmore*, 152 Ariz. 425, 733 P.2d 310, a case in which the marriage lasted sixteen months and an unequal property division was not upheld). Relying on *Toth*'s citation to *Whitmore*, Wife argues that her thirteen-month marriage precludes application of a *Toth* analysis. The citation to *Whitmore*, however, cannot be relied on for this proposition because the majority in *Toth* also distinguished *Whitmore* on the grounds it involved a prenuptial agreement, which controlled the character of jointly held property in that case. Further, the *Toth* court cited *Whitmore* as an example of when "other equities" come into play to make a division based solely on reimbursement inappropriate — in that case, a controlling prenuptial agreement; the court did not reference it as an example of the outer boundaries in applying a "length-of-marriage" analysis.

Regardless, the length of a marriage is a factor to be considered in balancing the equities of property division. In the case before us, while the legal duration of the marriage was just over one year, the record reflects that Husband moved out of the marital home less than eleven months after the wedding, and that the marital relationship was strained and deteriorating less than eight months after the couple exchanged vows. By almost any account this would be considered a short marriage, where there was insufficient time for other equities to tip the scale in favor of substantially equal distribution.

We conclude by emphasizing that in our view, a substantially unequal division of property must continue to represent a rare exception, lest it undermine the entire framework for dividing property during a marriage dissolution in Arizona. As such, this opinion should not be read as sanctioning automatic justification for an unequal division in any marriage of "short duration" where one spouse's sole and separate property was gifted to the community, as the equitable divestment of a gifted property interest will still be inappropriate in the vast majority of dissolution proceedings.

CONCLUSION

We concur with the family court's determination that this case involves circumstances that, like *Toth*, place it outside the general rule that an equitable property division must be substantially equal. Accordingly, we affirm the family court's ruling and hold that the court did not abuse its discretion in awarding to Husband all rights and interest in the Sugar Creek house or in allocating the community debts and assets.

Concurring: PHILIP HALL, Presiding Judge and MAURICE PORTLEY, Judge.

Discussion Question

1. What role does the length of the marriage play in deciding whether there should be unequal division of property?

---

2. Idaho: Many Statutory Factors

In Idaho, similar to Arizona, community property must be divided as the court *deems just*, and should be *substantially equally divided* unless there are circumstances demanding otherwise. Idaho Code §32-712(1)(a). Idaho Code §32-712 lists several factors that a court should consider in departing from the default rule of substantially equal division: (1) the duration of the marriage; (2) the existence of prenuptial agreements; (3) the age, health, occupation, amount and source of income, vocational skills, employability, and liabilities of each spouse; (4) the needs of each spouse; (5) whether the apportionment is in lieu of or in addition to maintenance;

(6) the present and potential earning capability of each party; and (7) retirement benefits. Idaho Code §32-712(1(b). Application of these factors can result in one spouse receiving a disproportionate portion of the community property and the other saddled with all the debts of the community.

SHURTLIFF v. SHURTLIFF

112 Idaho 1031, 739 P.2d 330 (1987)
Supreme Court of Idaho

HUNTLEY, Justice.

On February 14, 1959, Karen Mae Shurtliff and Donald K. Shurtliff were married. On April 13, 1984, Karen filed suit for divorce alleging that her husband had been guilty of adultery and extreme cruelty. Karen sought the following relief: (1) maintenance, including educational expenses; (2) a disparate division of community debts and assets between the parties; and (3) attorney fees and costs.

The record reveals that Mrs. Shurtliff had been a housewife and homemaker for the twenty-six year period of marriage. Mr. Shurtliff's job with the railroad, which currently pays over $54,000 a year, was the sole source of financial support. Further, Mr. Shurtliff totally controlled the finances and economic situation of the couple. Even though Mrs. Shurtliff had only an eleventh grade education, Mr. Shurtliff did not want her to pursue an education. In addition, he did not want her to seek employment outside the home, and during his wife's brief employment with American Micro Systems, Inc., he telephoned her employer stating she was quitting. The trial court found Mr. Shurtliff was guilty of adultery.

A disparate distribution of property was made. Mr. Shurtliff was required to pay all the community debts.1 Spousal support was set at $750.00 per month for five years and he was required to pay Karen's education expenses in the sum of $1,400 per year for five years. Mr. Shurtliff has appealed to the Supreme Court from the district court's affirmance of the trial court's judgment and decree of divorce.

* * *

[T]he appellant contends that the trial court erred in concluding that a disparate division of property was warranted. I.C. §32-712 lists several factors which may be considered in departing from the general rule of an equal division of property. The choice between substantial equality or disparate division of property is to be made by the trial judge based upon the factors set out in I.C. §32-712.

The disparity in the property division herein is due largely to the assignment of the community debts to Mr. Shurtliff. The question before this Court is whether, by doing so, the trial court abused its discretion. The findings of fact contain ample justification for the disparate division of property. The factors listed in I.C. §32-712 which justify disparate division in this case include the duration of marriage, employability of each spouse, and the present and potential earning capability of each party. Hence, the disparate property division cannot be deemed an abuse of discretion.

Further, the community debts totaled $24,612.85. The court ordered that the anticipated tax refunds of $8,400.00 for 1984 and $8,372.05 for 1983 be applied toward retirement of the community debt. The application of those refunds as directed by the court would have eliminated two-thirds of the debt. Since

Mr. Shurtliff violated the court order, neither applying the $16,772.05 to the debt nor accounting for it, he will have to finance or pay the debt from his monthly income, retiring it at $600 per month.

In conclusion, the grounds for divorce, the financial status of the parties, the respondent's need for support and further education, the relative earning capacities of the parties, and the status of community debts provide the trial court with adequate justification for its decision of a disparate property division and awarding maintenance to Mrs. Shurtliff. Therefore, the trial court decision is affirmed.

Costs and attorney fees to respondent.

SHEPARD, Chief Justice, dissenting.

Some of the more vocal and harsh critics of the appellate system of justice assert that the courts too often engage in "creative cowardice" in applying worn out aphorisms of the law such as "the findings are sustained by substantial and competent although conflicting evidence" as a method of avoiding the facing and dealing with difficult decisions. In the case at hand, I would suggest that an equally applicable axiom of the law provides that a decision of a trial court involving the exercise of discretion will not be sustained if that discretion has been abused.

In my view, the stark results of the instant case indicate that the majority opinion has ignored such an abuse of discretion. The defendant-appellant is of limited education, a locomotive engineer, and earns a take-home pay of approximately $2,500.00 per month. There is no showing that his income is subject to increase, but almost certainly his income will decrease due to his changed tax status. Nevertheless, he has been ordered to pay in excess of $85,000.00 over a period of five years. That obligation in large part results from the court's order that he support his former wife during, and pay the costs of, seven years of college education. A further part of the indebtedness results from the court's order requiring plaintiff-appellant to shoulder the approximately $24,000.00 of community indebtedness. Another part of the obligation consists of approximately $6,700.00 of attorney fees awarded to the plaintiff-respondent ex-wife. I would hold that those above-stated facts alone indicate an abuse of discretion on the part of the trial court.

One might assume, given the size of the obligation placed upon defendant-appellant, that the parties enjoyed some degree of affluence and property of some value. Such is not the case. After a marriage of 26 years the parties separated, and plaintiff-respondent wife sought a divorce. The record reveals that the sole community property of the parties was household goods and motor vehicles of a value of less than $10,000.00. That personal property was divided between the parties. Although the parties at one time owned a residence, the indebtedness thereon was not paid and the mortgage holder foreclosed. The record contains the inference that the equity of the parties is exceeded by the mortgage indebtedness, and hence defendant-appellant will be responsible for an additional unknown amount of community debt resulting from such foreclosure. The record discloses that the parties possessed no cash or other liquid assets, no insurance policies, no value in any real estate and only minimal personal property values. During the marriage the parties had gone through four bankruptcies, and a portion of the debt assigned to the defendant-appellant was payments on a then existing wage earner plan. Nevertheless, the trial court has ordered the defendant-appellant to pay approximately $85,000.00 during the course of five years.

I find no evidence that either of the parties is solely responsible for the lack of community assets, finances, or resources, and evidently during the marriage both parties enjoyed the available financial resources of the community. The children of the marriage have reached majority and are independent of the parties here.

At the time of the trial the plaintiff-respondent was a 46-year-old woman in good physical health, of substantial intellectual capacity, and she had regained her emotional stability. She had completed a two-year degree granting program at Idaho State University and was capable as a licensed practical nurse of earning at least $800.00 per month gross income. The costs of that program, together with her support during that time, was to be paid by the defendant-appellant.

Discussion Question

1. Do you think the trial court's disparate division of assigning all of the community debts totaling $24,612.85 to the husband was proper?

B.   UNEQUAL DIVISION AS AN EXCEPTION TO 50/50 DIVISION: THE NEVADA APPROACH

Nevada courts are instructed, to the extent practicable, to "[m]ake an *equal* disposition of the community property of the parties, except that the court may make an *unequal* disposition of the community property in such proportions as it *deems just* if the court finds a compelling reason to do so and sets forth in writing the reasons for making the unequal disposition." Nev. Rev. Stat. §125.150(1)(b) (emphasis added). The Nevada community property division statute was amended in October 1993 in response to confusion created by the Supreme Court of Nevada in *McNabney v. McNabney* (Nevada 1989). Notably, the prior version of the statute contained factors for courts to consider in deciding how to divide community property: the respective merits of the parties, the condition in which they will be left by the divorce, and who acquired the property. The major change, however, is that Nevada courts must now use the starting point of 50/50 division and provide a statement of reasons for deviating from this starting point.

McNABNEY v. McNABNEY

782 P.2d 1291 (1989)
Supreme Court of Nevada

SPRINGER, Justice.

The outcome of this appeal rests on the meaning of the words "just and equitable" as used in NRS 125.150(1). This statute relates to court distribution of community property between spouses in divorce cases.

> In granting a divorce, the court . . . shall make such disposition of . . . the community property of the parties . . . as appears *just and equitable*, having regard to the respective merits of the parties and to the condition in which they will be left by the divorce, and to the party through whom the property was acquired, and the burdens, if any, imposed upon it, for the benefit of the children.

NRS 125.150(1) (our emphasis).

The controversy here centers on the trial court's unequal but "just and equitable" division of one item of the parties' community property, a contingent legal fee received by the husband during the brief marriage of the parties.

The fee in question is to be received in the form of an annuity, payable in gradually increasing installments (presently $3,700.00 per month) until the year 2004. The fee is community property.

The trial court divided the other community property in an equal manner but determined that it would be just and equitable to award eighty percent of the legal fee to the husband. The trial court's determination was based on these facts:

1. The marriage was of short duration. Although the divorce was not granted until after three years of marriage, the couple parted after only two years of marriage.
2. The wife entered into the marriage, according to trial court findings, with "considerable separate estate" which included "income from rentals of her several separate properties and an investment account in excess of $100,000.00."
3. The wife "had been a well-paid federal government employee," was self supporting and neither "expected or depended upon" the husband for "economic or financial support before or during the marriage."
4. The trial court expressly found that after the divorce the wife will not require any financial assistance and will be able on her own to "maintain the same standard of living and lifestyle" that she had had.
5. With regard to the husband's income, the trial court found that "the monthly payments [of the annuity] constitute a substantial portion of [the husband's] law practice income."

The trial court could certainly have viewed this fee to have been a rare or once-in-a-lifetime emolument, which comprised, as expressly found by the court, a "substantial portion" of the husband's income. Of course, had there been children, had the wife been sick or disabled, or had the wife not have been financially independent, the equities would have been much different and not have justified this kind of distribution.

Persons of fair mind and disposition may reasonably conclude that the trial court's not wanting to deprive the husband of a substantial portion of his income and the court's wanting to give the husband a larger proportion of his earned fee were motivated by a sense of fairness and not by any thought of favoring one party or disfavoring the other. Most certainly the trial court's exercise of discretion in this regard was not "clearly erroneous" so as to require reversal.

The real question presented by this appeal is not whether the trial court's disposition was in fact "just and equitable," but, rather, whether the court had the power to divide this asset in a manner other than equally. If this were not the case, this appeal could be easily disposed of in summary fashion for it is fairly easy to conclude that the trial court's division of the husband's fee was not clearly erroneous. The wife centers her appeal not so much on the division itself but rather on the proposition that Nevada case law "mandates" that the division of all community property, and therefore the property in question, must be "essentially equal."

How the wife can maintain that the Nevada statute which requires a division of community property that is "just and equitable," really means a division that is "essentially equal" would be incomprehensible were it not for some possibly misleading language in Nevada case law. We will undertake to clarify any misunderstanding relative to this point.

That there has been a misunderstanding of some kind cannot be doubted. The trial judge himself questioned counsel as to whether he in fact had the power to "divide it unequally" and wondered if he was permitted in this case to make "an exception to the fifty-fifty rule." There is, of course, in Nevada, no "fifty-fifty rule" when it comes to the disposition of community property under NRS 125.150(1). The Nevada divorce statute directs only that a division of community property be *just and equitable* and that, in making such a division, the court must give due regard to the respective merits of the parties, to the condition in which they are left by the divorce and to who acquired the property. Therefore, it was quite proper for the trial court to decide that it did not have to make an equal, "fifty-fifty" division of this item of property, and it was not unreasonable for the trial court to have concluded that the husband merited or deserved to receive a larger proportion of his earned fee so that he would, like his wife, leave the marriage with an adequate income. Both parties were left by the trial court's action in sound economic circumstances, and the trial judge simply and properly found in accordance with the statute that the unequal division of this asset was just and equitable.

There is much precedent for the kind of equitable disposition that took place in this case. In *Herzog v. Herzog*, 69 Nev. 286, 249 P.2d 533 (1952), for example, this court stated with approval that "the trial court exercised its discretion by, in effect, awarding all of the community personal property to the husband. . . ." 69 Nev. at 290, 249 P.2d at 535. How, then, can the wife even think to urge upon this court, as she does, that "discretion has been consistently and clearly denied by the Supreme Court?" The answer may be, as observed by the trial court in this case, that "[t]he language of the statute has been ignored by the Supreme Court."

Certainly the bar has been beset by the uncertainties bearing on the question of equitable versus equal community property division. One Nevada Bar Journal article noted that "[i]n Nevada, the practitioner is unable to advise his or her client, with any certainty, as to what the law provides and how the trial court would review distribution under certain circumstances. The *confusion* lies in the contradiction between the distribution statute and the decisions of the Nevada Supreme Court." (Our emphasis). The author pinpoints the problem when he says

> By statute, Nevada is an equitable division community property state. This seemingly clear pronouncement of legislative intent is now brought into question by conflicting decisions of the appellate court and its apparent judicially created presumption that equal is equitable in most cases.

It is certainly true, as stated by Mr. Logar, that Nevada is by statute an "equitable distribution" jurisdiction, rather than an "equal distribution" jurisdiction, when it comes to distribution of community property. There is not, however, as suggested in the bar journal article, a real or "apparent judicially created presumption that equal is equitable in most cases." This court would not have taken it upon itself to make such a radical change in the law as to institute judicially a shift in the burden of proof in divorce cases in the manner done by statute in Idaho. The statute as it now reads requires the divorce court in making a division equitable to consider the merits of the parties, the condition in which they will be left by the divorce, the person who acquired the property and the needs of the children. NRS 125.150(1). An infinity of facts and circumstances bear upon these statutory considerations, and each case must be decided individually and on its own merits, although courts may use equal division of community property as a "starting point."[5] There is nothing in the statute that states or suggests that property must be divided evenly or that one party or the other should have an added burden of proof in establishing what is just and equitable.

As there is in Nevada no judicially created presumption favoring equal distribution of community property, neither is there a judicial "mandate" that community property must be divided in an "essentially equal manner." The trial judge in this case made a comment about the "contradiction between the distribution statute

---

5. Professor Mary Ann Glendon of Harvard Law School has called equitable distribution "discretionary distribution" because of the broad discretionary powers of judges to mete out "individualized justice" in divorce cases. Although this breadth of discretion can bring about abuses and injustices "[t]he vast majority of states allow the divorce court much flexibility in fashioning an appropriate division or distribution of property." Golden, *Equal Distribution of Property*, Family Law Series, Shepard's/McGraw Hill, p. 240 (1984).

Courts are virtually unanimous in holding that an equitable, just, or reasonable distribution does not necessarily mean an equal one. While an equal division may well prove to be an equitable one, the court is not compelled to make a 50-50 split. Moreover, there is no mathematical formula for deciding what is just and equitable. Each case must be decided on its own facts and circumstances, thus rendering precedents of little value in evaluating what kind of award is proper. For this reason it is "ill-advised and impossible for any court to set down a flat rule concerning property division upon divorce. *Golden*, at 241 (citations omitted).

Because of the very nature of community property, divorce court judges are likely in their deliberative processes to use equal division as a "starting point" for equitable distribution. (*See Golden, op. cit.*, p. 806). This is different from there being a legal presumption, where, as a matter of law, the spouse contesting equal division has the burden of overcoming a presumption. Using equal distribution of community property as a starting point "creates a particular structure for the judge's deliberative process but has no formal burden of proof attached to it." *Golden*, at 243. The "starting point" approach was criticized by the New Jersey Supreme Court in *Rothman v. Rothman*, 65 N.J. 219, 320 A.2d 496, 503 n. 6 (N.J.1974), because it seemed to be importing community property concepts into a common law state. Such objections obviously do not apply here.

Using equal division of community property as a starting point is not the same as there being a fifty-fifty "rule in most cases." *Weeks*. . . . Even "starting" at equal division has its problems. "One problem is that Family Court Judges tend to use a 50/50 rule of thumb in the division of marital property, which can leave the wife with insufficient compensation for her contribution to the marriage and for her diminished earning capacity due to conditions of the marriage. In some cases women ought to be awarded more than fifty percent for a truly equitable distribution, and thus a 50/50 split is not always a fair apportionment." *Final Report of the Rhode Island Committee on Women in the Courts*, p. 40 (June 1987).

Finally, laying too much stress on equal division may tend to favor the stronger party in divorce litigation. "To the party with fewer financial resources, the promise of equitable distribution is significant. In short, equitable distribution theoretically enhances the weaker party's negotiating position, encouraging a more equitable result to the divorce process." N. Perlberger, *Pennsylvania's Equitable Distribution: Progress or Confusion?*, 60 Temple L. Rev. 293 (1987).

and the decisions of the Supreme Court." Any such contradiction real or apparent is now eliminated.

A careful reading and review of our cases reveals that the confusion and contradiction between statute and decision probably find their origin in the case of *Weeks v. Weeks*, 75 Nev. 411, 415, 345 P.2d 228, 230 (1959). The unfortunate language in *Weeks* that has led to this apparent "contradiction" is this: "*Equal distribution of the community property appears to be the rule in most cases.*" (Our emphasis). This sentence says that when courts have divided community property, it *appears* that they usually, *i.e.*, in more than half the cases, distribute equally. The stated statistical estimate is probably true. After all, community property is, by definition, property owned in common by a husband and wife, with each having an undivided one-half interest. As a rule, courts, as was done with most of the community property in this particular case, have probably used equal division of community property as a starting point. That equal division of community property happens to be done as a rule certainly does not mean that there is any kind of imperative "fifty-fifty" legal rule of community property division which must be applied except when the one party who is seeking justice and equity is able to demonstrate the need for an unequal division. A *legal rule* as distinguished from a statement of statistical regularity is a "precept attaching a definite legal consequence to a definite, detailed state of facts." An example of a *legal rule* would be: "Divorce courts must divide community property equally between the parties." *Weeks* does not state such a legal rule; and if it had, it would have been, as already pointed out, in contravention of NRS 125.150(1). To put such a burden on one who is seeking what is just and equitable according to the terms of NRS 125.150(1) is to make a major change in the substantive law, a change that the court in *Weeks* should not, could not and did not effectuate.

We conclude that Nevada law most certainly does not, as contended by the wife, *mandate* "essentially equal" division of community property. A rigid "fifty-fifty rule" may obtain in "equal distribution" jurisdictions, but does not apply in Nevada, where the division must be "just and equitable." A fifty-fifty rule as a rule of law is inherently inconsistent with our statute. Any claimed "mandate" for an essentially equal division of community property is far too mechanical to allow for the broad discretion necessary in order to permit courts to make just and equitable divisions of property in divorce cases.

There was no need for the trial judge to pause, as he did, before deciding upon an unequal division of this community asset. Equal does not necessarily mean equitable. Countless examples can be brought to mind in which equal division is not equitable. The preeminent example is that of the wife and mother in a long-term marriage who has given up career opportunities to devote herself to her family. Very frequently justice and equity will require a divorce court to adjust community property in an unequal manner in these cases.

NRS 125.150(1) requires the divorce court to consider "the party through whom the property was acquired." This does not, of course, mean that in a community property state the party who acquires an item of community property is entitled by virtue of the acquisition to any greater or lesser share of the community property. "As a rule" the husband is more frequently the party who does the acquiring of community property. This obviously, by itself, entitles him to nothing. It is legitimate, however, as indicated by the wording of the statute, to consider who acquired the property when equitable considerations are being weighed. In a case like this one, where each party is economically self-sufficient, it is permissible to consider, as a factor in deciding how property is to be equitably distributed, how the property was acquired. If the wife had acquired a similar item of community property under comparable conditions, she, certainly, could be expected to seek an equitable but more than equal share.[7] If the court looked in this case to the manner in which the property was acquired and to the fact that while unequal distribution would have little or no effect on the wife's lifestyle, a different allocation would result in a substantial diminution in the husband's income and standard of living, then the unequal division decided upon would clearly be justified.

That the unequal division of the fee acquired by the husband was "clearly erroneous," which is to say *clearly* unjust and inequitable, is a conclusion that an appellate court should not reach in a case like this. That the mere failure to state reasons should be used as an excuse for reversing the judgment of the trial court is to ignore the basic fairness of the trial court's careful treatment of this case, the failure of the wife to preserve any error of this nature and the lack of any prejudice to the wife related to any failure on the part of the trial court to give a statement of reasons. There is no error on this record. The cross-appeal is dismissed; and the judgment of the trial court is affirmed.

MOWBRAY, J., and GUNDERSON, Senior Justice, concur.

YOUNG, Chief Justice, with whom STEFFEN, Justice, agrees, dissenting:

The district court classified the annuity as community property subject to disposition. It further found that awarding Laurence eighty percent and Gail twenty percent of the annuity was "just and equitable." However, the district court gave no specific reasons for this distribution. Instead, the court simply stated that it would not be just and equitable to divide the annuity equally.

At the time of the divorce trial, the annuity had a present value of approximately $713,000. By the trial court's distribution, Laurence would receive $570,000 and Gail $142,600 of the annuity's value as of March 1986. We agree with Gail that this division constituted an abuse of the trial court's discretion given the court's failure to set forth its reasons for the selected distribution scheme.

Nevada law provides for a disposition of community property "as appears just and equitable, having regard to the respective merits of the parties and to the condition in which they will be left by the divorce, and to the party through whom the property was acquired. . . ." NRS 125.150(1)(b). Our case law for nearly 30 years has reflected that "[e]qual distribution of the community property appears to be the rule in most cases." *Weeks v. Weeks*, 75 Nev. 411, 415, 345 P.2d 228, 230 (1959). We have consistently reaffirmed the general doctrine expressed in *Weeks*. We recently overturned a district court for ignoring the general principle announced by this court — equal division of community property as the rule — when neither the court nor the record provided a justification for disregarding appellant's community property interest in respondent's home.

---

7. An example comes to mind: If, say, during a short-term marriage the wife were to reap the financial rewards from a novel which had been many years in the writing and each party were economically self-sufficient at the time of the divorce, the court, in making a just and equitable distribution of the community property, could appropriately consider an award to the wife of a larger share of this asset.

The majority opinion concludes that the general rule is "an innocuous statistical observation." We disagree. Such a deprecatory label seems hardly appropriate when, in every decision in the last three decades we have held that under normal circumstances, equitable distribution requires an equal division of community assets. My brethren, who now undermine the *Weeks* rule, participated in many of these decisions. Heretofore, there has been no criticism of the holding in *Weeks* or its progeny. Moreover, although the majority opinion censures the initial presumption of an equal division, it offers no suggestions as to what guidelines the district courts should use when distributing community assets. There must be some starting point in the calculus of the trial judge. If a fifty-fifty figure is unsatisfactory to the majority, would a sixty-forty figure be preferable — or, should the ratio be determined on an ad hoc basis, after which the court could preclude rational review by merely uttering the mystical incantation that the division is "just and equitable."

The community property system is based upon the premise that spouses contribute equally to marriage and thus deserve to share equally in the resulting gains of marriage. *Marital Property Reform*, 23 B.C. L. Rev. 761, 771 (1982). As the majority opinion correctly states, "[c]ommunity property is, by definition, property owned in common by a husband and wife, each having an undivided one-half interest."[1] Accordingly, it is difficult to see how the starting place to determine a just and equitable distribution could be anything other than a fifty-fifty split.

Furthermore, after acknowledging that it is the husband who more frequently does the acquiring of community property, the majority states that it is legitimate to consider who acquired the property when equitable considerations are being weighed. While we may agree that it is appropriate to consider who acquired the property, it is precisely because wives less frequently do the acquiring that we believe anything other than an equal division starting point may well work an inequity for women.

According to the majority opinion, the record supports the trial court's conclusion that an equal division of the annuity income was not equitable. It lists the following three factors to justify the trial court's manifestly unequal eighty-twenty division: (1) the parties were married a relatively short period of time, approximately three years; (2) Gail can maintain the same standard of living and lifestyle that she had before and during marriage despite the unequal distribution of the annuity; and (3) the monthly annuity payments constitute a substantial portion of Laurence's law practice income.

We conclude that the reasons stated by the majority opinion for the eighty-twenty division do not justify the trial court's disposition of the annuity income. The factors listed by the majority are not persuasive in supporting a deviation from the general rule. Even though the parties were married only three years, Laurence clearly earned the annuity during his marriage to Gail. A relatively brief marriage does not alter the annuity's community property status, so it should not affect the distribution of the community assets.

Likewise, the second and third factors are of questionable relevance in dividing the annuity. The record indicates that both Laurence and Gail came into their marriage with considerable separate property. The record fails to show that either party requires the income from the annuity to maintain the standard of living enjoyed before and during marriage. Consequently, the last two factors do not justify the district court's deviation from an equal disposition of the annuity income.

If the gossamer reasons expressed by the trial court are deemed adequate to validate giving Laurence $570,000 and Gail $142,600 of what was clearly community property, we will establish precedent which may engender prolonged litigation, the principal beneficiaries of which will most likely be the lawyers, not the litigants. We will turn back the clock to the days prior to no-fault divorce when inordinate amounts of time and money were consumed in trying to show which spouse was guilty of greater fault.

STEFFEN, J., concurs.

Discussion Questions

1. Would the trial court have divided the legal fee differently if the wife did not work and was a stay-at-home mom?
2. Why do you think the Nevada Legislature amended §125.150?

C. THE ROLE OF FAULT IN DIVISION OF COMMUNITY PROPERTY: THE TEXAS AND WASHINGTON APPROACHES

1. Texas

Texas' general rule on property division states: "In a decree of divorce or annulment, the court shall order a division of the estate of the parties in a manner that the court *deems just and right*, having due regard for the rights of each party and any children of the marriage." Tex. Fam. Code §7.001 (emphasis added). Trial courts have discretion in dividing the community estate at divorce. One ground is "fault" in the break-up of the marriage. Other non-fault factors include the spouses' capacities and abilities, business opportunities, education, physical and financial conditions, disparities in ages and earning capacity, size of separate estates, and nature of the property.

The issue has arisen concerning the role of "fault" in the break-up of the marriage when a spouse is granted a divorce based on a "no-fault" ground only. In Texas, a no-fault ground was added to the Texas Family Code in 1969. It states that

> "On the petition of either party to a marriage, a divorce may be decreed without regard to fault if the marriage has become insupportable because of discord or conflict of personalities that destroys the legitimate ends of the marriage relationship and prevents any reasonable expectation of reconciliation." Vernon's Tex. Code Ann. §3.01.

In *Phillips v. Phillips* (Texas 2002), the wife Nancy alleged "insupportability" as the only ground for divorce, yet stated that she was entitled to a disproportionate part of the community property based on husband James' fault causing the break-up of the marriage. The Court of Appeals reached a split decision on the issue of whether fault may be considered by the trial court when the divorce is sought based on insupportability only.

PHILLIPS v. PHILLIPS

75 S.W.3d 564 (2002)
Court of Appeals of Texas

RONALD L. WALKER, Chief Justice.

James Drew Phillips appeals the final decree of divorce rendered by the trial court. Before us, James contends that the trial court abused its discretion in its division of the community estate of the parties, and that there was legally and factually insufficient evidence to support the trial court's division of the community estate. The record indicates that in her first amended petition for divorce, Nancy alleged insupportability as the only ground for divorce. Immediately after alleging insupportability, the following sentence appears: "The conduct of the Respondent has amounted to fault causing the break-up of the marriage, and therefore Petitioner is entitled to a disproportionate part of the community property." We are faced with what appears to be an issue of first impression: May "fault causing the break-up of the marriage" be considered by the trial court in its "just and right" division of the estate of the parties, when the petitioner sought divorce *only* on grounds of insupportability?

Trial was to the court without a jury. Following rendition of the decree of divorce, James filed a request for findings of fact and conclusions of law. Among the written findings of fact by the trial court, the following appears as finding number six: "The fault of Respondent James Drew Phillips caused the breakup of the marriage." James characterizes the testimony regarding his "fault" for the breakup of the marriage as "insignificant" so as to render the trial court's disproportionate award of the community estate to Nancy an abuse of discretion.

In a divorce proceeding, a trial court "shall order a division of the estate of the parties in a manner that the court deems just and right, having due regard for the rights of each party. . . ." TEX. FAM. CODE ANN. §7.001 (Vernon 1998). It is error for a trial court to sever the issue of divorce from the issue of property division, and until the property of the parties has been disposed of, no final divorce judgment exists. A trial court has broad discretion in making the division. A division of the community estate need not be equal, and the trial court may weigh many factors in reaching its decision. Among these many factors is the "fault" of either of the parties for the breakup of the marriage, if pleaded. However, even where "fault" is properly pleaded and proved, an unequal division of the community estate may not be awarded to punish the party at "fault." As the reviewing court, we must presume that the trial court properly exercised its discretion, and we may not disturb the trial court's property division unless it clearly abused its discretion. A court abuses its discretion when it acts without reference to any guiding rules or principles, in other words, when the act is arbitrary or unreasonable. Under an abuse of discretion standard, legal and factual insufficiency are not independent, reversible grounds of error but are relevant factors in assessing whether the trial court abused its discretion.

In the instant case, it is undisputed that the trial court awarded a disproportionate amount of the community estate to Nancy. Nancy contends the trial court properly awarded her approximately 60% of the community estate with the remaining 40% of the community estate going to James. In his brief, James contends that the division was even more lopsided in favor of Nancy and points out that he was awarded a mere 23.5% while Nancy was actually awarded 76.5%. Because the trial court entered a finding that James was at "fault" for the breakup of the marriage *and* awarded Nancy a disproportionate share of the community estate, we must initially examine whether the trial court abused its discretion in finding this fact before we move on to decide whether the trial court's ultimate property division was an abuse of discretion in violation of section 7.001 of the Family Code.

In both *Murff* and *Young,* the trial court was presented with petitions alleging statutory grounds for divorce, with the petition in *Murff* containing the additional "no fault" ground of insupportability. In the instant case, Nancy alleged only insupportability as the ground for divorce. Her rather conclusory allegation of "fault" for the breakup of the marriage was tied to her request for a disproportionate award of the community estate. An examination of the testimony in the record before us with regard to the "fault" allegation indicates that Nancy had suspicions as to James' marital infidelity but no direct evidence, and rather weak circumstantial evidence, supporting such suspicions. Furthermore, the decree of divorce is completely silent as to any reason for the dissolution of the marriage, simply decreeing that the parties "are divorced, and the marriage between them is dissolved." The findings of fact and conclusions of law are equally silent as to the grounds on which the trial court found the marriage should be dissolved, with no mention of the alleged ground of insupportability. As noted above, the trial court did find that the "fault" of James "caused the breakup of the marriage." It is clear to us that the substantive facts and holdings in both *Murff* and *Young* do not contemplate a case in which one or more *statutory* "fault" grounds for divorce are not at least pleaded and proved, yet the trial court nonetheless is permitted to consider "fault" in dividing the community estate. This, in essence, is appellee's position with regard to her "fault" argument. As we appreciate the background of the promulgation of the Texas Family Code, such a position presents us with what appears to be a lack of consistency for both parties and practitioners of family law.

We find support for this observation in two cases which give us both historical and legal perspective as to marital dissolution law in Texas. We first examine *Cusack v. Cusack*, 491 S.W.2d 714 (Tex. Civ. App.-Corpus Christi 1973, writ dism'd). *Cusack* contains the following discussion of divorce law in Texas and the historical underpinnings of the Texas Family Code and the "no fault" ground:

Until 1969, except for the above noted legislative enactments, Texas legislation on grounds for divorce remained virtually unchanged for over a hundred years. The adversary nature of divorce litigation remained, and ancient ecclesiastical grounds for separation based upon fault formed the core of substantive divorce law. It became apparent in the late 1960's that the existing grounds for divorce and the defenses thereto were no longer compatible with modern beliefs.

In keeping with the idea of a realistic marital code that would meet the needs of the twentieth century society, the Legislature, in 1969, enacted the Family Code, which became effective on January 1, 1970. A non-fault ground was added to the existing grounds for divorce. This new ground is found in §[3.01] of the Code, V.T.C.A., which reads, as follows:

> "On the petition of either party to a marriage, a divorce may be decreed without regard to fault if the marriage has become insupportable because of discord or conflict of personalities that destroys the legitimate ends of the marriage relationship and prevents any reasonable expectation of reconciliation."

Id. at 716-17. More to the point of our discussion was the *Cusack* Court's substantive analysis of the consequences of the legislature's enactment of the "no fault" insupportability ground in the context of the remaining traditional "fault" grounds of cruelty, adultery, abandonment, and felony conviction. We again reproduce the Court's excellent analysis of the effect of "no fault" insupportability in rocking the foundation of over one hundred years of divorce law in Texas:

> We construe §3.01 of the Code to be a ground for a divorce which is separate and independent from any other grounds provided by the Code. That section of the Code is clear, plain and unambiguous. Since divorces are granted only on statutory grounds, and as the Legislature was fully aware of the grounds for divorce that existed in 1969, when the Family Code was passed, it must be presumed that the Legislature was not satisfied with the existing traditional grounds therefor. We conclude that it was the intent of the Legislature to make a decree of divorce *mandatory* when a party to the marriage alleges *insupportability* and the conditions of the statute are met, *regardless of who is at fault*, on the theory that society will be better served by terminating marriages which have ceased to exist in fact. The courts have no right or prerogative to add to or take from such a legislative enactment, *or to construe it in such a way as to make it meaningless*. As we view the Code, when insupportability is relied on as a ground for divorce by the complaining spouse, if that ground is established by the evidence, a divorce must be granted the complaining party, *without regard as to whether either, both or neither of the parties are responsible for or caused the insupportability. Stecklein v. Stecklein*, 466 S.W.2d 421 (Tex. Civ. App.-San Antonio 1971, n.w.h.). It is not incumbent upon the plaintiff who brings the divorce action upon the ground of insupportability to show any misconduct on the part of the defendant, but it is only incumbent upon that spouse to establish by the evidence that a state of insupportability exists regardless of whether it is anyone's or no one's fault. Otherwise, the grounds for divorce would remain the same as they were prior to the passage of the Code, and the new ground would be of negligible force. It also occurs to us that §3.01 of the Code was incorporated therein as a new, independent and additional ground of divorce to render unnecessary the revealing to public gaze of sordid events that have come to mar two otherwise happy lives.

Id. at 717 (emphasis added).

The legislative intent of adding the insupportability ground to Texas marriage dissolution law, continues to find support in more recent case law. We, too, find that it was the intent of the legislature to make a decree of divorce *mandatory* when a party to the marriage alleges insupportability and establishes the statutory elements, *regardless of who is at fault*. By reasonable and logical extension, the above finding permits us to hold that when dissolution of marriage is sought *solely* on the ground of insupportability, evidence of "fault" becomes irrelevant as an analytical construct and may not be considered by the trial court in its "just and right" division of the community estate.

As we noted above, a trial court has broad discretion in dividing the community estate in a divorce action. The trial court exercises this discretion by considering many factors. Excluding the "fault" factor, the nonexclusive list includes the following: (1) the spouses' capacities and abilities, (2) business opportunities, (3) education, (4) relative physical conditions, (5) relative financial conditions and obligations, (6) disparity of ages, (7) sizes of separate estates, (8) the nature of the property, and (9) disparity in earning capacities or of incomes. *Id.* The trial court may also consider whether one of the parties to the marriage has wasted community assets. The fact that there are ten "non-fault" factors, as well as the fact that the list is nonexclusive, should continue to give a trial court very broad discretion in making its "just and right" division notwithstanding our holding that where insupportability is the sole ground pleaded, a trial court may not factor in "fault" in its "just and right" division of the community estate in order to award a disproportionate quantity of the community estate to one spouse.

Nevertheless, even if, as in the instant case, the petitioner has failed to both plead and prove a traditional "fault" ground for dissolution of the marriage resulting in the trial court's erroneously attributing "fault in the breakup of the marriage" to the respondent, said respondent must still demonstrate that the trial court abused its discretion in making its ultimate "just and right" division of the community estate. This is so because the trial court is still permitted to consider any other "non-fault" factor(s) in awarding a disproportionate amount of the community estate to one spouse.

We also find no abuse of discretion in the trial court's treatment of the retirement and Social Security issue. As mentioned above, the trial court may consider, among other things, the relative financial condition and disparity in earning capacities or of incomes in making a disproportionate award to one spouse. In the instant case, it was undisputed that while Nancy had worked as a teacher for twenty-nine years, her income at the time of trial was almost identical to that of James, who had been working for the Jasper school district in the capacity of Technology Director for four years at the time of trial. It would have been reasonable for the trial court to infer that James had the greater earning capacity as he had roughly the same salary as Nancy while having worked in his current job for only four years as compared to Nancy's twenty-nine years. Furthermore, as noted above, for the many years James was self-employed, he failed to put any money aside for retirement while Nancy had no choice but to contribute to retirement. We see no abuse of discretion in the trial court's valuation or treatment of the retirement and Social Security items.

Under the entirety of the record evidence before us, we cannot say that the trial court clearly abused its discretion in awarding Nancy a disproportionate share of the community estate. The trial court's division of the community estate was neither arbitrary nor unreasonable. James' two appellate issues are overruled. The trial court's decree of divorce will be affirmed.

Affirmed.

DAVID B. GAULTNEY, Justice, concurring.

I concur in the affirmance of the trial court's judgment. My disagreement is with the assertion that a trial judge has no discretion — under any circumstances, not just those at issue here — to consider conduct causing the divorce in making a just and right division of the property when a divorce is granted under section 6.001 of the Family Code. *See* Tex. Fam. Code Ann. §6.001 (Vernon 1998). I write separately because I believe a trial court should have discretion to consider proven fault.

Appellee pleaded fault as a basis for unequal division of the community property. Trial courts have wide discretion to consider a variety of factors in determining what is just and right in dividing community property. For example, in affirming a 72.9% award of community property to a wife one court noted "[a] key factor was [the husband's] abusive and violent nature, which ultimately contributed to the divorce." Similarly, in a divorce granted on grounds of insupportability, another court upheld the trial court's consideration of the fact that one spouse "was at fault in rendering the marriage insupportable." *See also Vautrain v. Vautrain,* 646 S.W.2d 309, 312 (Tex. App.-Fort Worth 1983, writ dism'd) (trial court may consider evidence of fault even if divorce granted on no fault grounds); *Clay v. Clay,* 550 S.W.2d 730, 734 (Tex. Civ. App.-Houston [1st Dist.] 1977, no writ) (cruelty considered in dividing property, even when the trial court granted divorce on insupportability).

What is "just and right" in dividing the property should not depend on the ground on which the divorce is granted; the just and right division of property is separate from the dissolution issue. If one spouse's conduct causes the destruction of the financial benefits of a particular marriage, benefits on which the other spouse relied, a trial court should have discretion to consider that factor in dividing the community estate — regardless of the basis for granting the divorce.

Discussion Questions

1. Why did Chief Judge Walker conclude that evidence of fault should not be considered when a divorce is sought on a no-fault ground only?

2. Why did concurring Judge Gaultney disagree with Judge Walker?

3. How will litigants approach the issue of fault in divorce proceedings in Beaumont, Texas?

---

2. Washington

Out of all of the "equitable" division jurisdictions, Washington takes the most unusual approach in dividing community property at divorce. Washington courts must divide property *justly* and *equitably* after considering all relevant factors, including: (1) the nature and extent of the community property; (2) the nature and extent of the separate property; (3) the duration of the marriage or domestic partnership; and (4) the economic circumstances of each spouse or domestic partner at the time the division of property is to become effective, including the desirability of awarding the family home or the right to live therein for reasonable periods to a spouse or domestic partner with whom the children reside the majority of the time. Wash. Rev.

Code Ann. §26.09.080. Unlike Arizona and Idaho, where "equitable" means "substantially equal" division, equitable division in Washington requires a fair, not necessarily an equal, division. See *In re Dalthorp*, 23 Wash. App. 904, 598 P.2d 788 (1979). Notably, the Washington statute allows a court to equitably divide the parties' separate property. As recognized by the Washington Supreme Court, the ultimate question in dividing property at divorce is whether the division is fair, just, and equitable; the characterization of the property is not necessarily controlling because all property, whether community or separate, is before the court for disposition. *Worthington v. Worthington*, 73 Wash. 2d 759, 440 P.2d 478 (1968).

The Washington statute also states that the court cannot consider "misconduct" when determining property division. Marital misconduct has been defined as "immoral or physically abusive conduct within the marital relationship and does not encompass gross fiscal improvidence, the squandering of marital assets or . . . the deliberate and unnecessary incurring of tax liabilities." *Marriage of Steadman*, 63 Wash. App. 523, 528, 821 P.2d 59 (1991). For example, the Washington Supreme Court in *Marriage of Muhammad* held that the trial court impermissibly based their disproportionate award of community property on the fact that the wife obtained a protection order against her husband that caused him to lose his job as a deputy sheriff. 153 Wash. 2d 795, 108 P.3d 779 (2005). Similarly, a trial court could not consider a husband's misconduct in molesting his former stepdaughters in determining the equitable distribution of community property. *Marriage of Urbana*, 147 Wash. App. 1, 195 P.3d 959 (2008).

MARRIAGE OF URBANA

195 P.3d 959 (2008)
Court of Appeals of Washington

Van Deren, C.J.

Robert Urbana appeals the trial court's division of the marital property in his dissolution from Elizabeth, arguing that it erred when it awarded Elizabeth a disproportionate share because it prospectively awarded child support for their child, A.R.U., it considered his marital misconduct, and it required him to support his stepchildren. Holding that the trial court abused its discretion, we vacate and remand to the trial court for further proceedings consistent with this opinion.

FACTS

I.   MARRIAGE AND SEPARATION

Robert and Elizabeth were married on January 27, 1996. Elizabeth had two daughters from a prior marriage and Robert and Elizabeth had a son, A.R.U., born on May 21, 1996. Robert and Elizabeth separated in June 2005 because Robert allegedly assaulted his eldest stepdaughter. Soon thereafter, both stepdaughters alleged that Robert had sexually molested them. Robert was subsequently convicted of three counts of second degree child molestation and one count of third degree child molestation. And the trial court sentenced Robert to 100 months' incarceration. The earliest date that Robert may be released from incarceration is December 20, 2011, when A.R.U. will be 15 years old.

II.   TEMPORARY PARENTING PLAN

When the parties separated, the trial court's temporary parenting plan required Robert to pay $254.00 per month as child support. At the time of the dissolution proceeding, he had paid only $27.00 and was $4,291.00 in arrears. Under the temporary parenting plan, Robert had residential time with A.R.U., but he failed to transfer A.R.U. properly back to Elizabeth and threatened Elizabeth in A.R.U.'s presence. Later the court terminated his contact with A.R.U.

III.   THE FAMILY HOME

When the couple married, they lived in Elizabeth's home in Portland until 1997, when they moved to Battle Ground, Washington. Before they moved, Robert performed some manual labor on Elizabeth's Portland home. Elizabeth netted $22,906.00 from the Portland home. The couple used those proceeds to pay community debts and to put $15,131.00 down on the Battle Ground home. Robert signed a quitclaim deed to Elizabeth when they purchased the Battle Ground home. Later, Elizabeth opened a $15,000.00 home equity line of credit on the Battle Ground home that the couple used to pay off bills and for vehicle repairs. When Robert and Elizabeth separated, Elizabeth still owed $10,509.00 on the home equity line of credit and $107,880.00 on the original home loan.

IV.   ELIZABETH'S EMPLOYMENT HISTORY

Elizabeth is employed by the City of Portland and earns a pension. In June 2001, Elizabeth quit her job and cashed out her entire pension, netting $53,458.00 after penalties and taxes, because the Battle Ground home was in foreclosure. She used approximately $4,000.00 to resolve the foreclosure. The family also took a vacation to Disneyland and, when Elizabeth's pension money ran out, she returned to work for the City of Portland where she has remained continuously employed. Shortly after the parties separated, Elizabeth's pension plan was valued at $5,453.00.

V.   ROBERT'S EMPLOYMENT HISTORY

During the marriage, Robert worked sporadically as a painter. Prior to the couple's marriage, when Robert was in his early twenties, he had a driving accident and his fifth and sixth neck vertebrae were compressed. As a result, he has degenerative arthritis. During the marriage, Robert had surgery for a double hernia and, after the surgery, his income dropped dramatically.

At the time of the dissolution proceeding, Robert was working while incarcerated and making $0.34 per hour for a maximum seven-hour day. Statutorily, the

Department of Corrections will allocate 15 percent of Robert's pay toward his child support obligation. RCW 72.09.111.8

VI.   OTHER FINANCIAL OBLIGATIONS

When the couple separated, they owed $500.00 on a credit card and $500.00 for vehicle repairs, $400.00 of which Elizabeth had paid off by the time of trial. Elizabeth also testified that Robert had written five checks that were returned for insufficient funds and that they owed $800.00 for mobile phone charges.

VII.   TRIAL COURT'S DECISION

The trial court ruled that the Battle Ground home was 87.9 percent community property and 12.1 percent Elizabeth's separate property. It found the fair market value of the home was $220,000.00. It subtracted the underlying mortgage of $108,000.00, leaving a net home value of $112,000.00. After applying the 87.9 percentage, it concluded that the value of the community portion was $98,448.00.

In reaching its decision on the property division, the trial court noted that Robert is currently incarcerated and had a record of sporadic employment during the marriage; whereas Elizabeth was steadily employed. It also stated that, while Elizabeth receives some child support for her daughters from her prior relationship, she will receive no support from Robert for A.R.U. The trial court also stated that it considered that, at or after the time of separation, Elizabeth discovered that Robert had been sexually abusing both of her daughters. The trial court concluded, "no child support order can be entered because [Robert] is unemployed. However, that factor does not have to be overlooked in the disposition of property in a divorce case such as this." Report of Proceedings (RP) at 114. It then awarded Elizabeth the Battle Ground home because she will be supporting herself and three children. In addition, it concluded that a fair and equitable division of the property, based on the parties' circumstances, was 20 percent of the community property to Robert and 80 percent to Elizabeth.

Robert appeals.[2]

ANALYSIS

Robert argues that the trial court erred in awarding a disproportionate share of the community property to Elizabeth because it must have included prospective child support for A.R.U. and it failed to base any such calculation on the statutory child support calculation guidelines. He also argues that the trial court may not divide property based on marital misconduct, nor can it consider support for former stepchildren when considering future economic circumstances of the parties.

---

2. Elizabeth waived her right to file a respondent's brief.

I.   STANDARD OF REVIEW—DISPOSITION OF PROPERTY

"A property division made during the dissolution of a marriage will be reversed on appeal only if there is a manifest abuse of discretion." A trial court abuses its discretion if its decision is manifestly unreasonable, based on untenable grounds, or based on untenable reasons. While the trial court "is not required to divide community property equally," if its dissolution "decree results in a patent disparity in the parties' economic circumstances," we will reverse its decision because the trial court will have committed a manifest abuse of discretion.

II.   DIVIDING PROPERTY AT DISSOLUTION

Robert notes that the trial court's findings and conclusions rely on case law that cites the former dissolution statute. When making the final just and equitable disposition of the marital property, the former dissolution statute, RCW 26.08.110 (1949), required the trial court to consider: (1) "the respective merits of the parties," (2) "the condition in which they will be left by such divorce or annulment," (3) "the party through whom the property was acquired," and (4) "the burdens imposed upon it for the benefit of the children." In 1973, the legislature enacted the new Dissolution of Marriage Act (Act), chapter 26.09 RCW.

RCW 26.09.080 replaced former RCW 26.08.110 and lists a nonexclusive set of factors that the trial court must consider when distributing the marital property. The underlying purpose of that act was "'to replace the concept of fault and substitute marriage failure or irretrievable breakdown as the basis for a decree dissolving a marriage.'"

When dividing the marital property, the trial court must consider "all relevant factors." Former RCW 26.09.080 (1989). This includes, but is not limited to:

(1) The nature and extent of the community property;
(2) The nature and extent of the separate property;
(3) The duration of the marriage; and
(4) The economic circumstances of each spouse at the time the division of property is to become effective, including the desirability of awarding the family home or the right to live therein for reasonable periods to a spouse with whom the children reside the majority of the time.

Former RCW 26.09.080.

These statutory factors are not limiting and the trial court may consider other factors such as "the health and ages of the parties, their prospects for future earnings, their education and employment histories, their necessities and financial abilities, their foreseeable future acquisitions and obligations, and whether the property to be divided should be attributed to the inheritance or efforts of one or both of the spouses."

"A fair and equitable division by a trial court 'does not require mathematical precision, but rather fairness, based upon a consideration of all the circumstances of the marriage, both past and present, and an evaluation of the future needs of the parties.'" And although the trial court may not give a singular factor greater weight than another, "the economic circumstances of each spouse upon dissolution [are] of 'paramount concern.'" In a dissolution action, the trial court must make a "just and equitable" distribution of the marital property "without regard to marital misconduct."

Contrary to Robert's assertion, under the new Act, the trial court may award a disproportionate share of the community property in lieu of future child support payments. But here, the trial court abused its discretion by not stating the basis of its property division, by not stating whether it intended to substitute property for child support, and by not quantifying the amount of child support satisfied by the disproportionate property division in Elizabeth's favor. Here, the trial court made no effort to quantify Robert's potential child support obligations during A.R.U.'s minority. Furthermore, the trial court did not quantify the community interest Robert gave up and, therefore, no credit can be calculated. Instead, the trial court completely extinguished Robert's child support obligation, which we do not permit.

Without findings of fact and conclusions of law allowing us to review the basis of its property division or quantify the value of property used to satisfy Robert's child support obligation, or to discern the trial court's intent with regard to child support, "the decree [has resulted] in a patent disparity in the parties' economic circumstances," and we must vacate the trial court's decree because it committed a manifest abuse of discretion.

We briefly address the following two issues because they are likely to arise on remand.

IV.   MISCONDUCT

Robert argues, "it is patently obvious that the court used the disproportionate award to punish the sex-offender husband." This argument is framed as one of misconduct, but is better articulated as an argument that the trial court abused its discretion by considering marital misconduct in dividing the community property.

"[M]arital misconduct which a court may not consider under RCW 26.09.080 refers to immoral or physically abusive conduct within the marital relationship and does not encompass gross fiscal improvidence, the squandering of marital assets or, . . . the deliberate and unnecessary incurring of tax liabilities." Certainly, Robert's abusive physical and sexual conduct toward his two stepdaughters amounts to marital misconduct.

The Washington State Supreme Court recently considered a trial court's disproportionate award of community property in light of the trial court's comments about the wife obtaining a protection order against her husband that caused him to lose his job as a deputy sheriff. *Muhammad*, 153 Wash. 2d at 804-05, 108 P.3d 779. The trial court noted that the wife "'sought to punish'" the husband and that she "had to 'recognize the consequences'" that were 'taken into consideration in terms of trying to make the distribution somewhat equitable.'" The Court held that a number of aspects of the property division illustrated that the trial court went beyond looking at the parties' economic circumstances and impermissibly assigned fault to the wife for seeking an order of protection.

Here, the trial court framed its findings in terms of the post dissolution economic circumstances of the parties, but commented on Robert's marital misconduct. For example, it found significant that Elizabeth "discovered that [Robert] had assaulted one of her daughters from a prior marriage and then later learned that [Robert] had molested both of her daughters from a prior marriage. [Robert] was sentenced for three counts of Child Molestation in the 2nd Degree and one count of Child Molestation in the 3rd Degree. [Robert] is presently incarcerated and his sentence is for 100 months."

This finding, considered in conjunction with an unexplained 20/80 percent split of community property, suggests that the trial court considered Robert's marital misconduct in dividing the property.

On remand, when distributing the marital assets, the trial court may consider the economic circumstances of the parties and the future earning potential of both Robert and Elizabeth. Furthermore, when calculating child support obligations, nothing requires the trial court to determine income solely on earned income or ignore a parent's other financial resources, such as dissolution awards, when one parent is incarcerated. But on remand, we caution the trial court only to consider the parents' economic circumstances and not to consider Robert's marital misconduct when distributing the marital assets.

We vacate and remand to the trial court for further proceedings consistent with this opinion.

We concur: BRIDGEWATER, and QUINN-BRINTNALL, JJ.

Discussion Questions

1. According to the Court of Appeals, what were the flaws in the trial court's division of community property?

2. On remand, could the trial court support its 80/20 division of community property by referring to the factors for "fair and equitable division"?

PROBLEM 14.1

Mark and Nancy have recently filed for divorce after many years of marriage. Mark is a doctor and supported the family and community while Nancy stayed at home and raised their three children. Nancy did not go to college and has not worked since she married Mark. During their marriage, they accumulated community property worth $500,000 which was all purchased using Mark's earnings he received during the marriage. Additionally, their home was purchased using Mark's earnings. How would each community property state divide the community property and home?

PROBLEM 14.2

Assume the same facts as above, but that the reason Mark and Nancy are divorcing is because of Mark's alcohol abuse and abuse toward Nancy. How will this change the division of their community property?

Table 14-1
Property Division at Divorce in Community Property States

State	Rule	Case/Statute
Arizona	Divides community property "equitably," which means "a substantially equal" division unless sound reason exists for another result. Courts may consider separate property contributions to acquisition of the property. Marital misconduct is a prohibited factor.	Arizona Revised Statutes §25-318(A)(2008). *Hatch v. Hatch*, 113 Ariz. 130, 547 P.2d 1044 (1976), division must be "substantially equal." *Marriage of Berger*, 680 P.2d 1217 (Ariz. App. 1983), contribution of separate funds supported unequal division.
California	Mandatory 50/50 division of community property.	Family Code §2550 (2009), "the court shall . . . divide the community estate of the parties equally."
Idaho	Divides community property as the court deems just which means "a substantially equal division, unless there are compelling reasons otherwise." Many factors can be considered as compelling reasons.	Idaho Code §32-712 (2010), many factors bearing on division: duration of the marriage, antenuptial agreement, age, health, occupation, income, liabilities, needs of each spouse, potential earning capability, retirement benefits.
Louisiana	Mandatory 50/50 division of community property.	Louisiana Civil Code §2336 (2002).
Nevada	Equal disposition of community property, except the court may make an unequal disposition as it deems just if there is a compelling reason to do so and explains the reasons in writing.	Nevada Revised Statutes §125.150(1)(b) (2007), *McNabney v. McNabney*, 782 P.2d 1291 (1989).
New Mexico	Mandatory 50/50 division of community property.	*Bustos v. Bustos*, 100 N.M. 556, 673 P.3d 1289 (1983).
Texas	Divides marital property as the court deems "just and right, having due regard for the rights of each party and any children of the marriage."	Vernon's Texas Statutes, Family Code §7.001 (1997), *Murff v. Murff*, 615 S.W.2d 696 (Tex. 1981), *Phillips v. Phillips*, 75 S.W.3d 564 (Ct. App. 2002).
Washington	Divides community and/or separate property as "shall appear just and equitable after considering all relevant factors, without regard to misconduct." Factors include nature and	West's Revised Code of Washington, Disposition of property and liabilities, §26.09.080 (2008), *Marriage of Muhammad*, 153 Wash. 2d 795, 108 P.2 779 (2005), *Marriage of*

State	Rule	Case/Statute
	extent of community/separate property, duration of the marriage and economic circumstances of each spouse, including awarding the family home to a spouse with whom the children reside.	*Urbana*, 195 P.3d 959 (Wash. App. 2008).
Wisconsin	Courts must determine which property is divisible or non-divisible property which includes inherited and gifted property. At divorce, property will be equitably distributed based on several factors and may include non-divisible property in case of hardship on the other party or the children of the marriage.	Wis. Stat. §767.61, *Grumbeck v. Grumbeck*, 296 Wis. 2d 611, 723 N.W.2d 778 (Ct. App. 2005) (absent special circumstances, marital estate should be evenly divided), *Bonnell v. Bonnell*, 117 Wis. 2d 241, 344 N.W.2d 123 (1984) (award of more to former wife was justified based on wife's health).

Chapter 15
Division of Community Property at Death

Let us return to our hypothetical couple George and Martha. They are now a very elderly couple and they have been advised that they should do some estate planning. When they consult a friend who is an elder law specialist, she explains some of the basics regarding their community property. Community property is owned by both George and Martha, so each is the owner of one-half of the community property. In all community property states, each spouse is entitled to dispose of his/her half of the community property by will. If George has a daughter from a prior marriage, he can devise his one-half of the community property to her through his will. If Martha has a son from a prior marriage, she can devise one-half of the community property to him through her will. If George dies first, one-half of the community property will go to Martha because she is the surviving spouse and one-half will go to George's daughter through his will. If Martha dies first, one-half of the community property will go to George because he is the surviving spouse and one-half will go to Martha's son through her will. If neither George nor Martha have a will (which is called dying intestate), the surviving spouse receives his/her one-half of the community property as the surviving spouse and, in most community property states, the surviving spouse receives the decedent's one-half.[1] It is imperative for George and Martha to indicate how they wish to dispose of their community property in case of death. Please note that it is possible for George and Martha to specify in their will that their interest in the community property go to the surviving spouse, if that is what they intend.

Let us say that George and Martha put off making wills and that George dies suddenly without a will. When Martha is going through his papers, she finds a life insurance policy for $100,000 and the beneficiary is George's daughter Diana. Also she finds that George has a bank account of $50,000 that was "in trust for my daughter Diana." Martha did not know about the insurance policy or the bank account. Let us also assume that George had no separate property. Thus we can assume that the premiums for the life insurance policy were paid from community property funds and that the funds in the bank account came from community

---

1. In Arizona, Louisiana, and Texas, the surviving spouse's right to receive the entire decedent's one-half of the community property depends on whether there is "issue" (loosely defined as children) of the decedent. See Ariz. Rev. Stat. §§14-3101, 14-2102, La. Civ. Code §§888-890, 1493-1496, 1621, Tex. Prob. Code 45.

property. We can already see a dispute brewing over the life insurance proceeds and the bank account. It is clear that George intended for Diana to receive $150,000 upon his death. It is also clear that Martha, as the surviving spouse, has a right to one-half of the community property upon George's death. The issue then is George's power over the other one-half of the community property. This may depend on the entire amount of community property in George's estate. In some community property states, like Arizona, Nevada, and Texas, the courts look at the total amount of the community property. This is called the aggregate theory of division of community property at death. In our case, if the community property totals $300,000, Martha will receive her one-half of $150,000 as surviving spouse. The other $150,000, which would have been George's right to devise through a will, will go to Diana as beneficiary of the life insurance and bank account. Under the aggregate theory, the surviving spouse's one-half of the community property is protected, but the decedent's intentions are carried out so long as that does not interfere with surviving spouse's rights. This theory is based on balancing the surviving spouse's interest in receiving one-half of the total community estate with the right of the decedent to give away his one-half share of the community property to someone other than his spouse.

In the other community property states, the item theory of division of community property at death is followed. That means that a surviving spouse has a one-half interest in each item of community property. Therefore, Martha has a right to one-half of the life insurance policy, $50,000, and one-half of the bank account, $25,000. Under this theory, George had no right to give away Martha's one-half of the community property without her written consent. Even though George had the right to give away his one-half through a will or a designation of a beneficiary of the life insurance or bank account, that right did not extend to Martha's one-half.

This chapter will include cases that illustrate the aggregate and item theory of division of community property at death, with an emphasis on life insurance proceeds. It will also deal with the effect of a divorce decree when a former spouse remains as the beneficiary of a life insurance policy. The chapter also raises the issues in the most unusual situation where a spouse who murdered his wife claims the proceeds of her life insurance policy.

A. THE AGGREGATE AND ITEM THEORIES OF DIVISION OF COMMUNITY PROPERTY AT DEATH

1. Aggregate Theory Applied

In *Estate of Kirkes*, 229 Ariz. 212, 273 P.3d 664 (2012), the Arizona Court of Appeals discusses the aggregate and item theories of division of community property at death. At issue was an individual retirement account (IRA) where the decedent had changed the beneficiary. Originally he had designated his wife as beneficiary but later he changed that to both his wife and son from a prior marriage, 83 percent to the son and 17 percent to his wife. In *Byrd v. Lanahan*, 205 Nev. 707, 783 P.2d 426 (1989), the Nevada Supreme Court applied the aggregate theory of division of community property at death. At issue was a $50,000 savings account that the decedent had opened in his name and later changed to a trust account for his daughter from a previous marriage. The trial court had awarded the proceeds of the account to the surviving spouse. The daughter appealed.

ESTATE OF KIRKES

229 Ariz. 212, 273 P.3d 664 (2012)
Arizona Court of Appeals

Howard, Chief Judge.

Appellant Joshua Kirkes appeals from the trial court's grant of partial summary judgment in favor of Gail Kirkes in the probate proceedings for the estate of Fred Kirkes. Joshua argues the trial court erred by determining that Gail was entitled to half of an individual retirement account (IRA) as community property and contends that instead she was entitled to fifty percent of the entire community property estate, not half of a particular item. For the following reasons we reverse the grant of partial summary judgment and remand for further proceedings.

FACTUAL AND PROCEDURAL BACKGROUND

The underlying facts are undisputed. Gail and Fred were married at the time of Fred's death. Joshua is Fred's son from a previous marriage. Fred named Gail as the sole beneficiary of his will. During the marriage, Fred created an IRA in his name and named Gail as the sole beneficiary. He then modified the IRA beneficiary designation, naming Joshua as beneficiary of eighty-three percent of the IRA and Gail as beneficiary of seventeen percent. Fred died. Both parties agree that all assets contained in the IRA are community property.

Gail filed a petition for declaration of rights, requesting the trial court invalidate the IRA beneficiary designation, which Joshua opposed. The parties filed cross-motions for partial summary judgment on the issue. The court granted Gail's motion and denied Joshua's, declaring Gail entitled to half of the IRA. The court issued a final judgment on the issue pursuant to Rule 54(b), Ariz. R. Civ. P., and this appeal followed.

DISCUSSION

* * *

Joshua argues the trial court erred by invalidating Fred's naming him as beneficiary of more than fifty percent of the IRA based on Gail's community property interest. He claims the court followed the item theory of division of community property at death, rather than the aggregate theory, asserting that Arizona has followed the aggregate theory. He asserts that under the aggregate theory the trial court should have determined whether Gail had received other property that compensated her for the diminished portion of the IRA.

Under the item theory of community property each spouse has "a one-half interest in each item of community property," whereas under the aggregate theory each spouse has "a one-half interest in the total community property when viewed in the aggregate." Charles E. Zalesky, *The Modified Item Theory: An Alternative Method of Dividing Community Property upon the Death of a Spouse*, 28 Idaho L. Rev. 1047, 1047-48 (1992). One drawback to the item theory is that it prevents the decedent from being able to convey completely a particular item of community property to a non-spouse and forces joint ownership of that item. *Id.* at 1051. This case, however, does not directly involve how a community property estate must be divided. Rather, it involves one spouse's attempted transfer of a community property IRA interest to a non-spouse.

A beneficiary designation in an IRA is an allowed non-probate, non-testamentary transfer. A.R.S. §14-6101(A). However, a spouse's right to transfer community property is subject to a fiduciary duty to the other spouse's interest in the property. *Mezey v. Fioramonti*, 204 Ariz. 599, ¶ 38, 65 P.3d 980, 989 (App. 2003), *overruled on other grounds by Bilke v. State*, 206 Ariz. 462, ¶ 28, 80 P.3d 269, 275 (2003). "[A]bsent intervening equities, a gift of substantial community property to a third person without the other spouse's consent may be revoked and set aside for the benefit of the aggrieved spouse." *Id., quoting Roselli v. Rio Cmtys. Serv. Station, Inc.,* 109 N.M. 509, 787 P.2d 428, 433 (1990).

We have not been directed to any Arizona statute or case that uses the terms "aggregate" or "item" theory in distributing a decedent's assets. Joshua, however, argues the legislature has "directed" that community interests in all assets be divided in the aggregate by adopting A.R.S. §14-3916. That statute states:

> In making a division or distribution of community property held in the decedent's estate, the personal representative may consider community property held outside the estate so that the division of community property held in the estate and outside the estate is based on equal value but is not necessarily proportionate.

§14-3916. And under A.R.S. §14-3101(A), "the surviving spouse's share of the community property is subject to [probate] administration." We agree with the trial court that §14-3916 does not control this case directly because we are not dealing with the distribution of estate assets. We further agree with the trial court that the statute's provision that the personal representative may consider whether the division of community property inside and outside the estate "is based on equal value but is not necessarily proportionate" is "enigmatic." But the statute clearly allows the personal representative to consider non-probate transfers of community property in distributing estate community property, thereby indicating the legislature considered the aggregate theory an acceptable method of distributing estate assets. But, by using the permissive "may," the legislature did not mandate that this theory be applied, even in distributing estate assets. Therefore, the statute, by itself, does not indicate that the court erred in using the item theory.

Although Arizona courts have not directly adopted either theory, they have dealt with the attempted alienation of more than a spouse's share of community property in the life-insurance context. In *Gristy v. Hudgens*, 23 Ariz. 339, 341, 348, 203 P. 569, 570, 572 (1922), *abrogated by Day v. Clark*, 36 Ariz. 353, 357, 285 P. 682, 683 (1930), the Arizona Supreme Court considered a case in which life-insurance premiums potentially had been paid with community-property funds, but a third party had been designated as the beneficiary. It held that even if the premiums had been paid with community property, any insurance benefits paid to a non-spouse did not defraud the wife, in part because there existed "no showing that the wife had not received even more than her share of the community property." *Gristy*, 23 Ariz. at 348, 203 P. at 572. Similarly, in *Gaethje v. Gaethje*, 7 Ariz. App. 544, 546, 441 P.2d 579, 581 (1968), this court was asked to determine the validity of a life-insurance policy beneficiary designation which named a son as the beneficiary instead of the deceased's spouse. We relied on *Gristy* in holding that when a deceased spouse has made a testamentary or non-testamentary provision for the surviving spouse, under which the surviving spouse receives at least half of the community property, "then there has been no 'fraud' upon [the surviving spouse's] rights and the designation of beneficiary should stand effective." *Gaethje*, 7 Ariz. App. at 547, 549, 441 P.2d at 582, 584. However, if the surviving spouse did not receive half the community property, then "there would be a constructive fraud upon [the surviving spouse's] rights and the designation would be ineffective to the extent of such constructive fraud." *Id.* at 549, 441 P.2d at 584.

In considering the benefits from a life-insurance policy, the Arizona Supreme Court recognized the method of allocating community property in *Gaethje* as "[o]ne approach approved in Arizona," but did not identify any other approved methods. *In re Estate of Alarcon*, 149 Ariz. 336, 339, 718 P.2d 989, 992 (1986). And this court repeatedly has cited the approach in *Gaethje* in subsequent cases concerning life-insurance proceeds. *See, e.g., In re Estate of Agans*, 196 Ariz. 367, ¶ 4, 998 P.2d 449, 450 (App. 1999); *Guerrero v. Guerrero*, 18 Ariz. App. 400, 402, 502 P.2d 1077, 1079 (1972), *abrogated by* §14-6101; *Carpenter v. Carpenter*, 150 Ariz. 130, 135, 722 P.2d 298, 303 (App. 1985), *vacated in part on other grounds by Carpenter v. Carpenter*, 150 Ariz. 62, 63, 722 P.2d 230, 231 (1986).

Gail, however, suggests the Arizona Supreme Court earlier implicitly had applied the item theory in *La Tourette v. La Tourette*, 15 Ariz. 200, 137 P. 426 (1914), *abrogated by Mortensen v. Knight*, 81 Ariz. 325, 331, 305 P.2d 463, 467 (1956). However, *La Tourette* did not address which theory to apply but instead set forth the rule that a wife had an interest in community property before her husband's death, although she acquired management and control of her share only at his death. 15 Ariz. at 207-08, 137 P. at 428-29. Thus, *La Tourette* is inapposite.

Gail also argues that in *In re Monaghan's Estate*, 65 Ariz. 9, 22-23, 173 P.2d 107, 115 (1946), our supreme court applied the item theory when it held that only the decedent's share of real property could be sold to pay probate expenses. However, the court considered only the issue of whether the wife's portion of community property could be sold to satisfy probate expenses; it did not consider or adopt either theory of community property disposition. *In re Monaghan's Estate*, 65 Ariz. at 22-23, 173 P.2d at 115. Gail further relies on *Propstra v. United States*, 680 F.2d 1248, 1250-51, 1251 n.3 (9th Cir. 1982), but that case dealt with valuation of an estate for federal tax purposes and not whether Arizona followed the "item" or "aggregate" method for determining community property interests in the administration of an estate. Furthermore, "federal decisions on state law issues do not bind us." *Dube v. Likins*, 216 Ariz. 406, ¶ 37, 167 P.3d 93, 104 (App. 2007). We conclude Arizona cases have adopted and relied on *Gaethje*'s approach in the context of life-insurance proceeds and have not clearly adopted or rejected an item theory.

Gail next contends that prior Arizona cases concerning life-insurance beneficiary designations should not control, because retirement accounts are of a "special nature." She argues retirement accounts are intended to provide financial security for a surviving spouse. She further suggests that we adopt a "modified item theory" in which most community property is distributed on an item basis, but fungible property is distributed on an aggregate basis. *See* Zalesky, *supra*, at 1067-70. Gail argues that the item theory should apply here again because of the special nature of retirement accounts.

However, both life-insurance policies and retirement-account beneficiary designations are methods of allocating assets for the future, and both may be used to provide for a surviving spouse. Moreover, both proceeds from life-insurance policies and IRA assets are fungible, in that they are money or may be sold easily. Even under a modified item theory, which we do not adopt here, fungible assets are divided in the aggregate. *Id.* Although Gail analogizes the IRA to other retirement plans governed by federal law, she concedes those statutes do not apply here. Therefore, Gail has failed to differentiate an IRA beneficiary designation from a life-insurance beneficiary designation or demonstrate that the item theory was properly employed here. Rather, applying the same rule that applies to a life-insurance beneficiary designation to an IRA beneficiary designation achieves consistency in related legal issues.

Gail further relies on a case from Louisiana in which the court differentiated between profit-sharing plans and life-insurance policies. *T.L. James & Co. v. Montgomery*, 332 So. 2d 834, 844-45 (La. 1975). But, in that case, the court acknowledged that the Louisiana Constitution and civil code always had treated life insurance distinctly and, therefore, the court did not apply general statutes and principles of law to life insurance. *Id.* at 845. Gail provides no authority for the proposition that Arizona historically has treated life-insurance policies in a distinct way. Instead, §14-6101(A) includes both individual retirement plans and insurance policies in its list of non-probate transfers which are non-testamentary. Thus, we would not find this Louisiana precedent to be persuasive in any event. *Ramsey v. Yavapai Family Advocacy Ctr.*, 225 Ariz. 132, ¶ 32, 235 P.3d 285, 294 (App. 2010).

One purpose of the probate code and related case law is to effect a decedent's intent in distributing property. A.R.S. §14-1102(B)(2); *In re Estate of Shumway*, 198 Ariz. 323, ¶ 7, 9 P.3d 1062, 1065 (2000). As the trial court found, Fred intended that Joshua receive eighty-three percent of the IRA and Gail receive seventeen percent. Employing the item theory here would defeat Fred's intent. Furthermore, Gail has failed to differentiate an IRA beneficiary designation from a life-insurance beneficiary designation; both direct the transfer of money to a recipient. Thus, we conclude the purpose expressed in §14-1102(B)(2), the reasoning in *Gaethje*, and the legislative intent expressed in §14-3916 control the IRA beneficiary designation here. We reverse the trial court's grant of summary judgment in favor of Gail.

Joshua argues the trial court erred by not granting his cross-motion for summary judgment, contending Gail did not present evidence the beneficiary designation resulted in a fraud on her interest. But under the IRA beneficiary designation, Joshua would receive more than fifty percent of a community asset. And, the law concerning this issue was unclear. The more equitable result is to allow both parties to marshal whatever evidence is relevant to the legal issue as clarified above.

CONCLUSION

For the foregoing reasons, we reverse the trial court's grant of summary judgment in favor of Gail and remand for proceedings consistent with this decision.

Concurring: PETER J. ECKERSTROM, Presiding Judge, and J. WILLIAM BRAMMER, JR., Judge.

Discussion Questions

1. How are IRA accounts and life insurance policies similar? Different?
2. Why did the Court of Appeals apply the aggregate theory to the IRA? What will happen on remand?

BYRD v. LANAHAN

105 Nev. 707, 783 P.2d 426
Supreme Court of Nevada

YOUNG, Chief Justice.

This appeal involves the disposition of the proceeds of a savings account established by Thomas J. Lanahan, deceased. Thomas executed a will in 1966 that devised and bequeathed all property owned by him, both real and personal, to his wife, Irene Lanahan, respondent and executrix of Thomas' estate. In November 1983, Thomas opened a $50,000 savings account at Nevada Savings and Loan Association (NSLA) in his name only. In November 1984, this account became a one-year certificate that was renewed for one year in November 1985. In September 1986, Thomas executed a document printed on an NSLA bank card, entitled "Change of Ownership." The card instructed the bank to change the ownership of his account to Thomas J. Lanahan as trustee for the appellant, Susan T. Lanahan Byrd, Thomas' daughter from a previous marriage. The original signature card was also changed to reflect the change in ownership. Thomas received all interest payments from this account until his death in January 1987. Neither Irene nor Susan had knowledge of the account or of the executed change of ownership card.

After Thomas died in January 1987, the bank refused to pay Irene the proceeds of the account because the account named Susan as beneficiary. The bank filed an interpleader action and a bench trial followed. At trial, Irene contended that Susan had no interest in or ownership of the savings account by virtue of the change of ownership card. Susan contended that in executing the change of ownership card, Thomas had created a valid Totten trust which he had not revoked before his death. The district court awarded the proceeds of the account to Irene as executrix, and Susan appealed.

Appellant contends that the district court erred in granting the proceeds of the account to Irene. Appellant asserts that she is the beneficiary of a valid Totten trust, recognized by caselaw and statute in Nevada, and that she is entitled to the entire proceeds of the savings account trust. We agree.

* * *

Additionally, the court may have reached its conclusion because it found that Totten trusts were not judicially recognized in Nevada. As articulated by the New York Court of Appeals, a Totten trust is a trust created by the

> deposit by one person of his own money in his own name as trustee for another. . . . It is a tentative trust, merely, *revocable at will,* until the depositor dies or completes the gift in his lifetime by some unequivocal act or declaration, such as delivery of the passbook or notice to the beneficiary. *In case the depositor dies before the beneficiary without revocation,* or some decisive act or declaration of disaffirmance, *the presumption arises that an absolute trust was created* as to the balance on hand at the death of the depositor.

In re Totten, 179 N.Y. 112, 71 N.E. 748, 752 (1904) (emphasis added).

* * *

Because the district court erred in impliedly concluding that Totten trusts are not valid in Nevada, we must determine whether the savings account in question was a valid Totten trust. To constitute a Totten trust, as with any trust, there must be an explicit declaration of trust or circumstances which show beyond doubt that a trust was intended to be created. *In re Madsen's Estate,* 48 Wash. 2d 675, 296 P.2d 518, 519 (1956).

In the present case, the account was designated Thomas Lanahan as trustee for Susan Lanahan Byrd and the signature card provided that the account was revocable by Thomas at any time and that the funds remaining after his death belonged to Susan as beneficiary. These provisions on the signature card clearly establish that a tentative trust was intended. Moreover, there is strong evidence of trust intent where, as here, the beneficiary is the daughter of the decedent by his former marriage and no provision was made for her in his will. Furthermore, there was no evidence of any objective contrary to establishing a trust. Finally, Irene testified at trial that Thomas had never established a similar trust account, indicating that he did not unintentionally create one for Susan.

The written declaration of trust on the bank signature card specifically identifies Thomas' intention to create a revocable trust for Susan. We hold that the signature card, together with the surrounding circumstances, is sufficient evidence to show Thomas' intention to create a trust in favor of Susan. Accordingly, we hold that the savings account was a valid Totten trust.

Nonetheless, respondent contends that the savings account signature card was invalid because NRS 123.230(2) prohibited Thomas from making a gift of community property without her consent.[2] However, under NRS 123.250(1)(b), each spouse has the power of testamentary disposition over his or her interest in the community property, with or without the other spouse's consent.[3] Respondent contends that Thomas' power of testamentary disposition was executed in her favor. Furthermore, because she maintains that the savings account signature card was not a valid testamentary instrument, respondent argues that it was not effective at disposing of Thomas' share of the community property. However, although a Totten trust is revocable during the decedent's life, it becomes effective as a testamentary disposition of the assets it contains at the donor's death.

We construe NRS 123.250(1)(b) to mean that each spouse may dispose of one-half of the total of all community property. The district court found that the total value of the community property at the time of Thomas' death was approximately $200,000. Thus, because the $50,000 in the trust account is less than half of $200,000, we hold that appellant is entitled to the entire proceeds of the valid Totten trust account.

Accordingly, we reverse the district court's order and grant the entire proceeds from the savings account to appellant.

STEFFEN, SPRINGER, MOWBRAY and ROSE, JJ., concur.

Discussion Questions

1. Why was the bank account created by the decedent a valid Totten Trust?
2. Why will the daughter Susan receive all the proceeds of the bank account?

---

2. Item Theory Applied

ESTATE OF MIRAMONTES-NAJERA

118 Cal. App. 4th 750, 13 Cal. Rptr. 3d 240 (2004)
California Court of Appeal

McCONNELL, P.J.

In *Estate of Wilson* (1986) 183 Cal. App. 3d 67, 68-69, 227 Cal. Rptr. 794, the court held that a surviving spouse who did not consent to transfers of community property

---

2. NRS 123.230(2) provides that "[n]either spouse may make a gift of community property without the express or implied consent of the other."
3. NRS 123.250(1) provides, in pertinent part:

　1. Upon the death of either husband or wife:
　(a) An undivided one-half interest in the community property is the property of the surviving spouse and his or her sole separate property.
　(b) The remaining interest is subject to the testamentary disposition of the decedent. . . .

into bank accounts for third persons may enforce his or her community property interest on an asset-by-asset basis, even though he or she is already receiving more than one-half of the total community property. In this case, we hold as a matter of first impression that in enacting Probate Code section 5021, the Legislature intended to codify, rather than nullify, the *Estate of Wilson* rule. Accordingly, we reverse orders denying Evangelina B. Miramontes' (Evangelina) petition under section 5021 to set aside the transfers of her community property interest in certain pay-on-death accounts, and remand the matter to the trial court with directions.

FACTUAL AND PROCEDURAL BACKGROUND

Evangelina and Raul Miramontes-Najera (Raul) married in Mexico in 1956. According to Evangelina's petition, they "entered into an express community property marriage." They were married until Raul's death in October 2000 in San Diego, California.

Beginning in June 1998, without Evangelina's consent, Raul transferred a total of $802,996 in community property funds into nine bank accounts payable on death to persons other than Evangelina. He transferred $100,000 into each of two money market accounts payable to, respectively, the minor children of Silvia Lizarraga Preciado (Silvia), Silvia Miramontes Lizarraga (young Silvia) and Adolfo Miramontes Lizarraga (Adolfo), and transferred $3,000 into a deposit certificate payable to young Silvia. In addition, Raul created six other accounts payable to third persons not involved in this appeal, consisting of $100,000 deposited in a money market account and $499,996 placed in five certificate of deposit accounts.

Raul had arranged to transfer all the community property by multiple nontestamentary means. Evangelina received community property having a total value of approximately $1.3 million, more than one-half of the value of the community property estate.

Evangelina petitioned the court under section 5021 for an order setting aside the transfer of one-half of the funds in each of the pay-on-death accounts. Citing *Estate of Wilson, supra*, 183 Cal. App. 3d 67, 227 Cal. Rptr. 794, she argued section 5021 requires the court to set aside her community interest separately as to each account, regardless of any other community property she received outside probate. The Lizarragas opposed the petition on the ground Evangelina had already received nonprobate transfers of community property exceeding her one-half interest in the community estate. They argued that in enacting section 5021, the Legislature intended to abrogate the holding in *Estate of Wilson*.

The court issued a letter ruling denying the petition "insofar as a blanket set aside of the . . . non-consensual transfers is concerned." The court determined section 5021 "empowers [it] to impose such terms, conditions and remedies as appear equitable under the circumstances of this case, and [it] will hear evidence and will exercise its equitable powers to make such an order that insures that each party — Petitioner and the decedent, have or have the right to dispose of one-half of their community property." The court also ruled that "[t]o the extent the evidence shows that Petitioner has received half or more of the community property she owned with decedent, none of the non-consensual transfers will be set aside."

After the interim order was issued, Evangelina conceded she received assets exceeding one-half of the community estate, including houses in California and Mexico, a condominium in Florida and "one of the California POD [pay-on-death] accounts." Accordingly, no evidentiary hearing was held. The court issued an order adopting and making final its previous findings and denying the petition as to all pay-on-death accounts.

DISCUSSION

* * *

II.   *ESTATE OF WILSON* AND SECTION 5021

A

"Upon the death of a married person, one-half of the community property belongs to the surviving spouse and the other half belongs to the decedent." (§100, subd. (a).) Each spouse has the right of testamentary disposition over his or her half of the community property. (*Tyre v. Aetna Life Ins. Co.* (1960) 54 Cal. 2d 399, 404-405, 6 Cal. Rptr. 13, 353 P.2d 725.)

In *Estate of Wilson, supra*, 183 Cal. App. 3d 67, 68-69, 227 Cal. Rptr. 794, the decedent, without his wife's consent, used community property to fund 10 Totten trust bank accounts for his children. After his death, she filed a petition in probate court claiming the right to all the decedent's community property. The objectors claimed she had no right to the children's accounts because their total funds were less than one-half of the total value of the community property. The court held: "[W]hen a spouse deposits community property funds in a bank account in his name as trustee for a third person, upon that spouse's death only one-half of the community property in the account is transmitted to the third person. The other one-half, being the surviving spouse's share of community property, goes to the survivor *even though he or she is already receiving more than one-half of the total community property of the parties.*" (Italics added.)

The court noted the meaning of the term "community property" in former section 201 (now §100, subd. (a)) was "not clearly indicate[d]," and the "phrase 'one-half of the community property' is, on its face, capable of meaning either one-half of the 'total value' of all community property or one-half of 'each item' of community property." (*Estate of Wilson, supra*, 183 Cal. App. 3d at p. 70, 227 Cal. Rptr. 794.) Based on case law, the court concluded the statute meant "the decedent has a right to dispose of only one-half of *each community property asset* to someone other than a spouse, although none of the cases directly hold[s] the decedent's right of disposition is so limited." (*Ibid.*, citing *Odone v. Marzocchi* (1949) 34 Cal. 2d 431, 439, 211 P.2d 297; *Trimble v. Trimble* (1933) 219 Cal. 340, 347, 26 P.2d 477; *Estate of Sweitzer* (1932) 215 Cal. 489, 493, 11 P.2d 633; *Tyre v. Aetna Life Ins. Co., supra*, 54 Cal. 2d 399, 403, 6 Cal. Rptr. 13, 353 P.2d 725.)

The court further explained: "The rationale of this rule is founded in the nature of community property. 'The respective interests of the husband and wife in community property during continuance of the marriage relation are present, existing and equal interests.' [Citation.] In other words, each spouse has a vested undivided one-half interest in the community property. Death of a spouse only dissolves the community; it does not affect the character of the property acquired or rights vested before the spouse's death. [Citations.] [¶] Because each asset is only half his or hers to give, a spouse cannot make a testamentary disposition to a third party of any specific item of community property except by a 'forced election' requiring the surviving spouse to elect to take under the testamentary scheme or to take his or her community property share. To give an example, one spouse cannot devise the family residence to a third party even if there are sufficient other community assets to counterbalance the gift's value, because each spouse only owns an undivided one-half interest in the residence. Obviously, *the decedent cannot give away more than he or she owns.* Indeed, it would be quite unfair to allow either spouse to give away an asset that both spouses treasure based merely on the contingency of who dies first. . . . [¶] Although this rule makes less practical sense in the context of fungible assets like money, . . . the same rule applies." (*Estate of Wilson, supra,* 183 Cal. App. 3d at pp. 72-73, 227 Cal. Rptr. 794, fns. omitted, italics added.)

> In 1992, the Legislature enacted section 5021, which provides at subdivision (a): In a proceeding to set aside a nonprobate transfer of community property on death made pursuant to a provision for transfer of the property executed by a married person without the written consent of the person's spouse, the court *shall set aside* the transfer as to the nonconsenting spouse's interest in the property, *subject to* terms and conditions or other remedies that appear equitable under the circumstances of the case, taking into account the rights of all interested persons." (§5021, subd. (a), italics added.) Section 5020 provides that a "provision for a nonprobate transfer of community property on death executed by a married person without the written consent of the person's spouse . . . is not effective as to the nonconsenting spouse's interest in the property.

The trial court essentially interpreted section 5021, subdivision (a) as abrogating the rule of *Estate of Wilson.* The court determined the statute's language "subject to terms and conditions or other remedies that appear equitable under the circumstances of the case" modifies the phrase "shall set aside," and gave it discretion to not set aside any portion of the pay-on-death accounts because Evangelina received at least one-half of the total value of the community estate. The court found it "is illogical to argue that a spouse has (pursuant to Probate Code, §100) the absolute right to give away his or her half of the community property by will, but cannot do so by another non-probate estate planning device such as a [pay-on-death] account or a joint tenant vesting," and the "correct interpretation of section 5021 enables the Court to make such orders as may be required to insure that each spouse may dispose of . . . half of the community property."

Statutory interpretation is a question of law we review independently. "'When interpreting a statute, we must ascertain legislative intent so as to effectuate the purpose of a particular law. Of course our first step in determining that intent is to scrutinize the actual words of the statute, giving them a plain and commonsense meaning. When the words are clear and unambiguous, there is no need for statutory construction or resort to other indicia of legislative intent, such as legislative history.'" When a statute is susceptible to more than one reasonable interpretation, we may consider a variety of extrinsic aids, such as the legislative history.

Generally, for purposes of statutory interpretation, "shall" is mandatory and "may" is permissive. Moreover, the Probate Code defines the term "shall" as "mandatory." Therefore, we should interpret the "shall set aside" language of section 5021, subdivision (a) as mandatory. If the "subject to" phrase in section 5021, subdivision (a) were interpreted to give courts discretion to not set aside nonconsensual transfers of community property on equitable grounds, the word "shall" would be meaningless. "In construing a statute we are required to give independent meaning and significance to each word, phrase, and sentence in a statute and to avoid an interpretation that makes any part of a statute meaningless."

Further, to any extent section 5021 is arguably ambiguous, the legislative history shows the Legislature intended to codify, rather than supplant, the holding in *Estate of Wilson, supra,* 183 Cal. App. 3d 67, 227 Cal. Rptr. 794. The California Law Revision Commission (the Commission) recommended section 5021, among other provisions, as a "codification of the general principles governing nonprobate transfers of community property." (Recommendation: Nonprobate Transfers of Community Property (Nov.1991) 21 Cal. Law Revision Com. Rep. (1991) p. 169 (Recommendation).) The Committee explained the legislation was intended to "resolve[ ] problems created by *Estate of MacDonald* [(1990)] 51 Cal. 3d 262, 272 Cal. Rptr. 153, 794 P.2d 911 . . . , in estate planning for married persons." (Recommendation, p. 165.) The Committee did not suggest it had any objection to *Estate of Wilson,* or that section 5021 was intended to nullify its holding. To the contrary, the Commission cited *Estate of Wilson* in explaining that under existing case law "after the death of a transferor, a donative transfer made without the required consent may be set aside as to the one-half interest of the nonconsenting spouse." (Recommendation, pp. 167 & fn. 4, 170 & fn. 8.)

The Commission did find that in some instances the *remedy* of recovery of one-half of a nonconsensual transfer is "unduly restrictive." (Recommendation, *supra,* 21 Cal. Law Revision Com. Rep., p. 170.) The Commission wrote that under subdivision (a) of section 5021, "the court has discretion to fashion an appropriate order, depending on the circumstances of the case. The order may, for example, provide for recovery of the value of the property rather than the particular item, or aggregate property received by a beneficiary instead of imposing a division by item." (Recommendation, p. 183.) This does not suggest a court has discretion to *deny* a surviving spouse's petition under section 5021 on equitable grounds. Rather, the Commission was concerned with an equitable remedy when nonconsensual transfers were of nonfungible assets, an issue discussed but not resolved in *Estate of Wilson, supra,* 183 Cal. App. 3d at p. 73, 227 Cal. Rptr. 794.

We conclude section 5021 codifies the *Estate of Wilson* rule, and Evangelina is entitled to one-half of the community property funds in each of the pay-on-death accounts Raul established, notwithstanding her previous receipt of more than one-half of the community estate. Because Evangelina did not consent to the transfers Raul made, the funds were "only . . . half his . . . to give." (*Estate of Wilson, supra,* 183

Cal. App. 3d at p. 72, 227 Cal. Rptr. 794.) However, because it appears she has already received funds from at least one of the accounts, we remand the matter to the trial court for a new hearing on the petition.

DISPOSITION

The orders are reversed and the matter is remanded to the trial court for further proceedings in accordance with this opinion. Evangelina is awarded costs on appeal.

We concur: BENKE and McINTYRE, JJ.

Discussion Questions

1. What is the main rationale for the item theory of division of community property at death?

2. Probate Code §5021 includes the phrase "subject to terms and conditions or other remedies that appear equitable under the circumstances of the case. . . ." According to the Court, when will "equitable remedies" apply?

B. LIFE INSURANCE PROCEEDS AND PROTECTING THE SURVIVING SPOUSE: THE TEXAS, NEW MEXICO, AND IDAHO APPROACHES

1. The Texas Approach: Was the Gift Unfair?

Although Texas law recognizes that a decedent may designate a beneficiary of a life insurance policy purchased with community property to someone other than the surviving spouse, that designation is subject to the trust relationship between the spouses regarding the community property. When the life insurance proceeds go to a third party, this may constitute actual or constructive fraud on the community, meaning that by designating someone else as beneficiary, the decedent has taken community property that should belong to the surviving spouse and given it to that third party. However, the beneficiary may receive the life insurance proceeds if the beneficiary can prove that the gift was fair. The beneficiary has the burden of proving fairness. The following cases, *Madrigal v. Madrigal*, 115 S.W.3d 32 (Tex. Ct. App. 2003), and *Estate of Vackar*, 345 S.W.3d 588 (Tex Ct. App. 2011), illustrate the "fairness" test that is the attempt to balance the rights of the surviving spouse and designated beneficiary.

MADRIGAL v. MADRIGAL

115 S.W.3d 32 (Tex. Ct. App. 2003)
Court of Appeals of Texas

PAUL W. GREEN, Justice.

Appellant Consuelo Martinez Madrigal (Consuelo) is the surviving spouse of Gregorio Madrigal, Sr. She appeals the trial court's judgment awarding the proceeds of Madrigal's life insurance policy to his former wife, appellee Concepcion Madrigal (Concepcion). Because Concepcion failed to show that the gift of the policy proceeds was fair to the community or that there are sufficient funds in Madrigal's community property interest to reimburse Consuelo for the gift, we reverse the trial court's judgment and render judgment in favor of Consuelo.

During his marriage to Consuelo, Madrigal acquired a life insurance policy as one of the benefits of his employment. Madrigal voluntarily paid additional premiums to obtain extra coverage. Madrigal named his former spouse, Concepcion, as the beneficiary of the policy, apparently without Consuelo's knowledge. The trial court awarded the entire proceeds to the designated beneficiary, Concepcion. On appeal Consuelo argues: (1) the evidence is legally and factually insufficient to support the trial court's award, thus conclusively establishing Consuelo was entitled to her community share of the proceeds; (2) the trial court improperly shifted the burden of proof to Consuelo, the surviving spouse; and (3) the trial court improperly substituted his subjective belief for uncontroverted evidence.

In reviewing a "no evidence" or legal sufficiency issue, we must view the evidence in a light that tends to support a finding of disputed fact and disregard all evidence and inferences to the contrary. If there is more than a scintilla of evidence to support the finding, it will be upheld. In reviewing a factual sufficiency point, we are required to weigh all of the evidence in the record. Findings may be overturned only if they are so against the great weight and preponderance of the evidence as to be clearly wrong and unjust.

Proceeds from a life insurance policy acquired as a benefit of employment during marriage are community property. *Korzekwa v. Prudential Ins. Co. of Amer.*, 669 S.W.2d 775, 777 (Tex. App. — San Antonio 1984, writ dism'd). The policy is the sole management community property of the employee spouse, and that spouse may designate the beneficiary of the policy. *Street v. Skipper*, 887 S.W.2d 78, 81 (Tex. App. — Fort Worth 1994, writ denied); *Murphy v. Metropolitan Life Ins. Co.*, 498 S.W.2d 278, 282 (Tex. Civ. App. — Houston [14th Dist.] 1973, writ ref'd n.r.e.). However, because a trust relationship exists between husband and wife regarding the community property controlled by each spouse, if the designation of a third-party beneficiary constitutes actual or constructive fraud on the community, proceeds may be awarded to the surviving spouse rather than the designated beneficiary. *See Murphy v. Metropolitan Life Ins. Co.*, 498 S.W.2d at 282; *Brownson v. New*, 259 S.W.2d 277, 281 (Tex. Civ. App. — San Antonio 1953, writ dism'd).

A surviving spouse establishes a prima facie case of constructive fraud on the community by proof that the life insurance policy was purchased with community funds for the benefit of a person outside the community. *Murphy*, 498 S.W.2d at 282; *Givens v. Girard Life Ins. Co.*, 480 S.W.2d 421, 426 (Tex. Civ. App. — Dallas 1972, writ ref'd n.r.e.) (no proof of fraudulent intent is required). The donor spouse or the designated beneficiary, seeking to overcome a prima facie case of fraud and sustain the gift, has the burden of proof to show that the disposition of the surviving spouse's one-half community interest is fair. *Korzekwa*, 669 S.W.2d at 777; *Givens*, 480 S.W.2d at 426. To determine whether a gift of proceeds is fair, the court may consider a number of factors, including: (1) the size of the gift in relation to the total size of the community estate; (2) the adequacy of the estate remaining to support the surviving spouse in spite of the gift; (3) the relationship of the donor to the donee; and (4) whether special circumstances existed to justify the gift. *Barnett v. Barnett*, 67 S.W.3d 107, 126 (Tex. 2001); *Street*, 887 S.W.2d at 81; *Korzekwa*, 669 S.W.2d at 777. The gift is generally allowed if the donor spouse has sufficient community property to reimburse the surviving spouse for the loss caused by the gift. *Korzekwa*, 669 S.W.2d at 778.[1]

In this case, there is no evidence of actual fraud; therefore, we must determine if the gift of proceeds to Concepcion resulted in constructive fraud on the community. *See Street*, 887 S.W.2d at 81. There is no dispute that the policy proceeds are community property. The record establishes a special relationship between Concepcion and the deceased through their three children. The parties stipulated that Consuelo will receive workmen's compensation survival benefits. In addition, she may receive retirement benefits through Madrigal's estate. However, the amounts of workmen's compensation or retirement benefits were not established. No other evidence was presented with regard to assets of Madrigal's estate. No evidence was presented as to: (1) the size of the gift in relation to the total size of the community estate, i.e., whether the community funds used were reasonable in proportion to the community assets remaining; or (2) the adequacy of the estate remaining to support the surviving spouse in spite of the gift. The total size of the community estate was not determinable from the evidence presented.

Without the missing evidence, Concepcion did not meet her burden to show the gift was fair or that Consuelo could be reimbursed from Madrigal's community interest. Accordingly, we reverse the trial court's judgment awarding the policy proceeds to Concepcion. We render judgment that Consuelo receive one-half of the policy proceeds, including any interest which may have accrued. Costs of the appeal are taxed against appellee Concepcion Madrigal.

ESTATE OF VACKAR

345 S.W.3d 588 (Tex Ct. App. 2011)
Court of Appeals of Texas

REBECCA SIMMONS, Justice.

Magdalen "Maggie" Marbry appeals the trial court's judgment, which invalidated the Statutory Durable Power of Attorney and Last Will and Testament of her

---

1. The defrauded spouse's right of recourse is first against the estate of the deceased spouse for reimbursement for his or her one-half interest in the funds disposed of in fraud. *Korzekwa*, 669 S.W.2d at 778. If there are insufficient assets in the deceased's estate, then the surviving spouse may pursue the proceeds of the policy, to the extent of her or his community interest, into the hands of the transferee. *Id.*

brother, Dennis Vackar. She also appeals the jury's finding that Dennis's gift of life insurance proceeds to her was unfair. We affirm in part and reverse in part.

BACKGROUND

On July 28, 2007, Dennis suffered a severe spinal injury when he fell approximately eight feet from the bucket of a front-end loader while he was trimming trees. At the time of the accident, Dennis was estranged from his wife of twenty-seven years, Betty Vackar. Their marriage had been "rocky" for at least five years. Dennis's relationship with his son, Dustin, was also estranged due to Dustin's relationship with his girlfriend and a prior physical altercation between him and Dustin; they had not truly spoken in approximately three years.

Betty believed that many of her marital problems were related to Dennis's close relationship with Maggie. Maggie was Dennis's confidant, and when Dennis was forced to choose between Maggie and Betty, he would choose Maggie. Betty was also annoyed that Dennis chose to travel every year with his sister instead of her.

In March of 2006, unbeknownst to Dennis, Betty began moving items out of the residence into a storage shed. Seven months later, while Dennis was traveling with Maggie in Morocco, Betty began moving personal items out of the residence into a one-bedroom apartment she had rented. When Dennis returned, Betty picked him up at the airport, drove him to their house, and told him that she had moved out. Betty and Dennis never lived together as husband and wife after October of 2006.

Immediately after falling, Dennis requested that Maggie and his brother Steve be contacted; he did not request that either Betty or Dustin be notified. A helicopter transported Dennis to University Hospital in San Antonio. As a result of the fall, Dennis suffered a serious spinal cord injury resulting in partial paralysis and the necessity of a ventilator. The hospital staff suggested to Dennis that he execute a medical power of attorney, and Dennis indicated that he wanted Maggie to be his agent. Dennis also requested that Maggie put her name on his checking account so that she could take care of his business while he was in the hospital.

Dennis executed a durable statutory power of attorney while in the hospital. Using the power of attorney and pursuant to Dennis's request, Maggie named herself as the beneficiary of Dennis's John Alden life insurance policy. Notably, prior to the accident, Dennis designated Maggie as the beneficiary of his retirement funds and a Dearborn life insurance policy. While at the hospital, he also executed a Last Will and Testament leaving all of his property to Maggie.

Dennis's health declined, and he was ultimately transferred to a rehabilitation facility. Following several months of care, Dennis decided to discontinue his treatment and withdraw all supportive care. Before discontinuing treatment, the hospital's medical ethics committee confirmed that Dennis was competent to make such a decision. Dennis died shortly after the hospital withdrew his life support.

Maggie filed an application in probate court to probate Dennis's Last Will and Testament. Betty and Dustin contested the will, alleging Dennis lacked testamentary capacity, and asserted that the will and the power of attorney were executed as a result of Maggie's undue influence. The jury found in Betty and Dustin's favor.

* * *

[The Court of Appeals held that Dennis's will and power of attorney were validly executed.]

* * *

FAIRNESS OF THE GIFT

The jury found that Maggie's receipt of $100,000.00 in proceeds from Dennis's John Alden life insurance policy was an unfair gift to Maggie from Dennis's and Betty's community estate. Maggie challenges the sufficiency of the evidence supporting this finding.

Proceeds from a life insurance policy acquired as a benefit of employment during marriage are community property. "The policy is the sole management community property of the employee spouse, and that spouse may designate the beneficiary of the policy." *Madrigal v. Madrigal,* 115 S.W.3d 32, 34-35 (Tex. App. — San Antonio 2003, no pet.). "However, because a trust relationship exists between husband and wife regarding the community property controlled by each spouse, if the designation of a third-party beneficiary constitutes actual or constructive fraud on the community, proceeds may be awarded to the surviving spouse rather than the designated beneficiary." *Id.*

A surviving spouse establishes a prima facie case of constructive fraud on the community with proof that the life insurance policy was purchased with community funds for the benefit of a person outside the community. *Murphy v. Metro. Life Ins. Co.,* 498 S.W.2d 278, 282 (Tex. Civ. App. — Houston [14th Dist.] 1973, writ ref'd n.r.e.). A donor or designated beneficiary seeking to overcome a prima facie case of fraud must prove that "the disposition of the surviving spouse's one-half community interest is fair." *See Madrigal,* 115 S.W.3d at 34-35. To determine whether a gift of proceeds is fair, a fact-finder considers: (1) the size of the gift in relation to the total size of the community estate; (2) the adequacy of the estate remaining to support the surviving spouse in spite of the gift; (3) the relationship of the donor to the donee; and (4) whether special circumstances existed to justify the gift. *Barnett v. Barnett,* 67 S.W.3d 107, 126 (Tex. 2001); *Madrigal,* 115 S.W.3d at 34-35. Whether a gift of life insurance proceeds is fair is generally a question of fact to be determined by the fact-finder.

Maggie argues that a gift of life insurance proceeds is fair as a matter of law if the surviving spouse receives more than half of the community estate. However, all of the cases Maggie relies upon affirmed findings that a gift was fair because the evidence presented at trial supported these findings. None holds that a gift from a community estate is fair to the donor's spouse as a matter of law if a spouse receives equal to or more than one half of the total community estate. *See Street,* 887 S.W.2d at 82; *Tabassi,* 737 S.W.2d at 616; *Horlock,* 533 S.W.2d at 55.

In *Murphy v. Metropolitan Life Insurance Co.,* the court held that the fact that a surviving spouse receives more than half of the community estate does not determine the fairness of a gift. 498 S.W.2d 278, 282 (Tex. Civ. App. — Houston [14th Dist.] 1973, writ ref'd n.r.e.). In *Murphy,* the decedent gave $12,500.00 in life insurance proceeds to his mother. *Id.* at 280. The trial court found that the gift constituted fraud on the community because it was not fair to the decedent's surviving spouse. *Id.* The Houston Court of Appeals affirmed this finding, despite the wife's receipt of over half of the community estate, reasoning that the gift was relatively large (about one-sixth of the community), the remainder of the community estate did not leave the wife with much financial security, the wife had no separate property, and she had three sons to raise and educate. *Id.* at 282. Based on this evidence, the court held that the trial court did not abuse its discretion in finding that the gift was unfair. *Id.*

Here, because Maggie does not contest that Dennis's John Alden insurance policy was a part of the community estate, Maggie had the burden to prove that Dennis's gift was fair. *See Madrigal,* 115 S.W.3d at 34-35. Maggie argues that the community estate is comprised of the following assets: a residence valued at $108,000.00; vehicles valued together at $21,500.00; an accidental death policy of $2,000.00; a Wells Fargo account with a balance of $20,000.00; the John Alden life insurance policy of $100,000.00; Betty's retirement of $18,000.00; Dennis's 401(k) of $11,000.00; and Dennis's pension, which Maggie calculates to be over $567,000.00. Maggie reaches the $567,000.00 figure by calculating Betty's life expectancy and multiplying the number of months by the monthly amount — around $2,000.00 — Betty will receive from Dennis's pension. However, Maggie failed to introduce at trial any evidence of Betty's life expectancy. Because the jury did not consider the pension election in light of the estimated length of Betty's life expectancy, Maggie failed to demonstrate that this amount is definitive of the size of the community estate. Therefore, the evidence as to the size of the gift in relation to the total size of the community estate or as to the adequacy of the estate remaining to support Betty was insufficient. Thus Maggie failed to meet her burden to show that the gift was fair as a matter of law. *See id.; see also Moore,* 576 S.W.2d at 695.

Moreover, even if Maggie had introduced evidence of Betty's life expectancy and the present value of the predicted total Betty would receive in monthly payments for Dennis's retirement, other evidence supports the jury's finding that the gift was unfair. Assuming that Betty would receive over $567,000.00 from Dennis's retirement, the John Alden proceeds comprise almost one-eighth of the community estate. Betty testified that she was disabled, that she was a bus driver paid on an hourly basis, and that Dennis's pension comprised almost half of her monthly income. Although Maggie was Dennis's sister and Dennis was estranged from Betty, the evidence also showed that Maggie had already received life insurance proceeds in excess of $300,000.00 from Dennis's other life insurance policy. Based on the foregoing, the evidence supported the jury's finding that the gift was unfair. *See Murphy, 498* S.W.2d at 282.

CONCLUSION

Therefore, we reverse and render judgment that Dennis's will and power of attorney were validly executed, but we affirm the judgment as far as it invalidates the gift of the John Alden life insurance policy.

Discussion Questions

1. Who is favored by the Texas formulation of the law regarding life insurance proceeds? The designated beneficiary or the surviving spouse?

2. Does Texas follow the aggregate theory or the item theory of division of community property at death?

---

2.   The New Mexico and Washington Approaches: Even a Former Spouse?

Let us return to our hypothetical couple George and Martha. George takes out a life insurance policy that is offered by his employer. He names Martha as the beneficiary. Later George and Martha divorce. The life insurance policy is not mentioned in the divorce decree. George does not change the designation of Martha as beneficiary. George dies. The question raised in the New Mexico case, *Matter of Schleis' Estate*, 97 N.M. 561, 642 P.2d 164 (1982), is whether the divorce has any effect on the life insurance policy. While reading this case, think about whether George's failure to change the beneficiary indicates his intention to keep Martha as beneficiary or whether this was an oversight and the life insurance proceeds should go through his estate to his heirs.

MATTER OF SCHLEIS' ESTATE

94 N.M. 561, 642 P.2d 164 (1982)
Supreme Court of New Mexico

PAYNE, Justice.

This appeal requires us to determine whether a divorce decree automatically severs an ex-spouse's beneficiary interest in an insurance policy. We hold that it does not.

Kathleen Haley and Stephen Schleis were married in 1975. During the marriage Stephen took out two insurance policies through his employer, naming Kathleen as beneficiary. On November 6, 1979, Stephen and Kathleen were divorced. The policies involved were term insurance and the period of coverage purchased with premium payments from the community funds had ended shortly after the divorce. Kathleen therefore retains no interest separate from her status as beneficiary. *Phillips v. Wellborn*, 89 N.M. 340, 552 P.2d 471 (1976).

In July, 1980, Stephen's personal representative moved for summary judgment on the proper distribution of the death benefits. The asserted grounds for the motion were first, that Stephen had designated a beneficiary for only one of the policies and second, that since the divorce decree gave Stephen all personal property in his possession, Kathleen was divested of her interest in the policies. Kathleen also moved for summary judgment in her favor. The district court granted summary judgment in favor of Stephen's estate, finding there were no issues of material fact. Kathleen appeals. We reverse.

Neither of the grounds asserted by Stephen's estate could support its motion for summary judgment in this case. His employer's practice was to require only one beneficiary designation no matter how many group policies were involved, unless separate beneficiaries were specifically desired. Under this procedure, Stephen's failure to make two beneficiary designations could not mean, as a matter of law, that he intended that proceeds of the second policy should go to his estate.

The estate's assertion that Kathleen was divested of her beneficiary interest in the policy because the divorce decree granted ownership of the policy to Stephen cannot be sustained. The estate relies on *Romero v. Melendez*, 83 N.M. 776, 498 P.2d 305 (1972). In *Romero*, we held that a wife's interest as beneficiary under a life insurance policy can be defeated by disposition of the policies in a divorce decree even though no change in beneficiary is made. We distinguished *Harris v. Harris*, 83 N.M. 441, 493 P.2d 407 (1972), which permitted a divorced wife to receive proceeds from a life insurance policy owned by her former husband, on grounds that the policy had not been disposed of in the decree. We reaffirm that the decree is dispositive, but feel it necessary to clarify what was meant in *Romero* and *Harris*.

The cases cited as authority for the *Romero* rule, *Brewer v. Brewer*, 239 Ark. 614, 390 S.W.2d 630 (1965); *Dudley v. Franklin Life Insurance Company*, 250 Or. 51, 440 P.2d 363 (1968), involved instances where the former wife specifically transferred and released any and all interest in the husband's policies and released him from any and all obligations which may have existed for any reason whatsoever. They were not cases in which the husband was merely given ownership of the policies. In *Romero* itself the decree "gave the decedent the policies as his sole and separate property and divested the appellant of any and all interest, including the expectancy as a beneficiary." *Id.* at 780, 498 P.2d 309. Thus, the *Romero* rule, which applies when policies are disposed of by a divorce decree, is limited to situations where the interest of the beneficiary spouse is specifically divested. Where the decree merely grants ownership of the policy to one spouse, without divesting the former spouse of the beneficiary interest, *Romero* does not govern.

Harris v. Harris, supra, sets forth the proper rule for situations where the insured spouse owns the policies, but where the beneficiary spouse is not specifically divested of any and all interest in the policies. Such ownership may be as a tenant in common when the decree does not grant ownership or as sole owner. In such situations, as *Harris* points out, the owner would have certain rights under the policy, including the right to change the beneficiary. Whoever is the named beneficiary owns the proceeds upon the happening of the contingency. The mere fact of a divorce has no effect upon the beneficiary's interest. 5 R. Anderson, *Couch on Insurance* 2d §29:4 (1960).

Accordingly, we hold that a divorce decree granting the insured spouse ownership of the policies does not, by itself, sever the beneficiary interest of a former spouse.

Such a beneficiary interest could be relinquished by clear and specific language releasing that interest in the insured spouse's policies. *Redd v. Brooke*, 604 P.2d 360 (Nev. 1980). However, if Kathleen never made such a release, her beneficiary interest could have been divested by Stephen's changing the beneficiary.

There is no evidence that Stephen complied with the policy's stated procedures for changing the beneficiary. The policy provided that a "change of beneficiary must be in writing(,) signed by the employee(,) and must be filed with the Company at its Head Office." Although the parties stipulated to the introduction of the policy as a part of the record on appeal, it appears that the trial court did not have the benefit of this policy provision in reaching its decision. We therefore do not base our decision on whether Stephen adhered to the policy provisions.

In order to change the beneficiaries, the insured generally must comply with procedures adopted by the insurer or imposed by statute. If no such procedures exist the courts may recognize a change desired by the insured if the intent is declared in an appropriate manner. See R. Anderson, *supra*, §§28:51-52.

Since no evidence of the policy requirements was introduced at trial, evidence of the insured's clear expression of intent combined with evidence of his reasonable efforts to change the beneficiary are necessary for the court to find a change of beneficiary. There is no such evidence in this record. Even if there were evidence that Stephen at some time expressed an intent to change the beneficiary, there is also evidence indicating expression of a contrary intent. Because we adopt the two-pronged test requiring a clear expression of intent coupled with reasonable efforts to effect the change of beneficiary, we conclude that Stephen never effectively changed the beneficiary.

On appeal, the parties have extensively addressed the issue of ownership, since the estate's claim that Stephen owned the policies was based in "catch-all" language in the divorce decree awarding him "the other personal property which is in his possession." This failure to specifically designate Stephen as owner of the life insurance policies is claimed to give Kathleen a continuing interest. While this argument may have been relevant through the term of coverage paid for by the community, there can be little question that once Stephen began paying for the insurance out of his separate funds and not under any obligation under the decree or other agreement, the policy belonged to Stephen. However, as we have shown, ownership is not the deciding factor.

Accordingly we reverse with instructions to enter judgment for the appellant.

EASLEY, C.J., and FEDERICI, J., concur.

Discussion Questions

1. In which situations will the divorce decree determine whether a former spouse who is designated as the beneficiary will receive the life insurance proceeds?

2. What if the decedent Stephen had written a letter to the insurance company that indicated he wanted to change the beneficiary from his former wife Kathleen to his sister Joan, but the letter was not processed by the insurance company?

Note: The holding in *Matter of Schleis' Estate* was reversed by the New Mexico Legislature in 1993, N.M. Stat. Ann. §45-2-804(B)(1)(a).

MEARNS v. SCHARBACH

103 Wash. App. 498 12 P.3d 1048 (2000)
Court of Appeals of Washington

KURTZ, C.J.

RCW 11.07.010 governs nonprobate assets upon dissolution or invalidation of marriage and revokes beneficiary designations naming the former spouse. This statute operates under the legal fiction that the former spouse, having died at the entry of the decree, does not survive the decedent. Applying RCW 11.07.010, the trial court here granted summary judgment awarding life insurance proceeds to the insured's children, Joel and Nanette Mearns, rather than the insured's former spouse, Christine Scharbach, who was named as the primary beneficiary in the policy. Ms. Scharbach appeals contending: (1) oral evidence is admissible to prove the insured's intent to maintain Ms. Scharbach as primary beneficiary after the divorce; (2) RCW 11.07.010 is unconstitutional when applied to insurance contracts made prior to the statute's enactment; and (3) RCW 11.07.010(2)(b)(ii) renders the automatic revocation provision inapplicable. We conclude RCW 11.07.010 automatically revoked the beneficiary designation naming Ms. Scharbach. We further conclude that the operation of RCW 11.07.010 does not unconstitutionally impair Mr. Mearns's contract with Guardian. We affirm.

FACTS

Christine Scharbach married Jerrold Mearns on March 5, 1982. Mr. Mearns applied for term life insurance in June 1992. The Guardian Life Insurance Company (Guardian) issued a renewable term policy on August 12, 1992. Mr. Mearns was designated as the "Owner" of the policy and the policy named "Christine A. Mearns, wife" as the "Primary Beneficiary." Mr. Mearns's two adult children, Joel C. Mearns and Nanette Mearns, were designated as the contingent beneficiaries. The policy renewed on a yearly basis. If the annual premium was not paid, the policy would lapse within 31 days of the expiration date. Mr. Mearns committed suicide on September 12, 1998, within the policy's grace period.

At the time of his death, Mr. Mearns was single, having divorced Ms. Scharbach on October 17, 1997. The Guardian policy was not mentioned in the decree of dissolution and Mr. Mearns did not change the beneficiary designation on the policy after the divorce. A few weeks after the divorce, Mr. Mearns called his insurance agent and cancelled a $200,000 term policy designating Ms. Scharbach as the primary beneficiary. Mr. Mearns and the agent also discussed the Guardian policy. Mr. Mearns told the insurance agent that he wanted to keep the policy. The agent reminded Mr. Mearns of the recent divorce and asked whether Mr. Mearns wanted to change the primary beneficiary to someone other than Ms. Scharbach. Mr. Mearns responded that he did not wish to make this change and that he wanted to leave the designation the way it was. Mr. Mearns never contacted the agent about changing the designation of the primary beneficiary.

In May 1998, seven months after the divorce, Mr. Mearns changed the beneficiaries on his retirement and life insurance policies held through his employer. He changed the designation from Ms. Scharbach to Joel Mearns and Nanette Mearns.

When making these changes, Mr. Mearns told the human resources consultant that he intended to change the beneficiaries from his former wife to his children on some, but not all, of his policies.

Joel Mearns administered his father's estate. Joel and Nanette were designated beneficiaries under their father's two policies through his employer. The Mearns children submitted claims to the Guardian policy even though the policy listed them as contingent beneficiaries. Ms. Scharbach also submitted a claim to Guardian for the proceeds of the policy. The Mearns children filed this action seeking the policy proceeds and Guardian interpleaded the money into court. The Mearns children filed a motion for summary judgment, but agreed to continue the motion to allow for discovery. Ms. Scharbach filed a cross-motion for summary judgment.

The court granted summary judgment in favor of the Mearns children, awarding them the policy proceeds. The court denied Ms. Scharbach's motion for summary judgment and motion for reconsideration. Ms. Scharbach appeals.

* * *

ANALYSIS

Does RCW 11.07.010 automatically revoke the beneficiary designation naming Ms. Scharbach?

Operation of RCW 11.07.010. RCW 11.07.010 reads in pertinent part as follows:

> (1) This section applies to all nonprobate assets, wherever situated, held at the time of entry by a superior court of this state of a decree of dissolution of marriage or a declaration of invalidity.
>
> (2) (a) *If a marriage is dissolved or invalidated, a provision made prior to that event that relates to the payment or transfer at death of the decedent's interest in a nonprobate asset in favor of or granting an interest or power to the decedent's former spouse is revoked. A provision affected by this section must be interpreted, and the nonprobate asset affected passes, as if the former spouse failed to survive the decedent, having died at the time of entry of the decree of dissolution or declaration of invalidity.*
>
> . . . .
>
> (5) As used in this section, "nonprobate asset" means those rights and interests of a person having beneficial ownership of an asset that pass on the person's death under only the following written instruments or arrangements other than the decedent's will:
>
> (a) A payable-on-death provision of a life insurance policy, employee benefit plan, annuity or similar contract, or individual retirement account.

(Emphasis added.)

RCW 11.07.010 was enacted in 1993, but its applicability is determined by the date of the decree of dissolution or declaration of invalidity. Specifically, RCW 11.07.010(6) provides:

> This section is remedial in nature and applies as of July 25, 1993, to decrees of dissolution and declarations of invalidity entered after July 24, 1993, and this section applies as of January 1, 1995, to decrees of dissolution and declarations of invalidity entered before July 25, 1993.

Mr. Mearns obtained the Guardian policy in 1992 and named "Christine A. Mearns, wife," as primary beneficiary. RCW 11.07.010 is applicable here because the decree of dissolution was entered on October 17, 1997.

RCW 11.07.010 provides that beneficiary designations made in favor of a spouse are revoked upon dissolution and that the nonprobate asset passes "as if the former spouse failed to survive the decedent, having died at the time of entry of the decree of dissolution or declaration of invalidity." RCW 11.07.010(2)(a). Hence, at Mr. Mearns's death, RCW 11.07.010(2)(a) created a legal fiction whereby Ms. Scharbach predeceased him. *See In re Estate of Egelhoff*, 139 Wash. 2d 557, 575, 989 P.2d 80 (1999), *cert. granted*, 530 U.S. 1242, 120 S. Ct. 2687, 147 L. Ed. 2d 960 (2000). As a result of this legal fiction, Ms. Scharbach's designation as primary beneficiary was revoked and the contingent beneficiaries were entitled to the insurance proceeds. Under RCW 11.07.010(2)(a), Ms. Scharbach cannot recover the policy proceeds because she is no longer a beneficiary under the policy. To maintain Ms. Scharbach as primary beneficiary, Mr. Mearns had to redesignate Ms. Scharbach as primary beneficiary after the decree of dissolution was entered.

Legislative purpose. Ms. Scharbach contends RCW 11.07.010 is a remedial statute that must be construed in light of its legislative purpose. Ms. Scharbach maintains that the sole purpose of the statute is to accomplish the deceased's intent. Ms. Scharbach suggests that an automatic revocation occurs only where there is no evidence indicating that the insured wished to retain the former spouse as a beneficiary of the nonprobate asset. In other words, Ms. Scharbach believes the statute is "automatic" in some circumstances but not others. She contends the statute does not apply here because there is evidence indicating that Mr. Mearns wished to retain her as a beneficiary under the policy.

RCW 11.07.010 was enacted in response to *Aetna Life Ins. Co. v. Wadsworth*, 102 Wash. 2d 652, 689 P.2d 46 (1984). The *Wadsworth* court concluded that a divorced husband's designation of his former wife as a beneficiary under his insurance policy was valid even though the divorce decree had specifically purported to divest his former wife of an interest in the policy. *Id.* at 663-64, 689 P.2d 46. The *Wadsworth* court adopted the following rule:

> To the extent no community property rights are invaded, the named beneficiary will generally be entitled to the proceeds. A dissolution decree will divest the former spouse of his or her expectancy as named beneficiary, however, if (1) the dissolution decree, in clear and specific language, states that the former spouse is to be divested of his or her expectancy as beneficiary *and* (2) the policy owner formally executes this stated intention to change the beneficiary within a reasonable time after the dissolution decree has been entered. Thus, if the insured spouse dies within this reasonable time period without formally executing the previously stated intention to change the beneficiary, the former spouse will not be entitled to the proceeds. After a reasonable time has passed, however, the clause in the dissolution decree will be ineffective and the former spouse, if named beneficiary, will be entitled to the proceeds. In any event, 1 year after dissolution, it shall be conclusively presumed that the policy owner intended to retain the named beneficiary as the one entitled to the proceeds.

Wadsworth, 102 Wash. 2d at 662-63, 689 P.2d 46. Applying this rule, the *Wadsworth* court determined that the former spouse was entitled to the life insurance proceeds because the language in the decree made no mention of the former spouse's expectancy as named beneficiary and over three years had passed between the date of dissolution and the date of the insured's death. *Id.* at 663-64, 689 P.2d 46.

The *Wadsworth* rule was adopted to "encourage individuals to consider carefully the disposition of life insurance policies in dissolution" and to "simplify the procedure of determining to whom life insurance proceeds are to be distributed." *Id.* at 663, 689 P.2d 46. But the result in *Wadsworth* was criticized as being contrary to what most divorcing couples would want. As a result, the Washington State Bar Association recommended the enactment of an automatic revocation provision. House Comm. on Judiciary, Final Bill Rep. SHB 1077, 53d Leg., Reg. Sess. (Wash. 1993).

Contrary to the assertions of Ms. Scharbach, RCW 11.07.010 does not seek merely to discern the intent of the insured. By adopting RCW 11.07.010, the Legislature sought to accomplish several purposes. First, the Legislature codified the assumption that divorcing couples want to change the beneficiary designations on nonprobate assets upon dissolution or invalidity of their marriage. Of equal importance, the Legislature chose to accomplish this goal by adopting an automatic revocation mechanism patterned after the revocation provisions applicable to wills. By choosing this mechanism, the legislators demonstrated their understanding that life insurance and other nonprobate assets are widely used as essential parts of estate planning and should be treated accordingly. Additionally, the adoption of a bright-line rule triggered by the date of dissolution or invalidation of marriage evinces a legislative intent to encourage couples to resolve estate planning questions when terminating their marital relationship.

In short, RCW 11.07.010 was adopted to achieve several purposes. The statute, as written, does not support Ms. Scharbach's argument that the statutory purpose was merely to discern the intent of the insured.

Ms. Scharbach next asserts that Mr. Mearns's oral statements are sufficient to negate the operation of the statute because the post-divorce designation here need not be in writing. Relying on Waldron v. Home Mut. Ins. Co., 16 Wash. 193, 196, 47 P. 425 (1896), Ms. Scharbach agrees that the requirement of a written designation is appropriate for wills, which must be in writing, but she asserts that this requirement is inappropriate for insurance policies, which can be oral. Stated differently, Ms. Scharbach maintains that the insurance revocation statute does not require that a post-divorce redesignation of a former spouse as a beneficiary must be in writing.

In the final bill report for RCW 11.07.010, legislators were informed that under the will revocation statute, RCW 11.12.051, a divorced testator could give a former spouse a gift under his or her will only by executing a new will following the divorce. By enacting RCW 11.07.010, the Legislature adopted a bright-line rule based on the will revocation statute. Acknowledging the importance of nonprobate instruments in estate planning, the Legislature determined that these instruments should be treated like wills. This legislative purpose is defeated if courts permit extrinsic oral testimony to negate the operation of the statute.

Moreover, the adoption of RCW 11.07.010 is also an extension of a portion of the *Wadsworth* rule. Under *Wadsworth*, the former spouse would not be entitled to the proceeds if the insured spouse died within a "reasonable time" after the entry of the dissolution decree without formally executing the previously stated intention to change the beneficiary. *Wadsworth*, 102 Wash. 2d at 663, 689 P.2d 46.

After considering the intent and operation of the insurance revocation statute, we conclude that any redesignation of Ms. Scharbach as a beneficiary had to be in writing. The evidence of oral statements made by Mr. Mearns is insufficient to contradict the operation of the statute. We note that this result is consistent with the Guardian policy, which also requires written changes as to the designation of a beneficiary.

Is RCW 11.07.010 unconstitutional as applied to beneficiary designations made prior to its enactment?

Ms. Scharbach contends that the retroactive application of RCW 11.07.010 unconstitutionally impairs Mr. Mearns's contract with Guardian. Ms. Scharbach maintains that Mr. Mearns entered into the insurance contract in 1992, naming Christine Mearns (Scharbach) as primary beneficiary and that he was unaware of the enactment of RCW 11.07.010 in 1993. Relying on *Whirlpool Corp. v. Ritter*, 929 F.2d 1318 (8th Cir. 1991), Ms. Scharbach contends that RCW 11.07.010 substantially impaired Guardian's contractual obligation to Mr. Mearns by disrupting the expectation that the proceeds would go to the named beneficiary.

* * *

Contract clause analysis. A statute is presumed constitutional and the party challenging the statute has the burden of proving its unconstitutionality. *Myers*, 133 Wash. 2d at 31, 941 P.2d 1102.

Both the federal and the state constitution prohibit the impairment of contractual obligations. U.S. Const. art. I, §10; Const. art. I, §23. The two clauses are substantially similar and are given the same effect. *Washington Fed'n of State Employees v. State*, 101 Wash. 2d 536, 539, 682 P.2d 869 (1984). "The threshold question is 'whether the state law has, in fact, operated as a substantial impairment of a contractual relationship.'" *Margola Assocs. v. City of Seattle*, 121 Wash. 2d 625, 653, 854 P.2d 23 (1993) (quoting *Allied Structural Steel Co. v. Spannaus*, 438 U.S. 234, 244, 98 S. Ct. 2716, 57 L. Ed. 2d 727 (1978)). The impairment is substantial if the complaining party relied upon the supplanted part of the contract. *Margola Assocs.*, 121 Wash. 2d at 653, 854 P.2d 23. However, legislation impairing contractual obligations may be upheld if the legislation advances a legitimate public purpose. *Birkenwald Distrib. Co. v. Heublein, Inc.*, 55 Wash. App. 1, 9, 776 P.2d 721 (1989). The severity of the impairment increases the level of scrutiny applied to the legislation in question. *Spannaus*, 438 U.S. at 245, 98 S. Ct. 2716.

In *Whirlpool*, a former spouse, Darleen Ritter, challenged the constitutionality of the Oklahoma insurance revocation statute. James and Darlene Ritter were married in 1972, and James enrolled in a group life insurance plan in 1985 and named Darlene as his beneficiary. *Whirlpool*, 929 F.2d at 1319. The Oklahoma Legislature passed an insurance revocation provision in 1987. Unlike the Washington statute which was triggered by the date of the entry of the dissolution decree or declaration of invalidity, the Oklahoma provision applied to life insurance contracts of any insured dying after November 1, 1987.[4] James and Darlene divorced in April 1989; three months later James died of a gunshot wound.

---

4. Contracts covered included "life insurance contracts, annuities, retirement arrangements, compensation agreements and other contracts designating a beneficiary of any right, property or money in the form of a death benefit." *Whirlpool Corp. v. Ritter*, 929 F.2d 1318, 1320 (8th Cir. 1991). The statute was later amended to apply to any contract of a decedent made after November 1, 1987. *Id.* at 1320 n.2.

Applying the contract clause analysis, the *Whirlpool* court determined that the Oklahoma insurance revocation statute impaired the insured's contract with the insurance company. The *Whirlpool* court further concluded that this impairment was substantial and that the statute, as applied retroactively, was "inappropriate in light of its intended purpose and underlying rationale." *Id.* at 1323.

We reach a different conclusion applying the contract clause analysis to the Washington insurance revocation statute. Legislation impairing contractual obligations may be upheld if the legislation advances a legitimate public purpose. *Birkenwald Distrib. Co.*, 55 Wash. App. at 9, 776 P.2d 721. The *Whirlpool* court determined that the intent of the Oklahoma statute was to discern the insured's intent after a divorce. The *Whirlpool* court also concluded that no general societal concerns were served by the statute's attempt to anticipate an insured's desire to change beneficiaries after the dissolution of a marriage. *Whirlpool*, 929 F.2d at 1322-23. In other words, the *Whirlpool* court viewed the Oklahoma statute as a new rule for interpreting insurance contracts and concluded that the statute was inappropriate as it would either effectuate or frustrate the insured's intent.

We view the purpose of our statute more broadly and conclude that it serves a legitimate public purpose. The Washington statute was not designed merely to provide guidance for the interpretation of an insured's intent with regard to the designation of a beneficiary in an insurance contract. RCW 11.07.010 serves a legitimate public purpose by applying will revocation principles to nonprobate assets and requiring that these assets be considered in the event of the dissolution or invalidation of a marriage. The Legislature accomplished this purpose by adopting an automatic revocation mechanism and linking the applicability of the statute to the date of the entry of the decree of dissolution or the declaration of invalidity. Comparing the public purposes advanced by RCW 11.07.010 with the level of the impairment to the insured's right to contract, we conclude RCW 11.07.010 is an exercise of legislative power designed to meet a legitimate public purpose.

Attorney Fees

This action was brought pursuant to RCW 11.96.070(2) which provides that a person with an interest in or right respecting the administration of a nonprobate asset may have a judicial proceeding for the declaration of rights or legal relations with respect to the nonprobate asset. The Mearns children seek an award of attorney fees from Ms. Scharbach under RCW 11.96.140 which permits a court to exercise its discretion and "order costs, including attorneys' fees, to be paid by any party to the proceedings or out of the assets of the estate or trust or nonprobate asset, as justice may require." Justice does not require that Ms. Scharbach pay the fees of the Mearns children for the privilege of litigating the difficult question presented in this appeal.

Affirmed.

Schultheis, J., and Kato, J., concur.

Discussion Questions

1. What was the purpose behind the enactment of RCW 11.07.010? How was that purpose accomplished?

2. Even though it was clear that Mr. Mearns wanted to keep his former wife as beneficiary, why didn't his intent control?

---

3. The Idaho Approach: Even a Slayer Spouse?

In community property states, the Supreme Courts of Arizona and Idaho have considered the issue of whether a spouse who murdered the decedent spouse is entitled to life insurance proceeds when designated as beneficiary of the policy. *Matter of Estate of Alarcon*, 149 Ariz. 336, 718 P.2d 989 (1986), *United Investors Life Ins. Co. v. Severson*, 143 Idaho 628, 151 P.3d 824 (2007). Even though the decedent spouse intended the surviving spouse to receive the benefits at the time the decedent designated the surviving spouse as beneficiary, it is obvious that intention would change if the decedent could be asked. The question had to be resolved at the state Supreme Court level and the guiding principle is that "no person shall be allowed to profit by his own wrong. . . ." Idaho Code §15-2-803(n).

UNITED INVESTORS LIFE INS. CO. v. SEVERSON

143 Idaho 628, 151 P.3d 824 (2007)
Supreme Court of Idaho

BURDICK, Justice.

This case asks the Court to decide whether I.C. §15-2-803 prevents a husband convicted of murdering his wife from acquiring one-half of his wife's life insurance proceeds. This case further asks the Court to decide whether the husband's appeal of his criminal conviction affects this civil proceeding and whether the application of the slayer statute in this instance is unconstitutional. We affirm the district court's order granting summary judgment.

II. FACTUAL AND PROCEDURAL BACKGROUND

Appellant Larry Severson (Severson) was found guilty of murder in the first degree and found guilty of the poisoning of his wife, Mary Severson (decedent). In August 2000 the decedent applied to United Investors Life Insurance Company (United Investors) for a term life insurance policy in which she listed Severson as the primary beneficiary and her mother, Respondent Carolyn Diaz (Diaz), as the contingent beneficiary. In October 2001 the decedent changed the primary beneficiary of her term life insurance policy to Diaz. The decedent died on February 15, 2002.

United Investors filed a complaint for interpleader on September 25, 2002, and filed the proceeds of the decedent's policy, $200,000, with the court. On July 28, 2003, the district court granted Diaz's motion for partial summary judgment holding that she is entitled to $100,000 of the proceeds because she is the beneficiary of the policy. That order did not make any final decision as to Severson's interest in or rights to the proceeds. Instead, the district court noted that it was undisputed that the policy premiums were derived from the community funds of the marriage between the decedent and Severson and that in Idaho, in such a case, at the death of the insured, one-half of the proceeds becomes vested in the surviving spouse. However, the court also noted that due to Idaho's slayer statute, I.C. §15-2-803, Severson may not be entitled to one-half of the proceeds if convicted of the murder of his wife.

On January 27, 2005, after Severson was convicted of first degree murder, the district court held that because Severson was the slayer of his wife I.C. §15-2-803(b) & (e) barred him from receiving any share of the insurance proceeds. Additionally, the district court ruled that pursuant to I.C. §15-2-803(e) the other half of the insurance proceeds should pass to the decedent's estate. Severson timely appealed the district court's decision.

III.   ANALYSIS

Severson argues that I.C. §15-2-803 does not prevent him from receiving one-half of the decedent's policy proceeds. Severson additionally argues that we should reverse the district court because he has appealed his criminal conviction and because the application of the slayer statute in this situation is unconstitutional. Finally, both parties request attorney's fees. We will address each argument in turn.

A.   I.C. §15-2-803 PREVENTS SEVERSON FROM RECEIVING
ANY OF THE DECEDENT'S POLICY PROCEEDS

Severson relies on *Travelers Insurance Co. v. Johnson,* 97 Idaho 336, 544 P.2d 294 (1975), to support his claim that he has a community property interest in one-half of the decedent's life insurance proceeds. According to *Travelers,* when certain requirements are met, including that a policy is acquired after marriage and the premiums are paid with community funds, that policy is community property. In such situations, the surviving spouse can void the gift of the proceeds "as to his half interest therein." Thus, one-half of the proceeds is the surviving spouse's own community property interest and the one-half that goes to the beneficiary is the interest of the decedent spouse. However, in this case, the surviving spouse is the "slayer" of the decedent spouse.

In *Travelers* we said that in a term life insurance policy the surviving spouse had no vested interest until the death of the insured. *Id.* at 340, 544 P.2d at 298. That is distinct from the situation where the marital community uses community property funds to purchase property in which both have a current vested interest; in that situation a spouse's community property interest does not depend upon the death of the other spouse. Therefore, the issue becomes whether any provision in Idaho's slayer statute prevents Severson from receiving proceeds of a policy in which he could have no vested interest until the death of the person whom he murdered.

1. I.C. §15-2-803(b) & (e)

The district court applied I.C. §15-2-803(b) & (e) to prevent Severson from receiving any of the proceeds. Both parties agree that I.C. §15-2-803(e) does not apply in this case.

Idaho Code §15-2-803(e) provides:

> Any community property which would have passed to or for the benefit of the slayer by devise, legacy or intestate succession from the decedent shall be distributed as if he had predeceased the decedent.

Idaho Code §15-2-803(e) does not apply to Severson because the one-half of the proceeds in question cannot be characterized as decedent's community property passing to Severson by "devise, legacy or intestate succession." Therefore, we hold that the application of I.C. §15-2-803(e) to Severson was error. Nonetheless, we will uphold a district court's decision if there is an alternative legal basis to support it.

2. I.C. §15-2-803(b) & (n)

The district court's grant of summary judgment can be upheld on the alternative basis that I.C. §15-2-803(b) & (n) prevent Severson from receiving any of the policy proceeds. "The Court will interpret [a] statute broadly to effectuate the intent of the legislature." In construing a statute, the Court "may examine the language used, the reasonableness of the proposed interpretations, and the policy behind the statute." The Court is to avoid an interpretation of a statute that leads to an absurd or harsh result.

Idaho Code §15-2-803(b) provides:

> No slayer shall in any way acquire any property or receive any benefit as a result of the death of the decedent, but such property shall pass as provided in the sections following.

Idaho Code §15-2-803(n) provides:

> This section shall not be considered penal in nature, but shall be construed broadly in order to effect the policy of this state that no person shall be allowed to profit by his own wrong, wherever committed.

The plain language of these subsections reveals the legislative intent that no slayer be allowed to acquire any property or receive any benefit as a result of the willful and unlawful killing of the decedent. Idaho Code §15-2-803(n) instructs the Court to construe the statute broadly in order to effectuate its purpose.

Idaho Code §15-2-803(b) flatly prohibits the slayer from acquiring any property or receiving any benefit as a result of the death of the decedent. Severson is not making a claim against the decedent's estate for his contribution to the policy premiums; he is making a claim on the policy proceeds. Had Severson not killed the decedent, the decedent would be alive and there would be no proceeds to receive. Hence, Severson would profit by the killing of the decedent if allowed to acquire any of the proceeds. This does not comport with the legislature's intent as expressed in I.C. §15-2-803(n). Nor is it in line with the I.C. §15-2-803(b) prohibition that a slayer not acquire any property or receive any benefit as a result of the death of the decedent.

Furthermore, had Severson been named as the policy's primary beneficiary, I.C. §15-2-803(j)(1) would have prevented Severson from receiving any proceeds. According to that subsection, had Severson been the primary beneficiary, the proceeds would have been paid to the secondary beneficiary and if there was no other beneficiary of the policy they would have gone to the decedent's estate. I.C. §15-2-803(j)(1). It would be an absurd result to interpret the slayer statute in a way that allows Severson to receive policy proceeds when he is not the policy's beneficiary but to prevent him from receiving policy proceeds when he is the policy's beneficiary.

Since to receive a share of the proceeds would be a benefit to Severson resulting from the decedent's death, we affirm summary judgment on the alternate grounds that I.C. §15-2-803(b) & (n) prevent Severson from receiving any of the policy proceeds. Additionally, we also reverse the district court's decision that one-half of the policy proceeds pass to the decedent's estate. We hold the terms of the policy control as I.C. §15-2-803(c)–(j) do not specifically apply and therefore the entire proceeds should be awarded to Diaz.

B.   SEVERSON'S APPEAL OF HIS CRIMINAL CONVICTION HAS NO EFFECT ON THIS CASE

C.   THE APPLICATION OF THE SLAYER STATUTE TO SEVERSON IS NOT UNCONSTITUTIONAL

D.   NEITHER EITHER PARTY SHOULD BE AWARDED ATTORNEY'S FEES

Diaz requests attorney's fees pursuant to I.C. §12-121 and I.C. §12-123 on the grounds that this appeal was brought frivolously. An award of attorney's fees under this set of statutes should be denied when the Court "cannot say that [the party's] legal argument . . . was so plainly fallacious as to be deemed frivolous, or that their case was not supported by a good faith argument for the extension or modification of the law in Idaho." *Hanf,* 120 Idaho at 370, 816 P.2d at 326. It cannot be said Severson brought this appeal frivolously as this is an issue of first impression and not a well settled area of law. Therefore, we also decline to award attorney's fees to Diaz.

IV.   Conclusion

We affirm the district court's grant of summary judgment on the alternate grounds that I.C. §15-2-803(b) & (n) prevent Severson from receiving any of the proceeds of the policy. We reverse the district court's decision that one-half of the policy proceeds pass to the decedent's estate and hold that the entire proceeds should pass according to the terms of the policy. We remand for proceedings in accordance with this opinion. Finally, we decline to award any party attorney's fees. Costs to Respondent.

Chief Justice SCHROEDER and Justices TROUT, EISMANN and JONES, concur.

Discussion Questions

1. On what basis could Severson claim that he was entitled to one-half of the life insurance proceeds?

2. If it is so clear that Severson should not be able to receive the life insurance proceeds, why did the Idaho Supreme Court decide that his appeal was not frivolous?

PROBLEM 15.1

During Alice and Bob's marriage, Alice opened a bank account for her brother Carl. Carl was younger than Alice. He had serious psychological problems and had never held a permanent job. Alice wanted to make sure that in the event that she died, Carl would have a significant nest egg to rely on. The bank account was in Alice's name "in trust for Carl." She did not tell Bob about the bank account that was funded from her community property earnings. Alice also made a will which stated that I "leave my interest in community property to my husband Bob." Alice was killed in an auto accident. The bank account had a balance of $100,000 at that time. The total community property estate at the time of Alice's death totaled $500,000. Bob is considering filing a lawsuit to receive one-half of the bank account, $50,000. Will Bob be entitled to $50,000 under the law of Nevada? California?

PROBLEM 15.2

Assume the same facts as Problem 15.1, except that Alice purchased a $100,000 life insurance policy from her community earnings and made Carl the beneficiary. How would a Texas court determine whether Carl will receive the proceeds of the insurance?

PROBLEM 15.3

When Ellen and Frank married, Frank took out a $100,000 term life insurance policy that was offered from his employer. He paid the premiums from his salary and he designated Ellen as the beneficiary. They divorced about a year ago and Frank married Gail. The divorce decree did not include any mention of the life insurance policy other than making Frank the owner of the policy. Frank continued to pay the premiums of that policy from his salary and did not change the beneficiary from Ellen. Frank died soon after his marriage to Gail. Ellen and Gail are both claiming the insurance proceeds. What argument supports Ellen's claim? Gail's claim? How would a New Mexico court decide?

PROBLEM 15.4

Assume the same facts as Problem 15.3, except that Frank had told his employer orally that he wanted to keep Ellen as the beneficiary of the policy. What is the result in Washington?

Table 15-1
Testamentary and Intestate Succession to Community Property
at Death in Community Property States

State	Rule	Case/Statute
Arizona	Each spouse is entitled to dispose of his/her half of community property by will upon death. If decedent's property is not disposed of by will or other nonprobate device, surviving spouse receives the decedent's half interest in the community property if decedent leaves no issue or all issue are also issue of the surviving spouse.	Ariz. Rev. Stat. §§14-3101 and 14-2102
California	Each spouse is entitled to dispose of his/her half of the community property and quasi-community property by will upon death. If decedent's property is not disposed of by will or other nonprobate device, surviving spouse receives the decedent's half-interest in the community property regardless of whether decedent leaves issue.	California Prob. Code §§100, 6101, and 6401
Idaho	Each spouse is entitled to dispose of his/her half of community and quasi-community property by will upon death. If decedent's property is not disposed of by will or other nonprobate device, surviving spouse receives the decedent's half-interest in the community property regardless of whether decedent leaves issue.	Idaho Code §§15-2-102, 15-2-201 and 15-3-101
Louisiana	Each spouse is entitled to dispose of his/her half of community by will upon death. If the couple acquired property while domiciled elsewhere that would have been community	La. Civ. Code §§888-890 (intestacy), §§2493-1496 and 1621 (forced heir), §§3526 (reclassification of property acquired elsewhere during marriage)

State	*Rule*	*Case/Statute*
	property had they been domiciled in Louisiana, Louisiana reclassifies this as community property at death. If decedent's property is not disposed of by will or other nonprobate device, surviving spouse receives the decedent's half-interest in the community property unless the decedent left issue. If decedent left issue, they get decedent's half-interest in the community property, but surviving spouse has a life estate (usufruct) in that half. *Note:* unlike any state in the country, Louisiana protects issue from disinheritance (even by will) at death of a parent unless there was just cause to have disinherited them for misconduct. Issue (called forced heirs) are entitled to a minimum share. At least one-quarter of decedent's estate must be preserved if there is one "forced heir" and half if there are two or more.	
Nevada	Each spouse is entitled to dispose of his/her half of community by will upon death. If decedent's property is not disposed of by will or other nonprobate device, surviving spouse receives the decedent's half-interest in the community property regardless of whether decedent leaves issue.	Nevada Revised Statutes §123-250
New Mexico	Each spouse is entitled to dispose of his/her half of community by will upon death. If decedent's property is not disposed of by will or other nonprobate device, surviving spouse receives the decedent's half-interest in the community property regardless of whether decedent leaves issue.	New Mex. Stat. Ann. §§45-3-101 and 45-2-102
Texas	Each spouse is entitled to dispose of his/her half of community by will upon death. If decedent's property is not disposed of by will or other nonprobate device, surviving spouse receives the decedent's half-interest in the community property if decedent leaves no issue or all issue are also issue of the surviving spouse.	Tex. Prob. Code §45 (after 2014, becomes Tex. Estates Code §201.003)

State	Rule	Case/Statute
Washington	Each spouse is entitled to dispose of his/her half of community by will upon death. If decedent's property is not disposed of by will or other nonprobate device, surviving spouse receives the decedent's half-interest in the community property regardless of whether decedent leaves issue.	RCW §§11.04.015, 26.16.030 and 26.16.230
Wisconsin	Each spouse is entitled to dispose of his/her half of the marital property by will, except the surviving spouse has an elective share to deferred marital property (which would have been marital property under Wisconsin's system when it was acquired). If decedent dies without a will, surviving spouse receives decedent's half interest in marital property if decedent leaves no issue or all issue are also issue of surviving spouse.	Wis. Stat. §§852.01. 861.02 (deferred marital property elective share)

Table 15-2
Division of Life Insurance Proceeds and Non-Testamentary Transfers at Death in Community Property States

State	Rule	Case/Statute
Arizona	Follows aggregate theory of division of community property at death, but item theory "not clearly adopted or rejected." A spouse's right to transfer community property is subject to a fiduciary duty. Absent intervening equities, a gift of substantial community property to a third person without the spouse's consent may be revoked and set aside for the benefit of the aggrieved spouse. If the surviving spouse did not receive half the community property, then there would be a constructive fraud upon the surviving spouse's right and the designation of beneficiary would be ineffective to the extent of the constructive fraud.	Ariz. Rev. Stat. §14-9316, *Gaethje v. Gaethje*, 7 Ariz. App. 544, 441 P.2d 579 (1968), *Estate of Kirkes*, 229 Ariz. 212, 273 P.3d 664 (Ct. App. 2012)
California	Follows the item theory of division of community property at death. Upon death of a married person, one-half of the community property belongs to the surviving spouse and one-half	California Probate Code §5021, codifying *Estate of Wilson*, 183 Cal. App. 3d 67, 227 Cal. Rptr. 794 (1986), *Estate of Miramontes-Najera*, 118 Cal. App. 4th 750,

State	Rule	Case/Statute
	belongs to the decedent. Each spouse has the right of testamentary disposition over his or her half of the community property. If a transfer of property is made without the written consent of the person's spouse, the court shall set aside the transfer as to the nonconsenting spouse's interest in the property. Discretion given to the court in some cases to aggregate property instead of imposing a division by item.	13 Cal. Rptr. 3d 240 (2004), *Estate of Resler*, 43 Cal. 2d 726, 278 P.2d 1 (1954)
Idaho	If life insurance policy premiums are paid from community funds during marriage, the surviving spouse has a vested interest in one-half of the proceeds upon the death of the insured. Named beneficiary of life insurance policy or IRA account can waive that interest in the policy through a property settlement upon divorce.	*Beneficial Life Ins. Co. v. Stoddard*, 95 Idaho 628, 516 P.2d 187 (1973), *Johnson v. Johnson*, 113 Idaho 602, 746 P.2d 1061 (1987)
Louisiana	Community property law does not apply to life insurance proceeds. Proceeds of life insurance, if payable to a named beneficiary other than the estate of the insured, are not considered to be a part of the estate of the insured. They do not come into existence during his life, never belong to him, and pass by virtue of the contractual agreement between the insured and the insurer to the beneficiary. Life insurance proceeds are not subject to Civil Code articles relating to donation inter vivos or mortis causa, nor are they subject to community claims or the laws regarding forced heirship.	*Demoruelle v. Allen*, 218 La. 603, 50 So. 2d 208 (Sup. Ct. 1950), *Fowler v. Fowler*, 861 So. 2d 181 (Sup. Ct. 2003), overruling *Thigpen v. Thigpen*, 231 La. 296, 91 So. 2d 126 (1937)
Nevada	Follows aggregate theory of division of community property at death. Upon death of either the husband or wife, an undivided one-half interest in the community property is the property of the surviving spouse. The remaining interest is subject to the testamentary disposition of the decedent. Validity of a Totten Trust recognized and proceeds with be the property of the beneficiary if less than one-half of the community property.	Nevada Revised Statutes §123-250(1)(a)–(b), *Byrd v. Lanahan*, 105 Nev. 707, 783 P.2d 426 (1989) (husband's savings account in trust for his daughter from a prior marriage entitled her to the entire proceeds because account was less than one-half of the community property)

State	Rule	Case/Statute
New Mexico	A divorce decree granting the insured spouse ownership of a life insurance policy revokes the interest of a former spouse who was designated as beneficiary. The insured owner has the right to change the beneficiary and divest the former spouse's interest in the proceeds of the policy.	*Matter of Schleis' Estate*, 97 N. M. 561, 642 P.2d 164 (1982), rev'd by statute, N.M.S.A. §45-2-804 (1993)
Texas	Follows modified item theory of division of community property at death. Proceeds of a life insurance policy acquired as a benefit of employment during marriage are community property. The employee spouse may designate the beneficiary of the policy. There is a trust relationship between the spouses regarding the community property controlled by each spouse. If the designation of a third-party beneficiary constitutes actual or constructive fraud on the community, proceeds may be awarded to the surviving spouse rather than the designated beneficiary. Designated beneficiary must prove that the disposition of the surviving spouse's one-half community interest is fair. Fairness is determined by (1) size of the gift in relation to the total size of the community estate, (2) the adequacy of the estate remaining to support the surviving spouse in spite of the gift, (3) relationship of the donor to the donee, and (4) whether special circumstances existed to justify the gift.	*Madrigal v. Madrigal*, 115 S.W. 3d 32 (Tex. Ct. App. 2003) (former wife of decedent did not prove gift of community life insurance to her was fair), *Estate of Vackar*, 345 S.W.3d 588 (Tex. Ct. App. 2011) (sister of decedent did not prove gift of community life insurance to her was fair)
Washington	Follows item theory of division of community property at death. Life insurance policy purchased with community funds during marriage is a community asset. A spouse may not make a gift of the entire community property without the consent of the other spouse. A decedent has the right to give one-half of the proceeds of a community property life insurance policy (or the community property portion of a policy) by designating as beneficiary a person or persons other than the spouse.	*Estate of Patton*, 6 Wash. App. 464, 494 P.2d 238 (1972), *Francis v. Francis*, 89 Wash. 2d 511, 573 P.2d 369 (1978), overruling *Occidental Life Ins. Co. v. Powers*, 192 Wash. 475, 74 P.2d 27 (1937), *Mearns v. Scharbach*, 103 Wash. App. 498, 12 P.3d 1048 (2000)

State	Rule	Case/Statute
Wisconsin	Follows item theory of division of marital property at death. Life insurance policy purchased during marriage is marital property and one purchased before marriage, where any premium is paid during marriage with marital funds, becomes mixed property. If insured names other spouse to receive proceeds at death, that is effective. But insured may only dispose of individual and marital property share of policy at death. A surviving spouse is entitled to his/her marital property share in the proceeds.	Wis. Stat. §766.61 & 860.01, *Bruskiewicz v. Bruskiewicz,* 344 Wis. 2d 125, 820 N.W.2d 157 (Ct. App. 2012) (unpublished)

Chapter 16

Moving to Another State: Conflicts of Laws

This chapter examines the issues that arise when a married couple moves from one state to another, a common occurrence in today's mobile society. It arises in two situations: when the move is from a common law state to a community property state and when the move is from one community property state to another community property state. The issue comes to the fore when the differences between the state laws will have a significant impact on the characterization and the division of the property accumulated during their marriage. It is especially acute when the move is from a common law state where a spouse's earnings are that spouse's property and the law of the common law state does not provide adequate protection for the non-earning spouse at divorce or death. When the move is from one community property state to another one, the differences may also affect how property is characterized at divorce. Thus, the courts' challenge is to resolve these "conflicts of laws."

There are two major theories to resolve these problems followed in community property states. The first is a traditional "conflicts of laws" approach. Under this approach, the character of the property is determined by the law of the state of acquisition. Therefore, if a married couple's earnings are the earner's property in a common law state, a community property state will respect that character even after the couple becomes domiciled in a community property state. In addition, the law of the common law state will be used to divide that property at divorce or distribute that property at death. To illustrate, let us return to our hypothetical couple, George and Martha. Assume that they acquired most of their wealth in a common law state where a spouse's earnings belong to the earner. In community property parlance, those earnings are separate property. If George was the breadwinner and Martha was not employed outside the home, their wealth would belong to George. If they move to a community property state, under traditional conflict of law analysis, the common law state's law would control the characterization of the property acquired during marriage. Thus, at divorce, if the common law state did not provide division of the property acquired from George's earnings, Martha would have no rights to the wealth accumulated during the marriage. The conflict with community property law is evident. In a community property state, earnings are community property and at divorce any property acquired with those earnings is community property. At divorce, in a community property state, the community property is either split 50/50 or equitably divided.

The second approach is the "quasi-community" property approach. In essence, the law of the community property state will control no matter where the property was acquired. That property, especially a spouse's earnings, is quasi-community property. Quasi-community property is defined as that property that would have been community property if acquired in a community property state. That means that even though the common law state would treat George's earnings as his property, a community property state would consider those earnings quasi-community property. That means that the character of George's earnings would be controlled by community property law not the law of where they were earned. If George and Martha divorced after moving to a community property state, quasi-community property would be divided according to the law of the community property state. Applying the law of the forum state is not uncommon in conflicts of law analysis. Applying the law of another forum raises difficulties for attorneys and judges who are not familiar with other systems and lack expertise in that law. Also, the legislature and courts in a community property state may favor the community property vision of equal ownership and resist application of common law principles that result in unfairness to a nonearning spouse. On the other hand, it is possible that the couple had the expectation that the law of where the property was acquired controlled. That is especially true when the marriage was a majority of the time in a common law state and the move to the community property state was for retirement or occurred soon before divorce.

A.   EXAMPLES OF THE "CONFLICTS OF LAW" AND QUASI-COMMUNITY APPROACHES

1.   Conflicts of Law Approach: Idaho

Most community property states have moved to a quasi-community property approach by enacting legislation that controls at divorce. However, Idaho and Nevada[1] follow the more traditional conflicts of law approach. The following Idaho case of *Berle v. Berle*, 97 Idaho 452, 546 P.2d 407 (1976), illustrates application of conflicts of law doctrine.

BERLE v. BERLE
97 Idaho 452, 546 P.2d 407 (1976)
Supreme Court of Idaho

McQUADE, Chief Justice.

The facts of this case are as follows. Plaintiff-appellant Winifred Berle (hereinafter appellant) and defendant-respondent Charles Berle (hereinafter respondent) were married in 1938 in the state of New Jersey. They lived in that state as husband and wife until October of 1971, when respondent left appellant in New Jersey and took up residence in Idaho. During their marriage, certain personal property

---

1. *Braddock v. Braddock*, 91 Nev. 735, 542 P.2d 1060 (1975) (Ohio law applied to character and division of community personal property at divorce).

consisting of securities and bank accounts was acquired by the parties. When respondent left New Jersey, he took this personal property with him and brought it to Idaho where it has remained ever since.

On November 30, 1971, respondent filed an action for divorce in Blaine County, Idaho. A copy of the complaint was personally served on appellant in New Jersey on December 9, 1971. Appellant applied for and received on December 17, 1971, a temporary restraining order from the Superior Court of New Jersey, Chancery Division–Essex County, enjoining respondent from further prosecution of his divorce action in Idaho. Notwithstanding this order, respondent obtained a decree of divorce in Idaho on January 6, 1972.[1]

Appellant did not make an appearance in the Idaho divorce proceedings, and her default was entered. The default judgment which was entered granted respondent a divorce from appellant; provided $250.00 per month alimony for the support and maintenance of appellant until such time as she might remarry, and awarded a 1966 Dodge Polara automobile to respondent as his "sole and separate" property. No disposition of other assets was made at that time.

Appellant brought this action in Twin Falls County against respondent seeking in count I of her complaint a division and distribution of the bank accounts and securities which were not disposed of at the time respondent's divorce decree was entered. In the alternative, in count II of her complaint, appellant seeks damages grounded in fraud. Her theory is that respondent's secretive actions and false statements led her to believe Idaho did not have jurisdiction to entertain respondent's divorce action at the time it was commenced in 1971, and that as a result of the respondent's fraudulent actions, she did not seek an equitable distribution of this personal property at the time respondent filed for divorce.

Respondent moved for judgment on the pleadings, or in the alternative, summary judgment, on the ground that there was no genuine issue as to any material fact and therefore he was entitled to judgment as a matter of law. The trial court deeming itself bound by the holdings of *Douglas v. Douglas,*[2] and *Peterson v. Peterson,*[3] granted the motion, dismissed the action with prejudice and entered judgment in the respondent's behalf. It ruled that the property in issue was under the law of New Jersey, respondent's "separate" property; that comity required the state of Idaho to denominate this personal property as respondent's "separate" property, and that under Idaho law, "separate" property was not subject to division between the parties in divorce proceedings. It is from the order granting summary judgment that appellant has brought this appeal.

Preliminarily, we must determine what effect, if any, the Blaine County divorce decree rendered on appellant's default, has in respect to her present claim for an equitable distribution of the marital property in respondent's possession at the time the decree was entered. Respondent contends that the doctrine of res judicata or collateral estoppel precludes appellant from asserting a claim to an equitable share of this property. We do not agree with this contention.

---

1. On July 9, 1973, a divorce was granted to appellant by the Superior Court of New Jersey, Chancery Division–Essex County, dissolving the marriage between appellant and respondent, and declaring that the Idaho divorce decree was null and void and of no effect in New Jersey. No award of property was made in that decree. Respondent was not personally served and did not make an appearance in that action. We need not decide whether this Court is obligated to give "full faith and credit" to the New Jersey judgment.

2. 22 Idaho 336, 125 P. 796 (1912).

3. 94 Idaho 187, 484 P.2d 736 (1971).

In his complaint in the divorce action respondent alleged that:

(D)uring the marriage of the parties, the following property has been accumulated:

(a) No real property
(b) Personal property

1. 1 1966 Dodge Polara automobile.
2. Certain items of personal property consisting of securities and bank accounts, all of which were acquired outside of the State of Idaho and while the Plaintiff was a resident of the State of New Jersey, all of which is Plaintiff's separate property and in whose name title to the same is vested.
3. Certain items of clothing, jewelry and miscellaneous personal effects belonging to the parties respectively, presently situated in the residence of the Defendant.

In the prayer part of his complaint, respondent requested that the marital bonds be severed; that he be awarded the automobile, that each of the parties be awarded those items of personal property consisting of clothing, jewelry and miscellaneous personal effects presently located at appellant's residence, that appellant be awarded alimony, and that the court grant such other and further relief as was equitable. No request was made for disposition of the securities and bank accounts mentioned in the complaint.

I.R.C.P. 54(c) provides in pertinent part:

A judgment by default shall not be different in kind from or exceed in amount that prayed for in the demand for judgment.

Although it was alleged in the complaint that during the marriage the parties had accumulated certain securities and bank accounts, the prayer for relief in respondent's complaint did not ask that he be awarded the securities and bank accounts. Therefore, the question of title over this property was never adjudicated in the divorce proceeding. In choosing not to respond to respondent's complaint, appellant had the right to assume that the judgment which would be entered following her default would embrace only the relief requested by the complaint, and that the relief granted would not exceed that prayed for therein. Accordingly, appellant is not barred from proceeding with her present action.

Appellant concedes that under the law of New Jersey (the state of marital domicile of the parties at the time the property was acquired), the property in issue during the existence of the marriage, would be denominated as the "separate" property of respondent. Appellant contends however that in determining the proper distribution of this property it was error to apply the law of this state, which prohibits the division of "separate" property upon a divorce, rather than the law of New Jersey, which recognizes the right of a spouse at the time of divorce to share in the distribution of this "separate" property. Appellant maintains that the concept of "separate" property in New Jersey differs significantly from the concept of "separate" property in Idaho. Therefore, appellant argues that it was wrong to apply an Idaho statute designed to govern the distribution of "separate" property, as that term is defined in this community property state, to the contested property, which being "separate" property under New Jersey law, carries with it the qualifications and incidents of ownership that that common-law jurisdiction attaches to it. We find this argument to be persuasive. Accordingly, we reverse the lower court's judgment and remand for a new trial.

The trial court found that the contested property was acquired by the parties while they were living together as man and wife in New Jersey. This finding is not disputed in this appeal. In accordance with New Jersey law, which does not recognize the concept of community property, this property was denominated as the "separate" property of respondent. However, under New Jersey law, this same "separate" property could be subject to an equitable distribution between the spouses on the occasion of a divorce. N.J.S.A. 2A:34-23 provides in pertinent part:

> In all actions where a judgment of divorce or divorce from bed and board is entered the court may make such award or awards to the parties, in addition to alimony and maintenance, to effectuate an equitable distribution of the property, both real and personal, which was legally and beneficially acquired by them or either of them during the marriage.

As noted by the New Jersey Supreme Court in construing this statute:

> A further question is presented when we consider assets that have come into the ownership of a spouse, or of both spouses jointly, during coverture. To the extent that such property is attributable to the expenditure of effort by either spouse, it clearly qualifies for distribution. Here we have principally in mind the earnings of husband or wife; such assets are certainly comprehended by the statute.[2]

Thus it is clear from both the statutory and case law of New Jersey, that the property in issue, despite its characterization during the existence of the marriage as respondent's "separate" property, could be subject to an equitable distribution upon a marital dissolution proceeding brought in that state. Appellant's interest in this "separate" property may be afforded protection under New Jersey law.[3] Had the property been acquired jointly by the parties while domiciled in this state, it clearly would have been deemed community property and subject to division upon a divorce.

We see no reason to defeat appellant's claim by applying an Idaho statute (I.C. §32-903) not designed to govern the property in issue. We find the reasoning of the Arizona appellate court in *Rau v. Rau*[4] to be of some assistance:

> We do not believe our legislature intended to prevent our divorce court from afecting the title to any and all property which under the law of the state of acquisition might bear the label "separate property." We construe the "separate property" as to which the statutory prohibition (in Arizona law) applies to be that defined in A.R.S. §25-213, subsec. A. To apply this restriction to "separate" estate acquired in a common-law jurisdiction only leads to unjust and unreasonable results. See de Funiak, *Conflict of Laws in the Community Property Field*, 7 Ariz. L. Rev. 50 (1965). When the restriction is limited to the statutory

2. Painter v. Painter, 65 N.J. 196, 320 A.2d 484, 493-94 (1974).

3. Professor Marsh has established as a qualified generalization that: "The wife's interest in the so-called statutory 'separate' property of the husband in a majority of common-law states is afforded a protection nearly equal to that given her interest in the community property acquired by the husband in the majority of community property jurisdictions." See Marsh, *Marital Property in Conflict of Law* at 45 (1952).

4. 6 Ariz. App. 362, 432 P.2d 910 (1967).

definition, the division made here does no violence to either the statutes of Arizona, or Illinois, and carries out the basic law of both jurisdictions that a fair division of marital property be made at time of divorce.[5]

We conclude that I.C. §32-903 prohibiting the distribution of "separate" property upon divorce is inapplicable, and cannot be utilized to defeat appellant's claim.[6]

In denying appellant's claim for an equitable share of the property, the trial court considered itself bound by the holdings of this Court in *Douglas v. Douglas, supra*, and in *Peterson v. Peterson, supra*. We believe that both Douglas and Peterson are distinguishable from the facts of this appeal, and are herefore not controlling.

In Douglas, the husband and wife were married in Colorado, and lived there for several years before moving to Idaho. Between the date of the marriage, and the time the parties relocated in Idaho, they accumulated real, personal, and mixed property which amounted to the sum of $13,050. Under Colorado law, this property was characterized as the husband's "separate" property. Upon arriving in Idaho, the husband invested this money in real estate in this state. The wife died a short time after the parties settled in Idaho. The wife's estate was administered on the theory that this real estate was community property. The husband challenged this, and brought a quiet title action to have this property declared to be his own "separate" property. The Court reversed the trial court which denied the husband's claim, and ruled in his favor.

Unlike the present appeal, where the property distribution law of New Jersey is before the Court, the opposite was true in Douglas. The contesting parties conceded that the property then in issue was the "separate" property of the husband under Colorado law. No attempt was made to show that the treatment of "separate" property in Colorado was any different from the treatment of "separate" property in Idaho. In the absence of evidence to the contrary, the Court correctly assumed that Colorado law with regard to the distribution of "separate" property was the same as Idaho law.

In *Peterson*, the wife was claiming an interest in Idaho real property which was given to the husband as a gift by his father while the parties were married and living in this state. The Restatement (Second) of Conflicts of Laws (1969) provides:

234. Effect of Marriage on an Interest of Land Later Acquired

(1) The effect of marriage upon an interest in land acquired by either of the spouses during coverture is determined by the law that would be applied by the courts of the situs.
(2) These courts would usually apply their own local law in determining such questions.

Under the law of the situs of the realty, which was Idaho, gifts to either spouse during marriage were the "separate" property of the acquiring spouse, not subject to distribution upon a divorce. Therefore the Court correctly denied the wife's claim

---

5. *I.d.* at 365, 432 P.2d at 913-14.
6. *Accord* Burton v. Burton, 23 Ariz. App. 159, 531 P.2d 204 (1975); contra Latterner v. Latterner, 121 Cal. App. 298, 8 P.2d 870 (1932).

to a share of the real property in Idaho acquired by the husband by way of a gift. The facts in *Peterson* distinguish it from the present appeal.

Our conclusion in this case does not penalize respondent for his relocation from New Jersey to Idaho, nor divest him of any property interest he might otherwise have. Upon remand, he will be awarded that to which he would be entitled under New Jersey law.

We reverse the trial court's judgment, and remand for a trial of the issues with instructions to divide the marital property in accordance with the applicable New Jersey law governing distribution of property upon divorce at the time respondent's divorce action was commenced.

Costs to appellant.

McFADDEN, DONALDSON and BAKES, JJ., concur.

SHEPARD, J., dissents without opinion.

Discussion Questions

1. What was the trial court's error in finding that Winifred had no rights to Charles's "separate" property at divorce?

2. How did the Supreme Court distinguish the earlier cases of *Douglas* and *Peterson*? What do you think will be the outcome of this case on remand?

---

2. Quasi-Community Property Approach: Texas Law at Divorce and Death

The Texas Legislature in 1981 adopted a "quasi-community property" statute, Texas Family Code §3.63(b), that applies at divorce. The statute overrides prior Texas law that used the traditional conflicts of law doctrine of applying the law of the place where the property was acquired. While reading the Texas case, *Ismail v. Ismail*, 702 S.W.2d 216 (Tex. Ct. App. 1985), note how the Court distinguishes California law and how the Court treats the constitutional issues regarding application of the Texas Code.

ISMAIL v. ISMAIL

702 S.W.2d 216 (1985)
Court of Appeals of Texas

WARREN, Justice.

This is a divorce case between two Egyptian citizens. The trial court granted the parties a divorce and divided certain property, including real property located in Egypt.

In six points of error, appellant contends that the trial court erred or abused its discretion: (1) in applying the Texas "quasi-community property statute" to this case, (2) in failing to decide this case under Egyptian law, (3) in failing to dismiss for forum non conveniens, (4) in dividing the alleged "quasi-community estate," (5) in awarding excessive attorney's fees to the appellee, and (6) in entering sanctions against the appellant.

Appellant and appellee, both Egyptian citizens, were married in July 1966. Shortly thereafter, they moved to Houston and lived there until 1972. During their stay in Houston, they both obtained permanent resident status (green cards), two children were born to them, and both received PhD degrees.

In 1972, the family returned to Egypt, but moved to England the following year. By the end of 1977, both were back in Egypt, and appellee was teaching at Al-Azhar University in Cairo. During that period, appellant bought Houston real estate, which is a subject of this appeal. The family lived together in Cairo until 1981, when appellee came back to Houston on a research fellowship. The fellowship was conditioned on appellee returning to Cairo and completing her research. Appellant accompanied appellee to Houston but only stayed long enough to rent an apartment, buy a car, and generally see that appellee was properly situated.

In December 1981, appellant began proceedings in Egypt to obtain permanent custody of the two children, who were living in Egypt. In January 1982, appellee filed for divorce in a Houston district court, seeking a division of the marital estate and custody of the two children. In May 1982, appellee returned to Egypt and resumed her position at Al-Azhar University. While there, she contested the custody suit and returned to Houston in July 1982, where she remained until the divorce trial.

In February 1982, appellant filed a general denial to appellee's divorce suit. From then until the decree was entered on August 9, 1984, both sides made extensive discovery, here and in Egypt. The trial court granted appellee a divorce, divided the property by giving appellee title to all Texas real property, her personal automobile, funds deposited in Texas bank accounts, and the personal property in her possession. Appellant was awarded all Egyptian real and personal property, all interest in certain business ventures, and all interest in pending lawsuits. Finally, the court awarded appellee $15,000 "as sanctions against appellant for his acts and omissions" as alleged by the wife, and $82,881.72 in attorney's fees. The court declined to decide child custody.

On August 21, 1984, the appellant requested that the court file findings of fact and conclusions of law. The same day, he filed his motion for extension of time in which to file findings of fact and conclusions of law. On September 10, 1984, he filed a motion for new trial. Neither the request for findings of fact and conclusions of law, nor the motion for new trial, was ever acted upon by the trial court.

I.   QUASI-COMMUNITY PROPERTY

In his first point of error, the appellant contends that the trial court erred in characterizing the Texas real estate as "quasi-community property" under section 3.63(b) of the Texas Family Code. In his fourth point of error, he contends that even if section 3.63(b) was properly applied in this case, the trial court abused its discretion in awarding all of the Texas realty to the appellee. That section, adopted in 1981, states:

> (b) In a decree of divorce or annulment the court shall also order a division of the following real and personal property, wherever situated, in a manner that the court deems just and right, having due regard for the rights of each party and any children of the marriage:
>
>> (1) property that was acquired by either spouse while domiciled elsewhere and that would have been community property if the spouse who acquired the property had been domiciled in this state at the time of the acquisition; or
>> (2) property that was acquired by either spouse in exchange for real or personal property, and that would have been community property if the spouse who acquired the property so exchanged had been domiciled in this state at the time of its acquisition.

Tex. Fam. Code Ann. sec. 3.63(b) (Vernon Supp. 1985). The appellant's arguments are essentially twofold: First, as a matter of statutory construction, section 3.63(b) does not apply to this case, since the appellee unilaterally moved to Texas; second, application of the statute in this case renders the statute unconstitutional.

The quasi-community property statute does not expressly limit its reach to situations where both spouses have migrated from a common law jurisdiction to Texas. Nonetheless, the appellant contends that the purpose of the statute is to remedy the inequities of prior decisions awarding all "common law separate property" acquired during the marriage to the acquiring spouse. He argues that where only one spouse migrates to Texas, the quasi-community property statute does not apply because the migrating spouse may enforce his or her rights to marital property by filing for divorce in the previous domicile. He further contends that because the appellee did not migrate from a common law jurisdiction (Egypt is neither a "community property" nor a "common law" jurisdiction), the statute does not apply.

We conclude that section 3.63(b) applies in the division of migratory spouses' property regardless of the nature of the previous domicile's legal system. This conclusion is supported by the plain meaning of the statute; it applies to property "wherever situated," acquired by either spouse while domiciled "elsewhere." Admittedly, the usual application of the statute will likely be in situations where the spouses were previously domiciled in a common law state. The legislative history of the provision indicates that this scenario was the primary focus of the legislation. See House Comm. on the Judiciary, Bill Analysis, Tex. H.B. 753, 67th Leg. (1981). No logic is given, however, to support the appellant's request that we limit the application of the statute to migrations from common law jurisdictions. The same potential problems exist in other migrations. The problems may even be exacerbated when the spouses migrate from a foreign country that has neither a common law nor a community property system. Moreover, applying the quasi-community property statute to migrations to Texas from all jurisdictions is the better rule in terms of uniformity and ease of application.

The appellant also argues that the statute should not be applied where only one spouse migrates to Texas. He contends that application of the statute in this context is unconstitutional. In support, he first cites California precedent for the proposition that the quasi-community property statute[1] only applies where both spouses have migrated to the community property state. *See In re Marriage of Roesch*, 83 Cal. App. 3d 96, 147 Cal. Rptr. 586 (Cal. Ct. App. 1978), *cert. denied*, 440 U.S. 915, 99 S. Ct. 1232, 59 L. Ed. 2d 465 (1979). *See also* Oldham, *Property Division in a Texas Divorce of a Migrant Spouse: Heads He Wins, Tails She Loses?* 19 Hous. L. Rev. 1, 25 n.134 (1981).

In *Roesch*, the California Court of Appeals held that its quasi-community property statute could be constitutionally applied only when two conditions were met: "(1) both parties have changed their domicile to California; and (2) subsequent to the change of domicile, the spouses sought in a California court legal alteration of their marital status." 83 Cal. App. 3d at 107, 147 Cal. Rptr. at 593; *see also Addison v. Addison*, 62 Cal. 2d 558, 399 P.2d 897, 43 Cal. Rptr. 97 (1965) (upholding the constitutionality of California's quasi-community property statute against constitutional attack based on (1) the due process clause's prohibition against legislation impinging upon "vested rights" via retroactive legislation and (2) the privileges and immunities clause of article IV of the United States Constitution). The *Roesch* court acknowledged that vested property rights may constitutionally be diminished by retroactive marital property legislation when demanded by a sufficiently important state interest. 83 Cal. App. 3d at 106, 147 Cal. Rptr. at 593. The court concluded, however, that the interest of California in the marital property was minimal and that the interest of Pennsylvania, the migrant spouse's previous domicile, was substantial. Finally, the *Roesch* court concluded that the non-migrant spouse (appellee) was sufficiently protected under the laws of Pennsylvania. *Id.* at 107, 147 Cal. Rptr. at 593. The *Roesch* court failed, however, to enunciate the precise rationale for its conclusion that application of the quasi-community property statute to a unilateral migration violated due process. *See* Oldham, *supra*, at 28 n.134. Professor Oldham noted:

> Unfortunately, the [*Roesch*] court did not state whether it believed that the application of the California law violated due process because California had no interest in the application of its law, or because California had insufficient contacts with the parties, or because California's contacts with the parties were so late in the chronology of the matter that the application of its law would constitute unfair surprise. The court also asserted that the wife was "entitled to the protection of the laws of [Pennsylvania]." This is, at best, a strange statement, since Pennsylvania law did not permit the equitable distribution of the spouses' property at divorce and gave the wife no protection.

Id.

The appellant also argues that the Texas Constitution[2] as interpreted by the Texas Supreme Court, prohibits the divestment of a spouse's "separate" property. In *Eggemeyer v. Eggemeyer*, 554 S.W.2d 137 (Tex. 1977), the court held that a trial court may not divest one spouse of his separate realty and transfer title to the other

---

1. See Cal. Civ. Code sec. 4803 (West 1970). The California Statute, enacted in 1961, is virtually identical to the Texas statute.

2. "No citizen of this State shall be deprived of life, liberty, property, privileges or immunities, or in any manner disfranchised, except by the due course of the law of the land." Tex. Const. art. I, sec. 19. The appellant is entitled to due process even though he is not a domiciliary of Texas. See *Pintor v. Martinez*, 202 S.W.2d 333, 335 (Tex. Civ. App. — Austin 1947, writ ref'd n.r.e.).

spouse. In *Cameron v. Cameron*, 641 S.W.2d 210 (Tex. 1982), the court adhered to the principle enunciated in *Eggemeyer* and concluded that art. 3.63(b) does not order division of what is considered "separate" property under community property law:

> [W]e hold that the property spouses acquire during marriage, except by gift, devise or descent should be divided upon divorce in Texas in the same manner as community property, irrespective of the domicile of the spouses when they acquire the property. *Id.* at 220. The appellant notes, however, that the *Cameron* court expressly held that its decision did not run afoul of the *Eggemeyer* prohibition against divestment because the Texas division of property in the case before it approximated a common law equitable distribution:

>> A Texas court that makes a distribution on divorce of the common law marital estate equivalent to what would occur in the common law jurisdiction where the couple was domiciled when they acquired the property, does not imp air the rights of spouses in the common law marital property. No divestment transpires because the acquiring spouse loses no more in a Texas divorce than he loses in a judgment rendered in an equitable distribution common law state. . . . Our judicial adoption of the quasi-community property amendment to Tex. Fam. Code Ann. sec. 3.63 does not violate article I, section 19 of the Texas Constitution.

Id. at 222-23 (citation omitted).

We conclude that the *Eggemeyer*, *Cameron*, and *Roesch* decisions do not prohibit application of the quasi-community property statute to this case. The real property that is the subject of this appeal is located in Texas. Texas obviously has a significant interest in controlling the disposition of property located within its boundaries, and indeed, Texas follows the general rule that marital rights of spouses in real property are determined by the law of the place where the land is situated. *See Commissioner v. Skaggs*, 122 F.2d 721, 723 (5th Cir. 1941), *cert. denied*, 315 U.S. 811, 62 S. Ct. 796, 86 L. Ed. 1210 (1942). Additionally, the appellant, unlike the non-migrant spouse in Roesch, has had other significant continuous business and personal contacts with Texas: the Ismails lived in Houston for six years, maintained bank accounts here, and traveled to Texas on various other occasions. Thus, from a due process perspective, appellant's contacts with Texas, when coupled with Texas' interest in protecting the migrant spouse in this case, warrant application of Texas law to the division of the Texas property.[3]

Also, we should not interpret the language of *Cameron* to hold that in every case where a party receives less in the Texas community property division than he or she would have received under the system of the previous domicile, the party

---

3. See Sampson, Interstate Spouses, *Interstate Property, and Divorce*, 13 Tex. Tech. L. Rev. 1285 (1982). It is arguable that a different outcome from that in *Roesch* is warranted in unilateral migratory divorces in Texas. Professor Sampson hypothesized:

> When the spouses reside in different states, the Texas outcome could well be exactly opposite from the *Roesch* decision under California law. After all, the California approach to dividing property is very different from the Texas formulation—a 50/50 split plus possible alimony versus equitable division and no alimony. Further, California law characterizes property earned or acquired after the spouses actually begin living separate and apart as separate. Texas law is exactly opposite. It is reasonable for a Texas court to equitably divide all the property before it, and in fact, this long has been the accepted procedure.

Id. at 1347-48. We should, however, heed the professor's admonition that "[p]redicting future applications of the quasi-community statute may be hazardous to one's health." *Id.* at 1346.

has been deprived of due process. Clearly, where the Texas division of property approximates what another domicile's law requires, the non-migrant spouse may not complain of divestment of "separate" property. But neither can the appellant in this case complain of an unconstitutional divestment of "separate" property under our state's constitution when, through his extensive contacts with this state, and through his personal appearance in this litigation, he has implicitly consented to Texas courts' exercising their jurisdiction in equitably dividing the marital property.

Finally, the appellant contends that the application of the quasi-community property statute is unconstitutional, since it constitutes a retroactive application of the statute. We reject this argument. First, the statute itself appears to have been enacted with the intent that it would apply retroactively. See Sampson, *supra*, at 1354. Second, an overriding public interest justifies application of section 3.63(b) of the Family Code to property acquired before the enactment of this statute. See *Cameron*, 641 S.W.2d at 219. If this court were to limit the effect of the statute to property acquired after the effective date of the statute, its remedial benefits would be lost for a generation of ill-fated marriages. Lastly, the Texas Supreme Court, in *Cameron*, judicially adopted section 3.63(b). That court's decision to adopt the statute retroactively is binding on this court.

We conclude that section 3.63(b) of the Texas Family Code applies to the facts presented in this case and that application of the statute in our case violates neither the United States nor the Texas constitutions. Finally, we overrule the appellant's fourth point of error, complaining of an abuse of discretion in the division of the marital property. The court awarded substantial property, both real and personal, located in Egypt to the appellant.

In considering whether or not the court abused its discretion in the division of property, it is the duty of the court to indulge every reasonable presumption in favor of a proper exercise of discretion by the trial court in dividing the property of the parties. *Thompson v. Thompson*, 380 S.W.2d 632, 636 (Tex. Civ. App.-Ft. Worth 1964, no writ). Further, the court may consider the value of real property lying outside of Texas in an equitable division of property. Texas courts do not assert jurisdiction to determine title to such land but may consider the foreign investment when dividing property. *See In re Read*, 634 S.W.2d 343, 348-349 (Tex. App.-Amarillo 1982, writ dism'd); *In re Glaze*, 605 S.W.2d 721, 724 (Tex. Civ. App.-Amarillo 1980, no writ). After reviewing the evidence, we note that the court considered in its award a substantial amount of property that was valued at over $2,000,000. Approximately one fourth of this amount, consisting of the property located in Houston, Texas, was awarded to the wife. The balance of the property was awarded to the husband. We find that the court did not abuse its discretion in its division of the property.

Appellant's first and fourth points of error are overruled.

* * *

II. CHOICE OF LAW

In his second point of error, the appellant argues that the trial court erred in deciding this case under Texas law because applicable choice of law principles, both traditional and those contained in the Restatement (Second) of Conflicts, dictate that this case be determined under Egyptian law. He cites *Orr v. Pope*, 400 S.W.2d 614 (Tex. Civ. App. — Amarillo 1966, no writ), and *Joiner v. Joiner*, 131 Tex. 27, 112 S.W.2d 1049 (1938). Both cases, decided long before the enactment of section 3.63(b), merely restate the rule of law that was the impetus for the enactment of the quasi-community property statute: Property acquired by a spouse when domiciled in another jurisdiction was, under pre-*Cameron* common law, characterized according to the previous domicile's laws.

The enactment of section 3.63(b), however, obviates the need to apply this anachronistic conflict-of-laws principle. See *Cameron*, 641 S.W.2d at 222. As Professor Sampson recently wrote:

> [Section 3.63(b)] constitutes a rejection of, or rather a substitution for, the standard conflict-of-laws solution. This remedy has become unworkable in modern mobile America. In short, a legislative solution has been provided to cut through the tangled jungle that has necessarily grown from the inherent limitations of the judge-created answer supplied by traditional conflict-of-laws theory.

Sampson, *supra* note 3, at 1344. Since the court properly applied section 3.63 (b) to this case, there was no error in refusing to apply Egyptian law.

Appellant's second point of error is overruled.

The part of the judgment awarding attorney's fees is reversed, severed, and remanded to the trial court for a hearing; the remainder of the judgment is affirmed.

Discussion Questions

1. Since the property awarded to the wife was acquired in Texas, what were the issues regarding application of the "quasi-community property" statute and how were they resolved?

2. What was husband's argument that Egyptian law should apply and did it succeed?

Two years after the decision in *Ismail*, the Texas Supreme Court took up the issue of whether the "quasi-community property" statute should also apply in death situations. This was a difficult argument to make since Texas Family Code §3.63(b) mentions only "a decree of divorce or annulment." However, the surviving spouse of Robert C. Hanau, Doris, made that argument in *Estate of Hanau v. Hanau*, 730 S.W.2d 663 (Tex. Sup. Ct. 1987). It was ultimately rejected. While reading the Court's decision, assess whether you agree with the Court's rationale.

ESTATE OF HANAU v. HANAU

730 S.W.2d 663 (1987)
Supreme Court of Texas

ROBERTSON, Justice.

This case involves the question of whether the rule announced in *Cameron v. Cameron*, 641 S.W.2d 210 (Tex. 1982) applies to probate as well as divorce matters.

Robert and Dorris Hanau were married in Illinois in 1974 and five years later moved to Texas. After moving here, Robert prepared a will leaving his separate property to his children by a prior marriage, and his community property to Dorris. Robert and Dorris each had substantial amounts of separate property before the marriage, and at all times kept such property under their own names. While married and in Illinois, Robert accumulated numerous shares of stock through the use of his separate property. Under Illinois common law, this would have remained his separate property. Robert died in Texas in 1982 and Dorris was granted letters testamentary on May 10, 1982. In February 1983, Dorris transferred large amounts of the estate's stock to the son, Steven, and the daughter, Leslie Ann. In May 1983, however, Steven brought an original petition seeking to have Dorris removed as execututrix, claiming that she was intentionally mismanaging and embezzling from the estate. Dorris soon thereafter filed an inventory and appraisal listing all of the property owned by Robert, claiming that all stocks obtained by Robert during their marriage were community property, even though they were originally acquired in a common law state. Thus, Dorris sought the return of some of the stock she had already delivered to the children. The parties stipulated that the stocks acquired before marriage were Robert's separate property and that stocks acquired while married in Texas were community property. The only question presented to the trial court was the status of those stocks bought during the marriage in Illinois using Robert's separate property.

The trial court severed the question of proper distribution of the assets and granted a partial summary judgment to Dorris on the characterization issue. The trial judge ruled that all the amounts that accrued during the marriage would be considered as community property in Texas, despite their characterization as separate property outside the state. He concluded that "the Texas Supreme Court in *Cameron v. Cameron* could not have intended to limit its new characterization of common law marital property to divorce proceedings, but rather intended that said characterization to be applied to any situation where the issue arose, including probate proceedings."

The court of appeals affirmed in part and reversed in part. 721 S.W.2d 515. The court determined that *Cameron* was not applicable to probate situations, rather it should be limited only to divorce matters. Therefore, the court held that most of the stocks should have been classified as separate property, and rendered judgment that they go to the son and daughter. The court did, however, affirm as to one specific stock (TransWorld) where it held that a proper tracing could not be shown so as to classify it as separate property. Both parties appeal here; Dorris as to the former holding, Steven as to the latter. We affirm in part and reverse and render in part.

In her application, Dorris relies exclusively on §3.63 of the Family Code and *Cameron v. Cameron*, 641 S.W.2d 210 (Tex. 1982). Dorris admits that *Cameron* dealt with divorce rather than probate, but argues that this court intended to make "a fundamental change in its characterization of common law marital property." She argues that a broad interpretation of the result in *Cameron* should be applied because no distinction can be made between dissolution of the marriage by death or divorce. We disagree.

The long-standing general rule is that property which is separate property in the state of the matrimonial domicile at the time of its acquisition will not be treated for probate purposes as though acquired in Texas. *Oliver v. Robertson*, 41 Tex. 422, 425 (1874); *McClain v. Holder*, 279 S.W.2d 105, 107 (Tex. Civ. App.-Galveston 1955, writ ref'd n.r.e.). In *Cameron*, we held, however, that separate property acquired in common law jurisdictions merits different treatment in the limited context of divorce or annulment. While there were solid reasons for creating the *Cameron* rule in those situations, the same rationales are not applicable to probate procedures.

In *Cameron*, this court used three bases for its holding. First, the court examined the laws of some of the other community property states, and agreed that a difference exists between common law marital property and the separate property of community property jurisdictions. This court cited to several cases, including *Rau v. Rau*, 6 Ariz. App. 362, 432 P.2d 910 (Ct. App. 1967), in support of its holding. In examining *Rau*, however, it is clear that the court there refused to apply the rule to probate cases because "the statutory regulation of rights of succession has been regarded as something apart from the determination of property rights between living persons." *Id.*, at 914. Furthermore, nothing in the other cases used for support in *Cameron* reveals an intent to extend the rule to probate cases in those jurisdictions. *See Hughes v. Hughes*, 91 N.M. 339, 573 P.2d 1194 (1978); *Berle v. Berle*, 97 Idaho 452, 546 P.2d 407 (1976). In fact, it appears that the only community property states which have extended the rule reach such a result based completely upon statutory authority. *See* California Prob. Code §66 (West 1985); Idaho Code §15-2-201 (1971). Thus, there is no case law or trend which supports change of the rule here.

The second basis used in *Cameron* was the Texas legislature's action in adopting §3.63 of the Family Code. Section 3.63 provides that a trial judge shall make a "just and right" division of property, which may include: "Property that was acquired by either spouse while domiciled elsewhere and that would have been community property if the spouse who acquired the property had been domiciled in the state at the time of the acquisition." Therefore, this court merely judicially adopted §3.63 into the substantive law of this State. Dorris suggests that we apply §3.63 to the probate situation, but by its own terms the Family Code provision applies only "in a decree of divorce or annulment." In addition, there is no provision similar to §3.63 in the Probate Code, nor in any other statute of this state, which would logically require us to follow her suggestion. Therefore, there is also a lack of statutory authority which mitigates against extending *Cameron*.

The final foundation in *Cameron* dealt with the necessity of giving the trial court the power to effect an equitable distribution of property. Without such power, unfair results could occur because one spouse's equitable share of the other spouse's separate property under common law might not be considered under our community property definition of separate property. The *Cameron* holding merely made such an interest in common law separate property one which is susceptible to a Texas trial court's equitable division. The key is that there is no similar right in a probate proceeding, nor is there any need for any. If there is a valid will, the will should usually be enforced regardless of the equity of the devises or bequests within. *Huffman v. Huffman*, 161 Tex. 267, 339 S.W.2d 885, 889 (1960) (while a court can relax rules of construction, it may not redraft a will). Similarly, if the property is to pass through intestacy, a specified statutory formula is invoked which operates without the need to make equitable determinations. *See* TEX. PROB. CODE ANN. §38 (Vernon 1980).

In sum, to extend *Cameron* would make a shambles of 150 years of Texas probate law, thus, without a clear showing of supporting case law, statutory authority or a clear need for such broad power in the trial court, we refuse to do so. Because the court of appeals refused to enlarge *Cameron*, its judgment on this point is affirmed.

In turning to the only other issue in this case, we must address whether the court of appeals erred in holding that the 200 shares of TransWorld stock were not properly traced.

* * *

Because the court of appeals' holding that the TransWorld stock was not properly traced was erroneous, we reverse the judgment of the court of appeals and render judgment that the TransWorld stock be transferred to Steven Hanau. The judgment is in all other things affirmed.

SPEARS, J., filed a concurring opinion.

SPEARS, Justice, concurring.

I concur in the result reached by the court. *Cameron v. Cameron*, 641 S.W.2d 210, 221-23 (Tex. 1982), was based in large part upon Section 3.63 of the Family Code which provided statutory authorization for the characterization of property acquired outside of Texas as quasi-community property. No such provision is present in the Probate Code; therefore, I concur.

The court's opinion creates two rules for the characterization of the same property. A husband and wife from a common law state could retire to Texas with the majority of their property characterized as the husband's separate marital property. If the wife brought divorce proceedings, the "separate" marital property would be characterized as quasi-community property under *Cameron* and Section 3.63 of the Family Code. The trial court would then be authorized to divide the marital property between the spouses in a manner that it deemed just and right. Under the majority's decision in this case, the same husband could execute a will devising all the "separate" marital property to a third party leaving the wife without any means of support after he dies.

Most jurisdictions have some method to protect the interest and insure the support of surviving spouses. This court's holding leaves surviving spouses without the protection afforded by either common law or community property statutory schemes in certain situations. Accordingly, I urge the Legislature to eliminate this illogical and potentially inequitable difference in the characterization of marital property by adopting a Probate Code section similar to Section 3.63 of the Family Code and the probate codes of other jurisdictions. *See* California Prob. Code §66 (West 1985); Idaho Code §15-2-201 (1971).

Discussion Questions

1. Why did the Supreme Court determine that the "quasi-community property" statute does not apply to a probate proceeding?

2. What was Justice Spears' objection to the majority opinion?

---

3. Quasi-Community Property Statutes: The Louisiana Approach

Along with California and Idaho, Louisiana's legislature has enacted quasi-community statutes that apply at divorce and at death. How the Louisiana quasi-community statute protects a surviving spouse's interest is illustrated by the following case, *In re Succession of Hubbard*, 803 So. 2d 1074 (La. Ct. App. 2001). While reading this case, think about whether the result reflects the decedent John's intent or whether it is the fair result.

IN RE SUCCESSION OF HUBBARD

803 So. 2d 1074 (2001)
Court of Appeal of Louisiana

KLINE, Judge.

This is an appeal by a surviving spouse from a judgment applying Florida law to award full ownership of shares of stock in decedent's name to the heirs of the deceased. For the reasons that follow, we reverse and remand.

FACTS AND PROCEDURAL HISTORY

John Wilson Hubbard and Ruth Vanhook Hubbard were married in Oklahoma on February 15, 1964. Mr. Hubbard went to work for Jacobs Engineering Company ("Jacobs") in 1971. The Hubbards moved to Florida and while employed by Jacobs, Mr. Hubbard enrolled in a "Thrift Savings Retirement Plan," which provided for the deduction of funds from his paychecks for investment in specified funds, including Jacobs stock. In conjunction with this retirement plan, Mr. Hubbard executed a document naming Ruth Hubbard as his primary beneficiary.

The Hubbards moved to Louisiana in May of 1976. Thereafter, Mr. Hubbard's employment with Jacobs terminated in July of 1976; he was re-hired and again terminated his employment with Jacobs in 1977. In settlement of his investments with the retirement plan, Mr. Hubbard received 188 shares of Jacobs stock and a check for the accumulated cash value of his account. At the time of his demise, the shares of stock had increased to some 2044 shares, by means of stock splits over the years; no new shares were purchased after Mr. Hubbard's employment with Jacobs ended.

Mr. Hubbard died on December 21, 1985. The succession proceeding was instituted September 22, 1998. Subsequently, a dispute arose between Ruth Hubbard and Mr. Hubbard's daughters from a prior marriage over the ownership of the Jacobs stock. The daughters filed a petition to be put in possession of Mr. Hubbard's separate property, namely, the Jacobs stock. After hearing the matter on November 16, 1999, the trial judge rendered judgment in favor of Mr. Hubbard's daughters, recognizing them as the sole owners of the Jacobs stock. From that judgment, Ruth Hubbard appeals, urging the following assignments of error:

> (1) The Trial Court erred in failing to adjudicate Ruth V. Hubbard as the owner of 100% of the Jacobs Engineering Group, Inc. stock pursuant to the "Multiple Beneficiary Designation" introduced into evidence as "H-2";
> (2) Alternatively, the Trial Court erred in holding that Florida laws, and particularly Florida Statute Sections 731.011 and 732.102, "have no bearing on this issue," i.e., the ownership of the stock.

DISCUSSION

Appellant urges this court to hold that since the shares of stock in question were the assets of the retirement plan, Mr. Hubbard's beneficiary designation should govern. In support of this position, the original beneficiary designation form executed by Mr. Hubbard was submitted into evidence before the trial court. This form states, "1, a Participant in the Jacobs Engineering Co. Thrift Savings Retirement Plan, hereby designate the person or persons whose names appear below as Beneficiary or Beneficiaries to receive, in the event of my death, if they are then living, amounts credited to my Accounts under said Plan." Ruth V. Hubbard was named thereunder as primary beneficiary, entitled to a one hundred percent share. Mr. Hubbard named his daughters, along with his step-daughters, and step-grandsons as contingent beneficiaries, each entitled to a contingent twenty percent or less share.

* * *

The testimony presented in this case established that upon termination of Mr. Hubbard's employment with Jacobs, he received a check for the cash accumulated in his account and the shares of stock at issue herein. The retirement account was effectively closed at that time. The beneficiary designation executed in conjunction therewith could have no effect on assets maintained outside of the account. Thus, the beneficiary designation can have no effect on the shares of stock that Mr. Hubbard personally received on the closing of his retirement account and were subsequently held by him.

We next examine what law should be applied to determine how the shares of stock devolve in Mr. Hubbard's intestate succession. In deciding to apply Florida law to the matter, the trial court relied on La. C.C. art. 3523, which provides as follows:

> *Except as otherwise provided in this Title*, the rights and obligations of spouses with regard to movables, wherever situated, acquired by either spouse during marriage are governed by the law of the domicile of the acquiring spouse at the time of acquisition.

(Emphasis added.) Our review of the choice of law provisions leads us to believe that La. C.C. art. 3526 is the more relevant article; it provides:

> Upon termination of the community, or dissolution by death or by divorce of the marriage of spouses either of whom is domiciled in this state, their respective rights and obligations with regard to immovables situated in this state and movables, wherever situated, that were acquired during the marriage by either spouse while domiciled in another state shall be determined as follows:
>
> > (1) Property that is classified as community property under the law of this state shall be treated as community property under that law; and
> >
> > (2) Property that is not classified as community property under the law of this state shall be treated as the separate property of the acquiring spouse. However, the other spouse shall be entitled, in value only, to the same rights with regard to this property as would be granted by the law of the state in which the acquiring spouse was domiciled at the time of acquisition.

(Emphasis added.)

The comments to article 3523 expressly state that one of the exceptions to that article is found in article 3526. La. C.C. art. 3523, comment (a). Similarly, the comments to article 3526 state that article 3526 derogates from the general principle of article 3523, and "prevails over it, being more specific." La. C.C. art. 3526, comment (a). The application of article 3526 is further explained by comments (b) through (f) as follows:

> (b) *Classification of property.* This Article envisions two separate mental steps. The first step is the classification of the property that falls within the scope of the Article as either "community property" or "separate property." This classification is to be conducted "under the law of this state," that is, the substantive rules Louisiana has devised for cases that do not contain any foreign elements. See, e.g., La. Civ. Code Arts. 2325-2437 (Rev. 1979). In other words, the classification is to be conducted as if the spouses were domiciled in Louisiana at all critical times. Aside from logistical simplicity, one reason for applying Louisiana law here is to avoid the anomaly of having to apply the law of a another state (e.g., a common-law separate-property state) to matters of classification when that state might not have any comparable scheme for classifying property.
>
> (c) *Distribution of property.* The second step is the determination of the respective rights of spouses with regard to the property that has been classified in the first step. For brevity's sake this step is called "distribution," although in actuality the property may not always be distributed. Although, as explained above, the classification of the property is governed exclusively by Louisiana law, the distribution of the property may be governed either by Louisiana law or by the law of another state.
>
> Subparagraph (1) applies to property that is classified as community property under Louisiana classification law and calls for the application of the same law for distributing that property at Louisiana's 50:50 ratio between the spouses or their successors. Subparagraph (2) applies to property classified as separate property under Louisiana law and calls for the application of the distribution law of the state where the acquiring spouse was domiciled at the time of acquisition. The reason for this difference is explained below.
>
> (d) Subparagraph (1): "Quasi-Community." Subparagraph (1) attempts to secure for the non-acquiring, formerly non-Louisianian, spouse the same protection as is provided by Louisiana substantive law for similarly situated Louisiana spouses. This scheme is similar to

Chapter 16. Moving to Another State: Conflicts of Laws

what is known in other states as the scheme of "quasi-community." One difference is that this provision is applicable to both divorce and death situations, whereas, with the exception of Idaho and California, other community property states confine their scheme to divorce situations only. See also §§17, 18 of the Uniform Marital Property Act. Another and more important difference stems from the fact that the quasi-community rule of subparagraph (1) is supplemented by the rule of subparagraph (2), which is explained infra.

(e) Subparagraph (2). Subparagraph (2) of this Article applies only to property that is not classified as community property under Louisiana substantive law. As long as the marriage lasts, this property is governed by the law designated by Article 3524 for immovables, and by Article 3523 for movables. Upon dissolution of the marriage, subparagraph (2) of this Article becomes operative and calls for the application of the distribution law of the state in which the acquiring spouse was domiciled at the time of acquisition. For similar results under the jurisprudence, see *Schueler v. Schueler*, 460 So. 2d 1120 (La. App. 2d Cir. 1985); *Gilbert v. Gilbert*, 442 So. 2d 1330 (La. App. 3rd Cir. 1983). See also *Hughes v. Hughes*, 91 N.M. 339, 573 P.2d 1194 (1978).

(f) The objective of subparagraph (2) is the same as that of subparagraph (1), namely to afford some protection to the non-acquiring spouse. Subparagraph (1) accomplishes this objective through the application of the community-property law of this state. Subparagraph (2) accomplishes the same objective through the application of the distribution laws of the domicile of the acquiring spouse at the time of acquisition. The co-existence of the two subparagraphs might create an impression of overprotection of the non-acquiring spouse. For a critique on exactly this point, see Reppy, "Louisiana's Proposed 'Hybrid' Quasi-Community Property Statute Could Cause Unfairness," 13(3) Comm. Prop. J. 1 (1986). For a response, see Symeonides, "In Search of New Choice-of-Law Solutions to Some Marital Property Problems of Migrant Spouses: A Response to the Critics," 13(3) Comm. Prop. J. 11 (1986).

Article 3526, as applied to the factual situation presented in this case, directs the district court to evaluate movable property, with respect to its classification as community or separate property, under the law of this state. The comments to article 3526 acknowledge such an approach is in derogation of article 3523, and indicate that the derogation is intended to protect the non-acquiring spouse.

In the face of such an express directive, the courts have no choice but to evaluate the shares of Jacobs stock, at issue in this case, in accordance with Louisiana law. Community property is defined by La. C.C. art. 2338 as comprising: "property acquired during the existence of the legal regime through the effort, skill, or industry of either spouse; property acquired with community things or with community and separate things, unless classified as separate property under Article 2341; property donated to the spouses jointly; natural and civil fruits of community property; damages awarded for loss or injury to a thing belonging to the community; and all other property not classified by law as separate property." In contrast, separate property is defined by La. C.C. art. 2341 as comprising: "property acquired by a spouse prior to the establishment of a community property regime; property acquired by a spouse with separate things or with separate and community things when the value of the community things is inconsequential in comparison with the value of the separate things used; property acquired by a spouse by inheritance or donation to him individually; damages awarded to a spouse in an action for breach of contract against the other spouse or for the loss sustained as a result of fraud or bad faith in the management of community property by the other spouse; damages or other indemnity awarded to a spouse in connection with the management of his separate property; and things acquired by a spouse as a result of a voluntary partition of the community during the existence of a community property regime." Things in the possession of a spouse during the existence of a community property regime are presumed to be community, though either spouse may prove that they are separate property. La. C.C. art. 2340.

Since the Jacobs stock was purchased with Mr. Hubbard's wages, which are considered community property under La. C.C. art. 2338, the stock must also be classified as community property. Therefore, the intestate succession provisions relative to community property, La. C.C. arts. 888-890, should be applied to determine the ownership of the Jacobs stock. The application of these provisions result in the inheritance by Mr. Hubbard's children of a one-half share of the Jacobs stock, with Mrs. Ruth Hubbard retaining a one-half share, as her community property interest in the community asset.

We reject the argument of appellees that application of the aforementioned conflict of laws provisions affects their property rights, which vested prior to the enactment of the law. As noted hereinabove, Mr. Hubbard died in 1985; however, the instant succession proceeding was not instituted until 1998. In the interim, 1991 La. Acts., No. 923 was enacted. Section 4 of Act 923 provides, "This Act shall become effective on January 1, 1992, and shall apply to all actions filed after that date." *See Kanz v. Wilson*, 96-0882, p. 10 (La. App. 1st Cir. 11/17/97), 703 So. 2d 1331, 1337.

Nevertheless, even where the legislature has expressed its intent to give a law retroactive effect, that law may not be applied retroactively if it would impair contractual obligations or disturb vested rights. *Morial v. Smith & Wesson Corporation*, 2000-1132, p. 9 (La. 4/3/01), 785 So. 2d 1, 10, *cert. denied*, 534 U.S. 951, 122 S. Ct. 346, 151 L. Ed. 2d 262 (2001). Because we find that the result would have been the same under the conflict of laws considerations in effect prior to the enactment of Act 923, and consequently, appellees had no greater rights thereunder than under current law, application of La. C.C. art. 3526 does not disturb any vested rights of appellees and is correctly applied herein.

* * *

CONCLUSION

Accordingly, the judgment of the trial court placing Mr. Hubbard's children in possession of one hundred percent of the Jacobs stock is reversed, and the matter is remanded for further proceedings consistent with the foregoing opinion. All costs of this appeal are assessed to appellees herein.

Reversed and remanded.

Discussion Questions

1. How did the Court of Appeals reach the conclusion that the Jacobs stock should be split between the surviving spouse Ruth and decedent John's daughters from a prior marriage?

2. What is the purpose of Louisiana's quasi-community property statute?

3. The Louisiana quasi-community statute is applicable at death and divorce: why doesn't it apply during the marriage?

B.   CONFLICTS ARISING WHEN MOVING FROM ONE COMMUNITY PROPERTY STATE TO ANOTHER COMMUNITY PROPERTY STATE

This entire book highlights the differences among the community property states with regard to specific issues. It is therefore inevitable that courts will be confronted with the problem of which law to apply in a case where two community property laws conflict. The case of *Martin v. Martin*, 156 Ariz. 440, 752 P.2d 1026 (Ct. App. 1986), pitted California law favored by the husband against Arizona law favored by the wife. Not surprisingly, the Arizona Court of Appeals applied the Arizona law concerning earnings during the period of separation.

MARTIN v. MARTIN
156 Ariz. 440, 752 P.2d 1026 (1986)
Court of Appeals of Arizona

BROOKS, Judge.

This is an appeal from a decree of dissolution distributing various marital assets between husband, a California resident, and wife, a resident of Arizona. The relevant facts are as follows.

Richard Martin (husband) and Mary Martin (wife) were married in Wyoming in 1950. Due to the nature of husband's work, the parties travelled extensively throughout the United States and the world. In August, 1979, the parties returned to the United States from Singapore, where husband had worked for Union Oil Company of California. The parties became domiciled in California, where husband's job was located. Shortly thereafter, they bought a townhouse in Prescott, Arizona as a planned retirement home. Wife moved into the Prescott townhouse in December, 1979, taking with her a substantial portion of the furnishings from the couple's California home. Husband remained in California, intending to join his wife in Prescott upon his planned retirement. During the period they remained separated, husband gave wife money for living expenses and payments on the townhouse mortgage. Things did not bode well for the marriage, however, and wife filed this action seeking dissolution of the marriage in 1982.

During the parties' three year separation prior to the action for dissolution, husband lived in California and worked for Union Oil Company. He maintained almost total control over the parties' extensive marital assets, sending only a fixed and relatively small monthly sum to his wife in Arizona. At no time has husband ever resided in Arizona.

At the conclusion of the evidence, the trial court found that certain shares of Gulf Oil stock and a partial interest in a trust known as the Dry Lake Farm trust, which husband claimed as his separate property, were in fact community property. The trial court also ruled that, under Arizona law, husband's post separation earnings in California were community property. After dividing the community assets and liabilities between the parties, the court awarded wife a money judgment in the amount of $46,688 "representing [her] share of the net community income" for the three years the parties were separated. The court also awarded a second money judgment in the amount of $9,473 to wife which represented funds in several joint savings accounts that husband depleted in order to make court-ordered spousal maintenance and attorney's fees payments to wife. Wife was also awarded $2,000 a month in spousal maintenance.

Husband now appeals alleging that the trial court made numerous errors in dividing the property between the parties and in awarding spousal maintenance to wife. We will address each of these allegations separately.

I.

Husband first contends that the trial court erred in finding that 100 shares of Gulf Oil stock and a 2/15 the interest in the Dry Lake Farm trust were community property. We disagree.

The record shows that husband received an initial one-fifth interest in the Dry Lake Farm trust as a gift in 1962. Wife properly concedes that this one-fifth interest is husband's separate property. Husband contends that he bought the 100 shares of Gulf Oil stock and the additional 2/15 the interest in the Dry Lake Farm trust with separate funds which he received as income from this initial one-fifth interest in the Dry Lake Farm trust. He argues, therefore, that the trial court erred in not finding that both the Gulf Oil stock and the 2/15 the interest in the Dry Lake Farm trust were his separate property.

Two hurdles confront husband's claim that the Gulf Oil stock and the 2/15 the interest in the Dry Lake Farm trust are his separate property. The first is that both assets were acquired during the marriage and are therefore presumed to be community property. Husband therefore has the burden of proving by clear, satisfactory, and convincing evidence that these assets were purchased with his separate funds. Secondly, in carrying this burden, husband is hindered by the fact that while the parties were residents of New Mexico, the income from husband's initial separate property interest in the Dry Lake Farm trust was deposited into a New Mexico joint bank account along with his regular salary, which was clearly community property. It was allegedly with these commingled funds that husband purchased the Gulf Oil stock and the additional 2/15 interest in the Dry Lake Farm trust. The law in Arizona is clear that where separate and community funds are so comingled that they become indistinguishable, they are presumed to be community property. The burden is then upon the party claiming a separate property interest in the funds to prove it, together with the amount, by clear and satisfactory evidence.

We find that husband has failed in his burden of proof. While he claims that he sufficiently traced the source of the funds used to purchase both the Gulf Oil stock and the additional interest in the Dry Lake Farm trust to his separate funds, our review of the record reveals quite the opposite. Husband's testimony at trial as to the source of the funds used to acquire these two assets was uncertain at best. Moreover, he was unable to produce any convincing documentation or records showing that the funds used to purchase these assets were traceable to his separate funds. We therefore affirm the trial court's ruling that both the 100 shares of Gulf Oil stock and the additional 2/15 interest in the Dry Lake Farm trust were community property.

II.

Husband next contends that the trial court erred by applying Arizona rather than California law to the issue of whether his post-separation earnings were separate or community property. Under A.R.S. §§25-211 and 25-213, post-separation earnings are community property in Arizona until a final decree of dissolution is entered. *Jurek v. Jurek*, 124 Ariz. 596, 606 P.2d 812 (1980); *Matter of Estate of Messer*, 118 Ariz. 291, 576 P.2d 150 (App. 1978). Under California law, however, such earnings are considered the separate property of the spouse who acquires them. Cal. Civ. Code §5118 (West 1983). We are thus confronted with a conflict of law question.

Husband contends that where parties are domiciled in different states when marital property is acquired, the law of the state where the acquiring spouse is domiciled at the time applies to determine the property's disposition upon dissolution. Restatement (Second) of Conflict of Laws, §258, comment c (1971). He claims that since wife was domiciled in Arizona and he was domiciled in California when the post-separation earnings were acquired, California law should be applied to characterize these earnings as his separate property.

While husband agrees that Arizona's quasi-community property law, 444 A.R.S. §25-318(A),[1] would normally supersede the Restatement's choice of law rule and convert his earnings into community property, *Woodward v. Woodward*, 117 Ariz. 148, 571 P.2d 294 (App. 1977), he argues that Arizona law should not apply where only one of the parties is domiciled in this state. In support of this argument, he relies on *In re Marriage of Roesch*, 83 Cal. App. 3d 96, 147 Cal. Rptr. 586 (App. 1978). In *Roesch*, the California Court of Appeals refused to apply California's quasi-community property law to a situation where only one of the parties was domiciled in that state. The court held that California law was applicable only where both spouses are domiciled in California. *Roesch*, 83 Cal. App. 3d at 107, 147 Cal. Rptr. at 593.

---

1. A.R.S. §25-318(A) states in pertinent part:

    In a proceeding for dissolution of the marriage . . . . property acquired by either spouse outside this state shall be deemed to be community property if the property would have been community property if acquired in this state.

Husband contends that since California's quasi-community property law is so similar to our own,[2] *see Sample v. Sample*, 135 Ariz. 599, 602, 663 P.2d 591, 594 (App. 1983), we should, by analogy, adopt California's view. Wife counters by arguing that this issue has already been decided against husband in *Woodward v. Woodward, supra.*

We begin our analysis by noting that Arizona has not decided the issue of whether our quasi-community property law supersedes the usual choice of law rule stated in comment c to the Restatement (Second) of Conflict of Laws §258 in cases such as the one at hand. Contrary to wife's claim, Woodward did not decide the issue. *Woodward* held only that where §25-318(A) applies, it necessarily supersedes the Restatement's choice of law rule. However, the issue of whether the statute applies where only one spouse is domiciled in Arizona was not addressed. The issue is thus one of first impression in this jurisdiction.

We are not persuaded that we should follow California's lead on this issue. It seems clear from our reading of *Roesch* that the court's refusal in that case to apply California's quasi-community property law to cases where only one spouse is domiciled there rests upon a misinterpretation of past California case law. The *Roesch* court refused to invoke California law where only one spouse was domiciled in that state because it was confronted with what it perceived to be constitutional limitations imposed in *Addison v. Addison*, 43 Cal. Rptr. 97, 399 P.2d 897 (1965). In *Addison*, the California Supreme Court addressed a constitutional challenge to California's quasi-community property statute. In upholding the statute's constitutionality, the *Addison* court simply interpreted the statute to mean that the concept of quasi-community property did not apply until a divorce action was filed in the California courts after both parties became domiciled there. *Id.* at 102, 399 P.2d at 902. The court then held that since something more than merely moving into California was required for the statute to apply — namely, that a divorce action be filed in the state court — the statute did not violate the federal privileges and immunities clause by disturbing the vested rights of other state's citizens. The court went on to hold that the statute did not violate federal due process because California had a compelling interest in the marital relationship and disposition of the marital property upon divorce. The California Court of Appeals in *Roesch*, however, broadly interpreted *Addison* as creating two constitutional prerequisites to the application of California's quasi-community property statute: 1) that both spouses be domiciled in California, and 2) that they seek a dissolution there. In refusing to invoke California's quasi-community property statute, the *Roesch* court declared:

---

2. California's quasi-community property law is embodied in Cal. Civ. Code §4803 (West 1970), which reads:

> As used in this part, "quasi-community property" means all real or personal property, wherever situated, heretofore or hereafter acquired in any of the following ways:
>> (a) By either spouse while domiciled elsewhere which would have been community property if the spouse who acquired the property had been domiciled in this state at the time of its acquisition.

Unless both of these conditions exist, the interest of the State of California in the status of the property of the spouses is insufficient to justify reclassification [by application of the quasi-community property statute] without violating the due process clause of the Fourteenth Amendment and the privileges and immunities clause . . . of the federal Constitution.

83 Cal. App. 3d at 107, 147 Cal. Rptr. at 593.

We do not find *Roesch* to be a proper interpretation of *Addison* and we decline to follow it. *Addison* did not seek to place constitutional restraints on the exercise of California's quasi-community property statute; rather, it only gave a statutory interpretation of what the court thought the statute itself required before the quasi-community property concept could be invoked. The court simply held that this interpretation of the statute's meaning would unquestionably pass constitutional muster. Nowhere did the court imply that the statute would be unconstitutional unless given such an interpretation. The court did not even address the issue of whether other interpretations of the statute were constitutionally permissible. To say, therefore, as *Roesch* does, that *Addison* created a two-pronged test for the constitutionality of applying the concept of quasi-community property misconstrues *Addison* and inflates its holding.

Moreover, while we note that the language of California's quasi-community property statute is very similar to our own, we decline to interpret our statute, as was done in *Addison*, to require both spouses to be domiciled here before the statute may be invoked. Indeed, no rationale was given by the *Addison* court as to why it interpreted California's statute in such a restrictive manner. It does not appear that the *Addison* court felt such an interpretation was necessary to uphold the statute's constitutionality since the court itself cast doubt upon the validity of the petitioner's constitutional challenge from the beginning. Such an interpretation is at odds with the broad language of both statutes. For instance, Arizona's statute, A.R.S. §25-318(A), provides that "property acquired by either spouse outside of this state" is subject to being treated as quasi-community property. This broad language clearly encompasses the facts of the instant case.

Furthermore, apart from the lack of any rationale in *Addison* for restricting the application of A.R.S. §25-318(A), we find that factors such as uniformity of result and judicial economy favor application of our quasi-community property law to all dissolution actions filed in this state. The alternative would be to apply the traditional Restatement choice of law rule to cases such as this. However, the Restatement rule has been criticized as "anachronistic" and "unworkable in modern mobile America." *Ismail v. Ismail*, 702 S.W.2d 216, 222 (Tex. App. 1985); *Sampson, Interstate Spouses, Interstate Property, and Divorce*, 13 Tex. Tech. L. Rev. 1285, 1344 (1982). Under the Restatement, a court may find itself with the task of applying various rules of disposition to different marital assets depending upon where each spouse was domiciled when the particular asset was acquired. For example, in the instant case, it is conceivable that husband could have been transferred to other states or countries — as he so often was in the past — after the parties separated. His post-separation earnings and any property acquired with them would thus be subject not only to California law (to the extent they were earned while he resided in California), but also to the law of the other jurisdictions. The problems that would confront a trial court in reaching a proper and equitable disposition of the marital estate in such a case can be readily appreciated. We believe that the trial court's task is sufficiently complicated without adding unnecessary burdens. From a choice of law standpoint, we therefore find that application of Arizona's quasi-community property law is the better approach in cases such as this. We hold, therefore, that A.R.S. §25-318(A) applies to this case and, under *Woodward, supra,* supersedes the usual choice of law rule stated in comment c to §258 of the *Restatement (Second) of Conflict of Laws.*

Without offering any particular legal analysis, husband next argues that such a blanket application of A.R.S. §25-318(A) may well give rise to constitutional problems. However, we believe that any question concerning the constitutionality of applying Arizona's quasi-community property law to a spouse who has never been domiciled here is subsumed by the issue of whether Arizona may acquire personal jurisdiction over such spouse.

The rule is well established that where Arizona has personal jurisdiction over both parties to a dissolution proceeding, it may apply its substantive law in dividing the marital property between the parties-even if that property is located in another state. *Auman v. Auman,* 134 Ariz. 40, 653 P.2d 688 (1982); *Bowart v. Bowart,* 128 Ariz. 331, 625 P.2d 920 (App. 1980). Whether Arizona courts may constitutionally exercise such personal jurisdiction over a non-resident spouse depends upon whether the spouse has sufficient minimum contacts with the state to justify being haled before an Arizona court. *Schilz v. Superior Court,* 144 Ariz. 65, 695 P.2d 1103 (1985); *Meyers v. Hamilton Corp.,* 143 Ariz. 249, 693 P.2d 904 (1984); *Rodriquez v. Rodriquez,* 8 Ariz. App. 5, 442 P.2d 169 (1968). In the case at hand, however, we need not address whether husband's contacts with Arizona were sufficient to properly subject him to personal jurisdiction in an Arizona court since he voluntarily submitted himself to such jurisdiction. As husband has consented to the Arizona court's jurisdiction, he cannot now claim that he is being treated unfairly by having Arizona's substantive law applied to the facts of this case. We find, therefore, that there is no constitutional infirmity in applying Arizona's quasi-community property law to the husband in this case. Consequently, we affirm the trial court's application of Arizona law to the issue of whether husband's post-separation earnings were community or separate property. Under Arizona law, they are clearly community property subject to division upon dissolution.

* * *

CONCLUSION

For the foregoing reasons, this case is remanded for entry of a revised judgment consistent with this opinion, together with such further proceedings, findings, and orders which the trial court deems necessary to adjust the rights and obligations of the parties in order to achieve a just and equitable result.

Given the substantial property distributed to each party in this case, in the exercise of our discretion, we deny the parties' respective motions for attorney's fees on appeal.

Reversed in part and remanded.

Discussion Questions

1. What is the difference between Arizona and California law regarding earnings during separation and why did wife Mary prefer Arizona law and husband Richard prefer California law?

2. What were Richard and Mary's arguments and which was accepted by the Court of Appeal? Explain the court's rationale.

PROBLEM 16.1

Diane and Edward were married in New Jersey, a common law state, and lived there for many years. Edward moved to Idaho recently and filed for divorce. At issue in the divorce is an account containing securities worth $300,000 that Edward brought with him to Idaho. The securities were purchased during their marriage with Edward's earnings. Under Idaho law, Edward's earnings would be characterized as community property and so would the securities purchased with those earnings. Under Idaho law, the court can only distribute community property and not separate property. Under New Jersey law, Edward's earnings and the securities would belong to him. Also, under New Jersey law, a court may equitably distribute "all property, both real and personal, which was acquired by them or either of them during marriage." Edward argues that New Jersey law controls the character of the property and Idaho law controls the division of property. Diane argues that the law of New Jersey should control both the character and division of the property. Explain what supports Edward's argument? Diane's argument? How should the court decide?

PROBLEM 16.2

Assume the same facts as Problem 16.1, except that the law of New Jersey excludes each spouse's earnings and purchases from those earnings from division at divorce. What will be the result?

PROBLEM 16.3

Assume the same facts as Problem 16.1, except that Idaho has passed the following statute: "In a divorce proceeding, property acquired by either spouse outside this state shall be deemed to be community property if the property would have been community property if acquired in this state." What will be the result?

Table 16-1
Conflicts of Law/Quasi-community Property in Community Property States

State	Rule	Case/Statute
Arizona	Quasi-community property approach at divorce, Conflicts of law approach at death.	Ariz. Rev. Stat. Ann. §25-318(A), *Rau v. Rau,* 6 Ariz. App. 362, 432 P.2d 910 (1967) (applied Illinois law)
California	Quasi-community property approach at divorce and death.	Cal. Fam. Code §§63, 125, 2550, Cal. Prob. Code §§66, 101, 6401
Idaho	Conflicts of law approach at divorce, Quasi-community approach at death.	*Berle v. Berle,* 97 Idaho 452, 546 P.2d 407 (1976), Idaho Code §15-2-201
Louisiana	Quasi-community property approach at divorce and death	La. Civ. Code Ann. §3526
Nevada	Conflicts of law approach at divorce and death.	*Braddock v. Braddock,* 91 Nev. 735, 542 P.2d 1061 (1975)
New Mexico	Quasi-community property approach at divorce, Conflicts of law approach at death.	N.M. Stat. Ann. §40-3-8(C)(1), *Hughes v. Hughes,* 91 N.M. 339, 573 P.2d 1194 (1978)
Texas	Quasi-community property approach at divorce, Conflicts of law approach at death.	Tex. Fam. Code Ann. §7.002, *Estate of Hanau v. Hanau,* 730 S.W.2d 663 (Tex. 1987)
Washington	Division of separate and community property at divorce would include "separate" property acquired in a common law state, Quasi-community property approach at death.	Wash. Rev. Code §§26.09.080, 26.16.220, 26.26.230

Chapter 17
Wisconsin Adopts Community Property

Wisconsin enacted the Wisconsin Marital Property Act (WMPA), which went into effect as of January 1, 1986. Even though the WMPA refers to marital property rather than community property, both the Wisconsin Legislature and the United States Internal Revenue Service recognized that Wisconsin joined the ranks of community property states.[1] However, it must be noted that Wisconsin's community property legislation applies only during marriage and at death. Regarding divorce, Wisconsin had passed divorce reform in 1977, changing title-based ownership of common law into equitable distribution principles.[2] As stated by the Wisconsin Court of Appeals in *Kuhlman v. Kuhlman*, 146 Wis. 2d 588, 432 N.W.2d 295 (1988),

> While some confusion is inevitable when courts, as they often do, refer to a divorcing couple's assets as "marital property," the reference is not to "marital property" as that term is defined in the Marital Property Act, but simply to division upon divorce within the meaning of sec. 767.255, Stats. The Marital Property Act, on the other hand, has nothing to do with division of property on dissolution of a marriage. It is concerned only with the spouses' ownership of property during the marriage and at their death.

Thus, the Wisconsin system starts with two ostensibly differing systems: (1) community property during marriage and at death and (2) equitable division of marital property at divorce. Marital property in one context may not have the same meaning as in another context.

A. WISCONSIN CHARACTERIZATION OF PROPERTY AT DIVORCE

Wisconsin's law regarding divorce does have an aspect of characterizing property before the trial court can exercise its discretion in dividing the marital property equitably. The following case, *Derr v. Derr*, 280 Wis. 2d 681, 696 N.W.2d 170 (Ct. App.

---

1. See Howard S. Erlanger and June M. Weisberger, *From Common Law Property to Community Property: Wisconsin's Marital Property Act Four Years Later*, 1990 Wis. L. Rev. 769, 769 n.2.
2. *Id.* at 771-772.

2005), illustrates the complexity of the characterization process. As you read the case, attempt to substitute typical community property terms of community and separate for the Wisconsin terms divisible and not divisible.

DERR v. DERR

289 Wis. 2d 681, 696 N.W.2d 170 (2005)
Wisconsin Court of Appeals

LUNDSTEN, J.

This is a divorce case involving challenges to property division and child support. With respect to property division, Michael Derr's appeal and Martha Derr's cross-appeal each challenge the circuit court's categorization of items as non-divisible. Martha argues that the court improperly categorized a gifted apartment building as Michael's non-divisible property. Michael contends the court improperly categorized a mortgage debt relating to the same apartment building as non-divisible. Michael also asserts the circuit court erred when it determined that he "wasted" $45,000 and counted that amount against him when dividing property. . . .

We conclude that the circuit court correctly categorized the apartment building as Michael's non-divisible property, but that the court should have deemed the mortgage debt a divisible debt. We also conclude that the circuit court properly determined that Michael wasted the $45,000. . . . Acordingly, we affirm in part, reverse in part, and remand with directions.

BACKGROUND

Michael and Martha married in 1990. They have one child, born in August 1993.

In 1994, Michael's parents gave him a 27-unit apartment building that was titled solely in Michael's name. In 1999, Michael and Martha borrowed $300,000 and used this borrowed money for the benefit of the marriage. The $300,000 loan was a mortgage equity loan using Michael's apartment building as collateral.[1] The mortgage note indicated that the loan was made to both Michael and Martha, and mortgage payments were made with marital funds. At the time of the divorce, the outstanding principal balance on the mortgage loan was $282,935 and the fair market value of the apartment building was $905,000.

During the marriage, Michael managed his 27-unit apartment building and other smaller apartment buildings. The rents from these properties appear to have been the major source of income for the family. At some point, Michael lost approximately $45,000 in a type of investing activity commonly referred to as "day trading."

---

1. The parties treat the 1999 loan as a simple equity loan that produced $300,000 in cash and debt for the family. They ignore any costs associated with closing the loan. It appears from the record and briefing that Michael had twice before secured mortgage loans in his name only on the apartment building. Despite this additional information, we follow the parties' lead and focus only on the 1999 loan and treat it as a simple transaction: a $300,000 equity loan with the apartment building as collateral, with the proceeds going to Michael and Martha, and with $300,000 of debt incurred by Michael and Martha.

In the divorce judgment, the circuit court categorized the 27-unit apartment building and the mortgage debt as Michael's non-divisible asset and non-divisible debt. The court also concluded that the $45,000 that Michael lost in day trading was "wasted" within the meaning of Wis. Stat. §767.275 (2003-04). The court took this "wasting" into account by allocating to Michael $45,000 that did not exist. The property division required that Michael pay Martha an equalizing payment of $157,417. . . . We refer to additional relevant facts as needed below.

DISCUSSION

I. CLASSIFICATION OF THE APARTMENT BUILDING AND THE RELATED MORTGAGE DEBT AS "DIVISIBLE" OR "NON-DIVISIBLE"

Michael's appeal and Martha's cross-appeal both address whether the 27-unit apartment building and the related mortgage debt were properly categorized as non-divisible under Wis. Stat. §767.255(2)(a). As set forth below, we conclude that the building is Michael's non-divisible asset, but that the debt is subject to division.

We think a full understanding of the terms and analyses we use to resolve these property division disputes requires that we first provide a summary of certain aspects of property division law and then explain the terms we have chosen to use and why we use them. We use the term "tracing" instead of using "identity" language and we explain the limited nature of the tracing inquiry. We also use "donative intent" instead of "character" terminology and explain the nature of this inquiry. What prompts us is the fact that several of Michael's and Martha's property division arguments employing "identity" and "character" terminology are either misdirected or confusing. We do not fault the parties. A reading of our twenty or so cases addressing Wis. Stat. §767.255(2)(a) and disputes involving divisible/non-divisible categorization leads to the conclusion that two phrases — "loss of identity" and "loss of character" — are the source of considerable confusion, largely because it is too easy to misunderstand what we mean when we use these non-descriptive phrases. For example, when cash is converted to stock, one might think the asset "lost its identity" as cash. Or, one might think the "character" of the asset changed from cash to stock. But a scrupulous student of our case law will recognize that both of these thoughts are off the mark. In fact, our example provides no clue about any change in "character" because it makes no reference to any factor relevant to donative intent. The example does show that there has been no "loss of identity," but only because identity is simply a matter of tracing and the stock traces directly to the cash. Before addressing the tracing and donative intent inquiries in more detail, we provide a brief overview of §767.255(2)(a).

A. Property Division Law and Wis. Stat. §767.255(2)(a)

We frequently say that a circuit court's decision on property division is discretionary. But a more precise statement is this: A circuit court's decision on how to divide *divisible* property is discretionary. This refinement is helpful because circuit courts are often required to resolve preliminary non-discretionary property division questions under Wis. Stat. §767.255(2)(a).

The general rule is that assets and debts acquired by either party before or during the marriage are divisible upon divorce. There is a statutory exception for property acquired (1) by gift, (2) by reason of death, or (3) with funds from either of the first two sources. Wis. Stat. §767.255(2)(a). Specifically, that statute provides that if a party acquires property:

1. As a gift from a person other than the other party.
2. By reason of the death of another. . . .
3. With funds acquired in a manner provided in subd. 1. or 2.

such property "is not subject to a property division." Wis. Stat. §767.255(2)(a).[3] As we shall see, the application of this subsection involves both fact finding and legal questions, but it does not involve the exercise of discretion.

When a party to a divorce asserts that property, or some part of the value of property, is not subject to division, that party has the burden of showing that the property is non-divisible at the time of the divorce. . . .

Notably, the categorization of property as non-divisible under Wis. Stat. §767.255(2)(a) does not necessarily dictate how such property will be treated when the court divides divisible property. Under some circumstances courts may

---

3. Wisconsin Stat. §767.255 reads, in pertinent part:

(1) Upon every judgment of annulment, divorce or legal separation, or in rendering a judgment in an action under §767.02(1)(h), the court shall divide the property of the parties and divest and transfer the title of any such property accordingly. . . .

(2)(a) Except as provided in par. (b), any property shown to have been acquired by either party prior to or during the course of the marriage in any of the following ways shall remain the property of that party and is not subject to a property division under this section:

1. As a gift from a person other than the other party.

2. By reason of the death of another, including, but not limited to, life insurance proceeds; payments made under a deferred employment benefit plan, as defined in §766.01(4)(a), or an individual retirement account; and property acquired by right of survivorship, by a trust distribution, by bequest or inheritance or by a payable on death or a transfer on death arrangement under ch. 705.

3. With funds acquired in a manner provided in subd. 1. or 2.

(b) Paragraph (a) does not apply if the court finds that refusal to divide the property will create a hardship on the other party or on the children of the marriage. If the court makes such a finding, the court may divest the party of the property in a fair and equitable manner.

(3) The court shall presume that all property not described in sub. (2)(a) is to be divided equally between the parties, but may alter this distribution without regard to marital misconduct after considering all of the following:

(a) The length of the marriage.

(b) The property brought to the marriage by each party.

(c) Whether one of the parties has substantial assets not subject to division by the court.

(d) The contribution of each party to the marriage, giving appropriate economic value to each party's contribution in homemaking and child care services.

. . . .

(m) Such other factors as the court may in each individual case determine to be relevant.

avoid "hardship" or inequities that might result from according property non-divisible status. Note the following examples:

- Under §767.255(2)(b), a court may treat non-divisible property as divisible property if failing to do so would "create a hardship on the other party or on the children of the marriage." The hardship exception involves both a legal question and the exercise of discretion. Once factual disputes are resolved, the existence of a "hardship" is a question of law. However, whether an identified "hardship" warrants the "invasion" of non-divisible property is a discretionary determination.
- Section 767.255(3)(c) authorizes circuit courts to consider "substantial" non-divisible property owned by one party when exercising discretion to divide divisible property.
- When making the discretionary decision whether to deviate from equal property division, a court may consider the fact that divisible property was generated in whole or in part by one party's donation of non-divisible property to the marriage.

Thus, in this area of divorce law, like others, there are sometimes different routes to the same result. Still, correctly categorizing property as divisible or non-divisible is important because it gives the circuit court the proper starting point for exercising discretion. Also, if the case is appealed, the correct categorization facilitates our review of the circuit court's exercise of discretion in dividing divisible property. When a reviewing court cannot tell from the record whether the circuit court would have assigned property in the same manner had the circuit court acted under a correct view of the divisible status of property, remand is necessary. As will be seen, that is what prompts remand in this case.

B. Identity/Tracing and Character/Donative Intent

In our case law addressing whether property is subject to division under Wis. Stat. §767.255(2)(a), we often speak of "identity" and "character" as if they constitute a complete two-pronged analysis. The following language is typical:

> The party seeking exclusion of inherited or gifted property must prove that it has retained its character and identity. Once the recipient of inherited property has met these requirements, the opposing party has the opportunity to establish by sufficient countervailing evidence the property is not inherited, or has otherwise lost its exempt status because its character or identity has not been preserved.

However, as set forth below, the "identity" and "character" inquiries do not comprise a test. Instead, they are labels for two distinct inquiries — tracing and donative intent — that may or may not fully resolve the divisible status of property at the time of a divorce.

1. Tracing

The "identity" inquiry "addresses whether the gifted or inherited asset has been preserved in some present identifiable form so that it can be meaningfully valued and assigned." *Brandt,* 145 Wis. 2d at 411, 427 N.W.2d 126. Thus, the "identity" inquiry is purely a matter of tracing; it is the job of determining the value and source of an asset or the value and source of a part of an asset. . . .[4]

In addition, case law holds that tracing produces an answer when the party asserting that an asset is non-divisible is *unable* to provide evidence that permits the tracing of an identifiable part of the asset to an original non-divisible asset. Our *Brandt* decision provides a good example. In *Brandt,* the wife deposited inherited non-divisible money in an investment account. Years later, at the time of the divorce, no part of the value of the account could be traced to the inherited non-divisible money because "countless" subsequent transactions, including withdrawals and deposits "from various sources, including both parties' salaries, gifts, other inheritances, and other joint and sole accounts," prevented the court from determining "with any degree of certainty" the current portion of the investment account attributable to the inherited money. The lesson of *Brandt* is that an asset is divisible if no identifiable part of that asset can be reliably traced and attributed to a non-divisible asset. . . .

Most important here, however, are cases demonstrating that tracing, by itself, does not answer whether a current asset, or any part of the value of a current asset, is divisible or non-divisible. Stated differently, tracing is nothing more than the exercise of following an asset trail. If an asset, or component part of an asset, can be traced to a source, we then rely on *other* principles and rules to determine whether the traced asset is divisible or non-divisible. In this regard, *Friebel* is instructive.

In *Friebel,* a wife funded an investment account with funds from three sources. The account earned interest and experienced realized and unrealized gains. We determined that all funds put into the account were non-divisible gifts owned by the wife and we engaged in tracing. That is, we identified the component parts of the current account and the source and value of those component parts as follows. At the time of the divorce the investment account balance was $153,654. Of that amount, $11,362 was attributable to interest income, $3,955 to realized gains, and $4,085 to unrealized gains. What remained was $134,252, comprised of original gifted funds. This completed the tracing analysis. We then applied other legal principles to decide whether these amounts were divisible. Of the $153,654 investment account balance, $134,252 was non-divisible because it was attributable to the original non-divisible gifts. The $11,362 portion of the balance was divisible because it was divisible interest income. . . We were unable to categorize the remainder — $3,955 in realized gains and $4,085 in unrealized gains — because of insufficient information. We remanded because we concluded that additional fact finding was needed to determine whether these amounts were attributable to divisible income or non-divisible appreciation.

---

4. We use the term "tracing" both because of its descriptive value and because tracing language has often been used in our "identity" discussions. *See, e.g., Krejci v. Krejci,* 2003 WI App. 160, ¶ 22, 266 Wis. 2d 284, 667 N.W.2d 780; *Preuss v. Preuss,* 195 Wis. 2d 95, 103, 536 N.W.2d 101 (Ct. App. 1995); *Brandt,* 145 Wis. 2d at 415-16, 427 N.W.2d 126; *Trattles v. Trattles,* 126 Wis. 2d 219, 227-28, 376 N.W.2d 379 (Ct. App. 1985); *Weiss v. Weiss,* 122 Wis. 2d 688, 694, 365 N.W.2d 608 (Ct. App. 1985); *see also Doerr v. Doerr, 189 Wis. 2d 112,* 133, 525 N.W.2d 745 (Ct. App. 1994); *Friebel v. Friebel,* 181 Wis. 2d 285, 301, 510 N.W.2d 767 (Ct. App. 1993). In his article on this topic in 1990, Judge Neal Nettesheim seemingly suggested that "tracing" is a helpful term when he used "identity/tracing" instead of just "identity." *See* Judge Neal Nettesheim, *Gifted and Inherited Property: To Divide or Not Divide?* 10 Wis. J. Fam. L., No. 4, 127, 141 (Oct. 1990).

We acknowledge that in *Friebel* our tracing exercise was interwoven with the rest of our analysis, and we sometimes used confusing language. Nonetheless, the tracing exercise was distinct from whether the traced components of the investment account were subject to division.

To summarize, in this opinion we use the term "tracing," instead of "identity" or "loss of identity." Tracing is the job of determining the value and source of an asset or the value and source of a part of an asset. Tracing is nothing more than the exercise of following an asset trail. Tracing does not, by itself, resolve whether an item is divisible under Wis. Stat. §767.255(2)(a), unless tracing is either the only disputed issue or the party asking the court to declare an asset non-divisible is unable to provide evidence that permits the tracing of an identifiable part of the asset to an original non-divisible asset.

2. Donative Intent

As pertains to Wis. Stat. §767.255(2)(a), the "character" inquiry involves no more and no less than determining whether the owning spouse intended to donate non-divisible property to the marriage, that is, did the owning spouse have donative intent. *See Finley v. Finley*, 2002 WI App. 144, ¶ 38, 256 Wis. 2d 508, 648 N.W.2d 536 (the character issue is whether "the owning spouse had a donative intent"); *Friebel*, 181 Wis. 2d at 298, 510 N.W.2d 767 (owning spouse "never demonstrated any donative intent with regard to the remaining assets in her investment account. Thus, her gifted property retained its character."); *Zirngibl v. Zirngibl*, 165 Wis. 2d 130, 136, 477 N.W.2d 637 (Ct. App. 1991) ("There is no dispute that the $16,167 was gifted property, that it went into a jointly titled bank account and that it was used to purchase the parties' residence. The dispute centers on the issue of donative intent."); *Popp v. Popp*, 146 Wis. 2d 778, 788, 432 N.W.2d 600 (Ct. App. 1988) ("Donative intent of the owner of the exempt property is an issue when deciding whether the character of the property has been changed."); *Brandt*, 145 Wis. 2d at 410-11, 427 N.W. 2d 126 ("the donative intent of the owner of the exempt property" is at issue in "character" cases).

"Character" is a label that fails to describe the pertinent inquiry. Unless one is steeped in "character" case law, neither "character" nor "loss of character" brings to mind donative intent. We think it apparent that "character" terminology just adds a layer of haze to a topic that is already sufficiently complicated. Why not cut to the quick and use the term "donative intent" when talking about donative intent? No reason comes to mind and, therefore, in this opinion we will, when possible, avoid the terms "character" and "loss of character" and instead speak directly in terms of donative intent.[5]

---

5. Also, we are cognizant that the term "tracing" is used to describe the identity inquiry in marital property cases under Wis. Stat. ch. 766. *See, e.g., Estate of Kobylski v. Hellstern*, 178 Wis. 2d 158, 174, 503 N.W.2d 369 (Ct. App. 1993); *Lloyd v. Lloyd*, 170 Wis. 2d 240, 257-58, 487 N.W.2d 647 (Ct. App. 1992). Indeed, in *Lloyd* we relied on *Brandt* for the definition of identity and we characterized the inquiry as "tracing." *Lloyd*, 170 Wis. 2d at 260, 487 N.W.2d 647. *Lloyd* could be read to suggest that the nature of the identity/tracing inquiry is the same in both the ch. 766 marital property context and the Wis. Stat. ch. 767 divorce context. *See Lloyd*, 170 Wis. 2d at 259-60, 487 N.W.2d 647. However, at least one other case might be read as suggesting the identity inquiry is somewhat different in the marital property context. *See Gardner v. Gardner*, 190 Wis. 2d 216, 236 n. 2, 527 N.W.2d 701 (Ct. App. 1994). Suffice to say that we speak in this opinion about the proper analysis only in divorce cases under ch. 767.

In order to properly analyze the parties' arguments on donative intent, we must first examine the nature of the inquiry in more detail. Although courts often — and correctly — resolve donative intent as a matter of law, by applying a legal presumption to undisputed historical facts, donative intent is ultimately a question of subjective donative intent.

The seminal case on donative intent is *Bonnell v. Bonnell*, 117 Wis. 2d 241, 344 N.W.2d 123 (1984). In *Bonnell*, the supreme court addressed whether inherited non-divisible property lost its "character" when it was transferred into joint tenancy. *Id.* at 245, 344 N.W.2d 123. It is evident that the supreme court treated donative intent as a factual issue involving subjective donative intent which, in *Bonnell*, had first been resolved by the circuit court. The Supreme Court explained:

> It is clear that Mrs. Bonnell intended to create a joint tenancy in the subject properties. This is evidenced by a deed executed on August 23, 1978, by Mr. and Mrs. Bonnell, transferring ownership to "John Bonnell and Betty Bonnell, husband and wife, as joint tenants with right of survivorship." Moreover, *the trial record supports the trial court's finding that Mrs. Bonnell intended to make a gift of the inherited property to Mr. Bonnell.*

Id. at 245-46, 344 N.W.2d 123 (citation omitted; emphasis added). Following this, the supreme court immediately quoted Mrs. Bonnell's own testimony indicating that she gave her property to the marriage to satisfy a demanding husband:

> "'Well, I got tired of hearing about how nothing was John's. I made out a will leaving everything to him if I died, but that didn't seem to satisfy him. I thought if [transferring to joint tenancy] would make him happy, why I would do that if I could find a lawyer to do it. . . . He didn't ask me in so many words, he just kept telling me that nothing was his.'"

Id. at 246, 344 N.W.2d 123. . . .

[I]n *Zirngibl*, 165 Wis. 2d 130, 477 N.W.2d 637, we treated donative intent as a question of subjective donative intent. In *Zirngibl*, a wife with non-divisible funds deposited those funds in a joint bank account and then the husband used the money to purchase a house for the family. We observed that these facts created a rebuttable presumption of donative intent, but then explained that the presumption had been overcome. Unbeknownst to the wife, the husband had titled the house in his name only. We affirmed the circuit court's implicit *factual* finding that the wife intended to give the money to the marriage only if it was used to purchase a home titled in both their names.

A prominent donative intent case is *Trattles v. Trattles*, 126 Wis. 2d 219, 376 N.W.2d 379 (Ct. App. 1985). In that case, we did not expressly address whether donative intent is a matter of subjective donative intent, but our decision assumed as much. We observed that it was surprising that the owning spouse never testified that she did not intend to make a gift, an obvious reference to the absence of subjective donative intent evidence. *Id.* at 224 n.3, 376 N.W.2d 379. We also explained that the presumption we employed was that the owning spouse "made a *conscious* . . . decision" to gift her property. *Id.* at 227, 376 N.W.2d 379 (emphasis added).

* * *

In any event, we are bound by the supreme court decisions in *Bonnell* . . . and, therefore, the donative intent inquiry under Wis. Stat. §767.255(2)(a) is directed at determining the owning party's subjective donative intent.

In *Trattles*, we first explained how the legal presumption works. When an owning spouse acts in a manner that would normally evince an intent to gift property to the marriage, donative intent is presumed, subject to rebuttal by "sufficient counter-vailing evidence." We are concluding in such cases that, in the absence of counter-vailing evidence, gifting is the only reasonable inference.

Our cases identify several situations that create a rebuttable presumption of donative intent.

Transferring non-divisible property to joint tenancy. In *Trattles*, we discussed *Bonnell* and explained that donative intent is presumed when an owning spouse transfers non-divisible property to joint tenancy.

Depositing non-divisible funds into a joint bank account. When non-divisible funds are deposited in a joint bank account, even for a short time, donative intent is presumed. *Finley*, 256 Wis. 2d 508, ¶¶ 38, 42, 648 N.W.2d 536 (the length of time the funds remain in the joint account, along with other evidence, is "part of the inquiry into whether the presumption of donative intent is rebutted by other evidence").

Using non-divisible funds to make purchases for the family. When non-divisible funds are expended to acquire property, goods, or services that are usually used for the mutual benefit of the parties, donative intent is presumed. *Trattles*, 126 Wis. 2d at 222, 225-27, 376 N.W.2d 379 (evidence that "gift proceeds were used to purchase household furnishings and effects, to pay for normal and usual household expenditures, [and] to pay for repairs, maintenance and improvement to the home the parties owned in joint tenancy" was presumptive evidence of donative intent).

Using non-divisible funds to make payments on a mortgage debt that was incurred to acquire jointly owned real estate. When non-divisible funds are used to make mortgage payments on a loan taken to acquire jointly owned real estate, donative intent is presumed.

When facts create a presumption of donative intent, rebuttal evidence may nonetheless show that the spouse did not intend to make a gift. Although the terminology we used in *Weberg v. Weberg*, 158 Wis. 2d 540, 463 N.W.2d 382 (Ct. App. 1990), is confusing, *Weberg* is nonetheless an example of a case in which the presumption was overcome. In *Weberg*, non-divisible funds deposited in a joint bank account remained non-divisible upon divorce because the circuit court believed the testimony of the owning spouse that the funds were held in the joint account only to protect the non-owning spouse if the owning spouse died. *Id.* at 550-52, 463 N.W.2d 382.

We glean from these cases and normal rules of appellate review the following. Circumstantial historical facts may give rise to the legal presumption that an owning spouse gifted property to the marriage. This presumption arises if the owning spouse acts in a manner that would normally evince an intent to gift. However, because donative intent is ultimately a question of subjective donative intent, other evidence may persuade a circuit court that the owning spouse consciously considered the matter and subjectively intended that gifting not occur. In this circumstance, donative intent is lacking and the property remains non-divisible. At the same time, circuit courts are not obliged to accept the testimony of an owning spouse about his or her subjective thoughts. If a circuit court makes an express factual finding that a spouse consciously did intend to gift or consciously intended no gift, we will accord that finding deference. If the court does not make an express factual finding, we will normally assume fact finding consistent with the court's ultimate decision. For example, if the record contains evidence of subjective thoughts tending to rebut a presumption of donative intent, if the circuit court makes no express findings regarding this rebuttal evidence, and if the circuit court determines there was a gift, then we will normally assume the circuit court implicitly found the rebuttal evidence lacking in credibility.

C. Application of the Law to This Case: The Apartment Building and the Mortgage Debt

The following facts and conclusions relating to the apartment building and the mortgage debt are undisputed:

* Michael and Martha married in 1990.
* In 1994, Michael's parents gave him a 27-unit apartment building, which was titled solely in Michael's name.
* Immediately following the gifting, the apartment building was Michael's non-divisible property.
* In 1999, Michael and Martha borrowed $300,000 and used this borrowed money for the benefit of the marriage.
* The $300,000 loan was a mortgage equity loan using Michael's apartment building as collateral.
* The mortgage note indicated that the loan was made to both Michael and Martha.
* Mortgage payments were made with marital funds.
* At the time of the divorce, the outstanding principal balance on the mortgage loan was $282,935.
* At the time of the divorce, the apartment building had a fair market value of $905,000.

The circuit court concluded that the apartment building was Michael's non-divisible property because it was gifted to Michael and because the apartment building did not subsequently lose either its "identity" or "character" during the marriage. The court treated the outstanding $282,935 mortgage debt as Michael's non-divisible debt.

Michael and Martha dispute whether the mortgage debt should be designated as divisible or non-divisible, and whether all or part of the apartment building was divisible property. For the reasons below, we conclude that the apartment building is Michael's non-divisible property, but that the mortgage debt is divisible.

1. The Mortgage Debt

Michael challenges the circuit court's decision that the remaining mortgage debt, $282,935, is his non-divisible debt. Before resolving this issue on its merits, we pause to reject Martha's contention that the circuit court's categorization of the debt as non-divisible was a discretionary decision.

Turning to the merits, Michael argues that the mortgage debt is a divisible debt because it was incurred to benefit the family. As Michael points out, it is undisputed that the $300,000 loan proceeds were used for the benefit of the family. Michael argues that the marriage received $300,000 in funds and a corresponding $300,000 debt. We understand Martha's response to be that nothing in Wis. Stat. §767.255(2)(a) suggests that it matters why a debt is incurred or what the borrowed money is used for.

We conclude that the mortgage debt is divisible because it is not exempt from division under Wis. Stat. §767.255(2)(a). The exemptions in this statute refer to "property" acquired by "gift" or "[b]y reason of . . . death" or acquired with "funds" from either of those sources. Regardless whether debt can ever be conferred by gift or by reason of death within the meaning of §767.255(2)(a), in this case the debt was not gifted to the parties, acquired by reason of death, or acquired with funds from either of those sources. Here, Michael and Martha took on the $300,000 debt in exchange for $300,000 in cash. It is true that Michael made the loan possible by putting equity in his apartment building at risk, but he did not in any meaningful sense "acquire" the debt with "funds acquired" from the gifted building from his parents, as those terms are used in §767.255(2)(a)3.[6]

We stress the limited nature of our holding. In this case, a gifted non-divisible asset was used as collateral for a loan. The marriage acquired an asset, $300,000 cash, and a debt of equal value. It was undisputed that the loaned money was used for the benefit of the marriage, that both parties were liable for the debt, and that marital funds were used to make payments on the debt. Under these circumstances, the debt is divisible.

2. The Apartment Building

The parties agree that the apartment building was Michael's non-divisible asset when he received it as a gift from his parents during the marriage. But they dispute whether the mortgage transaction and repayment of the mortgage debt with marital funds had the effect of converting Michael's apartment building to divisible property. Martha contends that the circuit court erred when it concluded that the apartment building was non-divisible. She argues that the building became wholly divisible because it lost both its "identity" and "character" as a result of the mortgage transaction. Michael takes the opposite view.

a. Tracing Inquiry Applied

With respect to tracing, there are no disputed historical facts. Thus, we address the tracing inquiry solely as a question of law. As set forth in . . . above, the tracing

---

6. Although Wis. Stat. §767.255(2)(a) does not on its face appear to contemplate an exemption for any debt, we do *not* hold that debt is never non-divisible. Several scenarios come to mind. Here are just two. First, suppose Michael had taken out an equity loan on his non-divisible apartment building, used the funds to repair the building, and made debt payments with inherited non-divisible money. Would the mortgage debt be divisible? Second, what would be the result if spouses divorced shortly after the husband sold a gifted non-divisible building for $200,000 and used that money as a down payment on a different $1,000,000 building, incurring $800,000 in mortgage debt in his name only and titling the building in his name only? Would the mortgage debt be divisible? Our opinion is not intended to suggest answers to these questions.

inquiry is the job of determining the value and source of an asset or the value and source of a part of an asset.

Martha's argument begins with the fact that the apartment building was used as collateral to secure the $300,000 mortgage loan and, therefore, to incur the corresponding $300,000 mortgage debt. She argues that the apartment building lost its "identity" because payments on the $300,000 mortgage debt were made with marital funds. Martha, relying on *Brandt*, states that "where marital funds are merged with a non-marital asset, unless the non-marital component of that asset can be traced, identified and valued, the asset must be considered a marital one." Martha complains that neither Michael nor the circuit court made a tracing effort and, therefore, the circuit court failed to determine how the mortgage payments related to the current net value of the apartment building.

As best we can tell, Martha's argument boils down to this: When debt payments made with marital funds increase the "net value" of an otherwise non-divisible asset, the marital payments destroy the "identity" of part or all of the non-divisible asset. Applied to this case, Martha contends that some undetermined part of the net value (fair market value minus the outstanding mortgage debt) of the apartment building is attributable to mortgage payments and, because mortgage payments were made with marital funds, some undetermined part of the net value of the building has been converted to divisible property. We are not persuaded.

To the extent Martha is arguing "loss of identity," she misapprehends the nature of the inquiry. As we have explained, identity is a matter of tracing. The mortgage payments made by the marriage reduced the mortgage debt from $300,000 to $282,935, a reduction of $17,065. Thus, a $17,065 reduction in mortgage debt is directly traceable to mortgage payments made with marital funds.

If Martha had properly applied the tracing inquiry to the undisputed facts, she would have easily traced the $17,065 figure. Further, she would presumably be arguing that the mortgage payments made with marital funds increased the "net value" of the apartment building by $17,065, thereby making this amount divisible. We resolved the tracing part of this argument in the last paragraph. But tracing does not tell us whether the $17,065 figure is divisible. We address that part of Martha's argument next.

b. Martha's "Net Value" Theory

* * *

Therefore, we reject Martha's argument that mortgage payments made with marital funds created equity in the apartment building belonging to the marriage.

c. Donative Intent Inquiry Applied

When addressing donative intent, we defer to a trial court's findings of historical fact unless those findings are clearly erroneous. Circumstantial historical facts may give rise to the presumption that an owning spouse gifted property to the marriage. This presumption arises if the owning spouse acts in a manner that would normally evince an intent to gift. The presumption is subject to rebuttal by "sufficient countervailing evidence." Because donative intent is ultimately a question of subjective donative intent, other evidence may persuade a circuit court that the owning spouse consciously considered the matter and subjectively intended that gifting not occur.

Martha, using "character" terminology, argues that Michael's entire apartment building lost its non-divisible character when he used the building for a marital purpose, that is, when he used it as collateral for the $300,000 equity loan. We understand Martha to be relying on *Finley*, *Friebel*, and *Trattles* for the following proposition: The presumption of donative intent arises when an owning party "uses" his or her non-divisible asset to acquire property for marital use. In each of those three cases, a spouse with non-divisible money (or non-divisible assets converted to money) used that non-divisible money to make purchases, make payments, or fund accounts for the benefit of the family. *Finley*, 256 Wis. 2d 508, ¶¶ 39-43, 648 N.W.2d 536; *Friebel*, 181 Wis. 2d at 298, 510 N.W.2d 767; *Trattles*, 126 Wis. 2d at 222, 224-27, 376 N.W.2d 379. Martha's argument hinges on her assertion that Michael similarly "used" his non-divisible apartment building when he used it as collateral to secure the $300,000 loan. She equates putting a non-divisible asset at risk by using it as collateral for a marital loan with selling the asset and then using the proceeds for a marital purpose.

To state Martha's argument clearly is to reveal its flaw. Michael's act of putting his building at risk to secure the mortgage loan does not evince an intent to give all or part of his building to the family. Such "use" of a non-divisible asset is far different than disposing of the asset in order to make a purchase for the family. Moreover, there is no testimony suggesting that Michael subjectively intended to donate his building to the family by allowing it to be used to secure the marital loan. We conclude that, without more, the act of putting property at risk by using it as collateral for a marital loan does not create a presumption that the owning spouse intended to donate part or all of the property to the marriage.

II. WASTING

* * *

In sum, the circuit court correctly concluded that Michael "wasted" the $45,000. The timing of the wasting is not critical here. As we explained in *Zabel*, Wis. Stat. §767.275 does not prevent a court from counting wasted assets against the at-fault party in a property division just because the waste did not occur within the one-year time frame in that statute.

* * *

CONCLUSION

We conclude that the circuit court correctly categorized the apartment building as Michael's non-divisible property, but that the court should have deemed the mortgage loan a divisible debt. We also conclude that the circuit court properly determined that Michael wasted the $45,000. Finally, we conclude that the court correctly determined Michael's income for purposes of child support. Accordingly, we affirm in part and reverse in part.

We remand because we cannot tell if the circuit court's erroneous categorization of the mortgage debt as non-divisible affected the property division. The circuit court believed that the divisible assets had a net value of $388,469 and awarded Martha 75% of this amount, that is, it awarded her $291,352 (.75 x $388,469). The court made this unequal property division because Michael had, in the court's words, a "very substantial asset not subject to division by the court, the [27-unit apartment building] with a net fair market value of $622,065." This $622,065 net equity was comprised of the apartment building's value, $905,000, less the outstanding mortgage debt, $282,935. Instead, the circuit court should have concluded that Michael had a non-divisible asset worth $905,000 and that the property subject to division had a net value of $105,534 ($388,469 less the mortgage debt of $282,935). The difference is that Michael actually has a more valuable non-divisible asset, but also the property subject to division is less. We understand that, as a practical matter, the circuit court needed to assign the mortgage debt to Michael because the building was Michael's non-divisible property. Still, we cannot tell if the court would have exercised its discretion in the same manner had it acted under a correct understanding of the divisible nature of the mortgage debt. On remand, the circuit court should exercise its discretion to divide divisible property in light of our categorization of the mortgage debt as divisible.

No costs to either party.

Judgment affirmed in part; reversed in part and cause remanded with directions; order affirmed.

Discussion Questions

1. What is the significance of the "character and identity" inquiry? How does a court determine if inherited or gifted property has retained or lost its character or identity?
2. What role does non-divisible property have in Wisconsin's equitable division of property at divorce?
3. What is the impact of the Court of Appeals' conclusion that the mortgage debt was divisible property?

B. WISCONSIN CHARACTERIZATION OF PROPERTY AT DEATH

Since the WMPA that establishes a community property system applies only during marriage and at death but not at divorce, the issues regarding characterization of property derive from a differing statutory scheme. As you read the following case, consider whether there is an overlap between the case law developed in the divorce context and that in the death scenario in *Estate of Kobylski*, 178 Wis. 2d 158, 503 N.W.2d 369 (Ct. App. 1993). Also, the *Kobylski* case illustrates how Wisconsin courts have referred to community property principles in traditional community property states to determine how to treat the use of community property funds to improve the separate property of one spouse.

ESTATE OF KOBYLSKI

178 Wis. 2d 158, 503 N.W.2d 369 (1993)
Wisconsin Court of Appeals

NETTESHEIM, Presiding Judge.

The principal issues on this appeal concern the "mixed property" provisions of sec. 766.63, Stats., of Wisconsin's Marital Property Act (MPA). Genevieve Hellstern's estate appeals from a judgment in favor of Genevieve's surviving husband, Geza Hellstern. The estate challenges the probate court's determination that a residence, titled in Genevieve's name and brought to the marriage by her, was reclassified to marital property pursuant to sec. 766.63 of the MPA. The estate also challenges the probate court's determination that Geza is not liable for the unpaid property taxes on the residence or for Genevieve's loan to him during the marriage for an automobile.

We reverse the probate court's ruling that the residence was reclassified to marital property and we remand for further proceedings on this issue. We also reverse and remand the court's ruling that Geza is not liable to the estate for the unpaid property taxes. We affirm the court's ruling that Geza is not liable to the estate for the automobile loan.

I. FACTS

Genevieve, age 58, and Geza, age 71, married on February 20, 1982. At that time, both were widowed and had children from their prior marriages. Their marriage produced no children.

At the time of the marriage, Genevieve owned a residence where she and her first husband had lived and raised their children. Genevieve and Geza lived in this residence for the duration of their marriage. Genevieve retained title to the property in her own name. During the marriage, Genevieve and Geza made several improvements to the residence that were paid for by funds from their joint checking and savings accounts. They also used these accounts to pay for property taxes, utilities, insurance and other household expenses. Additionally, Geza painted the interior and exterior of the residence, assisted Genevieve's son in enlarging the one-car garage, and did the yard work.

In addition to the residence, Genevieve brought to the marriage three certificates of deposit (CD's) valued at $10,000 each. Genevieve cashed one of the CD's during the marriage and later deposited the funds into a joint NOW account; the additional two CD's remained titled solely in Genevieve's name. In 1988, the spouses used

$9000 from the joint NOW account for the purchase of a 1987 Cadillac automobile that was titled in both of their names.

In June 1979, three years before Genevieve and Geza married, Genevieve executed her will which distributed her entire estate to her four children from her prior marriage. Following Genevieve's death in June 1990, Geza filed notice to take under the widower's election of deferred and augmented marital property. *See* secs. 861.02 and 861.03, Stats. Geza sought either:

> (1) reimbursement for the funds expended on the residence for improvements if the probate court ruled that the residence was Genevieve's nonmarital property, or (2) the value of his one-half marital interest in the residence if the court ruled that the residence was reclassified to marital property because he and Genevieve had contributed marital funds for improvements and because he also had applied uncompensated labor to improve the residence. The estate objected to Geza's claims.

The estate also filed claims against Geza for: (1) the unpaid property taxes on the residence which accrued after Genevieve's death while Geza was residing in the residence, and (2) the funds expended by Genevieve and Geza to purchase the Cadillac.

The probate court ruled in Geza's favor on all issues. The court held that the residence was mixed property under sec. 766.63, Stats., of the MPA because "substantive labor, efforts and marital cash were applied" during the marriage. The court further ruled that the residence was reclassified to marital property because "tracing is [not] possible." The court therefore awarded Geza the value of a one-half interest in the residence. Based on this conclusion, the court also denied the estate's claim against Geza for the residence's unpaid property taxes. Finally, the court denied the estate's claim for the $9000 allegedly loaned to Geza to purchase the 1987 Cadillac because the funds were drawn from a joint account and the vehicle was titled in both Genevieve's and Geza's names.

The estate appeals. Further facts will be provided as they become relevant to our discussion.

II. MARITAL PROPERTY LAW

A. STANDARD OF REVIEW

The estate argues that the probate court erred in its construction of the mixed property provisions, sec. 766.63, Stats., of the MPA. While the estate does not appear to challenge the court's determination that Genevieve and Geza mixed their marital and nonmarital property, the estate does dispute the court's further determination that tracing could not be performed and that, as a result, total reclassification of the asset occurred.

A trial court's tracing determination is a finding of fact that will be upheld unless clearly erroneous. *In re Lloyd*, 170 Wis. 2d 240, 251, 487 N.W.2d 647, 651 (Ct. App. 1992). However, whether the correctly found facts establish the property as marital or nonmarital is a question of law we review independently. Similarly, our application of ch. 766, Stats., to the facts also presents a question of law and we need not defer to the trial court's conclusion.

All property of married persons either is, or is presumed to be, marital property unless it is proven to be otherwise. Section 766.31(1) and (2), Stats. Likewise, any property determined not to be marital property is presumed to be deferred marital property and may be subject to a surviving spouse's elective rights under sec. 861.02, Stats. *See* sec. 858.01(2) Stats.; 1 K. Christiansen, F. Wm. Haberman, J. Haydon, D. Kinnamon, M. McGarity & M. Wilcox, Marital Property Law in Wisconsin §2.72b, at 2-116 (2d ed. 1986) [hereinafter Marital Property Law in Wisconsin]. At death, the deceased spouse may freely dispose of only the one-half interest the decedent owns in each item of marital property. The decedent may also dispose of the whole of each item of his or her nonmarital property. Sections 766.31(3) and 861.01, Stats.

Despite the MPA's presumption that all spousal property is marital, spouses are permitted to own individual and predetermination date property. *See* secs. 766.31(6) & (8), Stats. *See also* 1 Marital Property Law in Wisconsin §3.1, at 3-2 to 3-3. Predetermination date property is not individual property, or a type of individual property, nor does it imply a classification all its own.[1] However, during marriage, predetermination date property is treated as if it were individual property, and at death it may be subject to a deferred marital property analysis if the marital property presumption is overcome.[2]

The party challenging the marital property (or deferred marital property) presumption has the burden to establish that the property at issue is not marital. Demonstrating that the time, method or source of the property's acquisition establishes the property as nonmarital rebuts the presumption as to that item of property.

III.   The Residence

The probate court concluded that Genevieve's nonmarital residence was reclassified to marital property under sec. 766.63(1) and (2), Stats., because "substantive labor, efforts and marital cash were applied" during the marriage and "tracing is [not] possible . . . as unreimbursed labor is involved." We construe the court's ruling as resting upon two independent determinations under sec. 766.63:

> (1) Genevieve and Geza's use of their marital funds for improvements to the residence constituted a mixing of marital and nonmarital property which reclassified the residence to marital property pursuant to sec. 766.63(1) because its nonmarital component could not be traced, and (2) the application of Geza's substantial uncompensated labor to the

1. Under the act, "Property owned at a marriage which occurs after 12:01 a.m. on January 1, 1986, is individual property of the owning spouse if, at the marriage, both spouses are domiciled in this state." Section 766.31(6), Stats. In contrast, property *other than* that classified as individual under sec. 766.31(6) which is owned by either or both spouses at the determination date is referred to as predetermination date property. *See In re Lloyd,* 170 Wis. 2d 240, 253, 487 N.W.2d 647, 652 (Ct. App. 1992). *See also* 1 K. Christiansen, F. Wm. Haberman, J. Haydon, D. Kinnamon, M. McGarity & M. Wilcox, Marital Property Law in Wisconsin §2.70, at 2-111 to 2-112 (2d ed. 1986).

2. Deferred marital property is property acquired by the spouses while married and while ch. 766, Stats., does not apply, which would have been marital property if it were acquired when ch. 766 applied. Section 851.055, Stats. Any property determined not to be marital property is presumed to be deferred marital property unless the presumption is rebutted. *Lloyd,* 170 Wis. 2d at 255-56, 487 N.W.2d at 653.

residence served to reclassify the residence under sec. 766.63(2) because the value of the labor could not be traced. We address each of these determinations in turn.

A.   MIXING MARITAL PROPERTY WITH NONMARITAL PROPERTY PURSUANT TO SEC. 766.63(1), STATS.

1. Trial Court Ruling

The probate court made the following factual findings, none of which is disputed on appeal. Genevieve owned the residence when she and Geza married, and she retained title in her sole name during her life. During the marriage, Geza received a pension and social security, while Genevieve received social security and the interest from her CD's. Generally, all of Genevieve's and Geza's funds were deposited into and transferred between their joint savings and checking accounts to pay for property taxes, utilities, insurance and other related residence expenses. After their determination date,[7] the spouses paid $3970.08 from their joint checking account for improvements to the residence.

From these facts the probate court concluded that Geza and Genevieve's contribution of their marital funds to pay for the improvements constituted "mixing marital property with property other than marital property." *See* sec. 766.63(1), Stats. The court also concluded that tracing was not possible and therefore ruled that Genevieve's separately titled residence was reclassified to marital property.[8]

2. Statutory Presumption

Ordinarily, we would begin any classification discussion under the MPA with the statutory presumption that all spousal property is marital property. Section 766.31(2), Stats. However, Geza's argument is premised upon a *reclassification* claim—a contention which necessarily concedes on a threshold basis that the residence is Genevieve's nonmarital property. Thus, we begin our discussion in this case with the premise that the residence is Genevieve's nonmarital property and remained so unless reclassified.

3. Reclassification of Property Under the MPA

The MPA recognizes a variety of ways that reclassification may occur. Pursuant to sec. 766.31(10), Stats., a spouse may voluntarily reclassify his or her nonmarital property to marital property by, *inter alia*, gift, conveyance or marital property

---

7. The MPA generally first applies to spouses upon their determination date, which is the last to occur of the following: (1) marriage; (2) 12:01 a.m. on the date that both spouses are domiciled in Wisconsin; or (3) 12:01 a.m. on January 1, 1986. Sections 766.01(5) and 766.03(1), Stats. Genevieve and Geza were married in 1982 and domiciled in Wisconsin throughout the marriage. Thus, their determination date is January 1, 1986.

8. The probate court's conclusion that tracing was not possible was premised upon its finding that "unreimbursed labor is involved." The court does not appear to have directly ruled whether tracing was possible as to the marital funds which the spouses contributed to Genevieve's nonmarital residence. However, this exercise is required under sec. 766.63(1), Stats.

agreement.[9] Geza's claim, however, does not rest on this statute. Instead, he claims that the property was reclassified pursuant to the mixed property provisions of sec. 766.63, Stats., which recognizes another method by which reclassification can occur. Under this statute, nonmarital property is reclassified to marital property if the two are mixed to the point where the nonmarital component of the property cannot be traced. However, if the "component of the mixed property which is not marital property can be traced," reclassification does not result. *See* sec. 766.63(1).

4. Burden of Proof in a Mixed Property Proceeding

Geza's reclassification claim is based on "mixing." As with any claimant, we conclude that the burden to establish mixing is properly assigned to Geza. If this burden is satisfied, the marital asset is reclassified "*unless* the component of the mixed property which is not marital property can be traced." Section 766.63(1), Stats. (emphasis added). We think it logical that the party seeking to avoid reclassification by establishing tracing should carry the burden to do so.

5. Tracing

In *Lloyd*, we addressed the tracing rules applicable to a reclassification claim under sec. 766.63, Stats. *Lloyd*, 170 Wis. 2d at 257-60, 487 N.W.2d at 653-54. Borrowing from divorce property division law, we performed an identity analysis. *See id.* at 259-60, 487 N.W.2d at 654.

Identity addresses whether the nonmarital component has been preserved in some present identifiable form so that it can be meaningfully valued and assigned — in other words, "traced." Thus, where individual or predetermination date property is mixed with marital property, the critical inquiry is whether, despite mixing, the nonmarital component of the property can be identified and valued. Section 766.63(1), Stats. *See also Brandt v. Brandt,* 145 Wis. 2d 394, 412, 427 N.W.2d 126, 132 (Ct. App. 1988). At the same time, this inquiry is also used to determine the proportionate marital and nonmarital ownership. 1 MARITAL PROPERTY LAW IN WISCONSIN §3.20, at 3-7.

6. Analysis

We now turn to the application of the statute to the facts of this case. As we have previously noted, Geza had the burden of establishing mixing. At trial, the documentary evidence established the following payments, totaling $3970.08, by Genevieve and Geza from their joint checking account for the following "improvements" to the residence:

9. Section 766.31(10), Stats., also states that reclassification can occur by "written consent under §. 766.61(3)(e) or unilateral statement under §766.59 and, if the property is a security, as defined in §. 705.21(11), by an instrument, signed by both spouses, which conveys an interest in the security."

New siding and gutters	$1016.00
New siding and gutters	500.00
Wind damage	150.00
Carpet purchase	490.28
Carpet installation	250.50
Garage door purchase	440.00
Labor paid to Peter Kobylski (new 2-car garage)	300.00
Sewer till replacement	219.00
Concrete for new garage	122.06
Building material for new garage	482.24

By this undisputed documentary evidence, Geza established that his and Genevieve's marital property was mixed with Genevieve's nonmarital property. Thus, Geza met his burden to establish mixing under the statute. The question then becomes whether "the component of the mixed property which is not marital property can be traced." Section 766.63(1), Stats. As we have already held, this burden to establish tracing was on the estate.

Here, the same evidence which shows mixing also demonstrates that tracing can be easily accomplished. The "paper trail" of Geza and Genevieve's contribution of their marital funds to Genevieve's nonmarital residence provides a ready basis for segregating the nonmarital component of the marital property. Therefore, the estate met its burden of tracing the residence's nonmarital component. We conclude that the probate court erred when it concluded that tracing was not possible.

7. The Remedy When Tracing Can be Performed

This does not end our inquiry, however. As we have noted, sec. 766.63(1), Stats., precludes reclassification when tracing can be performed. However, the question remains as to what remedy *other than reclassification* the marital estate is entitled in such a setting. Wisconsin appellate courts have not yet addressed this question. Neither the mixed property statute, sec. 766.63(1), nor the "remedies" provision of the MPA, sec. 766.70, Stats., provides an express answer to this question. Since the trial court will have to address this question on remand in this case, we address it here.

The majority of community property states hold that when marital funds are used to improve the separate property of one of the spouses and tracing is established, the improvements acquire the classification of the underlying property. *See* 1 MARITAL PROPERTY LAW IN WISCONSIN §3.25c, at 3-45 to 3-47, supp. 3-21. However, the marital estate has a right of reimbursement for the funds expended by the community for the improvements. *See, e.g., Tester v. Tester,* 123 Ariz. 41, 597 P.2d 194, 197 (Ct. App. 1979); *Josephson v. Josephson,* 115 Idaho 1142, 772 P.2d 1236, 1240 (Ct. App. 1989); *McKey v. McKey,* 449 So. 2d 564, 566-67 (La. Ct. App. 1984); *Portillo v. Shappie,* 97 N.M. 59, 636 P.2d 878, 883 (1981); *Jones v. Davis,* 15 Wash. 2d 567, 131 P.2d 433, 434 (1942).

Many of the community property decisions which allow reimbursement, however, differ on whether the amount of reimbursement should be the actual amount expended by the community, the enhanced value attributable to the improvements, or whichever is less.[10] *See* 1 MARITAL PROPERTY LAW IN WISCONSIN §3.25c, at 3-45 to 3-47, supp. 3-21 to 3-22. *See also, e.g., Lawson v. Ridgeway,* 72 Ariz. 253, 233 P.2d 459, 464-65 (1951) (measure of the lien or right to reimbursement is the increase in value to the property and not the amount spent); *Josephson,* 772 P.2d at 1240 (measure of reimbursement is the increase in value of the property attributable to the community contribution, not the amount of the community contribution itself); *McKey,* 449 So. 2d at 566-67 (where community property is used to improve a spouse's separate property, measure of reimbursement is the actual amount expended by the community for the improvement, not the enhancement of value); *Anderson v. Gilliland,* 684 S.W.2d 673, 675 (Tex. 1985) (claim for reimbursement is measured by the enhanced value to the benefited estate); *Hale v. Hale,* 557 S.W.2d 614, 615 (Tex. Civ. Ct. App. 1977) (enhanced value of the property due to the improvements or cost, whichever is less).

In *Anderson,* the Texas Supreme Court had occasion to examine the measure of reimbursement for funds expended by the community to improve separate property of one of the spouses. There, the spouses spent $20,238 to build a home on a lot owned by the wife prior to the marriage. At the time of the husband's death, this improvement had increased the value of the wife's separate property by $54,000. The husband's estate sought to include in the estate one-half the reimbursement due the community for the improvements to the wife's separate property. After working its way through the Texas appellate system, the Texas Supreme Court ultimately ruled that a claim for reimbursement is measured by the enhancement in value to the benefited estate, stating:

> The "cost only" rule, if followed, would provide an easy-to-apply measure since it would not require proof of enhancement. However, such a rule would, in many instances, permit the owner of the benefited estate to be enriched at the expense of the contributing estate. This is true because the estate which contributes the capital necessary to construct the improvements would not share in the increase in value resulting from the investment. The "enhancement or cost, whichever is less" rule, however, would permit the benefited estate the maximum recovery at the expense of the contributing estate in all situations. This does not comport with equity.

Anderson, 684 S.W.2d at 675. *See also Portillo,* 636 P.2d at 883 (tying the community's recovery to the amount of money spent may produce results which, depending on the circumstances, would be unfair to either the separate estate or the community. By treating such expenditures as an equity investment of community funds, rather than a loan, the community shares in the fluctuations of the market, taking both the gains and the losses).

We are persuaded by the *Anderson/Portillo* rationale that measuring reimbursement by the enhancement in value to the property is more likely to ensure the equitable treatment of both the contributing estate and the benefited estate in most situations. The rule is sensible and consistent with the equitable principles

---

10. Section 766.70, Stats., is the remedies provision of the MPA. This statute provides, in part, that "a court may . . . determine rights of ownership in . . . marital property and the classification of all property of the spouses." Section 766.70(2). However, this general language does not advise whether the claimant's measure of relief is the amount of the claimant's contribution of marital funds, the enhanced value of the nonmarital asset due to such contribution, or some combination of both.

of our MPA, and we expressly adopt it here. *See* sec. 766.95, Stats. Where marital funds are used to improve the separate property of one of the spouses, a claim for reimbursement exists in favor of the marital estate measured by the property's enhanced value attributable to the improvements, not the amount of marital funds actually expended.[11] Thus, expenditures that relate merely to the maintenance of the property or which do not enhance the property's value are not to be considered. The party seeking such reimbursement has the burden of demonstrating that the improvement funds expended have enhanced the value of the spouse's separate property and the amount of enhancement. *See Tester*, 597 P.2d at 197; *Suter v. Suter*, 97 Idaho 461, 546 P.2d 1169, 1173 (1976); *Rogers v. Rogers*, 754 S.W.2d 236, 239-40 (Tex. Ct. App. 1988). This burden assignment is akin to the general rule that a claimant must prove damages. *See, e.g., Pleasure Time, Inc. v. Kuss*, 78 Wis. 2d 373, 387, 254 N.W.2d 463, 470 (1977); *Lindevig v. Dairy Equip. Co.*, 150 Wis. 2d 731, 735, 442 N.W.2d 504, 506 (Ct. App. 1989).

Having determined the appropriate legal test for the remedy, we now turn to the evidence in this case as it bears upon this question. Although the parties presented some evidence of the value of the residence at various times, the evidence does not expressly speak to the enhanced value attributable to the improvements. Since this is Geza's burden, we could visit this failure upon him with finality. However, since the probate court erred in its threshold determination that tracing could not be performed, and since this is the first Wisconsin appellate case to speak to this issue, we conclude that the fairer approach is to remand for further proceedings to allow the parties to present additional evidence on this question. Following such proceedings, the court shall determine which of the expenditures relate to mere maintenance of the property and which constitute improvements to the property. As to the latter, the court shall also determine the amount, if any, by which Genevieve and Geza's contributions of their marital property enhanced the value of the residence. The court shall then fix Geza's recovery accordingly.

B.   MIXING INDUSTRY WITH NONMARITAL PROPERTY PURSUANT TO SEC. 766.63(2), STATS.

1. The Statute and the Trial Court Ruling

Geza's claim also was made pursuant to sec. 766.63(2), Stats., which recognizes a second type of mixing: a spouse's contribution of uncompensated industry to the other spouse's nonmarital property. The statute provides:

> (2) Application by one spouse of substantial labor, effort, inventiveness, physical or intellectual skill, creativity or managerial activity to either spouse's property other than marital property creates marital property attributable to that application if both of the following apply:
>   (a) Reasonable compensation is not received for the application.
>   (b) Substantial appreciation of the property results from the application.

---

11. Of course, because a spouse may freely dispose of the one-half interest he or she has in each item of marital property, *Lloyd*, 170 Wis. 2d at 252, 487 N.W.2d at 651, a surviving spouse would only be entitled to one-half the reimbursement amount to which the marital estate is entitled.

It is important to note that, unlike subsec. (1) of the statute, this subsection *does not contemplate any reclassification of existing nonmarital property to marital property.* Rather, it contemplates *creation of a marital property interest attributable to the application of the industry.* In this case, therefore, Geza's industry created a marital property component in Genevieve's nonmarital residence if: (1) Geza applied *substantial* labor or skill to the residence, (2) Geza received no *reasonable* compensation for his efforts, and (3) the efforts produced a *substantial* appreciation of the residence.

Geza testified that during the marriage he painted the interior and exterior of the residence, assisted Genevieve's son in enlarging the one-car garage, and did the yard work around the residence. Further, he testified that he received no compensation from Genevieve for these efforts. The probate court held that these efforts constituted substantial uncompensated labor, serving to reclassify the entire residence to marital property. The court also held that "tracing is [not] possible . . . as unreimbursed labor is involved."

Regarding substantial appreciation, the probate court found that the residence was assessed at $73,644 in 1982, $63,596 in 1990, and was sold in 1991 for $79,500. Based upon the testimony of a real estate appraiser, the court also found that the residence's rental value increased from $450 a month in 1986 to $550 to $600 a month as of the time of Genevieve's death. The court concluded:

> It is obvious that the real estate did not significantly increase in value from 1986-1990. It slipped in value. Common sense and the increased rental value would dictate that by painting, residing and putting up a new garage Geza contributed to the utility and comfort of the home, although the market did not reflect this. At work here are market forces other than mere activity by Geza. (There is nothing to show that by adding the aluminum siding and a garage he damaged the property.)
>
> This is something not contemplated by the statute, market value drop not related to the activity of the non-owning spouse while substantive labor, efforts and marital cash were applied. I believe that §766.001 "liberal construction" and the presumption this property is marital aids Geza. I do not believe the [sic] tracing is possible here as unreimbursed labor is involved. Therefore, I believe that the home of the parties has become mixed under §766.63(1), (2)(a), and (b).

2. Industry Mixing and Burden of Proof

Before applying the statute to the facts, we first address burden of proof considerations in an "industry mixing" claim under sec. 766.63(2), Stats. Just as with a "property mixing" claim under subsec. (1), we conclude that an "industry mixing" claim under subsec. (2) requires the claimant to establish the contribution of the industry. This burden lies with Geza in this case.

However, unlike a subsec. (1) "property mixing" case in which the mixing produces reclassification of the property unless tracing can be performed, a subsec. (2) "industry mixing" case does not produce any reclassification. Instead, if mixing is established, the statute provides that marital property *is created* to the extent of the additional value of the property attributable to the industry. Thus, unlike a "property mixing" case, the statute does not require proof of tracing; rather, it presumes such as a matter of law if substantial appreciation can be established. Therefore, the burden does not shift to the other spouse to establish tracing.

We therefore conclude that the burden properly lies with the claimant (here, Geza) to satisfy all the elements of a "industry mixing" claim pursuant to sec. 766.63(2), Stats. Again, these elements are: (1) the application of substantial industry to the nonmarital asset, (2) no reasonable compensation for the industry, and (3) the industry must have produced a substantial appreciation of the nonmarital asset.

3. Analysis

We now apply the statute to the facts of this case. For two reasons, we conclude that certain of the probate court's findings do not satisfy the legal standard set out under sec. 766.63(2), Stats., and thus do not support its ultimate conclusion awarding Geza a marital property interest in the residence.

First, under the very words of the statute, the application of substantial uncompensated labor to a spouse's nonmarital property followed by substantial appreciation thereof does not serve to reclassify the whole or any portion of the property to marital property. *Rather, it creates marital property, and then only to the extent of the additional value of the property that is attributable to the substantial uncompensated labor.* Section 766.63(2), Stats. *See also* 1 MARITAL PROPERTY LAW IN WISCONSIN §3.27a, at 3-50. Thus, the probate court's conclusion that the property was totally reclassified was error.

Second, we conclude that certain of Geza's labors and efforts do not constitute the "substantial" contribution required by the statute. Although the statute offers no insight as to what constitutes "substantial" effort, §14 of the Uniform Marital Property Act is identical to sec. 766.63, Stats. The comment to §14 related to physical labor explains substantial effort as follows:

> The rule of the section is strict. It articulates a bias against creation of marital property from such an act unless the effort has been substantial and has been responsible for substantial appreciation. Routine, normal, and usual effort is not substantial. Though drawing a precise line as to what is substantial and what is not is not possible, the section does not create opportunity to translate for recognizing minimal effort to a property interest. The section is only satisfied by proof of (1) a truly substantial effort followed by (2) a truly substantial appreciation *attributable to the effort* for which (3) no reasonable compensation was received. . . . If the compensation was nominal or nonexistent, then the provisions of the section still require a showing that the effort was substantial and that substantial appreciation resulted from it. Otherwise there can be no quantification of the marital property created by the effort and the spouse expending the effort will simply have done so without anything demonstrable to show for it.

UNIF. MARITAL PROPERTY ACT §14 comment, 9A U.L.A. 131-32 (1987) (emphasis in original).

Under the facts of this case, we conclude that Geza's painting and yard work, without more, qualify only as routine, normal and usual maintenance of the property and did not operate to create a marital property component in Genevieve's nonmarital residence. *See* 1 MARITAL PROPERTY LAW IN WISCONSIN §3.27a, at 3-48. Therefore, we additionally reverse this portion of the probate court's ruling.

We do agree, however, with the probate court's conclusion that Geza's efforts and labors in enlarging the garage qualified as a "substantial" contribution of industry.

But this satisfies only half the statute since the industry must also produce a "substantial appreciation" of the nonmarital asset. Here, the probate court concluded that there was no evidence of an increase in market value. Nonetheless, the court reasoned that Geza had established substantial appreciation because his efforts had contributed to the "utility and comfort of the home." While the court's ruling was an attempt to do fairness, it does not comport with the statutory requirement of substantial appreciation. Fair or not, the legislature has decreed that the contributing party cannot recover for uncompensated substantial industry if there is no resulting substantial appreciation.

As with the preceding issue, we choose not to direct an outright reversal with finality on this issue. Instead, as with the preceding issue, we choose to remand for reconsideration and further evidence, if the parties wish, on the question of substantial appreciation. We do so for three reasons: (1) the probate court's threshold error in concluding that reclassification was the consequence of Geza's labor and efforts, (2) evidence in the record arguably bearing on substantial appreciation which the probate court did not expressly address, and (3) this is the first Wisconsin case to address this aspect of the MPA's mixed property provisions.

We therefore direct on remand that the probate court shall reconsider whether Geza's efforts and labor relating to the enlargement of the garage produced a substantial appreciation of the residence and, if so, to fix his recovery accordingly. As noted, the parties may supply further evidence to the court on this issue.

Discussion Questions

1. Why did the trial court reclassify Genevieve's "nonmarital residence" as "marital property"? Why did the Court of Appeals disagree?

2. Why did the Court of Appeals adopt the Texas approach to the measure of reimbursement for improvements with community funds to separate property?

3. Why did Geza fail on his "industry mixing" claim?

PROBLEM 17.1

When Susan's father died, she received an inheritance of $100,000. She deposited that money in a joint bank account with her husband Tom. They decided to use the money to buy a home in Green Bay. Since Tom handled most of the couple's financial affairs, he used the funds from the joint account to buy the home. Without telling Susan, he put the title in his name. They lived in the home for several years, but have recently filed for divorce. Susan found out that the house was in Tom's name and she told her attorney that she never intended for the home to belong to him. Because of the housing bubble, the home has not increased in value. What would be the "identity" and "character" of the home according to the standards in *Derr v. Derr*?

PROBLEM 17.2

Ann owned a home in Milwaukee before she married Bob. The title was in her name. The home was quite rundown. Because Bob was very handy, he completely renovated the home. He gutted the kitchen and installed all new appliances and cabinets. Also, he added a family room and two bedrooms. Bob used funds from their joint bank account where they had deposited their earnings. The renovations cost approximately $50,000. Ann died recently. Her children from a prior marriage are claiming that the home was nonmarital property. Bob is claiming that the home should be classified as marital property or that the marital estate has a right to reimbursement. There is evidence that the renovations increased the value of the home by $75,000. How would a court decide, applying the standards in *Estate of Kobylski?*

Table 17-1
Wisconsin Law on Property at Marriage, Divorce and Death

Term	Rule	Case/Statute
Common-law Marriage	Common-law marriage was abolished in Wisconsin in 1917.	*In re Van Schaick's Estate*, 256 Wis. 213, 40 N.W.2d 588 (1949)
Property Rights of Unmarried Cohabitants	No statutory right to property for unmarried cohabitants. Wisconsin Supreme Court has recognized protection for a cohabitant who relies on an express or implied in fact contract to share property. Claim must exist independently from the sexual relationship and is supported by separate consideration. Also available are claims for unjust enrichment and partition.	*Watts v. Watts*,137 Wis. 2d 506, 405 N.W.2d 303 (1987) Wis. Stat. ch. 770 (domestic partnership rights and obligations)
Premarital Agreements — Property and Spousal Support	Any agreement made by the parties before or during the marriage concerning any arrangement for property distribution; such agreements shall be binding upon the court except that so such agreement shall be binding where the terms of the agreement are inequitable as to either party. Modification or elimination of spousal support is permitted but may not result in a spouse having less than necessary and adequate support.	Wis. Stat. §§767.61(3)(L) (formerly §767.255(3)(L)), 766.68 (3)(d), (9), *Levy v. Levy*, 388 Wis. 2d 523, 388 N.W.2d 170 (1986) (premarital agreement intended to apply at death did not apply at divorce), *Krejci v. Krejci*, 266 Wis. 2d 284, 667 N.W.2d 780 (Ct. App. 2003) (enforcement of agreement would be inequitable)
Commingling	Non-divisible property (separate property) includes inherited and gifted property. At divorce, a party who asserts that the property is non-divisible has the	Wis. Stat. §767.255(2)(a), *Derr v. Derr*, 289 Wis. 2d 671, 696 N.W.2d 170 (Ct. App. 2005) (apartment building gifted to husband during marriage was

Term	Rule	Case/Statute
	burden of showing that it remains non-divisible at the time of divorce. That party must show that the property has retained its character and identity through tracing and lack of donative intent.	non-divisible asset), *Steinmann v. Steinmann*, 309 Wis. 2d 19, 749 N.W.2d 145 (2008) (tracing and transmutation can be used to characterize non-divisible property)
Joint Titles and Transmutation	Transfer of separately owned property into joint tenancy changes the character of ownership in the entire property into marital property that is subject to division at divorce. Joint tenancy and survivorship marital property are available in Wisconsin. Creation of joint tenancy requires a marital agreement.	Wis. Stat. §§767.255(2), 766.58-766.60, *Steinmann v. Steinmann*, 309 Wis. 2d 29, 749 N.W.2d 145 (2008)
Educational Degrees	Maintenance and property division statutes provide a flexible means by which the trial court may examine all the relevant circumstances of the particular case and can, in its discretion, award just compensation to a supporting spouse by using either maintenance or property division or both.	*Haugan v. Haugan*, 117 Wis. 2d 200, 343 N.W.2d 796 (1984)
Management and Control and Goodwill	A spouse, acting alone, may manage and control marital property held in that spouse's name alone or not held in the name of either spouse. Spouses may manage and control marital property held in the names of both spouses only if they act together. A spouse acting alone may give a third person marital property greater than $1,000 if the gift is reasonable in amount considering the economic position of the spouses. Salable professional goodwill may be included as divisible property at divorce.	Wis. Stat. §§766.51, 766.53, *McReath v. McReath*, 329 Wis. 2d 155, 789 N.W.2d 89 (Ct. App. 2010)
Separate Property Business	Application of one spouse of substantial labor, effort, inventiveness, physical or intellectual skill, creativity or managerial activity of either spouse's property	Wis. Stat. §766.63(2), *Haldemann v. Haldemann*, 145 Wis. 2d 296, 426 N.W.2d 107 (Ct. App. 1988)

Term	Rule	Case/Statute
	other than marital property creates marital property attributable to that application if both of the following apply: (1) reasonable compensation is not received and (2) substantial appreciation of the property results from the application.	
Creditors' Rights	An obligation incurred by a spouse in the interest of the marriage or the family may be satisfied only from all marital property and all other property of the incurring spouse.	Wis. Stat. §766.55, *Curda-Derickson v. Derickson*, 266 Wis. 2d 453, 668 N.W.2d 736 (Ct. App. 2003) (restitution order for husband's criminal conviction not a marital debt), *St. Mary's Hosp. Medical Center v. Brody*, 186 Wis. 2d 100, 519 N.W.2d 707 (Ct. App. 1994) (husband's medical expenses could be recovered from marital property)
Disability Insurance	When insurance proceeds compensate for the loss of a gifted asset, they are non-divisible. When insurance proceeds compensate for loss of income, they are divisible at divorce.	*Wright v. Wright*, 307 Wis. 2d 156, 747 N.W.2d 690 (Ct. App. 2007)
Putative Spouse Doctrine	A putative marriage is a marriage which has been solemnized in proper form and celebrated in good faith by one or both parties, but which, by reason of some legal infirmity, is either void or voidable.	*Xiong v. Xiong*, 255 Wis. 2d 693, 648 N.W.2d 900 (Ct. App. 2002) (for wrongful death action, the term spouse can include putative spouse)
Property Division at Divorce	Courts must determine which property is divisible or non-divisible property which includes inherited and gifted property. At divorce, property will be equitably distributed based on several factors and may include non-divisible property in case of hardship on the other party or the children of the marriage.	Wis. Stat. §767.61, *Grumbeck v. Grumbeck*, 296 Wis. 2d 611, 723 N.W.2d 778 (Ct. App. 2005) (absent special circumstances, marital estate should be evenly divided), *Bonnell v. Bonnell*, 117 Wis. 2d 241, 344 N.W.2d 123 (1984) (award of more to former wife was justified based on wife's health)
Property Division at Death	Each spouse is entitled to dispose of his/her half of the marital property by will, except the surviving spouse has an elective share to deferred marital property (which would have been marital property under Wisconsin's system when it was acquired). If decedent dies without	Wis. Stat. §§852.01. 861.02 (deferred marital property elective share)

Term	Rule	Case/Statute
	a will, surviving spouse receives decedent's half interest in marital property if decedent leaves no issue or all issue are also issue of surviving spouse.	
Life Insurance	Follows item theory of division of marital property at death. Life insurance policy purchased during marriage is marital property and one purchased before marriage, where any premium is paid during marriage with marital funds, becomes mixed property. If insured names other spouse to receive proceeds at death, that is effective. But insured may only dispose of individual and marital property share of policy at death. A surviving spouse is entitled to his/her marital property share in the proceeds.	Wis. Stat. §§766.61 & 860.01, *Bruskiewicz v. Bruskiewicz*, 344 Wis. 2d 125, 820 N.W.2d 157 (Ct. App. 2012) (unpublished)

Table of Cases (Alphabetical)

Principal cases are in italics

649

Table of Cases (By State)

Principal cases are in italics

Index